The Classics in the Middle Ages

medieval & renaissance texts & studies

VOLUME 69

The Classics in the Middle Ages

*Papers of the Twentieth Annual Conference
of the Center for Medieval and Early Renaissance Studies*

Edited by

Aldo S. Bernardo
Saul Levin

medieval & renaissance texts & studies
Center for Medieval & Early Renaissance Studies
Binghamton, New York
1990

© Copyright 1990
Center for Medieval and Early Renaissance Studies
State University of New York at Binghamton

Library of Congress Cataloging-in-Publication Data

State University of New York at Binghamton. Center for
　　Medieval and Early Renaissance Studies. Conference
　　(20th : 1986 : SUNY-Binghamton)
　　　The classics in the Middle Ages : papers of the
Twentieth Annual Conference of the Center for Medieval
and Early Renaissance Studies / edited by Aldo S. Bernardo
and Saul Levin.
　　　　p.　cm. — (Medieval & Renaissance texts & studies ;
v. 69)
　　　ISBN 0-86698-078-4
　　　1. Classical literature — Appreciation — Europe —
Congresses.
2. Civilization, Medieval — Classical influences — Congresses.
3. Literature, Medieval — Classical influences — Congresses.
4. Learning and scholarship — History — Medieval, 500-1500-
Congresses.　　5. Classicism — Europe — Congresses.
6. Middle Ages-Congresses.　　I. Bernardo, Aldo S.
II. Levin, Saul.　　III. Title.　　IV. Series: Medieval &
Renaissance texts & studies; v. 69.
PA3013.S73　1986
880.09′4′0902 — — dc20
　　　　　　　　　　　　　　　　　　　　　　　89-13083
　　　　　　　　　　　　　　　　　　　　　　　　　CIP

This book is made to last.
It is set in Baskerville, smythe-sewn,
and printed on acid-free paper
to library specifications.

Printed in the United States of America

Contents

Introduction *Aldo S. Bernardo*	3
Dionysiac Imagery in Coptic Textiles and Later Medieval Art *Susan Heuck Allen*	11
Gregory of Tours and the Classical Tradition *Paul J. Archambault*	25
An Early Humanist Invective Against Speculative Grammar *Monika Asztalos*	35
Those Books That Are Most Necessary for All Men to Know: The Classics and Late Ninth-Century England, A Reappraisal *Janet Bately*	45
The Role of the Papal Library in Saving Livy's Histories *Giuseppe Billanovich*	79
Cicero, Ambrose, and Stoic Ethics: Transmission or Transformation? *Marcia L. Colish*	95
Allegory and Invention: Levels of Meaning in Ancient and Medieval Rhetoric *Philip Damon*	113
Bernard Silvestris and the *Corpus* of the *Aeneid* *Marilynn Desmond*	129
The Heritage of Fulgentius *Robert Edwards*	141
Why We Can't "Do Without" Camille *Rebecca Gottlieb*	*153*
William of Malmesbury's Roman Models: Suetonius and Lucan *Joan Gluckauf Haahr*	165
Aeneas' Journey to the New Troy *Bernard F. Huppé*	175

Contents

Platonism in the Works of Pseudo-Dionysius 189
Andrew L. J. James

Language: Vehicle of the Classical Heritage 199
Henry and Renée Kahane

"Mirabilia urbis Romae" 207
Dale Kinney

The Classic Bond of Friendship in Boccaccio's Tito and Gisippo (*Decameron* 10.8) 223
Victoria Kirkham

Antiquity, the Middle Ages, and the Renaissance as Seen Through the Eyes of an Argentinian Scholar 237
Yakov Malkiel

Early Post-Byzantine Historiography 253
Marios Philippides

Michael of Ephesus and the History of Zoology 265
Anthony Preus

Petrarch's Scholarship in His *De remediis utriusque fortune*: A Preliminary Inquiry 283
Conrad H. Rawski

"Potens in opere et sermone": Philip, Bishop of Bayeux, and His Books 315
R. H. Rouse and M. A. Rouse

The Classics in Medieval Education 343
Aldo Scaglione

Apuleius in the Middle Ages 363
Carl C. Schlam

Aeneas in Fourteenth-Century England 371
Sharon Stevenson

The Classics: Episcopal Malice and Papal Piety 379
Edward A. Synan

Rome as "Region of Difference" in the Poetry of Hildebert of Lavardin 403
Charles Witke

Index 413

The Classics in the Middle Ages

Note on Latin Spelling

For the sake of reasonable consistency, since the contributors' own practice varied greatly (sometimes within the same paragraph), the editors decided on the following principles:

(1) Citations from classical Latin, unless embedded in a later text, should conform to the ancient orthography. Out of custom we retain the capitalization and punctuation that have developed in medieval and modern times.

(2) Citations from medieval and Renaissance texts should adhere to each author's own spelling, insofar as that may be represented in the best manuscripts and embodied in editions which do not deliberately classicize.[1] For clarity, however, words should be spelled out, even the ones usually abbreviated in manuscripts. The familiar ligature & for *et* may be either kept as is or resolved into the two letters.

(3) Along with an increasing number of Latinists, we reject the mistaken reforms of Ramus (1515–1572), who converted a mere positional variation in lettering between *u* and *v*, and between *i* and *j* (*v* at the beginning of a word, *j* after *i*), into a device for distinguishing sounds in the pronunciation of Latin, as it was then current especially among Frenchmen: *v* for a fricative consonant, *j* for an affricate (unlike the ancient semi-vocalic sounds). These changes were widely adopted from the seventeenth century on, and were indeed a boon to the modern languages. But their inappropriateness to Latin was demonstrated conclusively by scholars in the nineteenth century, and little by little the minuscule *v* and *j* (along with the capital U and J, which have no justification from any ancient model) are disappearing from well-edited Latin texts, dictionaries, and grammars. We retain them here only in quoting modern Latin, composed under the influence of Ramus' reforms. If applied to any earlier Latin, they simply misrepresent each author's own spelling, nor do they deserve respect as some sort of key to pronunciation—which, if it is of any interest, has to be investigated on other criteria.

---

[1] An example of a classicizing edition is Valentini and Zucchetti's "Mirabilia urbis Romae" (instead of "Rome"), cited frequently in Dale Kinney's article (note 12 ff.).

Introduction

There is much to be said for the contention that classical influences on medieval culture persisted in some form or other throughout the early and high Middle Ages, and that these influences eventually resulted — with Dante, Boccaccio, and especially Petrarch — in a wellspring which supplied the source for the birth of Humanism and the Renaissance. After the enthusiasm for antiquity displayed by Ambrose and Augustine, it was highly unlikely that classical authors would ever again suffer a major eclipse. To examine the extent of the influence of the classics in the Middle Ages was the purpose of the twentieth annual conference sponsored by the Center for Medieval and Early Renaissance Studies at the State University of New York at Binghamton in the fall of 1986.

By the middle of the fourteenth century the principal classical writers and thinkers had not only been studied and digested directly or indirectly, in whole or in part, but they were increasingly being viewed and analyzed within Christian parameters. Despite Dante's enormous respect for and devotion to Virgil, as a Christian Dante could not imagine the Roman poet's capacities extending beyond a vague awareness of the Christian Purgatory and the Garden of Eden. It was only with Petrarch that the twofold nature of the classical mind first began producing serious doubts in the conscience of a first-rate Christian author. From Augustine to St. Thomas the tradition held that while the classical mind had developed human reason to its fullest extent, it had lacked the dimension of the true faith, and had thus fallen short of its true potential. Petrarch was among the first devout Christian authors to question this tradition.

In a book on the evolution of the humanities, Robert E. Proctor shows the central role played by Petrarch in the birth of the *studia humanitatis* in the Renaissance.[1] According to Proctor, by turning inwardly as deeply as he did, Petrarch discovered that in their own way the classics had intuited certain truths that could provide Christians with great comfort and support in the face of the mysteries and sufferings of this life. Even before Petrarch's death Boccaccio was proclaiming that his dear friend had cleared the way leading back to the past and had cleansed "the Heliconian font of mud and swampy reeds [restoring] its waves to their pristine clarity," thereby not only bringing the name of poetry back into the light but making Parnassus and its heights accessible once again. Subsequent humanists, such as Leonardo Bruni and Rudolph Agricola, agreed with him, as did indeed Petrarch himself in *Seniles* 17.2, addressed to Boccaccio, in which he proudly acknowledges that, as the oldest and therefore the first scholar to do so, he had awakened minds to the study of the ancients both in and outside of Italy.

The more intimate Petrarch became with classical writers, the more he realized how, along with the early Fathers, they could help him mold and shape his own soul. He found them of great therapeutic value, as it were, in confronting the grief, bereavement, and fear that he so often experienced upon the deaths of a great number of his friends. The mystery of death in life never failed to inspire in him a deep anguish, intensified by feelings of anger and protest at what he viewed as the casual and utterly fortuitous nature of the deaths of his friends during such calamities as the plague of 1348. The frustration and disillusionment he experienced from his awareness that he could never seem to prepare himself for the unexpected blows of fate often resulted in an agony and anger toward himself that found release only in writing and reading. A deep sense of unexpected, inexplicable, and inescapable change haunted him even more than death. All of reality, both internal and external, seemed to be marked by transience, mutability, and incessant motion. He actually compared himself to Ulysses as he constantly moved from one place to another, from one project to another.

Petrarch understood that for the ancients, as for the medieval mind, peace and contentment could be found only by rising above the human and contemplating the eternal and unchanging heavens. He knew that, in his account of Scipio's dream, Cicero viewed this life as nothing more than a road or passageway to heaven; but he interpreted this to mean that a state of near-blessedness can be deserved and hoped for, if not actually attained, through human endeavor, even "while enclosed in the prison of the body," as he writes, adding that "there are times when this mortal life has some similarity to eternal life."[2] But while a mind such as Dante's was intent on portraying the finish of life's race, Petrarch's devoted all its emotional and creative energy into surviving the race. As Proctor maintains, "Petrarch was a deeply religious man. But he could not hear the word of God, at least as the scholastics preached it, in human life as he experienced it." So his was primarily a search for new ways of hearing and living God's word. Ultimately he had to learn to live with his confused and anguished state of mind, but he found no small consolation for his condition in the words and voices of the past which helped him become the physician to his own soul. Like the ill physician who feels his own pain, the words he read aloud "gradually sank down inside of me and pierced me there with their hidden points." Compared to gold, gems, and the like, "Books give us delight down to the very marrow of our bones...."[3] In describing to Boccaccio how his thousands of encounters with Virgil, Horace, Boethius, and Cicero had affected him, he writes: "These writings have entered into me so intimately, and are fixed not only in my memory but also in the marrow of my bones, and have so become one with my mind that even if I were never to read them again, they would remain embedded in me, having set their roots in the deepest part of my soul...."[4] One must agree with Proctor that the healing that came from such reading resulted not from being lifted outside of himself but from sinking deep down within.

In one of his polemical works Petrarch confesses that the kind of moral stimulation he sought was to be found primarily in Latin authors. Aristotle, for instance, made him feel more learned but not a better man. Aristotle does teach "what virtue is . . . but his lesson lacks those goads, those fiery appeals that incite the mind and direct it toward love of virtue and hatred of vice, or, at any rate, does not have enough such power." Latin writers, such as Cicero and Seneca, do have such power, "for they direct and drive deep into the heart the sharpest and most ardent stings of eloquence, by which the lazy are startled, the ailing kindled, the sleepy aroused, the weak made firmer, the fallen raised, and those attached to the earth lifted up to the highest thoughts and to honest desire. Then earthly things lose their attraction, vice, seen from up close, provokes an intense hatred of itself, while virtue . . . beheld by the mind's eye and contemplated in all its beauty and goodness . . . inspires a miraculous love of itself and of true wisdom."[5]

To study the lives of the ancients, for Petrarch, was like learning how to live. In a relatively early letter (*Fam.* 6.4), he defends the use of exempla, for which he had been criticized: "Next to experience itself, which is the best teacher of things, I would wager there is no better way to learn than by having the mind desire to emulate these greats as closely as possible. Therefore, just as I am grateful to all those authors I have read who afford me this opportunity to test myself with appropriate examples, so do I hope that those who read me will be grateful." There was, however, a very special process involved in Petrarch's kind of reading, a process whereby the ancients or their heroes were transformed from "manifestations of collective and normative categories of being into autonomous selves," to use Proctor's words. Petrarch was convinced that by pondering the deeds of unique individuals one could learn about oneself and thereby strengthen one's character; one could discover one's own lessons despite the entirely different lessons that one's sources might draw. For the ancients, the deeds of heroes were inspired by such outward-directed qualities as patriotism and manliness; Petrarch, instead, concentrated on the personal selves of those heroes. By using the heroic Romans as his guides in his attempts to strengthen his soul and character, he came to believe that they possessed an inner life similar to his own, though far more courageous. But whereas for the ancients such courage was outer-directed, for Petrarch it developed only through intense inner questioning and struggle of the will. Such a quest for the self was what was to lead him to what has been called "the discovery of the modern conscience," a conscience in crisis because of an innate irresoluteness regarding the role man was destined to play in this life over and above Christian providentiality.[6]

This brief analysis must suffice to show why and how Petrarch served as a wellspring for the many classical streams of thought and consciousness that flowed throughout the Middle Ages. The present proceedings examine several such streams. The essays include the eight invited papers read at the plenary sessions as well as a number of carefully refereed papers presented at the regular sessions. Because of the outstanding quality of the presentations dealing with Ovid, it was decided to publish them in a special issue of *Mediaevalia,* the primary journal of the Center.[7]

The eight plenary papers cover a considerable range of subjects, philological, philosophical, educational, political-social, and critical.

Giuseppe Billanovich traces the textual tradition of Livy's *Ab urbe condita* from its earliest form through the various papal and royal libraries and clerical scriptoria down to Petrarch. The core of the account is the role played by the Paduan, Lovato Lovati, and by the monastic library of Pomposa in the Po delta, whose rich holdings equalled those of the papal palace in Rome and the imperial palace in Bamberg in the eleventh century. With the schisms and other internal battles raging within the church throughout the twelfth and thirteenth centuries, Livy's history eventually reached Avignon, where Petrarch with the backing of the Colonna family and other influential friends was amazingly able to restore order to the textual tradition. As a result of such restoration, existing editions of the *Ab urbe condita* will require considerable revising.

By tracing the books owned by Philip, bishop of Bayeux, Richard and Mary Rouse show how the bishop may have played a significant role in the early and rapid dissemination of Roman and canon law among Anglo-Norman jurists. Philip's holdings in Roman law may indeed represent its first appearance in northern Europe. The collection also included many ancient and contemporary histories along with a number of classical and late classical works, some of which could be considered purveyors of a variety of classical verse forms. The essay, however, focuses on the way in which Philip's library holdings illuminate his role in establishing the importance of cathedral schools in the formation of the twelfth-century state.

In her paper Marcia Colish examines the manner in which the Stoic tradition was modified as it descended from the original Stoa through Cicero and to the Middle Ages by way of St. Ambrose. Her primary thesis is that a classical tradition such as Stoic ethics reveals its durability not in its being transmitted untouched by human hands, as it were, but in its persistence notwithstanding basic transformations. Both Cicero and Ambrose transformed the tradition rather extensively in order to make it conform to personal points of view. Such creative transformations of the classics, the paper argues, are as fully worthy of attention as their faithful preservation and use in a pure state, for they testify to the capacity of the classics to combine with other ingredients while yet holding their own.

Philip Damon's paper traces how distinctions between types of allegorical meaning descended from the most ancient commentators of Homer and Virgil down to Dante. By placing Siger of Brabant and Joachim of Flora in his "Allegory of Wisdom" in the circle of the Sun of his *Paradiso*, Dante, according to Damon, indicates his awareness of such distinctions.

Bernard Huppé concentrates primarily on a classical hero's journey through the Middle Ages and on the principal transformations and transmutations he underwent. Aeneas' voyage had gripped the medieval imagination since the earliest centuries of the Christian era, and had been cast in innumerable molds of the journey metaphor depicting man's basic condition as a pilgrim destined for a specific goal. From Rome to the New Albion (*Beowulf*), to Paris (Abelard's *Calamities*), to Troyes (Chrétien's *Erec* and *Lancelot*), to Orléans (*Romance of the Rose*), to Florence (*Vita nuova*), and finally to the New Troy, London (*Piers Plowman* and Chaucer's *Troilus*), the Virgilian hero reappears in various *personae* seeking some form of ultimate blessedness.

Janet Bately's essay provides fascinating insights into how the classical world was introduced to literate Anglo-Saxons in the late ninth century. She describes how, in mid-ninth century, Alfred, king of the West Saxons, in an attempt to restore the learning and wisdom of old to Anglo-Saxon England, sent out an appeal for help in the task of translating those books that were most necessary for all men to know. While he himself set about translating several early Christian works, including Boethius, others translated other books, likewise mostly religious, but including Orosius' *Historiarum aduersus paganos libri septem*. This last work drew almost all its material from classical sources, including Livy, Tacitus, Justin, and Eutropius, while Boethius' *De consolatione* contains numerous references to historical and mythological figures and to classical stories. The account of the influence exerted by these two books in introducing the educated Anglo-Saxon to classical civilization reveals the extensive efforts made in those early days to preserve such learning.

Aldo Scaglione discusses the manner in which ancient culture was transmitted from late-ancient schools through the medium of Anglo-Saxon monks in the form of the liberal arts, and especially the *triuium*, for the purpose of understanding the figures of speech in sacred writings. This, according to the author, contrasted sharply with the systematic attempt of the Renaissance to revive ancient culture in its original form. The prevalence of classical *auctores* in medieval schools is most revealing.

Edward Synan cites two interesting uses to which the classics were put in the twelfth century. The first is a goliardic poem by a fictitious "Bishop Goliath" which turns to the classics to validate the "bishop's" defense of Abelard's eloquence and learning against what the author considered the obscurantist religiosity of two monks, one of whom was known to have been St. Bernard. The second example treats of the pious use of the classics made by Pope Innocent III. Not only would the pope generally cite classics in his correspondence, but in a letter to an archbishop on a moral point he did not hesitate to cite Ovid's *Remedia amoris*. Even in his sermons he would cite a classical source side by side with St. Paul. It is clear that Innocent saw in pagan wisdom a valid anticipation of his own biblical and ecclesiastical faith.

The remaining papers complement the plenary papers by dealing with such disparate areas as language and grammar, zoology, and historiography. As the papers are presented alphabetically according to author, the reader will sense not only the pervasive impact of the classics on medieval culture, but why a dedicated man of letters such as Petrarch could say that the classics had penetrated the very marrow of his bones.

Aldo S. Bernardo

Notes

1. *Education's Great Amnesia: Reconsidering the Humanities from Petrarch to Freud, with a Curriculum for Today's Students* (Indianapolis: Indiana University Press, 1988). Citations from this work are taken from the typescript of either the preface or the chapter on Petrarch.

2. *De republica* 6.6; *Fam.* 4.2.

3. *Fam.* 3.18, in *Rerum familiarium libri I-VIII*, trans. Aldo S. Bernardo (Albany: SUNY Press, 1975).

4. *Fam.* 12.2, in *Letters on Familiar Matters: Rerum familiarium libri IX-XVI*, trans. Aldo S. Bernardo (Baltimore: Johns Hopkins University Press, 1982).

5. *De sui ipsius et multorum ignorantia*, in Francesco Petrarca, *Prose*, ed. G. Martellotti, P. G. Ricci, E. Carrara, and E. Bianchi (Milan-Naples: Ricciardi, 1955), 747.

6. Ugo Dotti, *Petrarca e la scoperta della coscienza moderna* (Milan: Feltrinelli, 1978); Aldo Scaglione, "Classical Heritage and Petrarchan Self-Consciousness in the Literary Emergence of the Interior 'I,'" *Altro Polo* 7 (1984): 23-24.

7. Warren Ginsberg, "Ovide and the Problem of Gender"; Frank T. Coulson, "The *Vulgate* Commentary on Ovid's *Metamorphoses*"; Ralph Hexter, "Medieval Articulations of Ovid's *Metamorphoses:* From Lactantian Segmentation to Arnulfian Allegory"; Gerald A. Bond, "Composing Yourself: Ovid's *Heroides*, Baudri of Bourgueil and the Problem of Persona"; Leslie Cahoon, "The Anxieties of Influence: Ovid's Reception by the Early Troubadours"; Barbara Nolan, "Ovid's *Heriodes* Contextualized: Foolish Love and Legitimate Marriage in the *Roman D'Enéas*"; Eric M. Steinle, "Versions of Authority in the *Roman de la Rose:* The Ovidian Pretext"; Teodolinda Barolini, "Arachne, Argus, and St. John: Transgressive Art in Dante and Ovid"; Rebecca S. Beal, "Dante in the Labyrinth"; Janet Levarie Smarr, "Ovid and Boccaccio; A Note on Self-Defense"; Thomas J. Hatton, "John Gower's Use of Ovid in Book III of the Confessio Amantis"; Sheila Delany, "The Naked Test: Chaucer's 'Thisbe,' the *Ovide Moralisé*, and the Problem of *Translatio Studii* in the *Legend of Good Women*"; John M. Fyler, "Love and the Declining World; Ovid, Genesis, and Chaucer."

Dionysiac Imagery in Coptic Textiles and Later Medieval Art

SUSAN HEUCK ALLEN

Dionysac iconography survived from the classical period into late antique and Coptic Egypt.[1] We can trace this continuity in the medium of woven textiles,[2] most of which were discovered in Egypt and date from the fourth to the seventh centuries. In the late antique world, Dionysos stood for the principle of fertility inherent in the grape, the life force in the vine itself.[3] The polarity of his dual nature (with divine sire and mortal mother) expressed itself in the creative and destructive characteristics of pleasure and brutality. As discussed below, scenes of Dionysos and his entourage, and imagery of the vine and grape harvest were especially popular. Previously employed by the Ptolemies in their ruler cult, Dionysos emerged as a politicized god of theatrical revels and triumphs. In the Early Christian era, Dionysos was identified as a martyred fertility god and hence as a prototype for Christ in Alexandrian iconography and literature. Though the survival of Dionysos' cult ended abruptly in the seventh century, the god's image resurfaced in the West in the later Middle Ages because of Carolingian and Ottonian interest in antiquity, the use of *spolia,* and the twelfth-century translation of Alexandrian Greek texts into Latin.

The Survival of Textiles

Coptic textiles are mainly preserved in the burial grounds and dumps of towns and monasteries. When Theodosius I (AD 379–395) passed legislation banning mummification, the inhabitants of Egypt began to bury their dead fully clothed. The dry sands of Egypt guaranteed the survival of the cloth. Representations of Dionysos are preserved on textiles of various types,[4] such as monumental wall hangings,[5] altar scarfs, and curtains.[6] These larger pieces, probably used for generations, and only later employed as burial wrappings for the dead, are usually not well-preserved. Whole tunics and ornaments, such as medallions,[7] square panels at shoulders, sleeves, or hems,[8] *claui* or vertical stripes from each shoulder, on the front and back, transverse bands at the neckline between the *claui,* and borders are found most frequently. Ornamented tunics, worn over a plain tunic, were the standard garment in late Roman times[9] for those who could afford them.[10] This tradition of ornamented tunics lasted from Roman Republican times until the Arab conquest.

Regional Techniques

Textiles were woven in several centers around the Mediterranean. The different materials and methods used in the weaving help separate various traditions and sources. For example, linen weaving, known in Egypt from Early Dynastic times[11] and incorporating tapestry-woven patterns in colored wool,[12] endured in Ptolemaic, Roman, and medieval Egypt.[13] In Diocletian's Edict of 301, the emperor ranked Alexandrian linen fifth in the Empire, also mentioning that the city produced a linen which imitated the fabrics of Tarsus in Cilicia.[14] The linen was woven by Roman weavers who formed a hereditary caste apart from the other weavers in quarters of Arsinoë and Theadelphia. Weavers were known by their district names, either Egyptian (Theban, Oxyrhynchite, Cynopolite) or foreign (Laconian, Lodix — for Laodicea) and their works were desired in both the East and the West. The vast majority of tapestries were of wool and undyed linen.[15] Numerous pieces from the fourth century and later seem to have been woven entirely of wool.[16] With the advent of the silk road of Central Asia, later caravans brought silk to weaving centers in Syria and the West. Very rarely, gold threads were incorporated into the designs.[17]

The tapestry-woven textiles fall into two main groups: polychrome and purple monochrome. In those of the latter group,[18] figures are articulated in purple wool and white or undyed linen threads. The style is basically linear, schematic and two-dimensional. One guild known expressly for the dying of purple cloth worked at Oxyrhynchus.[19] Those of the polychrome group are probably contemporary, possibly produced at the same atelier and presumably inspired by large scale paintings and mosaics.[20] One such atelier is suggested for the site of Herakleia Perinthos, located either near Constantinople or in the Faiyum.[21] It is posited that monumental wall-hangings or curtains of an illusionistic or painterly style were produced there in a factory under imperial control.

Evolution of the Ptolemaic Cult of Dionysos in Alexandria

Early in its history, Alexandria became the center of a ruler cult of Dionysos.[22] Ptolemy I Soter, Alexander's successor in Egypt, began to associate Dionysos with Alexander during his leader's lifetime in order to stress his own ties with the god.[23] In years following, Alexandria was increasingly associated with the god Dionysos, a tradition described by the court poets, writers, and guilds of Dionysiac artists of Ptolemy II Philadelphus in Alexandria and Ptolemais Hermiou. It was Philadelphus who was responsible for spreading the idea that Alexander had behaved in life as a Νέος Διόνυσος.[24] He also organized Dionysiac games[25] and the sumptuous New Year's procession which carried an effigy of the god reclining on the back of an elephant through the streets of Alexandria to honor the god to whom all others, including Zeus, were subordinated.[26] This festival is possibly echoed in the Triumph of Dionysos shown on the silver kantharos from the Walters Art Gallery.[27] It was his successor, Euergetes I, who first claimed descent from Dionysos and Hercules and thus began a tradition which endured until the Roman conquest.

Later still, Ptolemy IV Philopator transformed Alexandrian and tribal deme names into names of figures connected with Dionysos,[28] established the worship of Dionysos as a state cult and personally took part in the rites.[29] He had a leaf of ivy, symbolic of the god, tattooed on his body[30] and issued coins of Alexandria showing him in Dionysiac costume with ivy, staff, and fawnskin.[31] Clement of Alexandria notes that Ptolemy IV was called by the name of the god (*Protrepticus* 4.48) and there is evidence as well of an iconographical identification of Ptolemy IV Philopator with Dionysos[32] in the form of a terracotta head wearing a crown of ivy in the Benaki Collection;[33] a silver alabastron from Palaiokastro, Thessaly;[34] and the above-mentioned silver kantharos in Baltimore.[35] Moreover, later Ptolemies seem to have called themselves incarnations of the god, Νέος Διόνυσος.[36] Meanwhile, other Hellenistic rulers, such as Antiochus VI, Antiochus XII, Attalus I, and especially Mithridates I Eupator, tried with less success to strengthen their images and their pedigrees by similarly allying themselves with Dionysos.[37] These potentates desired to marshal the East as Alexander (Dionysos) had in their historical and legendary campaigns against India.[38] In the first century BC, Ptolemy Auletes and his daughter Cleopatra VII bore the titles Νέος Διόνυσος and Νέα 'Ισις.[39] Finally, in the last years of Ptolemaic supremacy, the same Cleopatra and Mark Antony espoused their Dionysiac connection in epiphanies in Ephesus where Antony was hailed as Dionysos by the inhabitants dressed as satyrs, maenads, and Pans.[40] Fraser has noted that "The devotion of the Ptolemies to Dionysos . . . forms by far the most significant link with the traditional gods of Greece [by means of] fabricated genealogy, the desire to associate with Alexander's Indian triumphs, patronage of the stage and the particular devotion of Philopator."[41] The use of Dionysos and his triumph as an imperial prototype continued with post-Ptolemaic rulers, such as the deified Augustus and the demi-gods Hercules and Bacchus, the Roman equivalent of Dionysos (Ovid *Ars Amatoria* 1.183–204), and in coin portraits, where the emperor is shown in a *biga* drawn by elephants.[42] Later Alexandrian coins of Domitian, Trajan, and Hadrian show the emperor in a *quadriga* drawn by elephants, thus continuing the imagery of the Dionysiac triumph.[43] When Julian the Apostate came to power, Themistius compared him to "Heracles and Dionysus of old who, being at once philosophers and kings, purged almost the whole earth and sea of the evils that infested them."[44]

Actually, several aspects of Dionysos evolved in Egypt: (1) the theatrical reveler, (2) political symbol, connected with the triumphs of the Ptolemies and later Romans,[45] as illustrated in later textiles,[46] and (3) the more personal fertility god of resurrection and immortality, identified with the martyred god Osiris. The connection of Dionysos with the fertility god Osiris is implicit in his function as the patron of grape cultivation. In the fifth century BC, Herodotus (*Historia* 2.42.2, 47–49), probably following Hecataeus, equates Demeter with Isis and Dionysos with Osiris. By the fourth century BC, he is further associated with the god of the netherworld, Hades or Pluton. In the Ptolemaic period, Dionysos assumed a very important role in the Memphite Serapeum[47] and some scholars believe that the religious equation of Dionysos with Osor-Hapi or Serapis reflects a deliberate policy of the Ptolemies.[48] This syncretism was then picked up by the later authors. In the first century BC, Diodorus, perhaps following Polybius, described the origin of human life in Egypt, then the introduction of civilization by Osiris, equated with Dionysos (1.15.6–8, 17–20.5 and 96.4–6). In the first century AD, Plutarch follows him in *De Iside et Osiride* 356B. This conflation of the two may be seen in the juxtaposition of Dionysos and Isis, consort of Osiris, in the fifth-century textile from Antinoë in the Louvre.[49] Furthermore, Shepherd has traced to Athenaeus (*Deipnosophistai* 5.198c) the odd iconographic detail of depicting Dionysos with the fertility symbol of the cornucopia[50] to the Dionysiac extravaganza of Ptolemy II and the year spirit, *Eniautos*.[51] Here, the two conceptions fostered by the Ptolemaic rulers come together most closely.

In the fourth through sixth centuries AD, the popularity of Dionysos was bolstered by a revival of Hellenistic literature through works such as the *Dionysiaca* of Nonnos from Panopolis (Akhmim) which was produced c. AD 500,[52] and the popularity of pagan sculptures, such as those at Ahnas.[53] The subsequent demise of the gods in Egypt was presaged in the activity of the monk Shenute who inveighed against his pagan contemporaries and their religion in the fifth century[54] and in Justinian's decree that the last temples be closed in AD 543.[55] Literary and artistic references to Dionysos were virtually extinguished with the sack of Alexandria in the seventh century.

Dionysos as a Precursor of Christological Imagery

During the late antique period certain pagan deities were taken up as prototypes for Christ.[56] The imagery of Dionysos in birth and death was appropriated by the Christians, just as the *Bacchae* of Euripides, which described the power and passion of Dionysos, was used as a model by the author of the *Christus Patiens*.[57] In this work the author employed the lamentation of Agaue over the body of her dead son (*Bacchae* 1280 ff.) for the scene where the Virgin weeps over Christ after the descent from the cross.[58] In the second century AD, the Christian apologist Justin Martyr wrote that demons, trying to deceive and seduce the unwary, mimicked the Old Testament prophets by having Dionysos fulfill that which was prophesied of Christ.[59] For Dionysos, like Christ, was killed and returned to life.[60] Hence Early Christian monuments, especially sarcophagi and funerary textiles associated with death and resurrection, often employed references to Dionysos.[61]

Sired by god and born of mortal, Dionysos partook of both divinity and humanity.[62] Because of this dual nature, the idea and the iconography of the birth of infant Dionysos was used as an appropriate model for the portrayal of the new infant god, Christ.[63] Both Nordhagen and Kitzinger have explored the iconography of the baby Dionysos.[64] The second-century Roman sarcophagus in the Capitoline Museum depicts the infant god bathed by two midwife/nymphs.[65] One woman is seated, holding the infant Dionysos, and the other, standing, pours water for the bath into the basin. In the fourth- to fifth-century Antinoë veil,[66] scenes from the story of Semele and the birth of Dionysos decorate a narrow upper frieze above the Triumph of Dionysos in the main scene. This follows the pattern of earlier sarcophagi, such as the Dionysiac sarcophagus in the Walters Art Gallery.[67] The bathing vignette on the Antinoë veil mirrors that on the Capitoline sarcophagus. On the left, a seated woman holds the infant while a standing servant rests her hand on the basin.[68] Weitzmann believes that a monumental painting served as prototype for both works.[69] In a fresco from the *Domus Aurea*,[70] the reclining figure of Semele resembles that of the Virgin on her couch so closely that Weitzmann has suggested that the entire scene of the birth of Dionysos may have served as a model for the Nativity of Castelseprio.[71] Peirce, Tyler, and Phillipart have pointed to the similarities in the representation of Semele struck by the lightning of her lover, Zeus (*Bacchae* 7–8 and 596 ff.), in the Antinoë veil,[72] and in the Christian portrayals of the Annunciation.[73] Nordhagen further suggests that Christian artists can be shown to have adopted the iconography of the divinely begotten Dionysos for the images of the infant Christ.[74]

Conversely, Dionysos is occasionally Christianized as in the sixth-century textile excavated at Akhmim, where a cross precedes the inscribed name Dionysos, next to a representation of the god with a panther.[75] On the same garment, the cross was also applied to an amphora held by a male god (Dionysos?) seated in the center of a roundel.[76] In this scene the negative aspects of the pagan god were exorcized while the positive powers were invoked by the cross and then incorporated into the Christian community.[77] Here, and in the lapidary of Kyranos, Dionysos was identified with Christ to heighten the potency of the image and the invocation. The Kyranides lapidary, essentially a medical treatise, was probably written during the second century in Alexandria.[78] It records the names of Aphrodite and Bacchus, Dionysiac festivals, and invocation formulae,[79] praising Dionysos and Christ in the same breath, while Christ is invoked with the language of the Bacchic rites εὐοῖ![80]

The importance of vine imagery to the god of wine who taught the cultivation of the grape does not need emphasizing.[81] In Hellenistic and late Roman art, Dionysos was often shown in the vineyard with maenads and satyrs. The grape harvest became a particularly popular theme on sarcophagi, such as that of Constantine, which shows *putti* gathering grapes.[82] Numerous Coptic textiles employ this grape harvesting theme, as in the transverse bands of the sixth-century tunic now in Brooklyn.[83] Here, figures harvest and drink in a vineyard. Beneath the scene in the center of the tunic, a cross was woven. On the reverse, it was removed. With this piece, it seems as if the Copts had again appropriated Dionysiac imagery, now evolved into an illustration of resurrection, of continuing life.

Not only a general symbol of resurrection and immortality, the vine was specifically taken up for new theology of the Christian Church. John 15:1–5 quotes Christ "I am the true vine . . . I am the vine, ye are the branches; He that abideth in me, and I in him, the same bringeth forth much fruit. . . ." Borrowing iconography from the god of wine and vine, Christ sets himself apart from the pagan rites by claiming to be the true god.[84] To drink wine meant to drink his blood; to eat bread, to feast on his body (Matthew 26:26-28). The Christian Eucharist in which the god was consumed was not new, but may have been partly derived from the idea of the ritual eating of raw flesh, the Dionysiac ὠμοφαγία of the Dionysiac mystery rites.[85] Later Christian authors explained the Dionysiac ritual or ὠμοφαγία as some would explain the Christian communion: it was merely a commemorative rite, in memory of the day when the infant Dionysus was himself torn apart and devoured by the Titans, as reenacted in the σπαραγμός of the cattle and Pentheus in the *Bacchae* (734 and 1125).[86]

It is not surprising, therefore, that textiles and equipment associated with the Eucharist, such as the Antioch Chalice, should have been covered with vine imagery.[87] Other liturgical implements, such as bronze incense burners and lamps, were decorated with a proliferation of vines and grapes. Moreover, the interiors of cathedrals and tombs were ornamented with vine scrolls and grape bunches, to evoke the theme of resurrection.[88] Yet all vines do not recall Dionysos directly. Such iconography refers most clearly to John 15:1. Both Tacitus and Plutarch comment on the Romans' confusing their wine god, Liber or Bacchus/Dionysos, with the god of the Jews because of the use of wine, music, and the vine in their cult (*Historiae* 5.1-13 and *Quaest. Conuiu.* 4.62).

The Triumph of Dionysos has also been shown to have influenced the iconography used to depict Christ in his chariot in the sixth-century, when it was used on a roundel now in Brooklyn.[89] The textile shows the upper body of a frontal rider with raised arms in a *biga*, a car drawn by two animals, interpreted by Thompson as panthers. This theme was probably borrowed from one of several sources: the Hellenistic Triumph of Dionysos or the Roman Imperial triumphs, the journey of Helios, or, possibly, the ascension of Alexander. The light blue nimbus of the figure bears a cross, and thus Riefstahl deduces that we have a representation of Christ as Helios at the moment of the Ascension. This representation, with its beardless Christ in a cruciform nimbus, is strikingly similar to a sixth-century Bawit fresco of the Ascension.[90] It also recalls the assimilation of the pagan sun god to the Christian deity in the third-century mosaic in the Iulii Mausoleum under St. Peter's in Rome, showing Christ-Helios born aloft in a quadriga.[91]

Frequently Coptic literary sources refer to Christ in a chariot. The apocryphal *Book of the Resurrection of Christ by Bartholemew the Apostle* recounts that during the Resurrection "Jesus rose and mounted into the chariot

18 Dionysiac Imagery

of the Cherubim." Later it mentions Christ appearing to Mary in the "chariot of His Father" as he was ascending. Furthermore, Bartholomew himself bears witness that he "beheld the Son of God on the chariot of the Cherubim."[92] It may be that the chariot of the Cherubim is represented here.[93] Certainly the Triumph of Dionysos was a well-known theme in the literature, art, and politics of Ptolemaic, Roman and Coptic Egypt. We can suppose that this iconography, so successful in the past, was adopted by the Christians.

Later Isolated Appearances in the West

Though representations of Dionysos appear sporadically in the West in the fourth through seventh centuries, no comparable examples in the East have survived. Between the seventh and eleventh centuries Dionysiac depictions seem to disappear in both East and West. In the West, earlier sculptures of Dionysos were occasionally reused or copied in religious sculpture and minor arts. In Aachen, Henry II (1002–1014) acquired sixth- to seventh-century Alexandrian ivories which he had inserted into the pulpit of the Cathedral.[94] These representations of Dionysos preserve the Praxitelean pose of Apollon Lykeios[95] popular in late antique, early Byzantine, and Coptic art. In both, the god is surrounded by vines. These *spolia* were signs of Henry's imperial ambitions; he used both antique and contemporary prototypes to identify with the world of antiquity. Also preserved within the Ottonian realm is a 1023 copy of the encyclopedic *De rerum naturis* of Rabanus Magnentius Maurus, archbishop of Mainz (784?–856), the Carolingian original of which has disappeared. In this work, Rabanus adapts the *Etymologiae* of Isidore of Seville.[96] In the best illustrated copy (*Cod. Casinensis*), Bacchus is shown in the presence of nine other gods, including his companion Pan.[97] Goldschmidt has shown that various elements of the illustration use classical prototypes.[98] As late as 1430, the illuminator of Palatinus 291 copied the same work of Rabanus Maurus, injecting contemporary flavor into figures which are clearly of classical descent.[99]

About 1180, the abbot of St. Denis gave his monks a fountain whose upper basin was oddly decorated with thirty heads of pagan gods, heroes of fables and ancient allegories.[100] Among these are Ceres, Bacchus, Pan, Jupiter, Juno, Thetis, Neptune, Paris and Helen, the elements, and the wolf and the lamb of fables. The inscription reads "*Labrum quod est in propilaeo fani diui Dionysii.*"[101] Adhémar rightly stresses the singularity of this composition of gods and heroes in the interior of an abbey cloister, a place destined for meditation and prayer.[102] He explains the presence of mythology in a religious context as a product of the new classicizing preference of the Scholastics.[103]

Throughout Europe, Roman monuments remained for medieval artists and patrons to view. These remains could be used as models in each case for historically circumscribed reasons, as in the ninth century. A century later, a Gothic artist, working on the portal of the Auxerre Cathedral,[104] imitated the pose of a faun from a Gallo-Roman pilaster in nearby Arlon.[105] Perhaps he was intrigued or challenged by the ancient work or perhaps he envisioned it as embodying the struggle of virtue over vice. For whichever reason, he sculpted a satyr killing a goat and Hercules with the lion in the midst of biblical scenes on the lower jamb of the portal.[106]

The one *spolium* which might consciously invoke Dionysos as Christ can be found on the thirteenth-century bookcover of the gospel of St. Lebuinus. A Roman gem of Bacchus set in the center of the cover of the Utrecht gospel shows continued appreciation, if not for the god himself, for the potency of classical images in general.[107] This chalcedony gem was probably carved between the first and third centuries of the Roman era, provenance unknown. The pudgy face of Bacchus is crowned with ivy leaves and schematic flowers bound by fillets and is quite similar to the depiction in a third- to fourth-century textile from Egypt.[108] Placed at the center of the cross, it recalls the identification of Christ with Dionysos one sees in the Kyranides lapidary, which was translated into Latin in the twelfth century and hence accessible to readers in the West.[109] One should note that other ancient gems were used similarly.[110] Despite ecclesiastical attempts to eradicate the pagan gods, Dionysos seems to have been revived, perhaps in his Christological aspect, in the thirteenth century, to which the Utrecht gospel may testify.

Through the agency of the Carolingian authors and the Ottonian collectors and copyists, works were brought to the West to inform the court and to strengthen the connection with antiquity inherent in imperial political ideologies. Moreover, the copying of illustrated manuscripts kept mythological images available. In the educated circles of the Scholastics, rare depictions of the gods of Virgil and Ovid were produced, while *spolia* and *mirabilia* were incorporated into Christian settings.

Notes

1. I should like to thank Charles Segal of the Department of Classics, Brown University and James Trilling of the Rhode Island School of Design for reading this essay and for adding their comments and suggestions. I also wish to thank

my husband Peter Allen and our daughter Emeline for their support and patience during this project.

2. Coptic *quft* or *qubt* from an Arabic corruption of the Greek word for Egypt, Αἴγυπτος has frequently been used to designate all Greco-Roman and medieval textiles, from late Roman to Islamic times, which were found in Egypt. The term groups together different styles, periods, and places of manufacture, although various schools and regional styles have been discerned. Since pagan and Christian practices coexisted during the fourth and fifth centuries (A. Momigliano, *The Conflict between Paganism and Christianity in the Fourth Century* [1963]), it is helpful to divide the textiles into late Roman and early Byzantine groups wherever possible (J. Trilling, *Roman Heritage: Textiles from Egypt and the Eastern Mediterranean 300–600 AD* [1982], 11), although for convenience I shall use the designation Coptic textiles for this catalogue. Although this study focuses on the medium of "Coptic" textiles, images from other media, such as limestone, bone, and ivory reliefs, repoussés, frescoes, and marble sarcophagi are occasionally discussed as *comparanda*.

3. F. Matz, *Die dionysischen Sarkophage (Die antiken Sarkophagreliefs* Bd. 4, T. 1-4; 1977), cat. no. 258.

4. Two fragments depict Dionysos, a maenad and satyr from a large composition, *Survival of the Gods: Classical Mythology in Medieval Art,* an exhibition by the Department of Art, Brown University, 1987, cat. nos. 6 and 7, pp. 38-41.

5. Frequently the hangings predate their burials and the ornaments antedate the garments onto which they were sewn. Dating them is difficult since most were dissociated from their archaeological context.

6. One example would be the large curtain decorated by medallions in the Brown exhibition *Survival of the Gods,* cat. no. 1, p. 28.

7. These types may be seen in Ibid., cat. nos. 1 and 10, pp. 28-29, 46-47.

8. Ibid., cat. nos. 5, 8, and 9, pp. 36-37, 42-45.

9. Deborah Thompson, *Coptic Textiles in the Brooklyn Museum* (1971), 2.

10. According to A. Johnson and L. West, *Byzantine Egypt: Economic Studies* (1949), 186, an embroidered tunic from the Faiyum cost 4,000 drachmas in the early fourth century.

11. Thompson (1971), 2.

12. One example would be the large curtain decorated by medallions as in note 6, pp. 27-28.

13. Resist-dyed linen fabrics, where designs were painted onto plain woven linen instead of being woven into the material, were also a well-known Egyptian specialty (Trilling [above, note 2], 102).

14. Johnson and West (above, note 10), 119-25.

15. Another Egyptian technique was that of weaving wool loops and cutting them to produce the effect of a mosaic, such as that used on the wall hanging of the Piping Maenad, Cleveland Museum of Art no. 68.74.

16. Yet Thompson states that after the Arab Conquest the weaving of textiles completely in wool became much more common. See Thompson (above, note 9), 2. Apparently wool was produced for the domestic market only (A. Badawy, *Coptic Art and Archaeology* [1978], 283 and *Age of Spirituality* [1979], cat. no. 125).

17. J. Beckwith, "Coptic Textiles," *Chemical Industry in Basle Review* 12.133 (1959): 7; A. Geijer and E. B. Thomas, "The Viminacium Gold Tapestry" *Meddelanden*

fran Lunds Universitets Historiska Museum (1964/1965): 235. In Athenaeus *Deipnosophistai* 5 [see note 26], Dionysos is described as wearing a purple cloak with golden embroidery in the *pompe* of Ptolemy Philadelphus.

18. Brown exhibition cat. nos. 8 and 9, pp. 42–45.
19. Oxyrhynchus Papyrus 1943, 5.
20. Brown exhibition cat. nos. 3 and 4, pp. 32–35.
21. See the discussion in Brown exhibition cat. no. 7, p. 40.
22. A. D. Nock, "Notes on Ruler-Cult," *Journal of Hellenic Studies* 48 (1928): 21–43.
23. L. Cerfaux and J. Tondriau, *Un Concurrent du Christianisme: le culte des souverains dans la civilisation gréco-romaine* (1957), 193.
24. Nock (1928), 21 ff.
25. Theocritus 17.112–14.
26. Athenaeus 5.197–202.
27. B. Segall, "Tradition und Neuschöpfung in der frühalexandrinischen Kunst," *Winckelmannsprogramm* (1966), 36 ff. Walters Art Gallery, Baltimore; acc. no. 57.929D.
28. P. M. Fraser, *Ptolemaic Alexandria* (1972), 1:203.
29. Athenaeus 5.196–203, 205e.
30. Fraser (1972), 2:347 n. 118: (*Etym. Mag. s.v.* Γάλλος).
31. F. Matz, "Der Gott des Elefantenwagen," *Akademie der Wissenschaften und der Literatur in Mainz, Abhandlungen der geistes- und sozialwissenschaftlichen Klasse* 10 (1952): 731 and R. S. Poole, *British Museum Catalogue of Coins. The Ptolemies* (1883), pl. 14, 6 f.; pl. 20, 6; pl. 24, 2 f.; pl. 27, 12.
32. Fraser (1972), 2:348 n. 119.
33. A. Adriani, "Sculture del Museo Greco-Romano," *Bulletin de la Société Royale d'Archéologie d'Alexandrie* 32 (1938): 106–11.
34. Segall (above, note 27), 36 ff.
35. Ibid.
36. F. Dvornik, *Early Christian and Byzantine Political Philosophy* (1966), 1:228.
37. Dvornik (1966), 235–39.
38. Dvornik (1966), 239.
39. Fraser (above, note 28), 1:244.
40. Plutarch *Ant.* 4.
41. Fraser (above, note 28), 1:205.
42. H. B. Mattingly, *Coins of the Roman Empire in the British Museum I* (1923), pls. 1, 5, 6, 19.
43. R. S. Poole, *Catalogue of the Coins of Alexandria in the British Museum* (1892), cat. no. 339, pl. xxvii, 508, 863.
44. Letter to Themistius, 253c–254a.
45. Athenaeus 5.198c, and possibly in the Baltimore silver *kantharos* (Segall, [1966], 36 ff.).
46. Brown Exhibition cat. nos. 8, and 9, pp. 42–45.
47. Fraser (above, note 28), I, 206.
48. Whereas the public dedications to Dionysos abound during this time, private dedications do not show a particular concentration on his cult, thus reaffirming the suggestion of state propaganda cultivated by the ruling regime (Fraser [above, note 28], 1:212).

49. P. du Bourget, *Catalogue des étoffes coptes* (1964), cat. no. B24.

50. Brown exhibition cat. no. 6, pp. 38-39.

51. Dorothy P. Shepherd "A Late Classical Tapestry," *Bulletin of the Cleveland Museum of Art* 63 (1976): 309-13. Also see Caroline Houser, ed., *Dionysos and his Circle: Ancient through Modern* (Cambridge, MA: The Fogg Art Museum, Harvard University Press, 1979) cat. no. 14, and the fourth century furniture inlays in Joseph Stryzgowski; *Catalogue général des Antiquitiés Egyptiennes du Musée du Caire*, vol. XII, *Koptische Kunst*. (Leipzig: Hiersemann, 1904), 183, fig. 237, cat. no. 7089, *Early Christian and Byzantine Art* [1947], cat. no. 71.1099).

52. This imitated the *Bacchae* of Euripides at a time when the memory of Greek tragedy was declining (E. R. Dodds ed. [1960], xxix).

53. E. Kitzinger, "Notes on Early Coptic Sculpture," *Archaeologia* 87 (1938): 193.

54. *Oeuvres,* É. C. Amélineau ed. (1907), 1:382 ff.

55. Also in the sixth-century Macarius of Antaiopolis, seventh-century Moses of Abydos and Pisentios of Coptos. See A. Badawy; *Coptic Art and Archaeology* (1978), 6-7.

56. A tradition arose that the death of Pan had occurred at the moment of Christ's crucifixion. See the discussion (cat. no. 5). Moreover, there exists a twelfth-century Byzantine gold signet ring with a Roman sard intaglio depicting Pan. The collar is inscribed with words from Psalm 26, "Lord, my light and my savior, whom shall I fear?" *Jewellery, Ancient to Modern* (1979), 153, cat. no. 430.

57. F. -L. Van Cleef, "The Pseudo-Gregorian Drama *Christos Paschon* in its Relation to the Text of Euripides," *Transactions of the Wisconsin Academy of Science, Arts and Letters* 8 (1888-91): 363-78 and A. Kirchoff, "Ein Supplement zu Euripides' *Bacchen,*" *Philologus* 8 (1953): 78-93. For bibliography on the question of authorship, see (above, note 52), lvi.

58. *Christus Patiens* 1247-1619.

59. Genesis 49:10. "A prince shall not fail from Juda, nor a ruler from his thighs, until He comes for whom it is reserved; and He shall be the expectation of the Gentiles, tying His foal to the vine, washing His robe in the blood of the grape," whereas Justin Martyr states "that Bacchus was the begotten son of Jupiter and that he discovered the vine (so they place wine in his mysteries), and taught that, after he was torn apart, he ascended into heaven." *Apology* chap. 54, trans. Thomas B. Falls (1948), 92.

60. Ibid. and *Dialogue with Trypho*, chap. 69.

61. See discussion by Richard Brilliant in *Age of Spirituality* (1979), 128, fig. 17.

62. H. Jeanmaire *Dionysos* (1951), 338 ff. and D. G. Rice and John Stambaugh, *Sources for the Study of Greek Religion* (1979), 39 discusses the tradition based on Plato's *Laws*.

63. Fr. W. F. von Bissing, *Mitteilungen der deutsches Instituts für ägyptische Altertumskunde* 7 (1937), 151 n. 1 to pl. 28 a-b.

64. P. J. Nordhagen, "The Origin of Washing the Child in the Nativity Scene," *Byzantinische Zeitschrift* 54 (1961): 333 ff., and E. Kitzinger, "The Hellenistic Heritage in Byzantine Art," *Dumbarton Oaks Papers* 17 (1963): 101-3.

65. Sir Henry Stuart-Jones, *A Catalogue of the Ancient Sculptures Preserved in the Municipal Collections of Rome: The Sculptures of the Museo Capirolino* (Oxford: The Clarendon Press, 1921), 117 pl. 24.

66. E. Guimet, *Les Portraits d'Antinoé au Musée Guimet* (1912), 19-20, pl. xiii. This was dated stylistically by H. Peirce and R. Tyler, *L'Art byzantin* (1932), 1:71.

67. K. Lehmann-Hartleben and E. C. Olsen, *Dionysiac Sarcophagi in Baltimore* (1942), fig. 7. Walters Art Gallery, Baltimore; acc. no. 23.31.

68. In the *Semele Hydrophoroi* the chorus are women who have brought water for the ceremonial washing of the infant.

69. K. Weitzmann, *The Fresco Cycle from S. Maria Castelseprio* (1951), 36-38, pls. 47-48 and Nordhagen (1961), 334 and Kitzinger (1963), 102.

70. Weitzmann (1951), 36-38 and pls. 47-48; G. Carletti and L. Mirri, *Le antiche camere delle Terme di Tito* (1776), pl. xvii.

71. Weitzmann (1951), 37, pls. 47-48.

72. Guimet (above, note 66), 19-20, pl. xiii.

73. Peirce and Tyler 71, no. 102 and H. Phillipart, "De Sémélé à la Madone," Ἀρχαιολογικὴ Ἐφημερίς (1937): 256 ff. Also see the Castelseprio Annunciation, Weitzmann (1951), 46.

74. Nordhagen (above, note 64), 333.

75. *Koptische Kunst: Christentum am Nil* (1963) cat. nos. 344, 358. Kunstmuseum Düsseldorf; acc. no. 12795.

76. Ibid., acc. no. 12790.

77. R. Berliner, "Tapestries from Egypt Influenced by Theatrical Performances," *Textile Museum Journal* 1 (1964): 38.

78. J. Evans, *Magical Jewels of the Middle Ages and Renaissance, Particularly in England* (1927), 18.

79. F. De Mely, *Les Lapidaires Grecs* (1902), 3:lxviii.

80. In remedy θ, Kyranos says, "Sage, an herb that is Dionysiac.... Clary [?] is a [holy] plant of Dionysos. Among Bacchants and Maenads the shoot itself is crushed in the wine-press. It is a plant of the earth which grows for the pleasure of men.... If anyone grinds four parts of this plant and four of the stone [thyrsite] and pronounces the Dionysiac formula and throws it into a jug of wine from which everyone drinks just one cup, upon drinking they will all go off as though drunk and thankful, saying 'Lord, you make us happy'.... If you throw into the wine the right eye of a tuna and pronounce the name of Dionysos.... The Dionysiac formula is this: 'Eï, eïris; short Christ Jesus; eïē, oiōo, a e ē ï l.' The veritable name is Hē-o-su or O-ō-b. Thus Harpocration, but Kyranos thus: 'Eïa baïcheu euïleu Dionysus'"; translated from the Greek (see De Mely [1902], 22-23; his French version, 48-49).

81. T. Hackens and R. Winkes, *Love for Antiquity* (1985), 54.

82. J. Beckwith, *Coptic Sculpture: 300-1300 A.D.* (London: A. Tiranti, 1963), fig. 1.

83. Deborah Thompson (1971). The Brooklyn Museum; gift of the Long Island Historical Society; acc. no. 26.746.

84. St. Paulinus of Nola writes "that He may look down from heaven and visit the vineyard where thy right has planted, so that I may adhere to the True Vine, and live as branches not to be lopped off for the fire, but pruned to bear fruit. May He who is the Vine and our Life ..." (Letter 19.3, p. 181).

85. *Bacchae* 138 and *Milet* 6.22.

86. E. R. Dodds, *The Greeks and the Irrational* (1951), 277; *Schol. Clem. Alex.* 92 P, vol. 1, Stahlin; Photius, s.v. νεβρίζειν; Firmicus Maternus, *Err. prof. rel.* 6. 5.

87. *Age of Spirituality*, 606-7. The Metropolitan Museum of Art; The Cloisters Collection, acc. no. 50.4

88. See fifth-century marble columns from Notre Dame de la Daurade,

Toulouse, France (Metropolitan Museum of Art 21.172), the marble parapet revetment from Daphne-Harbie near Antioch (Baltimore Museum of Art 44.170A), and the sixth-century tomb of Santa Costanza, and E. R. Goodenough, *Jewish Symbols in the Greco-Roman Period* (1956).

89. Brown exhibition cat. no. 10, pp. 46-47.

90. E. Riefstahl, "A Coptic Roundel in the Brooklyn Museum," *Bulletin of the Byzantine Institute* 2 (1950): 531-40.

91. E. Kirschbaum, *The Tombs of St. Peter and St. Paul* (1959), 144, 40-42, pl. iii.

92. This is summarized by M. R. James, *The Apocryphal New Testament* (1926), 181-93.

93. Riefstahl (1950), 538-39.

94. John Beckwith, *Captic Sculpture 300-1300*. (London: A. Tiranti, 1963), cat. nos. 101 and 102.

95. On Apollo Lykeios, please see G. E. Rizzo, *Prassitele* (Milan and Rome: Treves, Treccani, Tumminelli, 1932, 79-85.

96. A. M. Amelli, *Miniature sacre e profane dell'anno 1023, illustranti l'Enciclopedia medioevale di Rabano Mauro* (1896), pl. cxii.

97. Jean Seznec *The Survival of the Gods. The Mythological Tradition and its Place in Renaissance Art and Humanism,* (Princeton University Press, Bollingen Series XXXVIII, 1972). First published as "La survivance des antiques," *Studies of the Warburg Institute XI,* (London, 1940), 66-67, fig. 65.

98. A. Goldschmidt, "Frühmittelalterliche illustrierte Enzyklopädien," *Vorträge der Bibliothek Warburg* (1923-24), 215-16.

99. Seznec (1972), 88, fig. 66. Palatine Library, Vatican; no. 291.

100. Now in the École des Beaux Arts, Paris. Nearby in the treasury were cameos with ancient heads in profile on Cistercian miniatures. J. Adhémar, *Influences antiques dans l'art du Moyen Age Français* (1939), 265 n. 3.

101. J. Adhémar, "La Fontaine de St. Denis," *Revue Archéologique I* (1936), 224-32.

102. The only imitation of the basin was the baptismal font at Coucy de Chateau (Adhémar [1939], 266 n. 1).

103. Ibid., 266.

104. Ibid., pl. 117.

105. Ibid., 214 and pl. 116 and Louise Lefrançois-Pillon, "Sculptures de la Cathédrale d'Auxerre," *La Revue de l'art chrétien* (1905), 278-80.

106. Lefrançois-Pillon (1905), 278-80. Auxerre Cathedral; lower portion of northern jamb of central portal, west facade; Conservation des Antiquités et Objets d'Art de l'Yonne (France).

107. G. A. S. Snijder, "Antique and Medieval Gems on Book Covers at Utrecht," *Art Bulletin* 14 (1932): 5 ff. Utrecht, Rijksmuseum Het Catharijneconvent, ABM hs. 1. I thank Afuri Soeda for bringing this gem to my attention.

108. O. Wulff and W. F. Volbach, *Spätantike und koptische Stoffe aus ägyptischen Grabfunden in den staatlichen Museen* Berlin (1926), pl. 2, cat. no. 9247 S.2.

109. Joan Evans, *Magical Jewels of the Middle Ages and the Renaissance* (New York: Dover Publications, Inc. 1976), 18. First published in 1926 (Oxford: The Clarendon Press).

110. Here one should mention the curious use of a blue glass (?) bead of Livia from the first century as the head of Christ in the Heimann Cross, fabricated in the eleventh century. See *Ornamenta Ecclesiae,* Kunst und Künstler der Romanik in Koln, vol. 2 (Cologne, 1985), 207, 213.

Gregory of Tours and the Classical Tradition

PAUL J. ARCHAMBAULT

Readers of Gregory of Tours' *History of the Franks* have often taken his professions of literary incompetence literally, as they have his bleak vision of the state of literary culture in sixth-century Gaul. One remembers his general preface to the *History*, written in 573:

> The culture of liberal letters having declined, or more precisely being on its way to extinction . . ., when no grammarian skilled in dialectics could be found to write down the events [of our time] either in prose or in verse, many people were complaining repeatedly about this sad situation, saying: "Woe to our time, for the pursuit of letters has perished among us, and there is not a single man to be found among the people who might set down the present events on paper." Having constantly had to listen to these and similar complaints, I could not permit the quarrels of the wicked and the life of the righteous to be consigned to oblivion, wishing to keep alive the memory of those who have gone before us and instruct those who will come after us. Although my manner of speech is unpolished [*etsi incultu effatu*], I have been encouraged by the remarks which I have heard uttered by some of our people to the effect that few people understand a philosophizing speechifier [*philosophantem rethorem*], whereas many can follow a blunt speaker [*loquentem rusticum*].[1]

This, the most famous of Gregory's prefaces, is not the only one wherein he professes uncouthness of literary style. In his preface to the *Life of Saint Martin,* he tells of a dream, which occurred three times, wherein he is standing in the basilica of Saint Martin in mid-day, looking at "many lame people crushed under the weight of diverse sicknesses." As he looks on, his mother appears to him and asks him why he is so slow to write down the things that he sees. Gregory replies: "Mother, it's no secret to you that I am unschooled in letters [*inscius litterarum*]. Stupid and illiterate that I am, how could I dare publicize such admirable deeds as these? If only Severus or Paulinus were alive, or Fortunatus were here, to describe these things. But inept as I am for these matters, I'll attract attention if I attempt to write them down." His mother responds: "Don't you realize that in our case whoever speaks so that the masses of people can understand, exactly as you are able to speak, will be considered all the more illustrious? Don't hesitate, then, and don't balk at doing this: for if you keep silent about these things it will be criminal for you." Gregory obeys.[2]

In the preface to *The Glory of the Blessed Confessors,* Gregory subjects himself to the accusations of an imaginary interlocutor: "You have no valid way of making a point when you write. . . . You cannot even make out the nouns; you confuse masculines with feminines, feminines with neuters, neuters with masculines; even the prepositions, the proper use of which is sanctioned by the authority of illustrious writers, you don't put in their proper place most of the time. You even put accusatives in the place of ablatives, and conversely ablatives in the place of accusatives. Don't you think you will look like a lazy ox trying to do gymnastic exercises, or like a weighted-down donkey trying to run circles around a team of handball players?" Gregory answers his phantom accuser by saying: "It is your work I am doing [*opus uestrum facio*], and with my plainness [*rusticitatem*] I shall set your own talent to work. What I shall have written in an uncouth, curt and obscure style, you will then be able to expand into prolix pages of clear and brilliant verse."[3]

A century ago Gregory of Tours scholars usually took these professions of "rusticitas" literally and treated Gregory's Latin in terms of its avowed aberration from the rules of classical Latin grammar. In 1872, Gabriel Monod wrote a generally sympathetic but condescending study of Gregory of Tours as historian, and agreed that Gregory was right to complain about his incapacity to write correctly, "for his irregular style, a mixture of classical turns of phrase, ecclesiastical locutions and popular speech, though it was better understood by contemporaries than a correct Latin would have been, it is not so well understood by posterity. His grammar mistakes sometimes hinder the clarity of his phrasing, and the barbarity of his language cannot possibly have failed to make his thinking obscure."[4] Max Bonnet's study of 1890, *Le Latin de Grégoire de Tours* also treated Gregory's language as an aberration from a classical norm.[5] These late nineteenth-century normative views of grammar, combined with a positivistic faith in scientific progress and a neo-Kantian conception of moral rigor have, of course, been superseded. One almost envies the classical and Eurocentric smugness that could allow a Bonnet, for example, to scold Gregory as would a severe schoolmaster and to write: "A grammatical obligation, similar in origin and in nature to a moral obligation, manifests itself in the same way. . . . He [Gregory] remained ignorant all his life, and ignorant to such a point and in such subjects that today, with our [public] instruction so widespread and the exaggerated importance that we attach precisely to some of those subjects we find it very hard to believe the facts that prove this ignorance."[6]

Godefroy Kurth's two-volume study of the Frankish period, *Etudes franques,* appearing in 1919, contained a far greater sense of historical relativism and cultural modesty than had the works of Monod and Bonnet.[7] In an article on Gregory's Latin Kurth argued that far from being unlettered and rustic, Gregory knew Vergil (to the point of quoting or alluding to the *Aeneid* a total of thirty-five times), as well as Sallust and Aulus Gellius. Gregory, Kurth concluded, had far more knowledge of the classics than Monod and Bonnet had given him credit for.[8] Kurth may have been arguing in Gregory's favor, but he accepted the same classical parameters that had been set by his nineteenth-century predecessors. Even Erich Auerbach, in spite of his most sensitive treatment of Gregory's lively but confused Latin, feels he has to apologize for the sense of decadence and decline that is to be found in the *History of the Franks,* though he hastens to add that Gregory's vitality and historical sense compensate for his linguistic aberrations:

> His style is wholly different from that of the authors of late antiquity, even the Christians among them. A complete change has taken place since the days of Ammianus and Augustine. Of course, as has often been observed, it is a decadence, a decline in culture and verbal disposition; but it is not only that. It is an awakening of the directly sensible.[9]

In the light of recent research, Gregory of Tours' rhetorical skill and classical erudition have been judged more favorably than ever. In a summary piece on recent Gregory of Tours scholarship, Wallace-Hadrill wrote that "Gregory's profession of inelegance and incompetence is . . . a well tried device and need not detain us. He shows skill in handling the rhetorical cursus, and his powerful use of dialogue is something of his own. His Latin was what he meant it to be; it was realistic. Gregory's conscientious erudition has won the admiration of many scholars, and notably of Kurth and Levillian."[10]

No matter how sympathetic the scholar, the problem of Gregory's rapport with the classical tradition has been approached pretty much from the same norms and raised pretty much in the same terms: how much of the classical tradition is present in Gregory of Tours? Practically none, answered Monod and Bonnet; but scratch the surface a bit deeper, answer Kurth, Auerbach and Wallace-Hadrill, and you will find a great many classical allusions, a great deal of erudition, and, as Auerbach puts it, a "reawakening of the directly sensible." In each of these instances, scholars have posed the problem in intertextual, what Gerard Genette calls "palimpsest," terms: scratch the surface text, and see how much of the classical tradition is in the lower textual strata.[11]

In approaching the problem of Gregory's classical competence (or incompetence) scholars have never taken note of what is surely more than literary coincidence: Gregory's professions of *rusticitas* are inevitably inserted into prefaces of works that have no doubt already been written; and these are almost always written in dialogue form.[12] In the general preface to the *History of the Franks,* Gregory dialogues with the *plerique,* who complain that there is nobody around to set down the events of their time. In the preface to the *Life of Saint Martin,* Gregory dialogues with his mother. In the *Liber de gloria beatorum confessorum,* the dialogue occurs between Gregory and somebody [*aliquis*] who might tell him that his training is that of an illiterate peasant. In each case the dialogue is with an imagined interlocutor and set up on Gregory's own terms.

This use of the dialogue form in a preface provides the writer with a rhetorically acceptable manner of refuting implicit or explicit accusations of literary incompetence.[13] Gregory was sufficiently acquainted with Martianus Capella's *De nuptiis Philologiae et Mercurii* (which he once alludes to in the *History of the Franks*)[14] to know that an exordium has served its purpose if it makes the reader *attentum, docilem,* et *beniuolum.*[15] "We make him well-disposed," Martianus writes, "in either a material or a personal way . . . — in our own person if we commend what we have done well, or if we dilute or extenuate what is bad for our cause."[16] What better rhetorical instrument could Gregory make use of than the imaginary dialogue in order to deal with his alleged *rusticitas* and to "extenuate" his literary incompetence, particularly if the extenuation brings in something of a higher order?

These higher considerations are set forth by one of the voices in each of the dialogues we have mentioned: better a *loquens rusticus* than a *philosophans rethor,* better comprehensibility than elegance, better substance than form; better, in short, *sermo humilis* than *sermo sublimis.*[17] One preface of Gregory's, that of the *Libri miraculorum,* best shows that Gregory's use of the dialogue form in his prefaces was meant to oppose not merely two writing styles but two attitudes toward history and culture. No text of

Gregory's confronts Christian and classical pagan literature more dramatically than this one, especially in light of the very conscious allusion to Jerome's twenty-second letter in the opening sentence:

> The priest Jerome, a good doctor of the Church second only to the Apostle Paul, recalls how he was led before the tribunal of the Eternal Judge, and there submitted to a long torture because he had too often enjoyed reading the tricks of Cicero or the lies of Vergil. He confessed to the great Lord of all, before the holy angels, that from then on he would never read these things nor touch them again, unless they be judged worthy of God and fit for the edification of the Church. . . . For it does not behoove us to recall false fables, or to follow the wisdom of philosophers inimical to God, lest God taking notice, we be liable to eternal punishment; and my intention being to proclaim a few of the miracles of the saints, which up to now have remained hidden, I don't wish to be trapped, or tossed in these nets. It is not the flight of Saturn, nor the ire of Juno, nor the dalliances of Jove nor the revenge of Neptune nor the scepters of Aeolus that I plan to recall here; nor shall I commemorate the wars, shipwrecks, or reigns of Aeneas and his successors. I shall gloss over Cupid's mission, the charms of Ascanius; Dido's wedding, her tears, her bitter end; I'll not talk about the somber fore-court of Pluto, nor the rape of Proserpine, nor about the triple head of Cerberus. I'll not revive the speeches of Anchises, nor the wiles of the Ithacan [Ulysses], nor the tricks of Achilles nor the lies of Sinon. Nor shall I recount the advice of Laocoon, the strength of Amphitryo's son [Hercules] nor the encounters, flights, and final end of Janus. Nor shall I discourse about the shape of the Eumenides or of other assorted monsters, nor about the accounts of all other fables, which such and such an author has deceitfully recounted, or depicted in heroic verse. Rather, looking upon these things as if they were built upon the sand and soon to fall into ruin [*tanquam super arenam locata, et cito ruitura conspiciens*], let us go back, rather, to the divine miracles of the Gospel, of which John the Evangelist spoke when he said: "In the beginning was the Word."[18]

No preface, perhaps no text of Gregory's oeuvre illustrates his ambiguous attitude toward classical literature better than this one. This live, still fascinating but essentially dying tradition, he says, is to be perceived as built on sand and on the verge of ruin. To be sure, these titillating scenes from classical antiquity continue to exercise their hold, perhaps even to obsess him, else why should he describe them so graphically? If Gregory identifies as closely as he does with the Jerome of the twenty-second letter, it is no doubt that, like Jerome, he too may have to answer, in the waste of a delirious imagination, to God's accusation that he is a Ciceronian, not a Christian.[19]

Unlike the three prefaces discussed earlier, Gregory's preface to the *Libri miraculorum* is not constructed in dialogue form. It is, rather, written with conscious reference to Jerome's letter, which is implicitly dialogic in form and which contains the famous fragment of dialogue between Jerome and God in the desert.[20] Like Jerome's letter, the preface to the *Libri miraculorum* deals with the confrontation between classical and Christian literature, an issue still very much alive in the monastic schools of Gregory's time.[21] Like Jerome, Gregory seems slightly guilt-ridden by his inability to expel a total fascination with the beautiful lies (*fallacias*) of classical antiquity. Gregory's is the ambiguity so familiar to the great Christian educators of the earlier Patristic age who, like Basil, thought that the ears of Christian mariners should be stopped to the Sirens' song of classical literature, but that they, like Odysseus, might allow themselves to listen to these songs provided they were well secured to the mast of Christian faith.[22]

Gregory's ambiguous attitude toward and perception of the classical tradition raises the question of determining how much of that tradition is not only explicitly but implicitly present in the very forms of his own writing. It has already been noted that Gregory's prefaces follow the rules of *captatio beneuolentiae*, as set forth in a classical rhetorical manual of his time. But Gregory had also unconsciously absorbed far more of the classical rhetorical tradition than he ever would have suspected, particularly with regard to the art of historiography itself. As I have argued in another paper, the *History of the Franks* subscribes to a rhetorical mode found in much of classical historiography, in that it is written in the dominant mode of first-person discourse punctuated with third-person narrative, rather than the other way around. Like great historiographies such as those of Thucydides and Herodotus, the *History of the Franks* assumes from the very first pages the dominant mode of the first person, with large stretches of third person narrative.[23]

Gregory had another point in common with the classical historians: he took great pride in what he had written. One of the residually classical sides to his personality might perhaps be attributed to the patrician, senatorial rank which he came from: in spite of his protests of *rusticitas*, he expressly directed that not a single line of any of his works be destroyed. In the last chapter of the *History of the Franks*, he writes:

I have written ten books of history, seven books of miracles, one on the lives of the Fathers; I have written a book of commentaries on the Psalter, also a book on the Offices of the Church. And although I have written these books in a rather inelegant style [*stilo rusticiori*], I adjure all the priests of the Lord . . . if you are never to be condemned with the Devil as you withdraw from confusion from this Judgment—never allow these books to be effaced or rewritten, as if you were reading some parts and skipping some; but let them all remain whole and unblemished with you exactly as we left them. Even if, O Priest of God, whoever you are, our Martianus [Capella] has instructed you in the liberal arts,. . . even if you have been so drilled in these skills that my style is uncouth to you [*ut tibi stilus noster sit rusticus*], even then I beg you not to destroy what I've written. If you like something in this, however, I have no objection to your setting them to verse, but keep my work intact.[24]

Even in this farewell passage Gregory is (perhaps unconsciously) perpetuating a rule of classical rhetoric which allowed writers from time to time to list and comment on their lifetime's work. This rhetorical tradition, which Georg Misch called "Scriftsteller-Autobiographie," allowed scientific writers and orators to do what we might today call an intellectual autobiography.[25] Classical antecedents were well known. In *De diuinatione* Cicero had given a summary and critical evaluation of the major works of his which have allowed his fellow citizens to pursue in the way of noblest learning.[26] Around AD 190, Galen had written two short treatises summarizing the titles and contents of his own works, one called Περὶ τῶν ἰδίων βιβλίων γραφή (*On His Own Books*) and the other Περὶ τῆς τάξεως τῶν ἰδίων βιβλίων πρὸς Εὐγένιον (*On the Order of His Own Books, to Eugenius*).[27]

But Gregory managed to give even that classical tradition of *Schrifsteller-Autobiographie* a Christian twist. Classical authors like Cicero or Galen might have listed and commented upon their own works, but would they have consigned to hell anyone, even a bishop of God, who dared destroy a single line of theirs? No doubt Gregory found this type of entreaty in the *Church History* of Bishop Eusebius, who had himself taken the formula from St. Irenaeus, who was but imitating the formula of anathema to be found in the conclusion of the Book of Revelation. Looking back at his great work, which now lies finished before him, Gregory considered the possibility that some day a successor of his to the bishopric of Tours might find the subject matter of his work pleasurable but be put off by its artless presentation. If such a schooled prelate does arise,

Gregory will leave it to his discretion to decide whether to give the great subject of his work a more artful treatment, in verse form if possible. In this regard Gregory is earnestly clinging to a well-known classical opinion according to which artlessly written books, whether memoirs or commentaries, were considered raw material for a rhetor whose business it was to present them artfully. But one immediately notices how time has changed! If in Antiquity a writer of political memoirs pointed to the literary plainness of his work, that usually was one of those conventional expressions of modesty which meant exactly the opposite. With Gregory the whole traditional antithesis between what is "artless" and what is rhetorically accomplished is ultimately of no consequence. What really concerns him is the truth and the authentic transmission of the story he is telling. At a time when the chief concern of the Church in Gaul is to guard against fragmentation by combating the teachers of erroneous doctrine, especially the Arians, it is not at all contradictory that Gregory should write a history that he wants transmitted word for word;[28] and whether his disclaimers about the artlessness of his style are due to conflict, complex, or rhetorical modesty is an academically interesting question; but Gregory would surely have found it irrelevant.

Notes

1. Gregory of Tours, *Historiarum Libri Decem,* ed. Rudolph Buchner, 2 vols. (Berlin: Deutscher Verlag der Wissenschaften, 1955), 1:2. Unless otherwise indicated, all references to the Latin text of the *History of the Franks* will be to this edition. All English translations are my own.
2. "Epistola in Quatuor Libros de Virtutibus Sancti Martini Episcopi," in *Gregorii Turonensis Episcopi Opera Omnia, Patrologiae Cursus Completus,* ed. J. P. Migne (Paris: Petit-Montrouge, 1849), 71.911.
3. "Liber de Gloria Beatorum Confessorum," *Patrologiae Cursus Completus,* 71.829-30.
4. Gabriel Monod, *Etudes critiques sur les sources de l'histoire mérovingienne, Première partie: Introduction, Grégoire de Tours, Marius d' Avenches* (Paris: Librairie A. Franck, 1872), 110-11. Compare this other condescending judgment, 120: "Il est soumis aux illusions d'une imagination sensible à l'excès, comme il arrive fatalement à une époque où la foi est vive et où la science est morte."
5. Max Bonnet, *Le Latin de Grégoire de Tours* (Paris: Hachette, 1896), esp. 1-76. Gregory's Latin is treated throughout Bonnet's treatise as a charming but reprehensible deviation from absolute rule.
6. *Le Latin de Grégoire de Tours,* 43-44: "L'obligation grammaticale, semblable d'origine et de nature à l'obligation morale, se manifeste aussi de la même manière. Bien inférieure en dignité, elle n'est pas moins réelle." Cf. p. 76: "Il est resté ignorant toute sa vie, et ignorant à tel point et en de telles matières que de nos

jours, avec notre instruction si répandue . . . on a beaucoup de peine à croire les faits qui prouvent cette ignorance."

7. G. Kurth, *Etudes franques*, 2 vols. (Paris: H. Champion, 1919).

8. *Etudes franques*, 1:1-29.

9. E. Auerbach, *Mimesis*, trans. Willard R. Trask (Princeton: Princeton University Press, 1951; repr., 1968), 93-94.

10. J. M. Wallace-Hadrill, "The Work of Gregory of Tours in the Light of Modern Research," in *The Long-Haired Kings* (London: Methuen & Co., Ltd., 1962), 49-70.

11. Gerard Genette, *Palimpsestes: La Littérature au second degré* (Paris: Seuil, 1982). To paraphrase Genette (8), critics from Monod to Wallace-Hadrill have studied the problem of the transtextual relations between Gregory and the classical tradition in terms of *explicit* intertextuality only (references, allusions, etc.).

12. Gregory's prefaces have been edited and translated into English as separate pieces by William C. McDermott, in *Monks, Bishops, and Pagans: Christian Culture in Gaul and Italy* (Philadelphia: University of Pennsylvania Press, 1949; repr., 1975), 129-39.

13. According to Aristotle (*Rhetoric* 3.15.2-6), the exordium is the proper moment for a speaker to clear away attacks by accusers. Each of Gregory's prefaces is concerned with the refutation of an explicit accusation, usually assigned to an imaginary "other."

14. *Historiarum libri decem* 10.31 (Buchner 2:414): "Quod si te, o sacerdos Dei, quicumque es, Martianus noster septem disciplinis erudiuit. . . ."

15. Martianus Capella, *De nuptiis Philologiae et Mercurii*, ed. James Willis (Leipzig: Teubner, 1913), 545: "Exordium [orationis initium] est noscendae causae praeparans auditorem; eius uirtutes sunt tres: ut attentum, ut docilem, ut beniuolum faciat auditorem."

16. *De nuptiis* 545: "beniuolum aut a re aut a persona facimus, a persona autem aut nostra aut iudicum aut aduersariorum: a nostra, si quod fauorabile gessimus commendamus aut si quod obest causae diluimus uel extenuamus."

17. See Erich Auerbach, "Sermo Humilis," in *Literary Language and its Public in Late Latin Antiquity and in the Middle Ages*, trans. Ralph Manheim (London: Routledge and Kegan Paul, 1965), 27-66. In Christian literature throughout the Middle Ages, *sermo humilis* is victorious over *sermo sublimis* because it is, ultimately, the language of God. The leading idea in Auerbach's chapter on the subject was suggested to him by Benvenuto da Imola, the commentator on Dante: "Sermo diuinus est suauis et planus, non altus et superbus sicut sermo Virgilii et poetarum" (66).

18. Gregory of Tours, "Libri Miraculorum: Prooemium," in *Patrologiae Cursus Completus*, 71.705-6.

19. Cf. Saint Jerome, *Select Letters*, trans. F. A. Wright (London: William Heinemann, Ltd.; New York: G. P. Putnam's Sons, 1933), 124-29 and esp. 126. "Ciceronianus es, non Christianus."

20. Jerome's twenty-second letter (written in AD 384) is addressed to Eustochium, a young Christian woman of the Roman aristocracy, and assumes Eustochium's (spiritual) presence not merely as listener but as interlocutor (Jerome, *Select Letters*, 52-158). Jerome frequently puts first-person statements into Eustochium's mouth so that he can "respond" to them, e.g., 55: "You may say . . . what reward do I receive for this?"

21. Pierre Riché, *Education et culture dans l'occident barbare: VI-VIII* siècles* (Paris: Seuil, 1962), esp. 236–54. For an excellent study of that confrontation up to the early fifth century, see H. I. Marrou, *Historie de l'éducation dans l'antiquité*, 2 vols. (Paris: Seuil, 1948), 2:127–47.

22. Basil the Great, "To Young Men, on How They Might Derive Profit from Pagan Literature," in *Saint Basil. The Letters*, 4 vols., trans. R. J. Deferrari and M. R. P. McGuire (Cambridge, Mass.: Harvard University Press; London: W. Heinemann, Ltd., 1961), 388–89. Basil's main point is that much usefulness for the soul is to be derived from good pagan literature, but that when it is wicked, Christian young men should stop their ears "no less than Odysseus did, when he avoided the songs of the Sirens." Of course, Basil knew his *Odyssey* (12.39) well enough to realize that Odysseus had himself tied to the mast so as to *hear* the Sirens' song!

23. I am borrowing Gérard Genette's distinction between *discours* and *récit*, in "Frontières du récit," *Figures II* (Paris: Seuil, 1969), 49–69, and esp. 61–66. Ancient historiography assumed the dominant mode of first-person discourse, because good historical writing was assumed to require the highest rhetorical qualities (see Cicero, *De Oratore* 2.15.62). Of Thucydides Cicero said: "Omnes dicendi artificio, mea sententia, facile uicit" (*De Oratore* 26.13.55).

24. *Historiarum Libri Decem* 10.31 (Bucher 2:414).

25. Georg Misch, *A History of Autobiography in Antiquity*, trans. E. W. Davies, 2 vols. (Cambridge, Mass.: Harvard University Press, 1951), 1:326–39.

26. Cicero, *De Diuinatione* 2.1.

27. "Galeni de Libris Propriis Liber," in *Claudii Galeni Opera Omnia*, 20 vols., ed. C. G. Kühn (Hildesheim: Georg Olms Verlagsbuchhandlung, 1965), 19:8–48; "Galeni de Ordine Librorum Suorum ad Eugenium," 19:49–61.

28. For a discussion of the *History of the Franks* as "Schriftsteller Autobiographie," see Georg Misch, *Geschichte der Autobiographie*, 8 vols. (Frankfurt-am-Main: G. Schulte-Bulmke, 1955–67), 2:2. Hälfte, *Das Mittelalter: Die Frühzeit*, 366–74.

An Early Humanist Invective Against Speculative Grammar

MONIKA ASZTALOS

In the arts faculty of the medieval university, grammar was taught as a theoretical science. The grammarians did not teach the students how to express themselves correctly in Latin, but how to establish the universal features of language. Only by leaving aside the practical use of a language and investigating its universal and unchangeable causes could grammar live up to the Aristotelian definition of a speculative science.[1]

This theoretical bent is apparent in medieval commentaries on Priscian's *Institutiones grammaticae*, the grammatical textbook that followed the study of the more elementary Donatus in the arts curriculum. Robert Kilwardby, for example, who wrote his commentary around 1270, ignores most of Priscian's examples and concentrates instead on his general rules and definitions. Kilwardby's contemporary, Boethius of Dacia, complains in the introduction to his Priscian commentary that the value of the *Institutiones* is limited, since Priscian does not explain the causes of grammatical constructions but just corroborates them with authoritative statements of grammarians of Antiquity.[2]

In the fourteenth century, Priscian's *Institutiones* was replaced as a textbook and consequently as an object of commentary in certain universities by two grammars composed around 1200 in Latin verse: the *Doctrinale* of Alexander of Villedieu, which was based on Aristotle's doctrine on four causes and therefore more suitable for a philosophical approach to language, and the *Grecismus* of Eberhard of Béthune.[3] These works were both prescribed in the fourteenth century in the statutes of Paris and other universities that followed the Paris praxis.[4]

Boethius of Dacia is the first known representative of the so-called Modistic theory of grammar. According to the Modists, words are signs of mental concepts which in turn represent the objects of the real world. Put in modistic terminology, the *modi significandi* of words correspond to the *modi intelligendi* of concepts which in turn correspond the the *modi essendi* of things. The passage quoted earlier from Boethius of Dacia shows that the object of this kind of grammar, the so-called speculative grammar, was to investigate the causes of the observed grammatical forms and constructions. It concerned itself with general meanings, the ways in which words signify, that is to say with grammatical categories such as case, gender and tense.[5]

It seems that no important contributions were made to Modistic theory after Thomas of Erfurt around 1300, and it thus reached its maturity in only thirty years. During the fourteenth century the theory was attacked because of the ever-increasing complication of a terminological network that could not conceal the fact that the claimed correspondences between language, concepts and reality were not unproblematic.

The heaviest criticism came from the Nominalists, among others from Peter of Ailly in the last quarter of the fourteenth century. In his *Destructiones modorum significandi* he proves it unnecessary to posit the existence of any *modi significandi* beside the sign (the written or spoken word or the mental concept) and the thing signified.[6]

In spite of this criticism, lectures on Modistic theory were given until the sixteenth century, even if the theory was not enriched by any innovations, and its complex and intricate terminology made it an easy target for the attacks of the Humanists. But in their struggle against the Modists the Humanists in no way joined the army of the Nominalists. While the latter fought with the arms of their opponents by taking up arguments for the existence of *modi significandi* and proving them to lead to absurdities, the Humanists on the whole made no attempts to refute the Modistic theories, but simply proposed an educational reform where the philosophical approach to grammar would be replaced altogether by the study of the classical authors.[7]

This reform movement did not take place without opposition from members of the arts faculties of different universities. It was not only the teaching of grammar that was at stake, but the whole arts curriculum, since the use of logic in the first of the trivial sciences had hitherto provided a useful base for the study of logic and philosophy later on in the curriculum.[8] The concrete result of the Humanists' opposition to logic in grammar was that speculative grammar was no longer taught at the universities. The textbooks of Alexander of Villedieu and Eberhard of Béthune were also replaced by that of Priscian.

This new approach to the study of grammar originated in Italy, where Lorenzo Valla wrote his pioneer work *Elegantiae linguae Latinae* in 1444. At the end of the fifteenth century Germany became an important center for the reform movement.⁹ In his article "Logical Grammar, Grammatical Logic, and Humanism in Three German Universities,"¹⁰ Terrence Heath has described the development of the reform in Germany and its repercussions in three South German universities: Freiburg-im-Breisgau, Ingolstadt and Tübingen. He claims that in Northern Europe the reform followed a route that initially differed in some respects from the Italian movement. By editing a manuscript which has hitherto received little attention,¹¹ I have been able to refine Heath's picture and, if my assumptions prove to be correct, to provide further documentation as to what was actually going on in and around the arts faculties of Southern Germany in a period of radical change.

The manuscript in question once belonged to the Benedictine library in Seeligenstadt, whence it was transferred to Hanau during the Thirty Years War in order to remain safe from the pillaging Swedes. By one of fate's ironies, it was later given to a Swede who added it to the university library of Uppsala, where it is now found among the many manuscripts that were secured as war booty during the Thirty Years War from different European libraries.

The manuscript of 173 folios is an anonymous Latin grammar written after 1478, but not much later than 1500, by a Humanist, probably from Southern Germany. The *terminus post quem* is given by the author's quotations of the Italian Humanist Niccolò Perotti's *Cornucopiae,* which was completed in 1478. The illustrations of the manuscript and the watermarks of the paper point towards the 1490s. The German origin is assumed because of the many South German geographical names that figure as examples in grammatical constructions and of the Frankish dialect used in the German glosses.

This anonymous Latin grammar is based on the first sixteen books of Priscian's *Institutiones* which circulated separately during the middle ages under the name of *Priscianus maior.* The sections dealing with the eight parts of speech contain comprehensive Latin vocabularies, often provided with etymological annotations, explanations in Latin, and German translations. The Latin words in the vocabularies are often exemplified with quotations, mostly from classical Latin literature. A great number of the quotations are in fact taken from Priscian's *Institutiones.*

In the article mentioned above, Terrence Heath claims that the reorientation in grammar teaching in Northern Europe began in the famous schools of the Brethren of the Common Life in the Netherlands and Rhine Valley. An important center was Deventer, where teachers such as Alexander Hegius tried to revise the indigestible commentaries on Alexander's *Doctrinale.* Heath traces the beginnings of the reform back to Hegius' 1486 treatise *Inuectiua in modos significandi*, where he attacks the Modists by claiming that he who cannot speak or write correctly is unworthy of the name grammarian, no matter how much he talks about *modi significandi*.[12]

The author of the Uppsala manuscript gives detailed pedagogical instructions to the reader, who is supposed to be teaching grammar, explaining not only *what* should be taught but also *how* it should be taught. Like Alexander Hegius he launches some very sharp invectives against the Modists, and like most of the Humanists he makes no attempt to present a serious criticism of speculative grammar. Instead he rejects it on the ground that the subtle definitions cause dizziness, vertigo and nausea in the students and serve neither the acquisition of knowledge nor of scholarly honor.[13] In his eagerness to prove how the Modists destroy the sound Latin language, he produces a tirade in which he mixes metaphors to the extent that the Latin is hardly understandable: "In the first place the teacher shall avoid the fat and greasy definitions, which are so overfed that they produce nausea, and with which schoolmasters all over the world hitherto used to pollute and blacken the minds of the pupils as with a disgusting soot."[14]

The attempts of the Brethren of the Common Life to revise the *Doctrinale* naturally proved to be unsuccessful in the long run, since its logical framework was irreconcilable with the anti-logical approach of the Humanists. Nevertheless, the *Doctrinale* was not abandoned in the German universities, where the Brethren were very influential, before the beginning of the sixteenth century. Many of the Italian Humanists, on the other hand, had realized at a very early stage the incompatibility between the *Doctrinale* and their own outlook, and had taken the consequences by rejecting Alexander without further ado.[15]

The author of the Uppsala manuscript sides completely with the Italians on this point. He makes extensive use of Donatus, Servius, and especially Priscian, while Alexander is only quoted twice. He also quotes many of the Italian Humanist grammarians: Christoforo Landino, Giovanni Tortelli, Gasparino Barzizza, Niccolò Perotti, and, of course, Lorenzo Valla.[16] The abundant use of Italian works can be explained by the fact that Italian grammars became very popular in German universities at the end of the fifteenth century.[17] It thus seems that the author of our manuscript picked up the new Italian ideas at some Southern German university and delivered an attack on the Modists at approximately the same time (possibly even earlier) as Alexander Hegius, who has hitherto been regarded as the initiator of the reform in Germany. Heath described the teaching of the Brethren of the Common Life as an initial stage of the reform movement, but the Uppsala manuscript seems to indicate that Italian ideas could influence German universities independently of the Brethren.

It is possible to find more evidence in our manuscript of direct Italian influence. Terrence Heath points out that the grammatical works of Alexander Hegius and other Brethren of the Common Life have a clearly devotional character with many quotations from religious texts, and that they retain a moral standard by excluding the "amorous" poets.[18] Here again our author follows Italian praxis with an emphasis on classical examples, and he gives as many as thirty-one examples of grammatical constructions taken from Ovid's *Ars amatoria* and *Remedia amoris*, amorous poems if anything. As mentioned earlier, he often uses the same Latin examples as Priscian, but none of the examples from Ovid are to be found in the *Institutiones*. They obviously reflect his own reading preferences.

There is also evidence in the Uppsala manuscript that the author probably studied at a German university in the 1460s. The verb *restinguo* 'extinguish' is accompanied by a quotation from Sallust containing that word, and by the following remark: "Here magister Jacobus Publicii said in his lecture on Sallust that the verb *restinguam* can signify opposite things, so that it can signify indifferently *ussleschen* (extinguish) or *anczonden* (set on fire)."[19] This passage is obviously not a literary quotation but a report from a lecture on Sallust by the Spanish Humanist Jacobus Publicius. We know that Jacobus introduced classical literature into Germany and that during the period 1464-1470 he lectured in different German universities, such as Frankfurt, Basel, Louvain, Cologne, and Vienna. We also know that he had an interest in Sallust: in 1458 he asked Johannes Serra in Toulouse for an interpretation of two passages in Sallust's *Bellum Catilinae*. We can thus assume that the author of the Uppsala manuscript was active in some German university where he heard the visiting scholar and Humanist Jacobus Publicius lecturing on Sallust.[20]

The university connection of our author is further corroborated by the fact that he uses as grammatical examples the names of several towns in Germany, Bohemia, and the Low Countries where universities were founded at the end of the fourteenth century or in the fifteenth century: Mainz, Basel, Erfurt, Louvain, Würzburg, and Trier.

It is tempting to link the grammar of our manuscript to the arts faculty of some South German university. The only indication of the purpose of the manuscript is given in the instructions to the teacher, where the pupil is referred to as *nobilis puer*, which seems to indicate that the grammar was written on behalf of a nobleman for the teaching of his son. Here again we can find evidence that ties the text to the German universities. Many of them were in fact founded by dukes, and among them Ingolstadt provides an especially interesting example.[21] Johannes Turmair, also called Aventinus, was in 1508 appointed teacher for the duke of Wittelsbach's young sons Ernst and Ludwig, and in 1517 he published an expanded version of a text he had produced for their instruction in grammar. This Latin grammar was used as a textbook at the university of Ingolstadt for the next twenty years. The parallels with the Uppsala manuscript are striking: like our author, Aventinus used German, and drew grammatical charts and tables to facilitate the instruction. We must also keep in mind that the beginners at the university were not grown up, but boys of thirteen to fourteen years. In the statutes for the elementary grammar school, so-called pedagogium, at the university of Tübingen it was prescribed at the end of the fifteenth century that pupils who did not make progress would be physically punished, though not so much if they were ignorant in logic as if they were deficient in grammar.[22] On the whole it seems that the abolition of speculative grammar in the arts curriculum must have been a considerable relief for the young pupils. The author of the Uppsala manuscript refers to the definitions, divisions, and *modi significandi* as ferocious instruments of torture, an expression which is later echoed in Erasmus' famous complaint that in his youth pupils were tortured with *modi significandi* and "questions in virtue of what," *quaestiunculis ex qua ui,* while learning nothing but how to express themselves badly.[23]

The pedagogical zeal of our anonymous author is also shown in his acknowledgement of the difficulty of explaining metalinguistic notions to children and, not least, in the illustrations of the manuscript. The author consciously makes use of symbolic pictures to fortify the memory of the pupil: musical notes with different values are used to indicate long and short syllables of Latin words, death's heads and bones are used to indicate nonexistent forms such as imperative in the past tense, and the picture of a profusely bleeding eye pierced by a nail probably deterred any pupil from ever using a vocative form of *tuus*.[24] There are illustrations of hands with five case forms written on the five fingers. Only left hands are reproduced, probably because the pupil was supposed to write the forms in his own left hand. The author also remarks that the pupil shall constantly consult the notes on his hand.[25]

The emphasis on mnemotechnical devices and the use of frightening or amusing pictures to retain the attention of the pupil reflect the new emphasis on rhetoric among the trivial sciences at the cost of logic.

To sum up: Manuscript C 678 in Uppsala appears to be one of the earliest known documents of the grammatical reform that began in Germany at the end of the fifteenth century and lasted into the first decade of the sixteenth century. Its content shows a complete assimilation of the ideas of Italian Humanists at a time when most known documents in Germany still exhibit the characteristics of the teaching of the Brethren of the Common Life. The manuscript may also represent or reflect the grammar teaching at some young and dynamic German university founded by a duke. The teaching it reveals stands out as radical both in content and methods at a time when the unitary character of scholasticism was just beginning to break up and grammar was no longer seen as an introduction to logic and philosophy but to the study of the classics.

Notes

1. See J. Pinborg, *Die Entwicklung der Sprachtheorie im Mittelalter* (Münster Westfalen, 1967), 25.

2. *Boethii Daci Opera. Modi significandi siue Quaestiones super Priscianum maiorem*, ed. J. Pinborg and H. Roos, vol. 4 of *Corpus Philosophorum Danicorum Medii Aeui* (Copenhagan, 1969), 39.

3. See Ch. Thurot, *Extraits de divers manuscrits latins* (Paris, 1869; Unveränderter Nachdruck Frankfurt a. Main, 1964), 96-102.

4. In his bull *Parens scientiarum* from 1231, Gregory IX decreed that the masters of arts should always lecture on Priscian, and the statutes from 1252 and 1255 lay down that both *Priscianus maior* and *minor*, i.e., the first sixteen and the last two books of the *Institutiones*, should be lectured on. According to a document from before 1350, the artists had to attend lectures on Priscian at least three times during their period of studies. But the statutes of 1366 no longer mention Priscian, only the *Doctrinale* of Alexander of Villedieu and the *Grecismus* of Eberhard of Béthune. See *Chartularium Vniuersitatis Parisiensis*, ed. H. Denifle and Ae. Chatelain (Paris, 1889-97), 1: n. 79, n. 201, n. 246; 2: n. 1185; 3: n. 1319. In the case of the university of Toulouse, which was founded on the model of Paris, we can determine more closely when this change took place. The statutes for the Arts faculty of 1309 and 1313 mention only Priscian as a grammatical textbook, whereas a document from 1329 also includes Alexander's *Doctrinale* and Eberhard's *Grecismus*. See M. Fournier, *Statuts et privilèges des universités françaises* (Paris, 1890), 1: nn. 542, 544, 557. See also nn. 555 and 798.

5. Boethius of Dacia complains in the same passage about the limitations of Priscian, and it may be complaints of this sort that led to the change in the arts faculty of Paris, where Boethius was active and which remained the main center of the Modists. Oxford, on the other hand, never became a center of Modistic grammar theory, and therefore it is not surprising that its statutes only mention Priscian, never Alexander of Villedieu or Eberhard of Béthune. On speculative grammar, see Pinborg, *Die Entwicklung*; idem, *Logik und Semantik im Mittelalter*, (Stuttgart, 1972); G. L. Bursill-Hall, *Speculative Grammar of the Middle Ages* (Hague, 1972); R. W. Hunt, *The History of Grammar in the Middle Ages*, ed. G. L. Bursill-Hall (Amsterdam, 1980).

6. Pinborg, *Die Entwicklung* (see note 1), 202-7.

7. Ibid., 210-12.

8. T. Heath, "Logical Grammar, Grammatical Logic, and Humanism in Three German Universities," *Studies in the Renaissance* 18 (1971): 28 ff.

9. See E. Ising, *Die Herausbildung der Grammatik der Volkssprachen in Mittel- und Osteuropa. Studien über den Einfluss der lateinischen Elementargrammatik des Aelius Donatus De octo partibus orationis Ars minor* (Berlin, 1970), 53 f.

10. Ibid., 53 f.

11. University Library of Uppsala, C 678. See B. Stolt, "Das Werk eines pädagogischen Genies: die Ars minor des Donat im Codex Ups. C 678," *Daphnis* 8, no. 2 (1979): 309-20. It is misleading however to describe C 678 as a commentary on Donat's *Ars minor,* since it is based on the *Priscianus maior,* from which it also takes a great number of grammatical examples, whereas Donatus is only quoted a few times. I have prepared an edition of the text which will be published in Stockholm in 1989 together with a facsimile reproduction of the manuscript. The edition includes introductions on the date and origin of the manuscript as well as its sources and ideological context by myself, on its history and pedagogical value by B. Stolt, and on the German glosses by A. Stedje.

12. Heath, 17 ff.

13. Fol. 2v-3r (see note 14); fol. 4v: "Desitis ergo inconditis illis murmuribus quibus scolarum magistri pueros usque ad capitum uertigines fatigant, dicat preceptor puero docendo quod casus sex sunt"; fol. 5r: "Persona quid sit et unde dicta sit diffinicionibus operosis sudare student scolarum magistri, sed queso ut, talibus bractamentis neque ad doctrine laudem neque ad scientie acquisitionem usui futuris explosis, satis sit ingenioso magistro docendum puerum de sola personarum practica in modum ut sequitur instituisse."

14. Fol. 2v-3r: "In primis tamen fugiat nobilis filii preceptor adipatam et ad nauseam usque coactam diffinicionum crassitudinem, quibus ut feda quadam fuligine per scolarum magistros puerorum ingenia ubique gentium hactenus commaculari confuscarique usu ueniebat."

15. Heath, 17 ff.

16. Vergilius, *Opera cum tribus commentariis Servii, Aelii Donati et Christophori Landini* (Venice, c. 1491). Giovanni Tortelli's *De orthographia* was completed in 1448-53; see M. Rinaldi, "Fortuna e diffusione del *De Orthographia* di Giovanni Tortelli," *Italia Medioevale e Umanistica* 16 (1973): 227; Virginia Brown and Craig Kallendorf, "Two Humanist Annotators of Virgil: Coluccio Salutati and Giovanni Tortelli," in *Supplementum Festiuum: Studies in Honor of Paul Oskar Kristeller,* ed. J. Hankins, J. Manfasani, F. Purnell, Jr., Medieval & Renaissance Texts & Studies, vol. 49 (Binghamton, NY, 1987), 65-148. R. G. G. Mercer, *The Teaching of Gasparino Barzizza With Special Reference to his Place in Paduan Humanism* (London, 1979). Niccolò Perotti's *Rudimenta grammatices* appeared in 1468, his *Cornucopiae* in 1478; see G. Mercati, *Per la cronologia della vita e degli scritti di Niccolò Perotti* (Rome, 1925). Lorenzo Valla's *Elegantiae linguae Latinae* from 1444 was first printed in 1471.

17. Heath, 16 f.

18. Ibid., 21-26.

19. Fol.117r: "Hic magister Iacobus Publicii in lectione Sallustii dicebat uerbum 'restinguam' posse per contrarias significationes exponi, ut indifferenter significet ussleschen vel anczonden."

20. A. Sottili, "Note biografiche sui petrarchisti Giacomo Publicio e Guiniforte Barzizza e sull'umanista valenziano Giovanni Serra," *Petrarca 1304-1374. Beiträge zu Werk und Wirkung,* hrsg. von F. Schalk (Frankfurt a. Main, 1975), 270-86. L. Bertalot, "Humanistische Vorlesungsankündigungen in Deutschland im 15. Jahrhundert," *Zeitschrift für Geschichte der Erziehung und des Unterrichts* 5 (1919): 18.

21. Heath, 38 f.

22. J. Haller, *Die Anfänge der Universität Tübingen 1477-1517* (Nachdruck der Ausgabe Stuttgart, 1927; Aalen, 1970), 1:89 f., 2:30.

23. Erasmus, *De pueris statim ac liberaliter instituendis, Opera omnia* (Amsterdam, 1971), 1:2, 77.

24. Fol. 9v and passim.

25. Fol. 4v. See also B. Stolt, "Das Werk," 318; H. Hajdu, *Das mnemotechnischen Schrifttum des Mittelalters* (Vienna, 1936).

PLENARY LECTURE

Those Books That Are Most Necessary for All Men to Know: The Classics and Late Ninth-Century England, A Reappraisal

JANET BATELY

In the letter attached to the Old English version of Gregory's *Cura Pastoralis*,[1] Alfred, king of the West Saxons, sets out his aims and aspirations in undertaking the translation of this and other key Latin texts. According to the letter, his ultimate ambition was to restore wisdom and learning in the land and with it the general state of well-being which had characterized previous centuries. In the past, he says, Anglo-Saxon England prospered both in war and in wisdom: "ge mid wige ge mid wisdome."[2] But when he came to the throne of Wessex in 871, learning had so fallen off that there were very few people on this side of the Humber with a working knowledge of Latin. As a result everything had changed for the worse:

> Geðenc hwelc witu us ða becomon for ðisse worulde, ða ða we hit nohwæðer selfe ne lufodon ne eac oðrum monnum ne lefdon.[3]

Alfred's immediate aim was to set all young freeborn people to learning, until they could read English well, and then, to instruct a select few further in the Latin language. And in order to provide the students and other literate people with appropriate reading matter in the vernacular, he called on the recipients of his letter to help him in the task of translating those books that were most necessary for all men to know.[4]

Apart from the *Cura pastoralis*, the works that form the Alfredian canon are translations of the first fifty psalms and of the *De consolatione Philosophiae* of Boethius,[5] and a composite work based on Augustine's *Soliloquia* and *De uidendo Deo*, but deriving material and ideas also from Gregory and Jerome.[6] Other translations which date from the same period and appear to be either directly associated with Alfred or commissioned by him are Bishop Wærferth of Worcester's version of Gregory's *Dialogi libri IV* and the anonymous renderings of Orosius' *Historiarum aduersus paganos libri septem* and Bede's *Historia ecclesiastica*.[7]

Although none of the works translated are from the classical age, two of them were composed by late Latin authors well versed in the classics, whose knowledge is reflected in their writings. Boethius' *De consolatione* contains a number of references to historical and mythological figures and to classical stories that were still well known in the early sixth century. Orosius' *Historiarum aduersus paganos libri septem* draws almost all of its material from classical sources, using amongst other texts an epitome of Livy, and the histories of Tacitus, Justinus and Eutropius.[8] However, for neither author was a recounting of classical material a primary aim. Boethius, for instance, uses the myth of Orpheus in book 3, metre 12, to illustrate the dangers of looking backward—of pausing from the pursuit of good to turn back to earthly pursuits.

> Heu, noctis prope terminos
> Orpheus Eurydicen suam
> uidit, perdidit, occidit.
> Vos haec fabula respicit
> quicumque in superum diem
> mentem ducere quaeritis;
> nam qui Tartareum in specus
> uictus lumina flexerit,
> quicquid praecipuum trahit
> perdit, dum uidet inferos.[9]

The moral of book 4, metre 7, with its reference to the sacrifice of Iphigenia, the encounter between Ulysses and Polyphemus and the twelve labors of Hercules, is somewhat similar: people set on the path of increasing virtue must not hang back. Brutus, Cato and Fabricius owe their presence in book 2, metre 7, to the fact that Boethius wishes to illustrate the dubious value of reputation, which survives a person's death only for a short while. We still remember the names of these men, he says, but who knows now where their bones lie.

As for Paulus Orosius, he is not interested in history (or myth) for its own sake any more than Boethius is. Rather, in his seven books "against the pagans," he selects those incidents that illustrate his theme, that life before Christ was even more beset by calamities than life subsequently. So in book 2, chap. 18 he calls attention to the fact that, although he has discussed in so small a book and in so few words such a great number of events affecting many provinces, peoples and cities, he has set forth no deeds that did not also involve a great number of misfortunes: "non magis explicui actus operum, quam inplicui globos miseriarum," while in book

1, chap. 12 he confesses that he has had to leave out many details concerning even these:

> At ego nunc cogor fateri, me prospiciendi finis commodo de tanta malorum saeculi circumstantia praeterire pluria, cuncta breuiare. nequaquam enim tam densam aliquando siluam praetergredi possem, nisi etiam crebris interdum saltibus subuolarem.[10]

And, employing the rhetorical figure of *occupatio*, he goes on to list a number of people who committed disgraceful crimes about which — he says — he prefers to remain silent.[11]

Many stories are of course related in some detail; however, the bias is always there. It is the extent of the disasters in the Pyrrhic and Carthaginian wars that is of interest to Orosius, not the military tactics employed; it is Caesar's ruthlessness and his might in war, not his clemency towards his opponents that is a subject for report.[12] And because he can assume prior knowledge on the part of his readers, Orosius, like Boethius, is able throughout his work to sketch his stories lightly, omitting many details essential to the stories themselves but not to his main theme.[13]

The audiences for which Orosius and Boethius were writing were very different from the medieval readership of Alfred's time. For the latter a considerable filling in of detail relating to classical material was essential, if — in keeping with Alfred's plan — the books most necessary for all men to know were to be fully understood.[14] One of the most remarkable things about the Alfredian translations is the general awareness of classical civilization that they display and the extent to which Alfred and his colleagues were able both to achieve an understanding for themselves of what was in many ways alien source material, and to make it intelligible to others, to provide in the words of Alfred *andgit of andgiete*, that is, sense for sense:

> Siððan ic hie ða geliornod hæfde, swæ swæ ic hie forstod ond seæ ic hie andgitfullicost areccean meahte, ic hie on Englisc awende.[15]

Where did the translators acquire their additional information? According to the Welsh bishop Asser, Alfred's biographer, his patron compiled a handbook in which he collected *flosculos*, passages copied from various authors as he read,[16] and it may be that some of the classical material was assembled directly from classical texts in this way. It was, after all, nearly a century since Alcuin had argued that the study of secular literature and the liberal arts was the way by which Christians might ascend to the highest point of evangelical perfection, and it was some thirty years since the death of the continental scholar and copyist of classical texts,

Lupus of Ferrières (ob. c. 862).[17] Possible alternative sources would have been the collections of classical lore made by late Latin encyclopaedists such as Solinus and Isidore and by the mythographers, along with references to classical subjects by writers of commentaries such as Servius and Lactantius Placidus, and by Church Fathers such as Tertullian, Jerome, Augustine and Orosius — references which were also taken up by compilers of glossaries, scholiasts and other medieval Latin writers such as Hrabanus Maurus.[18] However, for some of their material, it may be that the Old English authors had to look no further than a glossed or interpolated copy of the Latin text that they were translating. So, for instance, in book 4, chap. 1, where Orosius refers merely to the ambiguous response — *responso ambiguo* — of the oracle when questioned by Pyrrhus, a number of manuscripts supply the wording given by Ennius and possibly handed down via the lost thirteenth book of Livy: "Aio te Aeacida Romanos uincere posse." Usually these words are inserted in the margin of the manuscript in which they are found; sometimes, however, they have actually been interpolated into the text.[19] Similarly, at the end of the account of the destruction of Sodom and Gomorrha, in book 1, chap. 3, a number of manuscripts include a description of Dead Sea Fruit, derived from Josephus by way of Hegesippus.[20]

Again, in the section on Alexander the Great in book 3, chaps. 19 and 20 of Orosius' History, where Orosius refers only to wars and expeditions and rivalries, the scribe of a version preserved in Universitätsbibliothek Uppsala (MS C 699, fols. 28^r.75^v), has first slightly abridged and reworded his exemplar and then abandoned his primary source completely, inserting a lengthy section based loosely on Julius Valerius, *Res gestae Alexandri Macedonis*. In this section he gives accounts of such matters as the egg which produced a baby dragon, the earthquake at Alexander's birth and the portent of the monstrous child that was half man, half beast, before reverting to the text of Orosius and book 3, chap. 21. He also follows Julius Valerius in attributing the murder of Alexander to an irate Antipater, whereas OH refers merely to the treachery of a servant.[21]

The examples given above are drawn from manuscripts of Orosius' *Historiarum aduersus paganos libri septem*, and, in the surviving copies of that work, glossing and interpolation are the exception rather than the rule. However, the evidence of a late ninth-century copy of a commentary on the first two books of Orosius, with duplicated lemmata, suggests that some heavily glossed manuscripts of this work must once have existed. Although the script of the Orosius commentary is continental minuscule, of the type used in Rheims, it was apparently copied from an insular exemplar.[22] So it is of particular relevance to a study of the knowledge of the classics in the British Isles in the late ninth century.

In the case of Boethius' *De consolatione*, on the other hand, there is conclusive evidence from the late ninth and early tenth centuries both of the established practice of heavy glossing and of the circulation of commentaries on the text. It is obvious that the work was widely used as a teaching text during that period.[23] However, of the commentaries so far identified, only one — that of the Anonymous of St. Gall — can, in the light of present knowledge, be safely claimed to have been in circulation in the late ninth century.[24] The precise date and interrelationships of two others — the commentary of Remigius[25] and the commentary in Vatican MS Lat. 3363 attributed by Troncarelli to Asser[26] — are still very much a matter of debate. The Vatican manuscript appears to have been in Britain by the late ninth century, while there are several versions of Remigius' commentary in tenth century English manuscripts.[27] Also unclear is the extent to which any of the surviving commentaries were dependent on older commentaries or teaching material now lost.[28] However, what is certain is that, in his additions to his text, King Alfred is directly indebted to none of them. So the commentaries will be referred to here by way of illustration, to demonstrate the kind of background knowledge that Alfred or his collaborators might have had access to, without ruling out the possibility that at least some of the material they contain could have been available both to him and to their compilers.

As recent studies have shown, the importance of the early Boethius commentaries was two-fold. They conveyed a mass of information and philosophy from the classical world to men whose culture had hitherto been largely biblical and liturgical; and they fostered an enlightened and liberal attitude to learning, particularly to secular learning. One of their major functions was to make available the rudiments of the ideas of the main philosophical schools; another was to provide etymologies for names; yet another, more immediately relevant to this paper, was to fill in the story or stories lying behind Boethius' historical and mythological allusions and to give a rationalization of the mythology. Not infrequently, allegorical explanations were provided and the moral or meaning of a tale spelt out.[29]

The Orosius commentary, in contrast, attempts no moral message. Apart from providing etymologies[30] and giving simple equivalents for difficult words and phrases, the author's main interest lies in the retelling of classical myths and tales that are only briefly alluded to by Orosius himself. So he relates the stories of Medea, of Pelops, of Ganymede, and explains the nature of the treachery of Mettus Fufetius and the sacrifice of Codrus,[31] who, he tells us, deliberately engineered his own death in order to ensure the supremacy of his own kingdom:

> *Codro moriente*: codrus athenensium rex fuit ⁊ cum inter phelopenses ⁊ athenenses bella gererentur ⁊ nullo modo potuissent conpesci responsum datum est ab apolline eorum fore uictoriam quorum rex manu hostium cecidisset cum ergo nemo auderet principem occidere codrus in modum rustici ueste sordida processit e castris ⁊ ostibus tanta gurgia ingesit ut mortem mere[re]tur ⁊ suis uictoriam prebuit.[32]

However, unlike the Boethius commentaries, the Orosius commentary is silent on the possible significance of the myths. And it had nothing to say about a number of individuals, including Liber Pater and Cincinnatus;[33] silence, in this case, implying absence of information.

The sources claimed by the Orosius commentary include Statius, Virgil, Dares Frigius and Isidore;[34] Remigius cites amongst his authorities Virgil, Ovid, Persius, Juvenal, Cicero, Lucan, Suetonius, Pliny, Solinus, Hyginus and Servius, to name just a few — though these are not always quoted at first hand.[35] Not named, but major sources of the Boethius commentaries, are the works of the mythographers and Isidore's *Etymologies*.[36]

The lists of sources given above are impressively long and at first sight appear to suggest very wide reading. In contrast, Alfred's classical knowledge as displayed in the Boethius appears to be slight. He has omitted altogether some of the historical, geographical and mythological details in his source; he has repeated others without further elucidation, and where he has provided amplification, it is often very brief and on occasion even inaccurate. So for instance in BC book 2, prose 6, §8, where Boethius tells of a certain freeman, tortured by a tyrant (referring to either Zeno and Nearchus or Anaxarches and Nicocreon), Alfred writes of Liberius, *sumum romaniscan æpelinge* (a certain Roman prince). However, here there are extenuating circumstances. Behind the reading *Liberius* (MS B *Tiberius*) must lie not Boethius' *liberum quendam* but an erroneous *Liberium quendam*, probably the result of either miscopying or misreading an abbreviation.[37]

However, as I have indicated, the authorities named by the commentators are not always quoted at first hand, while closer examination of the *Boethius* reveals the considerable skill with which the king has handled the allusions of his source and shows him to have been not without a certain understanding of, and sensitivity to, the full meaning of his text. He may not display the range of knowledge that the late ninth- and early tenth-centuries commentaries do. However, the wealth of information that they provide is to no small extent due to their encyclopaedic approach to their task and the freedom which their medium gives them to supply as much detail as they choose, regardless of its relevance to the immediate context. Fully to appreciate King Alfred's classical knowledge it is necessary to remember his immediate, and indeed his long-term, aims. And it is necessary to evaluate his silences as well as his words.

To begin with the silences. The majority of the references to historical characters omitted by Alfred occur in *De consolatione* book 1, and these have been removed simply as part of the very heavy cutting that was exercised by the king in the opening chapters of his work. Two long prose sections and a metre have been condensed into no more than seven sentences.[38] Apart from brief references to Boethius' contemporary Decoratus[39] and to Lucan's comment on Cato,[40] which have also been removed as a result of a general reshaping, the only other details of this type not taken over by Alfred are a reference to Paulus weeping tears of pity at all the disasters that had overwhelmed Perses,[41] and an allusion to the Roman general Fabricius.[42] Now Boethius uses the tale of Perses, last king of Macedonia, as an *exemplum* to illustrate the vagaries of Fortune, and continues with the well-known definition of tragedy: "Is not this what tragedy commemorates with its tears and tumult — the overthrow of happy realms by the random strokes of Fortune?"[43] Alfred, however, has deliberately transferred the speech in which the exemplum occurs from *Fortuna* to Wisdom — his name for Boethius' *Philosophia*[44] — a change which has necessitated a great deal of rewriting[45] — and, in the context, not of a capricious Fortune but of a kindly Wisdom, who is ever eager to succor the good in their need,[46] a reference to the miserable fate of Perses is no longer in the least appropriate.

It is possible of course that Alfred knew nothing at all of Perses or indeed of Cato other than what Boethius relates of them, and it is perhaps worth noting that the corresponding glosses in the commentaries provide no useful new information at these points: for instance, we are told that Cato laughed only once in his life — a detail hardly relevant to a passage on the transitoriness of reputation![47] In the case of Fabricius, however, there is a curious little piece of evidence which at the very least demonstrates that the king was not totally uninformed. In Alfred's version, the Roman general's name has been replaced by that of Weland, the great craftsman of Germanic legend: "Hwær synt nu þæs Welondes ban," asks the king, "oðð e hwa wat nu hwær hi wæron?"[48] This seems to be a deliberate attempt by Alfred to make Boethius' point about reputation accessible to an audience not familiar with the Roman celebrities listed by him—to arouse an emotional response in the way Boethius' poetry was intended to do just as the reworded passage, "Hu ne wæran þas gefyrn forðgewitene? ⁊ nan mon nat hwær hi nu sint. Hwæt is heora nu to lafe, butan se lytla hlisa ⁊ se nama mid faeum stafum awriten," appears to be intended to recall the themes of Old English elegiac poetry.[49]

However, buried in Alfred's comment is an echo of a comment on Fabricius from a Latin source: not the description of Fabricius refusing the enemy's gold which is given in a variety of forms by the commentaries and apparently derived from Servius on *Aeneid* 6, but an allusion found in some manuscripts of *De uiris illustribus* to Fabricius as being more difficult to shift from honesty than it is to move the sun from its course: "Ille est Fabricius, qui difficilius ab honestate quam sol a suo cursu auerti posset."[50] "Where are now the bones of the famous and wise goldsmith Weland?" asks Alfred, "I call him wise, for the man of skill can never lose his cunning and can no more be deprived of it, *ðe mon mæg þa sunnan awendan of hiere stede* [than the sun can be moved from its place]."[51] So Alfred had access to additional information about Fabricius, although he chose to remove the classical allusion and to adapt the comment.

Omission of mythological and geographical details can similarly be accounted for in terms of editorial responsibility. In the *De consolatione*, mythical material is concentrated in the metres. Alfred has provided renderings of Boethius' poems on the golden age, on Orpheus and on Ulysses and Circe, but he has written out references to the Trojan cycle and to the labors of Hercules from his prose version of book 4, metre 7, substituting unspecified wise men for the named classical heroes.[52] And book 5, metre 1, which uses a description of the relative positions of the rivers Tigris and Euphrates to illustrate the subordination of chance to the rule of law, is discarded altogether.[53]

It should be noted, however, that with a certain thriftiness akin to that shown in his handling of the Fabricius material, Alfred has transferred information about the Trojan War in book 4, metre 7 to his rendering of book 4, metre 3[54] and has used the information about Hercules' destruction of the hydra to expand a brief simile in book 4, prose 6, referring to the hydra as a serpent (*an nædre*), and adding by way of explanation that it had nine heads; if one of these heads was cut off, seven others grew in its place. He also adds the information that before burning it, Hercules covered the creature with wood.[55] The description of the hydra as having not fifty heads (as, for instance, in Mythographus 1),[56] nor a hundred (as in Ovid, *Metamorphoses* 9),[57] but nine is a feature of the accounts by Hyginus and Isidore.[58] In giving the replacement figure as seven, Alfred's text agrees with neither Ovid (where it is two) nor Isidore and Hyginus (where it is three). This could merely be due to careless copying; however, Mythographus 1 gives the figure seven as an alternative to his original figure of fifty—"uel, ut quidam dicunt, septem"—and it could therefore be misapplication of this last figure (for which I have not yet found a source) that could be responsible for Alfred's figure here. Interestingly, I have so far found a reference to the use of wood only in the twelfth-century manuscript of a Boethius commentary which Silk controversially attributes to the ninth-century scholar John Scotus, but this version makes no specific reference to the number of heads the hydra has.[59]

An appreciation of contextual propriety would seem also to have determined the extent of expansion and rewriting in those places where Boethius' allusions have been retained. Sometimes expansion is minimal. So, for instance, Aristotle and Epicurus are described as *uþwitan* ("philosophers"), Euripides as *mægister* ("teacher," "master"), Parmenides as *scop* (the OE equivalent of "poet"), and Antonius as *casere*.[60] Catullus is identified not with the poet, whose verse Boethius quotes, but with one of the consuls of that name and is accordingly described incorrectly as a "heretoga on Rome, swiðe gesceadwis mon" (the commentaries get it right), while Marcus Tullius is given his cognomen of Cicero and, like Cato, has both the rank of *heretoga* ("consul") and the designation *uþwita*.[61] Ptolemy was the author of books, in one of which he described the whole world, Homer was the teacher of Virgil, and Alcibiades was *æþelincg*.[62] The people who live beyond the Caucasus Mountains are Scythians; India is in the south-east of the world, while Thyle is in the north-west, having no night in the summer and no day in the winter.[63] As for the restricted space in the world available to mankind, this is due to the existence of zones of excessive cold and excessive heat: "hy hit ne magon eall gebugian, sum for hæto, sum for cile."[64] Apart from Orosius' *History*, Latin texts from which the bulk of this information could have been derived include the works of Pliny (possibly via Solinus),[65] Isidore,[66] Valerius Maximus,[67] Augustine,[68] and *De uiris illustribus*.[69] In none of the instances cited above would further information have been appropriate. Indeed the withholding of the major part of the additional material concerning Cicero until the second of two passages where his name is mentioned, demonstrates clearly Alfred's awareness of contextual propriety.[70]

Minimal expansion is also found in the story of Croesus and, again, appropriately so, since this story occurs alongside the story of Perses in that speech which Alfred transfers from Fortuna to Wisdom.[71] As a result it is only the second part of Boethius' exemplum—Croesus' fortunate escape from the pyre thanks to a shower of rain from heaven—that is relevant here, not his previous good fortune, or indeed his proverbial great wealth. Do you know, asks Wisdom, how I looked after the interests of Croesus, king of the Greeks, when Cyrus king of Persia had seized him and was intending to commit him to the flames: "Wast þu hu ic gewand ymb Croeses þearfe Creca cyninges, þa þa hine Cirus Pærsa cyning gefangen hæfde ₇ hine forbærnan wolde?" The corresponding Latin, book 2, prose 2, §11, has a statement by Fortune which refers to her inconstancy and asks, "An tu mores ignorabas meos? Nesciebas Croesum regem Lydorum Cyro paulo ante formidabilem mox deinde miserandum rogi flammis traditum misso caelitus imbre defensum?" The identification of Cyrus as king of the Persians is a commonplace in Latin texts, while the equation of Lydia with Greece may be due either to a misapprehension, or to the fact that that part of Asia Minor subsequently became part of the Byzantine empire.[72] As for Alfred's attribution of Croesus' delivery to divine intervention (by Wisdom), this could reflect knowledge of a version of the story in which the gods intervene. However, because of the presence of the ambiguous term *caelitus* in the *De consolatione*, we cannot rule out the possibility that it is merely an embroidery on the Latin text.

More attention, however, is paid to the story of Busiris. *De consolatione* book 2, prose 6, §10 says merely that "Busiridem accepimus necare hospites solitum ab Hercule hospite fuisse mactatum." The Boethius commentaries provide little additional detail at this point, though Remigius identifies Busiris as king of Egypt and quotes Virgil, while other versions cite Orosius.[74] Alfred, however, gives a fuller account. In addition to identifying the location as Egypt, he describes the form of killing as drowning in the Nile—perhaps inspired by the knowledge provided by Latin authors such as Hyginus, Servius and Augustine that Busiris was son of the water god Neptune,[75] and perhaps via a now lost intermediary source. We may compare this to the entry in the Orosius commentary, which also describes Busiris as sacrificing his guests to his lord, Neptune, and which says that Hercules proceeded to drown him in the Nile.[76] And since the point being illustrated is that great people are often done by as they did, expansion in this context is totally appropriate.

Other stories where expansion is both appropriate and found are accounts of the attack of the giants on heaven and of Nero's depravity. I shall return to Nero later. Of the giants the *De consolatione* book 3, prose 12, §24 says simply that the giants attacked heaven but were restrained: "Accepisti ... in fabulis lacessentes caelum Gigantes; sed illos quoque, uti condignum fuit, benigna fortitudo disposuit." The reference is used by way of illustration of Philosophy's point that God, the supreme good, is omnipotent. The commentaries fill in the details, probably from Mythographus 1—the giants were called Othus and Ephialtes and grew by nine fingers each month. They tried three times to overthrow Jupiter by piling mountain on to mountain and on the third attempt Jupiter destroyed them with a thunderbolt.[77]

Alfred agrees in some respects with the commentaries, but his material does not come from the mythographers, being instead of a type found in Ovid's *Fasti* and *Metamorphoses,* Servius, and Isidore. So Jove is son of heaven and the giants sons of earth (as it were sisters' sons). The giants were supposed to reign over the earth, but they resented Jove's control of heaven and wanted to destroy the heaven under him. Jove sent not the classical thunderbolt but a full-scale storm, with thunder and lightning and winds, and cast down the edifice that had been made, and killed the giants.[78] And Alfred goes on to compare this lying tale with a true story—"Ðyllica leasunga hi worhton, ⁊ meahton eaðe seggan soðspell, gif him pg leasunge næren swetran, ⁊ þeah swiðe gelic ðisum. Hi meahton seggan hwylc dysig Nefrod se gigant worhte. . ."—and turning to patristic sources, proceeds to insert a version of the story of Nimrod and the Tower of Babel.[79]

In this passage Jove is also described as son of Saturn and the highest of the gods according to *ealdum leasum spellum,* and a similar description, but with still further amplification—for instance, one of his sons was called Apollo and he was father of Circe, who in her turn was supposed to be a goddess—is given later, in Alfred's rendering of the story of Ulysses and Circe.[80] There, it provides necessary background to the story of Circe's supposed magical powers. Here, it serves as necessary background to an account whose falseness needs to be stressed. And it will be noted that Alfred's withholding of material from the first place where Jove is named in order to use it in the second is in keeping with his carefulness elsewhere—as, for instance, in his allusions to Cicero. Possible sources for this mythological information include Ovid, Isidore, and Hyginus.[81]

Contextually appropriate additions are also found in the stories of Damocles and Seneca. Of Seneca, Alfred says that when he found he had to die, then he offered all his wealth in return for his life, but the king would not accept it, nor would he grant him his life. When Seneca realized this, "þa geceas he him þone deað ðæt hie mon oflete blodes on ðæm earme; ⁊ ða dyde mon swa." Alfred's source for the details of Seneca's death appears to be Tacitus' *Annals*—though, according to Tacitus, Seneca cuts his own wrists and does not, as in Alfred's version, ask other people to carry out the act for him on a single arm. The commentaries also know something of the death of Seneca, telling of the cutting of veins in each of his arms. Remigius quotes Suetonius as an authority, though as Diane Bolton observes, only through recollection.[82] For the story of Damocles, the commentators' source seems to be Mythographus 1. Alfred's must have been very similar, but, as Joseph Wittig has pointed out, his version seems even closer to the account in Macrobius, which also includes direct speech.[83]

Perhaps the most interesting expansions, however, are to be found in book 3, metre 12 and book 4, metre 3. Alfred's rewriting of the metre on Orpheus and Eurydice and its treatment in the commentary versions have been dealt with in detail in an important article by Dr. Wittig.[84] The rewriting of the metre on Ulysses and Circe has a number of peculiar features; not the least being the distortion of the classical story whereby the transformation of Ulysses' companions into animals comes a considerable period of time after Ulysses met Circe and is inspired by the men's dissatisfaction at the delay in returning home. When Ulysses left Troy, says Alfred, he had no more than one ship. Then he was assailed by bad weather ("Ða gestod hine heah weder ⁊ stormsæ") and he was driven on to an island in the Mediterranean (*ðære Wendelsæ*), inhabited by a supposed goddess called Circe, who had a large band of thegns and other maidens. She immediately fell in love with him and he with her, so immoderately that for her sake he abandoned homeland and kindred. And he remained with her until his thegns could not stay any longer, but for love of their homeland and because of their exile decided to leave him. Then, says Alfred, according to the fable, Circe transformed them into animals.[85]

Because Boethius can assume that his audience is familiar with the whole story, the Latin metre concentrates on the transformation, with only a brief introduction setting the scene, and an even briefer aside *in medias res*, sketching in how Ulysses himself escaped Circe's magic.

> Sed licet uariis malis
> numen Arcadis alitis
> obsitum miserans ducem
> peste soluerit hospitis.

Alfred's interest is also centered on the transformation, and, thanks to his changes to the narrative, he does not have to repeat or explain Boethius' allusion to the winged god. His expansions and additions therefore are made to Boethius' introduction, while the account of the change of men into beasts and its moral implications is allowed neatly to round off the story. The king's sources for the additions to the Orpheus and

Eurydice story appear to be Ovid *Metamorphoses* 10, Virgil, *Aeneid* 4 and Fourth Georgic, and a commentary on Virgil such as that of Servius. He also makes use of material of the type found in Isidore's *Etymologiae*.[86] Details of the Ulysses and Circe story could have been taken directly from Ovid, *Metamorphoses* 14. Thus, for instance, the single ship, the identity of the *neritii ducis* and his status as ruler of Ithaca, Circe's numerous attendants, the mutual love and the lengthy stay (including by implication the abandoning by Ulysses of kingdom and kin for Circe's sake). As for the transformation of men into animals, it is tempting to associate this with another story in the same book of Ovid's *Metamorphoses*, where Diomedes' companions become disheartened and beg Diomedes to make an end of wandering: they too are transformed, though into birds not into animals.[87] Given the freedom with which Alfred and the author of the Orosius treat their Latin texts, it is not possible to determine whether the change is accidental, resulting from imperfect understanding or recollection, or deliberate.[88]

In his use of classical material, then, whether it comes directly from Boethius or is introduced from other sources, King Alfred shows restraint and discrimination. In contrast with the practice of the late ninth- and early tenth-century commentaries, there is in his translation no detail that is not contextually appropriate, no attempt at etymologizing, no offering of alternative comments, and there is a high degree of accuracy. The king is aware that the function of the mythological and historical material in the *De consolatione* is to provide illustration of Boethius' philosophical arguments and he observes the same rules as Boethius in his translation. In Orosius' *History* too, the classical material is used by way of illustration of Orosius' central theme—though here it is foregrounded. And the Latin author's selectivity again allows scope for the Old English translator to display his own knowledge of the classics. One of the first impressions that we get from his work is that this knowledge is in some ways slighter and more flawed than Alfred's. Thus, the translator appears to be unfamiliar with a number of the classical myths and legends alluded to in this source. The *quinquaginta parricidia* of the story of Danaus and Aegyptus is taken to be the slaying of fifty men by their own sons; Atreus and Thyestes are also guilty of killing their fathers, while, thanks to a misconstruing of the Latin, Oedipus is said to have not only murdered his father but also his step-father and his step-son.[89] The Minotaur is half-man, half-lion, a description which is possibly the result of careless reading of Isidore.[90] We may compare the Orosius commentary, which describes the sparing of Lynceus by Hypermnestra and gives the story of Pasiphae and the bull.[91] At the same time the author of the

Old English Orosius adds nothing to the stories of Ganymede and Pelops, although the commentary gives rough outlines of both.[92] However, this silence may be deliberate, since the two stories are part of a list, which the translator, following OH, says he does not intend to relate. On the other hand, the Old English author hints at knowledge of the story of Phaethon and the outcome of his attempt to drive the chariot of the sun, being aware that the latter suffered a mishap (*forscapung*);[93] he can identify Liber Pater as a god renowned for his military prowess, and he also seems to know something of the story of Deucalion and Pyrrha, though he describes Deucalion's flood as worldwide like Noah's.[94] Amon is described as son of Jove, who is the "highest god" of the Romans, while Alexander the Great's mother is said to have been accused of adultery with Nectanebus.[95] If we turn to the stories of Rome in its earliest days, then we find not only the same mixture of correct and incorrect information or deduction, but also much stronger evidence of knowledge of classical material other than that provided by the translator's primary source. So the stories of the rape of the Sabines and of Lucretia, which are only hinted at in Orosius' *History*, are related in some detail, and we are given a garbled account of the bravery of Mucius Scaevola in which it is Tarquin's men, not Mucius himself, who burn his hand, finger by finger.[96] The name of the dictator Cincinnatus is omitted, but the translator seems to have known something of Cincinnatus' reputation other than what is said in Orosius' *History*, since he describes him as *anne earmne mon*, a certain poor man.[97] In later sections notable additions include accounts of the deaths of Scipio, Cato and Cleopatra and of Caesar's behavior at the battle of Munda. So, for instance, Scipio upbraids the senate for its ingratitude and that very night the Romans are said to express their thanks for all his labors with a worse reward than he deserved, when they smother him in his bed.[98] Cleopatra puts *ipnalis seo naedre* to her arm because she thought it would be least sore there and the nature of that snake is that the creatures it bites end their lives in sleep,[99] while Caesar, expecting to be captured at Munda, "for þære ondrædinge þæs þe swiþor on þæt weorod þrong, for þon þe him wæs leofre þæt hiene mon ofsloge þonne hiene mon gebunde."[100]

All this addition is made appropriate by the change in approach of the Old English translator. Unlike Orosius, he is not concentrating on wickedness and the effects of wickedness, nor is he more interested in the disastrous outcome of battles than in their conduct, so the bravery of a Mucius and the clemency of a Caesar can be dwelt on and applauded and the stratagems of a Hannibal recounted.[101] Finally, like Alfred in the *Boethius*, the translator shows an understanding of classical life and culture which is not inconsiderable for his time. He is able to explain such terms as triumph, Vestal virgin, *Iani portae*.[102] And although, unlike some of the commentaries, he rarely gives etymologies, he has an explanation for the name Amazon as for the name Centaur.[103] As for his sources, the material he uses can be traced back to a variety of classical texts. For instance, as I have shown in detail elsewhere, details of military stratagems go back to Livy, Valerius Maximus, Sallust, and Frontinus; certain incidents in the life of Alexander are ultimately derived from Quintus Curtius and Julius Valerius, and additional material relating to Caesar, from Suetonius.[104] However, the style of translation is such that, as with Alfred's *Boethius*, it is often not possible to determine which of two or three potential classical or late Latin sources was actually used. So, for instance, the reference to Theseus as leading the attack at Marathon could have been derived from Pomponius Mela or from Lactantius Placidus, while details of Scipio's ruse at Utica could be derived from either Livy or Frontinus.[105] Information concerning Cincinnatus' poverty could have come from Valerius Maximus, or Augustine, and the stories of the rape of the Sabines and Lucretia contain details found in *De uiris illustribus*, Ovid's *Fasti*, Augustine's *De ciuitate Dei*, Eutropius, and scholia on Juvenal and Lucan. And, as I have argued elsewhere, it may be that at least some of the additions were acquired at second hand.[106] As we have seen, Alfred too may on occasion have been relying on imperfect recollection.

What I would like to focus attention on in conclusion are those instances where Alfred's *Boethius* refers to places, people and incidents mentioned also in either the Latin or the Old English versions of Orosius' *History* or both. It has been suggested that the translation of Boethius was made after that of Orosius and that Alfred was able to derive some of his additional information from that text. The evidence cited for this can be said to qualify as an instance of classical knowledge, since it relates to the sack of Rome in AD 410. This is the reference in both the *Boethius* and the *Orosius* to Rædgota and Eallerica as joint kings of the Goths at that time.

Thus, according to Dorothy Whitelock, Alfred "may owe something to the *Orosius*," because he "jumps from the mention of Rædgota and Eallerica, who occur at the end of the *Orosius*, direct to Theodoric, without any mention of the intervening history of the Goths. The form Rædgota is in both works, yet it is not the true Germanic equivalent of *Radagaisus*, which would be *Rædgar*."[107] The statement in the Boethius to which Dorothy Whitelock is referring occurs at the very beginning of the text:

> On ðære tide ðe Gotan of Sciððiu mægðe wið Romana rice gewin up ahofon, ⁊ mid heora cyningum, Rædgota ⁊ Eallerica wæron hatne, Romane burig abræcon, ⁊ eall Italia rice þæt is betwux þam muntum ⁊ Sicilia þam ealonde in anwald gerehton, ⁊ þa æfter þam foresprecenan cyningum Þeodric feng to Þam ilcan rice.[108]

The material in the *Old English Orosius* to which this statement appears to correspond occurs in two separate passages at the very end of that work. The first claims of Stileca that "for þæm feondscipe he forlet Gotan on Italie mid hiora twam ciningum, Alrican ⁊ Rædgotan."[109] The second describes the sack of Rome by Alrica, who is said to leave the city on the third day, and tells how Hettulf, kinsman of Alrica, married the sister of the emperor Honorius: "siþþan sæton þa Gotan þær on lande, sume be þæs caseres willan, sume his unwillan."[110] No more is said of the Gothic presence in Italy, the text ending with the extension of Gothic power to other lands. In Orosius' *History*, as Dorothy Whitelock's comment implies, Radagaisus and Alaric are referred to not together but separately; at the same time, more detail is given of the presence of the Goths in Italy.[111] However, the linking of Radagaisus and Alaric is not unique to the Old English translations. It is found, for instance, in the Chronicles of Prosper and of Cassiodorus. According to Cassiodorus, "His conss. Gothi Halarico et Radagaiso regibus ingrediuntur Italiam."[112] As for the origin of the Goths, in Scythia, this is a piece of information which must have been derived from a source other than either the Latin or the Old English version of Orosius' *History*.[113]

What is more, the leap from Radagaisus and Alaric to Theodoric in Alfred's *Boethius* is also easily explained without reference to either Latin or English versions of Orosius' *History*. In the first part of the compound sentence that opens the text, Alfred names Radagaisus and Alaric as representative of the beginning of the Gothic presence in Italy that provides the background to the tribulations of Boethius. In the third part, he refers to the Goth who was ruling Italy at the time when Boethius wrote the *De consolatione* and who was directly responsible for the latter's tribulations. The central section serves as a link between the first and last parts, briefly describing the conquest of the whole of Italy, including Sicily. Further details concerning Gothic history would be out of place here.

As for the form of the name *Rædgota*, for Latin *Radagaisus* or *Ragadaisus*,[114] the preservation of the names of a large number of continental rulers in *Widsith*—some of them with very peculiar spellings[115]—demonstrates that we cannot rule out the possibility of a vernacular tradition here. We may compare, for instance, the form *Beadeca* in *Widsith*, which editors take to be a variation on the historical *Baduila*.[116] So the evidence adduced for the dependence of Alfred's *Boethius* on the *OE Orosius* is, to say the least, inconclusive.

Other points of contact between Alfred's *Boethius* and the *Orosius* are the accounts of the deposing of Tarquinius Superbus and the story of Nero. BC book 2, prose 6 does not name Tarquin, claiming merely that "consulare imperium ... ob superbiam consulum uestri ueteres abolere cupiuerunt, qui ob eandem superbiam prius regium de ciuitate nomen abstulerant." Alfred, however, makes a specific reference to Tarquinius Superbus and seems also to be alluding to the subsequent attempts to restore the Tarquins and overthrow Brutus:

> ic wene ðæt þu mæge gemunan ðætte eowre eldran gio Romana witan on Torcwines dagum þæs ofermodan cyninges for his ofermettum þone cynelican naman of Romebyrig æresð adyon. Ond eft swa ilce þa heretogan ðe hine ær ut adrifon hi wolden eft ut adrifan for hiora ofermettum; ac hi ne meahton, forðæmþe se æftera anweald þara heretogena þæm romaniscum witum get wyrs licode þonne se ærra þara cyninga.[117]

We may compare the *Old English Orosius*, which replaces a brief allusion in its Latin source ("Tarquinii superbi regnum ... amissum ... non solum unius regis expulsio uerum etiam eiuratio regii nominis et potestatis") with a specific reference to Brutus and (Col)latinus as expelling Tarquinius Superbus and his son and all the royal family, and then follows its source in describing attempts by Brutus' sons and others to overthrow Brutus and restore the Roman monarchy.[118] However, the story was a commonplace in Latin literature, and there are a number of other possible sources for Alfred's brief comment, including the Latin version of Orosius.[119] It is indeed the *Historiarum aduersus paganos libri septem*, not its Old English translation, that could have furnished Alfred both with this and with another piece of additional information — that concerned Nero's depravity. A comparison of the two vernacular versions and their sources is illuminating. In his rendering of *De consolatione* book 2, metre 6,[120] Alfred follows Boethius in describing the murders committed by Nero, but adds to the list, in the metre, the killing of Nero's wife with a sword. He also inserts a reference to Nero's sexual depravity (*unryhthæmedu*) and he expands the brief allusion in his source to the burning of Rome, by detailing Nero's motive: Alfred says that Nero wished to see how it burned, how long and how brightly in comparison with Troy, a comment which recalls the entry in the Remigian commentary of Trier Sammelkodex

1093 "uolens uidere quantum fuerit troie incendium." However, Alfred does not go as far as the commentaries, with their reference to Nero carrying his mother into the flames on his back and leaving her there to perish, in imitation of Aeneas, who attempted unsuccessfully to save his aged father from the flames.[121]

The *Historiarum aduersus paganos libri septem* 7.7 also refers to the murder of Nero's wife, but not to the manner of her death, which Alfred describes as being put to the sword[122] — a claim which is not supported by classical sources, but might well show knowledge of the Pseudo-Senecan *Octauia* —[123] and it states that Nero caused Rome to be burned in order to be able to enjoy the spectacle. He himself viewed the conflagration from the lofty tower of Maecenas and while he enjoyed the beauty of the flames, it is said that he declaimed the *Iliad* in a tragedian's costume: "tragico habitu Iliadem decantabat." The Old English translator turns this into a dramatic account of how Nero "gestod himself on þæm hiehstan torre þe þærbinnan wæs 7 ongon wyrcan scopleoð be þæm bryne."[124]

Apart from the burning of Rome, the only other specific details the OE translator takes over from his source are references to the martyrdom of Peter and Paul—details which are not used by Alfred.

Similar general resemblances and similar differences can be cited regarding the references to Troy and the descriptions of Etna given in the two translations. Alfred tells of the war that lasted ten years (a piece of information which he may have transferred from BC book 4 metre 7, along with a reference to Agamemnon) and of the hundred ships (a piece of information to be found in many places, including Orosius' *History* and the *Old English Orosius*).[125] He concentrates on two of the Greeks involved in the war, Ulysses and Agamemnon, whom, following Dares Frigius or possibly Ovid, he names as the leader of the Greeks:[126]

> Hit gebyrede gio on Troiana gewinne þæt þær wæs an cyning þæs nama Aulixes; se hæfde twa þioda under þam kasere. Þa ðioda wæron hatene Iþacige 7 Retie, 7 þæs kaseres nama wæs Agamemnon. Da se Aulixes mid þam kasere to þam gefiohte for, þa hæfde he sume hundred scipa; þa wæron hi sume ten gear on þam gewinne.

The corresponding entry in OH 1.17.1 relates the "raptus Helenae coniuratio Graecorum et concursus mille nauium," the ten year siege ending in the fall of Troy, and cites Homer. The Old English version adds details of the identity of the two lovers who caused the war and reports the vow of the Greeks not to return until vengeance has been exacted.

Ær þæm þe Romeburg getimbred wære feower hunde wintrum ⁊ xxxgum wintra, gewearð þætte Alexander, Priamises sunu þæs cyninges, of Troiana þær byrig, genom þæs cyninges wif Monelaus, of Læcedemonia, Creca byrig, Elena. Ymb hie wearð þæt mære gewinn ⁊ þa miclan gefeoht Creca ⁊ Troiana, swa þætte Crecas hæfdon m scipa þara miclana dulmuna, ⁊ him betweonum gesworan þæt hie næfre noldon on cyþþe cuman ær hie hiora teonan gewræcen. ⁊ hi ða x gear ymbe þa burg sittende wæron ⁊ feohtende.

The translator also cites Homer as an authority. His secondary Latin source, however, like Alfred's, is probably ultimately Dares Frigius.[127]

As for the descriptions of Etna in the two works as the sulphur-exuding gate of hell, these have certain points of agreement not only with each other but also with material in Wærferth's translation of Gregory's *Dialogues*. Thus, beside Alfred's reference to "þæt fyr on þære helle, seo is on þam munte þe Ætne hate, on þam ieglande þe Sicilia hatte; se munt bið simle swelfe birnende, ⁊ ealla þa neahstowa þærymbutan forbærnð,"[128] and that of the *Orosius* to "Eþna þæt sweflene fyr which up of helle geate asprong on Sicilia þæm londe . . . ⁊ Sicilia fela ofslog mid bryne ⁊ mid stænce," and which every year is "bradre ⁊ bradre,"[129] we have:

in Siciliaea ofer ealle oðru land geoniað þa seaðas þara tintregena upp weallendum fyre. þa seaðas, þæs þe þa secgað þe hit witon, weaxað daga gehwilce ⁊ widiað; forþðon hit is genoh gewiss, þæt nealæcendum þam ænde þyses middaneardes swa myccle ma þa stowa þara tintregena beoð gesewene fram mannum, þæt hi widiað ⁊ openiað.[130]

Similarities between the *Boethius* and the *Orosius* here could be due either to knowledge by one translator of the other's work, to consultation between them, or merely to the use of a common source.[131] However, there is no indication of shared knowledge in the case of references to Hercules, to the status of the Roman gods, and to the stories of Busiris, Croesus and Regulus. Hercules is mentioned several times by both Boethius and Orosius. In the *Old English Orosius* he is described as *Ercol þone ent;* Alfred just as consistently refers to him as *Erculus Iobes sunu*.[132] For Alfred Jove and his family are kings and rulers who came to be worshipped after their death as gods; for the translator of Orosius, the pagan gods are demons.[133]

Similar differences in treatment appear in the two Old English versions of the stories of Busiris and Croesus. Alfred, as we have seen, enlarges considerably on the story of Busiris, but makes relatively minor additions to the story of Croesus.[134] The author of the *Old English Orosius*, on the other hand, adds nothing to his source in either case, apparently for contextual reasons. The reference to Busiris, for instance, follows Orosius' *History* in mentioning only Busiris' sacrifices, not his subsequent fate, and prompts the fictitious challenge by "Orosius": "I would like those people to answer me who say that things are now worse than they used to be" ("Ic wolde nu, cwæð Orosius, þæt me ða geandwyrdan þa þe secgað þæt þeos world sy nu wyrse on ðysan cristendome þonne hio ær on þæm hæþenscype wære").[135] As for the story of Croesus, this is subordinate in the Old English as in the Latin version of Orosius' *History* to the story of the fall of Babylon; moreover, because of a scribal error in the group of Latin manuscripts to which the exemplar of *Old English Orosius* belonged, Croesus is said actually to be killed by Cyrus.[136]

The story of Regulus' noble behavior when sent by his captors as an emissary to Rome and his refusal to embrace his family was a very well known one in classical times and was repeated by a number of patristic authors as well as the Boethius commentators.[137] But in the *De consolatione* and Alfred's *Boethius*, the story of Regulus serves as an exemplum, illustrating the dictum that a powerful man can do nothing to others that cannot also be done to him. Can that be power at all?[138] The insertion of additional information concerning Regulus' integrity and honor would clearly distract attention from the point at issue. So it is appropriate, and, I would venture to claim, surely deliberate that the only clarifying details used by Alfred are the description of Regulus as *heretoga* and identification of the *Poeni* as *Africanas* (available from many Latin sources including Orosius' *History*),[139] along with a mysterious reference to Regulus laying the bound prisoners in *balcan* (ridges?, heaps?), which may simply be artistic license. Paulus Orosius also seems anxious to avoid reporting any good of Regulus. In OH 4.20.1, he refers merely to the sending of Regulus as an ambassador, the rejection of the request for peace, and the dreadful death inflicted on the Roman general:

> Carthaginienses petendam esse pacem a Romanis decreuerunt. ad quam rem Atilium Regulum antea ducem Romanum, quem iam per quinque annos captiuum detinebant, inter ceteros legatos praecipue mittendum putauerunt: quem non impetrata pace ab Italia reuersum resectis palpebris inligatum in machina uigilando necauerunt.

In the Old English version, however, the shift of emphasis I mentioned earlier means that praise of Regulus is in order. And we find a somewhat garbled version of Regulus' oath to return and his arguments against the peace plan, with details which could have been drawn from a variety of sources including *De uiris illustribus,* Silius Italicus, Augustine, and Eutropius.[140] Other details which could have been derived from Orosius' *History* but not from the *Old English Orosius* are those relating correctly or incorrectly to Alcibiades,[141] Catullus,[142] and Cicero.[143]

The impression, then, is that Alfred and the translator of Orosius were both knowledgeable men. They were both in control of their texts. That is to say they had an overall strategy which determined the kind of additions and omissions that they made to their originals. Silence on their part therefore does not necessarily mean ignorance of the background of the stories and episodes alluded to in their sources. It is reasonable to suppose that their knowledge of classical material was greater than that which they convey in their translations. They have sought to understand their texts as fully as their limited resources would allow and, having understood them, they have attempted to render them word for word and sense for sense to the best of their ability.

And perhaps most significantly of all, the two men seem to have had access to different sources. Not only is there apparently no evidence of knowledge of the *Old English Orosius* in Alfred's *Boethius,* or of the *Boethius* in the *Orosius,* but there is also no convincing evidence that Ovid's *Metamorphoses,* one of the major secondary sources of the *Boethius,* was known to the translator of *Orosius*. In the light of our present knowledge, it seems unlikely that the translator of the Orosius could have been one of Alfred's helpers in translating Boethius. At the same time, it must be recognized that although they are writing for literate audiences and for people of fairly high social status, much of the additional material they provide is pretty basic. The audience is obviously not expected to know all the myths and has to be told that they are false stories. It is also not expected to understand even the most common terms, as, for instance, *consul,*[144] and, not surprisingly, it is expected to have little acquaintance with the geography of the world.[145] So to give their readership "full understanding" of what they are reading, the translators explain and elaborate. "Those books which are most necessary for all men to know" may not have included classical texts,[146] but the amount of insight into the classical world that the translators passed on to their readers was far from negligible. Asser tells of the excitement which Alfred felt when he first began to read and translate.[147] Through the activities and enterprise of the king and his colleagues, a not insubstantial glimpse of the brave new world which excited Alfred so much on that occasion was afforded to the literate if not latinate Anglo-Saxon of the late ninth century.

Notes

1. *King Alfred's West-Saxon Version of Gregory's Pastoral Care*, ed., Henry Sweet, EETS o.s. 45, 50 (1871; repr., 1958), 2-9. Alfred's translation is referred to in the footnotes as CP.
2. CP 3.8-9.
3. CP 5.5-6.
4. For recent discussions of the prefatory letter see Jennifer Morrish, "King Alfred's Letter as a Source on Learning in England in the Ninth Century," in *Studies in Earlier Old English Prose*, ed. Paul E. Szarmach (Albany: SUNY Press, 1986), 87-107, and Paul E. Szarmach, "The Meaning of Alfred's Preface to the Pastoral Care," *Medievalia* 6 (1982 for 1980): 57-86.
5. *Liber Psalmorum: The West-Saxon Psalms, being the Prose Portion, or the 'First Fifty' of the so-called Paris Psalter*, ed. James W. Bright and Robert L. Ramsay (Boston, 1907); *King Alfred's Old English version of Boethius' De Consolatione Philosophiae*, ed. Walter John Sedgefield (Oxford, 1899). Alfred's translation of Boethius is here referred to as Bo.
6. *King Alfred's version of St. Augustine's Soliloquies*, ed. Thomas A. Carnicelli (Harvard, 1969). For Alfred's sources see, esp., 28-37. See also Milton McC. Gatch, "King Alfred's Version of Augustine's *Soliloquies*. Some Suggestions on its Rationale and Unity," in *Studies*, ed. Szarmach, 17-49.
7. *Bischof Wærferths von Worcester Übersetzung der Dialoge Gregors des Grossen*, ed. Hans Hecht, Bibliothek der angelsächsischen Prosa, 5 (Leipzig, 1900, 1907; repr., Darmstadt, 1965); *The Old English Orosius*, ed. Janet Bately, EETS s.s. 6 (1980); *The Old English Version of Bede's Ecclesiastical History of the English People*, ed. T. Miller, EETS o.s. 95, 96 (1890-91; repr., 1959). For the Alfredian canon see Janet M. Bately, "Lexical Evidence for the Authorship of the Prose Psalms in the Paris Psalter," *Anglo-Saxon England* 10 (1982): 69-95. For the separateness of the *Orosius* and the *Bede* from the Alfredian canon see Elizabeth M. Liggins, "The Authorship of the Old English Orosius," *Anglia* 88 (1970): 289-322, and Janet M. Bately, "King Alfred and the Old English Translation of Orosius," ibid., 433-60. The *Old English Orosius* is referred to in the footnotes as Or and Wærferth's *Dialogues* as GD. For convenience I write of a single translator of Or, though the account of the voyages of Ohthere and Wulfstan has distinctive linguistic features, while the possibility of multiple authorship elsewhere cannot be ruled out.
8. For the *De consolatione* (referred to in the notes as BC) see Boethius, *De consolatione Philosophiae*, ed. Ludwig Bieler, CCSL 94 (Turnhout, 1957); for Orosius' *History* (OH) see *Pauli Orosii historiarum aduersus paganos libri septem*, ed. Karl Zangemeister, CSEL 5 (Vienna, 1882).
9. For the handling of Boethius's moral in the commentaries and in Bo see, e.g., Kurt Otten, *König Alfreds Boethius* (Tübingen, 1964), 133.
10. OH 2.18.4 and 1.12.1.
11. These include Tantalus, Pelops and Medea, for whom see further below.
12. See, e.g., OH 4, Pref. and 6.12. See further below.
13. See, e.g., OH 2.4.2, on the Sabine women (paraphrasing Virgil with the words *sine more raptas Sabinas*), and 2.4.12, on the rape of Lucretia (*adulteratae Lucretiae*).
14. It must be remembered that to understand a Latin text fully and to turn

it into the vernacular in a truly comprehensible way, the medieval translator had not merely to render word for word but also to act as a bridge, to mediate between two very different cultures. See Janet Bately, *The Literary Prose of King Alfred's Reign: Translation or Transformation* (London: King's College, 1980; repr. with addenda and corrigenda in *Old English Newsletter: Subsidia* 10 [SUNY-Binghamton: CEMERS, 1984]), and Gatch, "King Alfred's Version."

15. CP 7.19-20. In referring to translation word by word and sense by sense Alfred is echoing the words of his teacher Asser and of course earlier Latin authors including Gregory and Jerome. See *Asser's Life of King Alfred*, ed. W. H. Stevenson (Oxford, 1904), §77 and *Alfred the Great: Asser's "Life of King Alfred" and other contemporary sources*, translated with an introduction and notes by Simon Keynes and Michael Lapidge (Penguin Books, 1983), 259.

16. *Asser*, ed. Stevenson, §89.

17. See Jacqueline Beaumont, "The Latin Tradition of the *De Consolatione Philosophiae*," in *Boethius, His Life, Thought and Influence*, ed. Margaret Gibson (Oxford, 1981), 280. For an example of the work of Lupus of Ferrières see Charles Henry Beeson, *Lupus of Ferrières as Scribe and Text Critic* (Cambridge, Mass., 1930).

18. The number of classical manuscripts known to have been in England before AD 1100 is very small, and only two (an insular copy of Pliny and a continental copy of Cicero) survive from the period before 900. See Helmut Gneuss, "A Preliminary List of Manuscripts written or owned in English up to 1100," *Anglo-Saxon England* 9 (1981): items 838 and 423. Those later Latin writers who made extensive use of classical material are represented at this time only by Isidore, Servius and Martianus Capella. See Gneuss, "A Preliminary List," items 48, 96, 127, 821, 885 and 889. However, the absence of manuscript evidence for knowledge of such texts is in itself of no great significance, given the fact that were it not for the existence of the translations by Alfred and his contemporaries we would have had little or no evidence for knowledge of the works that they translated. See Gneuss, "A Preliminary List," items 581, 771, 820, 833, 894, and 908. The only complete copy of Orosius in an insular script to survive from the Anglo-Saxon period is Cambridge, Clare College MS 18 (Kk. 4.5). This dates from the late eleventh century and even allowing for collation and correction is not a very close relation of the text used by the translator of the OE Orosius: see Janet M. Bately, "King Alfred and the Latin Manuscripts of Orosius' History," *Classica et Medievalia* 22 (1961): 69-105. For fragments of two eighth-century manuscripts of Orosius, probably written in Northumbria, see Gneuss, "A Preliminary List," item 8. For a useful reminder that some of Alfred's circle had continental backgrounds and "contact with an intellectual tradition not represented in extant English manuscripts," see Joseph Wittig, "King Alfred's Boethius and its Latin Sources: A Reconsideration," *ASE* 11 (1983): 169 n. 33.

19. See Bately, "King Alfred and the Latin MSS of Orosius' History," 97 and idem, *The Old English Orosius*, 271. For another quotation from Ennius entered in the margin of MS St. Gall 621 by Ekkehart IV, see Otto Skutsch, *The Annals of Quintus Ennius* (Oxford, 1985), 25 f.

20. OH 1.5.10-11. Sweet adopts and prints this interpolation as part of his "Latin original." See *King Alfred's Orosius*, ed. Henry Sweet, EETS, o.s. 79 (London, 1883), 1.3; however, cf. *The OE Orosius*, ed. Bately, 212, note on 23.7-11.

For the distribution of the interpolation in the surviving Latin manuscripts, see Bately, "King Alfred and the Latin MSS of Orosius," 97.

21. See *Iuli Valeri Alexandri Polemi Res Gestae Alexandri Macedonis*, ed. B. Kuebler (Leipzig, 1888). Other inserted material concerns a prophecy by Daniel; the Alexander interpolation is followed by a short reference to the Parthian king Arsaces.

22. See Paul Lehmann, *Erforschung des Mittelalters* II (Stuttgart, 1959), 29–37. I am preparing an edition of this text, which is preserved in Rome, Vatican Library MS, Reginenses Latini 1650, fos. 1–10v.

23. See Beaumont, "The Latin Tradition," 278 ff., and D. K. Bolton, "The Study of the Consolation of Philosophy in Anglo-Saxon England," *Archives d'histoire doctrinale et littéraire du moyen age, Année 1977* (1978): 37.

24. See P. Courcelle, *La Consolation de Philosophie dans la tradition littéraire* (Paris, 1967), 260–67, and Beaumont, "The Latin Tradition," 282–84.

25. The date most usually given for Remigius' commentary on Boethius is 901-2 (see Courcelle, *La Consolation*, 241–69).

26. For arguments for and against a pre-tenth-century date for the small glossing hand of Vatican MS. Lat. 3363, see Fabio Troncarelli, "Per una ricerca sui commenti altomedievali al De Consolatione di Boezio," in *Miscellanea in Memoria di Giorgio Cencetti* (Turin, 1973), 363–80; idem, *Tradizioni perdute: la 'Consolatione Philosophiae' nell' alto medioevo* (Padua, 1981); and Wittig, "King Alfred's Boethius," 161 n. 20.

27. I agree with Wittig that none of the commentaries named above were used as sources by the Old English translators, though they occasionally contain shared or similar material. See Wittig (above, note 18) and Bolton (above, note 23), 33–78. For the problem of the relationship between Vat. Lat. 3363 and Remigius, see Bolton, 36, where it is pointed out that the Vatican glosses, which are "similar in many instances to the Remigian commentary, are closest and in many cases identical to the K version of the reviser [viz. Cambridge, University Library MS. Kk. III 21]. If the glosses are ninth-century in date, they could be a source for K." However, "if most of the glosses belong to the tenth century they derive from the commentaries of Remigius and his revisers." In the light of the findings of Wittig in his recent study, it is no longer possible to assert that "one source for Alfred's commentary was almost certainly the anon. of St. Gall."

28. See Courcelle (above, note 24), 261–63. It has been suggested that some of Alfred's helpers may have shared in the learning of the school at Rheims: see Wittig, 160 and n. 14; see also Diane Bolton, "Remigian Commentaries on the 'Consolation of Philosophy' and their Sources," *Traditio* 33 (1977): 389 and (above, note 23), 37.

29. For the material in this paragraph I am indebted to Bolton, "Remigian Commentaries," 45–46. See also the summary by Beaumont in *Boethius*, ed. Gibson, 282–95.

30. For example, f 5v "Amoyse id nomen famis. Amoisis id sine aqua." This etymology calls to mind Isidore's entry on Moses: "Moyses interpretatur sumptus ex aqua." See *Isidori Hispalensis Episcopi Etymologiarum siue Originum libri* 20, ed. W. M. Lindsay (Oxford, 1911; repr., 1971), 7.46.

31. Cf. OH 1.12.10, 1.12.3, 1.12.4, 2.4.10; 1.18.2. I refer for convience to a *single* author; however, since in several places there are two sets of lemmata and

glosses the scribe of Vat. Regin. Lat. 1650, or a predecessor, may well have been drawing his material from more than one source.

32. Fo. 7ᵛ: cf. OH 1.18.2 "Peloponnensium clades Codro moriente fractorum."

33. OH 1.9.4 and 2.12.7. See further below.

34. For instance, a gloss on OH 1.4.5 "quo praeter illam et Alexandrum" cites Virgilius; a gloss on 1.17.1 "concursus mille nauium" cites Dares Frigius, and a gloss on 1.4.3 "Zoroastrem," cites Isidore.

35. For instance, the entry on Seneca, attributed to Suetonius: see Bolton, "Remigian Commentaries," 383- 84.

36. See Bolton, "Remigian Commentaries," 381-94.

37. Bo 36.17. Cf. Trier Sammelkodex 1093, f. 130, "Hoc letitur [legitur?] fecisse Anaxagoras." The erroneous reading *Liberius* may have originated in misreading either of the five minims at the end of the word *liberum* or of an abbreviation for *um*. For a comparable confusion see the variants *Ignatus* and *Ignatius*, *Theodorius* and *Theodorus* in manuscripts of the *Anglo-Saxon Chronicle*. For the invention of a book called "Astralogium," see Bo 41.23 and BC 2, pr. 7, 3 "sicuti astrologicis demonstrationibus accepisti."

38. Cf. Bo chap. 3, §4 and BC 1, pr. 3, 1. m. 3 and 1. pr. 4. BC 1. pr. 3 and pr. 4 name amongst others Anaxagoras, Socrates, Zeno, Seneca, Cyprian, Gaius Caesar and Germanicus; cf. Vat. Lat. 3363 "Anaxagoras; hec omnia nomina grecorum philosophorum sunt."

39. BC 3, pr. 4, §4: "Tu quoque num tandem tot periculis adduci potuisti, ut cum Decorato gerere magistratum putares, cum in eo mentem nequissimi scurrae delatorisque respiceres?" Bo 62.12-14 replaces this by a general reference to the emperor's foolish favourites: "Ne wurde þu ðeah na adrifen from Ðeodrice, ne he ðe na ne forsawe, gif þe licode his dysig ⁊ his unrihtwisnes swa wel swa his dysegum deorlingum dyde."

40. BC 4, pr. 6, §33: "Et uictricem quidem causam dis, uictam uero Catoni placuisse familiaris noster Lucanus ammonuit." Alfred (132.24- 27) has chosen to write not in specific but in general terms: sometimes we judge a man in one way, he says, and God judges him in another. Sometimes we think he is better but God knows he is not so: "þæt is þonne þæt we ongitað hwilum mon on oðre wisan, on oðre hine God ongit. Hwilum we tiohhiað þæt he sie se betra, ⁊ þonne wat God þæt hit swa ne bið." Reference to Cato here would have demanded a lengthy explanation which would have detracted from, not reinforced, the point being made.

41. 2, pr. 2, §12 "Num te praeterit Paulum Persi regis a se capti calamitatibus pias impendisse lacrimas?"

42. 2, m. 7, 1.15 "Vbi nunc fidelis ossa Fabricii manent?"

43. BC 2, pr. 2, §12: "Quid tragoediarum clamor aliud deflet nisi indiscreto ictu fortunam felicia regna uertentem?"; cf. Bo 18.28-29, "Hwæt singað þa leoðwyrhtan oðres be ðisse woruld buton mislica hwearfunga þisse worulde." Cf. Isidore *Etymologiae* 18.44, where the writers of tragedies are described as *poetae*.

44. He also uses the term *Gesceadwisnes*, either alone or with *Wisdom*: see, e.g., 10.29-11.1 "se Wisdom þa ⁊ seo Gesceadwisnes him bliðum eahum on locodon" (var. *eagum onlocude*).

45. For this speech (BC 2, pr. 2; Bo 17.3-18.33), see, e.g., the comments by F. Anne Payne, *King Alfred and Boethius* (Wisconsin, 1968), esp. 80- 83.

46. "Hu ne wastu mine þeawas, hu georne ic symle wæs ymbe godra manna þearfe?", asks Wisdom in the parallel passage relating to Croesus (18.16-17): cf. BC 2, pr. 2, §11 "An tu mores ignorabas meos?", rounding off a reference to Fortune's wheel.

47. Cf., for instance, the Remigian commentary in Trier Sammelkodex 1093, f. 132v on Cato: "Cato leges duras instituit"; also Einseideln MS 179, f. 129 "Cato censorius semel in uita risit. moribus quoque fortissimus et castus et romanus." Of Aemilius Paulus MS Vat. Lat. 3363 says that "reputans sibi similia posse conti[n]gere miseratus est": see Troncarelli (above, note 26), 164.

48. Bo 46.20-21.

49. Bo 24-27. Cf. e.g., *The Wanderer*, lines 92-96. For the suggestion that the choice of Weland as a substitute for Fabricius might have been triggered by similarity between the name Fabricius and *faber*, see, e.g., Simeon Potter, "Commentary on King Alfred's Orosius," *Anglia* 71 (1952-3): 399. Another instance of Alfred's obvious desire to render BC comprehensible to readers with a very different background can be seen in Bo 34.20-30, where BC 2, pr. 6, §1 makes a comparison between rule by evil men and the effects of eruption or flood ("Quae si in improbissimum quemque ceciderunt, quae flammis Aetnae eructantibus, quod diluuium tantas strages dederint?"). Not only does Alfred add further details about Etna (see below) and restrict the *diluuia* of BC to Noah's flood, but he gives examples of typical wicked rulers (see below) and he introduces a new but totally familiar simile, concerning the spread of fire in a dry heathland:

> Hwæt, se eower wela þonne ⁊ se eower anweald, þe ge nu weorðscipe hatað, gif he becymð to þam eallra wyrrestan men, ⁊ to þam þe his eallra unweorðost bið, swa he nu dyde to þis ilcan Peodrice, ⁊ iu ær to Nerone þæm casere, ⁊ oft eac to mænegum hiora gelicum, hu ne wile he ðonne don swa hi dydon ⁊ get doð, ealle ða ricu þe him under bioð oððe awer on neaweste, forslean ⁊ forheregian, swæ swa fyres leg deð drigne hæðfeld, oððe eft se byrnenda swefel ðone munt bærnð þe we hatað Etne, se is on Sicilia ðæm ealonde; swiðe onlic ðæm miclan flode ðe giu on Noes dagum wæs.

50. *Liber de Viris Illustribus*, in *Sexti Aurelii Victoris Liber de Caesaribus*, ed. Fr. Pichmayer, rev. R. Gruendel (Leipzig, 1966), 35. The reference appears only in one group of manuscripts and is found also in the *Historia Miscella* now attributed to Landulphus: see *Historia Miscella*, ed. Franciscus Eyssenhardt (Berlin, 1869), chap., 18. See also Bately, "Evidence," 43. For entries in the commentaries see, e.g., *Seruii Grammatici qui Feruntur in Vergilii Carmina Commentarii*, ed. G. Thilo and H. Hagen (Leipzig, 1881; repr., Hildesheim, 1961), *Aen.* 6.844 "Fabricium paupertate gloriosum. hic est qui respondit legatis Samnitum aurum sibi offerentibus, Romanos non aurum habere uelle, sed aurum habentibus imperare."

51. Bo 46.17-20.

52. Bo 139.13-15: "hi wunnon æfter weorðscipe on þisse worulde, ⁊ tiolodon goodes hlisan mid goodum weorcum, ⁊ worhton goode bisne þæm þe æfter him wæron." Since Alfred's wise men "wuniað nu ofer ðæm tunglum on ecre eadignesse for hiora godum weorcum" (139.16-17), it is not surprising that the king

does not choose to refer to either Agamemnon, slayer of Iphigenia, or Ulysses, blinder of the Cyclops, or Hercules.

53. A reference to Vesuvius in BC 1, m. 4 also vanishes along with the rest of that metre. An omission of another kind concerns the name of a book: BC 3, pr. 9, §32, "ut in Timaeo Platoni . . . placet." Cf. Bo 79.4 "swa swa ure uðwita sæde, Plato," and the gloss "Timeo proprium nomen est. nomen libri" (Troncarelli, [above, note 26], 181). The names of other books are retained by Alfred and one is actually invented: cf. 140.9 *Fisica* and 41.23 *Astralogium* (for which see above).

54. Compare the reference to a ten year war and to *ultor Atrides* (i.e., Agamemnon) as leader of the Greeks in BC 4, m. 7 with Bo 115.15-19, and see further below.

55. Bo 127.7-14. cf. BC 4, pr. 6, §3 "uelut hydrae capita succrescant" and 4, m. 7, 1.22 "Hydra combusto periit ueneno."

56. *Scriptores Rerum Mythicarum Latini Tres*, ed. Georgius Henricus Bode (Celle, 1834; repr., Darmstadt, 1968), Mythographus 1.62: "quinquaginta . . . uel, ut quidam dicunt, septem,. . . uno caeso, tria capita crescebant."

57. P. *Ovidi Nasonis Metamorphoseon*, ed. R. Ehwald (Leipzig, 1925) 9.71-72.

58. See Hyginus, *Fabulae*, ed. H. J. Rose (Leiden, 1934), 30.3 "Hydra . . . cum capitibus nouem," and Isidore *Etymologiae* 11.3.34: "Hydram serpentem cum novem capitibus, quae Latine excetra dicitur, quos uno caeso tria capita excrescebant." The Remigian commentaries quote both Ovid and Mythographus 1: see Bolton (above, note 23), 74.

59. MS Oxford, Bodleian Lib., Digby 174, ed. E. T. Silk, *Saeculi Noni Auctoris in Boetii Consolationem Philosphiae Commentarius* (Rome, 1935), and, for a full bibliography of the controversy, Courcelle (above, note 24), 251 app.

60. Bo 73.1, 55.8, 70.30, 101.3 and 66.30 (referring to Antonius Caracalla). For reference to the philosophers see, e.g., Isidore *Etymologiae* 8.6, Augustine *De ciuitate Dei* 8.12. That Parmenides wrote poetry is a detail for which I have not yet found a Latin source (Cicero's account in *De natura Deorum* 1 describes him only as a philosopher); however, it may be that the Latin translation of the Greek proffered by Boethius—"rerum orbem mobilem rotat dum se immobilem ipsa conseruat"— may have indicated to King Alfred that he was dealing with poetry. Trier Sammelkodex 1093, fo 146^r, has the comment "graecus poeta fuit." That Antonius (*recte* Antoninus) was *casere* need be no more than a contextual guess, reinforced by knowledge that the Roman emperors included several men of that name, and a similar explanation may be put forward for the description of Euripides as Wisdom's *mægister* (Bo 70.30; BC 3, pr. 7, §6 *Euripidis mei*). Alfred also describes Seneca as *magister*, a term elsewhere in OE used of Aristotle. As for Plato as a philospher (Bo 79.4 "ure uðwitan . . . Plato"; BC 3, pr. 9, §32 *Platoni*) this is information previously provided by BC itself: see BC 1, pr. 3, §6.

61. Bo 61.24-25, 43.6-7 and 143.5-7. BC 2, pr. 7, §8 and 5, pr. 4, §1 refer to Cicero as M. Tullius. For this information see, e.g., *De Viris* §81 and cf. Trier Sammelkodex 1093, 131b "Ciceronem significat."

62. Bo 41.27-28, 72.30. For the information about Alcibiades see, e.g., Valerius Maximus, *Factorum et Dictorum Memorabilium*, ed. C. Kempf (Leipzig, 1888), 6.9. ext. 4. For Ptolemy as the author of a book on geography see, e.g., Capella, *De nuptiis* 6, §609 and 8, §813. That Virgil was Homer's disciple was a commonplace.

63. Bo 43.10, 67.32-68.2. For the information about the Scythians see, e.g., Isidore *Etymologiae* 14.8.2 and 14.3.31. Servius *Aen.* 4.367 refers merely to *Caucasus mons Scythiae*. For the position of India and Thyle see, e.g., Isidore *Etymologiae* 14.3.5 and 6.4; OH 1.2.13-15 and 79. For Thule's perpetual day alternating with perpetual night see *C. Plini Secundi naturalis historiae libri XXXVII*, ed. C. Mayhoff (Leipzig, 1906) 4.104, *C. Iulii Solini collectanea rerum memorabilium*, ed. T. Mommsen (Berlin, 1895; repr., 1958), 22.9; Isidore *Etymologiae* 14.6?, Capella, *De nuptiis* 6.602. For the persistence of this belief into the later Middle Ages see John Kirtland Wright, *The Geographical Lore of the Time of the Crusades. A Study in the History of Medieval Science and Tradition in Western Europe* (New York, 1925; repr., with a new introduction by Clarence J. Glacken, 1965), 241. Cf. the Remigian gloss, "Per Indiam intelligitur totius oriens. Thyle ultima est insularum in occidente in mari britannico, a qua unius diei nauigatione peruenitur ad mare congelatum," and the comment by the Irishman Dicuil, writing at the beginning of the ninth century, that the periods of continuous day and continuous night fall only around the summer and winter solstices (see *Dicuili liber de mensura orbis terrae*, ed. J. J. Tierney [Dublin, 1967], 12.8). Otten, *König Alfreds Boethius*, 128 n. 18 cites Isidore *Etymologiae* 14.4, but adds "der Wortlaut deckt sich wiederum nicht."

64. Bo 41.28-42.4: "Þær þu miht on geseon þæt eall moncynn ⁊ ealle netenu ne notigað nawer neah feorðan dæles þisse eorðan ðæs þe men gefaran magan, forþæmþe hy hit ne magon eall gebugian, sum for hæto, sum for cile; ⁊ þone mæstan dæl his hæfð sæ oferseten." See, e.g., Capella, *de Nuptiis* 6, §§602-8; Macrobius, *Commentariorum in somnium Scipionis libri II*, ed. Franciscus Eyssenhardt (Leipzig, 1893), 2.5. For later medieval versions of this belief see Wright, 156-65. With respect to this addition Otten (above, note 9), 128, quotes a gloss in Einsiedeln MS 127, but admits that this relates only to one small part of Alfred's new material.

65. See above, n. 63.
66. See above, nn. 57, 60 and 63.
67. See above, n. 62.
68. See above, n. 60.
69. See above, n. 61.
70. The first reference to Cicero is at Bo 43.5-7: "Hwæt, þu wast hu micel Romana rice wæs on Marcuses dagum þæs heretogan; se wæs oðre naman haten Tullius, ⁊ þriddan Cicero." This serves on the one hand to locate the event in history—in the time of the consul Cicero—and on the other to introduce a piece of information which happens to be recorded in one of his books. Cf. BC 2, pr. 7, §8: "Aetate denique M. Tullii, sic ut ipse quodam loco significat . . ." The second, at Bo 143.4-9, concentrates on Cicero as a wise man beset with a problem: "þis is sio ealde siofung þe þu longe siofodes, ⁊ manige eac ær ðe; þara wæs sum Marcus, oðre naman Tullius, þriddan naman he wæs gehaten Cicero; se wæs Romana heretoga; se wæs uðwita. Se wæs swiðe abisgod mid þære ilcan spræce, ac he hi ne meahte brengan to nanum ende." Cf. BC 5, pr. 4, §1 "Vetus, inquit, haec est de prouidentia querela M.que Tullio, cum diuinationem distribuit uehementer agitata tibique ipsi res diu prorsus multumque quaesita."

71. See above.

72. That Cyrus was king of the Persians is information found in the Bible as well as in classical and late Latin texts. Alfred's incorrect location of Lydia

in Greece may be the result of ignorance. See, however, Karl Heinz Schmidt, *König Alfreds Boethius-Bearbeitung* (Gottingen, 1934), 20, n. 1: "Überhaupt fasst Alfred den geographischen Begriff Griechenland sehr weit; ihm schwebte offenbar die Ausdehnung des späteren östromischen Reiches vor."

73. For a summary of the various versions of the Croesus story see the entry *Croesus* in Pauly-Wissowa, *Real-Encyclopädie der classischen Altertumswissenschaft*, Suppl. 5, 462. The Remigian commentaries here tell of Croesus' conversation with Solon, of a dream which he had, and of its subsequent fulfilment according to the interpretation given by his daughter. Vat. Lat. 3363 has a more unusual comment, which, in my view, is suspiciously close to an account in Justinus and OH of a ruse by Cyrus against not Croesus but Thamyris. Compare the text of Troncarelli (above, note 26), 63 and OH 2.7.

74. See, e.g., the Remigian commentary MS BN Lat. 6401A, "Busiridis rex fuit Aegipti qui triduo pastus [*lege* pastos] hospites immolabat. Postea immolatus e[s]t ab Hercule. Vel sacerdos Aegiptius uel rex cuius meminit Virgilius consul romanorum . . . Orosius refert has duas historias. iste namque solitus recipere hospites et interficere. et interfectus est. ab Hercule." I am indebted to Dr. Bolton for this material.

75. Servius *Georgics* 3.5: "Busiris rex fuit Aegypti: qui cum susceptos hospites immolaret ab Hercule interemptus est, cum etiam eum uoluisset occidere . . . et aliter: Busiris, Aegypti rex, omnibus annis Ioui hospites immolabat: nam per octo annos sterilitate Aegypto laborante, Pygmalion Cyprius finem futurum non ait, nisi sanguinis hospitis litatum fuisset . . ." etc. Hyginus *Fabulae* 56: "In Aegypto apud Busiridem Neptuni filium cum esset sterilitas et Aegyptus annis nouem siccitate exaruisset, ex Graecia augures conuocauit. Thrasis Pygmalionis fratris filius Busiridi monstrauit immolato hospite uenturos imbres, promissisque fidem ipse immolatus exhibuit."

76. See fo. 6^r, "Bossiridis in egypto rex fuit hospites suos neptuno domino suo immolabat. Cum hercules uenisset uincere [*lege* uinciri] passus est et admotus. Aris [*false punctuation*] subito uinculis ruptis bossiridem ipse more mactauit Nilo immolauit uelut enim ollim his ospites [= is hospites] immolabat simili exemplo. . . . damnatus est."

77. "Gigantes Othus et Ephialtes qui crescebant singulis mensibus nouem digitis, qui etiam conati sunt Iouem ter de sedis domicilio trahere ponentes montem supra montem, cum tertio quos ipse fulminauit" (quoted in Bolton [above, note 23], 43): see also Myth. 1.83.

78. Bo 98.26–99.3. For the giants as sons of earth see, e.g., Ovid *Metamorphoses* 1.157; Ovid *Fasti*, ed. Sir James George Frazer (London, 1976), 580; Isidore *Etymologiae* 11.3.13; and Mythographus 1.11. For the giants and Jove as sister's sons see, perhaps, Ovid *Metamorphoses* 9.498, where Saturn is said to be brother of Ops. For the attempt to storm heaven see Ovid *Fasti* 5.36–40, idem *Metamorphoses* 1.151–53 and cf. Isidore *Etymologiae* 9.2.135. For the giants' destruction by Jove's thunderbolt see Isidore *Etymologiae* 9.2.135 (of the Titans), Ovid *Metamorphoses* 1.154–55 and idem *Fasti* 5.35 f. (Servius and Hyginus attribute the destruction to Diana and/or Apollo). For the initial equality between heaven and earth, see Ovid *Fasti* 5.17–18.

79. Bo 99.4–17.

80. Bo 115.27–28; BC 4, m. 3. Circe is not named in the metre.

81. Cf. Ovid *Metamorphoses* 1.163, idem *Fasti* 4.203 f. and Isidore *Etymologiae* 8.11.33-34. For Phoebus Apollo (or Sol) as son of Jove see *Metamorphoses* 1.517, and 8.968, Isidore *Etymologiae* 8.11.33-34, Hyginus *Fabulae* 8.4. The description of Jupiter as son of Saturn and highest of the gods is a commonplace in classical texts. See further below.

82. Bo 66.27-29; *Commentarius*, ed. Silk, 134. See Janet Bately, "Evidence for knowledge of Latin literature in Old English," in *Sources of Anglo-Saxon Culture*, ed. Paul E. Szarmach, with the assistance of Virginia Darrow Oggins (Kalamazoo, 1986), 42, and Bolton, "Remigian Commentaries" (above, note 28), 383-84.

83. Bo 65.27-66.1. See Otten (above, note 9), 126, Wittig (above, note 18), 183-84, and Mythographus 1.218. Cf. BC 3, 5, §6: "Expertus sortis suae periculorum tyrannus regni metus pendentis supra uerticem gladii terrore simulauit"; Mythographus 1.218: "Dionysius tyrannus . . . Quadam autem die amicorum suorum quidam interrogauit, an esse felix? Qui ait: Quidni? iussitque illum residere in solio suo, indutum uestibus regiis sceptrumque tenentem; ac deinde gladium acutissimum, tenuissimo filo ligatum, super uerticem eius suspendi, et interrogauit eum, utrum sibi uideretur esse beatus? Qui respondit, nullo modo se esse beatum, qui aestimaret, se casu gladii cito moriturum. Cui Dionysius: Qualem tu, inquit, nunc habes timorem, talem ego assidue patior"; Macrobius *In Somnium Scipionis* 1.10.16: "Dionysius . . . gladium uagina raptum et a capulo de filo tenui pendentem mucrone demisso iussit familiaris illius capiti inter epulas imminere, cumque ille et Siculas et tyrannicas copias praesentis mortis periculo grauaretur, 'talis est,' inquit Dionysius. 'uita, quam beatam putabas: sic semper mortem nobis imminentem uidemus. æstima, quando esse felix poterit, qui timere non desinit.'"

84. Bo 101.22-103.13. See Wittig, (above, note 18).

85. Bo 115.13-116.26.

86. See Wittig, 185.

87. See Ovid *Metamorphoses* 14.241-65, 297-98, 308, 435-39. 483-509. For Ithaca as Ulysses' homeland see also Servius *Aen.* 2.44, Hyginus *Fabulae* 125, Dares, *De Excidio Troiae Historia*, ed. F. Meister (Leipzig, 1873) 15, also Ovid, *Metamorphoses* 18.711-12. In BC Ulysses is referred to merely as "Neritii ducis." At what stage the adjective *Neritius* was transformed into *Rhaetia* is not clear. However, either it happened after the identification with Ulysses was made, or knowledge of the story made identification of the hero (and the heroine) automatic. MS variants include the spellings *Naretii*, *Neretii* and *Nirettii*. Also from Ovid could be the location of the island in the Mediterranean. The major difference between Bo's account and those of both Ovid and Boethius is of course the chronology.

88. In an earlier paper ("Evidence" [above, note 7], 41) I commented that it was hard to see how Alfred could have told the story in this way had he known Ovid's version at first hand. However, it is perhaps not totally out of the question that the change should have been a deliberate one on Alfred's part. The dividing line between ignorance and inspired alteration is a very thin one. Cf. BC 2, m. 6 and Bo 39.16-30.

89. See Or. 28.6-9. Atreus and Thyestes in fact murdered their half-brother, Atreus subsequently killing both his own son and the sons of Thyestes. For a potential source for part of the story see Servius *Aen.* 1.568.

90. Or. 28.16: "Minotauro . . . þæt wæs healf mon, healf leo"; OH 1.13.2: "utrum fero homini an humanae bestiae aptius dicam nescio." Cf., e.g., Isidore, *Etymologiae* 11.3.9: "Alia . . . qui leonis habent uultum uel canis uel taurinum caput aut corpus, ut ex Pasiphae memorant genitum Minotaurum." The *OE Orosius* also incorrectly claims that *all* the noblest children of the Athenians were given to the Minotaur to eat.

91. See fo. 6^r.

92. See fo. 6^v.

93. See Or. 26.34 and cf. OH 1.10.19 "ridiculam Phaethontis fabulam." For the story of the destruction of Phaethon see, e.g., Isidore *Etymologiae* 16.8.6, "Phaethonte fulminis ictu interempto," and Ovid *Metamorphoses* 2.1-366; Hyginus *Fabulae* 152A. The noun *forscapung* is found only twice in OE, both instances occurring in Or. In view of the meaning "to transform" given to the corresponding verb in both Old and Middle English it is tempting to translate *forscapung* as "transformation" here, and to suppose that the author was aware that the story of Phaethon was told in Ovid's *Metamorphoses* but ignorant of the fact that he was actually destroyed. However, this sense does not appear appropriate to the second instance, in Or. 32.5, and indeed a meaning "mishap," "disastrous happening" is probably intended in both places.

94. See Or. 25.9, 24.32-25.6 and commentary on these lines.

95. Or. 69.20-28. Possible sources include Julius Valerius *Res gestae Alexandri Macedonis* 1.8 and Fulgentius, *De aetatibus mundi et hominis, Opera*, ed. R. Helm (Leipzig, 1898), 164.

96. See Or. 39.5-16, 40.4-12 and 41.1-11 and, for possible sources, see commentary on these lines.

97. Or. 50.3. For the association of Cincinnatus with the virtue of poverty see, e.g., Valerius Maximus 4.4 *De paupertate*, Augustine *De ciuitate Dei* 5.18, and Or. 118.24-119.8. That Scipio was strangled is suggested by Velleius Paterculus (*C. Vellei Paterculi ex Historiae Romanae Libris Duobus quae supersunt*, ed. C. Stegmann de Pritzwald (Leipzig, 1933; repr., Stuttgart, 1965) 2.4.5; see also *De uiris illustribus* 58.10 and Sidonius *Epistulae* 8.11, possibly following the now lost Livy 54 (see *Sidonius Apollinaris, Letters*, ed., O. M. Dalton, [Oxford, 1915]).

98. Or. 118.24-119.8 and commentary.

99. Or. 130.11 and commentary.

100. Or. 128.25-29. Or.'s description of Caesar's behavior could be based either on Frontinus (see *Iuli Frontini Strategematon Libri IV*, ed. G. Gundermann [Leipzig, 1888]) 2.8.13 "in primam aciem pedes prosiluit," or on similar statements in Florus (*L. Annaei Flori Epitomae Libri II*, ed. O Rossbach [Leipzig, 1896]) 2.8.82 and Velleius Paterculus, 2.4.3 — or of course the corresponding (now lost) book of Livy: cf. Periocha 115.

101. See, e.g., *The Old English Orosius*, ed. Bately, 41.1-9: 128.3-4 and 101.4-13, e.g., and commentary on these lines.

102. Ibid., 42.1-13, 60.8-10 and 59.3-11, and commentary on these lines.

103. Ibid., 29.35 and 28.16-21 and commentary on these lines.

104. Ibid., 106.7-11, 121.9-15 and commentary on these lines. For a detailed study see J. M. Bately, "The classical additions to the Old English Orosius," *England before the Conquest*, ed. P. Clemoes and K. Hughes, and idem, *The Old English Orosius*, commentary, passim.

105. See *The Old English Orosius*, 45.33-46.2; 106.13-30 and commentary on these lines.

106. Ibid., lxii-lxvii.

107. See D. Whitelock, "The Prose of Alfred's Reign," *Continuations and Beginnings*, ed. E. G. Stanley (London, 1966), 82 n. 398.

108. Bo 7.1-6. Cf. Chapter-headings 3.1-2 "Ærest hu Gotan gewunnon Romana rice, 7 hu Boetius hi wolde eft beræedan," suggesting that the author of the contents knew in addition that Theodoric was a Goth. This section, which deals with the life and death of Boethius, has of course no parallel in BC.

109. Or. 155.22-23.

110. Or. 156.11-23.

111. OH 7.37-43. Radagaisus and Alaric are, however, loosely linked in OH 7.37-38: "duo tunc Gothorum populi cum duobus potentissimis regibus suis per Romanas prouincias bacchabantur."

112. *Cassiodori Senatoris Chronica*, ed. T. Mommsen, *Monumenta Germaniae Historica, Auctores Antiquissimi XI. Chronicorum Minorum Saec. IV, V, VI, VII* (Berlin, 1961), 2.154. *Prosperi Tironis Epitoma Chronicon*, ibid., 1.464 refers to them as *duces*. See also *Consularia Italica*, ed. Mommsen, 1.299.

113. Although OH (but not Or.) describes Radagaisus as a Scythian (see, e.g., 7.37.5). For Gothia as part of Scythia see Isidore *Etymologiae* 14.4.3. See also Capella, *De nuptiis* 6 (§622). That the Goths conquered the whole of Italy including Sicily is not a claim found in OH or Or., though cf. OH 7.43.12 "in Siciliam Gothi transire conati."

114. For the variant forms *Radagaisus* and *Ragadaisus* see Bately, "King Alfred and the Latin Manuscripts," 102-3.

115. See *Widsith*, ed., Kemp Malone (Copenhagen, 1936; rev. ed. 1962). The form *Rædgota* could, however, have had another source. See Bately, "King Alfred and the Old English Translation of Orosius" (above, note 7), 438-39, where I have suggested that an original *Radagaisus* or *Ragadaisus* could have been modified as a result of incorrect incorporation of an interlinear gloss "Gotus" or "Gota" (i.e., a Goth). This modification of course could have taken place in any text at any time.

116. See *Widsith*, 1.112 and commentary, p. 130.

117. Bo 34.30-35.6.

118. Or. 40.1-14. Cf. OH 2.4.12-13.

119. See, e.g., OH 2.4.15-2.5.1-4. Cf. Remigius commentary, Trier Sammelkodex 1093 "filii Bruti, qui erant amici Tarquinii, uoluerunt eis urbem aperire; qua re comperta. . . ."

120. Bo 39.16-28. This is only one of several places where BC refers to Nero. See also Bo 34.24, 64.24, 66.23, 67.2. In most of the passages in question the only substantive detail that is added is the status of Nero as either *casere* or king (thus, e.g., Bo 66.23). The naming of Nero (along with Theodoric) as a typical evil ruler is an addition which seems to imply that some at least of the audience might be expected to recognise this figure. For Theodoric as evil see *Das Altenglische Martyrologium*, ed. Gunter Kotzor (Munich, 1981), 2.105.15-107.6. For the emperor Nero as an example of wickedness see, e.g., *The Scriptores Historiae Augustae*, ed. David Magie (London, 1953): *Diuus Aurelianus* 42.6.

121. See, e.g., Troncarelli (above, note 26), 171.

122. Bo 39.23-24.

123. Tacitus *Annals* 14.64 refers to two murdered wives — one (Octavia) who, having been bound, had her veins cut and was then smothered and decapitated, and one (Poppaea) who was kicked to death by her husband, when she was pregnant. However, in the anonymous tragedy *Octauia* a passage referring to Agrippina having being put to the sword ("non funesta uiolata manu/ remigis ante,/ mox et ferro lacerata diu/ saeui iacuit uictima nati?") is followed by a speech by Octavia in which she sees herself as being similarly sent to the gloomy shades by the tyrant. See *The Octavia*, ed. Lucile Yow Whitman (Bern and Stuttgart, 1978), ll. 954-59. I am indebted to participants at the conference for this reference.

124. Or. 137.19-27.

125. Bo 115.13-21; BC 4, m. 3 begins with a reference to "Vela neritii ducis." cf. 4, m. 7 "Bella bis quinis operatus annis / ultor Atrides Phrygiae ruinis / fratris amissos thalamos piauit."

126. Agamemnon is also alluded to (as *ultor Atrides*) in BC 4, m. 7 but not named, nor is his rank given. That Agamemnon was *casere* could be based on a description of him as *imperator*, as in Dares Frigius, or derived, by implication, from Ovid's *Metamorphoses*: see, e.g., *Metamorphoses* 12.626-28 and 12.276.

127. Or. 31.22-30. See Dares, *De Excidio Troie Historia*, also *The Old English Orosius*, ed. Bately, 222. The Orosius commentary also has a brief reference to the main protagonists in the story.

128. Bo 34.7-10. cf. BC 2, pr. 6, §1 "flammis Aetnae eructantibus."

129. Or. 50.25-30; cf. OH 2.14.3 *Aethna*.

130. GD 315.4; cf. *Gregorii Magni Dialogi Libri IV*, ed. U. Moricca (Rome, 1924), 4.36.

131. The description of Etna as exuding sulphur has many possible sources, including Servius *Aen.* 3.571. For the link with hell see, e.g., Isidore *Etymologiae* 14.8.14, "Mons Aethna ex igne et sulphure dictus; unde et Gehenna"; see also Bede, *De Natura Rerum, Patrologia Latina*, 90.276. The dangers of assuming shared knowledge is illustrated by recent comments on the reference to Titus in ASC and Or. See *The OE Orosius*, ed. Bately (above, note 7), xc-xci and 325.

132. Or. 30.15 and 72.7 "Ercol se ent"; Bo 36.33 and 127.11 "Erculus Iobes sunu." For the term *ent* see *The Old English Orosius*, ed. Bately, 30.15 and commentary, and cf. Augustine *De ciuitate Dei* 1.4.31 on *semideos*. For Hercules as son of Jove see, e.g., Ovid *Metamorphoses* 9.104.

133. See Bo 115.23-116.2 and Or. 24.11, 57.4-13, 84.7, 87.28 and 88.22 f. and cf. Isidore *Etymologiae* 8.11.1-4. For the gods as unclean see, e.g., Augustine *De ciuitate Dei* 2.26.

134. See above.

135. Or. 27.11-12; cf. OH 1.6.2, which merely enquires, "quod exsecrabile sine dubio hominibus uiderim an ipsis etiam diis exsecrabile uideretur."

136. According to OH 2.6.12, "ibi tunc Croesus ... cum ad auxiliandum Babyloniis uenisset, uictus sollicite in regnum refugit. Cyrus autem posteaquam Babylonam ut hostis inuasit ut uictor euertit ut rex disposuit, bellum transtulit in Lydiam." See Or. 44.7-11: "ða wæs Croesus se Liþa cyning mid firde gefaren Babylonium to fultume. Ac þa he wiste þæt hie him on nanum fultome beon ne mæhte, ₇ þæt seo burg abrocen wæs, he him hamweard ferde to his agnum

rice. ₇ him Cirus wæs æfterfylgende oþ he hiene gefeng ₇ ofslog," and cf. Orosius Commentary, fo. 9ᵛ "transtullit in lidiam: eoq; creoseus ad auxilium uenisset babilonis."

137. See e.g., the entries on MS BN Lat. 6401A and Cambridge University Library, MS Kk III 21, to be printed by Bolton in her forthcoming edition of the English tradition of Remigius. MS. Vat Lat. 3363 has material similar to the Remigian commentaries on Boethius and to Mythographus 1.219.

138. Bo 37.5-10, BC 2, pr. 6, §11.

139. See, e.g., OH 4.6.25 and 4.10.2 for consuls with the name Regulus. For the equation *Poeni: Africanas* see, e.g., Isidore *Etymologiae* 9.2.116 with 15.1.30.

140. See *The Old English Orosius,* ed. Bately (above, note 7), 95.21-96.5 and commentary on these lines.

141. Bo 72.30. Cf. OH 2.15.1, 16.2 etc. However, the description of Alcibiades as *æþeling* may reflect an allusion to his noble birth, as in Valerius Maximus 6.9 ext. 4, "Alcibiaden quasi duae fortunae partitae sunt, altera, quae ei nobilitatem eximiam, abundantes diuitiis . . . summa imperia . . ." Otten (above, note 9), 139, suggests influence by a comment such as "nobilem a terrenis desideriis expeditur [*lege* expeditum]" (Trier Sammelkodex 1093, fo. 130v, Einsiedeln MS. 179, fo. 129).

142. OH refers to a number of consuls by the name of Catullus: see, e.g., OH 4.8.5 and 4.11.6.

143. The details concerning Cicero are assembled all together in *De uiris illustribus,* §81. Cf. OH 6.6.1, where Marcus Tullius Cicero is referred to as consul. For a possible source for the incorrect reference to Brutus Cassius see Bately, "Evidence" (above, note 7), 44 and École de Médecine de Montpelier MS 358, fo. 27ʳ, *Commentarius in Bucolica et Georgica Virgilii:* "Tempore illo, gubernante Iulio Cesare imperium, regnauit Brutus Casius . . . et exortum est bellum inter Iulium Caesarem et Brutum Casium." I am indebted to H. T. Silverstein, "Chaucer's Brutus Cassius," *MLN* 47 (1932): 148-50 for this reference.

144. Bo identifies Latin *consul* with OE *heretoga,* Or with *ladteow*. See, e.g., Bo 7.11-12 "þa wæs sum consul, þæt we heretoha hataðˮ; Or. 40.12-14 "Him ða Romane æfter þæm ladteowas gesetton þe hie consulas heton, þæt heora rice heolde an gear an monn."

145. For the considerable body of additional information relating to geography see Janet Bately, "The Relationship between the Geographical Information in the OE Orosius and Latin Texts other than Orosius," *ASE* 1 (1972): 45-67.

146. We do not of course know whether Alfred had planned (or indeed caused to be made) translations of works other than those which have come down to us.

147. See *Asser,* ed. Stevenson, §87 f.

PLENARY LECTURE

The Role of the Papal Library in Saving Livy's Histories[1]

GIUSEPPE BILLANOVICH

(TRANSLATED BY GIOVANNI GULLACE AND RETA BERNARDO)

Armchair strategy or frontal attack? Many historians and philologists still ply their trade in the simplest, and most comfortable, manner: sitting in their armchairs and consulting books. They certainly have every right to do so, but in the meantime an infinite amount of material is hidden on ancient stones and in manuscripts and notary registers, despite industrial civilization having provided us grammarians with constantly improved means for research and study. It is true that recently Lowe and Kristeller, giants in the field, have published lasting monuments, *Codices Latini Antiquiores* and *Iter Italicum*. But for the most part, historians and philologists have taken less advantage of new developments than scientists, such as physicists, chemists, and physicians, or their cousins, archeologists and art historians. The richest mines, from the Vatican to the British Library, are filled with precious holdings that remain largely untouched. In particular, there are sources of texts essential to the restoration of classical and Christian works and to the reconstruction of events dominated by some of the great intellects of our civilization, such as Petrarch, Poliziano, and Erasmus. Let us take an important example and examine at some length the paths taken by Livy's histories over the course of a thousand years.

1. *Decades 1 and 3 and the Papal Library*

Nearly forty years ago, as a member of the prestigious Warburg Institute, I studied, or at least leafed through, nearly one thousand manuscripts in the British Library; during two fateful days I discovered that the entire manuscript Additional 19906 was written by the Paduan patriarch, Lovato Lovati, and that the young Petrarch had reconstructed and prodigiously restored in Harleian 2493 the entire corpus then available of the *Ab urbe condita* (i.e., the first, third, and fourth Decades).

I soon published this discovery, first in an article in the *Journal of the Warburg and Courtauld Institutes* entitled "Petrarch and the Textual Tradition of Livy," and then in the first half of *La tradizione del testo di Livio e le origini del umanesimo*, where I also included the complete facsimile of the three decades restored by Petrarch.[2]

Now I shall reveal other discoveries that are even more striking and sweeping. During the period when the Roman Empire was falling into barbarism, the mammoth structure of the *Ab urbe condita* was fractured. Fortunately, the illustrious Q. Aurelius Symmachus and others in his family, along with their relatives and collaborators, the Nicomachi, saved one section; this can clearly be seen in the signatures on the books of the first Decade. But after that, what happened? A century ago, Giovanni Battista de Rossi, a solitary pioneer and a stranger in his own country because of his political and religious convictions, meticulously examined the ancient papal library.[3] Though neither a professor nor a member of the Accademia de' Lincei, he investigated the catacombs, gathered Christian inscriptions, and collaborated with Theodor Mommsen in collecting many of the classical epigraphs in volume 6 of the *Corpus inscriptionum latinarum*. Because of the difficulty of navigating the dark seas of distant centuries without a catalogue as guide, and because of lack of interest, the papal library has been almost completely ignored. Thus, this important spiritual and philological depository remains a treasure galleon at the bottom of the ocean. Since the shadowy sixth and seventh centuries, the pontifical palace at St. John Lateran has had a large number of sacred and classical works and has distributed copies of them to monasteries and cathedrals, thereby disseminating them to the Christian world. Precisely because major sections of the *Ab urbe condita* were in the care of papal librarians, they have survived in good condition until the present.

It is common knowledge that an emperor or even an abbot on pilgrimage to Rome used to give the pontiff a Bible in beautiful script with fine illumination; for example, in 716 Abbot Ceolfrid brought the Amiatine Bible from England to Rome, and in 875 Charles the Bold brought the Bible, which is now in S. Paolo fuori le Mura, as well as the royal throne now in St. Peter's basilica, known as the "cathedra sancti Petri."[4] But we have yet to grasp the significant fact that popes, bishops, or lords customarily presented Livy's histories to emperors because it was the most comprehensive and respectable document supporting the empire's validity and the emperor's authority. This spectacle of popes as custodians of Livy's histories, who give copies of them in homage to emperors, is certainly not one that our Jacobin forefathers and liberal grandfathers would appreciate! In fact, they never did recognize this phenomenon because they who fail to seek do not find and they who do not wish to see do not see.

Quite early, the first Decade (the one put together by the Symmachi and the Nicomachi) and the archetype of the ordinary version of the third Decade became part of the papal library. Bernhard Bischoff, the leading expert of our day, has deduced that the latter was once owned by Charlemagne whose minister of culture, Alcuin, had had his monks at St. Martin de Tours make a copy of it in miniscule (now Vat. Reg. Lat. 762).[5] At the emperor's death on June 28, 814, his books by prearrangement were sold to give alms to the poor; as a result, the archetype for the Third Decade ended up in the monastery of Corbie, where it remained. To this we can now add that this archetype was given to Charlemagne by the pope — by Leo III, I believe, when he crowned him emperor on Christmas night in the year 800. Yet canons in the papal library also kept a copy of the venerable examplar, and thus the third Decade was passed on from two sources, the Corbie archetype (now Par. Lat. 5730) and more plentifully from the copy kept at the Vatican. Pope Leo III also gave Charlemagne a codex with the first decade, thereby broadening the history of Rome for him. It was that copy and two different texts of the Decade, which had remained at St. John Lateran, that produced offspring for the libraries of Christianity through two large families, λ and π.

The empire founded by Charlemagne was given new life by the Ottos, and through them the fortunes of the first, third, and fourth Decades of the *Ab urbe condita* were greatly improved. Since the distant reign of King Theodoric the cathedral of Verona had been a magnificent fortress, and in the interim had collected a large number of sacred and secular texts. Thus, it had preserved important readings of the first Decade in the Veronese palimpsest 40 along with nearly one half of the tradition in a codex still in majuscule. In 972, Ratherius, Verona's energetic bishop, had two copies in flowing Carolingian script made of the ancient codex; he kept the one which is now in Florence (Laur. 63, 19) in the cathedral, and presented the other in homage to his guests, Otto I and Otto II.

2. *Books 26–40 and the Papal Library*

The second half of the third Decade came down to us through a normal channel, a different and better one; yet its travels were so elusive that it is an editor's nightmare. Let us now clarify another tradition for books 26–30, something which will simultaneously shed light on the standard version of the fourth Decade. For we note a long-standing textual tradition in the papal holdings that combined books 26–40, namely, three volumes from the fifth century containing the pentads 26–30, 31–35, and 36–40. In Rome on May 21, 996, Pope Gregory V crowned his cousin Otto III as emperor; he also presented him with the last Decade in early uncial, which was still at St. John Lateran: this was the fourth Decade divided into two volumes.

In cathedral chancelleries it was common to work on the "restoration" of documents, while in monasteries and basilicas lives of the saints were periodically rewritten to improve their content, style, and handwriting. Similarly, the phenomenal "renouatio codicum," thus far given little heed by classical philologists, was a continual project in libraries with large holdings and in scriptoria. Consequently, deteriorating copies in obsolete scripts were periodically destroyed, i.e., sons devoured their fathers, that is to say, the copy of Livy in Carolingian script the damaged copies in majuscule. Thus, before the early pentads 31–35 and 36–40 were given to Otto III, custodians in the papal library transcribed the entire set in Carolingian: the first pentad (26–30) whose crumbling copy they let perish as was customary, and pentads 31–35 and 36–40. Later on, after Otto's successor, Henry II, had bequeathed to the newly-created and favored diocese of Bamberg the early fourth Decade given to Otto by the pope, together with other texts from the imperial treasure, the old text was recopied in the contemporary, pleasing Carolingian script; then, as usual, it lost all value and wound up in unbound fascicules, offering a wealth of parchment to generations of enthusiastic readers. Fragments of the fourth Decade in uncial, which had been used for binding in the Bamberg manuscript, were discovered only at the beginning of this century; they were immediately made public by the great paleographer and philologist, Ludwig Traube.[6]

Since researchers of the Livy tradition often found decades, but rarely pentads, they never suspected an anomalous set of circumstances affecting books 26–40. Instead, even for this lineage, the papal copy became the primary source, generating a second tradition for books 26–30 and the standard version for the fourth Decade. As early as the eleventh century, then, copies of the collection containing books 26–40 were brought from Rome to the great cathedrals of Chartres and Speyer; I have also used from the Archives of Nancy substantial fragments of a copy made in Rome during the same period. A little later, in the second half of the twelfth century, the Roman renaissance revitalized architecture and church decoration with a return to ancient or late-ancient models and revived sacred and classical studies. In fact, Rome was so vital during that period that, despite the turmoil due to the schism, copies of the first and third Decade were redone about mid-century at the papal residence; they were carefully corrected and enriched with curious, even unique, marginalia. These restructured Decades generated a host of descendants, primarily for the purpose of supplying monasteries and city churches in Rome with a history of ancient Rome; many of these restructured Decades still survive.

On the other hand, the fourth Decade attracted so few readers during this same period that recent intensive research has not uncovered a single copy dating from the twelfth and thirteenth centuries. And yet more than once during the eleventh and twelfth centuries, in order to compensate for this shortcoming (and this is something editors have never intuited), experienced papal librarians made use of their own collection of books 26-40 to correct errors which had troubled the standard text of the third Decade from the beginning and to fill lacunae which had crept into it. Thus, it is important that we avail ourselves of the vicissitudes in the Livy tradition and of other evidence in order to study the culture and philology that Rome, capital of Christianity, fostered for many centuries.

3. From Rome to Pomposa and from Pomposa to Padua

In the following century, the thirteenth, communes flourished in northern and central Italy, and in northeastern Italy the first examples of a new style of rhetoric and philology appeared. The Orlando of this exploit was the Paduan notary and judge, Lovato Lovati; he was born around 1240 and thus a contemporary of Dante's father, and died in 1309 when Petrarch was little more than an infant. In an uncultured age, Lovato was a man of formidable learning and a magnificent rhetorician. He trained as his successor Albertino Mussato, author of the tragedy *Ecerinis* and highly personalized histories, who was crowned poet and historian at the University of Padua in 1315. Lovato convinced his fellow townsmen that an ancient grave, recently discovered in Padua, dating back to the sixth century at the latest, was the tomb of the Trojan Antenor, the city's mythical founder. He also convinced them that the epigraph on a tombstone, which also reappeared at that time inscribed with the name of T. LIVIVS (CIL, 5.2865), was obviously the grave of their illustrious townsman [Titus] Livy. As a result of the discovery of the tomb and epigraph, he and his followers became the founders of the new disciplines of archeology and epigraphy.[7]

According to Strabo's testimony, during the golden age of Augustus, Padua was the third most important city in the empire, just after Rome and Cadiz. But the Lombard invasions in the seventh century and the Hungarian plunderings in the tenth had so depleted the central Veneto of ancient texts that Lovato had to acquire them outside his own commune. From the rich cathedral in prosperous Verona (some 80 kilometers to the west) he managed to obtain the poems, buried there, of the immortal Veronese, Catullus, as well as those of Ausonius.[8] Lovato also followed the torturous pilgrimage route to the south for nearly 100 kilometers and exploited the splendid library—as splendid as the basilica and campanile that are still standing—of the shrunken monastery of Pomposa in the Po delta. In what is now Additional 19906 of the British Library, of very modest appearance as literary texts usually were (and the reason too for its remaining hidden until recently despite its considerable value), he first transcribed, preciously reproducing certain characteristics of Carolingian script and orthography, Justin's *Epitome* from the *Philippic Histories* by Pompeius Trogus, taking it from a copy made at Pomposa in 1087 by the monk Teuzone from a version of Veronese origin.[9] He then transcribed the final section of Bede's *De temporum ratione*, likewise at Pomposa, while in the second part of the manuscript he transcribed a collection of his own poems and one of his *dictamina* using only Gothic writing and orthography.[10] From Pomposa he also took the only text of Seneca's tragedies in the codex called the *Etruscus* that has fortunately survived as Florence, Laur. 37, 13, now deservedly entitled *Pomposianus*. Lovato also acquired, like a Palladium for Padua, a restored set of the *Ab urbe condita* with a standard first Decade, the less well-known third, and the still unknown fourth. In the full heat of these remarkable discoveries, he wrote a biography of Livy and another of Seneca based on classical sources, literary and epigraphic, although these were questionable. Lovato's friends and followers from Padua, Verona, and Ferrara so exploited his version of the Decades that it multiplied like Abraham's offspring. A new era in civilization had begun; it was indeed the dawn of humanism.

During the eleventh century, the monastery of Pomposa had known its own golden age with nearly one hundred monks and three great abbots: St. Guido (1021-47), Mainardo (1047-56, 1063-73), and Girolamo (1078-1106). It enjoyed such close ties to the pontifical see and the papal library that Mainardo became a cardinal and librarian of the Roman church. Shortly thereafter, abbot Girolamo greatly increased its holdings, according to the testimony of a monk named Enrico in his letter of 1093; in its conclusion is given a list of about seventy codices recently acquired—the "armarium domini Hieronymi." Enrico listed three volumes of Seneca's works;[11] thus, Lovato surely must have appropriated the codex containing the tragedies. In fact, I suspect that the rest of the series was included, for the ancient Paduans knew them all—*Ad Lucilium, De beneficiis, De clementia*, and three other works. Enrico also catalogued the Justin of which Lovato made a copy, as well as the *Ab urbe condita*, accompanying it with the powerful comment, "Libri X. Liuii ab Vrbe condita: sed C.XL. adhuc desunt Pomposiano abbati quos reperire auide anhelat." Abbot Girolamo and his assistants had come upon the most widely known first Decade, as the title, *Ab urbe condita*, assures us; similar echoes of this may even be found in Enrico's letter. Yet his abbot "yearned" to recover the remaining 140 books of Livy.

In conclusion, then, as soon as the turmoil caused by the schism allowed (i.e., throughout the troubled twenty-year period from 1080-1100 when Archbishop Ghiberto of nearby Ravenna came to power as the antipope Clement III), after Enrico had written his letter and catalogue, abbot Girolamo satisfied his "greediness" before his death by recovering the third and fourth Decades, thereby making Pomposa the equal of the papal palace and imperial Bamberg. Both Decades were copied at the Lateran in truncated texts; they were found two centuries later by the similarly "greedy" Lovato who exported them.[12] Obviously, a detailed analysis of these transferrals of texts, from the Lateran to Pomposa and then from Pomposa to Padua, whose early threads we are beginning to uncover, will greatly expedite reconstruction of the libraries of the Lateran and Pomposa.

4. Petrarch and the Readers of Avignon

In the turmoil following the illustrious papacy of Innocent III (1198-1216), the pontifical archives and library were transferred for safekeeping from St. John Lateran to the Tower of the Frangipani. But shortly thereafter, with the election of Gregory IX in 1227, the Frangipani sided with Frederick II against the Church, and the pontifical documents and books were unfortunately dispersed. The papal library was later rebuilt through the persistent efforts of Boniface VIII (1294-1303), yet it developed very differently from the earlier one because it was inspired and nurtured by new interests and new books from the mendicant orders and universities, namely, theology, philosophy, and science. But Boniface's library was also plundered in 1320 at Assisi, once again by the Ghibellines. In the meantime, obligations and resources moved from the old to the new Rome where Livy's tradition was really revived, for books and men of talent flowed from the narrow borders of our Italian communes to Avignon when it became the papal see and capital of Christianity in 1306. The Maecenas of culture and art as well as the protector of the exiled Tuscan Guelphs was the Dominican cardinal, Niccolò da Prato. His inspiration and assistant was Simone d'Arezzo, a notary and papal writer; he has remained unknown until now because Italian scholars for the last two centuries have only been interested in writing the history of sonnets, while failing to define the importance of this able man in Italian and even European culture.

In 1310 the emperor Henry VII came to Italy, promising justice and peace, and in June 1311 Clement V chose Cardinal Niccolò da Prato as his legate to the imperial court. The cardinal soon became a close collaborator of the emperor and his companion during the visits and perils of the imperial journey. During the delays caused by the lengthy siege at Brescia, the cardinal and Simone d'Arezzo met Albertino Mussato, his commune's ambassador to Henry VII for the third time. After the fall of Brescia, the cardinal went to Genoa with the emperor, and there once again met Mussato who had returned as ambassador to the imperial court with Rolando da Piazzola, a scholar and Lovato's nephew; he remained at the court for one hundred days. In his *Historia Augusta*, Mussato states that Cardinal Niccolò seemed an important supporter of the emperor and of the Ghibellines, particularly the Tuscans.

Like the plots in old comedies, the knots in this intricate story now begin to unravel and revelations clarify certain events. Cardinal da Prato and Simone set their sights and minds precisely on the two masterpieces of Latin literature discovered and restored by Lovato, namely, Livy's histories and Seneca's tragedies. The reason for this was surely not an identical inspiration raining separately from the heavens upon Padua and Avignon, as has been the theory; rather it was due to information and urgings that Mussato and Rolando da Piazzola had given to Cardinal da Prato and Simone during their lengthy stay in 1311 at Henry's court. The two men had tried to win the cardinal's strong support for their endangered commune with literary gifts, and thus had turned over to Simone at least the text of the third Decade. On April 14, 1315, from Valence on the Rhone, Cardinal da Prato sent a letter, doubtless inspired and written by Simone, to his English confrère, Nicholas Trevet; it speaks of his reading Trevet's commentary on Boethius' *De consolatione* and his awareness of Trevet's commentary on Seneca's *Declamationes*. He also asks him to write a commentary on Seneca's difficult tragedies, for the two Senecas were still thought to be the same man.[13]

Seneca's tragedies soon became the breviary for the literati in northern Italy since Paduan rhetoricians made them the model for reading, scansion, correction and imitation. Lovato had explicated their metrics with his *Nota* on the iambic trimeter; and Mussato had imitated them in his tragedy *Ecerinis*. Lovato had also extracted some versions at Pomposa from the formidable Laur. 37,12 and had grafted them onto the opposing standard set of the tragedies (A), thus creating for readers between Padua and Venice the hybrid Σ.[14]

Trevet did accept the cardinal's invitation to write a commentary on Seneca's tragedies. He finished it so quickly that already on July 13, 1317 the papal library had in its possession a copy of his commentary on the *Declamationes* and a copy of his commentary on the tragedies which opened with a dedicatory letter to Cardinal Niccolò da Prato.[15] Moreover, in 1316, Trevet had sent to the newly-elected John XXII a commentary on Genesis. The pope then commissioned him to write a commentary on Livy's history, which Trevet completed within two years, "biennali labore"; he accomplished all this, seemingly, between 1316 and 1319.

While editors of Seneca's tragedies did avail themselves of the text offered by Trevet's commentary, Livy's editors have yet to consider Trevet's commentary on the Decades. Here now are some surprising facts. Trevet knew and commented only upon the first and third Decades. For the third Decade, he used the text discovered by Lovato, which certainly must have been copied for him somewhere between Avignon and England by Cardinal da Prato, or rather by the indefatigable Simone. If Simone only gave Trevet the third Decade, then, it was because he had yet to receive the still mysterious fourth Decade from Mussato and Rolando da Piazzola.[16] In fact, it should be explained that Lovato, and then his small academy, did not make public the new texts that they had found.

During this same period, chance had brought Petracco di Parenzo, an exiled White Guelph notary, from Florence to Avignon where he prospered under the patronage of Cardinal da Prato. Petracco sent his oldest son, Francesco, to study law at the nearby University of Montpellier and then at Bologna, the mother of universities for the study of law. There then occurred two periods, one in 1325 and the other in 1326, which were to be fateful for Francesco Petrarca and for European culture. In early 1325, the twenty-year old Francesco returned from Bologna to Avignon where he became a salaried employee of the noble Colonna family, which was powerful in Rome and Avignon; with his father's generous support, he acquired books and assembled in particular an admirable collection of poetic and grammatical texts, now in the Ambrosian Library in Milan, that is usually referred to as the "Ambrosian Virgil."[17] In the autumn, he did return to Bologna for his courses, but in 1326 Petracco died in Avignon; on April 26, his sons Francesco and Gherardo left Bologna and the university without degrees.

Landolfo Colonna had been a student at Bologna at least from 1269, and thus was nearly eighty at this time; he had acquired a reputation and benefices befitting his family's nobility and power. Most importantly, for some thirty years he had been a canon at Chartres where he generally resided, but several times he went to Avignon because of dealings with the Curia. Giovanni Colonna, his nephew and a Dominican friar, also stayed at Chartres as well as at Avignon where he formed a close friendship with Petrarch. Landolfo composed historical and juridical works, while Fra Giovanni wrote a *De uiris illustribus* and a *Mare historiarum*. Landolfo lovingly made use of the extensive library at the cathedral of Chartres; he obtained on loan "quendam librum Tyti Liuii," which he returned on December 16, 1303, and borrowed once again on November 12, 1309. In a biography of Livy in his *De uiris illustribus* Fra Giovanni made this statement: "Vidi tamen ego quartam decadem in archiuis ecclesie Carnotensis; sed littera adeo erat antiqua quod uix ab aliquo legi poterat." After the fourth Decade had entered the public domain, however, in redoing Livy's biography for the later *Mare historiarum*, Fra Giovanni eliminated this passage. Now we can identify the Chartres Livy as a copy of books 26–40 from the papal library.

Because of Cardinal da Prato's support, Simone d'Arezzo had received a canonry in thriving Verona; soon after the Cardinal's death at Avignon in March 1321, he moved there. Yet he continued to maintain such close ties with the Curia that he seems to have spent much of his rather lengthy leaves of absence during the period 1326–1335 in Avignon in order to tend to personal matters and to those of the Veronese church and clergy as well as to discuss books and projects with friends. The first leave that Simone obtained from his fellow canons was from November 3, 1326 to April 12, 1327. He doubtless took advantage of that leave to return to the Curia, since after a fast journey from Verona he was once again serving as a papal writer on November 17, 1326.[18]

Raymond de Soubiran, originally, I suppose, from the English fief of Gascony, was a professor of canon law at Toulouse and then a papal auditor and chaplain at the Avignon palace as well as an attorney for King Edward II of England. A business partner of Petracco di Parenzo, he was also a patron of his son, Francesco Petrarca, with whose help he studied Livy's histories, according to Petrarch's testimony in one of his letters (*Sen.* 16.1).

Petrarch's return to Avignon, temporarily in 1325 and permanently in 1326, was like a time bomb. The brilliant student from the most prestigious university of jurisprudence was immediately welcomed by older lawyers who sought to advance their position in juridical knowledge and practice through diligent study of rhetoric and history. As their leader and master, he immediately located a number of notable texts because of the golden shower of precious ancient codices raining upon the prelates and members of the Curia surrounding John XXII; these came from cathedral libraries accessible to canons and from libraries of deteriorating monasteries. Petrarch soon managed his resources so successfully and sharpened his talents so rapidly that the superhuman feat in 1325 of a law student in amassing the complex structure of his "Ambrosian Virgil" was surpassed by an even more prodigious accomplishment in 1326, something which fascinated and converted his sceptical friends: despite overwhelming financial difficulties, as a new cleric he was able to establish endless connections among the various branches of the tradition of the *Ab urbe condita*. Now as we, his enlightened descendants, subject his accomplishment to anatomical scrutiny, we too cannot help being amazed.

The youthful Petrarch began these studies in Avignon—and this has gone unnoticed—recovering ancient Roman remnants that were to prove valuable even for restoring Livy's tradition. I think that a Roman friend, perhaps his patron Bishop Giacomo Colonna, gave him a third Decade prepared in Rome some two centuries earlier. Consequently, because of the compressed form of gothic script and the prevalent university customs, Petrarch decided to combine the three Decades into one volume for the first time. He placed the old third Decade in the middle, and employed two copyists from central Italy to transcribe the first Decade, since the orthography of those from the Po valley, at least until the time of Guarino, was unacceptable south of the Rimini-La Spezia line.[19] Since he was working within the Roman circle, the transcription of this Decade also used the reading established at St. John Lateran some two centuries earlier.

Soon venerable elders arrived laden with gifts. In November 1326 Simone d'Arezzo brought from Verona to Avignon a copy of the powerful first Decade, the one prepared by Bishop Ratherius in the tenth century (now Laur. 63, 19). Petrarch heroically collated it, sprinkling essential variants that he found in it between the lines and in the margins of his own first Decade.[20] Simone also furnished a third Decade, the text of Lovato from Pomposa. During a fortunate stay in Cracow, I identified this third Decade in which some annotations by Petrarch had been added to the many written by Simone. Petrarch corrected all of his third Decade from Rome by comparing it to the one from Pomposa. At the same time Landolfo Colonna brought a copy of books 26-40 from Chartres to Avignon, which allowed Petrarch to make vital corrections in books 26–30 of his Harleian copy. In the Chartrian manuscript he also found the fourth Decade; meanwhile Simone brought a copy of Lovato's fourth Decade from Verona. The young magician then put together a longer version of the fourth Decade by inserting some of the variants from Pomposa into the text from Chartres. In addition, through conjecture, he was able to correct books 21–25 which were weak (weak because they derived from a single version); earlier and contemporary editors have often accepted these without knowing their source.[21] Because they did not know the identity of the genius who had prepared this version, they have failed to grasp the richness hidden in the young Petrarch's Harleian Livy. This is yet another reason why the three Decades need to be totally re-edited.

Landolfo Colonna worked along with Petrarch, and with his help prepared three Decades in a codex that has fortunately survived, Par. Lat. 5690. After Landolfo's death, Petrarch at first borrowed this codex from his patrons, the Colonnas, and later became its owner.

Shortly thereafter, around 1330, Petrarch came across the still unknown *Periochae* in the large market in Avignon; he made use of it to complete his restoration of the *Ab urbe condita*, giving a new number to each Decade and to each book. In addition, he was able to glean additional borrowings of the tradition for books 26–40. Perhaps their source was the codex recently found in the archives at Nancy? Encouraged by such rapid progress to lay aside his Harleian text, he made for himself a better version of Livy, which unfortunately is lost, although we can reconstruct it through its copies. These texts so patiently and skillfully reconstructed by Petrarch enabled Giovanni Boccaccio, many years before meeting Petrarch, yet already his admiring disciple, to translate into Italian Livy's third and fourth Decades.[22] There is little question that such intense philological labor on Livy's text contributed substantially to Petrarch's poetic skills in the vernacular: I can prove that as early as 1330 Petrarch had been gathering into a single volume poems which would eventually form, with some additions and corrections, the great collection of the *Rerum uulgarium fragmenta*.

A century later, through a providential course of events, the young Lorenzo Valla, prince of the new philology, came to possess the Harleian Livy (namely, the Livy reconstructed by Petrarch). He used it, adding copious notes, to prepare the superb *Emendationes in Liuium* which formed the conclusion to his *Antidotum in Facium*.[23]

5. The First Printed Editions: Conclusions

Finally, let us move from manuscripts to printed editions. During the height of humanism, the *Ab urbe condita* was a favorite work; consequently, it was in print early and frequently republished. Because its manuscript tradition has been explained in some detail, we are now in a position to understand its printing tradition. I have been able to identify a good portion of the texts of the *Ab urbe condita* and the *Periochae*, which that hero of first editions, Giovanni Andrea Bussi, Bishop of Aleria, prepared, meticulously corrected, and sent to be typeset, producing the first edition of Livy at Rome in 1469 or 1470. Now we realize that Bussi used the readings of the Decades recovered by Lovato at Pomposa and improved them with Petrarch's variants, while ignoring Valla's admirable speculations.

After many lost battles and conquered seigneuries, after the long-exploited Italian libraries had been drained, philological supremacy passed beyond the Alps, particularly to the Basel group led by Erasmus. Now too, we are able to understand the source of the borrowings with which Beatus Rhenanus and Sigismund Gelen in 1532 enriched the second edition by Froben. Using the codex given to Otto I and Otto II by Ratherius, which Hildebald, their imperial chancellor and bishop of Worms, had transferred to the Cathedral of Worms, they restored the first Decade. They also improved books 26–40 by using the copy that papal librarians had prepared for the younger and more grandiose cathedral of Speyer. All that is now needed is eyes and ears, for Roman pronunciation can be clearly seen in the orthography in some passages of this version, particularly in books 26–40, preserved in the papal household. Moreover, seven pieces of parchment written in uncial from the fifth century (now Vat. Lat. 10696), which include fragments of a unique version of Livy's book 34, were used, with commentaries attached early in the ninth century, to wrap relics in the Sancta Sanctorum chapel at St. John Lateran. All roads really do lead to Rome, in fact, to the Lateran!

Thus, the first Decade, the third Decade (with a double version for books 26–30), and the fourth Decade all found shelter at the Lateran. Perhaps the second Decade also found its way there, thereby completing the series? A pontiff between Odoacer and Theodoric—either Felix III (483- 492) or his successor Gelasius II (492–496)—made reference to the *Ab urbe condita* in a letter *Aduersus Andromachum*; no longer is the reference to a book, as in previous citations, but to a Decade, the second, reflecting the recent division. Did the papal library at that time have the second Decade, which later disappeared?

The belief persists that for centuries Italy had nurtured fewer writers and preserved fewer texts than France or Germany. It is true that Carolingian France and the Germany of the Holy Roman Empire were more powerful, and thus could more easily attract culture, that soft creature born and raised in the furrows of power and wealth. But relics of the Roman era always remained in Italy, for codices prepared by generations of people from Symmachus to Cassiodorus now seem to us as noble and sad as the more or less contemporary ruins scattered throughout the Aquileian countryside. Far more numerous than might be suspected, these codices even in adverse times were splendid artifacts in the most prosperous centers, particularly and especially in Rome, but also in Montecassino, Ravenna, Pomposa, Bobbio, Nonantola, Verona, and Milan, to cite only the names connected with the Livy tradition. We realize too that especially between the beginning of the ninth century and the beginning of the eleventh, i.e., from the foundation of the new western empire to the illustrious papacy of Innocent III, many copies of these books, and sometimes the originals, were part of the constant export trade with emperors, bishops, and abbots; thus, through a slow but continual dissemination, plants were generated in the nurseries of Christian civilization (the abbeys and cathedrals), particularly in France and Germany. Custodians in well-endowed libraries and busy scriptoria caused the dwindling of ancient Italian reserves by the periodic transfer of texts from old codices to new ones. Finally, as early as the thirteenth century and into the next one, eager Italian rhetoricians, both secular and religious, and notaries or secular clerics above all, drew the marrow from ancient classical and sacred texts which they found hidden in repositories; this process helped them create at a fantastic pace a new school, a new rhetoric, and a new literature. Yet precisely because they did plunder the repositories of cathedrals and monasteries, Italian antiquarians disseminated through theft and brutal transferrals many indigenous riches that were very old. Yet until now, estimates have been made on the basis of present holdings, even though these were inflated in the *Codices Latini Antiquiores*, leading to the conclusion that Romanic Italy had fewer codices than France and Germany. This is completely mistaken because Romanic Italy was doubly favored by numerous and conspicuous remains from classical civilization and by a widespread urban culture.

The edition of Livy must be redone, as must many editions of the classics, especially the Church Fathers. The history of humanism must also be researched and reshaped. There is sufficient work for us, and for our children and grandchildren!

Notes

1. An expanded Italian version of this essay appeared in *Studi petrarcheschi*, n.s., 3 (1986): 2-115 (published in 1988).
2. *Studi sul Petrarca* 9 (Padua, 1981).
3. G. B. de Rossi, "La biblioteca della Sede Apostolica," *Studi e documenti di storia e diritto* 5 (1884): 317-80.
4. M. Maccarrone, "La 'cathedra Sancti Petri' nel medioevo: da simbolo a reliquia," *Rivista di storia della Chiesa in Italia* 39 (1985): 349-447.
5. B. Bischoff, *Mittelalterliche Studien* (Stuttgart, 1966), 3:168; *Paläographie des römischen Altertums und des abendländischen Mittelalters* (Berlin, 1969), 257.
6. "Palaeographische Forschungen, Vierter Teil, Bamberger Fragmente der vierten Dekade des Livius," *Abhandlungen d.k. bayer. Ak. d. Wiss. zu München* 3 Kl., 24 1 (1904): 1-44.
7. L. Braccesi, *La leggenda di Antenore, Da Troia a Padova* (Padua, 1984); Billanovich, *La tradizione*, 1:48.
8. Billanovich, *La tradizione*, 1:273-81. See also Guido Billanovich, "'Veterum vestigia vatum' nei carmi dei preumanisti padovani ...," *Italia medioevale e umanistica* 1 (1958): 155-243.
9. Giuseppe Billanovich, "La biblioteca dei papi, la biblioteca di Pomposa e i libri di Lovato Lovati e del Petrarca," *La civiltà comacchiese e pomposiana dalle origini preistoriche al tardo medioevo* (Bologna, 1986), 619-23.
10. Guido Billanovich, "Preumanesimo padovano," *Storia della cultura veneta* 2 (Vicenza, 1976): 38-40.
11. A. Benati, "Presenza culturale di Pomposa nel Medio Evo," *Analecta Pomposiana* 1 (1965): 91-106.
12. Billanovich, *La tradizione*, 1:1-33, 282-334.
13. E. Franceschini, *Studi e note di filologia latina medievale* (Milan, 1938), 29-30; *Il commento di Nicola Triveth al Tieste di Seneca* (Milan, 1938), 1-8.
14. Giuseppe Billanovich, *I primi umanisti e le tradizioni dei classici latini* (Fribourg, 1953), 14-24.
15. M. Faucon, *La librairie des papes d'Avignon ...* (Paris, 1887), 25.
16. Giuseppe Billanovich, "Dal Livio di Raterio (Laur. 63, 19) al Livio del Petrarca (B.M., Harl. 2493)," *Italia medioevale e umanistica* 2 (1959): 158.
17. G. C. Alessio, G. Billanovich, Violetta de Angelis, "L' alba di Petrarca filologo: il Virgilio Ambrosiano," *Studi petrarcheschi*, n.s., 2 (1985): 15-84, and 3 (1986): 203-46.
18. L. Muttoni and C. Adami, "Un alleato del Petrarca: Simone d'Arezzo," *Italia medioevale e umanistica* 22 (1979): 171-222; and Muttoni, "Il cardinale Niccolò da Prato per il canonicato veronese di Simone d'Arezzo," *Italia medioevale e umanistica* 23 (1980): 377-79.
19. Billanovich, *La tradizione*, 1:11-12, 120.
20. Billanovich, "Dal Livio di Raterio," 158.
21. Billanovich, "Petrarch and the Textual Tradition ...," 14:175-77.
22. Giuseppe Billanovich, "Il Boccaccio, il Petrarca e le più antiche traduzioni in italiano delle *Decadi* di Tito Livio," *Giornale storico della letteratura italiana*, 130 (1953): 311-37; "Tito Livio, Petrarca, Boccaccio," *Archivio storico ticinese* 25 (1984):

3-10; Maria Teresa Casella, *Tra Petrarca e Boccaccio. I volgarizzamenti di Tito Livio e di Valerio Massimo*, Studi sul Petrarca 14 (Padua, 1982).

23. Laurentii Valle, *Antidotum in Facium*, ed. Mariangela Regoliosi, Thesaurus mundi 20 (Padua, 1981); Regoliosi, "Le congetture a Livio del Valla: metodi e problemi," in *Lorenzo Valla e l'umanesimo italiano, Atti del Convegno internazionale di studi umanistici (Parma, 18-19 ottobre 1984)*, ed. O. Besomi and M. Regoliosi, Medioevo e umanesimo 59 (Padua, 1986), 51-71.

PLENARY LECTURE

Cicero, Ambrose, and Stoic Ethics: Transmission or Transformation?

MARCIA L. COLISH

The title of this paper may require some explanation. It may, initially, sound strange, or provocative, to an audience familiar with the history of Greek philosophy in Rome and in the Latin church fathers, an audience familiar, as well, with the standard literature on the attitude of the church fathers toward classical thought. The red flag, of course, is the word "transformation." As for Cicero, the canonical approach to him is to see him not as a transformer of Greek philosophy but as a mere transmitter of it.[1] And, for his part, Ambrose is usually treated as having effected "an intellectual coup d'état" of Cicero's ethics, to use E. K. Rand's famous phrase.[2] According to this view, Ambrose allied Cicero's ideas with Christian ethics, without feeling any need for a constitutional rearrangement in the Ciceronian sector of his domain, following its annexation. What I hope to do in this paper is to convince you that Cicero did transform Stoic ethics rather than merely pass it along, wrapped in cellophane, untouched by human hands. I also hope to show you that Ambrose, in turn, transformed what he received from Cicero, subjecting both his mentor and Cicero's Stoic sources alike to his own point of view, and emerging with an amalgam of Stoicism and Christianity that bears a distinctive Ambrosian stamp. The term "transformation" in my title, then, is a brief way of stating the thesis I want to put forth.

At the same time, I want to defend this thesis as a building block in a larger thesis concerning the classical tradition in the Middle Ages. As we all know, the approach to this subject has undergone major shifts, ever since the "revolt of the medievalists" launched by Charles Homer Haskins and his contemporaries blew Jakob Burckhardt out of the water. Since Haskins' time, much effort has been applied to documenting the devotion of medieval thinkers to their Greek and Latin forebears. Classicists such as R. R. Bolgar, L. D. Reynolds, and N. G. Wilson have recast the medieval centuries, seeing them no longer as bottlenecks but as conduits, and even as the locus of strategic salvage operations, in keeping the classics pristine, uncorrupted, and available.[3] Literary historians such as Ernst Robert Curtius have emphasized the constancy and frequency with which medieval authors, in the vernacular as well as Latin, drew upon classical themes and *topoi*, and have read the Middle Ages as an authentic bridge between the ancient and modern worlds and as an integral part of a Western tradition whose fidelity to its classical roots is its very definition.[4]

Important as these perspectives have been in reshaping scholarly orientations toward the classical tradition in the Middle Ages, they still labor under the shadow of a bias—a classical bias, which gives them a distinctly monocular outlook. The commentators just mentioned reject the idea that the Middle Ages was a dark age to the extent, and just to the extent, that medieval thinkers got the classics right, understanding classical ideas and using them in classical ways, appreciating and imitating classical canons of taste, and trying to establish classical texts as correctly as they could.

Well, what is wrong with the classical bias? In my view, one of its major deficiencies is that it makes it difficult to explain why the classical tradition in Byzantium, which exhibits all the above-mentioned forms of fidelity and reverence for antiquity, turned out to be, in the long run, a fossil, a cultural icon, devotion to which was a manifestation of nostalgia, defeatism, and intellectual exhaustion. On the other hand, in the West, the classical tradition became an agent of change and a stimulus to cultural innovation. The path taken by the West becomes more comprehensible if we substitute for the classical bias a different way of looking at the survival and use of the classics. A number of recent scholars have offered suggestions that are pertinent here. Speaking, to be sure, about the Christian rather than the classical tradition, Jaroslav Pelikan has reminded us that a tradition remains vital only if it changes and develops, not if it stays the same. As he points out, the most exciting medieval developments in his field of study occurred in the spaces created by the perceived divergences and convergences between classicism and Christianity; the classical *lex speculandi* exerted no less an effect on the *lex credendi* than did the *lex orandi*.[5] At the same time, speaking about medieval lyric poetry, Peter Dronke has reminded us that the role of the classical tradition was not merely, or mainly, to provide poets with static models or standard motifs. In his words, the classical literary heritage supplied "oxygen, rather than bricks."[6]

I agree with Pelikan and Dronke and I think there is more to the as signment. Just as we need to move beyond the idea of the Middle Ages as a conveyer belt of classical sources, so we need to move beyond the idea that, in its interactions with sister traditions, classicism was a donor only. It was a beneficiary, as well. And, just as we need to surmount *Quellenforschung* and the analysis of the imitation of the classics, including an analysis of how their inspiration merged with the originality of medieval writers, we also need to compass the transformations which the classics themselves underwent in that process. For the interrelations involved were a two-way street. Dronke's oxygen metaphor is useful here. Oxygen sustains organic life, it enables dead matter to decompose, fire to burn, and metal to rust, only by uniting with other elements and forming new compounds in which the oxygen is changed, no less than they are. Its power to transform is a function of its capacity to be transformed. Shifting from Lavoisier to Erasmus, a figure we all feel more at home with, authority has a nose of wax, an attribute that enables it to continue in force as an authority. With respect to the classics in the Middle Ages, the plasticity of that nose, and the ways it was twisted, demand our attention no less than the constants of its physiognomy.

In stepping back from these broad concerns to the more immediate consideration of Cicero, Ambrose, and Stoic ethics, let me note that a major reason for choosing them is that they provide a clear, concise, and manageable means of illustrating what we can learn when we shift the focus from transmission to transformation. Let me also note, as we do so, that, for reasons of time, I will confine myself to the comparison of only two works—Cicero's *De officiis* and Ambrose's *De officiis ministrorum*. Ideally, of course, we should go farther, since each author treats Stoic ethics in other works as well, and because the two works in question can best be understood in the context of their author's *œuvre* as a whole. But, since a wider inquiry cannot be made here, the two works I have chosen have been selected for very obvious reasons. They are the longest, or the most mature, or the most important ethical treatises of Cicero and Ambrose. And Ambrose, in his *De officiis,* expressly acknowledges that Cicero's *De officiis* is his model,[7] which gives us a ready-made basis for comparison.

One of the issues I want to consider is how faithful Ambrose actually was to his announced model. This question is pretty easy to answer, since we have both texts and can compare them at will. For his part, Cicero also had an announced model for his *De officiis,* the middle Stoic Panaetius (second century BC), who wrote a book *On Duties,* which, Cicero tells us in his preface, he seeks to imitate and complete.[8] We are, however, not in a position to make a direct comparison between Cicero's *De officiis* and

Panaetius' *On Duties,* for the simple if regrettable reason that Panaetius' treatise is not extant. So we have to try to assess how faithful Cicero was to Panaetius in the light of information about Stoic ethics, and Panaetius' particular contributions to it, preserved in other sources.

Apart from this first problem, the inaccessibility of Panaetius' *On Duties,* there is still another problem, or, at least, a special "condition of labor" involved in treating Cicero's fidelity to his source. Although Cicero often makes prefatory statements in his philosophical works, telling the reader what to expect, these instructions cannot be taken at face value. In some works the prefaces serve the function of a *captatio beneuolentiae.* Most of the time, though, they serve the function of a smoke screen, clouding the reader's mind as to what is actually going on in the work. Often, for example, Cicero claims in his preface to be a mere doxographer, presenting what various philosophical schools have to say on some topic without giving his own opinion, when in fact he is manipulating the doctrines to support his own preferences. This lack of candor on Cicero's part affects his treatment of philosophy, and it in turn has a lot to do with Cicero's existential situation when he wrote his philosophical works.

Cicero had had a brilliant political career, culminating in the consulate, the highest office in the Roman republic.[9] But the rise of Julius Caesar relegated him to the status of a political outsider. Cicero was deprived of office and had to watch, from the sidelines, the change of the Roman polity from the republic, which he sought to defend, into an autocracy ruled by a usurper. It took Cicero about ten years to internalize the fact that his own career was over.[10] During his enforced retirement, he spent his time writing a series of philosophical works on political theory, law, theology, cosmology, and ethics. In these works he sought simultaneously to console himself, to advertise his own qualifications for public office, to attack his enemies, to advocate his republican views, and to develop a rationale for *otium litterarium* as the conduct of statecraft by other means. All of these concerns — the rhetorical, the personal, and the partisan — are present in the *De officiis,* as they are in the other works written in Cicero's retirement. At the same time, Cicero wrote the *De officiis* in order to take a definitive stand on ethics. The *De officiis* is his last work, coming at the end of a series of works that treat the same ethical themes, of which the most important are the *De finibus* and *Tusculan Disputations.* So, although the *De officiis* has an ostensibly narrow objective, a father's counsel dedicated to his son Marcus, it actually has deeper and broader aims.

Even so, Cicero is not necessarily elaborating on Panaetius, although that is what he says he is doing in the preface. Elsewhere in the *De officiis* he poses as an Academic Skeptic, saying that it would be presumptuous to seek anything but probabilities in the sphere of ethics.[11] Yet, throughout the *De officiis*, he posits and uses axiomatic ethical principles without raising any questions about their epistemological status. Similarly, although he is unquestionably dependent on Panaetius, Cicero injects a number of non-Stoic ideas into the *De officiis* which have the effect of altering Stoic morality dramatically. What emerges is a new Ciceronian ethic in which Stoicism is a critical ingredient but in which it is subordinated to insights derived from other philosophical schools, from traditional Roman values, and from Cicero's own personal political views.

Cicero's *De officiis* consists of three books, the first treating the *honestum*, or the highest good under the heading of the four cardinal virtues, the second treating the useful, or *utile*, and the third seeking to reconcile the two. The initial problem, and the language Cicero uses to formulate it, are Stoic.[12] As the Stoics saw it, the *honestum* is the *summum bonum*; indeed, it is the *unicum bonum*. The good is an end in itself and it can be defined as life in accordance with nature, or life in accordance with reason, which is the same thing. Nature is understood in a rationally normative manner. Evil, for the Stoics, is the irrational or the unnatural. Just as nature is rationalized in Stoic ethics, so is the psychology of ethical choices. Virtues spring from correct intellectual judgments; vices and passions spring from incorrect intellectual judgments.

Outside of good and evil, virtue and vice, the Stoics have a third ethical category, things indifferent, or the *adiaphora*. The *adiaphora* are morally neutral. Still, they may be graded into more, or less, preferable. They are acceptable to the extent that they do not conflict with virtue, and, when they are compatible with virtue, they may be conducive to it. But, the preferables remain neutral *en bloc*, and cannot be seen as subordinate grades of the good. They could be excised *en bloc* without affecting the good. The analysis of the preferables, the grading of them, and advice on how to make choices among them, are one of Panaetius' major contributions to Stoic ethics.[13] He elaborated this topic more fully than any other Stoic, in addition to developing a casuistical method for judging how the virtues should be manifested by people of different sexes, ages, and walks of life. He argued that virtue was possible for persons of any kind, although the way they went about it, and the preferables they chose, had to be assessed in the light of circumstantial and personal factors.

With this background in mind, it is easy to see how the Stoics would handle the problem which the *De officiis* sets out to solve. The *honestum*, for the Stoics, is the *summum bonum*. Virtues are ends in themselves. The *utilia* are the *adiaphora*, means to the end of virtue under certain circumstances, but morally neutral as a group. The applicability of the *utile* to the *honestum* depends on the *honestum*. The *honestum* is, and can be, the only criterion of the *utile*. Since the *honestum* is intrinsically good, and since it is the only good, it is the changeless norm by which the admissibility of the *utile* may be judged.

That is how a Stoic would handle the problem. But it is not how Cicero handles it. Instead, what he does is to lower the ceiling on the *honestum* and elevate the *utile* to the status of a moral criterion in its own right. He does this in each book of the *De officiis,* but differently in each. In book 1, he redefines the cardinal virtues in utilitarian terms. In book 2, using these newly redefined virtues, he argues that virtue is useful. And, in book 3, he turns the argument of book 2 around by arguing that vice is inexpedient. Now for a closer look at this strategy.

Cicero begins the scaling down and redefinition of the *honestum* in his treatment of the cardinal virtues in book 1. He starts by listing the standard four virtues that all Greek philosophers accepted as the cardinal virtues — wisdom, justice, fortitude, and temperance. But he does not give them consistently Stoic definitions, nor does he put them in a Stoic order of priority.[14] Instead of being ends in themselves, the virtues, as he judges them, are evaluated according to the criterion of their usefulness. And wisdom is not the reigning virtue, as it is for the Stoics; instead, justice is the leader, an Aristotelian preference, but one that Cicero likewise subjects to considerations of expediency.

Wisdom, he says, is not the leading virtue, since other virtues apply more directly "to the things on which the practicalities of life depend" (*quibus actio uitae continetur*). Still, wisdom has its usefulness in the avoidance of credulity and of excessive concern for subjects that are obscure or useless.[15] So, rather than itself judging what is useful, wisdom is subjected to the norm of utility. In defining justice, Cicero combines the traditional Platonic and Aristotelian *suum cuique* formula with an equally traditional protection of public and private rights drawn from Roman law. But, he adds the point that circumstances and necessities condition how both public and private rights are to be enforced. Cruelty may sometimes be just; and violence and guile, the techniques of the lion and the fox, may be required. In measuring our beneficence to others, we should be liberal to our friends, according to the services they have rendered or are likely to render "to our advantage" (*ad nostras utilitates*).[16] So, although justice is the paramount virtue, it too is judged according to expediency.

The same holds true for courage. Cicero agrees with the Stoics that, since virtue is essentially a fixed inner intellectual intention, courage can be expressed either in the active or the contemplative life — on the battlefield, in the courtroom, or in the study. All these applications of fortitude entail the same inner freedom from the passions, the Stoic state of *apatheia*. But courage is a good thing, he adds, because it endows its possessor with equanimity. It is also good because of the practical consequences it affords to its possessor. It enhances his wealth and position. The greatest acts of fortitude are thus both heroic, and "useful in the highest degree" (*maxime utiles*).[17] Finally, temperance is useful too, in that it enhances the reputation of its possessor and wins him public approval. In applying temperance to oneself, an area in which Cicero makes extensive use of Panaetian casuistry, one should remember, he counsels, that temperance is governed by *decorum*.[18] Another non-Panaetian note Cicero strikes on this topic can be seen in the fact that the vocational choices and lifestyles he assesses under the heading of temperance involve those confined to men only, implying that virtue is a purely masculine possibility.[19]

After observing Cicero judge the *honestum* according to the criterion of the *utile* in these redefinitions of the cardinal virtues in book 1, it is fairly easy to see how he will reconcile the good and the useful in books 2 and 3. A real reconciliation is not needed, for two obvious reasons: the *honestum* has now been defined as a species of the *utile*; and the *honestum* can now be explored, and exploited, as a means to the *utile*. In book 2, Cicero proves the latter point in two ways. First, he argues that useful things are valid ends. Just as he redefines the Stoic *honestum* downwards in book 1, so in book 2 he promotes the *utilia* upwards. No longer morally neutral *adiaphora*, they now become moral ends, and the goal of serving one's own advantage is rendered morally normative. All the virtues, and especially justice, now become valuable because they are advantageous. And, they are advantageous, says Cicero, because the possession of virtue wins respect and enables us to bend others to our own will more easily.[20] In book 3, Cicero continues to treat the *utile* as an end, but now argues not that virtue is expedient but that vice is inexpedient. Injuring others benefits neither the individual who commits an injury nor society at large, while moral obloquy brings disesteem and shame, not glory. Honesty is the best policy, Cicero concludes, for honesty is what gets results.[21]

Since Cicero has defined the *utile* as a worthy moral end and has evaluated the *honestum* as a means to that end, there is no real problem in reconciling them. This would be a problem, Cicero thinks, if the original Stoic conception of virtue had been left in place. But the transcendent, rational Stoic *summum bonum* is really far too inaccessible, he says. Even recognized exemplary characters, like Cato of Utica, cannot measure up to its demands, and have to settle for the more moderate goal of the duties, the *media officia*. These duties, too, like the redefined virtues, must be ordered to the *utile*. Cicero illustrates this point in good Stoic fashion, with the example of Hercules, toiling and suffering for the sake of others.[22] A man's duties are guided by what is useful, both to him and to others, and primarily by social utility, the norm to be followed if public and private interests do not happen to coincide. Even when one makes exceptions to the obligations flowing from duty, the spirit of the rule, that is, social utility, is the criterion Cicero invokes for departing from it.[23] While Cicero's discussion of the *officia* clearly shows that his utilitarianism is not an exercise in untrammelled pragmatism or a license for selfishness, it is equally clear, I think, that he has taken a giant step away from Stoic ethics and that he has virtually turned Panaetius inside out.

For all Cicero's dependence on Stoicism, then, his *De officiis* ends by reversing substantially the directionality of Panaetian ethics. Cicero categorically rejects the idea of the *adiaphora*. He redefines the *honestum* as a species of the *utile*. Having done this, he has to reject the Stoic idea of virtue as an end in itself, since the desire for the good, for the Stoics, cannot be virtuous if it is conditioned by any other goals. What Cicero does instead is to posit the intermediate goods or preferables as ends in themselves, making social utility the highest of these values. He retains an interest in Stoic *apatheia* and the inner state of autarchy as moral desiderata, as well as absorbing the casuistical method of Panaetius. But he makes these principles way-stations to a different destination. In one sense, the Ciceronian reconciliation of the *honestum* and the *utile* is achieved by treating them both as forms of the *utile*. In another sense, Cicero envisions the harmony between public and private interests as a function of the social and political framework in which he seeks to situate his ethics. Cicero implies the possibility of a utopia in which the *honestum* and the *utile* would be truly reciprocal, if not identical with each other and with Roman republican institutions. In the end, paradoxically enough, Cicero's transformation of Stoic ethics and his efforts to bring the Stoic *summum bonum* down to earth are tied to a political ideal that, in its own way and in Cicero's own time, was every bit as unattainable as the Stoic moral ideal he seeks to Romanize and to scale down to human size.

In moving from Cicero to Ambrose, we move from the first century BC to the fourth century AD, from paganism to Christianity, from the politician manqué to the ecclesiastical statesman in the thick of things as the bishop of a major metropolitan see in troubled times.[24] We also move from a *De officiis* that claims to be addressed to the author's son, but which has a much wider readership in view and the multiple aims of propaganda and self-advertisement as well as edification, to a *De officiis* written for the immediate and practical needs of the priests of Ambrose's diocese, and with no hidden agenda.

Despite these differences, Cicero's *De officiis* remained fresh and relevant to Ambrose and his contemporaries. It was read more extensively than any of Cicero's philosophical works; indeed, it was the most widely read work of ancient Latin prose from the classical period up through the Renaissance.[25] Cicero's *De officiis* seemed a perfectly natural choice for Ambrose when he sought a model for his book.[26] The question of whether a person could be a Christian and a Ciceronian at the same time never crossed his mind. Nor was he expressly concerned either with delineating the proper place of pagan thought in relation to Christianity or with formulating a systematic synthesis between them. Rather, Ambrose had a job to do in his *De officiis ministrorum*, and he did not hesitate to use whatever authentic wisdom there was in order to get that job done.

At the same time, it would be a mistake to see Ambrose as a mere pedagogical technician. He did have an authentic interest in ethics and psychology, and his approach often shows a decided originality, an independence from his sources, and a concern for the issues as such. His own reformulations of Stoic ethics involve not only his response to the Christian values he believed in and his practical reasons for writing his *De officiis ministrorum*. They also reflect both his attraction to non-Stoic philosophies and to a Stoicism more authentic in some respects than the Stoicism of Cicero. Even when he agrees with his mentor, his reasons for taking the line he takes are often diametrically opposed to Cicero's. Thus, in Ambrose's case, his particular transformation of Stoic ethics also involve his simultaneous dependence upon, and independence from, Cicero.

One of the most obvious dissimilarities between Cicero and Ambrose is stylistic—the fact that Ambrose illustrates his points with examples from biblical and Christian history. One of the most obvious similarities between the two thinkers is the formal one. Ambrose follows Cicero's scheme of organization. He presents a treatise in three books, dealing with the *honestum*, the *utile*, and their reconciliation. As with Cicero, Ambrose addresses the *honestum* in book 1 under the heading of the four cardinal virtues. And, as with Cicero, his initial definitions of those virtues are not entirely Stoic. But he departs from the Stoic definitions for completely different reasons.

Ambrose defines the *honestum* as "that which pertains to moral dignity and integrity in life" (*ad decus honestatemque uitae*) and the *utile* as "what pertains to the conveniences of life" (*ad uitae commoda*).[27] As his analysis proceeds, three strikingly non-Stoic features of his handling of these terms emerge, two of which are also non-Ciceronian. First, Ambrose follows Cicero in grading the *honesta,* as well as the *utilia.* Second, and this is intimately related to the first point, the reason why Ambrose grades the *honesta* is that he does not equate them with the *summum bonum.* Neither had Cicero, since he preferred to equate the *honestum* with the *media officia* and to place it under the judgment of the *utile.* For his part, Ambrose distinguishes the *honestum* from the *summum bonum* because, for him, the *summum bonum* is eternal beatitude. From the standpoint of the life to come, the *honestum* as well as the *utile* is an instrument, not an end. As he says,

> We posit the rule that nothing is fitting to right unless it is oriented toward future goods more than to present ones; and we state that nothing is useful unless it directs us to the grace of that life eternal, and not to the enjoyment of the present.[28]

Third, while Cicero departs from the Stoa in treating the advantages of this life as good and sufferings as evils, Ambrose departs from the Stoa by treating the advantages of this life as impediments and by treating suffering as having a redemptive potentiality.[29]

Ambrose includes the duties, both *perfecta* and *media,* which involve the apostolic counsels and the ordinary observance of the Ten Commandments, respectively. The *officia* of both sorts, he holds, are ordered to the virtues. Before addressing the virtues more specifically, Ambrose makes two general points about virtue that illustrate his practicality and the freedom with which he mingles Stoicism with other philosophies.[30] First, he remarks, following Panaetius, in discriminating among the duties the individual should consider his age, situation, and talents. Like Cicero, he omits the factor of sex, but for practical, not for conventional or sexist reasons: his book is for priests, an exclusively masculine occupational group. Second, Ambrose's Stoicism is susceptible of permeation by other philosophical traditions. He counsels *decorum* in the exercise of all the virtues, a wholly Stoic idea. At the same time, he interprets *decorum* in the light of the Aristotelian golden mean: "hold to the mean in all things" (*modum tenere in omnibus*), he counsels; and he describes virtue as an Aristotelian *habitus* that curbs nature,[31] rather than following the Stoic definition of virtue as *naturam sequi.*

Ambrose's definitions of the cardinal virtues themselves are also striking for their combination of originality and dependence, the originality stemming as much from his own insights as a psychologist as from an appeal to Christian values. In some ways, the definitions of the virtues in Ambrose that seem closest to Cicero's, at first glance, are the farthest from Cicero's, on closer inspection. Ambrose rejects both the Stoic preference for wisdom or prudence and the Aristotelian preference for justice as the paramount virtue. Instead, he makes temperance the key virtue.[32] He has two reasons for doing so, both original to Ambrose, and both reflecting the fact that his approach to virtue is not a formal or teleological one but, rather, a developmental and functional one. Self-discipline, he notes, precedes understanding in the acquisition of virtue. Men, and even children, can learn to control their impulses before they grasp the reason why they should do so. Thus, he concludes, temperance is prior to the other virtues in the temporal, or developmental, order. Secondly, temperance works through *decorum* in governing all the virtues. Tranquillity of mind, Ambrose points out, characterizes this process, whichever virtue is involved. Ambrose is clearly far less concerned with defining or analyzing the conditions of self-knowledge and self-rule that make this moral state possible than with describing the way it works. He is less interested in *decorum* and autarchy as psychic states, and how they are attained, than he is in the examination of the way they operate in action.

Ambrose's definition of wisdom is also innovative.[33] He does not associate this virtue with the possession of knowledge, whether speculative or practical. Instead, he associates it with the search for truth and with the desire for knowledge. Ambrose's reason for this definition is that he equates wisdom with the imperfect knowledge of faith available to man in this life, which will not be consummated except in heaven. Christianity clearly accounts for Ambrose's definition of wisdom, but both Christianity and a Stoicism more integral than Cicero's condition his treatment of justice. Superficially, Ambrose's definition of justice looks the same as Cicero's, combining the *suum cuique* formula with a concern for the common weal. But, Ambrose rapidly departs from Cicero in interpreting what the concern for the common weal entails, and how it should be expressed institutionally. Ambrose limits much more stringently than Cicero the sphere of private rights in relation to the public good.[34] He cites as a warrant for the common ownership of goods both the Stoic doctrine of natural equality and primal communism and the Christian's need to ground justice on charity and the apostolic counsels. Thus, for Ambrose, the right to private property is conventional, not natural or supernatural, and it must be suspended if it conflicts with the public good. Furthermore, the institutional expression of justice, for Ambrose, is neither the ideal Stoic cosmopolis ruled by natural law nor Cicero's ideal republic, but the Christian church as a visible community, where natural human bonds are strengthened and transcended by the bonds of faith and sacramental communion.[35] The final cardinal virtue, fortitude, shares for Ambrose the Stoic and Ciceronian ground of magnanimity, *magnitudo animi* as an inner intention.[36] Magnanimity irradiates all its various applications. But, since he is writing for priests, Ambrose omits the military expressions of this virtue and concentrates on its civilian forms.

Before leaving Ambrose's discussion of the virtues in book 1, it should be noted that there is one very striking area in which he is far more Stoic than Cicero. The Stoics taught that virtue was a fixed inner intention toward the good. A corollary of that idea, for the Stoics, is that all the virtues are one. The Stoics held that the possession of one virtue implies and entails the possession of the other virtues, since the same fixed inner intentionality is involved in any and all manifestations of virtue. Cicero agrees with the first premise, the idea that virtue is a fixed intentionality toward the good. But he rejects the corollary, the idea that he who possesses one virtue possesses them all. For his part, Ambrose argues in favor of the corollary as well as the premise on which it is based. He examines the interconnections of the four cardinal virtues with each other, and also argues for the interconnections of the three theological virtues of faith, hope, and charity with each other. He also stresses the interrelations of the two sets of virtues. For Ambrose, the cardinal virtues are modes by which the Christian virtues are expressed, while the Christian virtues supply the power that enables a person, psychically and spiritually, to meet the most rigorous demands of the cardinal virtues.[37]

If Ambrose redefines the *honestum* under the heading of the virtues in book 1, his redefinition of the *utile* in book 2 is even more extensive. The most original feature of his reformulation is that he does not associate the *utile* with worldly advantage at all.[38] The *utile* remains, to be sure, a means and not an end. Ambrose regards the *utile* as valuable to the extent that it leads to the virtues that, in turn, lead to eternal life. In this connection, Ambrose borrows Cicero's strategy in book 2 of the *De officiis* in arguing that virtue is useful. But, at the same time, he turns Cicero inside out. In a sense, both authors redefine the *honestum* as the *utile*. Cicero by rejecting the idea of virtue as an end in itself and Ambrose by treating the *honestum*, like the *utile*, as a means to the end of eternal life. At the same time, Ambrose reclassifies the *utile* as a species of the *honestum*, by removing it from the sphere of worldly advantage and by linking it, along with the *honestum*, to man's redemption.

With this foundation laid, Ambrose can make short work of reconciling the *honestum* and the *utile* in book 3. For him, this constitutes no real problem. He follows Cicero's technique of arguing that vice has no utility. But in contrast with Cicero, and in agreement with the Stoics, he views this as a false problem, although for different reasons. For the Stoics, the *utilia* are *adiaphora,* which may be graded but which are matters of indifference, distinct in kind from the *summum bonum.* For Ambrose, on the other hand, the *honestum* and the *utile* differ in degree, not in kind, since they are both understood with reference to the love of God and the pastoral responsibility borne by the clergy in drawing men to God.[39] In deciding on alternative courses of action, then, what is involved for Ambrose is not the greater or lesser preferability of either the *honestum* or the *utile* but the appeal to a different standard altogether: which course of action is more Christlike and more edifying to one's fellow man? This criterion, as Ambrose observes toward the end of book 3, is good, not only because it is Christian, but also because it is in conformity with nature, since men are bound by the law of nature to work for the common weal, which in this case means the redemption of one's fellow man. "The virtuous life is life in accordance with nature," he concludes, "because God made all things very good,"[40] an ethical formula that illustrates very nicely the parallels and intersections between the Stoic and Christian elements in Ambrose's *De officiis ministrorum.*

Ambrose rests the case there, and it is time for me to conclude as well. In the comparison of Ambrose's use of Stoic ethics with Cicero's, a number of points have now emerged. Neither author can be described as a slavish imitator of his sources. Each reworks his Stoic sources, combines them freely with other sources, and expresses the resulting amalgam in modes dictated by personal inclination as well as by professional or situational need. Cicero appropriates much from Panaetius, and Ambrose appropriates much from Cicero, as well as from other sources of Stoicism available to him. Although each author uses a format, a terminology, a schema, and a strategy of argument derived from his chosen model, each invests these borrowings with a very different content and meaning.

Ambrose makes some of the same substantive modifications of Stoic ethics as Cicero does, notably in his admission of Platonic and Aristotelian principles in defining justice and in counselling moderation. But Cicero and Ambrose make these changes for contrasting reasons. Cicero's goal is to soften the rigor and the austere rationalism of Stoic ethics. To this end, he accepts the infrarational faculties and activities of man, and bodily goods, as ethically relevant. On the other hand, while Ambrose also rejects the monistic rational psychology of the Stoa, he does so in order to underscore the distinction between soul and body, so as to elevate the soul above the body in light of the soul's eternal destiny. In effect, he uses a Platonic and Neoplatonic anthropology against the Stoa in the service of Christian ethical ends. Cicero, while he attacks the Stoic conception of the purely rational sage as an unattainable ideal, still adheres to the autarchic psychology of the Stoa as the strongest bulwark against the vicissitudes of fortune, and as the surest means of self-consolation. Ambrose retains the idealism of the Stoic sage in all its rigor, but energizes him and makes him capable of functioning through the liberating power of divine grace.

Ambrose, like Cicero, develops a hierarchy of virtues that departs from the Stoa. Cicero prefers the Aristotelian stress on justice, because of its orientation to the common weal, while Ambrose, thanks to his functional and developmental psychology, makes temperance the primary virtue. With the Stoics, Ambrose sees a unity among the cardinal virtues, not only because they operate in terms of each other, but also because they are grounded in the theological virtues and express them. Cicero is not as Stoic as Ambrose on this point, although both thinkers agree with the Stoic principle that virtue is a matter of inner intentionality, which can be manifested in various ways, respecting times, persons, and circumstances.

Both authors redefine the *honestum* and reject its identification with the Stoic *summum bonum*. Both coordinate the *honestum* and the *utile* by treating both of these ethical categories as useful. But Ambrose's definition of the *utile* orders the *utile*, like the *honestum*, to eternal life, while Cicero's definition of the *honestum* lowers the good to the duties that can serve man's worldly advantage. The result of Cicero's reformulation of the *honestum* and the *utile* is to assimilate the *honestum* to the *utile*; the result of Ambrose's handling of the same topic is exactly the reverse. Instead of bringing the Stoic sage down to earth, where his inner autonomy can be retained while its demands are moderated, Ambrose seeks to bring the Stoic sage into the fullness of being through Christian redemption, a process neither purely autonomous nor purely heteronomous. Cicero sees the setting for his transformation of the Stoic sage as an ideal republic whose earthly expression, with all its spots and wrinkles, had ceased to exist when he wrote his *De officiis*. Ambrose locates his transformation of the Stoic sage in a Christian community which few Christians, except the sporadic saints, have had the purity of heart to reify, and which the embattled Milanese church, even under his inspired leadership, did not approximate.

In presenting this analysis and comparison, I hope that I have succeeded in making the narrower case that both Cicero and Ambrose are far more than mere transmitters. Each, in his own way, transformed Stoic ethics, and these respective transformations testify to the creativity and flexibility of each thinker, and to his own intellectual, temperamental, and situational needs. I also hope that this particular case study helps to chart a part of the wider landscape in which I would like to position myself, in arguing for other creative transformations of the classics as a topic fully as worthy of attention as their faithful preservation and use in a pure state. For, with respect to Stoic ethics, the branch of the classical legacy examined here, the story I have outlined all too sketchily testifies both to the durability of Stoicism, the chief if not exclusive source of philosophical ethics for Cicero and Ambrose, and, equally, to its capacity to combine with other ingredients while yet holding its own. Both Cicero and Ambrose occupy an honorable place in the history of the Stoic tradition, not despite the fact that they transformed it in their own personal ways, but precisely because they did so.

Notes

Some of the material in this paper has been published, in a different form, in my book, *The Stoic Tradition from Antiquity to the Early Middle Ages*, 2 vols. (Leiden, 1985). I would like to thank the publisher, E. J. Brill, for permission to use it in the present format.

1. Good recent introductions to the literature on Cicero's relation to Greek philosophy include Karl Büchner, "Cicero, Grundzüge seines Wesens," in *Cicero*, Studien zur römischen Literatur, 2 (Wiesbaden, 1962), 1-24; A. E. Douglas, *Cicero* (Oxford, 1968); Olof Gigon, "Cicero und die griechische Philosophie," *Aufstieg und Niedergang der römischen Welt: Geschichte und Kultur Roms im Spiegel der neueren Forschung*, ed. Hildegard Temporini (Berlin, 1973), 1:4, 226-61; and Woldemar Görler, *Untersuchungen zu Ciceros Philosophie* (Heidelberg, 1974), 1-19. The fullest overall assessment of Cicero as a transmitter of Stoic ethics is Milton Valenti, *L'Ethique stoïcienne chez Cicéron* (Paris, 1956). For Cicero as a transmitter of Stoicisms more specifically in his *De officiis*, good recent statements of the standard view include Paolo Fedili, "Il 'De officiis' di Cicerone: Problemi e attegiamenti della critica moderna," *Aufstieg und Niedergang* 1:4, 376-87; Hans Armin Gärtner, *Cicero und Panaitios: Beobachtungen zu Ciceros De officiis*, Berichte der Heidelberger Akademie der Wissenschaften, philosophisch-historische Klasse, 5 (Heidelberg, 1974); and Georg Kilb, "Ethische Grundbegriffe der alten Stoa und ihre Übertragung durch Cicero," in *Das neue Cicerobild*, ed. Karl Büchner, Wege der Forschung, 27 (Darmstadt, 1971), 38-64. While emphasizing Cicero's debt to Platonism, the most recent statement of the question, Stephen Gersh, *Middle Platonism and Neoplatonism: The Latin Tradition* 2 vols. (Notre Dame, 1986), 1:71-72, retains the view that there are no fundamental departures from Panaetius in Cicero's *De officiis*. On the other hand, Andrew R. Dyck, "Notes on the Composition, Text, and Sources of Cicero's 'De Officiis,'" *Hermes* 112 (1984): 217-25 accents Cicero's freedom in the use of Panaetius. I would like to thank Robert Hardy for this reference.

2. Edward Kennard Rand, *Founders of the Middle Ages*, 2nd ed. (Cambridge, Mass., 1929; repr., New York, 1957), 79-83. The quotation is at p. 82. Rand is a close follower of Raymond Thamin, *Saint Ambroise et la morale chrétienne au IVe siècle: Étude comparée des traités "Des devoirs" de Cicéron et de Saint Ambroise* (Paris, 1895),

1 (the source of Rand's quotation), 201-309. Other late nineteenth-century proponents of this view include Paul Ewald, *Der Einfluss der stoisch-ciceronianischen Moral auf die Darstellung der Ethik bei Ambrosius* (Leipzig, 1881); and Theodor Schmidt, *Ambrosius, sein Werk de officiis libri III und die Stoa* (Augsburg, 1897). This position has been extremely durable. Its most self-assured recent restatement is Harald Hegendahl, *Latin Fathers and the Classics: A Study of the Apologists, Jerome, and Other Christian Writers*, Studia gracea et latina Gothoburgensia, 6 (Göteborg, 1958), 347-72. Others who follow suit include Pierre Courcelle, "Deux grands courants de pensée dans la littérature latine tardive: Stoïcisme et néo-platonisme," *Revue des études latines* 42 (1965): 123-24; Otto Hiltbrunner, "Die Schrift 'De officiis ministrorum' des hl. Ambrosius und ihr ciceronianisches Vorbild," *Gymnasium* 71 (1964): 174-89; J. T. Muckle, "The De Officiis Ministrorum of Saint Ambrose," *Mediaeval Studies* 1 (1939): 63-80; and Maurice Testard, "Étude sur la composition dans le *De officiis ministrorum* de Saint Ambroise de Milan," *Ambroise de Milan: XVIe centenaire de son élection épiscopale*, ed. Yves-Marie Duval (Paris, 1974), 155-97. More recently, Testard has agreed that Ambrose is not entirely faithful to Cicero. Without spelling out the details, he attributes this situation to errors and oversimplifications on Ambrose's part. See Testard, "Saint Ambroise et son modèle cicéronien dans le *De Officiis*," *Présence de Cicéron: Hommage au R.-P. M. Testard*, ed. Raymond Chevallier (Paris, 1984), 103-6. The best review of the literature on Ambrose's relation to Greek philosophy in general is Goulven Madec, *Saint Ambroise et la philosophie* (Paris, 1974), 13-17.

3. R. R. Bolgar, *The Classical Tradition and Its Beneficiaries* (Cambridge, 1958); L. D. Reynolds and N. G. Wilson, *Scribes & Scholars: A Guide to the Transmission of Greek & Latin Literature*, 2nd ed. (Oxford, 1975).

4. Ernst Robert Curtius, *European Literature and the Latin Middle Ages*, trans. Willard R. Trask (New York, 1953).

5. Jaroslav Pelikan, *The Vindication of Tradition* (New Haven, 1984), chap. 1 and 54-56, 60; *The Spirit of Medieval Theology*, The Etienne Gilson Series, 8 (Toronto, 1985), 7-12.

6. Peter Dronke, *Medieval Latin and the Rise of European Love Lyric*, 2 vols. (Oxford, 1965), 1:181. I would like to thank Robert B. Hardy for this reference.

7. Ambrose *De officiis ministrorum* 1.7.24, 1.8.25; *Patrologiae cursus completus, series latina* 16.

8. Cicero *De officiis* 1.2.2, 1.2.6, 1.2.7-1.3.10, ed. and trans. Walter Miller, Loeb Classical Library (Cambridge, Mass., 1961). See also *Ad Atticum* 420.4, ed. D. R. Shackleton Bailey, 6 vols. (Cambridge, 1965-68).

9. The best biographies of Cicero are Matthias Gelzer, *Cicero: Eine biographischer Versuch* (Wiesbaden, 1969); David Stockton, *Cicero: A Political Biography* (Oxford, 1971); and D. R. Shackleton Bailey, *Cicero* (London, 1971).

10. This point is brought out clearly by Otto Plasberg, *Cicero in seinen Werken und Briefen*, ed. Wilhelm Ax (Leipzig, 1926), 8-9. On Cicero's late works in relation to his life, the fullest treatment is Klaus Bringmann, *Untersuchungen zum späten Cicero* (Göttingen, 1971).

11. *De off.* 3.2.7-8, 3.4.20.

12. The best general study of Stoic ethics is Geneviève Rodis-Lewis, *La morale stoïcienne* (Paris, 1970). On the relations between physis and ethics, see Ernst Grumach, *Physis und Agathon in der alten Stoa* (Berlin, 1932), 1-43; Otto Rieth,

Grundbegriffe der stoischen Ethik: Eine traditionsgeschichtliche Untersuchung (Berlin, 1933); and Bohdan Wiśniewski, "Sur les origines du ὁμολογουμένως τῇ φύσει ζῆν des stoïciens," *Classica et Mediaevalia* 22 (1961): 106-16. On other related topics see I. G. Kidd, "The Relation of Stoic Intermediaries to the *Summum Bonum*, with Reference to Change in the Stoa," *Classical Quarterly* 49 (1955): 181-94; A. A. Long, "The Stoic Concept of Evil," *Philosophical Quarterly* 18 (1968): 329-48; Gérard Verbeke, "Ethische paideia in het latere Stoïcisme en het vroege Christendom," *Tijdschrift voor filosofie* 27 (1965): 3-53; and Nicholas P. White, "The Basis of Stoic Ethics," *Harvard Studies in Classical Philology* 83 (1979): 143-78. On the passions, *apatheia*, and moral choice see A. A. Long, "The Early Stoic Concept of Moral Choice," in *Images of Man in Ancient and Medieval Thought: Studia Gerardo Verbeke*, ed. F. Boissier, et al. (Leuven, 1976), 77-92; A. C. Lloyd, "Emotion and Decision in Stoic Psychology," and John M. Rist, "The Stoic Concept of Detachment," both in *The Stoics*, ed. John M. Rist (Berkeley, 1978), 233-46 and 259-72 respectively; and André-Jean Voelke, *L'Idée de volonté dans le stoïcisme* (Paris, 1973).

13. The most important general study of Panaetius is Modestus Van Straaten, *Panétius: Sa vie, ses écrits et sa doctrine avec une édition des fragments* (Amsterdam, 1946); other useful introductions include John M. Rist, *Stoic Philosophy* (Cambridge, 1969), 173-98; and Basile N. Tatakis, *Panétius de Rhodes, le fondateur du moyen stoïcisme: Sa vie et son œuvre* (Paris, 1931). Good studies of Panaetian casuistry and its relation to early Stoic ethics include A. A. Long, "Carneades and the Stoic Telos," *Phronesis* 12 (1967): 59-90; Gerhard Nebel, "Der Begriff des καθῆκον in der alten Stoa," *Hermes* 70 (1935): 439-60; Damianos Tsekourakis, *Studies in the Terminology of Early Stoic Ethics, Hermes*, Einzelschriften, 32 (Wiesbaden, 1974), chap. 1; and W. Wiersma, "Τέλος und καθῆκον in der alten Stoa," *Mnemosyne* 3:5 (1937): 219-28. Old but still basic is Raymond Thamin, *Un problème moral dans l'antiquité: Étude sur la casuistique stoïcienne* (Paris, 1884).

14. On this whole question see Helen F. North, "Canons and Hierarchies of the Cardinal Virtues in Greek and Latin Literature," in *The Classical Tradition: Literary and Historical Studies in Honor of Harry Caplan*, ed. Luitpold Wallach (Ithaca, 1966), 165-83.

15. *De off.* 1.5.17-1.6.19. The quotation is at 1.5.17.

16. *De off.* 1.7.20-1.17.58, 1.43.153-155, 1.45.157-158, 3.6.28. The quotation is at 1.14.45.

17. *De off.* 1.5.17, 1.19.62-1.26.92. The quotation is at 1.20.66.

18. *De off.* 1.27.93-1.30.106, 1.35.126-1.42.156.

19. *De off.* 1.42.150-151.

20. Esp. *De off.* 2.9.31-34, 2.11.39.

21. *De off.* 3.4.19-3.22.87.

22. For the more general point, *De off.* 3.3.12-3.4.17, 3.7.34-3.9.39. For the references to Hercules, 3.4.20, 3.5.21-3.6.29. See also 1.45.160.

23. *De off.* 3.6.30-32, 3.17.69.

24. The standard biography remains F. Homes Dudden, *The Life and Times of St. Ambrose*, 2 vols. (Oxford, 1935).

25. On the post-classical fortunes of Cicero's *De officiis*, see Fedeli, "Il 'De officiis' di Cicerone," *Aufstieg und Niedergang* 1:4, 376-86, 421-22; N. E. Nelson, "Cicero's *De Officiis* in Christian Thought: 300-1300," *Essays and Studies in English and Comparative Literature*, University of Michigan Publications, Language and Literature,

10 (Ann Arbor, 1933), 59, 64-79; Maurice Testard, intro. to his ed. of *Les devoirs,* livres 1-3, Collection des Universités de France, publiée sous le patronage de l'Association Guillaume Budé (Paris, 1965-70), 1:67-70. Less important but worth consulting are J. T. Muckle, "The Influence of Cicero in the Formation of Christian Culture," *Proceedings and Transactions of the Royal Society of Canada,* 3rd. ser., 42 (1948): 113-25; and Ettore Paratore, "Cicerone attraverso i secoli," *Marco Tullio Cicerone,* Scritti commemorativi pubblicati nel bimillenario della morte, Istituto di studi romani, Centro di studi ciceroniani (Firenze, 1961), 243-46.

26. Ambrose acknowledges his Ciceronian model overtly, *De off. min.* 1.7.24, 1.8.25. He also acknowledges at the same time that he has drawn directly on Panaetius, and that Biblical no less than classical authors have treated the topic of duty.

27. *De off. min.* 1.9.27; *PL* 16.31-32.

28. *De off. min.* 1.9.28; *PL* 16.32; "Nos autem nihil omnino quod deceat et honestum sit, futurorum magis quam praesentium metimur formula: nihilque utile quod ad uitae illius aeternae prosit gratiam definimus, non quod ad delectionem praesentis."

29. *De off.min.* 1.9.29.

30. *De off. min.* 1.17.65-1.24.105, 1.19.84.

31. *De off. min.* 1.20.89; *PL* 16.50.

32. *De off. min.* 1.24.115, 1.43.219-1.46.222. Ambrose provides a similar analysis of temperance in *De Iacob et beata uita* 1.2.5, ed. Carolus Schenkl, in Ambrose, *Opera,* ed. Schenkl et al., 7 vols. in 9, Corpus Scriptorum Ecclesiasticorum Latinorum, 32:1-2, 73 (Vienna, 1897-1968), 32:2.

33. *De off. min.* 1.20.89.

34. *De off. min.* 1.27.127-1.28.133, 1.30.143-1.32.169. On this point see the excellent recent studies by Louis J. Swift, "*Iustitia* and *ius privatum*: Ambrose on Private Property," *American Journal of Philology* 100 (1979): 176- 87; and Manfred Wacht, "Privateigentum bei Cicero und Ambrosius," *Jahrbuch für Antike und Christentum* 25 (1982): 28-64, the latter of which has a fine review of the literature on this subject, p. 29 n. 7.

35. *De off. min.* 1.29.142, 1.34.174.

36. *De off. min.* 1.20.89, 1.36.179-1.38.201.

37. *De. off. min.* 1.25.117-1.27.126, 1.50.251.

38. Esp. *De off.min.* 2.1.3-2.5.21, 2.6.22-2.7.29, 2.8.40-2.29.151.

39. *De off. min.* 3.2.8-9, 3.3.15.

40. *De off. min.* 3.4.28; *PL* 16.153: "Nam si honestas secundum naturam, omnia enim fecit Deus bona ualde. . . ." For the whole passage, 3.3.22-3.4.28.

PLENARY LECTURE

Allegory and Invention: Levels of Meaning in Ancient and Medieval Rhetoric

PHILIP DAMON

In his *Homerica Problemata*, the commentator Heraclitus defined allegory as a statement which says one thing and means another: ἄλλα μὲν ἀγορεύων, . . . ἕτερα δὲ ὧν λέγει σημαίνων (5.2). This was translated into Latin as *aliud dicere, aliud intendere* and passed on to the Middle Ages as one of the worst definitions in the history of rhetoric. The ways in which one thing can be said and another meant are many and various. They include metaphor, irony, paranomasia, parody, simple allusiveness, and ordinary conversational indirection. One result of this indiscrimination is that allegory has been used throughout its eventful history as a term for two quite antithetical processes. It frequently serves as the specification for a style of writing in which meanings are thought to be ostentatiously and even objectionably overdetermined. It is also applied to texts whose meanings are, or are at least supposed to be, problematically or mysteriously underdetermined. In an essay entitled "Allegory," Coleridge used the term to abuse parts of the *Faerie Queene* which he regarded as oppressive because of Spenser's determination to force ethical ideas on the reader by drawing narrative diagrams. The impulse toward explicitness, he complains, ruins the poetry. On the next page, however, he blames Tasso for having tried to turn *Jerusalem Delivered* into an allegory by claiming for it a hidden religious significance so dark that nobody but Tasso himself had ever noticed it. "Apollo be praised," he says, "not a thought like it would ever enter of its own accord into any mortal mind." Allegory is both the super-obvious and the impenetrably latent.

In the latter sense, it really belonged, throughout antiquity and the early Middle Ages, to the history of literary interpretation rather than the history of literature. Exegetes, Greek, Jewish, and Christian, found it necessary or convenient to read sacred or uniquely privileged texts as if they contained a hidden message directed specifically to them. It was not until the later Middle Ages and the Renaissance that European poets began to claim that they could themselves compose a dark conceit or *nascosa veritade* and veil their meanings in the systematically radical way that Spenser does in the *Faerie Queene* and Dante at least claimed to have done in his *Canzone* to the *donna gentile*. Martianus Capella's *Marriage of Mercury and Philology* contains some fairly esoteric doctrine, but its allegory of wisdom and the personifications who embody it are on the whole briskly explicit. Recent studies have shown that Prudentius' *Psychomachia* is theologically and architecturally denser than it once seemed to be, but its complexity does not compromise the extreme clarity of the allegorical action.[1] My intention is to trace out the emergence of the notion that a poet could, in the practice of his own craft and without supernatural direction, not merely write an obscure or difficult poem but carefully conceal a whole complex of meanings in a way that invites a search for it. I will try to situate this historical process within larger developments in rhetorical theory, and make it the occasion for some observations about Dante's allegory.

In the sixth book of *The Republic*, Socrates promises to exclude from the city all tales about fights among the gods either with hyponoia or without hyponoia. Hyponoia was a term with a fairly broad range of meaning. Aristotle observed that the comic writers of his own day preferred ὑπόνοια to the slapstick of Old Comedy, meaning that they employed innuendo. Socrates might therefore be saying that his citizens are not to be exposed even to bowdlerized accounts of the gods' misbehavior. But Philo of Alexandria regularly uses hyponoia to mean allegory. His phrase πρὸς τὴν ὑπόνοιαν, "according to the hyponoia" is always a warning that he is about to hit us with one of his astonishing spiritual interpretations. This is probably what Plato meant. He is ruling out indecorous tales about the gods even when they are accompanied by an improving allegorical gloss. The sort of thing he had in mind is found in a Homeric scholium probably written by Porphyry which tells us that there were three ways of dealing with Homer's Theomachy, the episode in the twentieth book of the *Iliad* which shows the gods descending to the Trojan Plain and belaboring each other in ordinary, awkward physical combat. One could, the scholiast says, excuse Homer by noting that he sang his songs a long time ago and that although he knew better himself, he had to adjust his picture of the gods to the limited understanding of a primitive audience. Alternatively, it could be argued that he earned his livelihood by performing for kings who regarded themselves as divine and that he flattered them by showing gods behaving as stupidly as they did themselves. Finally, the fight could be interpreted allegorically and its superficial crudities brushed aside as what a medieval exegete would call chaff. The passage, we are told, was sometimes read as an elemental conflict of the sort imagined in the cosmologies of Anaximander and Heraclitus. Apollo and Hephaistos are fire, Poseidon is water, Hera is air, and so forth. Alternatively, it was converted into a morally instructive psychomachia in which Aphrodite is passion, Ares violence, Hermes reason, and Leto forgetfulness. "This fashion of defending the text," says the scholiast, "is very ancient, going back to Theagenes of Rhegium, who was the first to write on Homer." Theagenes was regarded as the first Homeric commentator. He lived in the sixth century BC.

Whether he had a theory or a set of methodological principles we are not told. For signs of a reasoned, critically self-conscious account of Homer as allegorist we must wait for Neoplatonic commentators like Proclus, Heraclitus, and Porphyry himself, all of whom regard Homer as divinely inspired, mysteriously expressing profound spiritual truths through his accounts of violence and knavery. Like their fellow neoplatonist Philo, they believed that the godhead had spoken through their own great text and that it could be endlessly scanned for traces of what Philo called, "the pure unalloyed speech which is the Divine, too subtle for the hearing to catch but visible to the soul's sight." Porphyry's essay *De antro nympharum,* written in the second or third century, is a sensitive, learned, methodologically aware, and genuinely evocative neoplatonic allegory on the Ithacan cave which Odysseus enters before Athena changes him into an old man. Many people, Porphyry points out, had visited Ithaca and nobody had ever found a cave of this description on it. The cave is, moreover, a place of great cosmic importance—the point where gods go up and men come down—and it is not plausible to suppose that it would have been located in an out-of-the-way backwater like Ithaca. Read literally, the passage makes poor sense. Interpreted spiritually, it becomes a profound statement about metempsychosis made by a divinely inspired poet. Homer, Heraclitus says, is "the great hierophant who opens the celestial pathways which had before been closed to men."[2] "Absorbed by god," says Proclus, "and inspired by the Muses, he exposes the mysteries of the gods themselves. At this moment his poetry is inspired."[3] This is typical of allegorical theories up to and well beyond Augustine. The genuinely hidden as opposed to the merely metaphorical or metonymous was, until a comparatively late date, invariably taken to be the product of divine inspiration.

This is an awkwardly large generalization. I realize that there are some apparent exceptions, and since I can't cover them all, I will inspect a couple of the more obvious and representative ones. In his commentary on the *Dream of Scipio,* Macrobius says that the philosophers use fabulous narratives to conceal the truths of nature from the uninitiated. "They realize," he says, "that a clear and open exposition of herself is distasteful to Nature, who, just as she has withheld an understanding of herself from the uncouth senses of men by enveloping herself in variegated garments, has also desired to have her secrets handled by more prudent individuals through fabulous narratives. Similarly, her sacred rites are veiled in mysterious representations so that she may not have to show herself even to initiates. Only eminent men of superior intelligence gain a revelation of her truth; the others must satisfy their desire for worship with a ritual drama which prevents her secrets from becoming common."[4] This passage has regularly been cited as a precedent for twelfth and thirteenth century Neoplatonic ideas about allegory and specifically about the "veil"— the *integumentum* or *inuolucrum*—which was specifically contrasted with Scriptural *allegoria* and used to refer to the process by which a human poet artfully conceals secular, philosophical meanings in a text on his own, without divine inspiration. But this is not quite right. Macrobius distinguishes *narratio fabulosa* from fables like those of Aesop, framed tales in which both the frame and the contents of the frame are fictitious. Fabulous narrative, on the other hand, is a genre in which only the framework is a fiction and the contents are solidly and philosophically true, as in the *Dream of Scipio.* The dream is not an allegory but an exposition of cosmological doctrine beginning with a narrative introduction which suggests that it is only a story, a mere fable. Its truths are not veiled at all. Scipio's grandfather concludes by congratulating himself on the clarity of his exposition. The veil that Macrobius has in mind is the narrative introduction which, on his view, masks Cicero's didactic intentions. He was not talking about allegory.

The case of Vergil is more problematical. Attitudes toward him as a putative allegorist varied across time. In principle, a Christian could, for purposes of edification, do what he wanted to with a pagan poem, as Jerome pointed out in his remarks about spoiling the Egyptians. In practice, when it came to a reputation like Vergil's, there were usually some constraints, and questions of intention or inspiration were normally taken into account. During the later Middle Ages and the Renaissance, he was often given credit for various degrees of Christian insight into the supposedly prophetic bearings of the fourth Eclogue. Jean d' Outremeuse shows him converting the gentiles by preaching good trinitarian doctrine to them. Dante's Matilda says in so many words that Vergil had "dreamed" the Christian idea of salvation. The earlier, Patristic emphasis was rather different. Augustine maintained that Christ's coming had been foretold among the gentiles as well as the Jews. He believed that Vergil had heard a scrap of prophecy from the Cumaean Sibyl and had repeated it in a poem. The fourth Eclogue was, for him, the literal transcription of a report whose meaning the poet did not understand. The same kind of reserve appears in comment on Aeneas' descent to the underworld. It is frequently said that the Fathers, Lactantius in particular, allegorized this episode and indeed attributed allegorical intentions to Vergil, but this requires qualification. Lactantius takes the phrase at line 266, *Si mihi fas audita loqui,* "If it is permitted to tell what I have heard," to be Vergil's own assertion that he had picked up some pre-incarnational information — a *rumor obscurus* — about the resurrection and the Christian promise of immortality, but that his information on the subject was partial and imperfect. Lactantius' commentary on the *descensus Auerno* is not designed to recover a meaning which Vergil had hidden in his text but to show that it was a literally intended though garbled version of the truth. This applies not only to Christian significations but to pagan ones as well. Aeneas' choice of the right-hand road which leads to Elysium Lactantius interprets as a choice of *frugalitas* over *luxuria*. He then adds, quite correctly, that the image of the two roads was a well-known Pythagorean commonplace: a conventional and fully expressive metaphor.[5] He does not characteristically think of Vergil as hiding doctrine beneath his fable but as giving poetic expression to it. Servius, who was not fond of allegorical interpretation, admitted that some of the Eclogues did refer to the contemporary issue of agrarian redistribution. But he regarded this simply as Vergil's way of complaining about the loss of his farm without giving offence to the authorities. It was a commoner's tactful address to an Emperor, designed to deliver a message in socially appropriate terms and not to obscure it. There are, of course, many generalizing ancient parables and beast fables. Their form of statement is metaphorical and they are often called allegories, but their intention is, broadly speaking, to actualize and clarify meanings, not to conceal them. They are not the sort of thing I have in mind.

It is in the sixth century that we first find a commentator maintaining that a poet can systematically and pervasively conceal — really hide — important meanings in a text on his own, without divine help or special revelation. I refer to Fulgentius in his *De Continentia Vergiliana*.[6] This commentary on the *Aeneid* takes the form of a dream in which Vergil appears to the author and condescends to explain the meaning of his epic. The Christian dreamer's relationship to the pagan poet is, in its small way, reminiscent of Dante's situation in the dark wood. Vergil, sadly aware that his pupil has access to a wisdom higher than his own, undertakes to explain the truths which lie hidden beneath the heroic surface of his poem. The dreamer is eager to explore typological connections between these truths and Christian revelation, and although Vergil praises his efforts, he resolutely refuses to employ them in his own auto-interpretation. His wisdom, he says, was a mixture of the doctrine happily acquired from the Stoics and unhappily from the Epicureans, but such as it was, it was the wisdom available to him, and he placed it himself beneath the surface of his story of exile and warfare. He maintains that within the limits of his own dispensation he wrote a work of great profundity full of meanings long hidden from public apprehension. He hid them himself by his own rhetorical strategies, and the account he gives of them is a statement about his own poetic intentions.

He begins at the beginning with an analysis of *Arma uirumque,* explaining that by *arma* he meant fortitude and by *uirum* wisdom, which is to say that Aeneas combined the virtues of *sapientia* and *fortitudo.* When Fulgentius attempts a typological application by pointing out that Holy Scripture praises Christ's wisdom and fortitude, Vergil replies, "You know what the true God has taught you. Let me tell you what I had in mind." What he had in mind, we discover, was a complicated rhetorical strategy designed to capture the reader's benevolence for his hero. He describes the strategy in detail and concludes by asking, "Why shouldn't I have begun with *arma?*" The Christian may see other implications in the phrase, but Vergil is exclusively and assertively concerned with his own intentions. He says later on, "I didn't come here to tell you what I ought to have believed, but what I *did* believe."

The story of Aeneas was, he says, intended by himself as an allegory on the human condition and the three ages of man. Hidden beneath the story is an account of the passage from infancy through the intellectual awareness of maturity to the spiritual balance of old age. "Under the figure of a historical narrative I have displayed the whole state of man. First comes nature, second learning, third felicity." He maintains continuously and vigorously that the ideas installed beneath the heroic surface of the poem are his own ideas and that he put them there himself as part of his own grand rhetorical program. Fulgentius manages, on command, to stammer out a bald paraphrase of the first book, and then asks for an interpretation. "I would now like to know what sense you attribute to this." Vergil begins by saying, "I devised the shipwreck as an image of the perils of childbirth" and the rest of his self-exegesis insists heavily on his own authorial intentions. "I devised the golden bough," he says, "mindful that my mother once dreamed that she would give birth to a bough ... I described it as golden because I wanted to signify oratorical brilliance, mindful that when Diogenes the Cynic attacked Plato, he claimed to find nothing in his works but a golden tongue. I myself spoke in the Bucolics of ten golden apples, by which I meant the polished eloquence of the ten eclogues." The allegory derives from his own experience and his own personal associations, and he put it in his poem by himself. He ostentatiously disclaims any divine inspiration at all and insists on his poetic intentions as the source of the elaborate statement about man's fate which he concealed on principle and now, at last, reveals to Fulgentius.

Comparetti, whose *Vergil in the Middle Ages* contained the earliest detailed account of the medieval commentaries, regarded Fulgentius almost as a certifiable lunatic. "He may," he concluded, "be looked upon as the caricature of all who went before or followed after him in the field of allegorical interpretation."[7] Times have changed. A recent discussion contrasts the oddity of his approach to local detail with the broader attractiveness of his general interpretation.

> The ages-of-man theory, the view of epic as a step-by-step examination of the growth and maturation of man, which he derived from his method, persuaded and satisfied most of the Middle Ages — including such eminent minds as Petrarch's and Dante's — no doubt because he was not entirely wrong. Tracing the growth process from infancy may be a distortion, but it is a distortion of a process of intellectual maturation that is genuinely present in Vergil's text.[8]

Look in many a nineteenth century school edition and you will be told that Vergil was a great imitator of Homer. The *Iliad* devotes a book to the Funeral Games for Patroklos, and this is why the fifth book of the *Aeneid* includes something like Funeral Games for Anchises. Fulgentius, say what you will about his manner of formulating his insights, sees more than this. He sees growth and development and a partial recovery from the disaster at Carthage. He sees the beginnings of a rededication to ideals of his dead father. He sees a part of the process which will, in the sixth and seventh books, restore Aeneas' lost sense of mission. "In the fifth book, drawn by the contemplation of his father's memory, he occupies himself with the games of youth. What does this mean but that a mature man, having acquired prudence, will follow his father's example and exert himself bodily in noble enterprises." Allowance made for the ages of man business, this points to Aeneas' situation. Many a later commentator, has not, despite greater sobriety of statement, done as well.

Fulgentius' insights are the product of what may, I think, be called the discovery that a poet could, in the ordinary exercise of his art, conceal meanings in a way which had invariably been attributed to divine inspiration. I doubt whether the discovery should be taken for granted as a natural and expectable transference of interpretive methods from a sacred text to a profane one. It is often maintained that medieval readers, having been conditioned to believe that the divine Author intentionally hid the full meaning of his text, easily and almost automatically began to suppose that human authors could do the same. But Aquinas argued vigorously in the thirteenth century that human authors could *not* imitate God's style of allegory, and I would suppose that in the sixth there must have been inhibitions against imputing to a pagan poet a mode of composition which had always been associated with the voice of God. I surmise that positive stimulus was required for this reasonably momentous step, and that it (or some of it) was provided by a pervasive postclassical shift in literary analytical assumptions and a new way of reading literary texts. For Aristotle, and for Cicero after him, invention, the finding of convincing arguments to support a case, was a rhetorical and not a poetic procedure. Aristotle recognized that poets did imitate arguments in their poems, but he was prepared to maintain a crucial distinction. His term διάνοια, or "purpose," which Cicero translated as *sententia*, refers generally to the intellectual coherence of an argument and more specifically to a speaker's own manner of achieving coherence. It is necessary, Aristotle observed, for a narrative poet to be able to represent διάνοια, and he gives special praise to the speeches which Homer provides for Achilles. They are a major vehicle for the representation of his ἦθος, and Homer displays a mastery of rhetorical technique in inventing them for him. But coherent speeches do not, he insists, make a poem. For the poet, invention is not an end in itself but a means of imitation. Homer's representation of Achilles' διάνοια does not make him a rhetorician any more than Aeschylus' information about the Persian War makes him a historian. Speeches are not to be admired or interpreted as free-standing objects but as parts of a whole whose method is not rhetorical but poetic. Granted that Homer's are oratorically expressive, their interest and value must be investigated by methods belonging to the science of poetics and not of rhetoric. Homer would have made a great orator, but it is a bad mistake to take him for one.

    This genial principle, which a Homerist like Plato's Ion might have had some trouble grasping even in his own day, was totally submerged in the Latin tradition. The teaching of literature and the teaching of oratory were, in Cicero's time, kept separate. The grammarian would expound a text to his pupils and exclaim over its beauties. The teacher of rhetoric would offer training in declamation and argument. In the course of time, professional competition developed as grammarians began to require their students to declaim speeches excerpted form literary texts. "The teachers of literature are not content," says Quintilian, "to take the leavings of the rhetoricians but have extended their curricula to include declamation in character and deliberative argument." He thought that this was an unfortunate development, but it ultimately prevailed, with the result that categories of analysis and evaluation which Aristotle attached to public speaking gradually became attached to the study of poetry. In the fifth century, Tiberius Claudius Donatus argued that Vergil should not be taught by grammarians but by rhetoricians. For him, Vergil was himself the *summus rhetor*, the consummate orator, and it took a rhetorician to appreciate and to interpret his poem. "Virgilium non grammaticos sed oratores praecipuos tradere debuisse."[9] The corollary of this was the anti-Aristotelian proposition that the essence of Vergil's art was his ability to construct persuasive speeches. The invention of plausible arguments became (and remained for a long time) the theoretical essence of poetry. It was in his speeches that Vergil demonstrated his art most fully, and Donatus' own commentary is one long illustration of the error which Aristotle warned against: regarding an epic poem as a collection of orations connected by narrative.

The Sophists had defined rhetoric as the art of making the worse argument appear the better. Aristotle would not accept this formulation, but his strategies *were* designed to win cases. Quintilian, who had a lofty estimate of the orator's calling, conceded nevertheless that it was sometimes necessary for an orator to "support what is fallacious and deceive a judge in order to make justice prevail."[10] As the rhetorical approach increasingly dominated discussions of poetry, there was a movement away from the generalizing style of ancient literary comment toward a more closely detailed analysis intended to display the clever, lawyerly ingenuity of the poet. We are asked to admire the masterful way in which he shades the evidence and loads the dice in the interest of persuasion. His characters are seen as employing their rhetorical wiles on other characters and on *us*. For Donatus, Aeneas is essentially a defendant in the dock and by no means an obviously innocent one. Vergil is his advocate, a man pleading a difficult case. Both through the speeches he assigns to Aeneas and through his own comments, he manipulates our reactions in an effort to exculpate him. True appreciation of the poem depends on our ability to perceive the way in which he obfuscates the charges against his hero.

The charges were serious ones. Read Dares and Dictys, who were regarded as unimpeachable eyewitnesses, and you will find that as part of a generally suspicious performance at Troy, Aeneas conspired with

Antenor to betray the city to the Greeks. Poets were still worrying about this in the fourteenth century. Vergil was assumed to be doing his best to cover these matters up on behalf of his ancestor. Even on the doctored evidence, it remained clear to Donatus that Aeneas fled from Troy because he was unable to defend it. It was equally plain that the gods were against the Trojans and consequently against him, another incriminating fact. To a neutral observer, he says, he must appear as "a man who has led his life in such a way as to displease the gods even though he was the grandson of Zeus." We are more or less continuously asked to admire the way in which Vergil, by "wondrous art," minimizes these problems from the very beginning of the poem. "Like the consummate orator he is, he admits the charges which cannot be denied and then, having dealt with them, he converts them into occasions for praise. If anyone analyzes this passage carefully and diligently, he will find nothing that is not to be admired. It is replete with the art and subtlety of the orator."

Concerning Aeneas' account of the fall of Troy he says, "This is the subtle and artful speech of a man who was, after all, defeated, who knows himself to have been unable to defend his own city and who now wants to persuade the fearful Dido to accept him as the defender of *hers*." The argument, he says, "tends more toward exculpation than fraud," but fraud does not appear to be completely ruled out, and we are asked throughout to admire the indirection of Aeneas' approach—its lack of candor and straightforwardness. Dido is fooled into making her fatal decision as Aeneas uses the same oratorical sleights on her that Vergil himself uses on us. In the famous speech to his comrades beginning, "O passi grauiora," Aeneas is praised for speaking with "magno artis ingenio." He knows by now that he is hateful to his followers, who understand very well that he is responsible for most of their troubles. He therefore begins by calling them *socii*, cleverly suggesting that he is merely the sharer of their troubles rather than the cause of them. Vergil has become fundamentally a maker of speeches and an inventor of persuasive arguments. The reader's principal task is to detect the argumentative subtleties placed in his mouth by a narrator whose ability to conceal or confuse the facts of the case is the distinguishing feature of his art. I suspect that this broad shift in attitudes toward a special rhetorical conception of poetry encouraged Fulgentius' contention that Vergil had, in the exercise of his own art, concealed the full truth of his story. The idea of a genuinely multi-levelled secular allegory was associated with the post-classical notion that the poet is fundamentally an inventor of arguments, that his aim is persuasion, and that he is by artistic necessity a concealer of the full truth of his discourse.

Fulgentius' discovery, if we may call it that, had consequences. One careful twelfth-century reader of the *De continentia* was Bernardus Silvestris. Bernardus' own commentary on the first six books of the *Aeneid* is very Fulgentian.[11] He maintains that the poem is an allegory on man's progress from infancy to maturity. His interpretations of individual scenes are sometimes borrowed without major change from Fulgentius. His prefatory remarks are an authentic milestone in the history of literary exegisis and may fairly be said to make explicit the program which remains half-spoken in his source. "To the extent that he writes about the nature of human life," Bernardus says, "Vergil is a philosopher. His procedure is to describe allegorically by means of an integument what the human spirit does and endures while placed in the human body." Concerning integument, he says, "It is a type of exposition which wraps the apprehension of truth in a fictional narrative." A commentary on Martianus Capella which Juneau attributed to Bernardus distinguishes integument from allegory. Allegory is defined as a true historical narrative with a covert meaning. The example offered is Jacob's fight with the angel. Integument, on the other hand is a fabulous narrative containing *intellectum*, rational understanding, as in the story of Orpheus.[12] The distinction is between the hidden meanings of an inspired Scriptural text and those which a secular poet can conceal by the use of his own human intelligence. Bernardus did not invent this terminological distinction, but he was the first to make it this sharply within a specifically literary context. It is, like the commentary itself, a response to his reading of the *De continentia*. It is a theory about literary allegory drawn from Fulgentius' less systematic emphasis on the personal, secular inspiration of the hidden wisdom he detected in Vergil's poem.

Bernardus must have died about a hundred years before Dante was born. The dedicatory epistle to the *Paradiso*, which, if it is not by Dante, probably ought to have been, shares Bernardus' concern with the philosophical or sapiential value of the fictional or fabulous. So, with somewhat different emphases, do the *Vita Nuova*, the *Convivio*, and the *De uulgari eloquentia*. Like Bernardus, he uses the story of Orpheus in the *Convivio* to discriminate between Scriptural allegory and the *nascosa veritade*, the "hidden truth" of human poetry. It is widely thought to go without saying that Dante knew Fulgentius, and it has been suspected that he may have been thinking of him when he began the *Commedia* with an allusion to the ages of man and a dream-like encounter with Vergil. I want to offer a comment on the allegory of the *Commedia* in connection with what might be called the Bernardine or Fulgentian tradition of poetic allegory. Our contemporary understanding of this poem has been shaped by what may fairly be called the rediscovery of the fundamentally Augustinian inspiration of its allegorical style. One set of major documents in this rediscovery is Erich Auerbach's *Dante as Poet of the Secular World,* his essay "Figura," and his chapter "Farinata and Cavalcante" in *Mimesis.* Another is Charles Singleton's volumes of *Dante Studies* and his invaluable commentary. These have shown the extent to which Dante drew his theory and his practice of polysemous narrative from the Augustinian conception of biblical figurality — the notion that the Old Testament was a work in which, as Aquinas was to put it, "words mean things which in turn mean other things."[13] The Old Testament, having been written under divine inspiration, could evoke hidden meanings which had been structured into the fabric of sacred history by God himself. The story of Exodus, to use Dante's favorite example, could refer not only to the historical event but also to ideas about salvation, Christian morality, and eschatology which God had sacramentally installed within the event. This was, as Aquinas observed, something that no human author could do, but Dante found that he could at least evoke it, and that is what he does in the *Commedia,* presenting us with a densely textured, fully realized world which, relying on Scriptural reverberations, continuously points toward a complex of latent meanings beyond the narrated events. The critical emphasis on this method of allegorical composition has been enormously productive. It has been, perhaps, too productive, by which I mean that it has tended to monopolize the discussion and suggest an outline which is a shade too monolithic.

Auerbach's historicist persuasion led him to the view that the *Zeitgeist* manifested itself, to use his own phrase, "precisely and pregnantly," in every part of a serious literary work. In his analysis of *To the Lighthouse* in *Mimesis,* he maintained that the stylistic and historical implications he elicited from Mrs. Ramsay's impressionistic meditation could be found in any "random realistic text." Perhaps so, but my own sense of this novel is that the passages which put us inside the mind of Mrs. McNab "represent reality" rather differently, and I doubt whether they would have served Auerbach's purposes nearly as well as the one he selected. I do not think that the figural, scripturally based style of analysis he employs so brilliantly in analyzing the encounter with Farinata and Cavalcante in Hell can, as he seems to assert, be used with equally impressive results throughout the whole poem. There are important parts of the *Commedia* which actively and importantly resist the figural mode of interpretation in favor of other modes. I am not thinking of setpieces like the disturbance outside the City of Dis or the entrance into Purgatory, where Dante warns us that he is shifting momentarily to a more stiffly emblematic allegorical style. I mean that there are large, thematically central moments which insist rather in Spenser's manner that the narrative is informed by hidden meanings of the poet's own devising, ingeniously put there by himself for the discovery of the learned reader. Bernardus said that the subject of *integumentum* was Wisdom, and I want to look at what I will call Dante's Allegory of Wisdom, the Circle of the Sun in the *Paradiso*, the locus for the cardinal virtue of prudence or directive reason.

As usual in the *Paradiso*, Dante is presented here with statements and configurations which puzzle his understanding and, once resolved, lead to larger and more difficult puzzles, culminating in the one which passes all understanding. His two interlocutors among the Prudent are Saint Thomas Aquinas and Saint Bonaventure. Aquinas provides him with his first intellectual shock by introducing Solomon and saying of him that in matters of wisdom "no man ever rose to be a second," which is to say that he was the wisest man who ever lived. Dante, thinking of the unfallen Adam and Jesus, is puzzled, and Aquinas ultimately answers his unspoken question with a good scholastic distinction. Solomon was a king, he says, and I was referring to the kind of wisdom appropriate to a king. Solomon manifested it when, given a choice, he asked God not for spiritual enlightenment or philosophical understanding but for political expertise: "Teach me to rule my people." Before this verbal problem is solved, however, two situational ones have emerged. Among the twenty-four blessed exemplars of wisdom, Aquinas points out Siger of Brabant, the heretical Averroist whose doctrine of the double truth he had himself fought throughout his career. Siger had maintained that the Bible and Aristotle were both true, even when they contradicted each other. They need not and could not be harmonized, and the philosopher could discover final, irrefutable truths about the world and man without reference to revelation. Aquinas, who had voluminously maintained the contrary, now acknowledges him as a blessed fellow sage. Bonaventure, in his turn, points to Joachim of Flora, the heretical Franciscan who had been his own major headache. Joachim had prophesied the coming of a third age which would not repose, like the previous two, on law or grace, but on love. Man would, in this dispensation, reach perfection and become worthy of God's affection. Grace would no longer be necessary for salvation, and institutions designed to help acquire it, including the Church, would wither away and become purely spiritualized with no secular role at all. This view was anathema to Bonaventure and he devoted much of his energy as General of the Franciscans to combatting it. Here, in the circle of Wisdom, he, like Aquinas, collegially and problematically introduces his heretical antagonist as a colleague in wisdom.

126   Allegory and Invention

Etienne Gilson observed that Solomon, Siger, and Joachim, the circle's three personified puzzles, form a pattern: a king who desired only political or kingly wisdom; a philosopher who wanted only to philosophize; a prophet who foresaw a Church concerned exclusively with the spiritual.[14] This pattern is an allusion to the doctrine of the *De monarchia*, where Dante, in response to his own agonizing involvement in Italian politics, developed the theory of a universal monarchy in which full divine authority devolved directly and independently on the Emperor, the Pope, and the hypothetical Wise Man or Philosopher. The Emperor would, like Solomon, concern himself, as Emperor, exclusively with temporal affairs. The Pope would, as Joachim prophesied, keep his nose out of secular affairs in general and politics in particular. The Philosopher would, with divine approval, philosophize independently of both. This arrangement was Dante's own highly personal response to the turmoil which had ruined his own life and which preoccupies him throughout the *Commedia*. The first and basest soul he lays eyes on in the otherworld is Celestine V, whose resignation from the papacy made way for Boniface, whom Dante saw as the great betrayer of Florence and a principal cause of his own personal woes. He still has his mind on Celestine at the very end of the *Paradiso* as he prepares to look on the invisible things of God. And in the circle of the Prudent, the locus of directive reason, the virtue required to set the world to rights, he offers an ostentatiously rarefied allegory on his own political theory.

The *De monarchia* exudes on almost every page a powerful sense of personal discovery. Dante asks for God's help as an explorer might on beginning a dangerous journey into unknown territory, but he insists emphatically that it is his own powers of intellection and imagination that are being tested. He admits in the *Purgatorio* that he expects to pay a heavy price in the hereafter for his pride in his own artistic and intellectual accomplishments. His pride in the originality and the argumentative rigor of the *De monarchia* emerges from the first page on.

> All men on whom the Higher Nature has stamped the love of truth should especially concern themselves in laboring for posterity, in order that they may enrich future generations just as they themselves were made rich by the efforts of generations past. For that man who is so imbued with public teachings, but cares not to contribute something to the public good, is far in arrears of his duty .... Often meditating with myself upon these things, lest I should someday be found guilty of the charge of the buried talent, I desire for the public weal, not only to burgeon but to bear fruit, and to

establish truths unattempted by others. Therefore it is my purpose to bring it out from its hiding place, that I may both keep watch for the good of the world and be the first to win the palm of so great a prize for my own glory.

He is describing what he regards as a unique intellectual enterprise, the product of his personal experience and his private reflections upon it. His Allegory of Wisdom in the *Paradiso* is founded on what he unblushingly regarded as a major discovery of a singularly powerful and original mind: his own. Its form of statement—its intricately private and personal method of hiding meanings—reinforces this emphasis. Its figurative structure is less akin to the figural or biblical style of allegory, with its evocation of a shared, traditional set of associations, than to the intricacies of the Metaphysical poetic conceit whose ingenuities and rarefactions draw our attention as much to the mind of the poet as to the ostensible subject. The style of the passage is a part of its statement. The intricately wrought complex of latent meanings installed by the poet to challenge the reader's attention is in the intellectual tradition of Bernardus Silvestris. It is by no means certain that Dante would have scorned to acknowledge Fulgentius as a predecessor.

Notes

1. Macklin Smith, *Prudentius' Psychomachia: A Reexamination* (Princeton, 1976)
2. Heraclitus *Homerica Problemata* 76.1.
3. Proclus *In Rempublicam* 1.92.
4. Macrobius *In Somnium Scipionis* 2.17.
5. Lactantius *Institutiones* 7.22.1.
6. Fulgentius, *De continentia Vergiliana*, ed. R. Helm (Leipzig, 1898).
7. Domenico Comparetti, *Vergil in the Middle Ages*, trans. E. Benecke (New York, 1929), 108.
8. Earl G. Schreiber and Thomas E. Maresca, Introduction to Bernardus Silvestris' *Commentary on the First Six Books of Vergil's Aeneid* (Lincoln, Neb., 1979), 18.
9. Tiberius Claudius Donatus, *Interpretationes Vergilianae*, ed. H. Georgii (Leipzig, 1905–06), 1:4.
10. Quintilian *Institutio oratoria* 12.1.
11. *Commentum Bernardi Siluestris super sex libros Eneidos Vergilii*, ed. W. Reidel (Greifswald, 1924).
12. Edouard Jeanneau, "L'usage de la notion d'integumentum à travers les gloses de Guillaume de Conches," *Archives d'histoire doctrinale et littéraire du moyen âge* 32 (1957): 35.
13. *Summa Theologica*, quaest. 1, art. 10.
14. Etienne Gilson, *Dante et la philosophie* (Paris, 1939), 227 ff.

Bernard Silvestris and the *Corpus* of the *Aeneid*

MARILYNN DESMOND

In the commentary doubtfully attributed to Bernard Silvestris, the commentator—whether Bernard Silvestris, some other Bernard, or somebody else entirely—sets out to unwrap the *integument* of Vergil's text.[1] Bernard (as I will refer to this commentator) summarizes Vergil's intention in the *Aeneid*: "modus agendi talis est: integumento describit quid agat uel quid paciatur humanus spiritus in humano corpore temporaliter positus" (3)[2] ("his agenda is this: in an *integument* he describes what the human spirit does or what it endures while placed temporarily in the body"). Bernard goes on to define *integument*: "Integumentum est genus demonstrationis sub fabulosa narratione ueritatis inuoluens intellectum, unde etiam dicitur inuolucrum" (3) ("*integument* is a sort of presentation wrapping the comprehension of truth in a fictitious narrative, whence it is also called a wrapper [covering, envelope]"). The image of wrapping or covering represents the function of the *integument*, prompting one scholar at least to refer to the *integument* as a sort of "poetic cloak," and to describe the explication of a text as the activity of unwrapping or undressing the truth: "L'art du commentateur consiste à déshabiler la leçon philosophique, à lui enlever le manteau fabuleux qui la cache aux yeux du vulgaire et à la faire apparaître dans son authentique nudité."[3] Indeed, this characterization aptly describes a sort of "embodied logic"[4] visible in this commentary on the *Aeneid*: in unwrapping the "truth" of this text, the commentator finds under the *integument* an allegory based on a Platonic vision of the human body as a microcosm of the universe. Following twelfth-century allegorical practice, Bernard reads the universe represented in the *Aeneid* as a body, a reading informed by the vision of the world's body that dominates the *Timaeus*, especially the medieval Latin version of the *Timaeus*, which breaks off at p. 53 (Stephanus ed.) of the Greek text.[5] In this reading context, Aeneas' body itself becomes the locus of interpretation for the world's body.

Bernard's commentary proceeds from the assumption that as a philosopher, Vergil intends his text to be read according to a "natural order," which the commentator recuperates by reading the text as a representation of the development—psychologically and physically—of the body of Aeneas.[6] Thus Bernard glosses his etymological explanation of the name Eneas to emphasize the thematics of the body: "Dicitur autem Eneas quasi ennos demas, id est habitator corporis" (10). Bernard thereby justifies his interpretation of the *ordo naturalis* of Vergil's text as an allegory on the "ages of man." Such an interpretive framework, based on Fulgentius' fifth-century allegorical reading of the *Aeneid*,[7] allows the commentator to impose a biographical order on the plot of Vergil's text, whereby the temporal aspects of the plot of the *Aeneid* represent a biographical paradigm of the body. This reading strategy is visible in the actual presentation of the commentary: generally the plot of the *Aeneid* is announced in a skeletal summary (*continentia fabulosa*), followed by an interpretation (*expositio*) of it. Such developmental reading of the *Aeneid* finds book 1 to be an account of early childhood or the first age; the shipwreck becomes a figurative account of childbirth, a reading based on Fulgentius' allegorical interpretation of Vergil's narrative. Book 2 chronicles the second age "id est pueritie," the end of infancy when children begin to speak. Thus Aeneas' narration of his adventures at the beginning of *Aeneid* 2 marks his entrance into the second age. Book 3 illustrates the nature of adolescence, *natura adholecentie,* since the burning of the city in book 2 and the death of Anchises in book 3 represent the end of childhood. Book 4 chronicles the adventures of youth, *natura iuuentutis,* in its account of Aeneas' affair with Dido. The funeral games for Anchises in book 5 become an allegory of the age of manhood, *natura uirilis.* And finally, in book 6, the newly matured Aeneas enters the underworld to seek his father and to strengthen his virility, in terms of the commentator, to control his wandering spirit and to attempt to rule his desires with reason. Book 6, however, is so densely glossed that it resembles an autopsy more than an allegory. In order to elucidate the philosophy of book 6, the commentator resorts to an extremely dense etymological explanation of the words, as much as of the plot, of *Aeneid* 6. The density of such glosses causes the controlling allegory—the developmental look at the human spirit trapped in the body—to break down almost entirely. The commentary breaks off before it reaches the end of book 6, in contradiction to the commentator's introductory statement that he intended to take up the entire twelve books of the *Aeneid*.

This commentary on the *Aeneid* is permeated by an analogy of the body, an analogy that operates not only through the structuring paradigm that allows the *Aeneid* to be read developmentally along the "ages of man" model, but also through the cosmological, Platonic vision that allows the commentator to read the earth as a macrocosm of the human body. The commentary continually refers to the earth as a body:

> terre corpus ad modum humani corporis dispositum est. Quemadmodum in humano corpore sunt meatus humoris, id est uene, per quas sanguis desfluit et inde facto uulnere exilit, ita et in terra sunt uene quas cataractas uocant, per quas aqua deducitur et inde si fodiatur exilit. Item quemadmodum in humano corpore sunt arterie per quas hanelitus per corpus meat, ita in terra sunt cauerne per quas aer immittitur (8).

> The body of the earth is arranged in the manner of the human body. Just as in the human body there are passages for humors, that is, the veins, through which blood flows and from which it pours when a wound has occurred, just so, there are veins in the earth which they call cataracts, through which water is led and from which it springs if it is pierced. Likewise, just as in the human body there are windpipes through which the breath passes through the body, just so there are cavities in the earth through which air is admitted.

At this point, the veins in the body are compared to the cataracts in the earth, a comparison that uses the human body to describe the world's body. Bernard also compares the moisture of the body, the humors, to the sea: "Mare corpus humanum intelligitur quia ebrietates et libidines que per aquas intelliguntur ab eo defluunt et in eo sunt commotiones uitiorum et per ipsum ciborum et potus meatus fit" (10). ("The sea is understood to be the human body, because inebriations and desires which are understood to be the waters flow from it, and in it are the excitements of vices and through it are the passages of food and drink.") This analogy of the body is central to the strategy of this commentator; such comparisons can be found throughout the commentary. By locating the focus of the narrative of the *Aeneid* in the body of Aeneas and embedding the local concept of the body in a larger Platonic view of the world's body, the commentator produces a double focus by means of which he can elicit the philosophical meaning of the *corpus* of the *Aeneid*: the commentator unwraps the *corpus* of the text to disclose a representation of the figurative and philosophical potentials for meaning in the body, both the human body and the world's body.

The concept of the body that acts as a controlling analogy for this commentary also participates in a new mythology of the body. In the twelfth century, as a result of certain advances in the study of medicine, the concept of the medical body began to take on new meaning and thus provided a new frontier for the study of philosophy. This medicalization of the human body was initiated and encouraged by the growing collection of medical texts in Latin, translated from Greek and Arabic, particularly those attributed to Constantine Afer in the late eleventh century.[8] Enriched by these texts, medical education and practice were transformed in the early twelfth century, leading to a practical interest in human anatomy and the study of surgery, especially at Salerno.[9] At Chartres, the study of medicine was a branch of the study of philosophy, an institutional approach which led to the development of Bernard's analogy of the medical body as a microcosm of the cosmological body.[10] The study of the medical body was supported by the study of the elements in philosophical discourse,[11] as well as the study of human anatomy in medical texts. In addition, the development and practice of surgery, and the practice of dissecting the bodies of animals[12] produced a new discourse of the body that effectively complements the discourse of the world's body from Plato's *Timaeus*. The rather crude, non-poetic concept of the medical body as it develops in Bernard's commentary on the *Aeneid*, especially compared to the more philosophical and poetic description of the body as it develops in the *Cosmographia*,[13] is clearly based on the medical discourse of the twelfth century, discourse which enhances the mythic possibilities of the human body viewed as a microcosm of the world's body.

The medical body and the world's body, though basic to twelfth-century thought, would not appear to provide a meaningful context within which to read Vergil's *Aeneid*. Nonetheless, both the macrocosmic and the microcosmic *corpus* provide a framework for this commentary, a framework which illustrates Bernard's approach to reading as a form of scientific inquiry. The anthropomorphic qualities of this approach—to read the text as a *corpus* that participates in an elaborate macrocosmic view of the world—represent a sophisticated application of a particular *embodied logic,* as defined in sociological terms: "Human beings think nature and society with their bodies. That is to say, they first think the world and society as one giant body. In turn, the divisions of the body yield the divisions of the world and of society, of humans and of animals. Primitive classifications, therefore, followed an *embodied logic* of division of gender and kinship and replication."[14] The elaborate analogy of the body that permeates and controls Bernard's commentary is not an artifact of a primitive logic of reading, but a sophisticated assessment of both the act of reading and the experience of Vergil's narrative.

The assumptions Bernard makes in this commentary about the act of reading continually emphasize the perceptual potentials of the human body. This concept finds much fuller expression in the *Cosmographia*—a text securely attributed to Bernard Silvestris—where, in Brian Stock's terms, "Bernard's view may be described as sensorial and empirical perception, since the data from the external world, reflected directly by the senses, are analyzed by the brain, which in turn sends messages to the various parts of the body. This is essentially a physical approach and Bernard's debt to Galen is clear."[15] And Stock summarizes the philosophical potential of this approach: "Bernard sees man as a *sensilis mundus*, a sensorial cosmos. Man's senses are also directly related to the mechanical arts."[16] The reader, in Bernard's terms, "thinks the text" through his own gendered body, and he simultaneously subjects the body to interpretation. The body is both an instrument of interpretation and a locus of interpretation. As an interpretive approach to a complex narrative text, such a strategy actually foregrounds several thematic issues in Vergil's *Aeneid*.

Though reductive, Bernard's commentary provides a coherent frame within which to read the *Aeneid*, a text which generally resists thematically imposed coherence. Indeed, we might consider some of the very basic ways in which Vergil's Aeneas is shown to be trapped in his body.[17] Aeneas' initial appearance in the text emphasizes his physical vulnerability; thrashed about by the storm initiated by Juno, he first appears in a passage that exemplifies his corporeality when the narrator notes that his limbs fall slack with chill in response to the storm ("extemplo Aeneae soluuntur frigore membra" [1.92]). Several hundred lines later, he identifies himself and his band of Trojans in terms of physical weariness ("reliquias Danaum, terraeque marisque / omnibus exhaustos iam casibus" [1.598-99]). Throughout book 2, moreover, as he relates the fall of Troy, he characterizes the experience in terms of his own physical perceptions and sensorial responses; as he introduces his narration he emphatically notes his perceptual role: "quaeque ipse miserrima uidi / et quorum pars magna fui" (2.5-6). Aeneas' body has a definite thematic presence in the text; this is best seen when Aeneas himself sums up the heaviness of his weary flesh in book 6, when the whole idea of the transmigration of souls is presented to him, and he asks his father whether anyone would ever wish to return to his sluggish body. ("O pater, anne aliquas ad caelum hinc ire putandum est / sublimis animas iterumque ad tarda reuerti / corpora?" [719-21]).

Book 4, however, provides the most explosive potential for an investigation of the physiological reality of the body. In a particularly opaque and troubling presentation of Vergilian causality, Juno and Venus barter away Dido's body to insure peace, each for different reasons. Through the collusion of these two deities, another storm, cosmologically motivated by the will of the gods and parallel of course to the storm in book 1, forces Aeneas and Dido into the cave (*Aeneid* 4.160–72). There Juno provides the trappings of the wedding, and Aeneas and Dido clearly provide the physical consummation of a marriage. Vergil is appropriately elliptical about the cave scene. Although the narrative causality presented in the text proposes a divine cause in the will of the two goddesses, manifest in the storm that cosmologically motivates Aeneas and Dido to enter the cave, the scene itself cannot be fully explained on the "macrocosmic" level of the divine will personified by climatic forces. Vergil likewise forces us to remember Aeneas' humanity, his weariness and his natural affinities with Dido, aspects of his character that are forcefully illustrated throughout *Aeneid* 1. This microcosmic causality opens up a space for Bernard to impose his own medicalized explanation of the microcosmic causality implicit in the text:

> Tempestatibus et pluuiis ad cauernam compellitur, id est commotionibus carnis et affluentia humoris ex ciborum et potuum superfluitate prouenientis ad immundiciam carnis ducitur et libidinis. Que immundicia carnis cauea dicitur quia serenitatem mentis et discretionis obnubilat. Affluentia humoris ciborum et potuum taliter ad libidinis immundiciam ducit. In decoctione humoris quattuor sunt: liquor, fumus, spuma, fex. Decoctis ergo humoribus ciborum et potuum in cacabo stomachi fumus inde progrediens et, ut natura leuitatis exigit, ascendens ascendendo et per arterias colando rarior factus ad cerebrum uenit et animales uirtutes facit. Liquore uero membra coalescunt. Fex vero per inferiores meatus in secessum emittitur; spuma uero partim per sudores partim per foramina sensuum fluit. Cum autem spume nimia est superfluitas, quod contingit in crapulosis comestionibus et ebrietatibus, per uirilem uirgam quia uentri proxima est et subdita in sperma, id est semen uirile, conuersa emittitur. . . . Itaque ducunt pluuie Eneam ad caueam iungiturque Didoni et diu cum ea moratur (24).

> By storms and rain he is driven to the cave, that is by the excitements of the flesh and the influx of moisture arising from an excess of food and drink, he is led to the impurity of the flesh and of desire. The impurity of the flesh is said to be a cave because it beclouds the clearness of the mind and the discernment. The influx of the moisture of food and drink leads to the impurity of desire in the

following way. In the digestion of moisture there are four things: liquid, steam, foam and excrement. Therefore, when the humors of food and drink have been digested in the cooking pot of the stomach, steam is produced, and as the nature of lightness demands, it rises and in the course of rising and filtering through the arteries, it is thinned out; it comes to the brain and forms the animal powers. The members grow strong by the liquid. The excrement is sent out through the lower passages into the stool; the foam flows out partly through sweat, partly through the openings of the senses. When, however, the foam is too abundant, which comes to pass from gluttonous eating and drinking, then converted into sperm, that is, male seed, it is emitted through the male member because it is closest to the stomach and underneath it. . . . And so, the rains lead Aeneas to the cave and he is joined to Dido and for a while he remains with her.

This explanation is a classical description of the Galenic theory of the humors and their effects on the body, a theory made available in the texts translated by Constantine Afer, and basic to twelfth-century medical discourse. In *Aeneid* 4, Aeneas is ostensibly the victim of two deities; in Bernard's reading, he is a victim of his own body, a victimization emphasized by the medical/physiological explanations of the scene. Though Vergil had provided, among several causes, a cosmological explanation for the event based on the will of the goddesses, Bernard has simply taken this macrocosmic explanation, with its cosmologic potential, and translated it into a microcosmic explanation. For him the rain is a macrocosmic representation of the moisture in the body, since the theory of the humors could be used to explain climatic as well as medical disorders. In this commentary on the cave scene, Bernard has simply read Vergil's text as though it could be completely recuperated in terms of medical discourse. By emphasizing the physical over the divine motivation, Bernard is not only demonstrating his learning in philosophy and medicine; he is assigning specific causes to a narrative text that continually invites the reader to look for causes, then provides multiple and often contradictory or problematic causes. Far from imposing a reading on the text of the *Aeneid,* Bernard effectively focusses his audience's attention on primal or physiological explanations for events in Vergil's text. That he does so at the expense of Dido, who in this explanation becomes a personification of desire (*libido*), illustrates the gendered properties of the *corpus* of the *Aeneid*. In Vergil's narrative, mortal female bodies are disposable: Creusa, Dido, Amata, Camilla and Lavinia never succeed in the *Aeneid* in imposing their will on the events in which they participate. Indeed, Vergil presents mortal, female bodies as particularly permeable. Both Dido and Amata's predispositions are presented in vivid, corporeal and even medical imagery: they are infested, infected or wounded by the will of the gods. Dido's metaphoric wound is vividly expressed at the beginning of book 4 ("At regina graui iamdudum saucia cura / uulnus alit uenis et caeco carpitur igni" [1-2]), and evoked in the simile at 69-73, only to become "fulfilled" by the real wound at the end of the book. Amata's body likewise becomes infected with poison: "ac dum prima lues udo sublapsa ueneno / pertemptat sensus" (7.354-55); and the physical possession of Lavinia becomes the goal of the wars in Italy. The gender of the *corpus* of the *Aeneid* is decidedly male, and such a gendered world-view leads to Bernard's disposal of Dido as a figure for *libido*.

This commentary on the *Aeneid* ends abruptly in book 6 before Aeneas reaches the fields of Elysium. Of course, in *Aeneid* 6, the journey through the fields of Elysium represents the potential transcendence of the body by the spirit. But the transcendent vision of book 6 of the *Aeneid* does not hold up throughout the last six books of Vergil's text. At the end of book 6, Aeneas does not emerge with a philosophical vision that makes it possible for him to effectively transcend his corporeality in the course of the physical tasks that lie ahead for him. The body, not the spirit, remains the focus of the last six books of the *Aeneid*.

Though it is most certainly hopeless to speculate on the reasons for the abrupt end of this commentary, we may of course consider where such a commentary could have had it followed Aeneas out of the underworld and into the struggles of books 7-12. Vergil never provides, after the glimpse of the transmigration of the souls in book 6, any sort of comforting, transcendent vision for the text. The final scene of the epic depicts an intensely corporeal vision of the character of Aeneas feverishly inflamed by rage at the sight of Pallas' belt on Turnus' chest ("furiis accensus et ira / terribilis" [12.946-47]). The spirit remains trapped within the body throughout Vergil's *Aeneid*. Though Bernard's commentary would seem to emphasize the microcosmic vision over the macrocosmic, his commentary keeps us focussed on the body of the text and the body of Aeneas, a focus that endorses the problematic vision that develops in the last six books of Vergil's text, since the *Aeneid* provides no potential for truly transcending the body. Bernard's commentary, if it were to present a transcendent vision, would have to practically part company with the text. Indeed, the vision of transcending the *Aeneid*, produced by another poet in the next century, had to embody the poet himself and make him a guide through the underworld. For the embodied logic of

Vergil's text leaves us, like Aeneas, trapped in our own microcosmic physicality.

Notes

1. The attribution of this commentary to Bernard Silvestris is currently under debate. The editors of the recent edition of the commentary (Julian Ward Jones and Elizabeth Frances Jones, *The Commentary on the First Six Books of the Aeneid of Vergil Commonly Attributed to Bernardus Silvestris* [Lincoln and London: University of Nebraska Press, 1977]) state simply: "The authorship of Bernard may no longer be assumed," p. ix. Another Bernard—Bernard of Chartres—has been proposed as the author of this commentary, (see Jones and Jones, p. xi, and E. R. Smits, "New Evidence for the Authorship of the Commentary on the First Books of Vergil's Eneid Commonly Attributed to Bernardus Silvestris?" in *Non nova, sed nove: Mélanges de Civilisation médiévale dédiés à Willem Noomen*, ed. Martin Gosman and Jaap Van Os, Mediaevalia Groningana 5, [Groningen, 1984], 239–46). Yet another Bernard ("The Bernard who was sent by Gilbert Foliot to reform the Abbey of Cerne between 1145 and 1148") has been proposed as a possible author. See Christopher Baswell, "The Medieval Allegorization of the 'Aeneid': Ms Cambridge, Peterhouse 158," *Traditio* 41 (1985): 181–237.

2. Text of the commentary from Jones and Jones. Translations are my own. See also Earl G. Schreiber and Thomas E. Maresca, trans., *Commentary on the First Six Books of Vergil's Aeneid by Bernardus Silvestris* (Lincoln: University of Nebraska Press, 1979). Text of Vergil from P. Vergili Maronis, *Opera*, ed. R. A. B. Mynors (Oxford: Clarendon Press, 1969).

3. Edouard Jeauneau, "L'usage de la notion d'*integumentum* à travers les gloses de Guillaume de Conches," *Archives d'histoire doctrinale et littéraire du moyen âge* 22 (1957): 39. For a further discussion of *integument* see Winthrop Wetherbee, *Platonism and Poetry in the Twelfth Century; The Literary Influence of the School of Chartres* (Princeton University Press, 1972). Wetherbee discusses the Chartrian concept of *integumentum* in relation to the "Chartrian's reading of the Universe," 36–48.

4. For the concept of "embodied logic" on which this paper relies, see John O'Neill, *Five Bodies: The Human Shape of Modern Society* (Ithaca and London: Cornell University Press, 1985). O'Neill describes the embodied logic of our experience: "We are continuously caught up and engaged in the *embodied look of things*. . . . It is through our senses that we first appreciate and evaluate others. . . . What we see, hear, and feel of other persons is the first basis of our interaction with them" (22). O'Neill explicates five representations of the body that result from such "embodied logic": The World's Body, Social Bodies, The Body Politic, Consumer Bodies and Medical bodies. As we will see, the "embodied logic" of this commentary on the *Aeneid* depends on the representation of the world's body and the medical body.

5. For the Latin text and commentary of the medieval *Timaeus*, see J. H. Waszink, *Timaeus a Calcidio translatus commentarioque instructus* (London: The Warburg Institute, 1962). The medieval version of the *Timaeus* ends before the elaborate medical description of the body, beginning on 64 of the Greek. On the place of the *Timaeus* in Chartrian thought, see Wetherbee; Raymond Klibansky, "The School of Chartres," in *Twelfth-Century Europe and the Foundations*

of Modern Society, ed. M. Clagett, G. Post and R. Reynolds (Madison: The University of Wisconsin Press, 1961), 3-14; Richard McKeon, "Poetry and Philosophy in the Twelfth Century: The Renaissance of Rhetoric," *Modern Philology* 43 (1946): 217-34.

6. Bernard states Vergil's purpose: "Atque in hoc describendo naturali utitur ordine atque ita utrumque ordinem narrationis obseruat, artificialem poeta, naturalem philosophus" (3).

7. Fulgentius refers several times to medicine and physiology in relation to Vergil's poetry. He declares that Vergil was a "phisiognomicus et medicinalis" in the second book of the *Georgics* (84), and Fulgentius says that he himself has written a book of medical explanations (de medicinalibus causis) (92). See Fulgentius, *Opera,* ed. Rudolph Helm (Stuttgart: Teubner, 1898; repr., 1970). For a discussion of Bernardus' debt to Fulgentius, see J. Reginald O'Donnell, "The Sources and Meaning of Bernard Silvester's Commentary on the Aeneid," *Mediaeval Studies* 24 (1962): 233-49.

8. On Constantine Afer, see Paul Oskar Kristeller, "The School of Salerno: Its Development and Its Contribution to the History of Learning," *Studies in Renaissance Thought and Letters* (Rome: Edizioni di Storia e Letteratura, 1969), 508-10. For Constantine's influence on the medicine of the twelfth century, see Sudhoff, *Archiv für Geschichte der Medizin* 9 (1916): 348-56; H. Schipperges, *Sudhoffs Archiv für Geschichte der Medizin* 39 (1955): 62-67. A brief summary of Constantine's career can be found in Maurice Bassan, "Chaucer's 'Cursed Monk,' Constantinus Africanus," *Mediaeval Studies* 24 (1962): 127-38. See also G. Corner, *Anatomical Texts of the Earlier Middle Ages* (Washington: Carnegie Institute, 1927), 12-16. As Corner sums up Constantine's impact: "He gave the west . . . a great mass of important classical learning, in readable Latin, at a time when everything was ripe for growth. For a hundred years all western medical science grew out of these books" (14).

9. On the study of human anatomy in the Middle Ages, see T. V. N. Persaud, *Early History of Human Anatomy: From Antiquity to the Beginning of the Modern Era* (Springfield, Illinois: Charles C. Thomas, 1984), 70-88. See also G. Corner, "Twelfth-Century Texts: Demonstrations of Anatomy," *Anatomical Texts,* 19-30. Corner describes the Salernitan anatomical texts intended to be used in dissections of animals: "The three little books taken together give us a lively picture indeed of these men engaged in actual dissection of the animal body, surrounded by questioning pupils for whose benefit they try to fit their newly recovered relics of Galenic description to the pig's organs before them" (30).

10. See Brian Stock, *Myth and Science in the Twelfth Century* (Princeton: Princeton University Press, 1972). As Stock says of Bernard's intention in the *Cosmographia*: "He tried to bring together what he considered the two major sciences of his time, medicine and astronomy" (26). On the development of medical study at Chartres, see Loren MacKinney, *Early Medieval Medicine with Special Reference to France and Chartres* (Baltimore: Johns Hopkins Press, 1937), 115-51. MacKinney argues that the cathedral schools in France fostered an empirical approach to the study of medicine in the eleventh century.

11. On the connection between the theory of elements and medical discourse, see Richard McKeon, "Medicine and Philosophy in the Eleventh and Twelfth Centuries: The Problems of Elements," *The Thomist* 24 (1961): 211-56. As McKeon

states, "The theories of elements propounded in the medical works of the eleventh century and the cosmologies of the twelfth century likewise provide the principles of the relevant sciences" (213); "The medical writings which were translated during the eleventh century used elements more systematically to explain the phenomena of nature and provided greater precision of statement and more diversified data of application in the use of elements lent concreteness, specificity, and empirical detail to the consideration of the nature of things, but it is also accentuated the tendency to use a variety of structures or organisms as models for the universe, or to use the structure of the universe as a model for other lesser wholes, and therefore to analogize man and the universe (microcosm and macrocosm), human soul and world-soul, deliberate action and physical motion, in the treatment of cosmology, psychology, physiology, geography, and history. This merging of Platonism, the liberal arts and the new sciences was one of the distinguishing marks of the school of Chartres in the twelfth century" (231). See also Theodore Silverstein, "Guillaume de Conches and Nemesius of Enussa: On the sources of the 'New Science' of the Twelfth Century," *Harry Austryn Wolfson Jubilee Volume II* (Jerusalem: American Academy of Jewish Research, 1965), 719–34; Theodore Silverstein, "*Elementatum*: Its Appearance Among the Twelfth-Century Cosmogonists," *Mediaeval Studies* 16 (1954): 156–62.

12. The dissection of animals was certainly practiced in Salerno, if not in the north. As Kristeller summarizes the place of dissection and discussions of anatomy in medical texts in Salerno: "The extensive medical literature of the twelfth century obviously reflects a corresponding progress in medical teaching at Salerno. . . . The various treatises on anatomy clearly indicate the practice of anatomical demonstration in the classroom, based on the dissection of animal bodies" (512).

13. See chapter 13 of the *Cosmographia* (Bernardus Silvestris *Cosmographica*, ed. Peter Dronke [Leiden: Brill, 1978], 146–50). For a translation, see *The Cosmographia of Bernardus Silvestris*, trans. Winthrop Wetherbee (New York: Columbia University Press, 1973).

14. O'Neill (above, note 4), 28.

15. Stock (above, note 10), 259.

16. Ibid., 225.

17. For a thorough consideration of the corporal imagery in Vergil, see Philippe Heuzé, *L'image du corps dans l'œuvre de Vergile* (Rome: École Française de Rome, 1985).

The Heritage of Fulgentius

ROBERT EDWARDS

The sixth-century allegorical writer Fulgentius is an important, if at times problematic, figure in the transvaluation of the classics in later periods. He enjoyed a remarkably durable reputation among later writers in the Middle Ages and the Renaissance. Isidore of Seville and Rabanus Maurus, the major encyclopedists of the early Middle Ages, use him as a source for glosses and allegorical explanations, as do the three Vatican Mythographers who succeed him as a commentator on pagan myth. The Carolingian abbot Smaragdus of St. Michel counts Fulgentius among the Church Fathers whom he draws on to adorn his book "full of the flowers of allegories."[1] Max Laistner points out that Fulgentius' ornate style and exotic language influenced Carolingian writers to use rare words, mythological allusions, and etymologies in their compositions.[2] In the eleventh century, Sigebert of Gembloux mentions Fulgentius' *acumen ingenii* for interpreting pagan myths according to natural and moral philosophy in his *Mythologiae*.[3] Fulgentius' equally renowned treatment of Vergil and especially of the *Aeneid* (the *Vergiliana continentia*) inspired a similar commentary on Statius' *Thebaid*, which was ascribed to Fulgentius but arguably written by a later hand.[4] Literary historians credit Fulgentius in particular with introducing a sustained allegorical framework to contain the partial and fragmented glossings of Donatus, Servius, and Macrobius.[5]

The high estimate of Fulgentius in the Middle Ages is balanced, in some measure, by healthy skepticism, if not frank reservations. It is Boccaccio who reflects perhaps most clearly the divided response that some writers felt. Boccaccio praises Fulgentius as "doctor atque pontifex catholicus," but at several places in his *Genealogie deorum gentilium* he protests that he avoids the flights of fancy that often mark Fulgentius' search for obscure meanings in literary texts.[6] Nonetheless, Fulgentius remains a source for allegories for humanist scholars like Coluccio Salutati.[7] The Fulgentian thesis that the *Aeneid* outlines a scheme of moral development through the various ages of man establishes a framework for Mapheus Vegius to bring Vergil's epic to aesthetic and moral completeness by adding a Thirteenth Book.[8] The same thesis reappears in William Adlington's translation of Apuleius' *Metamorphoses* (1566): "this book of Lucius is a figure of man's life, and toucheth the nature and manners of mortal men, egging them forward from their asinine form to their human and perfect shape."[9]

The examples I have been citing give some indication of Fulgentius' stature as an authority for interpreting myth and poetry, but they tell relatively little about the kind of fascination he exercised over subsequent writers, about the qualities to which those writers responded while admitting that his interpretations could be hyperbolic and precious.[10] These are more subtle dimensions of literary influence than citation and testimony, but they offer a way of understanding the complex dialectic by which Christian culture assimilated classical literature. There are abundant sources on which a comparative study of this kind of influence might draw, such as Albericus of London's rewriting of the story of Syrophanes from the *Mythologiae* or John de Ridevall's extension of Fulgentius' moral iconography in the *Fulgentius metaforalis*.[11] But I shall confine myself to the commentary on the first six books of the *Aeneid* which is generally thought to have been written by the twelfth-century Platonist Bernardus Silvestris, for it is in the reading of Vergil that the assumptions and difficulties of Fulgentius' method stand out clearly.[12]

I have discussed at length in another paper the underlying assumptions of Fulgentius' *Mythologiae* and *Vergiliana continentia*.[13] Briefly, Fulgentius draws on the conventional distinction between things (*res*) and words (*uerba*) in classical linguistic theory, but he emphasizes the separation of the linguistic sign from the thing signified, of the proper from the figurative sense of words. Without claiming for pagan myths and secular texts the divine inspiration that Christian exegetes find in Scripture, he argues that a kind of philosophical truth exists apart from the surface of language. This truth provides the moral lessons which he takes as the figurative sense of classical myths.[14]

Furthermore, having established this separation of signs from referents, Fulgentius comes to equate the perception of hidden meaning with its actual presence. Reading is defined as an act of ingenuity and critical virtuosity. In the Prologue to book 2 of the *Mythologiae*, Fulgentius imagines it as a gymnastic arena (*arenam nostri studii* and *tui palestram ingenii*) where the reader can exercise and test his skill for seeing hidden significance: a space of play and moral rehearsal. Reading, then, is a conscious projection of ethical assumptions and associations onto the formal structure of the text; and it is made on the authority of moral truth, which resides outside the text and independent from the problems of literary representation. In the commentary on Vergil, Fulgentius dramatizes this style of reading and its potential for play by constructing an imagined dialogue with the poet, in which Vergil explains his intention to offer common-sense moralizing while the commentator summons the courage to explain the hidden truths of the poem to its author. What Fulgentius establishes in this fictive exchange is the proximity of discursive and interpretive writing to the mimetic and imaginative works that commentary is supposed to elucidate. Commentary and exegesis, he demonstrates, share important properties and formal characteristics with fictional discourse. Reading a text in the light of its ultimate reference, the interpreter subtly reshapes the original to reveal meaning beyond authorial or aesthetic intent.

In Bernardus' commentary, Fulgentius is a source for specific points of interpretation, and he lends the general notion that Vergil's poem incorporates the ages of man into its structure. Fulgentius' division between proper and figurative meanings reappears in the commentary, as does his insistence on the dual nature of the poet. In addition, Bernardus makes an effort to assimilate the techniques of Fulgentius' allegorizing to other literary authorities. Fulgentius had discussed Vergil as *uates*, but Bernardus adds Macrobius' testimony that a "twin doctrine" operates in the *Aeneid*, and he assigns Vergil the roles of "poeta et philosophus."[15] Like earlier commentators, Bernardus discovers a moral purpose in Aeneas' example of suffering, filial piety, and reverence, and he sees a caution against immoderate love in Aeneas' desire for Dido.[16] He also adapts Horace to redefine the poem's genre and bring it in line with Fulgentian moralizing. Reworking Horace's famous admonition that poets should instruct or entertain (*Ars Poetica* 333), he looks in the *Aeneid* for both the usefulness of satire and the delight of comedy; those two genres are then joined in yet a third form, historical writing. Although epic devices may afford heightened verbal adornment, Bernardus argues, Vergil's poem is related essentially to the functions of the middle style, which St. Augustine had earlier defined as praise and blame (*De doctrina christiana* 4.17-19) and which Fulgentius implied in stressing Vergil's adherence to the rules of praise.

Two radically divergent styles had helped to animate the *Vergiliana continentia* while remaining above the text which is their source of play. Fulgentius rehearses the lessons of the *grammatici*, while his Vergil expounds the original intention. By contrast, Bernardus uncovers two distinct orders within the text; he sees a rhetorical joining of artificial and natural order that mirrors the poet's dual roles. Vergil as poet, beginning "a medio narrationem," constructs an artificial order whose affinities, Bernardus remarks, are to Terence's comedies rather than the epics of Lucan and Statius. Meanwhile, as a philosopher, Vergil observes a natural order in treating "humane uite naturam" and setting down "quid paciatur humanus spiritus in humano corpore temporaliter positus" ("what the human spirit undergoes while temporarily placed in the human body" [3]). This description of the poem's rhetorical economy marks an advance over Fulgentius' view that philosophical meaning overarches the text. Like Macrobius who found four kinds of oratory combined in Vergil (*Saturnalia* 5.1.1–7), Bernardus argues for a coherent rhetorical organization of the poem in which the poet's dual roles and the narrative orders effect a synthesis of meaning. His argument, as Brian Stock notes, "is an attempt to integrate the creation of a literary work into the realm of experience" by employing moral and physical allegory.[17]

The concern with rhetorical order in the *Aeneid* leads Bernardus to speculate generally about the nature of language and particularly about its figurative use. Fulgentius' radical dislocation of signifier and signified had proceeded from his assumption that there is a disparity between authorial intention and hidden meaning: significance resides in a comprehensive philosophical system whose moral precepts are the things to which the text must ultimately refer; hence aesthetic unity is to be sought somewhere other than in the constructions of language itself. Bernardus formulates a different sort of problem by considering the various meanings that arise from the poetic fiction but still reflect a sense of *integritas*. He interprets Venus, for example, in her legitimate aspect as *musica mundana* (or the equal proportions of the cosmos or natural justice) and in her wanton aspect as cupidity. He then remarks: "Notandum est uero hoc in loco, quemadmodum in aliis misticis uoluminibus, ita et in hoc equiuocationes et multiuocationes esse et integumenta ad diuersa respicere" ("One must remember in this book as well as in other allegorical works that there are equivocations and multiple significations, and therefore one must interpret poetic fictions in diverse ways" [9]).

Bernardus is suggesting in a way that might anticipate modern views of language and signification that the problem of allegorical discourse does not lie chiefly in devising figurative meaning, as it had for Fulgentius, but in dealing with the literal text. Questions of denotation precede questions about the transferred sense. Much like his contemporary William of Conches who managed a deft balancing of the terms *integumen-*

tum (allegorical covering) and *ueritas* in his glosses, Bernardus links the fact of polysemous language to the existence of truth: "Hic autem diversus integumentorum respectus et multiplex designatio in omnibus misticis observari debet si in una vero veritas stare non poterit" ("Hence, one must pay attention to the diverse aspects of the poetic fictions and the multiple interpretations in all allegorical matters if in fact the truth cannot be established by a single interpretation" [9]). In other words, signs mark an approach toward the things that they are supposed to signify; they record an act of predication that somehow never achieves completion. A mythological figure like Jupiter, for instance, can be identified variously as fire, the human soul, the world soul, and a star. Rather than invoke meaning in a discrete act of perception, Bernardus chooses to see it evolve through a device of *multivocatio* which allows the *diversa nomina* of myth and poetry to flourish. The alternate names and identities of the gods reflect not the confusion of a fragmented system of correspondences but a spectrum of meaning accessible to the attentive reader.[18]

The implication of this shift away from Fulgentian allegory touches on the wider relations of allegory and poetry. Where language (*uerba*) no longer equals a thing signified (*res*), it begins to assume a function that has otherwise been assigned to myth. Modern interpreters regard the myth-making process as filling the gap between some present state of understanding and the unknown. The *diuersa nomina* come to represent a process of definition, a search for a middle term between words and things. To the extent that linguistic structures such as rhetorical order and repetitions operate in the play between words and things and thereby fill the gap, they, too, become mythological. Thus the effort to understand poetic language, and the larger structures it forms, moves forward by partial recognitions of meaning and a rough tracing of conceptual patterns that emerge as language continually falls short of enunciating completely what it sets out to say and name. And in this respect, one can see the great wisdom of Édouard Jeanneau's insisting that *integumentum*, the key term in Chartrian discussions about the nature of allegorical language, should be translated as 'myth.'[19] The wheat and chaff that fascinated writers from Augustine to Chaucer are not polarities of meaning so much as dialectical antitheses that permit the construction of meaning.

What I have been calling the mythological dimension of language proves important for Bernardus in establishing the epistemological and moral status of poetry. Interpretation shares with poetry the capacity to evoke meaning, and both enlist the reader as a collaborator. They also share the paradox of searching for a viable order of truth within fiction. This dilemma has its roots, of course, in antiquity, and it resurfaces in Macrobius and the writers of the High Middle Ages who assert the primacy of the *artes sermonciales* for all human understanding.[20] In the Vergil commentary, there is a powerful example of this paradox in book 6 where Bernardus treats the ekphrasis by which Vergil recounts the visual figures inscribed on the temple of Apollo. Bernardus treats this verbal portraiture as a *summa narrationis*. Returning to a distinction in Macrobius, he asserts, "Sunt namque poete ad philosophiam introductorii, unde uolumina eorum 'cunas nutricum' uocat Macrobius" ("Indeed, the poets introduce one to philosophy, whence Macrobius calls their volumes 'nurses' cradles' " [36]). Peter Dronke proposes that Bernardus' interpretation of the key phrase *cunas nutricum* is greatly influenced by William of Conches' own commentary on Macrobius.[21] Macrobius (*Commentum in Somnium Scipionis* 1.2.8) rejects fables that only delight the ear and are consequently diverting rather than instructive, but the Chartrian writers see the fables as part of a psychological and philosophical progression. Their view is in keeping with Fulgentius' notion of the ages and moral development of man.

Bernardus explains that this motif of progression is incorporated in the architectural structure of Apollo's temple, on whose exterior history and fable, the forms of discourse that Macrobius struggled to keep separate, are depicted as equivalents. Passing through the entrance way signifies the study of the arts and the authors ("in introitu ad artes, scilicet in auctoribus"). The temple itself signifies the philosophic arts. Therefore, Bernardus says, "quas qui ingressuri sunt oportet quod prius cernant picturas ante descriptas, id est ut dent operam istoriis et fabulis et hoc est quod in porticum ab introeuntibus cernuntur historie depicte et fabule" ("those about to enter should first see pictures made beforehand, i.e. they pay attention to stories and fables, and this is the reason why should pictorial history and fable are seen by those entering the partico" [36–37]).

This reading of the temple and its adornment reinforces the traditional division of learning into the Trivium and Quadrivium. But by seeing the authors as introductory and preparatory, Bernardus complicates the larger question of the status of poetry. Does poetry embody certain kinds of essential truths, or does it merely and inadequately point toward their existence, much as language only predicates the things it talks about? Is it a kind of knowledge or only a cipher of something beyond itself? Bernardus gives an answer that seems to resolve the question in the negative: "He fabule que sunt extra templum figurant omnes poetarum fabulas et ita non sunt mistice intelligende" ("These fables outside the temple represent all the fables of the poets and hence are not to be understood allegorically" [37]). His answer, however, is less direct and less dismissive of poetry than it might at first appear. The fables, he is careful to say, are a representation for all poetic fiction making, and they refer not to things in the world but to themselves. Like allegorical interpretation, they situate imaginative discourse within language, which follows similar codes and structures and makes the same uneasy claims to reach something beyond itself.

In following the logic of the architectural imagery, then, Bernardus has gone beyond Macrobius' original distinction between useful and diverting fictions to suggest that all poetic figments are incapable of being read in a figurative sense.[22] Although earlier he proposed that a story like that of Dido and Aeneas in book 4 can describe the youthful nature of man "manifeste ac mistica narratione" (24), he seems now to revoke the sanction for allegorical reading. Yet this seeming reversal marks something other than a contradiction or a lapse in his argument. In his glossing, Bernardus is trying to define the shifting limits for allegorical and poetic discourse. The cautionary nature of the example of book 4 and its ready transference to a moral *sententia* have to be taken, he suggests, on a different level from the approach to mystery and deeper philosophical truth in book 6. Much as Boethius' introduction to the essential reality of moral life and the cosmos can be said to begin with Lady Philosophy's banishing the Muses, the instruction of Aeneas and of Bernardus' searching reader demands the gesture of a radical break with earlier orders of knowledge. The moral lessons which the authors portray remain applicable to experience in the world, while the epic quest for truth (translatable into an act of reading) inquires into the causes of things. This is the distinction between moralizing and mystical meaning that Fulgentius plots in his dialogue with Vergil, but it emerges in Bernardus' commentary with greater subtlety and resonance than before.

This concern with the mythic function of language connects the commentary to Bernardus' own poetic work, especially his cosmological poem the *Cosmographia* (*De uniuersitate mundi*). Winthrop Wetherbee has remarked that there exists "a general relationship between the themes of the *Cosmographia* and the reading of the *Aeneid* presented in Bernardus' commentary."[23] For Bernardus, Aeneas' descent to the underworld is an introduction to philosophy as an all-encompassing field of knowledge, and it portrays the struggle of the intellect against vice and ignorance; similarly in the *Cosmographia* man must come to terms with destiny, order, and violence. Wetherbee says, "A long chain of fate and history depends from the first man, as Bernardus' Nature beholds him in the Table of Destiny, and there is, as in the world of Aeneas, a significant historical dimension to the universe of the *Cosmographia*. The challenge of destiny and the burden of experience seem to be inseminated in human life from the very beginning, and the conflict between order and violence in the history of man is foretold in the stars" (26).[24]

Bernardus' commentary and his epic poem depict mankind as a prototypical soul, seen at a moment before his own history, at an ethical and imaginative threshold where he must read his destiny and grasp the meaning of human action. By locating him at that boundary, both works transform Fulgentius' allegory, however. Man stands like Aeneas before the temple, but his work there is in earnest, not in play; it involves something more than the "gymnasium of ingenuity" where one practices the art of interpretation. Pierre Courcelle notes, moreover, that in manuscript miniatures depictions of Aeneas before the temple serve as a background for his meeting with the Sybil.[25] The conflation of the scenes intensifies Aeneas' confrontation with history, fate, and moral choice.

An even more suggestive staging of this scene occurs in Augustine's *Confessions*, in a passage where the author struggles to cancel the Vergilian source of his own moral definition (1.13). Augustine says that he repents memorizing the wanderings of Aeneas and lamenting Dido's suicide, and he contrasts the value of reading to the deception of poetry. He then adds, "at enim uela pendent liminibus grammaticarum scholarum, sed non illa magis honorem secreti quam tegimentum erroris significant" ("It is true that curtains are hung over the entrances to the schools where literature is taught, but they are not so much symbols in honour of mystery as veils concealing error").[26] The image Augustine evokes is the scene in which Aeneas stands before Apollo's temple, ready to penetrate the mystery represented by the Sybil. The formulation he gives this image (*uela liminibus*) both describes the moral enterprise of reading and registers the profound ambivalence it will have for Bernardus.

Notes

1. Smaragdus of St. Michel, "Collectiones in Epistolas et Euangelica quae per circuitum anni leguntur," in *Patrologia Latina* 102.13: "allegoriarum floribus plenum curaui colligere librum."
2. Max L. W. Laistner, "Fulgentius in the Carolingian Age," in *The Intellectual Heritage of the Early Middle Ages: Selected Essays by M. L. W. Laistner*, ed. Chester G. Starr (1957; repr., New York: Octagon Books, 1966), 204, 209.
3. Sigebert of Gembloux, *De scriptoribus ecclesiasticiss*, 28 (*PL* 160.554). Sigebert erroneously identifies Fulgentius with the bishop of Ruspe by the same name.
4. Fulgentius, *Opera*, ed. R. Helm, rev. Jean Préaux (1898; repr., Stuttgart:

Teubner, 1970), and Bernard Bischoff, *Mittelalterliche Studien*, 3 vols. (Stuttgart: Anton Hiersemann, 1967), 2:271.

5. O. B. Hardison, Jr., "Toward a History of Medieval Literary Criticism," *Medievalia et Humanistica*, n.s., no. 7 (1976): 5. See also Giuseppe Pennisi, *Fulgenzio e la "Expositio Sermonum Antiquorum"* (Firenze: Felice Le Monnier, 1963).

6. Giovanni Boccaccio, *Genealogie deorum gentilium*, ed. Vincenzo Romano, 2 vols. (Bari: Laterza, 1951), 2:736. Boccaccio refuses to cite Fulgentius' explanation of Chimera, saying that Fulgentius leaves more in obscurity on the literal level than he could ever explain below the surface (4.24). He dismisses Fulgentius' explanation of Castor and Pollux with the comment (11.7), "Posuissem Fulgentii expositionem, sed quoniam per sublimia uadit, omisi" ("I might have set forth Fulgentius' explanation, but I have omitted it because it rushes off into the sublime"). For translations of Fulgentius I use Leslie George Whitbread, *Fulgentius the Mythographer* (Columbus: Ohio State University Press, 1971).

7. Coluccio Salutati, *De Laboribus Herculis*, ed. B. L. Ullmann (Turin: Thesaurus Mundi, 1951).

8. Anna Cox Brinton, *Mapheus Vegius and his Thirteenth Book of the* Aeneid: *A Chapter on Vergil in the Renaissance* (Stanford: Stanford University Press, 1930), 24-40.

9. William Adlington, trans., *The Golden Ass of Lucius Apuleius*, ed. F. J. Harvey Darton (privately printed, n.d.), 14, 15, 18-20.

10. See the account in Domenico Comparetti, *Vergil in the Middle Ages*, trans. E. F. M. Benecke (1895; repr., London: George Allen & Unwin, Ltd., 1966).

11. Mythographus Tertius, *De diis gentium et illorum allegoris*, in *Scriptores Rerum Mythicarum Latini tres Romae nuper reperti*, ed. Georg H. Bode (1834; repr., Hildesheim: Georg Olms, 1968); and John de Ridevall, *Fulgentius Metaforalis: Ein Beitrag zur Geschichte der antiken Mythologie im Mittelalter*, ed. Hans Liebeschütz, Studien der Bibliothek Warburg, 4 (Leipzig: B. G. Teubner, 1926).

12. The attribution to Bernardus Silvestris is disputed by the commentary's latest editors. Julian Ward Jones and Elizabeth Frances Jones, eds., *The Commentary on the First Six Books of the "Aeneid" of Vergil Commonly Attributed to Bernardus Silvestris* (Lincoln: University of Nebraska Press, 1977). The evidence bearing on attribution is summarized in a review of the edition by Theodore Silverstein, *Speculum* 54 (1979): 154-57. Citation of the commentary will be made in the text with reference to the pages in the Jones's edition. The translation is that of Earl G. Schreiber and Thomas E. Maresca, *Commentary on The First Six Books of Vergil's* Aeneid *by Bernardus Silvestris* (Lincoln: University of Nebraska Press, 1979); some minor changes have been made for consistency.

13. Robert Edwards, "Fulgentius and the Collapse of Meaning," *Helios*, n.s., 3 (1976): 17-35.

14. Jean Pépin, *Mythe et Allégorie: Les origines grecques et les contestations judéo-chrétiennes* (Aubier: Editions Montaigne, 1958), 76-81 observes that the relation of sign to signifier underlies most allegorical systems; at issue here is not a semiotic structure but the disjunction within it. Fulgentius is the first mythographer to combine euhemerism and a philosophical interpretation; see Paule Demats, *Fabula: Trois études de mythographie antique et médiévale* (Geneva: Droz, 1973), 57-59.

15. John of Salisbury's *Polycraticus* similarly treats the ages of man (8.24) and the poet's dual role (2.15, 6.22).

16. Pierre Courcelle, *Lecteurs païens et lecteurs chrétiens de l'Énéide*, 2 vols. (Paris: Institut de France, 1984), 1:146.

17. Brian Stock, *Myth and Science in the Twelfth Century: A Study of Bernard Sylvester* (Princeton: Princeton University Press, 1972), 43.

18. In a commentary on Martianus Capella possibly written by Bernardus, these *equiuocationes et multiuocationes* are again said to give double and multiple meanings to the literal sense of the text. See Édouard Jeauneau, "L'usage de la notion d'*Integumentum* à' travers les gloses de Guillaume de Conches," *Archives d'histoire doctrinale et littéraire du Moyen Age* 32 (1957): 37-38; Stock, 36n-37 summarizes the evidence for and against attribution. Daniel Poirion, "De l' 'Énéide' à l' 'Eneas': mythologie ou moralisation," *Cahiers de la civilisation médiévale* 19 (1976): 226, notes the value of the mythographers as a source for the poetic transformations of mythology and for identifying new relations among symbols, images, and themes. Hans Robert Jauss, "Allégorie, 'remythisation' et nouveau mythe. Réflexions sur la captivité chrétienne de la mythologie au moyen age," in *Mélanges d'histoire littéraire, de linguistique et de philologie romanes offerts à Charles Rostaing*, ed. Jacques De Caluwé, Jean-Marie D'Heur, and René Dumas (Liège: Association des Romanistes de l'Université de Liège, 1974), 469-99, argues that the effort of allegorists to reduce classical myth to a static meaning succeeds conversely in offering new possibilities for myth in the High Middle Ages.

19. Édouard Jeauneau, "L'usage de la notion d'*Integumentum* à travers les gloses de Guillaume de Conches," 37-38. Peter Dronke has contended that the word designates both the outer covering of poetic fable and the meaning that the fable conveys; see *Fabula: Explorations into the Uses of Myth in Medieval Platonism*, Mittellateinische Studien und Texte, 9 (Leiden: E. J. Brill, 1974), 16-28.

20. See the discussion in R. Howard Bloch, *Etymologies and Genealogies: A Literary Anthropology of the French Middle Ages* (Chicago: University of Chicago Press, 1982).

21. *Fabula*, 17n.

22. J. Reginald O'Donnell, C.S.B., "The Sources and Meaning of Bernard Silvester's Commentary on the *Aeneid*," *Mediaeval Studies* 24 (1962): 247.

23. Winthrop Wetherbee, trans., *The* Cosmographia *of Bernardus Silvestris*, Records of Civilization, 89 (New York: Columbia University Press, 1973), 22-23.

24. The importance of Bernardus' commentary for Dante's sense of the soul's history is discussed by Theodore Silverstein, "Dante and Vergil the Mystic," *Harvard Studies and Notes in Philology and Literature* 14 (1932): 51-82; Giorgio Padoan, "Tradizione e fortuna del commento all' "Eneide" di Bernardo Silvestre," *Italia medioevale e umanistica* 3 (1960): 237-40; and David Thompson, "Dante and Bernard Silvestris," *Viator* no. 1 (1970): 203. Other examples of influence in medieval vernacular literature are more problematic to trace. John Gardner, "Fulgentius' *Expositio Vergiliana Continentia* and the Plan of *Beowulf*: Another Approach to the Poem's Style and Structure," *Papers on Language and Literature* 6 (1970): 227-62, argues for an impact on the Old English epic. Influence on the *Roman d'Eneas* is denied by Jean Frappier, "Remarques sur la peinture de la vie et des héros antiques dans la littérature française du XIIe et XIIIe siècle," in *L'humanisme médiéval dans les littératures romanes du XIIe au XIVe siècle*, ed. Anthime Fourrier, Actes et Colloques, 3, Université de Strasbourg (Paris: C. Klincksieck, 1964), 19; and Alfred Adler, "Eneas und Lavine: *Puer et Puella Senes*," *Romanische Forschungen* 71 (1959): 77-79. Raymond J. Cormier believes there are some reminiscences; see "The

Present State of Studies on the *Roman d'Eneas*," *Cultura Neolatina* 31 (1971): 33n; and *One Heart, One Mind: The Rebirth of Vergil's Hero in Medieval French Romance* (University, Mississippi: Romance Monographs, Inc., 1973), 183–87.

25. *Lecteurs païens et lecteurs chrétiens de l'Enéide*, 2:197, 223 (figs. 358, 396). Courcelle also notes that the ethical reading of book 6 of the *Aeneid* goes back as far as Seneca, who finds in it an example of Stoic heroism: "L'attitude de Sénèque à l'égard du livre VI est maintenant claire. Il s'intéresse exclusivement à la partie qui précède la descente aux Enfers, c'est-à-dire à ce qui concerne la conduite de l'homme. Énée est, à ses yeux, le type du Sage stoïcien" (1:425).

26. Saint Augustine, *Confessionum libri tredecim*, ed. Pius Knöll, CSEL 33 (Vienna: Tempsky, 1896; repr., New York: Johnson Reprint Corporation, 1962), 19; the translation is taken from *Confessions*, trans. R. S. Pine-Coffin (Baltimore: Penguin Books, 1973), 34.

Why We Can't "Do Without" Camille

REBECCA GOTTLIEB

Scholars who work on the anonymous twelfth-century romance entitled *Eneas* often compare it unfavorably with Virgil's *Aeneid*. Jessie Crosland demonstrates an extreme, although not unusual, version of this attitude,[1] which glorifies the Latin text and laments all *concessions* to medieval taste in the Old French version, including the portrait of Camille: "We would gladly have dispensed with the conventional description of Camilla and her ridiculous horse." The extremely detailed portrait of Camille does follow a "conventional" pattern for a description of a beautiful woman, but this passage illustrates specific poetic techniques which extend beyond the head-to-toe pattern and the usual adjectives to signal beauty. The portrait exemplifies the various ways in which the poet who composed the *Eneas* reads Virgil, for his[2] writing reflects his critical reading and his aesthetic judgments. The medieval poet can not "dispense with" the figure of Camille because he uses her portrait to mark an essential element in the structure of his poem, nor can we, as Crosland suggests, do without this remarkable description.

The convention in Old French literature which dictates that portraits of beautiful men or women begin with the top of the head and proceed downwards also establishes a tendency for these descriptions to exceed their ugly counterparts in length.[3] The length of a portrait and a person's beauty mark the person's importance. Camille's portrait has a higher degree of expansion than the portrait of Cerberus (in lines 2559 and following). In the *Aeneid* the encounter with Cerberus in book 6 is only a few lines shorter than the description of Camilla which concludes book 7, but in the twelfth-century version Camille occupies roughly three times as much space in the text as Cerberus. In both cases the poet elaborates on small details from Virgil,[4] but the exotic charms of Camilla merit even more expansion than the fascinating horror of Cerberus. The epithet *bellatrix* gives rise to a number of details:

She was of very great strength; there was no other woman with her knowledge. She was very wise, worthy, and courtly, and she possessed great wealth; she ruled her land marvelously well; she had always been brought up in warfare and she loved knightly behaviour and maintained it all her life ... she had ... esteem for bearing arms, fighting in tournaments, and jousting, striking with sword and with lance: there was no other woman of her valiance.

These characterisitics correspond to the attributes of a "chevalier," a knight who in many cases also rules as a feudal lord. The work appropriate for women, which this female warrior scorns, differs much less than the manner in which the two poets describe it. Virgil refers to the deity in charge of these occupations and the objects associated with them: the distaff and workbaskets of Minerva represent spinning and sewing. The Old French presentation specifies the activities: "she never cared for woman's work, neither spinning nor sewing." The medieval poet stretches out the oxymoron "adsueta ... proelia uirgo dura pati" to include a day-and-night opposition with the male and female: "by day she was a king, but by night a queen, never did a chambermaid or lady's maid go near her during the day, nor by night did any man ever enter into the bedroom where she was." The partially ironic suggestion of an unmarried queen emphasizes the oddity of this female in a typically male position, while the possibility of a joke about kings and chambermaids adds humor to this inversion of the sex roles.

After line 3982 the Old French appears to depart completely from Virgil's text. At the exact point where the formal portait begins the medieval poet starts to follow the typical twelfth-century outline[5] of a "marvelously beautiful" woman. Virgil does not specifically mention beauty in the passage on Camilla, but his beautiful description itself leaves us, like the medieval poet, with a strong impression that this extraordinary woman must be beautiful. The moral and physical portrait of Camille herself (lines 3959-4006), especially the "conventional" physical portion of it, replaces the double simile representing Camilla's speed (in *Aenied* 7.808-11). Virgil constructs the figure with an elaborate conditional sequence of tenses. Although no corresponding textual details exist in them, the functions of these passages resemble each other. Each reflects a writer's idea about the goals of the poetry he composes. Virgil sets his similes like jewels and he uses them to exhibit his technical skill. The fast dactylic meter of the lines in which Camilla skims over the "cornfields" and the "sea" culminates with a line which contains only two spondees: "ferret iter celeris nec tingeret aequore plantas."

The ability to compose a portait also constitutes an important technique, which mirrors a different conception of the poet's trade. The rich descriptions and details of the portraits, rather than extended similes or metaphors, decorate the twelfth-century narrative. This particular writer of Old French verse shows the delight he feels in this portrait when he uses a false paralipsis: "what could I tell about her beauty? In the very longest day of summer I would not be able to tell what the situation was with regard to the beauty which she had...."

Although his portrait is one of the longest in twelfth-century French[6] it does not take all day to read and portrays "the situation ... with regard to the beauty" of Camille thoroughly. His rhetorical denial actually expresses his confidence in his poetic and rhetorical skills. Another important technique of medieval rhetoric was *amplificatio*, but we do not need a lengthy proof of this particular poet's use of amplification!

At this point, when we might begin to think that all the details of the portrait would be completely independent of *Aeneid* 7, the poet includes two allusions to Virgil's text. Camilla wears "royal ... purple" while Camille has a "dress of black silk ... embroidered with gold." The correspondence between "regius ostro ... honos" and "porpre noir a or brodee" strikes us all the more forcefully because of the semantic drift of "porpre" which came to refer to a color which silk was often dyed. Both women have gold in their hair: "clasps interweave her hair with gold ... and she had golden hair, hanging down to her feet, she had braided it with a thread of gold...." The proximity of the hair to the silk dress strongly suggests that these details originate with Virgil. The straight parting of Camille's hair was mentioned (in line 3990) in its usual position, at the top of her head, but the specification of the hair's color and ornamentation does not occur until just before the depiction of the clothing. Virgil comments on these two aspects of Camilla's appearance in the opposite order, but they are adjacent (in *Aeneid* 7.814-16). The medieval poet's reversal of the order enables him to maintain a general head-to-toe direction and to lead into the elaborate clothing gradually.

The descriptions of the dress and of the magical cloak which Camille wears contain many fantastic details. The exotic aspects of Virgil's Camilla include her sex, her association with the "Volsci," her supernatural speed, and her weapons. Although no equivalents of "the Lycian quiver and the pastoral myrtle staff, tipped with a point" exist in the medieval text, it carries the marked sense of her otherness in its exoticism.

In the twelfth-century romance, Camille has a horse whose strangeness equals, or exceeds, that of her clothing:

There was never such a noble beast: its head was white as snow, the forelock was black, and the ears were both completely bright red, its neck was bay and very large, and the mane blue and green in tufts; it had a dappled grey right shoulder and the left was quite black; its front feet were like a wolf's and it was all brown on the sides; under the stomach it was like a hare and on the rump like a lion and it was all black under the saddle-bows; its two front legs were tawny and the two back ones red as blood; it had four completely white feet, one part of its tail was black and the other white and all curly, it had hollowed hoofs and slender legs: it was very well made and quite agile.

Since she has been transformed from a Volscian maiden into a female knight, the presence of a horse needs no explanation. This addition compensates for the absence of the details on her "running feet" and her "pastoral" weapon. Since she must have the equipment of a knight, including a horse, it will be just as strange and unusual as the "pastoralem praefixa cuspide myrtum." Although Crosland finds it "ridiculous," the horse represents a marvel of the type the medieval poet obviously relishes. When the virgin queen who is also a knight enters the city, the crowd reaction resembles that of the people in *Aeneid* 7 seeing a shepherdess turned warrior:

All the youths have poured out from the houses and the fields and a crowd of matrons admires her and they follow her with their eyes as she goes, gaping with minds astonished. . . .
Camille came magnificently into the army. . . . When she came journeying to Laurentum there was great tumult in the city, the townspeople climbed to the upper stories of their houses, noble ladies and maidens at the windows, and they were looking at the damsel who was so worthy and so beautiful. All the people who saw her held it to be a great marvel that she should ever fight, or joust, or knock down a knight.

Both of the reactions indicate the exotic and magical nature of this figure for whom others felt admiration. The fascination of both Camilla and Camille comes from the differences which separate them from the watching crowds and make them marvellous and astonishing. The place of the female at the end of the catalogue of enemy warriors or of knights serves to underline her double otherness. These passages portray not only a member of the opposing force, but also a woman. In both cases her sex marks the female warrior as an object whom others view as a "marvel," but the ratio between the descriptions of the male figures in the catalogue and the final woman changes dramatically from the *Aeneid* to the *Eneas*. In the Latin text she gets only slightly more attention than Turnus' other allies, although she receives structural emphasis because she appears at the very end of book 7. In the Old French she occupies roughly the same amount of space in the text as all the rest of the knights combined. This happens partially because the romance lacks the division into books. The end of a book occupies an important place in the structure of Virgil's epic. The length of a description represents an important feature within the structure of the *Eneas*. Both these techniques serve to focus attention on a figure destined to come to a glorious end. The two depictions prepare the episode in book 11 of the *Aeneid* and lines 6905 through 7724 of the romance. The image of Camille's remarkable tomb corresponds in its rich detail to her physical appearance. The portrait focuses attention on a figure, and its length indicates the person's future importance. The portrait of Camille conforms to twelfth-century convention rather than Virgil's text for a specific purpose. The conventional description gives the reader a clue to her importance later on in the romance; Virgil provides a similar clue by ending a book of his epic with the "uirgo . . . bellatrix."

Although the scope of this analysis does not permit extended discussion of the question of epic and romance genre distinctions, we have some indication that the *Eneas* represents a crucial step in the development from epic to romance[7] because it involves reading an epic and transforming it into a romance. We have seen how one reader who writes poetry uses his source, editing, omitting, contracting, expanding, adding, and innovating. Each omission and addition has its own aesthetic purpose. These techniques give us some indication of the poetic ideals[8] of the *romans d'antiquité*. The romance contains fewer characters and episodes than the *Aeneid* yet these appear in much greater detail.[9] Camilla appeals to the medieval imagination because Virgil's presentation marks her as exotic. Although this poet reads and interprets the *Aeneid* as he writes, he does not translate it in the modern sense. A modern term such as adaptation conveys the spirit of the medieval notion *translatio*. The adaptation of Virgil by this French poet shows which aspects of the *Aeneid* belong intrinsically to the rich context of myth and history of the literature of Augustan Rome and which elements fascinate the readers and poets of the twelfth century.

Notes

1. Jessie Crosland, "*Eneas* and the *Aeneid*," *Modern Language Review* 29 (1934): 283 ff.
2. I assume the medieval poet was a man, since female writers were so rare.
3. I describe these general tendencies based on Alice Colby-Hall, *The Portrait in Twelfth-Century French Literature* (Geneva: Dros, 1965). I have not yet read enough to assert it on my own authority, but Professor Colby-Hall has pointed out these trends not only in her book, but in class.
4. I do not have the time or the space to discuss whether this writer had what we think of as Virgil's *Aeneid* in front of him. He may have had a copy with commentaries or a Latin prose version. These possibilities do not substantially alter the impact of my analysis.
5. This concept reflects several suggestions of Professor Colby-Hall, made both in print and in person.
6. This generalization again shows my debt to *The Portrait in Twelfth-Century French Literature*.
7. R. W. Southern concludes *The Making of the Middle Ages* (New Haven: Yale University Press, 1953) with a chapter of that name.
8. For a slightly different view of this topic, see Daniel Poirion, "De l'*Énéide* à l' *Eneas:* mythologie et moralisation," *Cahiers de Civilisation Médiévale* 19 (1976): 213 ff.
9. For an excellent general analysis of the work's organization see Raymond J. Cormier, *One Heart, One Mind,* Romance Monographs, no. 3 (University, Mississippi, 1973).

Texts and Translations

Aeneid 7.803 ff.

>   Hos super aduenit Volsca de gente Camilla
> agmen agens equitum et florentis aere cateruas,
> bellatrix, non illa colo calathisue Mineruae
> femineas adsueta manus, sed proelia uirgo
> dura pati cursuque pedum praeuertere uentos.
> illa uel intactae segetis per summa uolaret
> gramina nec teneras cursu laesisset aristas,
> uel mare per medium fluctu suspensa tumenti
> ferret iter celeris nec tingeret aequore plantas.
> illam omnis tectis agrisque effusa iuuentus
> turbaque miratur matrum et prospectat euntem,
> attonitis inhians animis ut regius ostro
> uelet honos leuis umeros, ut fibula crinem
> auro internectat, Lyciam ut gerat ipsa pharetram
> et pastoralem praefixa cuspide myrtum.

In addition to these came Camilla, of the Volscian people, leading a column of horsemen and troops brilliant in bronze armour, a warrrior, she has not accustomed her woman's hands to the distaff and workbaskets of Minerva, but, although a virgin, is accustomed to endure harsh battles and to outstrip the wind with running feet [the running of her feet]. She might fly across the highest blades of the unreaped cornfields and not have harmed the tender ears with her running, or across the middle of the sea, poised on the swelling flow, she might take her journey and not have dipped her swift soles in the water. All the youths have poured out from the houses and the fields and a crowd of matrons admires her and they follow her with their eyes as she goes, gaping with minds astonished at how royal splendour clothes her smooth shoulders with purple, how clasps interweave her hair with gold, how she bears the Lycian quiver and the pastoral myrtle staff, tipped with a point.

Eneas v. 3959 ff.

    Enprés i vint une meschine,
qui de Vulcane estoit reïne;
Camille ot nom las damoisselle,
a mervoille par estoit bele
et molt estoit de grant poeir;
ne fu feme de son savoir.
Molt ert sage, proz, et cortoise   3965
et molt demenot grant richoise;
a mervoille tenoit bien terre;
et fu toz tens norrie an guerre
et molt ama chevalerie
et maintint la tote sa vie.   3970
Onc d'ovre a feme ne ot cure,
ne de filer ne de costure;
mialz prisoit armes a porter,
a tornoier et a joster,
ferir d'espee et de lance: 3975
ne fu feme de sa vaillance.
Lo jor ert rois, la nuit raïne
ja chamberiere ne meschine
anviron li le jor n'alast,
ne je la nuit nus hom n'entrast   3980
dedanz la chambre ou ele estoit;
tant sagement se contenoit
n'en darriere ne en davant,

que ne en fet ne en samblant
i peüst an noter folie 3985
je tant n'eüst vers li envie.
De biauté n'ert o li igaus
nule feme qui fust mortaus;
lo front ot blanc et bien traitiz,
la greve droite an la vertiz, 3990
les sorciz noirs et bien dolgiez,
les ielz rianz et trestoz liez;
biaus ert li nes, anprés la face,
car plus blanche ert que nois ne glace;
entremellee ert la color 3995
avenalment o la blanchor;
molt ot bien faite la bochete,
n'ert gaires granz mais petitete,
menu serrees ot les denz,
plus reluisent que nus argenz. 4000
Que diroie de sa beauté?
An tot lo plus lonc jor d'esté
ne diroie ce qu'en estoit
de la biauté qu'ele avoit,
ne de ses mors, de sa bonté 4005
qui vallent mielz que la bialté.
  Molt par ert bele la raïne.
Vers l'ost chevalche la meschine;
chevous ot sors, lons jusqu'as piez,
a un fil d'or les ot treciez; 4010
bien fu la dame estroit vestue
de porpre noir a sa chair nue;
la porpre fu a or broudee,
par grant entante fu ovree:
trois faees serors la firent, 4015
an une chanbre la tissirent;
chascune d'els s'i essaia
et son savoir i demostra
et firent i poissons marages,
oissiaus volanz, bestes salvages. 4020
Vestue an fu estroitement;
dessus fu ceinte cointement
d'une sozceinte a or broudee;
menuëment ert botonee.

Chaucie fu d'un siglaton; 4025
si soller furent d'un peisson
de cent colors menu veiriez;
a or furent li liepiez.
Li mantiaus fu riches et chiers
et fu toz fez a eschaquiers; 4030
l'un tavel ert de blanc hermine
et l'autre ert de gole martrine;
vols fu de porpre esperital,
li tassel furent a esmal,
li or les fu mervoilles biaus 4035
et fu de gorges d'uns oisiaus
ki sollent pondre al fonz de mer
et sor l'onde sollent cover;
cent toises covent an parfont;
de si chaude nature sont 4040
que, se desus lor oes seoient,
de lor chalor toz les ardroient;
bien fu or lez de ces oisiaus,
desi qu'a terre li mantiaus.
Ele an ot antroverz les pans, 4045
que li parut li destre flans,
et chevalchot un palefroi
qui soz li moine grant estroi.
Unques ne fu tant gente beste:
come noif ot blanche la teste, 4050
lo top ot noir, et les oroilles
ot ambedos totes vermoilles,
lo col ot bai et fu bien gros,
les crins indes et vers par flos;
tote ot vaire l'espalle destre 4055
et bien noire fu la senestre;
les piez devant ot lovinez
et fu toz bruns par les costez;
soz le vantre fu leporins
et sor la crope leonins 4060
et fu toz noirs desoz les auves;
les dos james devant ot falves,
le dos desriers vermalz com sans;
les quatre piez ot trestoz blans,
noire ot la coe une partie, 4065

l'altre blanche, tote crespie,
lo pié copé, les james plates:
molt fu bien faiz et bien aates.
Li palefroiz fu bien anblanz,
et li froins fu molt avenans;   4070
de fin or ert li cheveçaus,
fet a pierres et a esmaus,
et les regnes de fin argent,
bien treciees menuëment;
la sele ert bone, et li arçon   4075
furent de l'ovre Salemon,
a entaille de blanc ivoire;
l'entaille an ert a or trifoire;
de porpre fu la couverture
et tote l'autre afautreüre,   4080
et d'un buen cerf andous les cengles,
de bon orfrois les contrecengles;
li estrié furent de fin or,
li petriaus valut un tresor.
Camille vint molt richement   4085
an l'ost et amena grant gent:
bien ot o soi de chevaliers
desi que a quatre milliers.
Quant a Laurente vint errant,
temolte ot an la vile grant,   4090
borjois monterent sus as estres,
dames, meschines as fenestres,
et esgardoient la pucelle
qui tant ert proz et tant ert bele.
A grant mervoille lo tenoient   4095
tote la gent qui la veoient,
qu'el se deüst onques cambatre,
joster ne chevalier abatre.

After this came a maiden who was queen of Vulcane; the damsel was called Camille, she was very marvelously beautiful and she was of very great strength; there was no other woman with her knowledge (3964). She was very wise, worthy, and courtly, and she possessed great wealth; she ruled her land marvelously well; she had always been brought up in warfare and she loved knightly behaviour and maintained it all her life (3970). She never cared for woman's work, neither spinning nor sewing; she had higher esteem for bearing arms, fighting in tournaments, and jousting, striking with sword and with lance: there was no other woman of her valiance (3976). By day she was a king, but by night a queen, never did a chambermaid or a lady's maid go near her during the day, nor by night did any man ever enter into the bedroom where she was; she conducted herself so wisely, both openly and secretly, that nobody could remark any foolishness in her action[s] or in her expression, no matter how much envy he felt towards her (3986). No woman who was mortal was equal to her in beauty, she had a white and well-shaped forehead, a straight part on the top of her head, black and very delicate eyebrows, laughing and completely happy eyes (3992); her nose was beautiful, along with her face because it was whiter than snow or ice; the color was mixed together becomingly with the whiteness, she had a very well-made little mouth, it was scarcely large; rather it was small and pretty, her teeth were very close together, they shone more than any silver (4000). What could I tell about her beauty? In the very longest day of summer, I would not be able to tell what the situation was with regard to the beauty which she had or with regard to her manners, or her goodness, which are worth more than beauty.

The queen was very, very beautiful. The maiden rides towards the army, she had golden hair, hanging down to her feet, she had braided it with a thread of gold (4010); she was wearing a tight dress of black silk on her bare flesh; the silk was embroidered with gold, it was worked with great attention: three fairy sisters made it, they wove it in a chamber; each one of them tested herself in it and showed her knowledge in it and they made fish of the sea on it, flying birds, and wild beasts (4020). She was dressed tightly in it and over it was girded elegantly with a belt embroidered with gold, the dress was buttoned up with many buttons placed close to each other. She wore hose of delicate silk; her shoes were from a fish whose skin was made iridescent by a hundred colors; the ribbons [shoelaces!] were of gold (4028). Her cloak was rich and costly and was made all in checks; one square was of white ermine and the next was of red fur from a marten's throat; it was covered with heavenly silk, the clasps were enameled, the border was marvelously beautiful and was from the throats of birds who are accustomed to lay eggs at the bottom of the sea and to sit on them on top of the waves; they hatch [them] a hundred fathoms deep; they are of such a hot nature that, if they were to sit on their eggs they would burn them up with their heat (4042); the cloak was bordered with these birds down to the ground. She had the sections of it partially open so that her right side appeared, and she rode on a palfrey which showed great spirit under her (4048). There was never such a noble beast: its head was white as snow, the forelock was black, and the ears were both completely bright red, its neck was bay and very large, and the mane blue and green in tufts; it had a dappled grey right shoulder and the left was quite black (4056); its front feet were like a wolf's and it was all brown on the sides; under the stomach it was like a hare and on the rump like a lion and it was all black under the saddlebows (4061); its two front legs were tawny and the two back ones red as blood; it had four completely white feet, one part of it's tail was black and the other white and all curly, it had hollowed hoofs and slender legs: it was very well-made and quite agile (4068). The palfrey ambled very well, its bridle was very becoming; the headstall was of pure gold, made with precious stones and enamels, and the reins were of pure silver, very finely braided; the saddle was good and the saddlebows were Solomon-work in an arcade pattern, work of carved white ivory; the carving was overlaid with gold (4078); the cover and all the other padding were of silk, and both the saddle-girths were of good deer-hide and the surcingles were of good orphrey; the stirrups were of pure gold and the chest-strap was worth a treasure.

Camille came magnificently into the army and brought many people: indeed she had with her as many as four thousand knights (4088). When she came journeying to Laurentum there was great tumult in the city, the townspeople climbed to the upper stories of their houses, noble ladies and maidens at the windows, and they were looking at the damsel who was so worthy and so beautiful. All the people who saw her held it to be a great marvel that she should ever fight, or joust, or knock down a knight.

I am greatly indebted to Frederick Ahl, Alice Colby-Hall, and Nita Krevans for their help with the translations of these passages. I also consulted the following editions, translations and commentaries:

Eneas. Edited by J. -J. Salverda de Grave. Paris: Champion, 1929.

Eneas. Translated and with notes by John A. Yunck. New York: Columbia University Press, 1974.

Faral, Edmond. *Recherches sur les sources latines des contes et romans courtois du moyen age.* Paris: Champion, 1983.

Maronis, P. Vergili. *Aeneidos* Libri VII-VIII. Edited and with commentary by C. J. Fordyce. Oxford University Press, 1977.

Virgil, *Aeneid* VII-XII. Edited and with notes by R. D. Williams. London: MacMillan, 1972.

William of Malmesbury's Roman Models: Suetonius and Lucan

JOAN GLUCKAUF HAAHR

When William of Malmesbury set out to write a history of England from the beginnings to his own day, he was able to claim with some confidence that aside from Bede's "clear and captivating" model, there had been no lucid and comprehensive history of the English nation. Not that he was unaware of his predecessors' efforts! In his preface to the *Gesta regum*, William mentioned Æthelward and "those notices written in the vernacular tongue after the manner of a chronicle," as well as Eadmer's *Historia nouorum*. Subsequent references show his familiarity with the British histories of Gildas and Nennius as well as numerous foreign chronicles: "I have studiously sought for chronicles far and near," he wrote, although "I have scarcely profited anything by this industry. For perusing them all, I still remained poor in information" (GR Prol. bk. 2; G-94).[1]

What Bede had provided for the early years of English history, and what William wanted for later centuries, was a synthesis of the annal, of which the *Anglo-Saxon Chronicle* was the best example, with a more reflective and instructional narrative of past events. For William, the bare record of the Chronicle, valuable as it was for its rescue from oblivion of events after Bede, was but the skeleton of historical writing. He disparaged the work of Æthelward for its crude Latin and simple aim. While he admired the eloquence and lucidity of the *Historia nouorum*, he lamented the sketchy treatment Eadmer accorded to events before the Conquest. "Thus from the time of Bede," wrote William, "there is a period of two-hundred and twenty-three years left unnoticed . . . so that the regular series of time, unsupported by a connected relation, halts in the middle" (GR Prol. 1; G-2). William's ambition was to fill the gap, "to season," as he said, "the crude materials" of the Chronicle "with Roman art." As Bede had done, or Gildas, of whom William had a high opinion (describing him as "an historian neither unlearned nor inelegant, to whom the Britons are indebted for whatever notice they obtain among other nations" [GR no. 20; G-22]), William hoped to present a narrative which would both illuminate the past logically and consistently and create a new fund for moral teaching and example. Lacking English and Norman models, he would turn for narrative and ideological guidance to Roman writers. In this paper, I would like to concentrate on the influence of two of those writers: Suetonius and Lucan.

Despite William's professed aim of clear and coherent narrative, parts of the *Gesta regum* are notable for their seeming lack of order and rather desultory chronology. In his introduction to the Rolls edition, Bishop William Stubbs wrote: "It must be that our author was resolutely determined that his work should be read not as a book of reference but as a literary production that would not allow skipping. I know no book that stands more in need of a perfect index."[2] The books to which Stubbs particularly referred, books 4 and 5, dealt with recent or contemporary events for which William had few, if any, written sources. Marie Schütt, in 1931, was the first to suggest that their seeming lack of unity, their incoherence and awkward transitions may derive from that very "Roman art" to which William had referred so admiringly.[3] Perhaps William's model, in writing of William II and Henry I, the kings who ruled in his lifetime, was not traditional history at all but rather the somewhat eccentric "biographical" form devised by Suetonius for the *Vitae Caesarum*.

For all the deficiencies of his style and idiosyncracies of his method, Suetonius' influence on imperial biography had continued through the end of the classical era.[4] Even in the early medieval period, the basic structure of Suetonian biography, which derived from Greek and Latin panegyrical oratory as discussed by Cicero and Quintilian (among others), continued to have some influence, although only a single western European manuscript of the *Vitae Caesarum* (at Fulda) seems to have survived in the "dark ages." For Christian biographers, however, concerned not so much with historical accuracy or personal idiosyncrasy as with hagiographic formulae, the Suetonian model, with its emphasis on the often scandalous minutiae of imperial corruption, was less relevant.

In fact, there are a few medieval examples of Suetonian-influenced historical writing. The most notable is probably Einhard (who had read the manuscript at Fulda); writing shortly after Charlemagne's death, he made the emperor a composite of several Roman emperors, although the *Vita Caroli,* as panegyric, lacks much of the wit and color which characterize the less flattering *Vitae Caesarum*.[5] Asser, too, in the *Vita Alfredi,* followed Suetonian form, although it is possible that he knew only Einhard's *Vita,* not the Fulda manuscript itself.[6]

What, then, of William of Malmesbury? We know that he had read Einhard's *Vita*, to which he not only referred explicitly in the *Gesta regum* (GR no. 68; G-63-64) but imitated closely in his own *Vita Wulfstani*. Can we claim that William, like Einhard, may have had first-hand knowledge of the Suetonian text? There is, to be sure, circumstantial evidence only: on the one hand his remarkable work as monastic librarian; on the other his apparent debt to Suetonian form and rhetoric, which seems to exceed what he would have been able to pick up from Einhard and Asser alone.

How did the *Vitae Caesarum* differ from other histories? Its characteristic and distinctive rhetorical feature was the arrangement of biographical information under a series of standard headings both explicit and implicit. Many Latin prose writers, and even some poets, used this device (called *partitio* or *diuisio*) to some extent, but Suetonius developed a biographical formula based on the arrangement of such topics as family and birth, childhood and education, early career, accession, imperial acts, *mores* (appearance and character), and death into a fairly standard format (although, in some of the later *Lives*, what had originally been a method of classification developed into a mannerism more perplexing than helpful, with a list of headings followed by all topics scrambled haphazardly together without order or transition).

William of Malmesbury adopted and modified the Suetonian format, using the headings as logical aids in arranging a great quantity of biographical information.[7] Thus his account of the reign of William Rufus in book 4 begins not with the king's accession but with his birth and genealogy. His early boyhood and youth are described, his accession to the throne, the subsequent rebellion of the nobles, and his conflicts with his brother Robert and their resolution. There follows a section on *mores*, or private life, which afforded William an opportunity for the kind of moral analysis he saw as central to historical writing. After accounts of Rufus' quarrels with Anselm and various natural events (earthquakes, storms, a comet) portending the king's imminent end, there follows the final Suetonian *diuisio* of death and post-mortem evaluation.

The account of the reign of Henry I in book 5 similarly follows the Suetonian model: birth and education; early manhood and accession (including the death of William the Conqueror); deeds at home and abroad, *mores* (physical appearance and character); family, including brief biographies of his wife and children. However, since Henry was still alive at the time William completed the first recension of the fifth book, the book ends not with Henry's death, but with an account of the investiture controversy and a description of celebrated ecclesiastical figures of the day. Nor did William, in his later revisions of the text, take account of the king's death, probably because, with the arrangement of events topical rather than chronological, he would have had to distribute the events of the last ten years of Henry's reign under various appropriate headings and thus radically revise the narrative.[8]

Book 3 of the *Gesta regum*, devoted to William the Conqueror and far more coherent than its successors, is an example of medieval historical writing at its best. The book, proceeding for the most part in orderly chronological fashion, uses traditional techniques of historiography. Yet here too we see the informing influence of the Suetonian biographical divisions: we move from accounts of the Conqueror's parents, birth and boyhood through his youth, knighthood and early military victories, both domestic and foreign. The heart of the book is devoted to his claim to the English throne, the battle of Hastings, and his conflicts with the English barons. William next appears as king, and we read of his dispositions at home and abroad; we are introduced to his most prominent courtiers, and learn the state of foreign affairs during his reign. A section on *mores* (private life, character, appearance) precedes the account of his last days and death. The biographical narrative of book 3 is, however, interrupted at several points with more traditional historical narrative: William of Malmesbury supplements his account of the Conqueror's relations with the Church with an analysis of contemporary affairs at Rome and the papacy of Hildebrand; he surveys important religious events during and immediately following the Conqueror's reign, and even includes a short life of Berengarius of Tours, probably the most prominent ecclesiastical figure of the late eleventh century.

Without a direct citation, it is impossible to do more than suggest William of Malmesbury's acquaintance with the actual text of the *Vitae Caesarum*. In fact, even his skillful adaptation of the Suetonian narrative model does no more than demonstrate his acquaintance with techniques of Suetonian biography which may indeed have come from an intermediate source (especially Einhard). What gives added force to the suggestion of direct Suetonian influence, however, are several explicit echoes of the Suetonian text which do not appear in the *Vita Caroli*. The physical description of William Rufus, for example, incorporates details from Suetonius' lives of Augustus, Claudius, Vespasian, and Titus.[9] Rufus is described:

> ... colore rufo, crine subflauo, fronte fenestrata, oculo uario, quibusdam intermicantibus guttis distincto; praecipuo robore, quanquam non magnae staturae, et uentre paulo proiectiore. Eloquentiae

nullae, sed titubantia linguae notabilis, maxime cum ira succresceret (GR no. 321).

... his complexion florid, his hair yellow; of open countenance; different colored eyes, varying with certain glittering specks; of astonishing strength though not very tall, and his belly slightly projecting; of no eloquence but remarkable for hesitation of speech, especially when angry (G-341).

A comparison with Suetonius' *Titus* reveals both echoes and significant modifications:

forma egregia et cui non minus auctoritatis inesset quam gratiae, praecipuum robur, quamquam neque procera statura et uentre paulo proiectiore.... Armorum et equitandi peritissimus. Latine Graeceque uel in orando uel in fingendis poematibus promptus et facilis ad extemporalitatem usque" (Titus 3, 1 ff.).

He had a handsome person, in which there was no less dignity than grace, and was uncommonly strong although he was not very tall and his belly projecting.... Skillful in arms and horsemanship, he made speeches and wrote verses in Latin and Greek with ease and readiness, and even off-hand.

Note that William may be using the Suetonian passage as inspiration for his own commentary even when he alters it.

An anecdote which may derive from Suetonius occurs in William of Malmesbury's account of William the Conqueror's disembarcation at Hastings. In stepping off his ship, the Conqueror slipped and fell, but a nearby soldier interpreted the misstep favorably: "In egressu nauis pede lapsus, euentum in melius commutauit, acclamante sibi proxime milite, 'tenes,' inquit, 'Angliam, comes, rex futurus ...'" (GR no. 238) ("As he disembarked he slipped down, but turned the accident to his advantage; a soldier who stood near calling out to him, 'you hold England, my lord, its future king ...'" [G-274]). The anecdote does not appear in the usual sources of the Conqueror's life, William of Poitiers or William of Jumièges, nor in any other medieval account of the landing preceding that in the *Gesta regum*. A similar story does appear, however, in Suetonius' life of Julius Caesar (59), where an identical stumble is turned to identical advantage (in almost identical language) although by Caesar himself: "Prolapsus etiam in egressu nauis uerso ad melius omine: teneo te, inquit, Africa." ("Even when he had a fall as he disembarked, he gave the omen a favorable turn by crying 'I hold thee fast, Africa!'") To be sure, analogous stories are told in two other classical works familiar to William of Malmesbury: Frontinus' *Strategemata* (of which a transcription survives in William's own hand),[10] and Nepotianus' *epitome* of Valerius Maximus (to which William referred a friend in the preface to his compilation of classical quotations called *Polyhistor*). In Frontinus, the story is told (with slight variations) both of Caesar (who reassures himself) and Scipio (who reassures his men). In Nepotianus, the story is told only of Scipio. Whatever the specific source, it seems likely that William of Malmesbury resurrected the story from ancient writers, combining the two motifs of favorable omen and reassurance of the soldiers, and attributed the revised story to the Conqueror. (Incidentally, the combined motif was to reappear several times in the twelfth and thirteenth centuries — most strangely, perhaps, in a version, identical to William's, in Snorri Sturlason's account of St. Olaf's landing at Saelà in the *Heimskringla*.)[11]

Unlike Suetonius, whose history was little known, Lucan was widely read. The *Pharsalia* became an important model for a rhetoric of history and its phrases enlivened the style of saints' lives and other ecclesiastical biographies as well as histories proper. Lucan seems to have been known in England at least from the seventh century.[12] Aldheim, who was abbot of Malmesbury and had studied with Theodore and Hadrian at Canterbury, used ten citations from the *Pharsalia* as metrical examples in his *Epistle to Acircius*, although these may have been obtained at second-hand. Bede quoted Lucan directly, although infrequently. The library at York founded by Egbert included Lucan among its authors, according to Alcuin's poetic catalogue: *"Maro Virgilius, Statius, Lucanus."* Not until the eleventh century, however, did the name of Lucan appear again in Anglo-Norman writings, when Æthelward quoted him as an authority on barbaric tribes. By the twelfth century, copies of Lucan were probably to be found in most monastic libraries, and the *Pharsalia* and the *Aeneid* were held to be of equal merit.[13] Lucan's epic formed an important part of the curriculum in the monastic schools, and is fairly represented in *florilegia* and annotated manuscripts.

Lines from the *Pharsalia* are quoted or paraphrased by numerous medieval English historians, including Henry of Huntington, Orderic Vitalis, Richard of Dyon, Benedict of Peterborough and Geoffrey of Monmouth. William of Malmesbury, however, did not merely cite Lucan but made frequent casual allusions to the text. Within two pages in the fourth book, for example, are three unmistakable echoes:

". . . *fames, quae tuta etiam expugnare solet* . . ." (GR no. 362) (". . . famine, which usually conquers even what is safe . . .").

"*Expugnat quae tuta, fames . . .*" (*Phars.* 4.410) ("Famine, which conquers what is safe . . .").

". . . *et esurire sustinebat prolato ieiunus uenditor auro . . .*" (GR no. 362) (". . . and when gold has been brought forward, the seller, though hungry, put up with his hunger . . ." [literally: "endured to hunger"]).

"*Non dest prolato ieiunus uenditor auro*" (*Phars.* 4.96–97) ("when gold has been brought forward, the seller, though hungry, is present" [literally: "is not missing"]).

". . . *cum bello infestatis cresceret inedia, inedia semper magnorum comes prima malorum*" (GR no. 364) (". . . when hunger increased for those who had been attacked in the war, hunger, always the first companion of great evils").

"*Iamque comes semper magnorum prima malorum / saeua fames aderat*" (*Phars.* 4.93–94) ("And now savage hunger approached, always the first companion of great evils").

Other brief allusions, both direct and indirect, are sprinkled throughout the *Gesta regum*.[14] More interesting than these, however, is William's use of Lucan as an aid in characterizing William Rufus. He had, as we have seen, modeled Rufus' physical description on Suetonius' *Titus*. From Lucan's portrait of Caesar, intemperate, occasionally magnanimous and always fearless, William borrowed incidents which he attributed to the even more passionate and unrestrained English king. In one notable incident, Rufus, hearing that the city of Mans, which he had recently added to his lands, was being besieged, hurried to the sea despite admonitions from his men that he wait. He arrived at the coast during a storm but forbade any delay, admonishing the frightened sailors: "I have never heard of any king perishing by shipwreck; no, weigh anchor immediately, and you shall see the elements conspire to obey me" (GR no. 320; *Phars.* 5.591–92). Upon landing, he heard that the besiegers had retreated. The instigator, Helias, was brought before the king who, echoing Caesar's words to Domitius, "Et nihil hac uenia, si uiceris, ipse paciscor" (*Phars.* 2.515) ("And if you should conquer, I stipulate nothing for myself because of this pardon"), let him escape: ". . . nihil, si me uiceris, pro hac uenia tecum paciscar" ("If you should conquer me, I would stipulate nothing with you in return for this pardon") (GR no. 320). William added this postscript to the narrative:

> Who could believe this of an unlettered man? And perhaps there may be some person who, from reading Lucan, may falsely suppose that William borrowed these examples from Julius Caesar; but he had neither inclination nor leisure to attend to learning; it was rather the innate warmth of his temper and his conscious valor which

prompted him to such expressions. And, indeed, if our religion would allow it, as the soul of Euphorbus was said to have passed into Pythagoras of Samos, so might it equally be asserted that the soul of Julius Caesar had migrated into King William (GR no. 320; G-341).

Given his consistently evident disdain for William Rufus, it is hard to believe he was not being ironic.

William of Malmesbury continually demonstrated his familiarity with ancient writers. The *Gesta regum* is crowded with classical allusions and citations. His subsequent editions and commentaries on the works of classical writers (Frontinus, Vegetius, Eutropius, Jordanes, Dares Phrygius, Cato, Martianus Capella, Cassiodorus, Cicero) in addition to the wide-ranging *Polyhistor* (described on its final leaf as "Malmesbury on the memorable sayings and doings of the philosophers") attest to his undiminished interest in ancient literature, notwithstanding his apparent concentration, in later years, on works of *lectio diuina*.[15] For it is clear that when he had no English or continental sources on which to draw for narrative and ideological inspiration, he went easily and naturally to Roman models.

Notes

1. Latin quotations from the *Gesta regum* are from Bishop William Stubbs' edition from the Rolls Series, *Williemi Malmesbiriensis monachi De gestis regum Anglorum; Historiae nouellae*, Chronicles and Memorials of Great Britain and Ireland during the Middle Ages, no. 90 (London: Great Britain Public Record Office, 1887-89), referred to in the text as GR followed by the article number. English quotations are from J. A. Giles' translation, *William of Malmesbury's Chronicle of the Kings of England* (London: H. G. Bohn, 1847; repr., 1904, 1968), referred to as G followed by the page number.

2. Stubbs, 2:cxxxiii.

3. Marie Schütt, "The Literary Form of William of Malmesbury's *Gesta regum*," *English Historical Review* 46 (1931): 255-60.

4. Marius Maximus continued the series of *Caesars* (a work now lost) in the following century. The Augustan *Lives* of the third century are somewhat indebted to Suetonius, as are Eutropius, Aurelius Victor, and other fourth-century imperial biographers. See G. B. Townend, "Suetonius and his Influence," in *Latin Biography*, ed. T. A. Dorey (London: Routledge and K. Paul, 1967), 96-97.

5. Townend, 98.

6. See Marie Schütt, "The Literary Form of Asser's *Vita Alfredi*," *EHR* 83 (1957): 209-20.

7. See D. H. Farmer, "Two Biographies by William of Malmesbury," in *Latin Biography*, 157-76.

8. Schütt, "The Literary Form . . . *Gesta regum*," 259.

9. Townend, 107.
10. Lincoln College, Oxford, Latin MS. 100.
11. See Ove Moberg, "Olav Haraldssons Hemkomst. En historiografisk undersökning," *Historisk Tidsskrift* (Oslo) 32 (1942): 545-75.
12. For information about Lucan's influence in England, I am indebted to George M. Logan, who has kindly let me refer to the chapter on the Middle Ages in his unpublished doctoral thesis "Lucan and England" (Harvard, 1967).
13. See David Knowles, *The Monastic Order in England* (Cambridge: Cambridge Univ. Press), 526.
14. Elsewhere Herbert Losinga, in a paraphrase from Lucan, was compared to Curio ("Fuitque Herbertus mutatus, ut Lucanus de Curione dixit, 'momentum et mutatio rerum' ") ("Herbert, when he changed, as Lucan said about Curio, was 'the turning point and change of events'"). GR no. 339 paraphrasing *Phars.* 4.819: "momentumque fuit mutatus Curio rerum" ("And Curio, when he changed, was the turning point and change of events"). The Turks, in a somewhat problematic passage, were referred to as slaves " 'ignorantque,' ut Lucanus ait, ideo 'datos ne quisquam seruiat enses' " (GR no. 360) ("and they do not know, as Lucan says, 'that swords have been given' just 'so that no one should be a slave'" [*Phars.* 4.579]).
Baldwin, during the seige of Ramlah, emulated a military stratagem used by Lucan's Caesar, an incident absent from William's source, Fulcher of Chartres. Disregarding the "mad impetuosity" of the Saracens, Baldwin delayed entering the field until the enemy, having wearied of waiting, withdrew, and Baldwin was able to defeat those remaining (GR no. 381: *Phars.* 4.281-85). An adage from Lucan, "cupias quodcumque necesse est" ("may you desire whatever is inevitable") (*Phars.* 4.487) was quoted in the preface to book 2 of the *Gesta regum*. In describing Canute's motives in attacking the Swedes at the battle of Helgeå, William's "nam nescia eius stare loco, nec contenta Danamarchia quam auito, et Anglia quam bellico jure obtinebat, martem in Sweuos transtulit" ("For his [valor], unable to stand still, not satisfied with the Denmark which he obtained through ancestral right and the England which he obtained through right of war, brought war upon the Swedes") (GR no. 181) may be an echo of Lucan's "sed non in Caesare tantum / nomen erat nec fama ducis, sed nescia uirtus / stare loco, solusque pudor non uincere bello" ("But in Caesar there was not only the name and fame of a general, but also valor unable to stand still, and his only shame was not to conquer through warfare".) (*Phars.* 1.144-45). The parallel, incidentally, may have been picked up from William by Snorri 4 Sturlason. See Ove Moberg, *Olav Haraldsson, Knut den Store och Sverige* (Lund: C. W. K. Gleerup, 1941).
15. In the dedication to his *Commentary* on the *Lamentations of Jeremiah*, written after 1135, William wrote, "Formerly, when I amused myself with history, the delightful material matched my youthful years and happy lot. But now my greater age and less happy fortune demand that a different kind of work be written. Its principle scope will be to turn our hearts away from the world and enkindle them for God. Until now we have lived too much for ourselves; henceforth let us live for our Creator." However, the commentary itself contains citations from the *Disticha Catonis,* Themistius, Aristotle, the Physiologus, Virgil, Lucan and Seneca, among others. See Hugh Farmer, "William of Malmesbury's *Commentary on Lamentations,*" *Studia Monastica* 4.2 (1962): 288-89, and the same author's "William of Malmesbury's Life and Works," *Journal of Ecclesiastical History* 11 (1962): 39-54.

PLENARY LECTURE

Aeneas' Journey to the New Troy

BERNARD F. HUPPÉ

Vergil on wings of magic traveled widely through medieval literature. His most famous journey, which has been traced in detail, took him to Florence, which he visited in the persona of Dante's guide through Hell. The itinerary of Vergil's Aeneas, however, has been followed in much less detail. Because the voyager, Aeneas, has been so transformed and transmuted on the forge of medieval poetic genius, there are gaps in our recognition of the way his voyage gripped the Medieval imagination. This voyage, thus transmuted, took him from Rome to the New Albion (in *Beowulf*); later to Paris (in Abelard's *Calamities*) and (in Chrétien's *Erec*) to Troyes; later yet but still in France, his voyage reappears, transmuted almost beyond recognition, as a dreamer's pilgrimage in the *Roman de la Rose*; in Florence it reappears in the *Vita Nuova* as the inner journey of Dante to the new beginning when he will find in Vergil, a guide to the Beatrice of the New Jerusalem. Finally, in the limited itinerary I chronicle, the voyage reappears in the New Troy, London, as the inner search for the Truth in Trinity of the dreamer Will in *Piers Plowman,* and as the journeys of the narrative persona and of the hero in Chaucer's *Troilus*.

This peregrination may appear to be merely whimsical unless a fundamental truth about the survival of the classics in medieval literature is remembered. This obvious truth is that Latin literature is like the language in which it was written, a language that never needed a medieval "renaissance" because its life was continuous. On the one hand, it remained, only slightly altered, as the medieval koine of the Church and of the literate laity; on the other hand it remained, although responsive to the genius of a people, transmuted into the various vulgates. Similarly, the Latin classics were continuously transcribed, and the creation of literature in Latin continued in an unbroken line. The future life of its tradition, however, belonged to the poets of the vulgar languages and the Germanic. These poets were not heedless of the Latin literary tradition, which, for them, was continuous. Great poets, however, are not name-droppers, transcribers, or makers of quotations. They are nourished on the literature of their past, but they transform this literature into nourishment for their own generation and attune it to the central problems of their own time. What is then of chief importance in the study of the continuity of the past is not external identification, naming, but the discovery of the process of transformation by which the old becomes the new.

Thus, to give a modern example, what is important to know about Joyce's *Ulysses* is not its title and its hints of an Odyssean structure, but its transformation, transmutation of the wily Odysseus into the wily Leopold Bloom. Suppose Joyce had called his book *Dublin on Bloomsday* or *Stephen Meets Leopold* and had given no hint of its Odyssean scheme. Would the novel be any less a remembrance of poetry past, transformed to create the conscience of a race? It would have been a little harder to trace its ancestry, but the effort to understand his work through comprehension of the manner of his transmutation would have been merely more difficult, not less significant for our understanding.

Joyce transmutes the *Odyssey* by recasting Odysseus as Leopold Bloom and narrowing his journey in space to the streets of Dublin and in time to a single day. More important for our illustrative purposes is that his transmutation involves making one thing mean another; that is, his use of word play, paronomasia, as functional metaphor to reveal that nothing is as it seems. And as Joyce transmuted the *Odyssey,* the medieval poets transmuted the *Aeneid* in order to re-create the conscience of their race, but with the basic difference that their method was not paronomasiac but allegorical.

The distinction and relationship between allegory and word play is worth pursuing because it may take us closer to an understanding of the medieval poet's methodology. The difference between the two is, in fact, a difference only in degree. Word play and allegory share the same basic definition; both say one thing and mean another, except that in allegory the other thing meant must be ethically or metaphysically significant, whereas in word play (if defined as the lowest form of humor) no significant meaning need be revealed beyond the demonstration of skill in verbal gymnastics. Although allegory and word play are related in the perception that word or thing may not be what it seems, their kinship is broken when word play is not seen as functional in adding depth of signification. The kinship exists, then, only when word play is not classified as the lowest form of humor, revealing nothing beyond the display of verbal prestidigitation.

In addition, word play must be perceived as intentionally significant or it loses its functional relation to allegory. Such unintended saying of one thing and meaning something else may be found in an advertisement, 11 August, 1986, by Eastern Maine Tech of its Fall curriculum. There, after Heating and before Machine Tool, Humanities is listed with the following offerings:

Business Communication
Communications I
Economics
Freshman Composition
Introductory Psychology
Oral Communications
Public Relations

Clearly Eastern Maine Tech is advertising one thing and offering another, but the only significance to be attached is that benighted ignorance has found a home, or that the word, Humanities, has become current as an incantatory force. It may be, of course, that a deeper significance is to be found, as with the opening of Genesis, in the ordering of words, with the list of Humanities offerings climactically concluding with Public Relations. Perhaps the Humanist may learn, after all these years, whither he has been tending, and find his true social function. Because such profound meaning could not be intended, it may be ruled out as accidental signification. The perception of intention, as with the exegete's reading of the first verse of Genesis, is essential to the functional relation of word play to allegory.

What Joyce intended by his word play I do not pretend to understand with any coherent and communicable decisiveness; it may well be that a metaphoric irony in the essence of things is all he wished to signify, and that he is not an allegorist. For in allegory the other thing that is meant must have a referent which can be coherently determined and communicated. That meaning must be clear and be agreed upon by poet and audience, however opaque the paronomasiac vehicle may be by which allegory conveys its message. The vehicle of word play may lead simply, as with Cummings, to "somewhere i have never traveled, gladly beyond any experience," or, with Conrad, to "misty halos made visible by the spectral illumination of moonshine." Conversely it may lead to allegory, as in *Piers Plowman*; the title is itself a prime example of allegorical word play.

A pedestrian little story may perhaps define the distinction and relationship I am trying to establish. In Portland, Maine, where I once lived,

I used to walk past a saloon evocatively called "The Last Chance." When, after an absence, I walked past it again it had become, even more evocatively, a "Redemption Center." The Dickensian realist might have seen this simply as suggesting a story of social significance, perhaps with Mr. Micawber as its hero. Joyce, in turn, might have perceived the paronomasiac irony that empty bottles had found a home in the place where they had been emptied. For me, however, attuned by indoctrination to the allegorical possibilities inherent in word play, the experience suggested that if Dante had not had his vision of Beatrice he might well have found here a sufficient inspiration for the *Divine Comedy*.

These attitudes reasonably deduced from my pedestrian experience inform us first of the gap that divides realism from Joycean word play and the latter from allegory. More than this, the very different perceptions of the same thing (or word) suggest that in addition to the requirement that allegory to succeed must have a referent of shared meaning between author and audience, allegory, to be possible, must also have a social climate which is hospitable to the perception that word and thing may express a metaphysical reality behind appearance. The literary climate of the nineteenth century was realistic. Thus, for example, when George Meredith made an early, and I think, successful venture into allegory in his *The Shaving of Shagpat,* his attempt fell on deaf ears, so that he never ventured upon allegory again, but was content to promote a metaphoric level of understanding. The twentieth century continues to be realistic in its perception of what is valid in literary experience; Chaucer, as a "realist," is acclaimed, but *Piers Plowman* remains largely ignored by the general literate public.

Charles Dickens provides in *Bleak House* an illuminating example of the contempt of the realist for word play and allegory which makes them rest uneasily in the modern world. "Allegory," he says, "makes the head ache — as would seem to be Allegory's object always, more or less." Dickens certainly avoids this cause for headaches, and the allegory he cites is a figure on a ceiling painting in the chambers of the sinister attorney, Mr. Tulkinghorn, and its only functional use is dramatically to point a finger at the murdered occupant. Indeed Dickens shows himself so capable of avoiding headaches that he succeeds in making even Personification, the staple of allegory, both non-allegorical and rhetorically realistic when elsewhere in *Bleak House* he describes a coal grate as "pinched in the middle as if Poverty had gripped it." One need only think of the figure of Poverty in the *Roman de la Rose* or in *Piers Plowman* to recognize the enormous gulf between realist and allegorical perceptions and modes.

I do not know of the incidence of headaches among the serious readers of the Middle Ages, although it is true that Boccaccio speaks of sleepless nights spent in the unraveling of the web of poetry, its allegorical veil; but I do believe that the medieval penchant for allegory was not merely masochistic and that it sprang from a felt need to explain and exposit the world of their configuration. This configuration was essentially an Augustinian transformation of Platonism. It is based on the understanding that there is one Ideal, one Truth which could be approached through faith in Christ and the Christian interpretation of the message of Scripture. The world hides this Truth, and man's language may equally mislead. Only through exegetical interpretation of deed and word might the Truth be revealed. It is for this reason that biblical exegesis was the central intellectual preoccupation of the Middle Ages, and that poetry was considered valid only in so far as it conformed to its scriptural model.

That is why the pervasive influence of Vergil's *Aeneid* on Medieval literature can only be understood when it is recognized that a derived allegorical meaning is central to the power of its inspiration for the medieval poet. Such allegorical interpretation, as we know, exists in Christian commentary on the *Aeneid*, in particular, Fulgentius' *Expositio Vergilianae Continentiae*. Fulgentius, if tradition is correct, was an African episcopal contemporary of St. Augustine. Although his direct influence on any given poet is not possible to determine with certainty, he does provide, at the least, a general sense of the manner in which Vergil, apart from the sonorous magic of his verse, may have inspired a medieval poet.

That Fulgentius' *Exposition* is headache-producing is evidenced in the outburst by Ramsay, one of Dickens' contemporaries, who writes of it: "The absurdity of this piece is so glaring, that, had it been composed in a different age, we should have pronounced it to be a tedious and exaggerated burlesque."[1] The *Exposition* is, indeed, so glaringly, gratuitously allegorical as to be an affront to any common-sensical reader of the *Aeneid*, for whom its absurdity could only be explained by its having been written in the benighted darkness of the Augustinian twilight. Fulgentius' *Exposition*, in which "Vergil" is made to be the expositor, begins with an attribution of auctorial intent not likely to produce recognition in the reader of Vergil's epic, only an invitation to laughter or annoyance: "Thus I [Vergil] begin by saying 'This is a tale of arms and man,' indicating manliness by 'arms' and wisdom by 'man,' for all perfection depends on manliness of body and wisdom of mind."[2] From this follows his exposition of the allegorical significance of the *Aeneid* as the journey of a man to wisdom, evidenced, for example, by the conquest of Turnus, the "furious rage" which the wise man overcomes. Stated thus baldly, how could medieval poets have been taken in, have found inspiration in such trash?

Unless we are prepared to dismiss these poets as not very bright or as benighted by the dark age in which they lived, unenlightened by the glorious Renaissance and the fruits of nineteenth-century scholarship, we must find some answers. One such answer is to be found in recognizing that Augustinian Christianity permeated their lives in a way very difficult for the modern positivist to comprehend. Thus, as Barbara Tuchman says, "The hardest task today for a person who endeavors to understand the medieval world is to realize the extent to which the doctrines, dogmas, and controversies of the Christian Church enveloped and absorbed all mental activity."[3] Her reminder, given in 1956, may no longer be necessary, but the need to keep it in mind remains for modern readers, however well-informed and open-minded they may be, particularly when we still hear voices heralding Marie de France or Jean de Meun as sexual celebrants, forerunners of that sexual religion of which Hugh Hefner is a high priest.

It is also highly possible that a common-sensical realist may miss the subtlety of Fulgentius' exposition of the *Aeneid*. Certainly his point will be missed if it is not recognized that Fulgentius takes his stance from a basic proposition about pagan literature, one which Augustine formulated in his *De doctrina,* for example, and one which saved the classics from the destructive impulses of the narrowly puritanical and provided a means for the medieval poet to find inspiration in a poet who, however great and effective, remained suspect as a pagan.

The proposition (which scarcely needs repeating), simply stated, is that a Vergil, let us say, was inspired to recognize the truth—a Truth, however, beyond his comprehension, because he was unillumined by Faith. His was the gold which the Israelites saved from the Egyptians, making it godly. Fulgentius' exposition clearly echoes this doctrine in revealing that "Vergil's" pagan interpretation of the gold of the "golden bough" as signifying "knowledge," is ultimately empty because it fails to recognize that such gold is an abomination unless redeemed by Christian revelation. Fulgentius' purpose is to capture the gold of the *Aeneid* and redeem it through Christian interpretation. For Fulgentius, the mythographer, the pagan "Vergil" had been inspired to create the *Aeneid* in order to disclose the tripartite journey of man's life: "There is a threefold progression in human life: to possess, to control, to ornament," i.e., to attain to the prosperity of wisdom. Thus, implicit in the *Aeneid* for Fulgentius is the revelation that man's life is an inner journey, which should have its end in the attainment of wisdom. Fulgentius, however, in his interrogation of his "Vergil" reveals the Christian sentence of the *Aeneid*: man's journey in life should have its end in blessedness, the attainment not of Rome, but the heavenly Jerusalem. This perception of the sentence of the epic as a spiritual journey, the *itinerarium mentis ad deum,* is a vital seed bed for the flowering of medieval story and allegory.

There is more than this, however, in Fulgentius' *Exposition,* for in it he creates a kind of implicit "dream vision" in which he as very humble enquiring persona asks the most magisterial persona of Vergil to exposit his epic. In the process, which is more than a little comic, it is revealed that in comparison to Christian rhetoric, pagan rhetoric is empty, even Vergilian rhetoric, the highest achievement of which the pagan is capable. The pose of "Fulgentius" is that of an awed student sitting at the feet of the all-knowing poetic master, and "Vergil" accepts the role, which is then undermined by humble Christian commentary. Thus, early on "Fulgentius" accepts "Vergil's" assumption that he is a neophyte to whom the master will try to propound matters which will probably be beyond his comprehension, but his abject humility is given an ironic twist when "Fulgentius" juxtaposes Christian inspiration, the hem of Christ's garment, and "Vergil's" assumption of all-knowing pagan wisdom. Again, "Vergil," beginning his exposition, makes the magisterial sign, the first two fingers making a one, and the thumb binding the other two to make a three, a magisterial sign that is, unbeknownst to him, a symbol of the Trinity.

For one other instance, in a manner reminiscent of the mass of commentary on the opening of Genesis, where rhetorical analysis reveals the Trinity, "Vergil" explains the rhetorical design of "arms" preceding "man": "wisdom controls manliness, yet the soul's wisdom stems from manliness." Fulgentius in his reply, however, cites Psalm 1:1 to show how "the higher wisdom of God" employs more brilliantly the same rhetorical principle to reveal that the soul's wisdom stems from "blessedness," not "manliness": "Beatus uir, qui non abiit in consilio impiorum." "Vergil" acknowledges the superior rhetoric of revelation, but when pushed to explain what is the end of his threefold progression, he can do no better than to affirm that Aeneas' achievement of wisdom means the attainment of philosophical prosperity. Not having Faith, he cannot realize that beyond philosophic attainment is the blessedness of the attainment of Charity, through Faith and Hope.

This "Fulgentian" perception of Vergil and his *Aeneid* gives due reverence to the power and inspiration of the poetry, but reserves its fullness of meaning for Christian understanding. It is a perception which reverberates through medieval literature, reaching the high plateau of the *Di-*

vine Comedy, the vision of a journey to the heavenly Jerusalem of the blessed, with Vergil as necessarily superseded guide. Before turning to specific instances, however, it seems best to face a nagging question: does such inspiration testify to Vergilian continuity or to its perversion? To face this question, I am afraid, is not to answer it. It might be possible for someone better equipped than I to argue that Fulgentius carries on one aspect of classical literature, a rhetorical extravagance foreign to the Ciceronian, but a legitimate part of that literature. Such matters are beyond anything but my pure conjecture, and I do not know if Fulgentius represents a continuation of one side of classical literature, or is simply a perversion of it. The problem in intellectual history is troubling, but I must be content to affirm what is indisputable: that the *Aeneid* had a continuous history of vital life, not only in the echoes of verses translated from it, but in functional inspiration; that, like the Latin language itself, it remained at the heart of the matter whether as perversion or transformation.

With this problem tabled, it is possible to begin tracing a partial itinerary of Aeneas' journey on the vehicle of "Fulgentian" interpretation through some major medieval poetry, exclusive of the *Divine Comedy*, where Vergil himself appears as persona. We begin early in the Middle Ages with *Beowulf* in the New Albion, Britain, where, we are told (in *Gawain and the Green Knight*), the noble Trojan, Brutus, found the home to which he gave his name:

> Sithen the sege and the assaut watz sesed at Troye ...
> & fer ouer the French flod Felix Brutus
> On mony bonkkes ful brode Bretayn he settez,
>
>   with wynne.

Although the influence of the *Aeneid* on the phrasing of several passages in *Beowulf* has long been recognized, it was John Gardner, with creative perception, who first posited that, "In *Beowulf*, the basic Fulgentian scheme of the *Aeneid* [the tripartite journey] appears intact, with the important exception that the ending of *Beowulf* is tragic."[4] Although at first glance the exception he points to seems to be not merely important but critical to the acceptance of the Fulgentian scheme as inspiration for *Beowulf*, yet on reflection the difference in endings appears to be implicit in the scheme; that is, the journey of man's day has two, and only two, directions: one that leads to the heavenly Jerusalem, the other to the diabolical Babylon. Thus implicit in the *itinerarium mentis ad deum* is its opposite, the *itinerarium mentis ad diabolum*. Comedy and tragedy, in a classical definition, are basically distinguished by their directions to an end: in comedy man rises; in tragedy he falls. They are the balanced contraries of man's function and purpose in the world. If Aeneas' rise is seen in Christian commentary as an emblem of the journey to blessedness, then the fall of Beowulf may be seen as an emblem of the necessary doom of the pagan hero. In other words, Aeneas may stand for, emblemize, the voyager to Jerusalem, as Vergil may emblemize an inspiration capable of enlightenment through Faith. Neither, however, can in themselves achieve salvation: Vergil must remain behind in Dante's journey, and Beowulf, the pagan hero, is the actuality of Aeneas, his reality, not his Christian emblem.[5]

Supporting the proposition that the Fulgentian scheme inspired the form of *Beowulf* is the suggestion that I have made elsewhere that Fulgentius may well have provided the *Beowulf* poet with the method he employed to solve the difficult problem of making his hero appear praiseworthy and his society worthy of credence in the very process of revealing that the social ideals of his pagan hero are wrong and can only lead to damnation. In the "Vergil" of Fulgentius' exposition, a persona who has celebrated a pagan hero without realizing his implicit revelation of Christian truth, the *Beowulf* poet might well have found the solution to his problem: he could create a fictive Germanic master poet as narrator-persona to celebrate a hero whose doom only the Christian author-persona and his audience could comprehend. It is for this reason that there are two unmistakably different voices in *Beowulf*; and this design, very possibly suggested to the poet by the Fulgentian *Aeneid,* provided him not only with purple passages to adorn his verse, but also with a basic sentential scheme and design for development: if Vergil's verses rang in the poet's ear, his mind was engaged with the Fulgentian "Vergil" who celebrated a journey which only the Christian could ultimately understand.

Our itinerary now hurdles some centuries and stops next at Paris in the twelfth century with Abelard, philosophical genius, born adversary of academic bureaucracy, celebrated by votaries of romance for his transcendent love for Heloise, his star-crossed fate lamented, his renunciation deplored. The Fulgentian *itinerarium mentis* of Aeneas reappears in Abelard's *Calamities,* which begins with a picture of himself, in a modernized version of Vergil's *arma,* setting out on his life's journey, wandering about "the provinces" seeking tournaments of disputations, a knight-errant of logic, his mind his armor. In addition to his reclothing of the Vergilian journey in the current fashion of chivalry, Abelard further complicated the Fulgentian journey by setting it in the mode of the consolation, made memorable by Boethius, and in the manner of the confession, immortalized by Augustine. Both consolation and confession are in themselves forms of the *itinerarium mentis ad deum*: the consolation reveals how a man may find his way out of calamity to the peace of God, and the confession shows how man finds direction by indirection, the truth through error. Thus Abelard offers consolation in the confession of his life as knight-errant of the mind, falling through pride and passion and achieving wisdom through his own Mercury, the amazing grace of his emasculation and the burning of his book, which leads to the founding for Heloise of the Paraclete, the earthly vision of the heavenly Jerusalem.

We come next in the same century to Chrétien in Troyes, a city whose name catches the Fulgentian ear and the allegorical eye. In his *Erec* Chrétien writes a chivalric tale set in the Arthurian never-never land: Erec, a knightly "Aeneas," through uxoriousness is made recreant, but through battle and rational love finds his way home. And this homecoming is symbolized by his coronation and enrobement in the Quadrivium, the knowledge of external reality (things), to which he could not have passed until he was master of the Trivium, the knowledge of himself (word); that is to say, he has attained the wisdom which enables him to govern himself and thus others. Such a design could certainly have been suggested by Fulgentius' *Exposition,* where "Vergil" explains that book 2 of his *Aeneid* allegorically expresses "infancy" in the figure of Cupid's triumph over Aeneas, "for the way of an infant is always to covet and desire," i.e., Aeneas has been cupidinous, cherishing Dido more than duty. Books 3 and 4 follow with allegorical representations of childhood and adolescence, a rejection of "control" which leads to the dominance of passion, until Mercury, "the god of the intellect," urges youth to abandon passion; book 5, in turn, reveals "a man of prudent maturity, exercising the body in deeds of valor," so that Aeneas, having done with youthful passion, may come to Apollo, "studious learning," and may take "counsel on the course of his future life," that is, for Fulgentius, the direction of the contrite heart to God. Armed now with the golden bough of learning—that learning which, for the Christian, reinforces revealed truth—Aeneas in books 7 and 8, having disciplined the will and made learning supreme, comes to wisdom. The Fulgentian journey provides the basic scheme of Erec's journey in which he recovers from passion, and through the right exercise of arms achieves the learning that leads to wisdom and the possibility of his becoming a true Christian king.

The "tragic" counterpart to Chrétien's "comic" *Erec* is his *Lancelot,* a tale of a knight of the highest achievement, shipwrecked on the shore of his Dido, Guinevere, a shipwreck from which Mercury does not save him, so that he becomes symbolically imprisoned, never to escape if the tragic implications of unrescued shipwreck are fulfilled, or to escape through love, a possibility which can exist only in the land of heart's desire where the romantic and bathetic imagination lives. Chrétien seems to have provided both endings, leaving his readers to decide between romantic illusion and sober Fulgentian-Vergilian truth.

In the thirteenth century, when Romanesque has become Gothic, the tragic counterpart to the comic journey reappears in the *Roman de la Rose*, with important innovations. What in the twelfth century is clothed as confessional and consolatory autobiography, or as a romance of knight-errantry, now becomes entirely allegorical, the dream vision of a first-person narrator. The symbolic becomes the essence, and the complication to our understanding is the dream itself and how it is to be interpreted. How easy it is to be misled by what is funny in the *Roman*, by what appears to be good-natured celebration of youthful passion, is testified to by the history of modern commentary on the poem, which tends to overlook the dire forebodings conveyed. Not to linger, however, it is sufficient to note the fact that the dream ends in a nightmare of the deflowering of the rose, an act of fornication described in blasphemous metaphor gone mad, a shipwreck of language. For the romantic triumph of young love in the language of Fulgentian commentary is indeed a "shipwreck"—a dream from which there is no escape except through Mercury, who has come to the author but not to his dreamer—at least unless he awakes.

Dante at the end of the century and the opening of the next in his *Vita Nuova* employs the journey theme in the Abelardian mode of consolatory confession, but in the manner of the *Roman de la Rose* as an *itinerarium mentis* told in a series of dreams and visions and couched in elaborate functional word play, ringing the changes on *vita nuova* and number symbolism generally. By indirection "Dante" finds direction; like Aeneas he casts aside his youthful passion, and, heedful of Mercury, enters into the "vita nuova" of maturity, prepared to meet his Apollo, "Vergil," and begin his journey to Beatrice.

We come finally to the latter half of the fourteenth century. This was an autumnal time, very like our own; a time of fruition and of premonition of change. Even the attempt to define it reveals an irreconcilable conflict between conservative and revolutionary attitudes: to the former it appears as the radiant twilight of the Middle Ages; to the latter it will appear as the bright dawn of the Renaissance and the modern world to come. Both will agree, however, that in England it was a time of high literary achievement. This achievement includes some reclothings of the journey motif in modes reflective of its age. Thus, in *Gawain and the Green*

Knight the chivalric mode of *Erec* reappears, but modified to reflect a consciousness of the unresolved, of dubious battle. Gawain is sorely tempted by Cupid, but unlike Erec he does not fall to his cupidinous arrows, but to another cupidity, the desire to maintain his courtly reputation and, in obedience to nature, to save his life—in doing which he accepts a false faith in the power of the magic of the girdle. The green knight's axe teaches him to know himself, and thenceforward Gawain wears the girdle to remind himself always of his fallibility and of his need never to give credence to anything but true faith.

In the New Troy Langland modified and elaborated the mode of the dream vision journey of the mind. In *Piers Plowman* the will of man, personified as the dreamer, Will, journeys "wide in the world," loses his way more than once, finds his Mercury, Reason, who introduces him to his Apollo, Piers Plowman, who is Peter, the apostolic representative of Christ. But in a poem reflective of its age Will must still learn through error and failure that words hide more than they reveal, that everything is dubious but Truth, which is most difficult to discover in a world of appearances, that it is beyond belief hard to attain to that wisdom which leads to blessedness. His *itinerarium* comes to no resolution; rather, the dream ends with Conscience in the face of the world's betrayal becoming a pilgrim again in search of Piers Plowman, and the poem ends with the dreamer, Will, awakening to Conscience's prayer for Grace sounding in his ears. Langland does not, I think, leave a counsel of despair, but the message that the Fulgentian-Vergilian journey to find God has no end on earth, but must continue, generation after generation, for each human, remorselessly, interminably, forever recapitulated, whether *in malo* or *in bono*. Jerusalem is not Rome and cannot be found except in the craving of man to find his home, which only through Grace and unrelenting effort he can do.

Finally, still in the New Troy, Chaucer remembering the fall of the ancient city, and Aeneas' journey not to Rome but to the city that will not fall, Jerusalem, in his *Troilus* carries off the spectacular *tour de force* of combining both the comic and the tragic journeys. His narrator is a figure of fun, full of pride in his rhetorical skill, a kind of comic "Vergil" who, with approving sympathy, celebrates the tragic journey of Troilus. In this journey Troilus is shipwrecked on the shore of his Dido, Criseyde, never to find his way home until it is too late and he is dead, an heroic suicide. Only then does he look back on "this litel spot of erthhe," to perceive too late that the world is "wrecched" and that all is "vanite," except for the journey to "the pleyn felicite that is in the hevene above." And only then, when it is too late to cast off passion, does his Mercury come to him to lead him where it is "sorted hym to dwelle." And only then does our comic "Vergil" rise to the height of his author's Christian understanding as he damns the love he has so much admired, makes his solemn warning to "yonge fresshe folkes," and concludes with his version of Dante's great prayer to the Trinity. In the *Troilus,* then, if I am right, there are two roads, two creative echoes of Fulgentius' Vergil and his *Aeneid,* a testament to its power to evoke a recreation of the conscience of a race, that conscience which in the late fourteenth century is full of the sound of dubious battle.

My sketch of the itinerary of Aeneas' journey as recreated by the genius of the Middle Ages is ended, and there remains either the fear that I have provided only a Dickensian headache, or the hope that it will be a reminder of places already visited, and will set free the store of memories to fill in the blanks and make of this itinerary a prolegomenon to a definitive understanding of the way in which the Latin classics were shaped, molded, and transformed in the forge of the great medieval poets.

Notes

1. "Fulgentius" in W. Smith's *Dictionary of Greek and Roman Biography and Mythology* (London, 1846).

2. This and subsequent translations are by Leslie G. Whitbread, *Fulgentius the Mythographer* (Columbus: Ohio State University Press, 1971).

3. Barbara Tuchman, *Bible and Sword* (New York: New York University Press, 1956), 17.

4. John Gardner, *Construction of Christian Poetry in Old English* (Carbondale: Southern Illinois University Press, 1975), 56.

5. Bernard F. Huppé, *The Hero in the Earthly City,* Medieval & Renaissance Texts & Studies, vol. 33 (Binghamton, NY, 1984).

Platonism in the Works of Pseudo-Dionysius

ANDREW L. J. JAMES

In the Middle Ages, which some have called "the Age of Faith," but which others—notably artists in the Italian Renaissance—preferred to look upon as a "Dark Age," the majority did not know how to read. Today, it is estimated that perhaps sixty million adult Americans cannot read a newspaper with comprehension, and now there is a laser disk with an estimated sixty-two *million* extant Greek words extending from the time of Homer to the time of Justinian the Great.[2] Of those words, most Americans—however literate—can read exactly none.

In western Europe a little Greek learning was kept alive, during the first Dark Age, in Ireland;[3] this learning came into the European mainstream via Irish missionaries. One Irishman of importance to our discussion is Johannes Scotus Erigena: John the Scot, born in Ireland. He is important, because he was one of the translators of Pseudo-Dionysius, thereby becoming one of the transmitters of Dionysian thought to France, and hence to the western world.

Franz H. Bäuml has said: "Obviously, the reception, the understanding of written texts, as of everything else, is conditioned by the expectations of the perceiver, which are formed by prior experience."[4] As it happened, in the fifth century, a Syrian monk wrote books in such learned Greek that his contemporaries believed him to be the person he claimed to be: St. Paul's convert from Mars Hill, in first-century Athens, mentioned in Acts 17:34. Many wanted to believe he was who he said he was, because what he said served their own purposes.

Those who received his writings with joy needed them to combat such iconoclasts as Eusebius the historian had been. Though questions arose about the genuineness of Dionysius' works, almost as soon as they appeared,[5] they laid the foundation for the Church's acceptance of images. It was not until 1895 that two Roman Catholic scholars conclusively proved that Dionysius the Areopagite and the man who wrote the pseudepigrapha attributed to Dionysius cannot have been the same man.[6]

The pseudepigrapha had been accepted almost as though they were Holy Scripture.[7] Pope St. Gregory the Great introduced those writings to the West,[8] and at the Lateran Synod of 649, Pope St. Martin fulsomely referred to them.[9] St. Maximus the Confessor spoke of "the God-revealer (Θεοφάντωρ) and great Areopagite, Saint Dionysius."[10]

His works actually represent a form of Christianized Proclus,[11] and were more seriously flawed than the Fathers were willing to admit.[12] The Fathers failed to condemn Dionysius' thinking—which introduces irrationality as mystically acceptable Christianity, and comes heavily tainted with Monophysitism—since some relished what he said, thinking he was someone from the first century who spoke approvingly of images, associating God Himself with artistic representation. He did this by continually referring to God as the transcendently Beautiful/Good, a Form which, necessarily, must be called "It," since, like all Forms, it is impersonal. To Dionysius, this Form was the Form of Forms.

Now there are those who would maintain that Plato did not deal with the Beautiful and Good in an extensive manner, and that therefore, any fully developed Platonic doctrine which chiefly concerns itself with the Beautiful/Good is hybrid Plato. But Plato's concepts grew, just as ours do, and in the *Kratylos* he reached the position (which he states as a question):

> May we say there is something which is beauty itself or good itself, and so also for each of the things that is?[13]

Then, having considered the above, he says:

> But if the knower lasts and what is to be known awaits, and if the beautiful and the good and each of these existences is, then I cannot think that they resemble a rushing and shifting . . . unhealthy and flowing, like leaky pots or people with catarrh. . . .[14]

That is, if there are Forms of all else, there may also be forms of the Beautiful and Good. And having said that, he reached a conclusion:

> But at any rate the appearances appear thus to me, that the idea of good is seen last and hardest among known things; but when it is seen we must infer that it is the cause of all that is right and fair to everything. . . .[15]

In Dionysian thought there is no such probing; rather the Forms of Good and Beauty not only exist, they are one with each other; indeed, they the Form of Forms, because the Beautiful/Good is God Himself/ Itself.

The difficulty with that thought is that it violates something in the Platonic doctrine of Forms, since paradigmatic forms must stay apart as definitional principles to be arrived at by reflection. As Rudolph Weingartner put it: "To understand these forms is to understand the permanent structures of the things we observe in the world of becoming."[16] Obviously, nothing physical is permanent, and, if Dionysius was a Christian who believed that God had become Man, and that man (Jesus) changed, why then, the Form of Forms must also be seen to be changing, unless we are to hold (as Monophysites do) that Jesus' fleshly appearance was merely an appearance.

Dionysius' Form of Forms does stay apart, because It lives on a plane of darkness where there is utterly nothing, saving Itself. It calls all things into being, all things turn towards It, in a form of erotic yearning, seeking union with It, through union with that which is beautiful in the physical world. In that way, the multiplication of beautiful things is explained, though the One Beautiful/Good, alone, is utterly beautiful, eternally good, and supersubstantially *The* Beautiful/Good.

Plato was unwilling to dismiss the notion that there might be such a thing as a Form for Mud, Hair, and Dirt.[17] That being so, he would have been hard put to deny the possibility of a Form of Good and Beauty. It seems natural that any concern for the Beautiful/Good should ultimately lead to an artistic expression, yet, for Plato, there was little to be said for imitative art, since he looked upon it as τέχνη "the manufacture of an object."

If, as Plato seemed to suppose, the world of the senses is only half-real, and man is born so circumstanced that he takes these shams for reality, then the "proper" thing for man to do is to put away these physical things. Hence, Plato admonishes us to abandon the senses and seek knowledge through the soul alone.[18]

It is at this point that Plato and Pseudo-Dionysius are closest—whatever the apparent contradiction of using artistic metaphors for Platonic thought—since Dionysius develops a philosophical position that the highest form of "knowing" is *not* to know, but to be "locked in the blind embraces with the Rays of Unapproachable Light" in which the soul experiences God (Whom Dionysius here describes as Light, in order to express a belief that all existent things have part of that Light), and comes to experience Θέωσις—which may perhaps best be translated into artificial English as "engodment." One comes to be like God, or godlike, in a state which Dionysius called Θεοειδής.

Plato names the meanest part of the soul (ἐπιθυμητικόν) "the seat of desire,"[19] and seems to damn desire as a dangerous redundancy; presumably, what is damnable about desire is that it arises from the senses. Yet Dionysius uses the senses, as John the Scot put it, as a *manductio*[20] — a manual guide — to lead the soul to the one Beautiful/Good.

Curiously, when Dionysius discusses the Beautiful/Good in the longest of his passages on It, (chapter 4, paragraph 7, of *On the Divine Names*)[21] he uses Plato's own pun from *Symposium* saying that the One Beautiful/Good "summons all things to fare unto itself (from whence it hath the name of 'fairness'). . . ."[22] Apparently, he saw no "incorrect" Platonism in his thinking.

Three other passages from Dionysius can be quoted to demonstrate an interweaving of Platonism as it developed by the Middle Platonists:

On the Celestial Hierarchy, 2.4:

It is not possible for our minds to reproduce without material, and contemplate the heavenly hierarchies other than by using material means. For the thinking man, phenomenal beauties become images of invisible beauty. Sensual fragrances are reflections of the non-material source of brilliance.[23]

On the Ecclesiastical Hierarchy, 4.3:

. . . in sensible images, if the painter looks without interruption at the archetypal form, neither distracted by any other visible thing nor splitting his attention toward anything else, then he will, so to speak, duplicate the persons painted and will show the true in the similitude, the archetype in the image, the one in the other, except for their different essences (or natures).[24]

And *The Mystical Theology,* 2.1:

Unto this darkness which is beyond Light we pray that we may come, and may attain unto vision through the loss of sight and knowledge, and that in ceasing thus to see or to know, we may learn to know that which is beyond all perception and understanding, for this emptying of our faculties is true sight and knowledge, and that we may offer Him that hymnody which we shall do by denying or removing all things that are — like as men who, carving a statue out of marble, remove all the impediments that hinder the clear perceptive [sic] of the latent image and by this mere removal display the hidden beauty . . . ascending upwards from particular to Universal conceptions we strip off all qualities in order that we may attain a naked knowledge of that Unknowing which in all existent things is enwrapped by all objects of knowledge, and that we may begin to see that super-essential Darkness which is hidden by all the light that is in existent things.[25]

Thus, Dionysius carries Plato's concept of rising from lesser to greater perception, by means, first, of material things—that is the love of beautiful bodies—to a love of beautiful ideas, to its ultimate conclusion and we strip off all qualities, all physical attachment, giving up even the use of words and figures of speech to understand what the mind cannot grasp, to become one with the One in that Darkness which is beyond the meretricious gaudiness of the light of this world.[26] And we know the One, by knowledge which is gained through Infinite Ignorance, when one is locked in the Blind Embrace of the One Beautiful/Good.

Orthodox Christian Fathers have taught, since Dionysius, that it is possible for holy artists to create images which reflect the nature of the One Beautiful/Good, as in a process of divine emanation or energy. And though Dionysius developed a doctrine which holds that God is similar to Himself and to nothing else, yet God also grants to those whom He will the grace to develop the greatest similitude with Him. If such a person were trained to look, spiritually, without interruption at the Archetype, he might reproduce It, as it were, in images.

Dionysius held that: "Visible images are imitations of the invisible, the one in the other, differing only in their different essences."[27] Thus, Dionysius raises τέχνη to the level of the sublime, where it participates, actively, in the changeless life of the Beautiful/Good. And while this is inconsistent with what Plato thought of art, it is born of his mind; this thinking is a linked sequence with Platonic thought, and becomes one with it, as a form-class.[28]

The form-class to which this Platonic thought belongs is epistomological: How do we know what we know? For Paul Rorem, examining Dionysius' thought, God's relationship with us is epistemological, in that:

> God "descends" and multiplies Himself to become accessible to a "divided" human mind, and the latter, by interpreting symbols, receives "the single true, pure and coherent knowledge."[29]

Was it not Proclus who said: "If God should wish to turn towards Himself He would have to make an image of Himself, lest, being boundless, He step out upon nothing, and plunge the world into darkness"?[30]

Hence, if Plato calls upon us to put off sensual learning, and learn only through the soul, any image which portrays for us the imageless God must be God-revealed and speak to us through dematerializing the physical world. This is precisely what Byzantine art came to do, accenting the mathematical proportions of dematerialized human and natural forms and the symbolic reference of iconographic signs.

Somehow this seems an appropriate artistic response to Platonism, since, for Plato, a work of art was valued in proportion to the amount of the theoretical, especially the mathematical, to be found in it.[31]

Perhaps the ultimate meeting place for the union of art and the form-class begun in Plato's intellectual anagogical progression towards higher and higher appreciation of reality is the Byzantine icon, in which He Who Is, the One, the Beautiful/Good becomes manifest to us and in turn becomes part of the same anagogical process, as part of the linked solution leading the mind upward towards that Plane of Darkness where Plato said the soul comes to rest in the presence of beauty, in communion and contemplation, and achieves immortality, where Dionysius the Areopagite claims the light of matter vanishes, and God is all in all.

Notes

1. Will and Ariel Durant use this phrase to designate the Middle Ages, in *The Story of Civilization*, vol. 4 (New York: Simon and Shuster, 1967).

2. The disk is appropriately called *Thesaurus Linguae Graecae;* "In Brief: Computers & Technology," *The Chronicle of Higher Education*, 18 June 1986, 30.

3. Sir Kenneth Clark, in his book *Civilisation* (New York: Harper and Row Publishers, 1969), 7 f., explains that a boat-load of scholars escaping Europe in 550 came to Ireland, and established such unlikely places as Skelling Michael, on the west coast, on a bluff seven hundred feet above the sea.

4. Franz H. Bauml, "Varieties and Consequences of Medieval Literacy and Illiteracy," *Speculum* 55, no. 2 (1980): 253.

5. Josef Pieper, *Scholasticism: Personalities and Problems of Medieval Philosophy* (New York: McGraw-Hill, 1964), 47. This questioning may have come about as a result of one glaring anachronism, in *On the Divine Names*, in which Dionysius refers to St. Ignatius of Antioch, who died at Rome in about 115 AD, as "Ignatius the divine" (C. E. Rolt, *The Divine Names and the Mystical Theology* [London: S. P. C. K., 1920; repr. 1940], 194). It is altogether unlikely that a first-century convert in Athens could have known a man several generations later in Antioch.

6. See David Baumgardt, *Great Western Mystics* (New York: Columbia University Press, 1961), 41; *The Oxford Dictionary of the Christian Church*, ed. F. L. Cross (London: Oxford University Press, 1958), 40 f.; and David Knowles, *The Evolution of Medieval Thought* (Baltimore: The Helicon Press, 1962), 56.

7. Joseph Pieper, quoting Hegel, *Sämtliche Werke*, ed. H. Glockner, 19:199; *Scholasticism*, 48.

8. "Un Saint, Grégoire le Grand, qui fin du sixième siècle ... annonce à l'Occident les écrits d'un Denys presenté par les Grecs comme le membre de l'Areopage converti par Saint Paul"; *Dionysiaca*, ed. by Philippe Chevallier et al. (Paris: Desclée de Brouwer & Cie, Editeurs, 1937), lxv.

9. "Cinquante ans plus tard, c'est un pape et un saint, Martin I, qui fonde solennellement l'autorité doctrinale de Denys et crée son magistère. A trois reprises, au synode du Latran en 649, Denys est à l'honneur, sur les lèvres du Pontife Roman." Ibid., lxvii. This synod established Pseudo-Dionysius' authority as "uncontested"; see *Oxford Dictionary of the Christian Church*, 403.

10. *Omnia Opera, Patrologia Graeca*, 90. col. 1260 (also 84).

11. Alfred E. Taylor, *Platonism and Its Influence* (New York: Cooper Square Publishers, Inc., 1963), 19; and also C. E. Rolt, "Introduction," *On the Divine Names* and *The Mystical Theology*, 1.

12. Jaroslav Pelikan says that ". . . most of the doctrines on account of which the Second Council of Constantinople anathematized Origen were far less dangerous to the tradition of catholic orthodoxy than was the Crypto-Origenism canonized in the works of Dionysius the Areopagite." "The Emergence of the Catholic Tradition, (100–600)," *The Christian Tradition, A History of the Development of Doctrine* (Chicago: The University of Chicago Press, 1971), 1:348.

13. *Kratylos* 439c-d.

14. Ibid.

15. Ibid.

16. Rudolph H. Weingartner, *The Unity of Platonic Dialogue* (Indianapolis: Bobbs-Merrill Co., Inc., 1973), 140 f. But he also asserts: "The fact, therefore—and it is not a matter of controversy—that Plato's conception of dialectic underwent important changes in the course of this long career creates a presumption that he modified his conception of the forms as well." Ibid. With references to Plato on art and the consistency of what he would have others believe, Richard Robinson holds that "On the face of it . . . there is an inconsistency between Plato's principles and his practice about images." *Plato's Earlier Dialectics*, 2nd ed. (Oxford: The Clarendon Press, 1966), 220. Plato spoke as though he would never use images, but he uses them all the time; even his word εἶδος, "Form" is, at final analysis, an image. Tertullian claimed εἶδος is the diminutive for εἴδωλον, from which we take the word "idol." "Early Latin Theology," *The Library of Christian Classics*, ed. S. L. Greenslade (Philadelphia: Westminster Press, 1956), 5:85.

17. *Parmenides* 130c, 135; though Socrates maintains that these are doubtful Forms, since they are " . . . just the things we see; it would surely be too absurd to suppose they have a form." But he confesses that he is sometimes troubled by doubt, whether ". . . what is true in one case may not be true in all."

18. *Kratylos* 432c; but also *Symposium* 209e, 212a has Socrates discussing one of the principle points of this paper, that a young man's concept of beauty, as it grows from awareness of the beauty of one body, to the beauty shared by all bodies, to awareness of the beauty of laws and customs, he comes to the beauty of knowledge, then, after he has participated in discourses in philosophy, he comes to a vision of the eternal, changeless, pure, and unqualifiedly beautiful, the source of the ultimate μάθημα, the last step in the soul's progress in Eros, to rest in the presence of this beauty, in communion and contemplation—and thus reaches "immortality."

19. *The Republic*, passim; actually, ἐπιθυμητικόν which means "coveting, lusting after a thing," comes from the verb ἐπιθυμέω: "to set one's heart upon," and thus participant in an incipient ὕβρις which is what is being condemned by Plato. See Liddell and Scott *An Intermediate Greek-English Lexicon*, 7th ed., (Oxford: The Clarendon Press, 1972), 292.

20. Johannes Scotus, "Expositiones super Ierarchiam Caelestem S. Dionysii," *Patrologia Latina* 192 (1865), 138c.

21. The following is the text of *The Divine Names*, chap. 4, paragraph 7, in full:

> This Good is described by the Sacred Writers as Beautiful and as Beauty, as Love or Beloved, and by all other Divine titles which befit Its beautifying and gracious fairness. Now there is a distinction between the titles "Beautiful" and "Beauty" applied to the all-embracing Cause. For we universally distinguish these two titles as meaning respectively the qualities shared and the objects which share therein. We give the name of "beautiful" to that which shares in the quality of beauty, and we give the name of "Beauty" to that common quality by which all beautiful things are beautiful. But the Super-Essential Beautiful is called "Beauty" because of that quality which It imparts to all things severally according to their nature, and because It is the Cause of the harmony and splendour in all things, flashing forth upon them all, like light, the beautifying communications of its originating ray; and because it summons all things to fare unto Itself (from whence It hath the name of "Fairness") and because It draws all things together in a state of mutual interpretation. And It is called "Beautiful" because It is All-Beautiful and more than Beautiful, and is eternally, unvaryingly, unchangeably Beautiful; incapable of birth or death or growth or decay; and not beautiful in one part and foul in another; or yet beautiful in one place and not in another (as if it were beautiful for some but not beautiful for others); nay, on the contrary, It is, in Itself and by Itself, uniquely and eternally beautiful, and from beforehand It contains in a transcendent manner the originating beauty of everything that is beautiful. For in the simple and supernatural nature belonging to the order of beautiful things, all beauty and all that is beautiful hath its unique and pre-existent Cause. From this Beautiful all things possess their existence, each kind being beautiful in its own manner, and the Beautiful causes the harmonies and sympathies and communities of all things. And by the Beautiful all things are united together and the Beautiful is the beginning of all things, as being the Creative Cause which moves the world and holds all things in existence by their yearning for their own Beauty. And It is the Goal of all things, and their Beloved, as being their Final Cause (for 'tis the desire of the Beautiful that brings them all into existence), and It is their Exemplar from which they derive their definite limits; and hence the Beautiful is the same as the Good, inasmuch as all things, in all causation, desire the Beautiful and Good; nor is there anything in the world but hath a share in the Beautiful and Good, for Non-Existence is itself beautiful and good when, by the Negation of all Attributes it is ascribed Super-Essentially to God. This One Good and Beautiful is in Its oneness the Cause of all the many beautiful and good things. Hence comes the bare existence of all things and hence their unions, their differentiations, their identities, their differences, their similarities, their dissimilarities, their communions of opposite things, the unconfused distinctions of their interpenetrating elements; the providences of the Superiors, the interdependence of the Coordinates, the response of the Inferiors, the states of

permanence wherein all keep their own identity. And hence again the intercommunion of all things according to the power of each; their harmonies and sympathies (which do not merge them) and the coordinations of the whole universe; the mixture of elements therein and the indestructible lineament of things; the ceaseless succession of the recreative process in Minds and Souls and in Bodies; for all have rest and movement in That Which, above all rest and all movement, grounds each one in its own natural laws and moves each one to its own proper movement (Rolt [above, note 5]), 95-98.

22. *Symposium* 210-11, trans. B. Jowett, intro. Louise R. Loomis (New York: W. J. Black, 1942).
23. Quoted from Gerhart B. Ladner, "The Image Concept," *Dumbarton Oaks Papers*, 7 (Cambridge: Harvard University Press, 1957), 13.
24. Wladyslaw Tatarkiewicz, *History of Aesthetics*, ed. C. Barret, trans. R. M. Montgomery (The Hague: Mouton Publishers, 1970), 2:34.
25. Rolt, 194-96.
26. This is at least similar to what Plato called "immortality" in *Symposium* 209e-212a.
27. Tatarkiewicz, 34, quoting the disputed "Letter X."
28. George Kubler, *The Shape of Time* (New Haven: Yale University Press, 1960), 33 ff, discusses "form-class" as a linked solution to a given problem, each successive stage being an extension of the solution through time. Though it is not necessarily possible to retrace the stages back to the first solution; all subsequent addenda are part of the form-class, if they use matter from any previous solution.
29. Paul Rorem, *Biblical and Liturgical Symbols within Pseudo-Dionysian Synthesis* (Toronto: Pontifical Institute of Medieval Studies, 1984), 61. Rorem thus ignores the notion in *Mystical Theology* 2.1, that we put away all symbols, by the loss of sight and of knowledge.
30. Proclus Diadochus, *In Platonis Timaeum Commentaria*, ed. E. Diehl (Lipsiae: B. G. Teubner, 1903), the translation is my own. Plato, in *Kratylos* 432c, indicates there can be such a thing as a "correct image," εἰχόνος ὀρθότης, and in 435c he says a likeness is a better way of revealing something than a conventional symbol which does not resemble it. Which, though faint praise indeed, nevertheless grudgingly speaks of images with approval. In *Sophist* 240a he defines an εἴδωλον as "another one such as the true one and likened thereto." It seems probable that Proclus meant something of the same here.
31. "So bestimmt sich also der Wert einer künstlerischen Schöpfung, nicht anders als der Wert einer wissenschaftlichen Untersuchung, für Plato nach dem Mass theoretischer, und zwar besonders mathematischer Einsicht, die in ihr invertiert worden ist. . . ." Erwin Panofsky, *Idea, Ein Beitrag zur Begriffsgeschichte der alteren Kunsttheorie* (Berlin: Verlag Bruno Hessling, 1960), 3. However, in chapter 1, footnote 6, Panofsky notes that for Plato the concept εὕρεσις is not so much "eine Erfindung"—an "invention"—as it is a "eine Entdeckung ewiger und allgemeingültiger Prinzipien"—a "discovery" of eternal and universal principles.

Language: Vehicle of the Classical Heritage

HENRY AND RENÉE KAHANE

With the breakdown of the Roman Empire, Western linguistic culture changed radically. In all provinces from which the legions were called home, the use of Latin faded away. But in the areas in which the legions stayed beyond the fourth century, Latin continued as the dominant language together with, in a bilingual system, the regional vernacular. In such context Latin, through a stage of creolization, became a new language with its own structure. It integrated phonological and lexical features of the native language, usually subsumed as substratum influences. The entire early phase of the Romance languages, which lasted from, say, the fourth to the ninth century, was involved in this evolution: Proto-Romance was, depending on the area, Latino-Italic, Latino-Celtic, or Latino-Iberian.

But new states, above all the Carolingian Empire, developed on the ruins of the Imperium Romanum, and they were in need, as all organized societies are, of a linguistic standard for their worldly and their spiritual administrations. Latin, predominantly, filled the gap, and this revival of Latin to function as a standard became a mark of Western civilization. Through a chain of such revivals, which we call Renaissances and which cover about a millenium, that heritage was enriched, with each phase being centered on specific objectives and features of language.

(a) The *Carolingian Renaissance* organized the teaching of Latin. Grammatical categories and a grammatical system were established, and the sentence was given its dominant role. Above all, language took on its function as the distinctive feature of societal structure for high and low.

(b) The *Twelfth-Century Renaissance,* with its scholastic methods, gave attention to rhetoric with application to epistolography for official, legal, and business purposes. Lexicology developed with the abstraction of meaning from context. Translation from Greek and Arabic into Latin was a lively business, resting on the strictest literalness, *uerbum in uerbum.*

(c) In the *Italian Renaissance,* the life style of its glamorous protagonist, the Humanist, was tied to Latin; and *his* linguistic problems have remained those of Western society. His linguistic experience, with Latin *and* the vernacular, was that of bilingualism. His Latin was a revived classical Latin, which conferred elite status on him. The acquisition of classical Latin was an experience of synchrony, with the absorption of rules; and of diachrony, with the imitation of the models of ages past.

(d) The primarily *German Renaissance,* which reached from the latter part of the eighteenth to the early nineteenth century and is often subsumed under the heading of *Klassik und Romantik,* was dominated, in linguistic matters, by Wilhelm von Humboldt. Humboldt's classical training and erudition (his *Alterthumskunde*) was a fruitful soil for his linguistic thinking. The three basic concepts of Humboldt's linguistic thinking are fundamentally humanistic. (1) Language creates our world-view: each language, in its particular way, through its categories, semantic fields, syntactic models, transposes the world into thought. (2) Language is not ἔργον but ἐνέργεια, not static but dynamic; ἐνέργεια refers to man's creative ability, the cognitive process, the self-realization of the ego. (3) Language has an *innere Sprachform,* inner form, often explained as system, sometimes as the semantic feature of language.

Now, this extraordinary linguistic heritage, the Latin superstratum, accumulated over the centuries, a cherished possession and mark of the educated, was bound to have its impact on the vernacular with which it co-existed in some form of diglossia. The process of the integration of the prestige language into the vernacular, known as "nativization," displays, broadly speaking, two patterns, *overt* and *covert.*

"Overt" subsumes those borrowed features which the educated speaker, at least during their early presence in the target language, may relate to the source language. It refers above all to lexemes, and furthermore, to affixes and morpho-syntactical structures.

The lexical borrowings commonly correlate with the domains typical of the traditions of the superstratum culture, and therefore are well represented in its language. Rosenfeld (1974) offers a detailed description of the profuse Humanistic impact on the German language, with examples from the fifteenth and sixteenth centuries. The German vocabulary does not measure up to the Latin, and the Humanists' familiarity with Latin tempted them to blend Latin words into their vernacular. The terminologies of all fields involving intellect and education are permeated by Latinisms: religion and ethics; the sciences, medicine, and law; literature, the arts, and theatre; grammar and school.

In the school, for example, the predominance of Latin was so strong that the neologisms of that domain were Latinisms. Since the sixteenth century, the teacher of Latin is called *Professor,* the headmaster, *Rektor,* and the collective of teachers and students, *Fakultät.* The pupils' activities included *studieren, diktieren, memorieren, präparieren, definieren.* Incidentally, in these and hundreds of similar German Latinisms the infix *-ier-,* inserted between the root and the personal ending, renders, in typical Lingua Franca fashion, the Old French infinitive suffix *-ier.*

Humanistic German, beyond lexical borrowings, copied also morpho-syntactical features of Latin. The fifteenth-century translator Niklas von Wyle sought to create an elegant German prose style through a direct imitation of Latin constructions. The construction known as "accusatiuus cum infinitiuo" is a case in point: he renders Lat. *ille feminam dicebat animal esse,* meaning "he said a woman to be an animal," by *er sprach ain frowen sin ain tiere.*

Affixes are a third pattern of overt borrowing. They represent a feature commonly transmitted through a prestige language, and the Carolingian Renaissance offers a superb example. The key terms behind Charlemagne's achievement are essentially deverbatives with some such meaning as "creative," preceded by the prefix *re-* "back, again." Its very consistency marks this pattern of compounding as the hypernym, the common denominator, of the set of examples. Charlemagne's imperial bull of 803 reveals the strategy: it reads, on the reverse, *Renouatio Romani Imperii,* "renewal of the Roman Empire." The meaning of *re-* is elusive, somewhere on the continuum "return" / "blending of then and now" / "new beginning." Thus, von den Steinen (1965) understands it as "back," a new beginning realized through restoring the indelible values of the past; Ladner (1966) underlines the Carolingian fusion of past and present; Ohnsorge (1958) stresses the futuristic component and sees in the bull a hidden program, the upgrading of the Roman Empire through the Franks. The following is a roster of the pertinent lexemes: *renouatio / regeneratio / restitutio / reuocatio / reparatio.* The documentation of these key terms, which we owe to Alcuin, the mentor and spokesman of Charlemagne's reformatory work, circumscribes the heritage as a multi-faceted mission. The Church convened in 794, "to renew, *ad renouandum,* the status of the

Church." Among the King's obligations is that of *ecclesias renouare* "to restore churches." The war against the heathens was a *restitutio* of divine order. The secular ruler has to refurbish, *renouare*, those laws that have fallen into decay. As to his scholasic reform, Charles himself proudly mentions his endeavors "to restore, *reparare*, the forgotten training of letters." Alcuin translated the revival of literacy into language planning: he wants the classical heritage to be renewed, *renouari*, and the practice of Latin to be restored, *redintegrari*.

Renouatio, in short, evolved as a blending of tradition and emancipation, and it forecast the course by which Latinity was to be kept alive. It is the story of a profound impact on Western culture, all tied to the prefix *re-*.

"Covert," in contrast to this overwhelming infiltration of Latin, refers to such forms of its nativization which do not readily appear as foreign. The feature known as "calque" is typical in this respect. "Calque" denotes a foreignism nativized through literal translation, morpheme by morpheme. Concepts snappily expressed in Latin are transferred by copying their semantic constituents. Early German Humanism offers good examples of this mode of adaptation (Rosenfeld 434): *colloquium/mitredung / concordia/einherzigkeit / desperatio/misshoffnung*. Frequently, in a variation of this technique of disguised adoption, the Latinism is introduced in the form of a binomial, in which the foreign element is coupled with and interpreted by its native synonym (Rosenfeld 416): *rumors und geschrays / wane und oppinion / red und oracion*.

So far, we have described the Latin heritage as a process: Latin lexemes and Latin structural features being nativized in the Western languages. But what began as the massive impact of a prestigious superstratum ended up with a lasting and vital function in both the development and the typology of the target languages.

As to its role in the development of the Western languages, Latin fared like all prestige languages: the period of glamour is followed by one of decline, due to popular linguistic pressures, but the decline, which terminates the stage of diglossia, is largely ostensible: in reality, the new standard incorporates features of the former prestige language. All over the West (as pointed out by Auerbach [1965]) the linguistic standardization which evolved with the rise of the middle class turned into a compromise between Latin and the respective vernacular. This rapprochement was the great achievement of the Renaissance. It transformed the medieval elite into the modern educated European public. Hall (1974) formulated the conversion succinctly as "Humanism in the vernacular." Migliorini (1960), who analyzed the case of Italy, saw the function of the Latinisms as "raising the *volgare* to the dignity of Latin."

By stressing the role of Latin in the process of standardization, we considered it in relation to the pertinent native languages. But then, one may take Latin, the prestige language, and its impact as a monolithic and unified event. The shared experience welded Western civilization — independently of the varying patterns of genetic relationship — into a community of linguistic education and orientation which shares the style of writing, the abstract lexicon, and the ways of metaphorization. This linguistic bond has repeatedly been emphasized. Let us mention the SAE, *Standard Average European,* of Whorf (1941), centered on the Latin tradition in our language and culture complex; Weinrich's *Europäische Bildgemeinschaft,* the European metaphoric community (1976); and Munske's *Common European Humanism* and *European-Atlantic Sprachbund* (1982).

The commonness of abstract conceptualization is well evidenced by the lexicological model of doublets. Doublets are two different forms of the same morpheme: one is inherited and nativized according to the rules of phonological change, while the other is borrowed, preserving more or less its original shape. Paradoxically, the borrowed form — historically the later — tends to reflect the earlier stage. Thus Lat. *pensare* "to weigh" yields, with regular loss of Lat. *n* before *s,* synonymous Fr. *peser;* but the original form, with its nasal, reappears via Church Latin in Fr. *penser* "to think," It. *pensare,* Sp. *pensar,* Eng. *pensive.* And then, this difference of forms is correlated with a semantic difference. The borrowed forms, distinct from the "folksy" ones, represent a good deal of the "bookish" lexicon common to the Western world. Semantically, the "folksy" forms retain their concrete use, whereas the "bookish" forms have often turned into metaphors based on the literal meaning. "Thinking," in our example, is perceived as "weighing the pro against the contra." Doublets are particularly numerous in the Romance languages and in English. French, according to the recent monograph by Reiner (1980), displays about six thousand of them.

So far, then, we have tried to outline the role that the Latin heritage played, and is still playing, in our linguistic culture. But by inheriting Latin, we inherited "for free," that is, without being aware of it, that other classical language, which meant to the Romans about the same that Latin means to us. We are speaking, of course, about, in Paul Friedlander's phrasing, "the Greek behind Latin." In short, the Latin embedded in our Western Languages functioned as the carrier of a substantial measure of Greek features. Indeed, Berschin (1980) describes the Latinity of the Middle Ages strictly from a Greek perspective, explicitly and significantly entitling his study *Griechisch-lateinisches Mittelalter.*

For six centuries, from the third BC to the third AD, the educated Roman was bilingual — able to speak, read, and write Greek in addition to Latin. The ideal Roman, as Toynbee (1973) notes, had to know Latin in order to participate in the world's government and Greek in order to participate in the world's cultural life. Greek was a status symbol. The Greek tradition was stable among the aristocracy and the upper bourgeoisie, not only in Rome but also in the provinces, particularly in Gaul. Greek remained, furthermore, the base language of professions such as medicine, philosophy and rhetoric, and the language of the nascent Christian religion. With the expansion of Latin in the papal chancellery, Greek began to lose ground; by the end of the fourth century, the Christians rejected Greek as a symbol of pagan tradition. The powerful superstratum of the Germanic invasions had a devastating effect on the survival of Greek. The Greek instruction of the young broke down in the provinces. By the end of the sixth century, Greek, as a living prestige language, was gone, even in Italy.

But just as, a millenium later, the standardization of the Western languages resulted from a blending of the vernaculars and the Latin heritage, so in the final stages of the ancient world the literary-colloquial level, the literary standard resulted from a blending of Vulgar Latin and the Greek heritage. The Latin Bible translation, e.g., rested on a high degree of Hellenization. Bonfante (1960) considers Italian "a synthesis of Greek and Latin"; Bartoli (1925) evokes a blending of *spirito greco* and *materia latina;* Coseriu (1971) sees in the Greek impact the central problem of so-called Vulgar Latin, i.e., the foundation of the Romance languages.

Our Greek heritage, linguistically speaking, is everywhere behind the Latin word. The great Greek gift was their ability to grasp abstract concepts and to name them through the metaphorization of concrete processes. Their linguistic genius is still a living heritage. If we take, as an illustration, the field of "literary judgement" (analyzed by Van Hook [1905]), the metaphorization went clearly, in a chain of translations, *from* Greek *through* Latin *into* the modern languages. A small sample, with English representing the modern languages, will provide an idea of that extraordinary tradition. The stimuli for metaphorization rest in the everyday experience of man: in nature, the human body, social status, and arts and crafts: Gr. καθαρός / Lat. *pūrus* / Eng. *clear;* Gr. ἀνθηρός / Lat. *flōridus* / Eng. *flowery;* Gr. ξηρός / Lat. *āridus* or *siccus* / Eng. *dry;* Gr. δημώδης / Lat. *uulgāris* / Eng. *folksy;* Gr. πτωχός / Lat. *inops* / Eng. *poor;* Gr. λεῖος / Lat. *lēuis* / Eng. *smooth.*

Looking back, then, the classical heritage, here seen as linguistic heritage, came to us as an incisive feature of medieval civilization: medieval Latinity. Its foundation rested in the Carolingian revival and grew through the succession of the Renaissances. At the dawn of the modern age, with the recession of the diglossia and with language in the hands of the Humanists, the Greco-Latin heritage became a vital feature in the evolution of the Western standards. In sociolinguistic terms, the level of literacy, first represented by medieval Latinity, and, from the Renaissance on, by the literary standards based on the nativized Latinity, turned into a mark of our complex social structure. What in the diglossic system of the Middle Ages had been the prestige language became, with the sixteenth century, a linguistic subcode which we may label παιδεία, education, and which stands out against the *naturalness* of everyday speech. This model of our linguistic culture represents, we may assuredly state, the most incisive and the most lasting impact of our classical heritage.

References

We drew on five of our own studies:

Kahane, Henry and Renée. 1979. "Decline and Survival of Western Prestige Languages." *Language* 55:183-94.
———. 1983a. "Humanistic Linguistics." *Journal of Aesthetic Education* 17:65-89. Report of a 1980 publication.
———. 1983b. "Paideia, A Linguistic Subcode." In *Language Change*, edited by I. Rauch and C. F. Carr. Bloomington, Ind. Report of a 1980 publication.
———. 1984. "Linguistic Aspects of Sociopolitical Keywords." *Language Problems and Language Planning* 8:143-60.
———, Henry. 1986. "A Typology of the Prestige Language." *Language* 62:495-508.

Auerbach, Erich. 1965. *Literary Language and its Public in Late Latin Antiquity and in the Middle Ages*. Translated by R. Mannheim. London.
Bartoli, Matteo. 1925. *Introduzione alla Neolinguistica*. Biblioteca dell' Archivum Romanicum, ser. 2, vol. 12. Genève.
Berschin, Walter. 1980. *Griechisch-lateinisches Mittelalter*. Bern.
Bonfante, Giuliano. 1960. "Les rapports linguistiques entre la Grèce et l'Italie." In *Hommage à Léon Herrmann*. Collection Latomus 44. Bruxelles-Berchem.
Coseriu, Eugenio. 1971. "Das Problem des griechischen Einflusses auf das Vulgärlatein." In *Sprache und Geschichte: Festschrift für Harri Meier*. München.
Friedlander, Paul. 1943-44. "The Greek behind Latin." *Classical Journal* 39:270-77.
Hall, Robert A., Jr. 1974. *External History of the Romance Languages*. New York.
Ladner, Gerhart. 1966. "Erneuerung." In *Reallexikon für Antike und Christentum*, edited by Th. Klauser. 6:240-75. Leipzig.
Migliorini, Bruno. 1960. *Storia della lingua italiana*. 3rd ed. Firenze.
Munske, Horst H. 1982. "Die Rolle des Lateins als Superstratum im Deutschen und in anderen germanischen Sprachen." In *Die Leistung der Strataforschung und der Kreolistik*, edited by Sture Ureland. Linguistische Arbeiten, 125. Tübingen.
Ohnsorge, Werner. 1958. "Renouatio Regni Francorum." In Ohnsorge, *Abendland und Byzanz*. Weimar.

Reiner, Erwin. 1980. *Die etymologischen Dubletten des Französischen.* Wein.
Rosenfeld, Hans-Friedrich. 1974. "Humanistische Strömungen (1350-1600)." In *Deutsche Wortgeschichte,* I, edited by F. Maurer and H. Rupp. Grundriss der germanischen Philologie, 17:1. Berlin.
Toynbee, Arnold. 1973. *Constantine Porphyrogenitus and his World.* London.
Van Hook, Larue. 1905. "The Metaphorical Terminology of Greek Rhetoric and Literary Criticism." Ph.D diss., University of Chicago.
von den Steinen, Wolfram. 1965. "Der Neubeginn." *Karl der Grosse: Lebenswerk und Nachleben,* edited by Braunfels et al. Düsseldorf, 1965-68, 2:9-27.
Weinrich, Harald. 1976. *Sprache in Texten.* Stuttgart.
Whorf, Benjamin. 1956. "The Relation of Habitual Thought and Behavior to Language." In *Language, Thought and Reality,* edited by John B. Carroll. Cambridge, Mass. Reprint of a 1941 study.

"Mirabilia urbis Romae"

DALE KINNEY

Among historians of medieval art the question of the "classics" is conventionally subsumed by the discussion of "renascences." Unlike ancient writing, ancient art did not have a continuous afterlife in the middle ages. Whereas some corpus of pre-Christian Latin literature was always studied in medieval schools as the prerequisite to learned reading and composition, ancient art served no such exemplary purpose. The visual arts were craft traditions passed on from one living practitioner to another, and mosaicists, enamel makers, ivory carvers, and silver- and goldsmiths had nothing mechanical to learn from marble sarcophagi and bronze statues. The art forms of antiquity and of the Christian middle ages were disjunctive; therefore, the periodic reappearances of ancient media (cast bronze), artistic genres or categories (equestrian statues, figured columns), or representational techniques (damp-fold drapery, chiaroscuro modelling, spatial "illusionism") are plausibly explained as acts of deliberate re-creation. Constellations of such acts appear as "revivals," "rebirths," "renascences": transitory predecessors of the definitive Renaissance that occurred in the Italian Quattrocento.[1] Deliberate acts imply motivation, and medieval renascences are generally perceived as programmatic, the products of agendas that were overtly cultural or political or (most frequently) both.[2]

Imbedded in these formulations is a definition of art-historical "classics" which is not easy to extract. Most art historians, I think, would concur in Curtius' judgement based on literature, that a concept of "classical" determined, as ours is, by distinctions of quality and age did not exist in the Middle Ages.[3] Yet the same art historians will assert the ability of medieval artists to recover "the essential principle of classical statuary"; to recreate a "classical spirit"; to achieve "intrinsic classicism."[4] These are modern phrases and they elicit qualities that undeniably are present to the modern eye. Certain medieval works of art do display an indisputable affective resemblance to extant Roman statues, sarcophagi, and works of minor art. Doubtful, however, is the perception and intention of that resemblance from a medieval point of view. Where there is no recognized body of "classics," can there be a recognition of "classical" qualities and ideals?[5]

"Classical" is an abstraction based on impressions gleaned from thousands of ancient objects most of which were recovered after 1400 CE. The corpus of ancient works of art available before then was neither large nor representative. It was created by unrecorded processes of natural attrition and systematic elimination. Wall painting, by virtue of its materials the least durable of the major art forms, had a negligible rate of survival; and while much has been written about the influence of Roman illusionism on medieval painting, one can scarcely name a single Roman mural which medieval or Byzantine artists could have seen. Bronze was melted down, and marble statues were smashed on principle or ground up for lime dust. The only category of sculpture which survived in large numbers was sarcophagi, and it was largely from sarcophagi that classical art began to be recreated in the Italian Renaissance.[6]

Enormous quantities of statuary must have been destroyed in the early Middle Ages by Christians acting in the belief that three-dimensional sculpture was blasphemous at best, and at worst demonic. This history was transmitted synecdochically in the legend that the pagan statues of Rome were all mutilated by Pope Gregory I: "In order that the seeds of the old heresies should not multiply, he [Gregory] caused all the heads and limbs of the statues of the demons to be broken, so that from the crushed roots of heresy, the palm of Christian truth might more fully manifest itself."[7] Buddensieg traced this legend to Martinus Polonus in the thirteenth century, and beyond that to two twelfth-century antecedents: the approving statements by John of Salisbury that the same pope burned the Palatine and Capitoline libraries, and a story in the "Mirabilia urbis Romae" that Pope Gregory I destroyed the colossus of Nero.[8] This account seems difficult to reconcile with Panofsky's apotheosis of John as the "greatest mediaeval champion" of humanism, and with the often repeated characterization of the "Mirabilia urbis Romae" as an early expression of a new, positive, humanistic attraction to the material remains of ancient Rome.[9]

The modern scholarly reconstruction of the medieval appreciation of ancient statuary rests largely on works of art: the objects in which the "classical spirit" seems to "breathe."[10] The Mirabilia urbis Romae (MuR) is a rare example of a different sort of testimony: a verbal reaction to antique artifacts. Until recently it was barely distinguished from a later work with a similar title, the "Narracio de mirabilibus urbis Romae" by Magister Gregorius, but this has been remedied lately, notably by Master Gregory's translator John Osborne.[11] A comparative analysis of the descriptions of ancient statues in these two texts should illuminate the terms on which medieval spectators approached and comprehended the relicts of classical art.

"Mirabilia urbis Romae" is the editorial title of what might best be called a sacro-historical topography. The original untitled composition is generally ascribed to Benedict, Canon of St. Peter's Basilica, who also wrote a papal *ordo* for Cardinal Guido di Città di Castello between 1140 and 1143. Regardless of authorship, the MuR is dated by internal evidence to just the same years.[12] It has three parts: chapters 1-10, an enumeration of ancient public structures according to type (gates, bridges, *thermae*, etc.); chapters 11-18, tales pertaining to important landmarks; chapters 19-31, an enumeration of ancient buildings in topographical order.[13] The author claims a straightforward purpose for his work:

> There were these and many other temples, and palaces of emperors, consuls, senators, and prefects of the time of the pagans in this city of Rome . . . We have taken care to commit to writing, as best we could, for the memory of future generations how great was the beauty of their gold and silver, bronze and ivory and precious stones.[14]

Panofsky, for one, seems to have taken this at face value.[15] Other scholars have detected a subtext which makes the MuR a political polemic.[16] Another view is that it was written for pilgrims, as a guidebook.[17]

Whatever its intention, the text has a clearly perceptible pattern of exposition.[18] The last two sections continually demonstrate the connection between past and present Rome:

> (chap. 28) On the Esquiline Hill was a temple of Marius, which now is called "Cimbrum" because he conquered the Cimbri. In the palace of Licinius a temple of Honor and Diana. Where S. Maria Maggiore is, was a temple of Cybele. Where S. Pietro in Vincoli is, was a temple of Venus. At S. Maria in Fonte a temple of Faunus . . . .[19]

The connection of past and present was necessarily of pagan and Christian. Repeatedly their succession is shown to be providential, or portentously revealed. This seems to be the point of the stories told in chapters 11, 12, 16, and 18, and these chapters establish the perspective from which to understand the lists of topographical coincidences that follow. One of the stories is constructed around a famous statue group, the Horse Tamers of the Quirinal Hill (figs. 1-3):

> The Marble Horses; to what purpose they were made nude, and the men nude, and what they are counting... In the time of the Emperor Tiberius there came to Rome two young philosophers, Praxiteles and Phidias. The Emperor, seeing them to be of great wisdom, kept them dear in his palace.

The philosophers claim that they can tell the emperor what he thinks when they are not with him, and when they succeed in this feat he makes them a monument:

> ... naked horses that stamp the earth, that is the powerful princes of the secular realm, who rule over the men of this world. A most powerful king will come who will climb upon the horses, that is on the power of the princes of this world... They who stand semi-naked next to the horses, with arms raised and fingers bent, are counting those which were to be. And just as they are nude, so all worldly knowledge is naked and open to their minds (*nuda et aperta est mentibus eorum*).[20]

The colossal marble horsemen stood (as they still stand) in the area of the Baths of Constantine, on bases with the false late antique inscriptions OPVS FIDIAE and OPVS PRAXITELIS[21] (fig. 3). The latter apparently provided the medieval interpreter's point of departure. He did not know that Phidias and Praxiteles were sculptors; this would be rediscovered by Petrarch two centuries later.[22] He probably did know a medieval legend that they were magicians.[23] With magicians transformed to philosophers, an allegorical interpretation of the statues' most conspicuous features (nudity and pose) yielded a perfectly coherent *lectio christiana* culminating, as Panofsky observed, in a paraphrase of the Epistle to the Hebrews.[24]

The author of this interpretation appears to have had no acquaintance with the classics, much less a perception of "classical." Yet among the acknowledged sources of the MuR the only one cited by name is Ovid's *Fasti*, which is elaborately credited three times: "sicut dicit Ouidius in libro Faustorum [!]," "sicut repperitur in marthi[ro]logio Ouidii de Faustis," "sicut dicit Ouidius in Fastis."[25] Though in one case the allusion is too vague to be traceable and in another it is inaccurate, other unacknowledged parallels confirm that the twelfth-century author did read the classical poem.[26] Its ostensible use to him was as a source of factual information, but in that capacity the *Fasti* would serve poorly, and most

Fig. 1. Horse Tamer, "Opus Phidiae." Rome, Piazza del Quirinale (photo: Deutsches Archäologisches Institut, Rome, Neg. 75.594).

Fig. 2. Horse Tamer, "Opus Praxitelis." Rome, Piazza del Quirinale (photo: Deutsches Archäologisches Institut, Rome, Neg. 75.589).

Fig. 3. Horse Tamers, c. 1565. E. Du Pérac, *Disegni de le ruine di Roma e come anticamente erono,* fol. 37r (from facsimile edition of 1963, with introduction by R. Wittkower; photo: Michael Pirrocco).

of the topographical material in the MuR can be traced to other, more suitable sources.²⁷ There is a larger correspondence between the ancient poem and the medieval guidebook, however, such that the one almost seems a response to the other. The *Fasti* concerns itself with the religious topography of the city of Rome; so does the MuR. A web of myth, history, and ritual is spun on the arbitrary frame of the calendar in the *Fasti*, of the regions in the MuR. In the *Fasti* mythological figures and events are treated historically, and historical figures mythologically; the same is true in the MuR. Classicists will find this comparison galling because the language of the MuR is so crude, and its composition so banal. But the nature of the fiction is very similar. The fictional character of the MuR is often counted against it, but it is futile to disparage as fantasy a work whose self-proclaimed literary model begins with an apparition of Janus.²⁸ It is we who are fantastic, in imagining that the MuR is history and expecting it to conform to history's conventions.

The MuR is very selective in its attention to sculpture. The Marble Horsemen and the bronze "caballus Constantini" (equestrian Marcus Aurelius) are treated at length, but otherwise few images are mentioned, and none is analyzed.²⁹ The idol "which stood on the top of the Colosseum" is listed, but *pace* Buddensieg its destruction is not explicitly referred to, and there is no mention of Pope Gregory I.³⁰ It is Master Gregory who ascribes the demolition to his papal namesake, while other medieval sources credit the act to Pope Sylvester.³¹

Master Gregory was an Englishman who travelled to Rome about a century after the first edition of the MuR, carrying a good schoolman's baggage full of sentences from Lucan, Virgil, and Ovid which he enjoyed matching to the physical "wonders" of the city.³² His "Narracio" takes the form of a letter to friends at home, describing the marvels he encountered and not incidentally his success in identifying their historical origins and meaning. Master Gregory fits the model of "renascence" much better than the author of the MuR; in fact he fits Panofsky's model perfectly, for he does exactly what later humanists would do, only not consistently and not nearly as well.

Although his description of a marble Venus is almost a cliché, I repeat it here because it so nicely illustrates the contrast with the MuR. The object in question is thought by some to have been the Capitoline Venus (figs. 4-5), but the hypothesis is neither likely (the Capitoline Venus is known to have been excavated under Pope Clement X [1670-1676]) nor necessary. Written texts and drawings record several statues of the *pudica* type that were known to fourteenth-century antiquarians and fifteenth-century artists, and Master Gregory's statue should probably be sought among them.³³ Whatever he saw, he liked it very much:

Fig. 4. "Capitoline" Venus. Rome, Musei Capitolini, Inv. 409.

Fig. 5. "Capitoline" Venus. Rome, Musei Capitolini, Inv. 409.

This statue, dedicated by the Romans to Venus, stems from the myth which relates that in a rash competition she, along with Juno and Pallas, displayed herself naked to Paris. Contemplating her, the thoughtless judge said: "In our judgement Venus conquers both."

This image is made from Parian marble with such wonderful and intricate skill, that she seems more like a living creature than a statue; indeed she seems to blush in her nakedness, a reddish tinge coloring her face, and it appears to those who take a close look that blood flows in her snowy complexion. Because of this wonderful image, and perhaps some magic spell that I'm unaware of, I was drawn back three times to look at it despite the fact that it was two stades distant from my inn.[34]

Knowing Ovid, Master Gregory was able to endow the ancient statue with an appropriate—though false—literary content.[35] In Panofsky's formulation, he thereby reintegrated classical form and classical content, a feat which most of his contemporaries were unable or unwilling to accomplish.[36] He did this, however, without exhibiting any discernible perception of a category of classical art. To him the marble female was not a normative artistic achievement but a wonder, created with "inexplicable skill"; and in its unaccustomed naturalism it exerted a nameless power.[37] A viewer with a notion of classical art would have recognized the attraction as aesthetic, but Master Gregory, deliberately or not, gives the impression that his feeling had a more carnal stimulus. Nor does he seem to have recognized a principle in his easy matching of the statue with a myth. This transpires from his account of the marble horsemen, which follows immediately upon the Venus:

> Close by there are two marble horses of incredible size and skillful composition. It is said that they represent the first mathematicians, to whom horses were assigned because of the quickness of their intellects.[38]

When his memory did not produce a classical subject for the statues, Master Gregory readily abandoned humanistic integration for ahistorical speculation. He accepted the premise of the MuR, that the statues were gnomic portraits. To him, their "counting" gesture suggested that the heroes must have been mathematicians, and a suitable allegorization of the horses followed from that.

The question posed at the outset was whether, in the absence of a perceived body of classical art, there could be a recognition of classical qualities and ideals. My answer would be yes and no. "No" in the case of the MuR, not because of any intrinsic impossibility but because of the author's peculiar understanding of Roman antiquities: as oracular texts in which the record of Providence could be read by those who knew how, and as relics of a chosen moment in the city's millennial history. A qualified "yes" in the case of Master Gregory, who patently appreciated some qualities, like naturalism and the artistic dissemblance of materials, that came to be regarded as essential characteristics of classical art. But he could not name them, and naming, many would argue, is the central and indispensable act of recognition.

Notes

1. For western Europe, the definitive formulation is by Erwin Panofsky, *Renaissance and Renascences in Western Art* (1960; repr., London: Paladin, 1970), 42-113. A Byzantine analogue is the "Macedonian Renaissance" defined by Kurt Weitzmann: "The Character and Intellectual Origins of the Macedonian Renaissance" (1963), reprinted in *Studies in Classical and Byzantine Manuscript Illumination*, ed. Herbert L. Kessler (Chicago and London: University of Chicago Press, 1971), 176-223. "Illusionism" as an index of revival is effectively discussed by Ernst Kitzinger, *Byzantine Art in the Making* (Cambridge, MA: Harvard University Press, 1977).

2. Panofsky, 42-113; Roberto Weiss, *The Renaissance Discovery of Classical Antiquity* (New York: Humanities Press, 1969), 1-15; Michael Greenhalgh, *The Classical Tradition in Art* (London: Duckworth, 1978), 19-33.

3. Ernst Robert Curtius, *European Literature and the Latin Middle Ages*, trans. Willard R. Trask (1953; repr., Princeton: Princeton University Press, 1973), 49.

4. Panofsky, 60, 62; Greenhalgh, 29.

5. For a discussion of the same question in different terms see Nora Nercessian, "Renaissance, residues, and other remains," *Res* 5 (1983): 23-29. A demonstration that the ability to conceptualize abstract "classical" qualities distinguished the Italian Quattrocento is made by P. Bober in Phyllis Pray Bober and Ruth Rubinstein, *Renaissance Artists & Antique Sculpture* (London: Harvey Miller Publishers and Oxford University Press, 1986), 31-40.

6. Bober and Rubinstein, 31.

7. Martinus Polonus (d. 1278), translated by Tilmann Buddensieg, "Gregory the Great, the Destroyer of Pagan Idols," *Journal of the Warburg and Courtauld Institutes* 28 (1965): 47.

8. Buddensieg, 46-47.

9. Panofsky, 68, 73; Robert L. Benson, "Political *Renovatio*: Two Models from Roman Antiquity," in *Renaissance and Renewal in the Twelfth Century*, ed. Robert L. Benson and Giles Constable with Carol D. Lanham (Cambridge, MA: Harvard University Press, 1982), 352-55; Herbert Bloch, "The New Fascination with Ancient Rome," in *Renaissance and Renewal*, 632.

10. Greenhalgh, 29.

11. *Master Gregorius. The Marvels of Rome*, trans. with introduction and commentary by John Osborne (Toronto: Pontifical Institute of Mediaeval Studies, 1987),

8-10; John Osborne, "Magister Gregorius and the 'Mirabilia' Tradition," in *Rome, Tradition, Innovation and Renewal,* ed. Clifford M. Brown et al., in press. See also Greenhalgh, 49-50; Nercessian, 29 ("a stunning difference").

12. "Mirabilia urbis Romae," ed. Roberto Valentini and Giuseppe Zucchetti, *Codice topografico della città di Roma* 3 (Fonti per la storia d'Italia [vol. 80]; Rome: Tipografia del Senato, 1946), 17-65. On the date and authorship: ibid., 5-6; Paul Fabre and Louis Duchesne, *Le Liber Censuum de l'Eglise romaine* (Paris: Ernest Thorin, 1910), 1: 3-4, 32-35. The attribution to Canon Benedict was questioned but not, in my opinion, disproved by Bernhard Schimmelpfennig, *Die Zeremonienbücher der römischen Kurie im Mittelalter* (Tübingen: M. Niemeyer, 1973), 6-15. Following Schimmelpfennig is Ingo Herklotz, "Der Campus lateranensis im Mittelalter," *Römisches Jahrbuch für Kunstgeschichte* 22 (1985): 25 n. 129.

13. The first section contains two Christian categories, "cimiteria" and "loca quae inueniuntur in passionibus sanctorum." The second section contains two anomalous chapters: an account of the offices of "judges" (chap. 13) and a description of columns (chap. 14) that seems to belong in section one.

14. MuR c. 32, ed. Valentini and Zucchetti, 65.

15. Panofsky, 73; cf. Benson (above, note 9), 353 ("the tendency of the *Mirabilia* is archaeological and historical").

16. Every possible stance, pro-papal, pro-imperial, and pro-senate, has been claimed. The most extended analyses favor a senatorial bias: Herklotz, 26-28; Richard Krautheimer, *Rome. Profile of a City, 312-1308* (Princeton: Princeton University Press, 1980), 198-99. Ernst Kitzinger calls the MuR "political archaeology" on behalf of Pope Innocent II: "The Arts as Aspects of a Renaissance: Rome and Italy," in *Renaissance and Renewal,* 648. According to Weiss, 6-7, "the *Mirabilia* . . . obviously breathes the consciousness of the city's imperial destiny. . . ." Valentini and Zucchetti, 7, suggest a more generalized political inspiration: "lo spirito della *renovatio* dei tempi di Ottone III è ancora vivo ed efficiente. Proprio allora Roma si ordinava a comune. . . ." Similarly Percy Ernst Schramm, *Kaiser, Könige und Päpste* (Stuttgart: Anton Hiersemann, 1969), 3:355.

17. Bloch (above, note 9), 632; Nercessian, 28.

18. The pattern has been observed and discussed by Max Manitius, *Geschichte der lateinischen Literatur des Mittelalters* (Munich: C. H. Beck, 1931), 3:245-46; Maurilio Adriani, "Paganesimo e cristianesimo nei *Mirabilia Urbis Romae,*" *Studi romani* 8 (1960): 535-47; Robert Brentano, *Rome before Avignon* (New York: Basic Books, Inc., 1974), 76-80; Nercessian, 28-29; Osborne, *Master Gregorius,* 9-10, and "Magister Gregorius and the 'Mirabilia' Tradition" (above, note 11).

19. MuR c. 28, ed. Valentini and Zucchetti, 60.

20. MuR c. 12, ed. Valentini and Zucchetti, 30-31.

21. Bober and Rubinstein, 159-61, no. 125. Note that in fig. 3 the draftsman has reversed the positions of the inscriptions.

22. Arnold Nesselrath, in *Da Pisanello alla nascita dei Musei Capitolini. L'Antico a Roma alla vigilia del Rinascimento* (Milan: Arnoldo Mondadori; Rome: De Luca, 1988), 197.

23. Phoebe A. Sherman (Sheftel), "The Dioscuri of Monte Cavallo" (M.A. thesis, Columbia University, 1967), 48. I am grateful to Dr. Sheftel for loaning me a copy of her thesis.

24. *Ad Hebraeos* 4.13: "omnia autem nuda et aperta sunt oculis eius, ad quem

[= Deum] nobis sermo." Erwin Panofsky, *Studies in Iconology* (1962; repr., New York: Harper and Row, 1972), 155-56 n. 93.

25. MuR cc. 21, 23, 24, ed. Valentini and Zucchetti (above, note 12) 47, 52, 56.

26. Claimed references: MuR c. 21: "[templa] ad quae confluebant Romanae uirgines cum uotis," too vague to be traced (Valentini and Zucchetti, 47 n. 2). MuR c. 23: "In summitate arcis . . . fuit templum Iouis et Monetae," cf. *Fasti* 6.73-74: "aurea possedit socio Capitolia templo / mater et, ut debet, cum Ioue summa tenet" and 6.183: "arce quoque in summa Iunoni templa Monetae." MuR c. 24: "templum Iani, qui praeuidet annum in principio et in fine," cf. *Fasti* 1.65-66 "Iani biceps, anni tacite labentis origo, / solus de superis qui tua terga uides." Unacknowledged parallels: MuR c. 23: "cathedra pontificum paganorum, ubi senatores posuerunt Iulium Caesarem in cathedra sexta die infra mensem martium," cf. *Fasti* 3.419-20 (the 6th of March): "Caesaris innumeris . . . / accessit titulis pontificalis honor." MuR 29: "In Auentino templum Mercurii aspiciens in circo," cf. *Fasti* 5.669: "templa tibi posuere patres spectantia Circum." MuR 29: "et templum Palladis," cf. *Fasti* 6.728: "coepit Auentina Pallas in arce coeli." MuR 29: "et fons Mercurii, ubi mercatores accipiebant responsa," cf. *Fasti* 5.673, 675 ff.: "est aqua Mercurii portae uicina Capenae . . . huc uenit incinctus tunica mercator et urna. . . ." MuR c. 31: "Foris portam Appiam templum Martis," cf. *Fasti* 6.191-92: ". . . Marti festa est, quem prospicit extra / appositum Tectae porta Capena uiae." The edition of the *Fasti* cited here is vol. 5 of the Loeb Classical Library *Ovid*, trans. Sir James George Frazer (Cambridge, MA: Harvard University Press; London: William Heinemann Ltd., 1976).

27. Valentini and Zucchetti, 9: ". . . antichi regionari, ignoti cataloghi topografici, antica letteratura agiografica, sermonari, compendi di storia romana, biografie nel *Liber Pontificalis*. . . ."

28. E.g., Greenhalgh, 48: "a typical medieval propensity to deal in fantasy rather than in fact." Contrast Nercessian (above, note 11), 28: "the actualization of the past;" Adriani (above, note 18), 536; Brentano, 79-80. Adriani focuses most clearly on the mythopoeic character of the MuR.

29. MuR c. 16: a mythical statue of Cybele mentioned also in c. 19; c. 21: gold peacocks, a bull, and four bronze horses once on the Mausoleum of Hadrian; c. 22: statues of gods in the Mausoleum of Augustus, and two bronze bulls once on the facade of the Pantheon; c. 24: a *simulacrum* of Mars, and a relief on the triumphal arch of Tiberius; c. 25: a *simulacrum* of the Sun that stood on the Colosseum; c. 28: *simulacra* of Saturn and Bacchus (actually river gods, now on the Capitoline Hill). The "caballus Constantini" is the subject of c. 15. I will discuss it in a separate study devoted to the critical fortune of this equestrian statue.

30. MuR c. 25, ed. Valentini and Zucchetti (above, note 12), 58.

31. Osborne, *Master Gregorius* (above, note 11), 23, 50-51; Nesselrath (above note 22), 218-21, no. 67.

32. Osborne, *Master Gregorius*, 1-15.

33. Osborne, *Master Gregorius*, 59, follows Rushforth who suggested the identification of Master Gregory's Venus with the Capitolina. Maria Grazia Tolomeo Speranza, in *Da Pisanello alla nascita*, 176, points out the weakness of the thesis and reproduces some fourteenth- and fifteenth-century witnesses of other statues. Of particular interest is a *pudica* seen in a private collection in Florence by Ben-

venuto Rambaldi da Imalo; see also Bober and Rubinstein, 59-60. A second-century Venus in the Vatican (Bober and Rubinstein, 61-62, no. 16) has a dedicatory inscription on its base, in accordance with the first sentence of Master Gregory's description.

34. Trans. Osborne, *Master Gregorius,* 26. For the Latin text see *Magister Gregorius (12ᵉ ou 13ᵉ siècle). Narracio de mirabilibus urbis Rome,* ed. R. B. C. Huygens (Leiden: E. J. Brill, 1970), 20.

35. The Ovidian reference is to the *Art of Love* (1.248); Osborne, *Master Gregorius,* 26, 59.

36. Panofsky, *Renaissance and Renascences,* 82-113.

37. Magister Gregorius, ed. Huygens, 20: "tam miro et inexplicabili perfecta est artificio." Cf. Panofsky, *Renaissance and Renascences,* 112.

38. Trans. Osborne, *Master Gregorius,* 26.

The Classic Bond of Friendship in Boccaccio's Tito and Gisippo (*Decameron* 10.8)

VICTORIA KIRKHAM

The long tale of Tito and Gisippo, Boccaccio's account of a "classical" friendship, strikes modern readers as one of his least successful *novelle*. But this story had powerful appeal in the Renaissance, and Boccaccio himself considered it a privileged component of the *Decameron,* since he put it antepenultimate in the anthology. Tito and Gisippo join company with Torello and Saladino, Gualtieri and Griselda, creating the trio of heroic couples whose virtues cap the day that crowns the book. The last characters to appear in the *Decameron* from ancient times, theirs is a story that unfolds during the Golden Age of Latin culture, a historical milieu and ethical climate that heralds the Christian era.

Set between Athens and Rome under the triumvirate of Octavian, the eighth story on Day Ten has as its theme the holy bond of friendship. A young Roman patrician, Tito Quinzio Fulvo, sent to Athens to study, stays with his father's best friend, Cremete, and becomes bosom friends with Cremete's son, Gisippo. Together the youths learn philosophy with Aristippo. After Cremete dies, Gisippo is affianced, but Tito falls passionately in love with the lady, Sofronia. Tito agonizes over the dilemma: if love is all-powerful, can friendship be stronger? To save Tito from his mortal lovesickness, Gisippo decides to give him his bride. The two devise a plan whereby on the wedding night, in the darkness of the chamber, Tito will consummate the marriage in place of the groom, Gisippo. This *ménage-à-trois* continues for some time, unbeknownst to anyone else — including Sofronia, until the death of Tito's father recalls him to Rome. Now the truth must be revealed. Sofronia and her family are furious, but Tito delivers an eloquent oration, successfully defending the ruse. He returns with Sofronia to Rome, where Gisippo, reduced to impoverished exile by the scandal, arrives for help. But when Tito, living in high estate, appears to snub Gisippo, the latter, in despair, allows himself

224 Friendship in Boccaccio

to be arrested for a murder he did not commit. As he is sentenced to death by crucifixion, Tito happens on the scene, this time recognizing miserable Gisippo, and to save him, claims that he, Tito, committed the crime. Meanwhile, the real murderer, moved by compassion for the two innocent friends, comes forward and confesses. Octavian summons and pardons all three, Tito marries his sister to Gisippo, and everyone lives happily ever after.

This tale enjoys a status unique in the *Decameron* on several scores. Second-longest of the stories (outdistanced only by the scholar's vengeance on the widow), its leading men are given leave for speaking to the most extraordinary lengths. Although Tedaldo (3.7) and Ghismonda (4.1) are almost as multiloquent in their apologies, Tito's defense of his secret marriage to Sofronia sets the record for the book's single longest speech. It is no mean distinction in a narrative territory populated by nearly 350 characters rarely reluctant to talk.[1]

Chronological setting further gives an unusual identity to the ninety-eighth *novella*. Among a handful of tales not set historically within one, or at most two, generations before the Black Death of 1348, it alone is entirely classical in period, location, and cast. As he launches Filomena into her narration of the events proper, Boccaccio is emphatically precise about where we are and when:

> You must know, then, that at the time when Octavianus Caesar (not yet styled Augustus) ruled the Roman Empire in the office called Triumvirate, there was in Rome a gentleman called Publius Quintius Fulvus, who, having a son of marvellous understanding, by name Titus Quintius Fulvus. . . .[2]

Since Octavian became a triumvir in 43 BC and sole ruler in 30 BC, our story takes place during the years between 43 BC and 30 BC.

Finally, I see Tito and Gisippo's case as singular because they have suffered such a painful fall from grace with the reading public. Their story was among the top three from the *Decameron* in Renaissance Europe (Sorieri 99). The others, Ghismonda and Tancredi, and Griselda and Gualtieri, are still subjects of lively interest. But ideal friendship seems not to have the enduring appeal of fornication with hints of incest or sado-masochistical marriage.

Of the modern commentators, some say the story is disadvantaged to begin with since it belongs to the Tenth Day, where the *Decameron*'s atmosphere becomes cold and artificial (Russo; Padoan 1964, 167–68), and the actors' behavior verges on the monstrous (Battaglia 510). Others object that an overdose of analysis, intellectual and psychological, spoils this tale (Scaglione 74; Getto 225); or, they regret that Boccaccio was not able to create a realistic situation here, the ultimate failure for a writer of fiction. Rather, being best at describing his own times, he could only make these remote, ancient characters come out "draped with philosophy like antique statuary" (Muscetta 293) in a story stale, forced, and "bogged down" in oratory (Cavallini 138). Referring to the "frigid solemnity" of its structure, Salvatore Battaglia (487–522) gives the *novella* a particularly thorough roasting. He finds it the least approachable in the entire *Decameron,* one whose protagonists operate more like con-men ("patenti bricconi") than gentlemen, their behavior verging on idiotic criminality.[3]

Boccaccio, though, not to speak of his Renaissance readers, must have thought otherwise. For him, Tito and Gisippo are models of magnanimity and generosity, motif of the *Decameron*'s final day. Their well-planned response to an unlucky circumstance resolves a life-threatening conflict, reconfirming what Cicero had called that "natural fraternity" where men are united by reason and speech (*De officiis* 1.16). Tito and Gisippo should be read, not as miscreants in a morally repugnant situation, but as exemplars of the most noble classical virtue, friendship. Filomena eulogizes its powers in her rhetorically elevated summation, powers comparable in secular terms to those of Christian *caritas:*

> A most sacred thing, then, is friendship and worthy not only of especial reverence, but to be commended with perpetual praise, as the most discreet mother of magnanimity and honor, the sister of gratitude and charity and the enemy of hatred and avarice, always, without waiting to be entreated, ready virtuously to do to others that which it would have done to itself.

Friends, she finally asserts, are more precious and more loyal than whomever we know in any other personal relationships, even immediate family. On this note the story ends:

> Let men, then, covet a multitude of kinsmen, troops of brethren and children galore and add, by dint of wealth, to the number of their servitors, considering not that every one of these, who and whatsoever he may be, is more fearful of every least danger of his own than careful to do away the great perils from father or brother or master, whereas we see a friend do altogether the contrary.[4]

Bizarre peripeties in Filomena's tale dramatize classical definitions of friendship to which her closing remarks allude. A first-century Roman exponent of the tradition on which Boccaccio capitalizes, author of a factual cache that was a medieval favorite, is Valerius Maximus. Discussing this virtue in typically axiomatic form, Valerius affirms that true friends prove themselves in adversity, not prosperity. The bond of friendship is stronger than consanguinity because we have the latter by destiny, but the former is voluntary. Various examples illustrate his *dicta*. First among the foreigners are the Pythagoreans Damon and Phintias. When Dionysius of Syracuse condemned one to death, the other came as surety until his friend had set his affairs in order and returned to be executed at the appointed time. The tyrant was so impressed that he asked to become a third member in their friendship (4.7.1).

Tito and Gisippo, literary descendants of Damon and Phintias, stalwartly withstand trials imposed by Fortune. For the dying Tito's sake Gisippo sacrifices his betrothed, his reputation, his inheritance, and his fatherland. For Gisippo, Tito offers himself to the pretorian crucifier, then gives the homeless, destitute Athenian his own sister as wife, and makes him partner in all his property. To Roman and Greek, who defied the marriage contracted by Gisippo's family, friendship is the ultimate allegiance. It must take precedence over more ordinary "relationships" among kith and kin, as Filomena had pointed out in her finale. So Gisippo would rather surrender his wife than his friend: "I should not, perhaps, be so free to do this, were wives as scarce and as hard to find as friends; however, as I can very easily find me another wife, but not another friend, I had rather . . . transfer her than lose you."[5]

Who else belongs to Tito and Gisippo's spiritual ancestry? We can pursue the genealogy, turning first to other works by Boccaccio himself. In his *Filocolo*, a learned romance written fifteen to twenty years before the *Decameron*, is to be found a set piece on the subject of friendship. Florio mourns the death of his dear companion, the knight Ascalion:

> Some seek to praise for supreme friendship that of Pylades and Orestes, others boast with wonder of that that between Theseus and Pirithous, and many argue that between Achilles and Patroclus was greater than any other; and the supreme poet Maro places that of Nisus and Euryalus above others in his song, and there are those who say that of Damon and Pythias had exceeded all others; but none of those who say this has known ours. Certainly none can be compared with that which you have had toward me.[6]

Closer to the *Decameron* is Boccaccio's letter of 1348 to the poet, Zanobi da Strada. The epistle opens with reverent praise for friendship: "Quam pium quam sanctum quam uenerabile sit amicitie numen, quis posset uerbis debitis explicare? Non ego" ("Who could describe with fitting words how pious, how holy, how venerable friendship is? Not I") (Boccaccio

1928). Words, needless to say, do not entirely fail the writer, though, who goes on to marshal some sterling examples: Damon and Phintias, Theseus and Pirithous, Nisus and Euryalus. What we have in both cases is a catalogue, names of the male couples most memorable in world history for their unswerving reciprocal devotion.

To this canon, whose members were all Greek by birth, must be added another duo of Roman origin. I refer to Publius Scipio Africanus and Gaius Laelius, celebrated subjects of Cicero's *De amicitia*. Cicero imagines that after Publius Scipio has died, Laelius, for the benefit of his two sons-in-law, recreates the picture of their friendship. Expressing the wish that its memory might always endure, he continues, "this thought is the more pleasing to me because in the whole range of history only three or four pairs of friends are mentioned; and I venture to hope that among such instances the friendship of Scipio and Laelius will be known to posterity."[7]

Although Laelius does not name them, Cicero would have had in mind a list identical to Boccaccio's, minus one couple whose fame rests on Virgil, the Trojans Euryalus and Nisus. When Boccaccio shaped the tale of Tito and Gisippo, his aim was to admit one more rare pair into the cycle he had inherited from antiquity. Going the ancients one better, though, he devises a "mixed" partnership, half Greek and half Roman, uniting "animo romano e senno ateniese" ("Roman spirit and Athenian wisdom") (10.8.55).

That his bid to enter them in friendship's hall of fame succeeded we know from the story's remarkable diffusion. Spurred as much by Filippo Beroaldo's Latin translation of the early 1490s as circulation of the Tuscan *Decameron* itself, Tito and Gisippo's popularity carried them throughout Europe to destinations ranging from Matteo Bandello to Ludovico Ariosto to British balladry to the plays of Hans Sachs (Sorieri). Boccaccio would have been pleased to discover that his mark had, for example, made its way into the *Faerie Queene*, where, in the Temple of Venus, Spenser visualizes an elect company of truest friends. Its members, Biblical as well as classical, number Hercules and Hylas, Jonathan and David, Theseus and Pirithous, Pylades and Orestes, Titus and Gesippus, Damon and Pythias: "all these and all that ever had been tyde / in bands of friendship, there did live forever" (4.10.27).

When read in light of the ancient literature on friendship, Tito and Gisippo reassume an identity that would have been taken for granted by their Renaissance interpretative community—not as hypocrites or con-men, but paragons of a virtue that is the cement of society. At the head of the tradition stands Aristotle, whom Boccaccio cites in several works on the three types of friendship (*Ethics* 8). His earliest treatment of the Aristotelian trinity, friendship for the sake of pleasure, for the sake of utility, and for the sake of virtue, occurs in a key passage of the *Filocolo*, Fiammetta's central ruling in the love debate (4.44). Speaking in medieval terms of "amore," not "amicizia" literally, she asserts, like Aristotle, the superiority of virtuous friendship over ties cultivated for pleasure or utility:

> Love takes three forms, and through these three all things are loved.... The first of these three is called honest love: this is the good and right and loyal love which ought to be embraced by all, as a matter of habit. This is what holds the supreme and original creator bound to his creatures, and they to him. Because of this the heavens, the world, realms, provinces, and cities remain in place. Because of this we deserve to become eternal possessors of the celestial realms. Without this, we lose whatever we have the potential to do well.[8]

For the Middle Ages it was Aristotle who had first seen in friendship the noble, binding force necessary for life and civic unity. He attributed to it a special kinship with just government, for both serve the common advantage. Perfect friendship, he acknowledged, is rare, since it can exist only between men of virtue, who are few, and it cannot ripen until they have eaten the proverbial peck of salt together.

Cicero's Laelius develops this line of reasoning when he holds, "nisi in bonis amicitiam esse non posse" ("friendship cannot exist except between good men") (5), for "nec sine uirtute amicitia esse ullo pacto potest" ("without virtue friendship cannot exist at all") (6). By his etymology, which plays in Fiammetta's pronouncement on "love," "amicitia" derives from "amor": "Amor enim, ex quo amicitia nominata est, princeps est ad beneuolentiam coniungendam" (8). A natural urge, it is best practiced by the wealthy and powerful, since they are the most self-sufficient, hence most given to generosity. Hypocrisy, flattery, or feigning are far from faithful friends, who mirror each other in a "rivalry of virtue" (9), and are always there when Fortune is fickle. Pure and faultless friendship subdues the passions, self-serving by definition, and promotes justice, creating the human bonds necessary for cohesion of household and state.

Scions of patrician households, closer than blood brothers, Tito and Gisippo, who vie to outdo each other in ascending tests of virtue, answer ideals in Cicero's *De amicitia*. Likewise they conform to specifications in the same philosopher's treatise on moral duty, *De officiis*. It is summoned to our attention by a signal at the beginning of Boccaccio's story (Branca 1976, 1532):

You must know, then, that at the time when Octavianus Caesar (not yet styled Augustus) ruled the Roman Empire in the office called Triumvirate, there was in Rome a gentleman called Publius Quintius Fulvus, who, having a son of marvellous understanding, by name Titus Quintius Fulvus, sent him to Athens to study philosophy and commended him as most he might to a nobleman there called Chremes, his very old friend.

Cicero opens the *De officiis* by addressing the person for whom he writes, his son: "Quanquam te, Marce fili, annum iam audientem Cratippum, idque Athenis, abundare oportet praeceptis institutisque philosophiae" ("My dear Marcus, you have now been studying a full year under Cratippus, and that too in Athens, and you should be fully equipped with the practical precepts and the principles of philosophy"). Like Marcus junior, who left Rome to learn with Cratippus, so the younger Tito is sent by his father to study in Athens under Aristippo.

In this treatise, following the Stoics, Cicero investigates three questions: Is an act morally right or wrong? Is it expedient? When the good and the expedient conflict, how do we chose? Now Boccaccio's *novella* raises precisely such concerns. To a reader like Battaglia, the supposed heroes are really scoundrels because they put the expedient above the good, abetting Tito's lust at the expense of Sofronia's dignity and Gisippo's honor. Still, does Tito's appetite really triumph, as Giuseppe Mazzotta has very recently argued (254–60), in a solution to the friends' dilemma that is at best darkly ambivalent, at worst, an act of violence and self-delusion?

With Cicero in mind, we can, I think, take a brighter view of the story's ambiguities. Deliberate to be sure, they are meant more to dazzle than to disturb. Reason, not passion—community, not selfishness—are the powers that win out in Boccaccio's plot. From the first word of its rubric, "Sofronia,"[9] the tale emphasizes rational endeavor. Her name (formed from the Greek adjective σωφρον-), means "soundness of mind," hence "wisdom" (Mazzotta 257; Deligiorgis 223). Tito and Gisippo, who both desire her, pursue wisdom twice over while students of philosophy in Athens, city of Minerva and wisdom.[10]

Steeped in this atmosphere, Tito does not, after all, succumb to the fatal threat of his *coup-de-foudre* for Sofronia. As he mentally struggles with the dilemma, intellect tells him what is right: "dà luogo alla ragione, raffrena il concupiscibile appetito, tempera i disideri non sani" ("Make way for reason, bridle your concupiscent appetite, temper your unwholesome desires" [translation mine]). Alone, however, he has not sufficient strength of will, and had not the selfless friend heroically come to his rescue, the outcome of their conflict would have been, if not Tito's suicide, at least adultery. As Cicero puts it, men united by ties of goodwill "will first of all subdue the passions," for "Friendship was given to us by nature as the handmaid of virtue, not as a comrade of vice; because virtue cannot attain her highest aims unattended, but only in union and fellowship with another."[11] In Boccaccio's story, amity assures probity; the heroic triumphs over the erotic. Tito's love can be accommodated to marriage, which, as the life-affirming "tie that binds," is the most basic unit of political cohesion and harmony.[12]

More than anything else, what makes the dominance of reason evident in this tale is the predominance of logical discourse, particularly Tito's *apologia*, a *tour-de-force* of epideictic oratory. Mario Baratto (73, 34–42) is quite right to pick out rhetoric as the story's real protagonist. Balm and protection for storms of the soul, it is the rational word that rules this tale. Gisippo must persuade Tito to accept Sofronia, then Tito must convert her family from fury to reason ("ramarichii, più da furia che da ragione incitati"), persuading them that friendship led to the right decision, one optimally expedient *and* good. Through painstaking elaboration of his medieval source tales,[13] Boccaccio recreates for the moderns a classical mythos of friendship, a Ciceronian ideal of style, and a Stoical philosophy of life.

I should like to add a note on nomenclature and dates in *Decameron* 10.8. Some of the characters' names, beginning with Sofronia's, have allusive value in accordance with the traditional norm, "Nomina sunt consequentia rerum." Gisippo's father, Cremete, has a congener in Chremes, one of the two father-friends from Terence's *Andria*, men who had in turn inherited the bond from their fathers before them. Aristippo, preceptor to Tito and Gisippo, has a name aristocratic in ring. Belonging to a real Greek philosopher of the fifth century BC, it is used once before in the *Decameron* for "un nobilissimo uomo," the Cypriot father of Cimone (5.1.3).[14] Tito's agnomen Quinzio attaches him, by a fictitious branch, to an illustrious Roman family, the "gens Quintia" (Branca 1976, 1532).

These allusions, clearly, enhance the story's classical flavor. Others, terms that conjure the ghost of Dante, function differently. Consider Octavian, whose role in this *novella*, the "octave" on its day, calls attention both to the number 8 and the future emperor's name. Why did Boccaccio set *Decameron* 10.8 specifically during the triumvirate of "Octavian Cesare"? The period, as Filomena's exordium qualifies it, is significant for what it precedes: "Nel tempo adunque che Ottavian Cesare, *non ancora chiamato Augusto* [*not yet styled Augustus*] . . . lo' mperio di Roma reggeva."

Octavian the triumvir became Octavian Augustus, that same emperor under whom our world reached the providentially ordained time for Christ's Incarnation. This is, in other words, not just a Roman setting. To be more precise, it is a pre-Christian setting. Octavian, the crucifixion to which Gisippo is sentenced, and his rescue by a man called Tito all point forward to the Christian era—Christ's Coming, His sacrifice on the cross, and the avenging of it by Emperor Titus.[15]

So, too, does the number 8 adumbrate His Coming as an emblem of baptism, resurrection, and life eternal (Hopper 77, 114; Meyer 140–41). Its salvational semantics find expression in the tremendously popular twelfth-century *Speculum humane saluationis,* where Advent, 8, and Octavian all symbolically converge. The eighth chapter of this historiated encyclopedia is illustrated by the Nativity. Three typologically parallel pictures accompany that scene: Pharoah's cup-bearer dreaming of the vine, Aaron's rod, and the Tiburtine Sibyl foretelling Christ's birth to the Roman Emperor Octavian (Robb 26).

Octavian, who ruled as Caesar Augustus when Christ was born, had in medieval memory a second connection with the Nativity: he had been vouchsafed a vision of the Child's Advent. The story, widely known in varying versions narrated by writers and painters alike, would have been familiar to Boccaccio from both the *Mirabilia urbis Rome* and *Legenda aurea.* According to the latter, when the Roman Senate wanted to deify the Emperor for having brought the world to peace, he wisely inquired of the Sibyl whether there would one day be born a man greater than he. In response, there came an amazing apparition of the Virgin, holding her infant Son, on a heavenly altar in the noonday sky. That miracle gave its name to the spot where Octavian stood, now the Church of Aracoeli.[16]

Tito and Gisippo, whose era overlaps with the Golden Age of Latin literature, Octavian's privileged rule, and the *pax Romana,* embody the historical culmination of pagan culture. Friends, orators, and Stoic philosophers, they come as close to being Christian as conceivably possible, by nation, epoch, and ethics. Emblems of Hellenic and Latin civilization at its finest moment, they are a fitting pair for the closing sequence in the *Decameron*'s magnificent finale.

Notes

1. The census estimate is from Bergin (1977). Battaglia notes that Tito's speech is longest (1965, 517). For a study of that speech in context with the talk of other *Decameron* characters, see Kirkham (1987). Successful speeches may even depend on silence, a case in point being Zima's ingenious monologue (Forni 1986).

2. I quote from the John Payne translation of the *Decameron* (revised by Charles S. Singleton [1982]). *Dec.* 10.8.5: "Nel tempo adunque che Ottavian Cesare, non ancora chiamato Augusto ma nello uficio chiamato triumvirato, lo 'mperio di Roma reggeva, fu in Roma un gentile uomo chiamato Publio Quinzio Fulvo; il quale avendo un suo figliuolo, Tito Quinzio Fulvo nominato, di maraviglioso ingegno, a imprender filosofia il mandò a Atene."

3. For the condemnation, which accompanies an excellent close study of this tale's relationship to its source tale in the *Disciplina clericalis*, see Battaglia 487 ff.

4. *Dec.* 10.8.111: "Santissima cosa adunque è l'amistà, e non solamente di singular reverenzia degna ma d'essere con perpetua laude commendata, sì come discretissima madre di magnificenzia e d'onestà, sorella di gratitudine e di carità, e d'odio e d'avarizia nemica, sempre, senza priego aspettar, pronta a quello in altrui virtuosamente operare che in sé vorebbe che fosse operato"; *Dec.* 10.8.119: "Disiderino adunque gli uomini la moltitudine de' consorti, le turbe de' fratelli e la gran quantità de' figliuoli e con gli lor denari il numero de' servidori s'acrescano; e non guardino, qualunque s'è l'un di questi, ogni menomo suo pericolo più temere che sollecitudine aver di tor via i grandi del padre o del fratello e del signore, dove tutto il contrario far si vede all'amico."

5. *Dec.* 10.8.38: "forse così liberal non sarei, se così rade o con quella difficultà le mogli si trovasser che si truovan gli amici: e per ciò, potend'io legerissimamente altra moglie trovare ma non altro amico, io voglio innanzi . . . transmutarla che perder te."

6. *Filoc.* 5.75.4: "Alcuni vogliono lodare per amicizia grandissima quella di Filade e d'Oreste, altri quella di Teseo e di Peritoo mirabilemente vantano, e molti quella d'Achille e di Patrocolo mostrano maggiore che altra; e Maro, sommo poeta, quella di Niso e di Eurialo cantando sopra l'altre pone, e tali sono che recitano quella di Damone e di Fizia avere tutte l'altre passate: ma niuno di quelli che questo dicono la nostra ha conosciuta."

7. *De amicitia* 4: "eo mihi magis est cordi, quod ex omnibus saeculis uix tria aut quattuor nominantur paria amicorum, quo in genere sperare uideor Scipionis et Laeli amicitiam notam posteritati fore."

8. *Filoc.* 4.44: "amore è di tre maniere, per le quali tre, tutte le cose sono amate. . . . La prima delle quali tre si chiama amore onesto: questo è il buono e il diritto e il leale amore, il quale da tutti abitualmente dee eser preso. Questo il sommo e primo creatore tiene lui alle sue creature congiunto, e loro a lui congiunge. Per questo i cieli, il mondo, i reami, le province e le città permangono in istato. Per questo meritiamo noi di divenire etterni possessori de' celestiali regni. Sanza questo è perduto ciò che noi abbiamo in potenza di ben fare."

9. The full rubric is unusually long, anticipating complexities of plot: "Sofronia, credendosi esser moglie di Gisippo, è moglie di Tito Quinzio Fulvo e con lui se ne va a Roma, dove Gisippo in povero stato arriva; e credendo da Tito esser disprezzato sé avere uno uomo ucciso, per morire, afferma; Tito, riconosciutolo, per iscamparlo dice sé averlo morto; il che colui che fatto l'avea vedendo se stesso manifesta; per la qual cosa da Ottaviano tutti sono liberati, e Tito dà a Gisippo la sorella per moglie e con lui comunica ogni suo bene."

10. Athens is a prominent symbol of wisdom in Boccaccio's epic, the *Teseida*, and returns more than once in later works with the same essential identity. In the *Decameron* itself (Concl. 21), Athens again crops up as learning center. Its culture is also remembered in *De casibus uirorum illustrium* 1.10: "Athene ciuitas,

phylosophorum poetarum et oratorum olim egregia altrix" ("the city of Athens, who once nourished philosophers, poets, and orators"). Cf. *De mulieribus claris* 6.7: "Ob tot comperta, prodiga deitatum largitrix, antiquitas eidem [=Athenis] sapientie numen attribuit" ("For all her discoveries the ancients, generous bestowers of divinity, attributed to Athens the numen of wisdom").

11. *De amicitia* 22: "Virtutum amicitia adiutrix a natura data est, non uitiorum comes, ut, quoniam solitaria non posset uirtus ad ea quae summa sunt peruenire, coniuncta et consociata cum altera perueniret."

12. Branca (1981, 105-6) sees 10.8 as an antiphrastically obscene situation; the adultery that could have been exploited for comic or tragic purposes is transformed by Boccaccio into a heroic example of virtue. Greene writes of marriage as a form of accommodation in the *Decameron*. Cavallini (127-45) agrees that the story expresses "an authentic ideal" for Boccaccio; and so does Cottino-Jones (175), who speaks of an "apotheosis of friendship." More on the relationship of reason to appetites in the *Decameron* can be found in Kirkham (1985).

13. See Battaglia (1965, 519). A complementary discussion of the story's antecedent in Alexander de Bernay can be found in Sorieri.

14. Mazzotta (1986, 255-57) takes Aristippo as an emblem of ethical hedonism, basing his argument on tradition in the Church Fathers. I prefer to see the story's hedonism as a danger surmounted by reason and ethical Stoicism. Athenian philosophy always seems to be positive in potential for Boccaccio.

15. The Dantesque undertexts here include, beyond *De Monarchia*, *Purg.* 7.4-6: "Anzi che a questo monte fosser volte / l'anime degne di salire a Dio, / fur l'ossa mie per Ottavian sepolte"; *Purg* 21, 82-84: "Nel tempo che 'l buon Tito, con l'aiuto / dell sommo rege, vendicò le fora / onde uscì 'l sangue per Giuda venduto."

16. Graf devotes an entire chapter to Octavian Augustus and his medieval mystique (1:308-31). The vision of Augustus receives prominent attention in *The Marvels of Rome*, where it heads the list of the city's monuments (2.1). In the *Golden Legend*, Jacobus da Varagine affirms (Dec. 25) that the Nativity was revealed to "every class of creatures, from the stones, which are at the bottom of the scale of creation, to the angels, who are at its summit." To Octavian the revelation came as follows: "Now on the day of the Nativity the Sibyl was alone with the emperor, when at high noon, she saw a golden ring appear around the sun. In the middle of the circle stood a Virgin, of wondrous beauty, holding a child upon her bosom. The Sibyl showed this wonder to Caesar; and a voice was heard which said: 'This woman is the Altar of Heaven (Ara Coeli)!' And the Sibyl said to him: 'This child will be greater than thou.' Thus the room where this miracle took place was consecrated to the Holy Virgin; and upon the site the church of Santa Maria in Ara Coeli stands today." The theme flourished in the visual arts from the thirteenth through sixteenth centuries (Kirschbaum 1:226-27). Among those who painted the scene was Rogier van der Weyden, who illustrates the belief that the Church of Aracoeli was built over Augustus' palace chamber, the spot where he had his vision (Knauer).

Bibliography

Baratto, Mario. 1970. *Realtà e stile nel Decameron*. Vicenza: Neri Pozza.
Battaglia, Salvatore. 1965. *La coscienza letteraria del medioevo*. Naples: Liguori.
Bergin, Thomas G. 1977. "An Introduction to Boccaccio." In Giovanni Boccac-

cio, *The Decameron*. Selected and translated by Mark Musa and Peter E. Bondanella. New York: Norton.

Boccaccio, Giovanni. 1928. *Opere latine minori*. Edited by Aldo Francesco Massèra. Bari: Laterza.

———. 1967a. *Filocolo*. Edited by A. E. Quaglio. In *Tutte le opere*, vol. 1. Milan: Mondadori.

———. 1967b. *De mulieribus claris*. Edited by Vittorio Zaccaria. In *Tutte le opere*, vol. 10. Milan: Mondadori.

———. 1972. *The Decameron*. Translated by G. H. McWilliam. Penguin.

———. 1976. *Decameron*. Edited with commentary by Vittore Branca. In *Tutte le opere*, vol. 4. Milan: Mondadori.

———. 1982. *The Decameron*. Translated by John Payne. Revised and with a commentary by Charles S. Singleton. 3 vols. Berkeley: Univ. of California.

———. 1983. *De casibus uirorum illustrium*. Edited by Pier Giorgio Ricci and Vittorio Zaccaria. In *Tutte le opere*, vol. 9. Milan: Mondadori.

———. 1985. *Filocolo*. Translated by Donald Cheney with Thomas Bergin. New York: Garland Publishing.

Branca, Vittore. 1981. *Boccaccio medievale*. 5th ed. rev. Florence: Sansoni.

Cavallini, Giorgio. 1980. *La decima giornata del "Decameron"*. Rome: Bulzoni.

Cicero. 1913. *De officiis*. Translated by Walter Miller. Loeb Series. Cambridge, Mass.: Harvard Univ.

———. 1923. *De amicitia*. In *De senectute, De amicitia, De divinatione*. Translated by William Armistead Falconer. Loeb Series. Cambridge, Mass.: Harvard Univ.

Cottino-Jones, Marga. 1982. *Order from Chaos. Social and Esthetic Harmonics in Boccaccio's Decameron*. Washington, D.C.: Univ. Press of America.

Deligiorgis, Stavros. 1975. *Narrative Intellection in the Decameron*. Iowa City: Univ. of Iowa.

Forni, Pier Massimo. 1986. "Zima sermocinante (*Decameron* III, 5)." *Giornale storico della letteratura italiana*, vol., 163, no. 521:63–74.

Getto, Giovanni. 1972. *Vita di forme e forme di vita nel Decameron*. Turin: Petrini.

Graf, Arturo. 1882. *Roma nella memoria e nelle immaginazioni del Medio Evo*. 2 vols. Turin: Ermanno Loescher.

Jacobus da Varagine. 1941. *The Golden Legend*. Translated by Granger Ryan and Helmut Ripperger. New York: Longmans, Green and Co.

Kirkham, Victoria. 1974. "Reckoning with Boccaccio's *Questioni d'amore*." *MLN*, vol. 89, no. 1:47–59.

———. 1985. "An Allegorically Tempered Decameron." *Italica*, vol. 62, no. 1:1–23.

———. 1987. "The Word, the Flesh, and the *Decameron*." *Romance Philology*, vol. 41, no. 2:127–49.

Kirschbaum, Engelbert, S. J., ed. 1968–76. *Lexikon der Christliche Ikonographie*. 8 vols. Rome: Herder.

Knauer, Elfrieda. 1970. "A CVBICVLO AVGVSTORVM. Bemerkungen zu Rogier van der Weydens Bladelin-Altar." *Zeitschrift für Kunstgeschichte*. vol. 33, no. 4:332–39.

Mazzotta, Giuseppe. 1986. *The World at Play in Boccaccio's Decameron*. Princeton: Princeton Univ. Press.

Meyer, Heinz. 1975. *Die Zahlenallegorese im Mittelalter. Methode und Gebrauch*. Munich: Wilhelm Fink.

Muscetta, Carlo. 1972. *Boccaccio.* Bari: Laterza.
Nichols, Francis Morgan, ed., trans. 1986. *The Marvels of Rome,* 2nd ed. Introduction by Eileen Gardener. New York: Italica Press.
Padoan, Giorgio. 1964. "Mondo aristocratico e mondo comunale nell'ideologia e nell'arte di Giovanni Boccaccio." *Studi sul Boccaccio,* vol. 2:81–216.
Robb, David M. 1973. *The Art of the Illuminated Manuscript.* Philadelphia: Art Alliance.
Russo, Vittorio. 1965. "Il senso del tragico nel *Decameron.*" *Filologia e letteratura,* vol. 2:29–83.
Scaglione, Aldo. 1963. Reprint. 1976. *Nature and Love in the Late Middle Ages.* Westport, Conn.: Greenwood Press.
Sorieri, Louis. 1937. *Boccaccio's Story of "Tito and Gisippo" in European Literature.* Comparative Literature Series. New York: Institute of French Studies.
Valerio Massimo. 1972. *Fatti e detti memorabili.* 2 vols. Milan: Rizzoli.

Antiquity, the Middle Ages, and the Renaissance as Seen Through the Eyes of an Argentinian Scholar

(The Buenos Aires Years of María Rosa Lida de Malkiel, 1910–62)

YAKOV MALKIEL

Counter to first appearances, classical studies do have roots or, at least, rootlets in certain cultural centers and *milieux* of Spanish America—from the Mexican and the Caribbean areas all the way to southcentral Chile and Argentina. However, these roots, in addition to being scattered, uneven, and subject to numerous discomforting political and economic fluctuations and upheavals, are also essentially heterogeneous, a circumstance that further weakens their chance of producing, in the end, clusters of beautiful blossoms.

In a conservative country, such as Colombia or Ecuador, the local tradition of classical research, to the extent that it jells in publications, is—as one would expect—more Latin- than Greek-oriented. Also, it goes back in a fairly straight line, all across the nineteenth century, to a late-colonial pattern of cultural preference and, even farther back, to a period of flowering of Humanistic concerns in Renaissance and post-Renaissance Spain, in such centers of learning as the universities of Salamanca and Alcalá— the not unworthy counterparts of Italy's Pavia and Padua. Modern-day studies of this sort, emanating from, say, Bogotá or Quito, have traditionally not at all been taken into account by the far more advanced classicists active in countries like Sweden, Germany, Italy, France, England, and the United States, to cite just a few examples.

In countries of intensive immigration, waves of newcomers, ever since the late nineteenth century, have contained a few younger individuals either fully trained in classics by distinguished European universities or, at least, displaying a strong disposition (starting with the right bent of intellectual curiosity) for a classically-colored program of training or, if need be, for self-education in humanities. Understandably, Chile thus established a strong link with German research centers, which set the tone for a while (cf. Federico Hanssen and Rodolfo Lenz); and in the so-called La Plata zone, which encompasses Uruguay and a big chunk of Argentina (including the province and the capital city of Buenos Aires), the influx of Italians, not a few of them from Genoa, endowed with such knowledge, such heritage, and such leanings produced a similar result. Everywhere, straight medieval studies were completely lacking; nor can one speak of serious Renaissance studies exceeding the bounds of preoccupation with the Golden Age of metropolitan Spanish literature and its colonial offshoots.

Argentina was a relative newcomer to this situation; neighbors sometimes enviously viewed her as a *nouveau riche;* whether one does or does not agree, by 1925 Buenos Aires was on its way to evolving into a major cultural center fit to compete with Madrid and Barcelona in sheer local and imported talent and in dynamism, if not in the holdings of its archives and libraries (except for material useful for local history). Gradually, the Faculty of Letters of the country's leading university could afford to establish a very few endowed chairs and to launch a well-equipped and progressively-managed "Instituto de Filología" (with "philology" still defined as, fundamentally, an ensemble of inquiries into Spanish language and literature, both metropolitan and overseas).

In the late twenties and early thirties, a number of gifted people — practically all of them men — started getting together, informally, at this focal point, in a few other comparably active centers and in offices of imaginative book and newspaper publishers. Contacts with potential sponsors and benefactors were also established. An elite of distinguished, widely-traveled, and, as a result, cosmopolitan local *lumbreras* ("luminaries") was joined by a trickle of faculty members from the nearby La Plata University, comfortably located, as we would say, "within commuting distance," much as some Berkeleyans and a handful of Stanfordites have made it a habit of coming together — preferably in San Francisco.

At that dramatic moment, in 1936, the Spanish Civil War exploded, bringing in its wake, over a period of three horror-laden years, waves not only of politicians, but also of writers, artists, actors, scientists, and, yes, scholars to the shores of Latin America, with Buenos Aires and Mexico City competing for supremacy in acts of hospitality. Immediately afterward came World War II, with other waves of displaced or persecuted persons asking for asylum — among them both celebrities and virtual unknowns. Included in their number were scholars who, in their home countries, had been beneficiaries of a broad humanistic training, such as Paul Bénichou. Other refugees could boast a high-level specialization in classics and historical linguistics — a description fitting the likable, well-established Torinese Benvenuto A. Terracini. A still distinctly young Juan (or Joan) Corominas arrived with credentials as a Romance philologist whose expertise bridged the domains of Castilian and Catalan. In sum, famous practitioners of humanities, whether aged or still fairly young, writers whose names the intellectuals among *porteños* (as the inhabitants of Buenos Aires have been traditionally called — from *puerto* "sea or river port") had previously gleaned only from books and journals, were now among them, often destitute, sometimes eagerly waiting for temporary appointments, and, in any event, invariably ready to engage in stimulating discussions. This was an intellectually lively, unexpectedly rewarding period.

Among the daily witnesses to this unprecedented fermentation was a group of three young, talented and promising siblings, born into a hardworking family of Jewish immigrants, from the Polish sector of Eastern Europe (to be exact, the father from the Russian, the mother from the Austrian zone), the Lidas: two brothers, already born in the Old World, and a younger sister, a native of the Argentine Republic. The older brother, Emilio, after successfully graduating from high school, opted for a medical career. After earning his doctorate, and specializing as a research pathologist, he worked twelve years as an assistant to the Nobel Prize-winning local expert Bernardo Alberto Houssay (1887–1971) and eventually settled down as a highly regarded, many-sided, and successful practitioner. Raimundo became a student of philosophy (with emphasis on esthetics), a refined and influential literary critic, an exceptionally well-informed literary historian, and a deft translator and polyglot to boot. His interests stretched from the seventeenth to the nineteenth centuries, and his favorite genre was the essay. Raimundo's academic itinerary was complicated enough, leading from the La Plata University via Mexico City's long-established Colegio de México to Ohio State and eventually to Harvard, where in the end he earned a coveted endowed chair in the Romance department. Not exactly blessed with physical robustness, he died of a heart attack, pathetically enough, a few days after reaching the retirement age, in 1978. To this day, he is fondly remembered by former students for his special skill in initiating talented neophytes into the art of textual analysis and the *métier* of meticulous, yet somehow light-winged, scholarly writing, be the text at issue in a sophisticated Baroque or an arcane modernist key. The daughter, six years younger than Emilio and only two years younger than Raimundo, was María Rosa.

Despite severely limited resources, the parents honestly tried to give their three children, who turned out to be model students at their respective schools, the expected musical education (through piano-playing) and a modicum of tutorial exposure to traditional Jewish learning, including some reading knowledge of Hebrew. Because of the absence of qualified mentors, the results turned out to be less than satisfactory. In later life María Rosa would bitterly reproach herself for her failure, at that early stage, to have acquired familiarity at first hand with Old Testament Hebrew; reading the Septuagint or the Vulgate, she finally understood, was no substitute. On the other hand, the model high school that María Rosa attended — an institution at which not a few university professors had been invited to teach certain classes — offered her many intellectual rewards, besides tokens of recognition for accomplishments and the chance to meet superior young women of entirely different family roots and ethnic strains. Her teachers showed the same diversity of backgrounds, and even of accents. She excelled in mathematics and in Latin, and learned impeccable Spanish, both literary and colloquial, which she obviously could not hear at home. Latin and Spanish, including the latter's earlier varieties, absorbed from self-immersion in medieval and Golden Age literature, became the objects of a real infatuation. Her precocious excitement about a dead language may be traced to the convergence of two forces: in a Romance country, Latin, in a way, represents the idealized version, the primeval form of the local vernacular; in addition, functionally, the intensive study of a highly respected dead language, such as Latin, involves a suitable substitute — subconscious, of course — for the atavistic craving for Hebrew in a Jewish family hypersensitive to such values. Riding the crest of this infatuation, María Rosa, as an autodidact, acquired the knowledge of classical Greek — not a required subject in a women's lyceum. As an adolescent, María Rosa, along with her best friend, meanwhile devoured certain masterpieces of Spanish literature excluded from the curriculum, such as *La Celestina,* a late-fifteenth-century play hardly recommended for children, which subsequently was to keep her busy for fifteen long years. With her brothers, María Rosa discovered the existence of second-hand bookstores, into which one could profitably sink some of the money the children were receiving from their parents for candy. This is how nineteenth-century and modern literature came to their attention. Raimundo's and María Rosa's responses to this rich store of challenges and temptations were different: he was the artistically more gifted of the two and the one more spontaneous in his responses to musical and poetic stimuli; she was more disciplined and methodic in her commitments, and less spoiled by premature applause.

With María Rosa's interests, from adolescence, so sharply profiled in the direction of classical antiquity, it was a foregone conclusion that she would major in Latin and Greek language and literature at the local

"Faculty of Philosophy and Letters"—the label under which humanities were conventionally and conveniently subsumed. This she actually did, and her academic record was so consistently excellent that, in the end, she received a university medal. From this widely-publicized episode some observers drew the inaccurate conclusion that she was a grade-conscious perfectionist hungry for recognition and immediate success. Actually, she was very shy and conspicuously free from vanity—but she was responsible (never a drifter), uncompromising about standards of performance, and loyal to her commitments.

The university curriculum was quite inflexible in those days, a situation which had its share of advantages. Since the classicists, among María Rosa's teachers, were for the most part nonentities, the fact that certain obligatory courses in psychology, logic, and Spanish philology happened to be taught by competent and stimulating professors, a few of whom had studied abroad or themselves had come from abroad and, as a result, knew about such novelties as symbolic logic or stylistic analysis of literary texts, was unquestionably beneficial. There were also extracurricular compensations: her closest friend, Francisca Chica Salas, was a talented poet and, through her inspired writing, acquainted her with certain creative and modernist aspects of literary work.

Upon graduating, María Rosa soon discovered that, despite the fanfares of commencement exercises, the doors failed to fly open for the daughter of immigrant parents. To be sure, she was allowed to teach some high school classes, but not in her favorite subjects. The unimaginative Classics Department, placed under pressure to entrust her with some rewarding research project, found nothing more exciting to offer her than routine translation jobs: she was to cast into Spanish some article or monograph by a foreign authority (say, Wilamowitz-Möllendorf); then her translation job would be filed and catalogued, remaining unpublished and practically inaccessible to others. She did perfect, in this fashion, her reading knowledge of scholarly German, English, and French prose (not to mention Italian), but little else was achieved, and frustration ensued.

A dramatic turning point, after this fairly dreary lustrum, came in the early and mid thirties when Amado Alonso, the dynamic director of the Spanish-culture-oriented "Instituto de Filología," also a brilliant organizer and talent scout, decided to break these doldrums. He wrote to his great teacher in Madrid, Ramón Menéndez Pidal, a man of exceptional far-sightedness and richly deserved influence, who, on the spur of the moment, invited in a flattering letter (preserved to this day in the Lida Archive) a barely twenty-three year old woman virtually unknown overseas to become a regular book reviewer for the newly-founded Madrid journal in classical studies, *Emerita* (named after a Roman city in Spain, *Mérida* at present), an offer which María Rosa promptly and cheerfully accepted, honoring her pledge until the outbreak of the Civil War in mid-1936. She specialized in assessing books (often technical) written in German, including O. Körner's *Die Sinnesempfindungen in Ilias und Odyssee*, K. Keyssner's *Gottesvorstellung und Lebensauffassung im griechischen Hymnus*, and even the opening volume of Walde-Hofmann's *Lateinisches etymologisches Wörterbuch* — as well as current volumes of standard-setting German-language journals; say, *Hermes* and *Glotta*. This service, which went beyond summarizing, she performed with increasing skill and finesse.

Next, Alonso's senior friend and close associate in several intellectual ventures, Pedro Henríquez Ureña, was just launching an attractive series of books — typographically tasteful, but also philologically exacting — masterpieces of all ages, of potential appeal to the sophisticated general reader steeped in the Spanish tradition of *belles lettres:* namely, the "Cien obras maestras . . .," i.e., world literature's one hundred indisputable masterpieces, the whole translated into enjoyable Spanish and provided with appropriate introductions and, where necessary, comments. María Rosa's generous share in this undertaking was to open many doors for her. The prefatory notes from her pen — to Plutarch's *Parallel Lives,* to the *Aeneid,* to Horace's *Odes* and *Epodes,* plus the same Augustan poet's *Satires* and *Epistles* — were designedly succinct; but her total involvement went much farther. Since not a few of the translations at issue stemmed from writers of distinctly earlier periods, inspired, to be sure, but untrained in rigorous textual criticism and unequipped with modern tools (the work on the Virgil texts, for example, had been carried out by Eduardo de Ochoa, a fairly obscure nineteenth-century figure), María Rosa assumed the additional responsibility for tacitly weeding out all sorts of errors and misunderstandings, and thus, in the process, learning the art of editorial discretion.

This was not all. Either Alonso or Henríquez Ureña, or both, acting in friendly conspiracy, established the much needed contact with the Argentine Academy of Letters (Academia Argentina de Letras), whose Bulletin was in the hands of editors casting about for excellent contributions, including essays on Greek and Latin mythology and literature phrased, to be sure, with amenity, but by writers endowed with the requisite technical knowledge. In this medium, María Rosa, after receiving the proper dosage of encouragement, began to publish some of the earliest samples of her independent research, for example, such pieces as "A Woman Confronts the Issue of Language: Some Opinions of Antiquity and of the

Renaissance" (1937). Other items, including two extended essays, mutually complementary, on Helen of Troy, made their appearance that same year, in comparably excellent Buenos Aires journals — one unabashedly skewed in the direction of broad-gauged scholarship (*Cursos y conferencias* . . .), the other purely literary and, on purpose, distanced from academia (*Sur*, the favorite outlet of Jorge Luis Borges). A note on Sappho, still in 1937, saw the light of day in Havana's *Revista Cubana*, tone-setting and cosmopolitan at the time. The following year, a high-level alumni journal became the vehicle for one of María Rosa's occasional attempts to trespass on the domain of linguistics: "Spanish Hellenisms, as Viewed by Juan de Valdés." The latter writer, a noted figure of Hispano-Italian Humanism, was the author of the long unpublished *Dialogue on Language* (ca. 1530), conducted in the Platonic manner.

Even more important in its eventual consequences than this well-intentioned and adroitly-executed maneuvering on the part of Alonso is what he undertook for his former prize-pupil within the framework of the institute entrusted to his care. He scored two successes. First, he managed to have María Rosa appointed, not just for one year, but for an indefinite period of time, if only on a part-time basis, as a librarian and cataloguer of all incoming books and periodicals, an activity which quickly gave her a panoramic view of relevant goings-on the world over. Second, he arranged for her to receive a comparably long-term, university-sponsored research fellowship; the officially approved project — which we, at present, might be tempted to call an academic exercise in comparative literature — was to determine the angle at which antique texts were seen and, in the end, partially assimilated by Spain's medieval and Golden Age (that is, Renaissance and Baroque) writers. What Alonso probably had in mind was the sort of "Toposforschung" very fashionable on the European continent in those years, its chief exponent being the brilliant but sometimes whimsical Bonn professor Ernst Robert Curtius. By way of prelude, María Rosa began to plough methodically through the writings — long familiar to her, of course, as a lay reader — by Spain's foremost fiction writers and playwrights of the sixteenth and seventeenth centuries (say, Cervantes and the inexhaustible Lope de Vega), annotating in her notebooks the occurrence of certain mythological and historical names, resemblances of plots and personages to those pervading the known or merely suspected Greek and Latin models of those texts, favorite similes, metaphors, and invocations traceable to prototypes very distant in time, and the like, with increasingly heavy emphasis not on mere recurrences, but also on both patent and subtle discrepancies.

For a while, the Middle Ages interested her little, even though she had

had, from adolescence, a few favorite writers in that epoch, especially that elusive early fourteenth-century figure, Juan Ruiz, the Archpriest of a small town called Hita, a writer of genius about whose identity and real life, intriguingly enough, practically nothing was known a half-century ago, and little more is known at present, except what could be conjectured—but are such conjectures legitimate?—from a single long unpublished poem, a strange blend of different genres, the *Libro de buen amor* (*The Book of Good Love*). A paleographically sound edition of the text, on the strength of three basic manuscripts, had been in existence since ca. 1900, prepared by a scrupulous French scholar, J. Ducamin; but now a much younger scholar, Félix Lecoy, also a youthful, witty, and erudite Frenchman, presented an elegantly worded, cogently reasoned book-length monograph, in which Ruiz's heavy dependence on antique models was painstakingly elucidated. The reading of this 1938 book, entitled *Recherches sur le "Libro de buen amor,"* became a major experience for María Rosa, who appreciated the underlying philosophy of analysis and eagerly learned some of the techniques applied.

As if to show his mettle as an imaginative, ever alert initiator, Alonso quickly realized by 1939 that, with the collapse of the short-lived Spanish Republic and with the threat of a new war hanging over most of Europe, the golden opportunity had arrived for him to launch a first-rate scholarly quarterly from his safe headquarters in far-off Buenos Aires. His flair for the realities of life told him that Volume I, and especially the opening issue, had to look impressive. For the lead article, on the side of linguistics, he had elicited a manuscript from his former Madrid teacher, a seasoned phonetician with leanings toward synchrony, Tomás Navarro; what about the literary side? For the sake of perfect balance and, at the same time, polarization, the companion piece had better come from a young woman versed in diachronic textual analysis. At this juncture, María Rosa's topos studies, which had been quietly maturing over a period of three or four years, came in handy, fitting the description of the *desideratum* as snugly as could have been wished for. The forty-three page space for the concluding article in the inaugural number of the *Revista de Filología Hispánica* (such was the name of the newborn journal) was consequently filled with a small florilegium of her inquiries into the survival and transmutation of Graeco-Latin themes and structural patterns in Spanish lyrical poetry, surveyed across the ages; for example, the nightingale of Virgil's *Georgics* and the topic of the wounded stag at a spring of water. The critic-historian's own style had meanwhile been polished to a fine sheen—it was elegant but shorn of clogging rhetoric and cumbersome pedantry, a classic of scholarly prose in its own right. Later,

Marcel Bataillon, in his necrological essay on the author, described the impression that this particular many-splendored paper—so much unlike what European readers had long been accustomed to coming across in Latin American publications—had made on him and on his circle of friends in France on the eve of the war; and I readily confess my own excitement when it came to my attention in New York the following year. Actually, it was Tomás Navarro who showed it to me on the occasion of my first visit, with trepidation, to Columbia.

With so many successes—all of them richly deserved and overdue, but still unexpected and overwhelming in their cumulative effect—scored in a matter of years, there clearly could be no talk of letting María Rosa continue her teaching in a drab high school environment. In the absence of a suitable opening at a university level, María Rosa Lida, by 1941, secured the position of a professor of classical Greek language and literature at the local pedagogical institute—one of the continent's finest teachers' colleges, where she saw herself surrounded by distinguished colleagues and well-prepared, appreciative students. Three years later, this initial appointment was so expanded and re-defined as to include a year-round course on medieval Spanish literature. These activities were to last until adverse circumstances forced her to leave the country—as it turned out, not temporarily (the way she had assumed), but for good.

It can be safely stated that the period between 1940 and 1947 represents the segment of maximum intellectual and even sheer physical concentration in the scholar's life under scrutiny. The succession of these eight years also corresponds to her optimal period for examining, through the prism of literature, the multi-layered relations between antique, medieval, and Renaissance cultures, with special but at no time exclusive, attention to Spain. Only samples of this sustained interest can be subjected here to a brief examination—instead of the leisurely inquiry which they deserve.

The "Defense of Dido in Spanish Literature" (1942; revised and expanded edition, 1974) involves an attempt to show that the portrait of the Virgilian heroine emerges rather different from the brush strokes of the Spanish Golden Ages poets than it does from those of their Italian and French contemporaries. Given the continuity of Virgil's ubiquitous prestige and influence over the ages, this was a sort of well-chosen laboratory case for testing various ideas that had been raying out from Madrid, where scholars of the caliber of R. Menéndez Pidal and Américo Castro had been emphasizing certain pervasive features of Spanish literature and thought prevalent until the Enlightenment, with special attention to, first, a kind of crass realism known under the label of *verismo* ("unvarnished truth to bare facts") and, second, a clearly recognizable moralizing vein, involving a stance very closely akin to a didactic attitude—highly typical of medieval culture everywhere over the West. Unlike the situation in Italy and France, where with the close of the Middle Ages representative writers ceased to be, preeminently, teachers and preachers, the moralizing-didactic slant lingered on in Spain and Portugal, over-ruling—even at the height of the Renaissance—the predominantly or strictly esthetic, rather than judgmental, approach, bequeathed by ancient Greece to postmedieval France and Italy.

Precisely what does the key phrase "the defense of Dido" mean? There existed a strong medieval tradition in the West purporting to demonstrate that Virgil—in the last analysis, because he was a pagan—had behaved like a liar in reporting in his *Aeneid* that Dido, upon learning that she had been treacherously abandoned by that fugitive from captured Troy, Aeneas, out of grief and frustration and unfulfilled passionate love, had committed suicide, dramatically using a sword Aeneas had left behind. To cite just one characteristically explicit condemnation of Virgil, allegedly the real culprit in this context, a Spanish mid-sixteenth-century writer like Gonzalo Fernández de Oviedo would use the verse and the attached exegetic prose sections of his *Quincuágenas* to drive home the point that Dido plunged the sword into her lovely body to protect her uxorial fidelity to her first husband, Sychaeus, thus eschewing any harassment by, and refusing to become the spouse of, King Iarbas. Fernández de Oviedo explicitly extolled the Queen of Carthage's virtue and chastity, castigating Virgil for his vile mendacity. In this he unwittingly carried on a tradition strongly rooted in medieval Europe, but generally rejected with the advent of the Renaissance, although he was sophisticated enough to summon the support of Petrarch, whose verses he quoted: "Poi vidi tra le donne peregrine / quella per lo suo dilecto e fido / sposo, *non per Enea,* vuol se ir al fine: / Taccia il volgo ignorante: i' dico Dido, / cui studio d'honestade a morte spinse, / non vano amor. . . ."

The lone exception from this belligerently moralistic, anti-Virgilian stance, María Rosa Lida argues, was Cervantes, in his pastoral novel *La Galatea,* in his oft-neglected poetic *œuvre,* and especially in *Don Quixote,* where he struck an ironic rather than apologetic attitude toward the protagonists of the *Aeneid,* and in the process specifically portrayed Dido as having succumbed to Aeneas' blandishments in a cave ("adó la hermosa Dido fue rendida / al querer del troyano desterrado," par. (Epistle to Mateo Vázquez); ". . . la cueva donde el traydor y atrevido Eneas gozó a la hermosa y piadosa Dido," (*D.Q.,* part 2, chap. 48). Cervantes thus emerges, from María Rosa Lida's sharply-pointed analysis, as by far the most "European" of all Spanish Golden Age writers—artistically the equal of the versatile and inspired playwright Lope de Vega, but intellectually his superior here and in comparable contexts, having successfully overcome any residual dependence on the medieval consensus.

A whole cluster of studies sprang into existence centering around the figure of King Alexander of Macedonia. These investigations came to fruition in the post-Buenos Aires segment of the author's short life, including the years when she was aware of her impending doom; but they are traceable to much earlier preoccupations. They yielded one book, whose title does not immediately reveal its link to this topic, plus two articles mutually complementary. Of these, one—strictly, a review article—bore on a young Englishman's, sadly, posthumous inquiry of considerable weight, namely, George Cary's *The Medieval Alexander*, while its counterpart concerned itself with stray or detailed references to the Alexander legend in representative works of older Spanish literature. Surveying succinctly not the thirteenth-century *Libro* (or *Poema*) *de Alexandre*, but the sundry briefer accounts of and allusions to the world conqueror in the less obviously relevant prose and verse texts, with heavy emphasis on the fifteenth century, María Rosa showed the fascination of this gallery of pictures through its dual partnership in the declining Middle Ages and the stirrings of pre-Renaissance. Alexander, one learns, was seen as a symbol of generosity and chivalrous behavior in late medieval Spain, a country whose culture was beholden to the Middle Latin and Old French interpretations of the personality of the King of Macedonia. Yet, here and there, an affinity with the Near Eastern, principally Arabic, portrait of Alexander suddenly comes into view, as when, in the play *La Celestina*, an erudite servant, Sempronio, likens the monarch to the biblical Nimrod, crediting them both with a burning desire to conquer not only the globe, but heaven as well.

What the Middle Ages principally associated with Alexander's meteoric career and subsequent unceasing glory was the very concept of richly deserved fame. It is thus hardly surprising that a separate book-length project on this central idea should, I repeat, before long have jelled, under the slightly infelicitous, because too modest, title of *La idea de la fama en la Edad Media castellana,* cutting loose—but not entirely so—from the ensemble of her studies attuned to the Alexander theme. The book saw the light of day in 1952; it is, incidentally, the only one from her pen that has been translated—I might as well add, magisterially translated—into French by her junior friend Sylvia Roubaud [-Bénichou] (1968). This posthumous venture bears a more specific and explicit title than the original: *L'idée de la gloire dans la tradition occidentale: Antiquité, Moyen Âge occidental, Castille.* The study is tripartite, but the partition is not the same as in the earlier inquiry into Dido.

The introductory section ably summarizes knowledge then available on fame in antiquity, with concentration on Roman literature, from Ennius via Lucretius and Cicero all the way to Livy, Persius, Juvenal, Macrobius, and Boethius. The middle section takes the reader to Christianized Europe, from St. Augustine through Thomas Aquinas to Dante and beyond, paying heightened attention to masterpieces of French literature: the *Life of St. Alexis,* the *Rose,* the courtly romances, plus, of course, Gautier de Châtillon's *Alexandreis* all come to the fore, with appropriate attention to medieval England, especially Joseph of Exeter's *De bello Troiano* and Walter Map's *De nugis curialium;* here Ernst Robert Curtius' pioneering writings must have paved the road for her. The third part, the longest and by far the most original, examines the reactions of the older Spanish texts, one by one, to the challenge, not to say seduction, of heroic achievement, the *hazaña,* with the incrustation of thirty pages on the *Libro de Alexandre* representing, as one would expect, the single most delicately nuanced analysis. The succession of critically-slanted miniatures extends as far as Juan de Mena and Jorge Manrique, or mid- and late-fifteenth-century fame, *à propos* of both of whom the author was treading ground very familiar to herself. The balance sheet contained a flat denial of the widespread assumption of the early modern age's abrupt return to antiquity: "La soif de renom / qui caractérise le début de l'Âge moderne constitue l'aboutissement ... d'une évolution continue tout au long du Moyen Âge, et non un retour à l'Antiquité sans lien avec le proche passé médiéval" (285).

One regrets that the ensemble of María Rosa's Alexander studies has remained incomplete through postponement and, in the end, omission, of the Renaissance and Baroque periods. She whetted the reader's appetite, making him eager to learn whether the trajectory of this motif paralleled, or deviated from, the Dido topos.

While classical antiquity, incontrovertibly, remains the fountainhead of most of Spain's medieval and Renaissance culture, it need not have been the sole or, in any single instance, the predominant force. What lends Spanish letters, time and again, a touch of pleasing exoticism is, precisely, the existence of important rival strains, specifically, the Muslim and the Jewish; within the latter, one actually discovers two varieties: the share of the thoroughly assimilated, converted Jew, often the child, grandchild, or great-grandchild of forcibly baptized professors of the Jewish faith, and the semi-assimilated Jew, who could have become an accomplished master of the Spanish language, even a classic, but whose world view continued to be that of a Jew rather than a Catholic. This highly complex state of affairs involves a real challenge to the experienced explorer; beginners had better stay away from it. Some of these problems titillated María Rosa's imagination already during her Buenos Aires years; of the importance of others she grew aware during the subsequent period of her intellectual growth, which one associates chiefly with Berkeley and, for two brief periods, with Harvard.

Only a few random examples can be very briefly provided here. The classical and, above all, medieval Latin sources of Juan Ruiz's *Libro de buen amor* had already been laid bare, we recall, by Félix Lecoy; in her editorial venture, in two major articles (of which the second and more important falls into her later years), and in a string of book reviews (not all of them flattering), María Rosa rounded out Lecoy's discoveries, but she also believed she had recognized in the bizarre sequence of confessions by the author's "persona," interwoven with fables, prayers, and burlesque interludes, the trace of a Semitic cultural tradition, entirely alien to the Hellenic heritage. In this she was not alone; her senior friend and former teacher, Américo Castro, in a sensationally influential, existentialist book-length study published in 1948, had proposed an Arabic model for this deviant structural pattern. Though a great admirer of Castro's, María Rosa accepted only one half of his thinking, namely the recognition of an Oriental ingredient; as a substitute for the Arabic source, however, she eventually proposed a medieval Hebrew crazy-quilt narrative pattern, the *mugāma,* a thesis that was to run into considerable critical opposition.

The most enigmatic poet of the Spanish pre-Renaissance, Juan de Mena, was doubly obscure: to crack his numerous historical and mythological allusions, a reader had to be himself a scholar steeped in what we might be tempted to call archeological erudition. The second element of that obscurity which surrounded Mena's comet-like appearance in the mid-fifteenth century is the parsimoniousness of information about his life and activities, as if a matter of deliberate self-effacement were involved. Also, María Rosa noted an almost pervasive absence of allusions to Christian symbolism in his prose and poetry. All of this did not necessarily make a crypto-Jew out of Mena; but he could, at least, have been a very lukewarm Christian, who sought in his self-imposed immersion in pagan antiquity a sort of escape from the, to him, obtrusive ubiquitous pressure of a thoroughly Christian environment. While María Rosa's technically brilliant disentanglement of Mena's unyieldingly learned, heavily allusive style won unanimous and instant applause, her more daring attempt to place the elusive poet in a concrete socio-historical context, amid reluctant New Christians, was received with considerable (and, I incline to think, undeserved) skepticism.

Finally, it could happen that the antique source at issue itself involved a blend of pagan, or free-thinking, Hellenistic culture with a liberalized Judaic tradition, whether the meeting place was Alexandria or Hellenized Imperial Rome. The two obvious figures to be watched very closely, so far as possible subsequent repercussions of their—incidentally, disparate— approaches were concerned, were, as one might have guessed, the philosopher-theologian Philo and the historian Flavius Josephus. On Philo we have, from María Rosa's pen, only two short, if sparkling, essays; but Josephus' legacy developed into a life-long concern, which for a while came close to yielding a *magnum opus,* and which only a constellation of adverse circumstances prevented from springing into existence in the form aimed at (even so, the fragments salvaged amount to an aggregate of almost a thousand pages), just as a cruel doom ultimately hindered the scholar from writing the book that, in the concluding years of her life, was uppermost on her mind: the book on Fray Luis de León, the late-sixteenth-century Catholic friar, inspired poet, master of prose, and professor of Hebrew, Greek, and Latin at the venerable University of Salamanca, who was accused by the Inquisition of Judaizing leanings and incarcerated.

But examining María Rosa Lida de Malkiel's American period as well as her plans for the future might threaten to induce me to transcend without warrant the self-chosen modest scope of this pen portrait.

References

Alonso, Amado. 1935. *El problema de la lengua en América.* Madrid: Espasa-Calpe.
Bataillon, Marcel. 1963. "María Rosa Lida de Malkiel (1910–1962)." *Bulletin hispanique* 65:189–91.
Bénichou, Paul. 1968. *Creación poética en el romancero tradicional.* Madrid: Gredos.
Caro, Miguel Antonio. 1951. *Versiones latinas,* ed. J. M. Rivas Sacconi. Bogotá: Instituto Caro y Cuervo.
Cary, George. 1956 (repr., 1967). *The Medieval Alexander,* ed. D. J. A. Ross. Cambridge: Cambridge University Press.
Castro, Américo. 1948. *España en su historia: cristianos, moros y judíos.* Buenos Aires: Losada.
Corominas, Juan, ed. 1941–46. *Anales del Instituto de Lingüística de Cuyo.* Mendoza, Arg.
Curtius, Ernst Robert. 1948. *Europäische Literatur und lateinisches Mittelalter.* Bern: Francke.
Chica Salas, Francisca. 1941. *El límite.* Buenos Aires: F. A. Columbo.

Ducamin, Jean, ed. 1901. *"Libro de buen amor"; texte du XIVe siècle.* . . . Bibliothèque méridionale, 1:6. Toulouse: A. Privat; Paris: A. Picard.
Emérita: Boletín de lingüística y filología clásica. Vols. 1-5. 1933-37. Madrid: Junta para ampliación de estudios. Centro de estudios históricos.
Fernández de Oviedo (y Valdés), Gonzalo [1478-1557]. 1880. *Las quinquágenas de la nobleza de España,* ed. Vicente de la Fuente. Madrid: Real Academia de la Historia.
Henríquez Ureña, Pedro, ed. 1938-42. *Las cien obras maestras de la literatura y del pensamiento universal.* 34 vols. Buenos Aires: Losada.
Keyssner, Karl. 1932. *Gottesvorstellung und Lebensauffassung im griechischen Hymnus.* Würzburger Studien zur Altertumswissenschaft, vol. 2. Stuttgart: W. Kohlhammer.
Koerner, Otto. 1932. *Die Sinnesempfindungen in Ilias und Odyssee.* Jena: Gustav Fischer.
Lecoy, Félix. 1938. *Recherches sur le "Libro de buen amor" de Juan Ruiz.* Paris: E. Droz.
Lerner, Lía Schwartz. 1981. "Un vasto proyecto recuperado: los estudios sobre Josefo de María Rosa Lida de Malkiel." *Romance Philology* 35:374-88.
Lida (de Malkiel), María Rosa. 1937a. "Helena en los poemas homéricos." *Cursos y conferencias* 11:113-40.
———. 1937b. "La mujer ante el lenguaje; algunas opiniones de la Antigüedad y del Renacimiento." *Boletín de la Academia Argentina de Letras* 5:18:237-48.
———. 1937c. "El mito de Helena." *Sur* 7:39:65-75.
———. 1937d. "Cómo era Safo." *Revista Cubana* 8:22-24:85-89.
———. 1938a. "Los grecismos del español según Juan de Valdés." *Boletín del Colegio de Graduados* . . . (B.A.) 7:23:53-57.
———. 1938b. Introduction (pp. 7-15) to Publio Virgilio Marón, *La Eneida,* trans. E. de Ochoa. In Las cien obras maestras . . ., dir. P. Henríquez Ureña, no. 3. Buenos Aires: Losada.
———. 1939. "Transmisión y recreación de temas grecolatinos en la poesía lírica española." *Revista de Filología Hispánica* 1:20-63.
———. 1940a. "Notas para la interpretación, influencia, fuentes y texto del *Libro de buen amor.*" *Revista de Filología Hispánica* 2:105-50.
———. 1940b. "Horacio en la literatura mundial." [Review of E. Castle et al., *Orazio nella letteratura mondiale* (Roma, 1936),] *Revista de Filología Hispánica* 2:370-78.
———. 1941a. "Para la biografía de Juan de Mena." *Revista de Filología Hispánica* 3:150-54.
———. 1941b. "La sabiduría humana y la sabiduría divina: historia de una frase y de una actitud" [Filón], *La Nación* (B.A.), Suplemento literario, April 13, p. 1a.
———. 1941c. *"Libro de buen amor"; selección.* Edición con estudio y notas por. . . . Colección de textos literarios, dir. A. Alonso. Buenos Aires: Losada.
———. 1942a. "Una copla de Jorge Manrique y la tradición de Filón en la literatura española." *Revista de Filología Hispánica* 4:152-71.
———. 1942b. "Dido y su defensa en la literatura española." *Revista de filología hispánica* 4:209-52, 313-82, 5:45-50.
———. 1944a. "Dido en la poesía de Chaucer." *Orígenes* (Havana) 1:3-14.
———. 1944b. *Introducción al teatro de Sófocles.* Buenos Aires: Losada.
———. 1946. Preface. *Bibliografía de Amado Alonso: homenaje de sus discípulos* (Buenos Aires, 1946), 13-20.
———. 1949. "La prosa de Juan de Mena." *Boletín de la Academia Argentina de Letras* 18:69:393-432.

———. 1950. *Juan de Mena, poeta del Prerrenacimiento español*. México, D. F.: Publicaciones de la *NRFH* (Fondo de cultura económica).

———. 1952a. "La métrica de la Biblia: un motivo de Josefo y San Jerónimo en la literatura española." In *Estudios hispánicos: Homenaje a Archer M. Huntington* (Wellesley College), 335-59.

———. 1952b. *La idea de la fama en la Edad Media Castellana*. México, D. F.: Fondo de cultura económica.

———. 1956a. "Una conversación con Pedro Henríquez Ureña." *Gaceta* (México, D. F.) 3:21:4a-c.

———. 1956b. "Alejandro en Jerusalén." *Romance Philology* 10:185-96.

———. 1959a. Nuevas notas para la interpretación del *Libro de buen amor*." *Nueva Revista de Filología Hispánica* 13:17-82.

———. 1959b. "Josefo en la *General Estoria*." In *Hispanic Studies in Honour of I. González Llubera* (Oxford), 163-81.

———. 1962a. "La leyenda de Alejandro en la literatura medieval." [Review of G. Cary, *The Medieval Alexander* (Cambridge, 1956).] *Romance Philology* 15:311-18.

———. 1962b. "Datos para la leyenda de Alejandro en la Edad Media castellana." *Romance Philology* 15:412-23.

———. 1968. *L'idée de la gloire dans la tradition occidentale: Antiquité, Moyen Âge occidental, Castille*. Trans. Sylvia Roubaud. Paris: Librairie C. Klincksieck.

———. 1970. "Las infancias de Moisés y otros tres estudios: en torno al influjo de Josefo en la literatura española." *Romance Philology* 23:412-48.

———. 1972. "En torno a Josefo y su influencia: Precursores e inventores." In *Studia Hispanica in Honorem R[afael] Lapesa* 1:15-61. Madrid: Gredos.

———. 1973. *Juan Ruiz: Selección del "Libro de buen amor" y estudios críticos*. Buenos Aires: EUDEBA

———. 1974. *Dido en la literatura española: su retrato y defensa*. Támesis Books, A37. London: Támesis.

———. 1975. *La tradición clásica en España*. Barcelona: Ariel.

Lida, Raimundo. 1958. *Letras hispánicas: estudios, esquemas*. México, D.F.: Fondo de cultura económica.

Navarro Tomás, Tomás. 1939. "El grupo fónico como unidad melódica." *Nueva Revista de Filología Hispánica* 1:1-19.

Oroz, Rodolfo. 1932 rev. 2nd edn., 1950. *Gramática latina, con notas lingüísticas*. Santiago de Chile: Nascimento.

Revista de Filología Hispánica, ed. A. Alonso. 1939-46. 8 vols. Buenos Aires: Instituto de Filología.

Terracini, A. Benvenuto. 1951. *Conflictos de lengua y de cultura*. Buenos Aires: Ediciones Imán.

Valdés, Juan de. 1940. *"Diálogo de la lengua"; selección, estudio y notas*, ed. Rafael Lapesa. Zaragoza: Editorial Ebro.

Walde, Alois, and J. B. Hofmann. 1938. *Lateinisches etymologisches Wörterbuch*. vol. 1. Heidelberg: C. Winter.

———. 1973. *Juan Ruiz: Selección del "Libro de buen amor" y estudios críticos*. Buenos Aires: EUDEBA

———. 1974. *Dido en la literatura española: su retrato y defensa*. Támesis Books, A37. London: Támesis.

———. 1975. *La tradición clásica en España*. Barcelona: Ariel.

Early Post-Byzantine Historiography

MARIOS PHILIPPIDES

During the revival of classical scholarship in the tenth century, historiography began to flourish once more and became one of the more successful genres of the so-called First Byzantine Renaissance.[1] Most Byzantine historians composed their works in an archaic idiom which had roots in the classical and Hellenistic periods, as most medieval authors in Greece based their compositions on the models that have been provided long ago by the ancient masters.[2] In practical terms, this conservative trait of medieval Greek historiography meant that very few individuals could understand, let alone appreciate, contemporary historical works. The medieval West employed Latin as its educated language; in a similar fashion, in the East, ancient Greek became the standard medium for the composition of serious literature.

During the last period of Byzantium's independent existence, the so-called Palaeologan era (1261–1453), we encounter a peak in the adoration of the ancient Greek past.[3] At this time a literary environment was created which was comparable to a virtual renaissance; it has been justly called the forerunner of Western humanism.[4] In the literature of this era emphasis was placed squarely on Byzantium's heritage from ancient Hellas, and continuity from antiquity to the present was stressed, in opposition to the policies and wishes of the Orthodox Church, which had traditionally and consistently opposed the Hellenic-pagan elements in Greek society.[5]

Yet this Palaeologan interlude did not last long. In its brief span individuals with unique talents and exceptional abilities flourished. Their erudition and scholarly contributions can be easily seen in the achievements of the Greek scholars who fled from Greece to Italy shortly before, during, and after the Ottoman annexation of the Balkan peninsula in the middle of the fifteenth century. Thus such impressive humanists as Cardinal Bessarion or Cardinal Isidore of Kiev established themselves in Italy and left their imprint on Western humanism.[6] Similarly, less known but equally important scholars who sought refuge in the west assisted in the production of the early editions of Aldus Manutius in Venice.[7]

Yet in the mainland of Greece the Palaeologan renaissance came to an abrupt end, and the revival of ancient Greek thought and style in contemporary literature experienced a decline, as most scholars had either fled to Italy and to the West or entered the service of the Greek Patriarchate of Constantinople-Istanbul. During the period of the Ottoman domination, the Patriarchate, which heavily depended on the good will of the reigning sultans, discouraged any attempts to come to terms with Western Catholicism and continued to express its opposition to the revival of the classical tradition, as it had done in the Byzantine period. And as the Greek Patriarchate came to exercise immense influence over the Greek subject population of the Ottoman sultan, any literary connection with ancient Hellas or pagan Rome was viewed with suspicion, in spite of the fact that in the West the spirit of humanism had resulted in the virtual adoration of antiquity.[8]

Before the Ottoman conquest, accounts of contemporary events were composed by numerous historians in the Palaeologan era. Their narratives cover the period between 1261–1360. Strictly speaking, Byzantine historiography ends ca. 1360 with the work of Nikephoros Gregoras and the memoirs of Emperor John VI Kantakouzenos. Apparently, no individual was subsequently inspired to write an account of the events that dealt with the gradual loss of territory to the Ottoman Turks after the middle of the fourteenth century. The next group of historians appears long after Kantakouzenos and immediately after the fall of Constantinople to the Ottoman Turks (1453); they worked under Ottoman rule in the East or in Greek-speaking areas that were still under Frankish lordship.[9]

Thus Byzantine historiography survives in the works of the so-called "historians of the fall": Doukas, Khalkokondyles, Kritoboulos, and Sphrantzes. Their generation had witnessed the climax of the monumental struggle between East and West that finally ended with the spectacular loss of Constantinople, an event that fired the imagination of the Western humanists and prompted such important individuals as Aeneas Sylvius Piccolomini (the later Pope Pius II) to claim that this "was the second death of Homer and Plato."[10] The historians of the fall had also observed the loss of all Greek independent states, in addition to the fall of Constantinople: the Ottoman conquest of the despotate of the Morea (the Peloponnese) and the annexation of the "empire" of Trebizond.

The main theme of these historians of the Quattrocento was the loss of Greece to the Turks, and their method of composition was destined to dominate Greek and, to a certain extent, Italian historiography throughout the sixteenth and seventeenth centuries, especially since Europe became extremely interested in the rise of the Ottoman Turks.[11] Thus the historians of the fall served as guides and as primary sources; particularly influential in the sixteenth century were the works composed by George Sphrantzes and by Laonikos (i.e., Nikolaos) Khalkokondyles; the latter was used as a source by various Italian authors (including Francesco Sansovino and Paolo Giovio) and by the anonymous author of the Greek Chronicle[12] known as the *Barberini Codex 111*, while Sphrantzes' account[13] was elaborated into the celebrated *Chronicon Maius*.

Sphrantzes' authentic work, the *Chronicon Minus*, is an annalistic summary of the events that this author had personally witnessed. Since he had been the childhood friend and intended μέγας λογοθέτης of Constantine XI Dragaš Palaeologus, the despot of the Morea and last Greek emperor of Byzantine Constantinople, and had actually participated in the events, his composition is of primary importance for the history of the last years of Byzantium. The *Minus* of Sphrantzes shows no debt to antiquity. It is a simple, chronological account of events, lacking digressions or inquiries into the nature of history. In other words, this author declined to imitate the models from antiquity, such as Herodotus, Polybius, or Thucydides, who had been used by other Byzantine authors. Moreover, Sphrantzes' language displays no conscious imitation of Attic Greek, the standard style of Byzantine historians, who cultivated the obscure and archaic turns of phrases of the archaic idiom to such an elaborate degree that it very frequently resulted in the distortion of logical syntax. Thus Sphrantzes' account is composed in the simple, spoken idiom of the fifteenth century, without any literary pretensions.

There is another work traditionally attributed to the pen of Sphrantzes; it is known as the *Chronicon Maius*. This is a more ambitious composition, written in the traditional form of a major history. Its language and treatment of the subject matter imitate ancient models. It was believed for a long time that the *Minus* represented the bare notes that Sphrantzes had collected during his life, which he eventually amplified and incorporated into the *Maius*. This last work, however, has been recently shown to be a sixteenth-century fabrication by Makarios Melissenos-Melissourgos, the well-known forger of Palaeologan chrysobulls. The forger was active in Italy, especially in the Greek community of Naples, one century after the death of Sphrantzes.[14] The authentic account, the *Minus*, shows that Sphrantzes was a realistic individual, who was inclined to attribute the fall of Constantinople to the blunders of Byzantine foreign policy and diplomacy and not to Fortune or to Divine Providence. The sixteenth-century elaborator, however, reverts to the traditional explanation and assigns the fall of Constantinople to "sins" and to the abstraction of the medieval *Fortuna* or Τύχη, a concept that goes all the way back to the writings of Polybius.[15]

Doukas, the second major historian of the fall, spent most of his life in the island of Lesbos.[16] Like Sphrantzes, Doukas composed his history in an idiom that was not directly derived from ancient Greek literature. Yet his presentation of the material betrays a debt to antiquity. Doukas chose to present his work in the form of a "universal" history, a genre that had been popular since the Hellenistic period. Even though he is innovative in his idiom and his lively style is marked by a number of neologisms, the influence from ancient writers can be constantly detected in Doukas' passages, especially in the treatment of certain *topoi* such as portents of impending disasters.

Michael Kritoboulos[17] and Laonikos Khalkokondyles[18] seem to have been realistic individuals, who tried to demonstrate that empires are destined to succeed one another and that the conquest of Byzantium by the Ottoman Turks was inevitable. They believed in the presence of Τύχη-*Fortuna* and its influence in the course of history and not in the Christian concept of Providence or Divine Punishment. Their focus was the death of East Rome; yet they also went to great lengths to discuss the rise of the Ottoman Turks in detail. Thus Khalkokondyles' narrative is an early, if not the earliest, representative of the genre that became so popular in the early Italian Renaissance, as it dealt with the origins and the rise of the *Gran Turco*.[19]

In the works of Kritoboulos and Khalkokondyles, the classical tendencies of late Byzantine historiography are clearly in evidence. Both historians follow the structure of ancient compositions. Kritoboulos employed Thucydides as his model for his style while Khalkokondyles' idol was obviously Herodotus. In fact, Khalkokondyles' work, it may be argued, is so consciously modelled after Herodotus that it does not even qualify as a historical work, as it is more of an ethnographical study. It is, in the final analysis, a late medieval treatment of "exotic" people, from the Byzantine point of view. While this "history" is ultimately concerned with the Ottoman conquest of Greece, of Serbia, of Bosnia, of Albania, and of the Balkan peninsula in general, Khalkokondyles has included, in the form of very long, detailed digressions, material on the West (i.e., Italy, France, England, Spain, and Portugal), on the North (i.e., Russia, Prussia, Germany, Transylvania, Lithuania, Hungary, and

Wallachia), on the East (i.e., the Mongols, the Arabs, the Turks, the Persians, and the Indians), and on the South (i.e., Egypt, Libya, and the land of the Moors). Unlike Herodotus, however, Khalkokondyles does not seem to have personally visited any of these "exotic" places that he describes in detail, with the notable exception of Italy, where members of his family had settled. Thus he relied on informants for his account of the West, while for his material on the East there is reason to believe that he consulted with members of the Ottoman Porte and Turks who had settled in the Balkans.

Khalkokondyles was a member of an old aristocratic Athenian family. In his youth he had received a solid classical education at the capital of the despotate of the Morea, Mistra, during the zenith of the Palaeologan revival of Hellenic culture. The father of western archaeology and the well-known humanist, Cyriacus of Ancona, had personally made his acquaintance at Mistra and had commented on his erudition.[20] Part of his active years Khalkokondyles spent at Mistra, which had served as the center of the late Byzantine renaissance, and he had also studied under the famous Neoplatonist, George Gemistos Plethon.[21]

While Khalkokondyles' theme and treatment of the subject are strongly reminiscent of Herodotus, his literary style is modelled, to a great extent, on Thucydides. Thus his language remains within the standards of Byzantine composition, which, as we have seen, traditionally admired and imitated the ancient masters. It is the focus of his narrative, however, that marks Khalkokondyles as an innovator, as he has broken free from the Byzantine past. Neither Byzantium (as is the case in Doukas' work) nor Mehmed II, the conqueror of Byzantium (as is the case with Kritoboulos), is the center of his history. His theme consists of the origins and rise of the Ottoman Turks and of the creation of their *imperium*, in general. He further exhibits a keen interest in Europe and in western affairs, a subject which had been thoroughly neglected by most Byzantine historians and had received passing mention only when the Byzantine empire was directly involved.

Khalkokondyles' familiarity with ancient authors and his admiration of Hellas are clearly evidenced in the opening passages of Book 1. He attempts to correct the prevalent notion that the Byzantines were exclusively "Roman" or "Christian," an appellation that had been favored and fostered by the Greek Church. Khalkokondyles states in no uncertain terms that the Byzantines were Greeks and revives the ancient term: Hellenes.[22] In the Byzantine period this term was equivalent to "pagan" or "non-Christian"; (thus, in an earlier period, the Byzantines referred to the Arabs as "Hellenes"). Moreover, Khalkokondyles is one of the first

Greek scholars to suggest that the sack of Constantinople by the Ottoman Turks in 1453 amounted to an Asiatic revenge for the destruction of Troy by the Hellenes in antiquity, an αἴτιον that was eventually to become the standard explanation in Western humanistic texts.[23]

Thus, in terms of structure, Khalkokondyles is Herodotean; not only does he treat his subject matter in the tradition of an ethnographer but he also echoes the old Herodotean theme of the struggle of the East versus the West; both he and his predecessor, Herodotus, sought clues for the origins of the monumental conflict in the remote past and they take us back to the Homeric legends. Khalkokondyles cannot be separated from ancient Greek literature.

Yet, even though he qualifies as the last Athenian historian,[24] in the classical sense, he also deserves to be called the "first Athenian historian of the modern period," as he is aware of the Ottoman empire and of the importance of the West.[25] Thus he is a typical humanist who has managed to free himself from the ethnocentricity of medieval Byzantium and from its insistence on the existence of a single, undivided Roman-Christian empire, known as the οἰκουμένη.

The sixteenth century witnessed an increasing interest in the origins of the Ottoman Turks and in the formation of their empire.[26] While, in the East, Ottoman chronicles were being compiled, numerous histories and biographies of the sultans began to appear in Italy. Some were written in Latin and others in Italian. The work of Khalkokondyles became one of the primary sources for such accounts. Because he had employed the difficult linguistic idiom of Herodotus and Thucydides, in Italy his work could be readily understood. The irony is that it could not be easily read by the average Greek speaker of the sixteenth century. Thus it is possible that his account was paraphrased into Modern Greek, although no example of such a rendition is extant. Such a paraphrase, however, could have served as the basic guide and source of the so-called *Barberini Codex 111*, whose anonymous author was clearly familiar with the contents of Khalkokondyles' history. It is also evident that this author of the *Codex 111* was not educated and could not have understood the archaic idiom of Khalkokondyles' text.

Nowadays it has become possible for us to distinguish two traditions of post-Byzantine historiography in the fifteenth, sixteenth, and seventeenth centuries. One school was centered in Constantinople-Istanbul and in areas that were directly under Ottoman administration and under the jurisdiction of the Greek Patriarchate; this school produced histories and works with a heavy ecclesiastical emphasis, following the Christian traditions and ideals that had been established by the clergy throughout the Middle Ages.[27] More or less, this school remained within the Byzantine tradition and produced such works as the chronicle(s) attributed to Manuel Malaxos, an important composition by Damascenus the Studite, the anonymous Ἔκθεσις Χρονική, and a poem attributed to an official of the Great Church by the name of Hierax.[28]

The second school of historiography flourished in Greek-speaking areas that were not under direct Ottoman control, i.e., mainly the Greek communities in Italy, where the full impact of the Italian Renaissance and of Western humanism could be felt. The two outstanding productions of this school are the *Chronicon Maius* and the *Barberini Codex 111*; the latter has secular origins and is not concerned with religious matters at all. The basic source for both productions goes back to the fifteenth century work of the Palaeologan humanist, Laonikos Khalkokondyles. It is indicative of the Dark Age of Modern Greece (as this early period under the Ottoman sultans is called) that no comparable accounts were produced in the Balkan peninsula. After all, the subjugated Greeks had not been afforded the opportunity to be directly exposed to the Italian Renaissance, and the Palaeologan revival of Hellas and its humanism had been all but forgotten.

The influence of the West in Greek culture during the fifteenth century had been on the rise before the Turkish conquest. Both the *Barberini Codex 111* and the *Chronicon Maius* have employed as their source, in their accounts of the siege and sack of Constantinople (1453), a Latin letter that had been composed by an eye-witness, Bishop Leonardo of Chios.[29] In earlier periods the use of primary Latin-European sources for the composition of history had been unthinkable in Byzantium. It was only in the Palaeologan era that Byzantine intellectuals began to pay serious attention to the literature and thought of the West. Yet even scholars in the Palaeologan era never went so far as to employ Latin histories, chronicles, or documents as primary sources. Translations of Latin works into Greek, especially in poetry and theology, were not unknown in Byzantium. Early examples of such translation include the Greek versions of Cicero, Caesar, Ovid, Boethius, and Augustine. During the Palaeologan era, Demetrios Kydones, a member of the imperial court of John VI Kantakouzenos, translated into Greek works by Anselm of Canterbury, Augustine, and Thomas Aquinas.[30] Influence from Western popular culture was further on the rise, as is evidenced in the Byzantine chivalric romances, some of which clearly imply thorough familiarity with their European counterparts of the late Middle Ages.[31]

The fact that some Greek authors in the sixteenth and seventeenth centuries used a Latin source (or even perhaps an Italian translation of this Latin source) in accounts of the fall of Constantinople may be regarded as a natural step towards the recognition of Western historiography. This school of Western Greek historiography had the background of the Italian humanism of the Quattrocento and of the Palaeologan Renaissance. By contrast, the Eastern Greek school of historiography in Constantinople-Istanbul of the sixteenth century failed to take into account or to utilize Western sources and documents, thus returning to the rules of medieval, Byzantine historiography. Although this school seems to have made extensive use of Ottoman sources, it was not influenced by contemporary western methods in the composition of history.

Thus, in the final analysis, the Western school was both an innovator and, to a certain degree, the natural continuator of the Palaeologan tradition and humanism which had briefly flourished shortly before the Ottoman conquest of the Balkan peninsula. Under the influence of humanism and through the revival of ancient Greek literature in Italy, the Western school was able to utilize the spirit and the tools that became available in the Italian Renaissance, making improvements on the rules of composition that had been established in Byzantium during the Middle Ages. By contrast, the Eastern school of the Patriarchate remained firmly within the Byzantine tradition, failing to take advantage of the Palaeologan Renaissance or of Western humanism. It is not an accident that during the seventeenth and eighteenth centuries parents in Greece sent their children to study in Greek schools that had been established in the Greek community of Venice and elsewhere in Italy.[32] By that late date it had become evident that the "marriage" of traditional Byzantine culture and Western humanism had been successful, while the "pure" Byzantine tradition that was maintained in a conservative manner by the Patriarchate of Istanbul was viewed by the Greeks as monolithic, inadequate, and in need of innovation. These trends are already evident in the early history of the two schools of historiography in the fifteenth and sixteenth centuries.

Notes

1. In general, cf. W. Treadgold, ed., *Renaissances before the Renaissance: Cultural Revivals of Late Antiquity and the Middle Ages* (Stanford, 1984); P. Lemerle, *Le premier Humanisme byzantin. Notes et remarques sur enseignement et culture à Byzance des origines au XVe siècle* (Paris, 1971); and N. G. Wilson, *Scholars of Byzantium* (Baltimore, 1983).

2. Cf. R. Browning, "The Language of Byzantine Literature," in *The "Past" in Medieval and Modern Greek Culture* (Βυζαντινὰ καὶ Μεταβυζαντινά 1, ed. S. Vryonis) (Malibu, 1978), 103–35; H. Hunger, *Die hochsprachliche profane Literatur der Byzan-*

tiner, 2 vols. (Munich, 1973); idem, "Klassizistische Tendenzen in der byzantinschen Literatur des 14. J.h.," *Actes du XIV*ᵉ *Congrès International des études byzantines* (Bucharest, 1974), 139-51; and G. L. Kustas, "Literature and History in Byzantium," Βυζαντινὰ καὶ Μεταβυζαντινά 1 (1978): 51-71.

3. S. Runciman, *The Last Byzantine Renaissance* (Cambridge, 1970); I. Ševčenko, "The Palaeologan Renaissance," in Treadgold (above, n. 1), 144-73; and D. M. Nicol, *Church and Society in the Last Centuries of Byzantium. The Birbeck Lectures* (Cambridge, 1979), chap. 4.

4. On the Greek Church in this late period, cf. S. Runciman, *The Great Church in Captivity. A Study of the Patriarchate of Constantinople from the Eve of the Turkish Conquest to the Greek War of Independence* (Cambridge, 1968).

5. On the Greek refugee scholars, cf. D. J. Geanakoplos, *Greek Scholars in Venice* (Cambridge, Mass. 1962) (repr. as *Byzantium and the Renaissance: Greek Scholars in Venice* [Hamden, Conn. 1972]); idem, *Interaction of the "Sibling" Byzantine and Western Cultures in the Middle Ages and Italian Renaissance (330-1660)* (New Haven and London, 1976); and K. M. Setton, "The Byzantine Background to the Italian Renaissance," *Proceedings of the American Philosophical Society* 100 (1956): 1-76.

6. L. Labowsky, "Il Cardinale Bessarione e gli inizi della Biblioteca Marciana," in *Venezia e l'Oriente fra tardo Medio Evo e Rinascimento*, ed. A. Pertusi (Venice, 1966), 159-82; idem, "Bessarion Studies," *Medieval and Renaissance Studies* 5 (1961): 108-62; A. Pertusi, *Storiografia umanistica e mondo bizantino* (Palermo, 1967); A. A. Kyrou, *Bessarion, the Greek*, 2 vols. (Athens, 1947) (in Greek); and Z. V. Udalcova, "Žizn' i dejatelnost' Vissariona Nikejskogo," *Vizantijskij Vremennik* 37 (1967): 74-97.

7. C. Dionisotti, "Aldo Manuzio Umanista," in *Umanesimo Europeo e Umanesimo Veneziano* (Florence, 1963), 213-43; D. J. Geanakoplos, "Erasmus and the Aldine Academy of Venice: A Neglected Chapter in the Transmission of Greco-Byzantine Learning to the West," *Greek, Roman, and Byzantine Studies* 3 (1966): 107-34; and P. Kristeller, "The Renaissance and Byzantine Learning," in *Renaissance Concepts of Man* (New York, 1972), 64-110.

8. In general, cf. C. Th. Dimaras, *A History of Modern Greek Literature* (Albany, 1973) and Runciman (above, n. 4).

9. Cf. Nicol (above, n. 3), 121-30.

10. Latin text in Pertusi, *La Caduta di Constantinopoli*, vol. 2: *L'Eco nel Mondo* (Verona, 1976), 46: "secunda mors ista Homero est, secundus Platoni obitus," and 54: "nunc ergo et Homero et Pindaro et Menandro et omnibus illustrioribus poetis secunda mors erit."

11. E. Cochrane, *Historians and Historiography in the Italian Renaissance* (Chicago and London, 1981); also cf. M. L. King, *Venetian Humanism in an Age of Patrician Dominance* (Princeton, 1986).

12. M. Philippides, trans., *Byzantium, Europe, and the Early Ottoman Sultans: An Anonymous Greek Chronicle of the Seventeenth Century (The Barberini Codex 111)*, forthcoming. On this matter, cf. E. Zachariadou, *The Chronicle of the Turkish Sultans and its Italian Prototype* (Thessalonica, 1966) (in Greek).

13. M. Philippides, trans., *The Fall of the Byzantine Empire: A Chronicle by George Sphrantzes, 1401-1477* (Amherst, 1980).

14. M. Philippides, "The Fall of Constantinople 1453: Bishop Leonard and the Greek Accounts," *Greek, Roman, and Byzantine Studies* 22 (1981): 287-300; idem,

"An 'Unknown' Source for Book III of the *Chronicon Maius* by Pseudo-Sphrantzes," *BSEB* 10 (1983): 174-83; and idem, "Contemporary Research on the Texts of Sphrantzes," *Parnassos* 25 (1983): 94-99 (in Greek).

15. For the development of Tyche as a force in history, cf. J. Hornblower, *Hieronymus of Cardia* (Oxford, 1981).

16. H. J. Magoulias, trans., *Decline and Fall of Byzantium to the Ottoman Turks by Doukas* (Detroit, 1975). Kritoboulos managed to impress, with his erudition, the well-known antiquarian and "father of archaeology" Cyriacus of Ancona, who met him in the island of Imbros on Sept. 28, 1444. Cyriacus said of him: ". . . uiro cum docto et Imbrioti nobili Hermodoro Michaeli Critobulo. . . ."

17. English translation (based on an older French translation and not on the original Greek) by C. T. Riggs, *The History of Mehmed the Conqueror by Kritovoulos* (Princeton, 1954; repr., Westport, Conn. 1974).

18. M. Philippides, trans., *The Rise of the Ottoman Sultans by Laonikos [Nikolaos] Khalkokondyles*, forthcoming.

19. Cochrane (above, n. 11).

20. On this family, cf. W. Miller, "The Last Athenian Historian: Laonikos Chalkokondyles," *JHS* 42 (1922): 35-49. Laonikos' kinsman was the well-known Demetrius Chalco[co]ndyles, who played an important role in Italy, through his numerous editions of ancient Greek authors and because of his teaching activities in Florence, Padua, and Milan, three of the main centers of Italian humanism; cf. Geanakoplos, *Interaction* (above, n. 5), chap. 13. On Cyriacus' meeting with Laonikos, cf. K. M. Setton, *The Papacy and the Levant, 1204-1571*, vol. 2: *The Fifteenth Century* (Philadelphia, 1976), 97. Cyriacus' text has been published in R. Sabbadini, "Ciriaco d'Ancona e la sua descrizione autografa del Peloponneso trasmessa da Leonardo Botta," in *Miscellanea A. Ceriani* (Milan, 1910), 203, 204. Cyriacus describes Laonikos as a young man "egregie latinis acque grecis eruditum."

21. Plethon was probably the most ambitious thinker in all of Byzantine history. His views on religion, which promoted a syncretism of ancient cults with Islam, Christianity, and Jewish traditions, brought him into conflict with the Greek Church. After his death, most of his writings were condemned and burned by his old student George Kourtetsis Scholarius, who, under the name of Gennadius II, was the first patriarch of Istanbul under the Ottoman sultans.

22. 1.3: "At Byzantium Greeks mingled with Romans and since the Greeks were more numerous by far, the Greek language and customs prevailed with the passage of time. Retaining, however, the ancient appelation out of respect for tradition, the emperors of Byzantium called themselves 'kings and emperors of the Romans' and never 'emperors of the Greeks'. . . . So much for the Greeks and for the difference with the Romans. I have pointed out the errors in regard to the appellation of the empire."

23. 8.7: "It seems to me that this misfortune [sc. the sack of Constantinople by the Turks] surpasses all others throughout the world in terms of human suffering. It almost equals the fate of Ilium. In fact, it has been suggested that the barbarians [sc. the Turks] were avenging Ilium. The Romans are of the opinion that in this manner the Greeks finally atoned for the suffering that they had caused at Ilium." The identification of the Turks with the ancient Trojans was assisted by the fact that in the Middle Ages the Turks were known as *Teucri* in Latin docu-

ments. The same term had been employed in antiquity by Vergil to designate the Trojans. Cf. S. Runciman, "Teucri and Turci," in *Medieval and Middle Eastern Studies in Honor of Aziz Suryal Atiya*, ed. A. Hanna (Leiden, 1972), 344-48.

24. Miller (above, n. 20) sees Laonikos as the last Athenian historian.

25. A. E. Vacalopoulos, *Origins of the Greek Nation: The Byzantine Period, 1204-1461* (New Brunswick, 1970), considers Laonikos as the first historian of modern Greece.

26. Cochrane (above, n. 11).

27. For this tradition, cf. M. Philippides, "Patriarchal Chronicles of the Sixteenth Century," *GRBS* 25 (1984): 87-94.

28. For a new edition (with English translation) of this text, cf. M. Philippides, *Emperors, Patriarchs, and Sultans of Constantinople: An Anonymous Greek Chronicle of the Sixteenth Century (The Ekthesis Khronike)*, forthcoming.

29. Philippides (above, n. 14).

30. Ibid., 300 n. 31.

31. H.-G. Beck, *Geschichte der byzantinischen Volksliteratur* (Munich, 1971).

32. For the Greek communities in Renaissance Italy, cf., among others, Geanakoplos (above, n. 5), *Interaction*, pt. 2; I. K. Khasiotes, "La comunità greca di Napoli e i moti insurrezionali nella penisola balkanica meridionale durante la seconda metà del XVI secolo," *Balkan Studies* 10 (1969): 279-80; N. Tomadakes, "I Greci a Milano: Nota," *Istituto Lombardo (Rendiconti, Classe di Lettere)* 101 (1967): 568-80; and J. Veloudes, *The Orthodox Greek Community of Venice* (Venice, 1893) (in Greek).

Michael of Ephesus and the History of Zoology[1]

ANTHONY PREUS

The history of zoology has not been as thoroughly studied as the histories of several other sciences; in particular, relatively little attention has been paid to the transmission and interpretation of ancient biological texts during the medieval period.[2] Consequently, it remains difficult to determine whether the scientific study of zoology has had a history which may be characterized as a more or less continuous evolution since the time of Aristotle, or as a series of relatively discrete paradigms, separated by conceptual revolutions.

My objective in the present essay is to present a preliminary assessment of the place of Michael of Ephesus in the history of zoology. As we will see in more detail below, Michael wrote commentaries on several of Aristotle's biological works during the period AD 1117–1138. To inquire about Michael's role in the history of zoology is in a way to inquire more widely about the role in intellectual history of commentaries upon classic authors. In the present instance, we need to say something about the character of Aristotle's zoology in its historical setting, then ask about the relationships of his work to later zoological investigations. Has zoology shown a continuous line of development since Aristotle's work, or have there been significant conceptual shifts? Michael's commentaries may mark a case in point.

Certainly we have learned to expect that the history of science has been marked by epistemological breaks. In the English-speaking world, Thomas Kuhn[3] is perhaps the best-known advocate of the theory that human understanding has progressed by a series of radical restructurings of the terms of understanding; in France, Gaston Bachelard[4] distinguished features of "science" from "pre-science" in such a way that it turns out that all of the ancients were by definition "pre-scientific," and his views dominate the discipline of the history of science in France today. The "revolutionary" interpretation of science, and of many other aspects of western culture, has been made into a generalized interpretive position by Michel Foucault[5] and his many disciples. According to the "revolutionary" interpretation, modern biology in particular could not have begun seriously before the work of Charles Darwin and Gregor Mendel, or even Watson, Crick, and Monod. The "revolutionaries" often say that what the ancients did was "conceptually interesting," but they deny that it belongs to the same enterprise as twentieth-century biology. To express the point in the French way, there have been "epistemological breaks" between the time of Aristotle and our own epoch.[6] We cannot begin to understand the "science" of an ancient writer like Aristotle, for example, without approaching his writings "archaeologically," reconstructing the meaning of his work within its context rather than in terms of our own habits of thought.

But we may well be tempted to see the history of biology, especially, as continuous rather than discontinuous, and that continuity may be thought to go back far beyond Aristotle, back to our most primitive ancestors and perhaps even to impulses expressed by our pre-human primate forebears: when Ernst Mayr saw a film of one of Jane Goodall's chimpanzees carefully inspecting a dead rodent, he remarked that we were having a look at "the first zoologist."[7] If chimpanzees may have a scientific curiosity about other species of animal, *a fortiori* we may expect the impulse to understand the living world to be nearly universal in the human race. Our human ancestors often observed their animal prey quite precisely, as we can see in the cave paintings at Lascaux; in classical antiquity, we find considerable understanding of human anatomy in the Homeric poems. The line between good observation, a persistent curiosity concerning the bodies of men and animals, on the one hand, and an organized methodology which we, from our perspective, will be prepared to call by the honorific term "science," is by no means easy to draw. From the point of view of observational natural history, the development of thought from primitive times to the present might well be seen as a continuous process, without serious "epistemological breaks." The development of biological knowledge might be interpreted as a continuity, rather than as a series of discontinuous episodes.

If there was a revolution in zoological thought, the line between pre-science and science may well have come in the works of Aristotle; Aristotle's approach to the animal world does seem radically different from the mythic and visionary interpretations which preceded it — I think particularly of Empedocles' *On Nature* and Plato's *Timaeus*. Aristotle's advance was not simply one of looking at the animals themselves — certainly Empedocles and his contemporaries looked at animals, though perhaps not as many nor as carefully as Aristotle; nor was it simply a matter of having a comprehensive theory within which zoological observations both past and future could be accommodated — one may well argue that Plato provided such a theory. No, Aristotle is a zoological revolutionary because his motive for looking at animals is radically different from the motives of all his known predecessors: he investigated animals with the belief that his metaphysical theory would be validated by biological observations; observation of the living world was for him necessarily interconnected with the construction of an account of being and becoming.

Aristotle believed that any adequate ontological theory had to account for the observed processes and varieties of life; he was confident that his ontology could do that, and that the competing ontologies of Democritus and Plato could not. As we see repeatedly in Aristotle's zoological books, and elsewhere in the corpus, he was testing the atomistic and idealist accounts of nature against the phenomena of nature and finding them deficient, while he claimed that his own metaphysical system was supported by observation.

Because Aristotle's zoological investigations were motivated by, and resulted in, metaphysical speculations, those investigations did not exactly result in what Thomas Kuhn calls "normal science"; members of the Peripatetic school pursued certain investigations with the metaphysical motivations more or less intact, and some, whether Aristotelians or not, started from his work for the sake of pragmatic applications. We may mention Theophrastus' botanical investigations under both headings, the medical tradition's reliance on Aristotle's results under the pragmatic heading, and perhaps the work of some of the earlier Peripatetics in addition to Theophrastus under the metaphysical head. In general, however, the metaphysical problems which had motivated Aristotle did not have the same significance after he had completed his work; he had succeeded in establishing his doctrine of οὐσία, partially by means of his biological investigations, and subsequent philosophers either worked within the structure of Aristotle's logical and metaphysical works, or explained their departures from that structure on non-biological grounds. The debates between Peripatetic, Academic, Stoic, and Epicurean ontologies were not seen as turning, in any significant way, on the findings of empirical zoology. Consequently those debates did not motivate people to pursue empirical zoological investigations.

Of ancient writers, only Galen seems to have had an interest in Aristotle's peculiar blend of zoological and ontological problems; we see that interest pursued particularly in Galen's *De usu partium*.[8] But just as it is difficult to find many who combined zoological and ontological investigations between the time of the early Lyceum and the time of Galen, so it is difficult to find any real successors to Galen in this respect, at least until Ibn Sina in Persia and perhaps Michael of Ephesus in Byzantium. Aristotle's zoological works did not establish a "normal science," not because they were somehow defective and "prescientific" in the Bachelardian sense, but because a quarter-century after his death no investigators continued within the guidelines which he had laid down.

Since Aristotle's zoology did not become "normal science" in the Kuhnian sense, later developments in zoology, as different from Aristotle's structure as they may appear, do not constitute a "scientific revolution," since the Aristotelian structure *in zoology* was never so normative that alternative methodologies had any trouble establishing themselves. We need only look at the encyclopedism, without explanatory content, of Pliny's *Natural History*, the professed atomism of the physician Asclepiades, the pandemic stoicism criticized by Galen, and Galen's own profession of Platonism and his persistent critiques of Aristotle's anatomical and physiological errors.[9] There was no ancient revolt against the dominance of Aristotle's zoology because it was never dominant.

Certainly none of the ancient commentators appears to have cared enough about Aristotle's biological works to have devoted a commentary to any of those books. Alexander of Aphrodisias, John Philoponus,[10] Simplicius, and the others, all found other parts of Aristotle's work much more engrossing. Perhaps they did not know how to deal with the fact that scientific understanding of many of the phenomena had actually progressed significantly since Aristotle's day. For example, Galen had demonstrated conclusively that the governing part of the soul is to be found in the brain, rather than in the heart; Alexander's attempts to disprove cephalocentrism (in his *De anima*[11]) were spirited, even courageous, but were doomed to failure. For the commentators of late antiquity, it would have been necessary either to explicate Aristotle's text while persistently ignoring the results of more recent medical investigations, or to spend their time correcting the many errors of detail in Aristotle's accounts; they seem to have had little enthusiasm for either task, since their own philosophical goals could not be served through either enterprise. In a sense, the properly philosophical results of Aristotle's biological investigations had been assimilated fairly thoroughly by the early Stoics (this has been shown in detail by David Hahm in his book on Stoic science),[12] and were understood even more deeply by the Middle Platonists and Neoplatonists, though that understanding did not lead them to carry out any further empirical investigation.[13]

I would suggest that the commentators of late antiquity had relatively little interest in Aristotle's biological works because the philosophical problems with which they were struggling did not demand practical biological investigation; Aristotle's own empirical investigations had been sufficient to establish the crucial metaphysical points, and once those points were established, few cared to reopen the biological questions. Perhaps this suggestion may appear essentially *ex post facto*, but it does remind us that Aristotle's zoology did not have the status of dogma in antiquity; consequently no one in antiquity could have mounted a scientific revolution against it.

Of course we do find biological scientists in the *modern* era who represent themselves as revolting against the dominance of Aristotle; for that revolution to make sense, Aristotle's work would have to have been elevated to dominance at some time more than a thousand years after his death. At least two moving causes of such an elevation might be traced: First, it might be argued that the resurgence of interest in Aristotle's biology stems ultimately from the writings of the Islamic medical writers, especially Ibn Sina, and their impact on the Latin west, as well as from the increasing interest in the Aristotelian texts upon which the Muslim writers had built their science. Second, it might be argued that the development of Renaissance biology stems ultimately from the activities of several twelfth- and thirteenth-century Christian Aristotelians: the commentaries of Michael of Ephesus in Byzantium (and their ultimate translation into Latin); the very real biological interests of Albert the Great, and the apparent interest of his most famous student, Thomas Aquinas; and perhaps most important of all, the translations of most of the biological works made directly from the Greek by William of Moerbeke. No doubt Renaissance biological investigations had roots both in the Islamic tradition and in the Byzantine tradition, and they sprouted in the relatively fertile soil of the young schools of the Latin-writing High Middle Ages.

To trace such possible connections we would have to look at the extent of teaching of the biological texts in the universities of Bologna, Paris, Oxford, Basel, and of course Padua. We will return to investigate those connections toward the end of this essay. To anticipate, we may say that seventeenth-century biology was to a large extent inspired by Aristotle's work, and could be said to be in a sense Aristotelian. In the early modern period, there were several revolts against some aspects of seventeenth-century Aristotelian biology, so that one may want to say that there was an Aristotelian paradigm which inspired some opposition. However, it is necessary to point out that modern biological Aristotelianism was not temporally continuous with Aristotle's work, since centuries passed when no one did any significant Aristotelian biological investigation — and probably Renaissance Aristotelianism was conceptually discontinuous as well, in that scientists were responding to issues quite different from those which Aristotle posed to himself. But that becomes a more subtle question than I wish to treat in this paper.

Michael of Ephesus

One may argue that the history of zoology has been marked by paradigmatic shifts, or that it has been a continuous evolution of understanding based ultimately upon principles not very dissimilar from those propounded by Aristotle, or that it has been a series of more or less disjointed episodes, dominated by a few individual investigators each of whom worked as if without progenitors and without issue. However one characterizes the history of zoology, one ought to take account of the place in that history of Michael of Ephesus.

Michael of Ephesus was a member of the circle of Anna Comnena, along with Eustratius; he would have been working approximately in the years 1117 to 1138 or so.[14] We have from his hand commentaries on the *De partibus animalium*, the *De generatione animalium*, most of the *Parua naturalia* including the *De motu animalium* and *De incessu animalium;* we also have his commentaries on the *Politics* and *Sophistical Refutations,* at least, and very likely (as argued by Paul Mercken)[15] he contributed importantly to the commentary on the *Nicomachean Ethics* composed by several hands, and translated by Grosseteste into Latin. According to George Tornikes, in his Eulogy of Anna Comnena, Michael complained that she was the "cause of his blindness, because he had worked night after night, without sleep, commanded by her to write commentaries on the works of Aristotle; the use of candles had caused drying of the eyes."[16]

Why did the Byzantine princess, author of the *Alexiad,* command at least one of her entourage to comment upon the works of Aristotle? Was it because the dominant philosophy in Byzantium was a kind of Platonism, and she, being out of power, thought that perhaps Plato's closest critic would give her some support for her bid for the throne? Was it an attempt to resurrect an image of Hellas which had been only very incompletely recovered by the classicists of the stripe of Arethas and Psellos? Was it an attempt to develop a kind of philosophical prestige for her party in the face of overwhelming competition both from within and from outside the Byzantine empire? We cannot tell. But we can assert that the efforts of Anna Comnena and her group did contribute to the rebirth of interest in Aristotle's works, both in the establishment of an acceptable text which could then be recopied and indeed translated into Latin, and so on, and in the interpretation of texts which had never been commented upon in any detail since their composition fourteen hundred years before.

Michael does not pretend to be a biological scientist, nor indeed any other kind of scientist; he is not uninterested in what Aristotle has to say, but he very rarely indeed has anything to add from his own observation, and in fact he seems to be completely unaware of biological facts which were well-known to the medical writers of his own day. Michael's efforts are commonly "philological" in character, that is, he often paraphrases into a language which would be clearer for his contemporaries, and he often makes textual conjectures when the manuscript with which he was working does not seem to make sense. Michael also draws comparisons with other works of Aristotle—he knows the corpus rather well, and seems able to quote fairly accurately from memory, when he does not actually look up the passage to quote it verbatim. He also likes to draw from the works of Alexander of Aphrodisias, whom he regards (with considerable justice) as the most reliable of the ancient commentators. One might even say that Michael's own motivations for his work must have included the ambition of developing commentaries on the model of Alexander's for the works which neither Alexander nor the other ancient commentators had written about. And unlike the ancient commentators (as I would speculate), Michael is not deterred from commenting upon Aristotle's works by difficulties of dealing with Aristotle's factual shortcomings, since Michael seems largely unaware, or otherwise nonchalant, about any progress in empirical investigation in the intervening fourteen centuries. Nor is Michael deterred by a metaphysical standpoint which has been subtly shifted away from the issues with which Aristotle was concerned; Michael is more curious about the discursive content of the works upon which he comments than seeking involvement with the same issues in the same spirit as the original author. For Michael, the Aristotelian texts are intriguingly intricate puzzles, challenges to an intellectual exercise.

The Generation of the Eyes in Aristotle and Michael: A Sample

a) A translation of Aristotle, *Generation of Animals* 2.6, 743b32.[17]

What happens in the case of the eyes of animals is something of a puzzle. In land animals, water animals, and birds alike, the eyes start out appearing very large, yet they are the last of all the parts to be completely formed, for they shrink up in the meantime. The reason is that the sense-organ of the eyes is indeed, like the other sense-organs, set upon passages; but whereas the sense-organ of touch and of taste is immediately a body or some part of the body of animals, and smell and hearing are passages full of connate pneuma, connecting with the outer air and terminating at the small blood vessels around the brain which extend to it from the heart, the eye, by contrast, is the only one of the sense-organs which has a special body of its own. It is fluid and cold; and unlike the other parts which are present in their places potentially to begin with and later on come to be formed in actuality, this one is not there at the start, but it is produced by the purest part of the liquid around the brain being secreted off through those passages which are to be observed leading from them to the meninx around the brain. Evidence for this is that beside the brain there is no part in the head except the eye which is cold and fluid. So it is from necessity that this region gets large at first but shrinks later on; because the same happens to the brain: at first this is fluid and large, but as evaporation and concoction proceed it becomes more solid and shrinks; so does the size of the eyes. At the beginning the head is very large, on account of the brain, and the eyes, as we see, appear large on account of the fluid in them. But the eyes are the last of all to reach their completion, because the brain (on which they depend) does not set at all easily; it is quite late before it ceases to be so cold and fluid; and this is true of all animals that have a brain, especially of man. That is why the *bregma* (anterior fontanelle) is the last of the bones to be formed: even after the embryos are brought to birth, this bone is still soft in the case of children. The reason why this occurs especially in man is that in man the brain is more fluid and greater in volume than in any other animal, and the reason of this, in its turn, is that the heat in the heart is purest in man. The fineness of the blend in man is shown by his possession of intellect: man is the most intelligent of animals. Even children, however, for a considerable period lack full control over their heads. This is due to the weight of the brain, and the same may be said of those parts of the body which have to move. It is quite late before the principle of movement gets control over the upper parts; and its control over those parts (such as the legs) whose movement is not closely connected with it is achieved last of all. Another such part is the eyelid. Now as Nature does nothing that is superfluous or pointless, it is plain that she will not do anything too late or too soon, for in that case what was done would be either pointless or superfluous. Therefore the separation of the eyelids and the ability to move them must coincide in time. Thus the completion of the formation of the eyes comes late, because of the large amount of concoction required by the brain, and it comes last, after all the other parts, because the movement must be very strong and powerful in order to move parts which are so far away from the first principle, and so much subjected to cold. That such is the nature of the eyelids is shown by the fact that even if a very little heaviness affects the head through sleep or intoxication or anything of that sort, we are unable to raise the eyelids although their weight is very little.

b) Some comments on *GA* 2.6, 743b33-744b9.

This passage is not untypical of Aristotle's usual way of carrying out biological investigation. We see in it several characteristic features: for one, Aristotle is solving an explanatory puzzle (an ἀπορία)—his biological works are often structured around interlocking puzzles. Then too, his response to this puzzle is in two parts: one part gives a "material" explanation: because the eyes are made out of the same material as the brain, they may be expected to behave similarly to the brain, and another part gives a teleological explanation: there is no point in the eye being fully developed until the animal can open its eyes, and control of the eyelids develops relatively late, as part of distal motor control. Another striking feature of the passage is the accuracy of the observation of fetal development, that the eyes develop from the brain, and actually change their location during the embryological process. We may also note the inaccuracy of the observation that the eyes "shrink"—they only appear to become smaller, as they achieve a relatively *much* larger size than the other parts of the head early on, and then the other parts catch up as development continues. Aristotle does not pull out a calipers and measure. We also see here how Aristotle essentially ignores evidence for the cephalocentric theory and maintains his cardiocentric theory through thick as well as through thin; indeed he turns the observations concerning the development for the eyes, which might well be thought good evidence for cephalocentrism, into evidence for cardiocentrism, a neat rhetorical trick.

Aristotle does not directly attack any of his predecessors in the passage; I think that none of them had the observational data available to pose to themselves the question discussed in the passage. So far as his successors are concerned, Galen (in *De usu partium* VIII) uses Aristotle's observations in this passage to defend cephalocentrism against cardiocentrism, but he also develops Aristotle's theory of connate pneuma to the point that he assumes that connate pneuma must be the body for every sense organ; consequently Galen asserts that the optic nerves are *hollow*, and even says that he has poked a hog bristle down an optic nerve; this assertion is in turn challenged by Fabricius of Aquapendente, in *De uisione* (1600).

But let us turn to Michael's commentary.

c) Michael of Ephesus' Commentary on *GA* 2.6, 743b32ff.[18]

"They are . . . formed" means "completion belongs to them." "In the meantime" refers to the time in which the other parts are formed; for since the heart is completed first of all, and the eyes last of all, there is a certain intermediate time during which the others are completed. "Shrink" perhaps means "become shorter."

The puzzle is something like this: why do the eyes appear very large at the beginning, when they are also undifferentiated and just as incomplete as all the other parts except the heart, but in the intervening time they become smaller in length, and at last they themselves are perfected in minute detail. Having stated the problem, he solves it, saying that "the reason" for what happens "is that the sense-organ of the eyes" (meaning by "sense-organ" the crystalline part — for the optical power is in this; "eyes" include the membranes surrounding them) is "set upon passages," that is to say it lies at the end and completion of blood vessels; for he calls them "passages"; so the reason for what happens is that the crystalline is and lies at the end and completion of blood vessels, but the crystalline is peculiar and different from the other sense-organs. He adds how it is different from those constructions: "this one is not there at the start." For it is not like the sense-organs of the other senses, e.g., passages or bodies, which are present right from the start as something sketched and being potentially this thing; so the crystalline too is present from the start potentially, then later comes to be actually, but not like the sense organs of the others, since in this case the purest part of the fluidity of the brain which has been completed and come to be in actuality is secreted and carried through the blood vessels to the membranes. So that since the brain is at first large and fluid, necessarily also this sort of crystalline must be large and have size and mass, and because it must be large, also the membranes in which it is must be large, but later it must shrink and become smaller, both it and the membranes, because the brain too later contracts and is completed. For "complete" is when the entire embryo is completed, and it is entirely completed when the so-called *bregma* has hardened.

[113] That is the sense, but the text runs something like this: now the sense organ "of touch and of taste is the body or some part of the body," adding "some part of the body" because he does not mean that the flesh or its analogue is the sense-organ, but rather the pneuma indwelling in all the flesh. In the passage "smell and hearing are passages," "their sense-organs" is to be understood, I think, so that filled out it would say "as for smell and hearing, their sense-organs are passages" "connecting with the outer air." That would be the continuation of the text. Smell and hearing are generated from the heart, but their sense-organs are passages (meaning by "passages" the nostrils and ears), which passages touch the outer air because they are not empty, but are filled with connate pneuma. For there is in them, as is said in the *De anima* (cf. 2.8, 9) and *On Sense and Sensibles* (cf. 5) indwelling pneuma, which connate pneuma extends to the blood vessels around the brain; for the pneuma goes this far, but no further.

In the passage, "which are observed leading from them to the meninx around the brain," "from them" means "from the eyes" and "meninx" the membrane which surrounds the brain; for the blood vessels terminate in this meninx, and do not extend into the depth, so to speak, of the brain.

At "evidence for this" he means for his claim that the purest part of the fluidity of the brain is secreted. He has chosen to say that "the heat in the heart is purest in man" instead of "hottest" since it is tempered by the brain; a sign of that is that the intellect is well tempered (finely blended). At "the same may be said of those parts of the body which must move," by "parts" he means, for example, hands, feet, and eyelids; for children cannot at first control these parts and do what they want with them; otherwise they would grasp things and walk. They do not control them because the source of movement, i.e., the heart or the soul in the heart, controls the upper parts slowly and late, and last of all the parts controls those which are not directly connected with it. For the eyelids are separated from it and are almost by themselves, and the same goes for the limbs, e.g., the feet. Now since nature makes nothing superfluous, she makes the animal able to move its eyelids neither sooner nor later than she makes the eyes. If she did make them, that is to say if she completed the eyes absolutely, but the animal were not able to move the eyelids, the eyes would have been completed in vain. [114] Thus the eyes are completed at the same time as one is able to move the eyelids and separate the upper from the lower. Clearly children have their eyes incomplete when they are born. They are able to move the eyelids last because "the movement must be very strong and powerful in order to move parts which are so far away from the first principle," i.e., if the moving principle were not very powerful, it would not be able to move the eyelids and the other parts, because they are so far from it; later it becomes very powerful and strong, since later it must move both the limbs and the eyelids. It is clear that even later something having very little weight indeed, even something light, is able to master the eyelids so that nature is hardly able to move them, not only at the beginning but also later, so nature is able to move them and master them only slowly.

d) Comments on Michael's Commentary.

We notice that Michael has surreptitiously introduced two bits of Galenism into his commentary: that the actual sense organ of vision is the "crystalline," i.e., the lens—that is something which one might derive from Galen (*De usu partium* 10.1: it is the "principle organ" of vision), and that *every* sense depends upon connate pneuma—in the passage, Aristotle asserts only that hollow parts of the nostrils and ears contain connate pneuma. In fact, in the *De anima*, when discussing smell and hearing in 2.8–9, Aristotle uses the word *pneuma* only to refer to "breath," and never alludes to "connate pneuma" as the organ of sense in these cases—he says indeed that the organ of hearing, and of smell, is *air*, trapped in internal cavities, but that's quite another matter ultimately. I think that much the same thing can be said of *Sense and Sensibles* 5. But if we look at the *De anima* by Alexander of Aphrodisias, and at his commentary on the *Sense and Sensibles*, we find a theory of connate pneuma which is much more developed than in Aristotle's own treatises. Alexander's commentaries are *direct* sources for Michael.

Michael's knowledge of Galen is at best second-hand, and definitely very limited, since his account of the "passages" is mistaken in that it differs substantially from Aristotle's account, and it also differs significantly from the Galenic version. Aristotle certainly distinguishes those passages from blood vessels (since they are continuous with the brain, not with the heart), and Galen clearly identifies the passages as optic nerves: Michael simply takes them as blood vessels, which shows that he has never been close to a dissection of an animal's head.

Michael: A Link in a Continuous Chain, or Something Else?

One way that Michael may be considered a "link in the chain" of the history of biology is through his influence upon subsequent biological investigation: if later writers saw their own work on biological issues as a continuity of something to which Michael had contributed, that would tend to support that interpretation.

There are some possible medieval successors of Michael. We may note, for example, James of Venice, the first translator into Latin of several of Aristotle's writings. James worked in Constantinople just at the time when Michael was working there; in fact, Michael had finished his commentaries on the *Parua naturalia* and *Sophistical Refutations* not long before James did commentaries on those treatises.[19] One might well investigate whether James used Michael's *Parua naturalia*.

Also William of Moerbeke, in the middle of the thirteenth century, translated Aristotle's biological treatises from Greek to Latin.[20] Very likely the Greek text of Aristotle which William used included that established by Michael, and he would have had Michael's commentaries available to him as well. He worked in Nicaea, the location of the school of Nicephorus Blemmydes from 1224 to 1236, and Nicephorus used the materials generated by Michael and his colleagues. Of course the influence of Moerbeke's translation was enormous: Albertus Magnus first commented on Aristotle's biology on the basis of Michael Scot's translation of the Arabic version, but after 1260, Albertus used the Moerbeke translation and possibly the Michael commentary as well.[21]

Michael's commentaries became more widely known during the Renaissance. At the end of the fifteenth and beginning of the sixteenth century, the University of Padua was the center for translation and commentary on many of the Aristotelian texts, including the biological, and the home of the scholars who published the texts, translations, and commentaries, in nearby Venice. Nicolas Leonicus Thomaeus (1456–1531) was professor of Greek at Padua from 1497; he had a major hand in the publication of many of Aristotle's works (and other ancient texts), both in Greek and in Latin translation. He also published a commentary on the *Parua naturalia,* including the *De motu animalium* and *De incessu animalium,* in Venice (1523); this was little more than a direct translation of Michael's commentary on those treatises. This commentary was reprinted several times, including Florence (1527) and Paris (1530 and 1541). Leonicus also did the *Parts of Animals*, published in Venice (1540), Basel (1541), Paris (1542). The 1541 Basel edition included a translation of Michael's commentaries on the *Parua naturalia* by Conrad Gesner.

Among the texts of Michael's commentaries, published in Greek, at the beginning of the sixteenth century, we may mention the *Parua naturalia* commentary of 1527 and frequently thereafter, the *Parts of Animals* (Florence, 1548), and the *Generation of Animals* (ascribed to Philoponus; Venice, 1526). Evangelista Lungus Asulanus translated Michael's commentaries on the *Parua naturalia* etc. under the title *Scholia Michaelis Ephesii in Aristotelis Opuscula Aliquot Non Ante e Graeco in Latinum Conuersa*, in Venice, 1552. Michael's commentary on the *Parts of Animals* was retranslated by Dominico Monthesauro (i.e., after the Leonicus version of 1541) and published in Basel, 1559.

No doubt this quick survey of Renaissance texts of Michael is only partial, but it is sufficient to make the general point that Michael's commentaries were available, both in Greek and in Latin, to scholars in the sixteenth and seventeenth centuries, and furthermore that they must have been read, since some of the commentaries went through several editions in various cities, and some of them were translated more than once during the sixteenth century.

Let us turn to look at the biologists who may have been aware of Michael's commentaries. In Padua, there had been scientific study of biology and medicine since the thirteenth century, in the days of Pietro d'Abano (1257-1315),[22] but the period of the publication of the text and translation of Michael's commentaries on the biological works was also a period of flourishing of Aristotelian biology in Italy. To mention just a few names: Andreas Vesalius (1514-1564),[23] Franciscus Piccolomini (1520-1604),[24] Andreas Caesalpinus (1525-1603),[25] Jacob Zabarella (1532-1589), and Hieronymus Fabricius of Aquapendente (1537-1619).

In 1600, William Harvey came to Padua to study biology, and he later said that his two inspirations were Aristotle and Fabricius.[26] Some might want to say that Harvey's discovery of the circulation of the blood was a "Copernican Revolution" in biology, but for Harvey himself it was the working out of essentially Aristotelian ideas.

It is not possible to tell what influence Michael's commentaries themselves had upon the development of the biology of Vesalius, Fabricius, and Harvey, but we can say that Michael's preservation of the Aristotelian text, and his participation in the tradition, must have made it more available to the Renaissance investigators.

Some Provisional Findings

I sometimes get the impression that the discontinuists think of scientific theories on a rather close analogy with biological evolution: they imagine that a particular "normal science" is a bit like a species of animal, and that when another "normal science" comes along, the earlier version is likely to be soon extinct. Once the dinosaurs are extinct, nothing else which comes into being is precisely a dinosaur. Similarly, according to the discontinuist thesis, once Aristotelian biology stopped being done in antiquity, nothing else which came into existence later could be a truly Aristotelian biology. But I do think that continuism and discontinuism in the history of scientific theories are really quite different, after all, from continuism and discontinuism in biological evolution. When a scientific theory or methodology has been set aside, it always remains possible for someone to take it up again, even centuries later. The question remains, when someone does take it up again, is it going to be the same thing, or something quite different really from its original nature?

Michael looked again at Aristotle's biological writings after centuries of neglect. When Michael turned to those books, probably no one else in the Greek world was reading them. Of course there had been interest in them in the Muslim world; Ibn Sina and Ibn Rushd read the biological works carefully, and that interest carried over into the Latin West, which first became acquainted with some of Aristotle's biological ideas through those Arabic-speaking physician-philosophers, and through the translations of the Arabic text of Aristotle's biology into Latin by Michael Scot. But also between Galen and Ibn Sina there is a caesura of considerable proportions, with minimally few and minor figures in the gap. We may also remark that in the centuries since Michael commented on Aristotle's biological works, those books have reappeared on the stage of scientific investigation more than once. If we think about these historical moments in relation to the discussion between continuists and discontinuists in the philosophy of the history of science, we must wonder whether the reappearance of elements of a theory is evidence for or against the continuous life of that theory. Certainly the case of Michael is not *clear* evidence for either thesis.

Michael's motivations in reading and commenting upon Aristotle's biological works are obviously radically different from Aristotle's original motivations in writing them. One may say that that contrast is between "science" and "scholarship." Aristotle was, by modern standards of scholarship, not a very good scholar: so far as can be determined, he systematically misrepresented the philosophical positions of all of his predecessors, including that of Plato, whom he knew well for twenty years. It is not so strange that a creative philosopher should misrepresent his predecessors—look at Bertrand Russell's *History of Western Philosophy* for another example. Michael is not a marvelous scholar either, but he has essentially scholarly motivations—accuracy of representation is his goal. We have already claimed that Aristotle should be counted as a "scientist," in some sense of that honorific word, and in the same generalized sense of "scientist," Michael is not a scientist at all. Michael is not motivated to represent the state of knowledge of a topic in his own day: if he introduces alien material into his interpretation of Aristotle's text, it is by accident, unintentionally, as in his reference to the crystalline part of the eye.

In a more general sense, our little exercise has demonstrated the simultaneous perishability and imperishability of ἐπιστήμη, even if we cannot definitively translate ἐπιστήμη as "science" or "knowledge."

On the one hand, those who ignored Aristotle's investigations missed out on some remarkable observations and discoveries, and even some who read those texts failed to see some of what was there, as Michael fails to understand that Aristotle has observed what Herophilus and then Galen realized was the optic nerve. On the other hand, those who did read Aristotle attentively could easily be led astray on many points: Michael, like Alexander of Aphrodisias, defends cardiocentrism long after it had been conclusively refuted, and even Galen is so convinced that the nerves must contain *pneuma* that he thinks himself to observe that the optic nerve is hollow.

Scientific observation and explanation, once written down, survives at least as long as the text survives and is understood. Aristotle's biological work survives as a challenge, as a standard, as a warning, as a puzzle, depending upon the age and the men who read it. Similarly Michael's commentaries survive at least as a warning and as a puzzle, if not as a standard, for our modern age of scholarship and of science.

Notes

1. An earlier version of this paper was presented at the USF-Tampa conference on "Byzantine Philosophy and Culture," 7 November 1986. It has been extensively revised for this volume.

2. A notable recent exception is James Scanlan, M.D., *Albert the Great, Man and Beast, De animalibus (Books 22–26)*, Medieval & Renaissance Texts & Studies, vol. 47 (Binghamton, N.Y., 1987). Of course a rather large bibliography may be constructed, but nothing comparable to the bibliography of physics and astronomy during the middle ages.

3. T. Kuhn, *The Structure of Scientific Revolutions* (Chicago, 1962; second edition, 1970). For an application to ancient science, see G. E. R. Lloyd, *Science, Folklore and Ideology* (Cambridge, 1983), 117.

4. Gaston Bachelard, *La Formation de l'esprit scientifique*, 6th ed. (Paris, 1969). An extended example of the application of Bachelard's ideas to ancient science may be found in Louis Bourgey, *Observation et expérience chez les médecins de la collection hippocratique* (Paris, 1953); Bachelard's theories are applied to Aristotle by

Robert Joly, "La biologie d'Aristote," *Revue Philosophique* 158.6 (1968): 219–53. Pierre Pellegrin, *Aristotle's Classification of Animals*, trans. A. Preus (Berkeley, 1987), does not reject the Bachelardian approach.

5. Michel Foucault, *Les mots et les choses* (Paris, 1966), trans. *The Order of Things* (New York, 1971).

6. See Pellegrin, 40.

7. Mayr told this story himself at a conference on Aristotle's zoology at Williams College in 1984.

8. See Paul Moraux, "Galen and Aristotle's *De partibus animalium*" in *Aristotle on Nature and Living Things*, ed. Allan Gotthelf (Pittsburgh, 1985), 327–44.

9. See especially Galen, *On the Doctrines of Hippocrates and Plato*, ed. and trans. Phillip De Lacy (Berlin, 1978).

10. Michael of Ephesus' commentary on Aristotle's *De generatione animalium* was attributed to Philoponus from the Renaissance to relatively recent times. The confusion may stem from the fact that Philoponus did write a commentary on Aristotle's *De generatione et corruptione* (as well as on the *De anima*, for example). It is clear from the first couple of pages of the commentary on the *De geneiatione animalium* that its author had already commented upon several other biological treatises of Aristotle, including the *De partibus animalium*, and that description fits only Michael, surely not Philoponus. See especially *In GA* 2.12–16, where the author says that it has been his custom to discuss everything in detail, but in this commentary he will give up that habit, concentrating on things especially needing discussion. That describes Michael's commentaries on the other biological works, but not Philoponus' commentaries. Also, anyone who has read Philoponus' commentary on the *De anima* for example, and any of Michael's commentaries will recognize immediately that the language of the *In GA* is typical of Michael, not of Philoponus.

11. See Athanasios P. Fotinis, *The De Anima of Alexander of Aphrodisias* (Washington, DC, 1979).

12. David Hahm, *The Origins of Stoic Cosmology* (Athens, Ohio, 1977).

13. See my "Plotinus and Biology," in *Neoplatonism and Nature*, ed. Baine Harris, forthcoming.

14. See my *Aristotle and Michael of Ephesus on the Movement and Progression of Animals* (Hildesheim, 1981); the introduction deals with the question of Michael's place in the Byzantine tradition in more detail than is appropriate in the present essay. Michael's dates were established by R. Browning, "An Unpublished Funeral Oration on Anna Comnena," *Cambridge Philological Society, Proceedings* 188 (1962): 1–12. For other general studies of the period, see Paul Lemerle, *Le premier humanisme byzantin* (Paris, 1971), and Basile Tatakis, *La philosophie byzantine* (Paris, 1959).

15. Paul Mercken, *Eustratius on Book I and Anonymous Scholia on Books II, III, and IV, The Greek Commentators on the Nicomachean Ethics of Aristotle in the Latin Translations of Robert Grosseteste, Bishop of Lincoln,* Corpus Latinum Commentariorum in Aristotelem Graecorum (Brussels, 1974).

16. Jean Darrouzes, *Georges et Demetrios Tornikes, Lettres et Discours* (Paris, 1970), 283.

17. This translation is based on that by A. L. Peck, in the Loeb *Generation of Animals* (London, 1953); it is included here for the convenience of the reader.

18. Michael of Ephesus *In libros de generatione animalium commentaria* (attributed previously to John Philoponus), commenting on *GA* II.6, 743b32, Michael Hay

duck, ed. (Berlin 1903), 112, line 6 ff.; translated by A. Preus. Hayduck's page numbers are in brackets.

19. See L. Minio-Paluello, "Jacobus Veneticus Grecus," *Traditio* 8 (1952): 265-304; L. M. De Rijk, *Logica Modernorum* (Assen, 1979), 1:100-105, and 1:222, and my *Aristotle and Michael of Ephesus*, 13.

20. For an account of Moerbeke's writings, see Pierre Thillet, *Alexandre d'Aphrodise, de Fato ad Imperatores, version de Guillaume de Moerbeke* (Paris, 1963) 28 ff. Moerbeke's translation of Aristotle's *De motu animalium* is printed by Luigi Torraca, *Aristotele de Motu Animalium* (Naples, 1958).

21. For a discussion of some evidence of Albert's use of the commentary on the *De motu animalium*, see my *Aristotle and Michael of Ephesus*, 15 ff.

22. See J. H. Randall, Jr., "The Development of Scientific Method in the School of Padua," *J. Hist. Ideas* 1 (1940): 177 ff.

23. Cf. *De fabrica humani corporis*, first edition (Padua, 1543).

24. See Walter Pagel, *New Light on William Harvey* (Basel, 1976) 38-39.

25. See Andreae Caesalpini Aretini, *Peripateticarum Quaestionum Libri Quinque* (Venice, 1571; photoreproduced, Bruxelles, 1973). This work deals with a wide range of controversial issues in Aristotelian philosophy; book 5 turns to biological questions, including the generation of animals and the role of the heart in the bodily economy.

26. See Walter Pagel, *William Harvey's Biological Ideas* (Basel, 1967); and *New Light*.

Petrarch's Scholarship in His *De remediis utriusque fortune:* A Preliminary Inquiry

CONRAD H. RAWSKI

1. Rationale

The scholarship "of Francesco Petrarca—philosopher, orator, and eminent poet, champion and restorer of a new flowering of literature and of the Latin tongue, which was corrupted and nearly buried by centuries of dreadful barbarity"; in whose works "you will find, beside the precepts of theology, and natural and moral philosophy, an encyclopedia of the liberal arts, a treasure trove of history, and the divine power of poetry, equalled by grandeur of style" (as the Basel, 1554 and 1581 editions of his *Opera omnia* noted on their title pages)[1] —was evident and recognized since the early 1340s, when the *Priuilegium lauree domini Francisci petrarche* awarded him at his coronation as poet laureate in Rome, April 8, 1341, referred to him as *magnus Poeta & historicus*, designated him *magister*, and bestowed upon him the right to lecture and debate at the university *tam in dicta arte poetica quam in dicta historica arte*.[2] Boccaccio, Petrarch's earliest panegyrist, praised him as a devoted, erudite, creative scholar and researcher of exceptionally clear mind and discerning intellect.[3] It is Petrarch who inspired, and in many ways anticipated, his scholarly activities and efforts and those of the following generation that centered around the transmission of literature and knowledge.[4] Petrarch was forever concerned with the enduring past, the continuity of knowledge which, as the most precious heritage of his generation of latecomers, was to be rediscovered, cherished, and made available by scholarship and learning— the late Rudolph Pfeiffer's Augustinian concept of a *philologia perennis*,[5] that would dispel the gloom of ignorance, so that our grandchildren should be able to "walk back into the pure radiance of the past."[6]

The scope of Petrarch's interests has been mapped and analyzed in terms of the five *studia humanitatis*[7] by Paul Oskar Kristeller, and further pursued in related studies.[8] His scholarship in the narrower sense of a sum total of activities constituting "the art of understanding, explaining, and restoring the literary tradition,"[9] has been probed since the days of Pierre de Nolhac and Remigio Sabbadini.[10] Led by the work of Petrarchan scholars and editors like Billanovich, Wilkins, Ullman, Festa, Rossi, Bosco, and Martellotti — to name only a few outstanding Petrarchists of our time[11] — a host of studies have explored specific facets of Petrarch's scholarship as evidenced in his texts, and his work of textual criticism, interpretation, and historical reconstruction — the "correction" and "conjecture" E. J. Kenney has spoken of.[12] A summary overview of these activities and their historical dynamics remains to be written. But it is self-evident that this literature represents the trends of interest and emphasis in today's studies of the Latin Petrarch.

And it is here that the rationale for this modest effort presents itself. As the *magnum opus* of Petrarch's later years, his *De remediis utriusque Fortune* — Remedies for Fortune Fair and Foul, in two books comprising some 250 dialogues between Reason and the four passions, Joy, Hope or Desire, Sorrow, and Fear, which occupied him from about 1354 to 1366 and later — ranks significantly in the canon of his works, even if we are unaware of the many relationships, essential, but seldom explored, between the *De remediis* and some of his other works, foremost among them, the *Secretum*, the *De uita solitaria*, *De ocio*, the invective *De sui ipsius*, and, both, the epistolae *Ad Familiares* and *Seniles*.[13] But the *De remediis* text has not received adequate attention and remains, as Pier Giorgio Ricci pointed out some thirty years ago, the one most neglected by Petrarchan students.[14] In our days the single major effort of "any substance"[15] devoted to the *De remediis* is Klaus Heitmann's *Studie* of 1958, and even this magisterial dissertation, bringing together a wealth of detail, fails to offer any systematic purview of the scholarly apparatus of Petrarch's text.[16]

The present paper, which represents only a first step toward a needed, critical, i.e., comparative, examination in detail, is based on my forthcoming English edition of the *De remediis*,[17] which has been under way, off and on, ever since I published *Petrarch: Four Dialogues for Scholars* nearly twenty years ago[18] — testimony, perhaps, for both my faltering energies and the demands of Petrarch's massive text.

2. *Citation and Quotation*

We may begin our inquiry with an examination of the ways Petrarch cites and quotes in the *De remediis* (henceforth referred to as *DR*, and cited by book, dialogue, and line). I shall use "cite" and "citation" for authors and works mentioned or alluded to in Petrarch's text, reserving "quote" and "quotation" for works actual text portions of which are used in the *DR*.

Unlike Jean de Hesdin, the learned opponent of his last invective, *Contra eum* (1373),[19] the Petrarch of the *DR*, more often than not, fails to identify his references with great care. This may have to do with Petrarch's purpose as far as his text and his readership or audience is concerned, or it may somehow be linked to the literary genre involved: Petrarch appears more careful in a modern sense in some of his other works, particularly so in *De ocio*.[20] Be that as it may, *precise citations*, such as, e.g.,

"Varro wrote a satire, which is called Menippean, *On the Duty of a Husband*. There you can read the short but effective advice of this great scholar regarding this matter" *DR* 2.19.28,[21]

or, less elaborate,

"Lactantius, in Book Two of his *Institutions*" 1.13.32,[22]
"Seneca, who mentions in his *quaestiones naturales*" 2.19.35,[23] and
"[Severus Alexander],"
"as Aelius Lampridius wrote about him" 2.60.24,[24]

are greatly outnumbered by *casual citations* of the type,

"in Cicero's words" 1.34.2,
"this sentence by Augustine" 1.22.96,
"about whom Sallust wrote" 1.29.69
"I agree with Pliny and believe with him" 1.37.19,
"Seneca said" 2.13.169,

or formulaic and descriptive references, which abound.

Petrarch uses frequently the old *formulaic citations*, which hearken back to late Antiquity,[25] early writers like the otherwise bibliographically meticulous Lactantius, and classifications like Isidore, *Etym.* 8.7, De poetis,[26] and which continued to be used as late as Salutati's generation: e.g., with varying consistency:

"the poet" (most often for Virgil),
"the lyrical poet" (most often for Horace),
"the satiric poet" (Juvenal or Persius),
"the comic poet" (Terence), etc.

Even the time-honored periphrasis *ille sapiens uir*—that wise man (2.79.98) appears not infrequently.[27] Serving as an example of the practice is 2.13.35-65, where Reason, the principal colloquist in the *DR*, refers to "your satiric poet (Juvenal) . . . the wise man of the Hebrews (Proverbs) . . . another of your poets, call him now satiric or lyrical (Horace) . . . the wise man from abroad (Proverbs) . . . your orator (Cicero) . . . the ecclesiastical orator" (conflating Eccles. 10, 9 and 10). These labels may be extended into *descriptive citations,* such as

"The poet versed in nature's lore" (Lucretius) 2.90.232
"another great and ancient author" (referring to a passage in Cicero's letters to Brutus) 1.Pref.87,
"the advice of that excellent counsellor" (Seneca) 1.38.56,
"your neighbor in Verona" (Pliny)[28] 1.64.39,
"the greatest historian about the greatest war ever fought" (Livy and the second Punic war) 1.103.22,
"two glorious princes of this earth and the true faith" (St. Paul, St. Peter) 2.7.45,
"the prophetess guided by divine counsel," 2.90.232 (who turns out to be Anna of 1 Reg. 2.10) and
"that old man who abounded in livestock," 1.59.37 (referring to Job 1:3).

And then there are the many *unidentified references,* some indicated by phrases, such as,

"by him who said" 1.1.20,
"someone has said" 1.51.18,
"and something (someone) else" 2.95.8,
"one of those of whom is written (of whom has been sung)" 1.69.35; 1.107.13,
"and this ... and that ... and this, by another" 2.13.95,
"as someone has said not altogether inelegantly," which, in 2.88.30, introduces a self-quotation,[29] or,
"the poetic phrase proved true" 2.70.60, and
"which is acknowledged in this distich ... whence this ... ," referring to the much discussed Martial distichs, 1.64.60-67[30]

and many more without indication of any kind: the text simply incorporates a quotation or quotations varying in length, rarely, if ever, set off in the original text,[31] often in *cento*-like fashion (as in 1.18.39-43, and 56-64, quoting Suetonius, 2 [*Aug.*] 76 and 77,[32] on the frugal eating habits of emperor Augustus, or the Scriptural composite, 2.126.9-13) from a key text that is (1.2.52-59)[33] or is not (1.112.54-59, and 2.115.36, both based on Cicero, *De diu.* 1.1.1) adduced verbatim.

These anonymous quotations may be of a relatively simple nature, as, e.g., the Socrates story in 2.67.58, which comes from Cicero's *Tusculan Disputations* (5.37.108), or the parallel stories of Hadrian and Tiberius in 1.101.119, involving two texts (*Hist. Aug., Hadr.,* 17.1; and Suetonius, 3 [*Tib.*] 61), or, they may use and reproduce *res* and *uerba*—content and form of the key text in extended fasion, as shown in tables 1 and 2.

In places, Reason seems to challenge the reader *sub specie ludi,* to use Huizinga's phrase,[34] to identify a quotation or allusion.[35] Most frequently, however, texts by other writers are used, with what appears to us today as random freedom and little concern for intellectual property or originality.

Table 1

Seneca *De tranqu. animi*		*DR* 1.43
5; 7	Books used for show and decoration	1-9; 143-55
6	Excess in anything becomes a fault	23-56
5	The forty thousand books of Ptolemy Philadelphus	28-35
4; 6	Owners of countless books looking at the outsides of their volumes	47-56; 116-20
4	Many books a burden to students	129-41

Table 2

Seneca *Nat. quaest.* 6		*DR* 2.91
1, 1-3, 13	Earthquakes in Pompeii, Herculaneum, Naples, Campania, Achaia, Macedonia, and Asia Minor	30-37
1, 4-7, 10-15	Omnipresence of quakes—no place to hide	11-16, 56-57, 59-63
1, 5, 15, 6	The earth no longer solid	13-14, 63-69
	Subterranean shelter against thunder and lightning	7-11
1, 8-9	Death amounts to the same thing everywhere	49-50
2, 8 2, 1; 3, 2	Earthquakes occur seldom	23-27
2, 1	Dangers on all sides	17-23
2, 7	A joy to die in a grand manner	51-52

This practice is not characteristic of the *DR* or Petrarchan quotation habits alone. It is engaged in throughout the medieval literature, which cited fully when authority was desirable, but sought accomplishment and originality in the utilization of materials—not in the materials into which the scholarly author immersed himself, making them his own. The age-old notions of *translatio, imitatio,* and *aemulatio,* with the aspiration of equalling or outdoing the ancients, that ultimately are involved here,[36] cannot be adequately discussed in this limited paper. The basic viewpoint of the period as to the immediate concerns regarding citation and quotation is bluntly expressed by John of Salisbury in his *Policraticus* of AD 1159:[37]

> I have been careful to insert pertinent text passages by various authors that come to mind as helpful and gratifying, sometimes without naming the authors—this because I know most of them are quite familiar to you (i.e., Thomas Becket, Archbishop of Canterbury), who is exceptionally versed in literature, and might induce those who are less knowledgeable to further assiduous reading. If in these texts there should be anything that is far reliable from truth, I believe that I should be forgiven, since I do not promise that all that is written here is true, but, rather, that it will be useful to the reader, whether it is true or false. . . . The greater part of what I present here belongs to others, save for the fact that I make my own whatever is well said somewhere else, and express it in my own words for brevity's sake, or in the words of the original for reasons of authenticity. And since I have started to reveal the secrets of my mind—let me disclose my arrogance still further: I consider all those whose words or deeds I encounter in the field of philosophy to be my vassals, and, what is more, claim them as my servants, so that instead of me they—as they have been reported—should oppose the cries of detractors.

Petrarch, well aware of the practices of scholarly retention and recall, which included making a *sententia* (in his case a phrase by Heraclitus) one's own by repeating it often,[38] discussed his active immersion into his favorite texts in several places[39]—nowhere more fiercely defensive than in *Fam.* 5.18, written in 1343 to Guido Sette:[40]

> Though I am all in one piece, thus far, I have always believed with Domitian that "nothing is more pleasing than beauty, but nothing shorter-lived."[41] *I was,* indeed, *born to a greater destiny than to be a slave to my body.* You say, "Seneca said this."[42] Who denies it? And I say it, and many will say it after me, and, perhaps, many said it before

him—and whoever will have said it, will have said distinguished and noble words, provided he did not lie. Not only have I said this, but I shall say what follows, and, in both instances, I know that I am not lying, and do hope that I am not in error. Far be it from me to dread the day of death because of love of my body or a desire for this life, since I have adopted for my own use what has been most truthfully said by another—that *what is being called our life, really is death.*[43]

Apart from the obvious pitfalls of *ex post facto* identification, the use of unidentified references, be they now quotations or paraphrases, creates further problems for the modern researcher.

There is the problem of sources cited or quoted within a key text. Often, Petrarch adopts such a reference and cites Herodotus and Varro based on Aulus Gellius (1.23.7-14; 2.19.25, and 2.104.47), Aristophanes, on Valerius Maximus (2.39.68), Plutarch *via* Lactantius (1.15.69-71) Ennius *via* Cicero (2.82.37), and Plato from sources ranging from Cicero (e.g, 1.15.44-50; 2.48.14) and Seneca (1.16.80-81; 2.5.76-77) to Valerius Maximus, Augustine (2.15.64-66; 2.75.25-30), and, probably, John of Salisbury[44]—which poses a perennial *caveat* for the eager interpreter.[45]

And there is the problem of the *topics*. In Petrarch's times these fundamental formulas of rhetoric and literary deportment—Cicero had called them the *seats of an argument*[46]—represented a long established repertory comprising age old traditions and practices—Ernst Robert Curtius' *Vorratsmagazin*—the stockroom of the house of intellect[47]—many items of which had long since become staples of discourse, literary expression, and exposition. It provided also a convenient memory aid for filing away pertinent quotations, phrases, maxims, and examples, and therefore played an important part in the writer's craft.[48] Table 3 reviews parallels between texts by Cicero and Augustine, and Reason's account of the beauties of nature in 2.93.40-171. But the invocation of nature and the superiority of man within the realm of nature is an ancient literary topic.[49] Characteristic features of this topic, for instance, catalog-like enumerations of component parts (e.g., trees, streams, meteorological phenomena, etc.),[50] promptly appear in Petrarch's text; and they remind us that, notwithstanding established lines of reference, such as Petrarch's conversance with both Cicero's *De natura deorum* and Augustine's *De ciuitate Dei*,[51] any number of source relationships may obtain, which, with old vintage topics such as this—topics controlling a whole "literature" of their own that predated Petrarch's generation by centuries[52]—included familiarity by acquaintance, as it were, because the topic and its motifs had become part and parcel of intellectual heritage and literary decorum.[53] Conversely, adherence to a closely literal interpretation of a topical passage may lead the modern reader to erroneous results (cf. 2.93.27–34).

Table 3

DR 2, 93, lines		Cicero, De nat. deor. 2	Augustine, De ciu. Dei 22.24, LCL, Green, pp.
40	roots and herbs	62, 156	334
41	flowers, scents, colors, tastes & sounds	39, 98; 56, 140–58, 146	334
42–43	living creatures	60, 151; 62, 158 (De leg. 1.8.25)	334
45–52	the earth (hills, dales, glens, streams) and the oceans	39, 98–100	334, 336
52–54	country and cities, wilderness	39, 98–99	
54–62	firmament; sun, moon, and stars	39, 101–15; 62, 155	334
104–06	majesty of man redeemed	(De leg. 1.8.25)	338
119–31	man's mind	59, 147	328, 330
132–41	the many arts; condiments; medicine	60, 150–52; (De leg. 1.8.25–26)	326, 328, 336
146–56	erectness, mind, mien	56, 140–41; (De leg. 1.9.26–27)	330, 332, 334
164–71	man uses all parts of nature	60, 151; 61, 154–64, 162	228

3. Authors and Works

L'Antiquité a été révélée à Pétrarque par ses écrivains, et l'histoire de sa bibliothèque, si on pouvait l'avoir complète, serait l'histoire même de son esprit.

— Pierre de Nolhac

Now that we have examined come of the bibliographical nether regions of the *DR*, we must turn to the data thus revealed — to those writers, as

Petrarch notes in his prefatory letter to Azzo da Correggio that preceeds *DR*, book 1,

> hundreds of years before our time, who still live and dwell with us, and talk to us with divine intellect in their great books. Amidst the perpetual turmoil of our mind, like so many bright stars fixed on the firmament of truth, like so many pleasant and favorable breezes, like so many eager and skilled sailors, they point us to the port of rest and guide the limp sails of our hopes and the helm of our wavering soul until such time as it can check and control its judgments, battered by such great storms.[54]

Arranging in descending frequency the authors and collections referred to and used in the *DR*, we find the following:

Table 4
Authors and Collections Cited and Quoted in the *DR*[55]
(*=included in Petrarch's lists of his favorite books, Paris, B. N. lat. 2201)

Vulgate	138	Jerome	4
* Cicero	113	Josephus Flavius	4
* Seneca	41	* Justin-Trogus	4
* Virgil	40	Claudian	3
* Horace	38	Q. Curtius Rufus	3
* Juvenal	29	* Firmicus Maternus	
* Suetonius	27	(*Mathesis*)	3
Pliny	25	Lucretius	3
* Aristotle	18	Orosius	3
* Augustine	18	Dicaearchus	2
* Ovid	17	Hecaton	2
* Lucan	16	Heraclitus	2
* Statius (*Theb.*)	14	Herodotus	2
* Sallust	13	Innocent III (*De miseria*)	2
* Valerius Maximus	12	John Chrysostom (*Quod*	
Historia Augusta	12	*nemo laeditur nisi a se ipso*)	2
Plato	11	Publilius Syrus	2
Terence	10	Seneca Rhetor (*Controu.*)	2
* Livy	6	Theophrastus	2
* Macrobius (*Saturn.*)	6	Varro (Menippean Satires)	2
Plutarch	6	Vitruvius	2
Lactantius (*Diu. inst.*)	5	Accius	1
Apuleius	4	Ambrose (*De exc. frat.*	
* Aulus Gellius	4	*sui Sat.*)	1

Aristophanes	1		Euripides	3
Asclepius	1		Persius	2
Ausonius (*Lud. sept. sap.*)	1		Plautus	2
Eusebius	1		Zeno, the Stoic	2
Martial	1		Athanasius	1
Origen	1		Bernard of Clairvaux	1
Pacuvius	1		Hippocrates	1
Plautus	1		Propertius	1
Quintilian	1		Roscius	1
Solinus	1		Sappho	1
Just referred to:			Valerius Flaccus	1
Epicurus	9		Xenophon	1
Catullus	4		Zeno of Elea	1

Sayings, allusions, echoes, and reminiscences from:

Aristotle, Augustine, Boethius, *Cons. phil.*, Cicero, Isidore, *Etym.*, and similar handbooks, John of Salisbury, *Policrat.*, Macrobius, *Comm. Somn. Scip.*, Jacobus de Voragine, *Legenda aurea*, or Saints' lives from various, often overlapping, sources (e.g., Paulus Presbyter, *Vita Ambrosii* and *Legenda aurea* [2.26.27-30], or Jerome, *Vita Malchi* [2.7.27-28]).

Detail: The Works in Descending Order of Frequency

Vulgate	Psalms		Malachi
	Ecclesiasticus		Luke
	Proverbs		Philippians
	Job		Hebrews
	Sapientia (Wisdom		Isaiah
	of Solomon)		Micah
	Corinthians		Habakkuk
	Exodus		John
	Romans		Acts
	Regna (=Samuel		Thessalonians
	and Kings)	Cicero	* *Tusculanae*
	Ecclesiastes		*disputationes*
	James		* *De officiis*
	Matthew		* *De re publica* vi
	Genesis		* *De amicitia*
	Numbers		*De finibus*
	Deuteronomy		* *De diuinatione*

(Cicero)	* De senectute * De natura deorum Ad Brutum Partitiones oratoriae Philippicae Ad Atticum Ad Quintum fratrem * De inuidia Epistolae ad familiares (?) * Paradoxa Stoicorum * (Rhetorica : cf. Ullman [1955], 122) Pro Ligario Pro Roscio comico	Ovid Plato	Augustine * Confessiones * De ciuitate Dei De uera religione * Metamorphoses Ars amatoria Fasti Remedium amoris Tristia Theaetetus Res publica Apologia "Epigramma eroticum" Leges Phaedrus
Seneca	* Epistulae * De tranquillitate animi De beneficiis De ira Naturales quaestiones Apocolocynthosis: Ludus de morte Claudii De matrimonio fragmentum * De remediis fortuitorum	Terence Livy (Livy)	Timaeus Andria Adelphoe Eunuchus Heauton timorumenos 5.55; 28.43-6; 30.14.11; 34.4.1-3, Belli ciuilis libri 112, as in Seneca, De tranquillitate 9.5. On this, Billanovich (1981), 120-27 on Brit. Mus. Harl.
Virgil	Aeneis Georgica Eclogae		2493; Reynolds & Wilson (1974), 114;
Horace	Carmen saeculare Carmina Epistulae Ars poetica Saturae Epodi	Apuleius Jerome	Mann (1984), 29. Metamorphoses Florida Aduersus Iouinianum Epistula 22
Aristotle	* Ethica Nicomachea Politica Rhetorica De caelo (?)	 Claudian	In Matthaeum Vita Malchi (?) De bello Gildonico In Rufinium

Petrarch's favorite books and literary apparatus have been most fully discussed by Nolhac and Ullman.[56] In the parts that apply, our tabulation bears out the quasi-statistics of their findings.[57] Nearly all the favorites of Petrarch's youth appear in the core-repertory of the *DR*. The quantitative aspects, as such, remain unchanged. The Scriptural references are dominated by the Psalms, Ecclesiasticus, Proverbs, and Job; the patristic ones by Augustine's *Confessions* and *De ciuitate Dei*. When it comes to the literary sources of Antiquity, the strongest emphasis is on Cicero in general, and the *Tusculan Disputations* in particular. As Pierre de Nolhac said long ago: "les Tusculanes sont l'ouvrage philosophique que Pétrarque a le plus souvent cité."[58]

Absent from the *DR* repertory are Cicero's *Academica* and Seneca's *De clementia,* the poets Propertius and Persius, who are mentioned, and Tibullus, who is not; the grammarians; Martianus Capella and Cassiodorus; and the historians, Cornelius Nepos, Aurelius Victor, Velleius Paterculus, Eutropius, Rufus Festus, Hyginus, Pomponius Mela, and Dares and Dictys. The absence of any reference to Boethius' *De consolatione Philosophiae* may seem surprising in view of the fact that the Consolation appears in the lists of Petrarch's favorite books, and that the *DR* is a book in the Boethian tradition.[59] Petrarch may have regarded the Consolation, which he cherished as the work of a holy, learned man[60] — like Isidore's *Etymologiae,* which he had consulted since childhood, but stylishly protested to "use but rarely"[61] — as being among the *opera communia* — works found in many places and widely accessible.[62]

More noteworthy may be the two quotations from Vitruvius (*De archit.* 6, Pref.) in 2.9.43-71. Besides the marginal note in the Ambrosian Virgil discussed by Nolhac,[63] these passages represent the only quotations from Vitruvius in Petrarchan texts known thus far.[64] Noteworthy also are the specific and unidentified references to Flavius Josephus, who is not often adduced in Petrarchan texts,[65] such as *DR* 1.69.123 (*auctor expressior sit Iosephus*) to *Jewish Antiqu.* 11.2; *DR* 2.90.78 (*qui . . . apud Iosephum legis*), and the allusion in *DR* 1.112.113, both, to *Jewish Antiqu.* 18.7.195-204.[66] And there is also in 1.23.85, what seems to be a reference to Plato's *Republic* 4.424.b-c. This could be added as a second passage to the well-known remarks about *Republic* 3.398 a, in *Contra medicum* 3.270-275, based on Cicero, *Tusc. disp.* 2.11.27, and Augustine, *De ciu. Dei* 8.13,[67] provided we do not consider it as echoing *Republic* 3.398c-403 c, the sequence to the text referred to in *Contra medicum*. Both alternatives would suggest that Petrarch's knowledge of the *Republic* text did extend further than hitherto assumed.

Another unidentified quotation of interest occurs in 2.7.81-84:

And also this piece of advice, which is widely quoted and most appropriate to human needs: Desire to do what needs must be done.[68] This way you elude the compelling force of necessity itself.[69]

This relates to some fifteen *DR* passages on "do willingly what needs must be done," *necessitas, uim necessitatis,* and "the wise man has learned to consent to things that he cannot resist."[70] Our quotation and the majority of related text passages invoke Seneca, *Ep.* 54.7:

> the wise man does nothing unwillingly. He escapes necessity, because he wills to do what necessity is about to force upon him,

which in turn, points to Cicero, *Ep. fam.* 4.9.12:

> ... it has ever been considered the mark of a wise man to yield to circumstances, in other words, to bow to the inevitable.[71]

However, much further inquiry is needed in order to establish whether our quotation paraphrases in maxim fashion the Stoic concept,[72] or constitutes a unique echo of Cicero's *Ad familiares,* nearly half a century prior to Coluccio Salutati's copy of 1392.[73]

The literary repertoire of the *DR* is carefully selected and utilized to body forth or to support the argument at hand in various ways, ranging from full quotations to terse text references, allusions, and formulaic lists. The wealth of subjects discussed in the 122 dialogues of book 1, and the 132 dialogues of book 2,[74] has been summarized by Ernest Hatch Wilkins in this resounding *enumeratio*:

> Among the topics treated in the first Book are bodily beauty, health and speed, eloquence, noble birth, banquets, personal adornment, fragrances, singing, dancing, ball playing, dice and chess, hunting, palatial abodes, furniture, jewels, books, the title Doctor, wealth, gardens, elephants, camels and monkeys, dowries, wives, children, teachers, students, fair weather, travel by sea, release from prison, popular favor, high office, warfare, vengeance, alchemy, and soothsayers. Among those treated in the second Book are ugliness, weakness, illness, base birth, poverty, servants, importunate neighbors, shipwreck, theft, overcrowded houses, imprisonment, exile, old age, gout, sleeplessness, bad dreams, earthquakes, toothache, blindness, deafness, the seven deadly sins, and the fear of death.[75]

There is hardly any need to stress the degree of familiarity and control required to bring to bear meaningfully on such a text the many sources that we have recorded.

4. Subsidia

Among the customary supports of the scholarly apparatus was noting and note taking, which *Augustinus* recommends to *Franciscus* in Petrarch's *Secretum*:

> But you, if you make precise notes at the proper places, will gather the fruit of your reading.[76]

Augustinus anticipates the program of the *DR* when he continues:

> Whenever in your reading any wholesome maxims occur, by which you feel the mind is bestirred or bridled, do not just depend on the powers of your intellect, but enshrine them in the recesses of your memory and try all you can to make them your friends, so that like an experienced physician you have the remedy, so to speak, written in your head, no matter where or when some urgent case of illness may befall. For there are some afflictions of the mind, in which, like in those of the body, delay is so pernicious that whoever defers the remedy destroys all hope for a cure.[77]

A related practice was text annotation. Like his scholarly forebears and peers, Petrarch inserted marginalia and glosses into many of the books in his library and referred to these *postillae* when composing his text (see fig. 1).[78]

[i. Jul. Caes., 64:]
in mare. nando per ducentos passus euasit ad
proximam nauem elata leua. ne libelli quos tene
bat madefierent. paludamentum mordicus trahens
ne spolio poteretur hostis.   De probatione et disci
[65:] Militem neque a moribus   plina eius in milites.
neque a fortuna probabat. sed tantum a uiribus trac
tabatque pari seueritate atque indulgentia. non enim
ubique ac semper. sed cum hostis in proximo esset coherce
bat tum maxime exactor grauissimus discipline.
ut neque itineris neque prelii tempus denuntiaret sed par
atum et intentum momentis omnibus quo uellet:
subito educeret. Quod etiam sine causa plerumque faciebat
precipue pluuiis ac festis diebus. ac subinde se ob
seruandum repente interdiu uel nocte subtrahebat.   admonens
augebatque iter: ut serius subsequentes defatiga
ret.   De eodem.

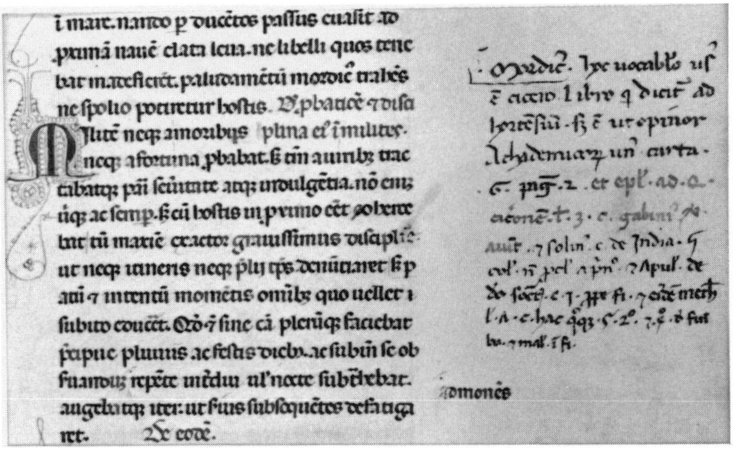

Fig. 1. Petrarch's Suetonius, *De XII Caesaribus*. Oxford, Exeter Coll. 186, f. 8r: Iul. Caes. 64–65, with marginal notes by Petrarch. (Billanovich [1960], 28–58; Mann [1975] 494–95, no. 256.) Courtesy of the Librarian, Exeter College, Oxford.

Mordicus. Hoc uocabulo usus
est cicero libro qui dicitur ad
hortensium. sed est ut opinor
Achademicorum unus carta.
vi pagina 2^1 et epystolis[2] .ad. Q.
ciceronem libro 3 capitulo Gabinius uersu
Aiunt.[3] et Solinus capitulo de India 5
columna non procul a principio.[4] et Apuleius de
deo socratis. capitulo 1 prope finem.[5] et eiusdem Metamorphoseon
libro 7, capitulo *hac quoque.* par. 2^6 .et.quarto de Finibus
bonorum et malorum. in fine.[7]

admonens
1. *Acad.* 2 (Priora), 16, 51; LCL, p. 530.
2. Petrarch's spelling, *Fam.* 1, 1, 9, 14, 20, 31, 32, 42, etc.
3. *Ad Quintum fratrem* 3.4.2; LCL, p. 587.
4. *Collect.* 52, 41 (T. Mommsen, 1895).
5. *De deo Socr.* Prol. 4 (P. Thomas, 1908).
6. *Metam.* 8.23; LCL, p. 382. Cf. Billanovich (1960), 38, n. 5.
7. *De fin.* 4.28, 78; LCL, 386, at the end of book 4.

Less familiar to us moderns are the *loci* and *imagines* of artificial memory, which, Reason informs us in 1.8, had been invented by Simonides of Ceos,[79] and was discounted by Themistocles who, when offered instruction in the art of memory, said he would rather learn the art of forgetfulness[80] — a reply that

> applies to nearly everyone, since all of you learn what you should forget and forget what you should learn, waste your memory on matters best consigned to oblivion, and, dissatisfied with the limits of nature, turn this madness into an art[81]

— that is a memory strengthened by *inductio quaedam et ratio praeceptionis* — a kind of training and system of discipline.[82] Mnemonic techniques constituted an important tool of scholarship in an age of manuscript books and precious few means of bibliographic control.[83] They ordered references and text passages, topics, and examples, and undoubtedly assisted in the *DR* with the compilation of encyclopedic summaries, such as cases of parricide (1.52); cases of rape (1.72); and of adultery and sexual incontinence (2.21); people with abnormal dentition (2.94); accomplishments by men of advanced age (2.101); famous men who died away from home (2.125), etc.

Specific evidence for Petrarch's use of associative recall in one form or another are the recurring sequential patterns of citations and quotations. In 1.95, Reason quotes Laberius,[84] followed by quotes from Ovid and Ennius.[85] In 2.82.34-45, the same sequence of quotations (Laberius-Ovid-Ennius) recurs and is enlarged by an additional quotation from Cicero, *De off.* 2.7.24. In *Sen.* 14, 1 (1581: 374), the great treatise on princely government for Francesco da Carrara,[86] the sequence of quotations is as follows: Laberius — Cicero, *De off.* 2.7.24 — Ennius, plus an unidentified quotation from Accius, *Trag.* 203, which is used by Cicero, Seneca, and Suetonius,[87] and recurs in both, Petrarch's *Fam.* 12.3.16, and the invective *Contra quendam* (*Prose* [1955], 708).

Exempla, and related lists, such as the recitals of ancient cities destroyed,[88] point to a similar template of en bloc citation. When the subject is physical beauty and its value, Spurina, the Tuscan youth who preferred self-mutilation to the allure of his handsome face, will be mentioned. When Reason addresses supreme happiness, Diagoras of Rhodes, who died of joy, is bound to come up.[89] The element of static redundancy that is inherent in such patterning is part of the didactic purpose of the text.[90] "Yes," says Reason in reference to the Laberius-Ovid-Ennius-Cicero quote in 2.82, "I repeat the same thing many times, because the subject requires it"[91] — and, concerning Spurina, in 2.78.28:

> have you forgotten the young man I have mentioned twice before in this conversation?[92]

In the *DR* Petrarch employs these techniques with great skill, as he links his knowledge and interests as a historian, student of literature, and philological and textual critic into the making of his huge guide book, depicting in a text to be argued with, this life's alternatives for those who seek a basis for right action. Whether he deals with historical facts, like the chronological sequence of Roman emperors (from 27 BC to AD 423, in 1.96.81-100); the birth places of classical authors (2.125); or Roman antiquities (1.118); the choice of words in a text (2.19.28); the divergent viewpoints on a subject expressed by several authors (2.118) or in several passages by the same author (2.98), or states his own opinions at a text (2.98, 99, 118; and 1.2.87, as below and note 96) — he displays a tremendous command of the sources that reverberate throughout the *DR*. The stress is on the text.[93] And while Reason and her creator impress upon the general reader the ethical quest of reading for action,[94] Petrarch's text attests in passage after passage to the textual immersion — and fascination — of rigorous scholarship.[95]

Some passages, such as Varro on an irksome wife (2.19.28), mentioned earlier (and note 21), are quite detailed and learned. Some reveal the debate *in his own bosom* (e.g., 2.81.151) between the thoughtful reader and his text:

> Seneca wrote [*Ep.* 66.2]:
> The poet who sang
> *gratior et pulchro ueniens e corpore uirtus* —
> worth is more pleasing in a form that's fair [Virgil, *Aeneid* 5.344],
> is, in my opinion, mistaken.
> It seems to me that poet could be criticized with more justification had he said *maior* — greater, or *perfectior* — more perfect, or *altior* — of a higher degree. But he said *gratior* — more pleasing, and thus refers not to *uirtus* — worth itself, but to the judgment of the beholders. Therefore, Virgil, the poet who wrote this, does not seem wrong to me.[96]

Only seldom does Petrarch's scholarly concern weigh heavily and strike us, who are strangers to his cosmos, as dry and pedantic — while most of the time we find in his text the savoring of connoisseurship and the precision of inquiry, both of which resound in Reason's remark on the *homo erectus* topic:

> And, though all other animals are prone, and fix their
> gaze upon the earth, he gave to man an uplifted face
> and bade him stand erect and turn his eyes to heaven,
> as Ovid so beautifully says, although Cicero said it before him.[97]

Abbreviations

Works by Petrarch

1492	*De remediis utriusque Fortune,* edition by Niccolò Lucaro, Cremona: Bernard de Misintis & Caesar Parmensis.
1554 and 1581	*Francisci Petrarchae Florentini — Opera quae extant omnia ...,* Basel.
Prose (1955)	Francesco Petrarca: *Prose.* Ed. G. Martellotti et al. Milan, Ricciardi.
Rime (1951)	Francesco Petrarca: *Rime, Trionfi e Poesie latine.* Ed. F. Neri et al. Milan, Ricciardi.
Africa	*Africa.* Ed. N. Festa, Edizione nazionale, vol. 1. Florence: Sansoni, 1926.
Contra eum	*Inuectiua contra eum qui maledixit Italie.* Ed. E. Cocchia in his "Magistri Iohannis de Hysdinio Inuectiua contra Fr. Petrarcham et Fr. Petrarchae Contra cuiusdam Galli calumnias apologia," in Società Reale di Napoli, R. Accademia di Archeologia, Lettere e Belle Arti, *Atti,* n.s., 7 (1920): 93–202; parts, ed. P. G. Ricci, in *Prose (1955),* 768–807.
Contra med.	*Inuectiue contra medicum.* Ed. P. G. Ricci. Rome: Ediz. di Storia e Letteratura, 1950.
Contra quendam	*Inuectiua contra quendam magni status hominem sed nullius scientie aut uirtutis.* Ed. P. G. Ricci: Florence: Le Monnier, 1949.
De sui ipsius	*De sui ipsius et multorum ignorantia.* Ed. L. M. Capelli. Paris: H. Champion, 1906.
De uita sol.	*De uita solitaria.* Ed. G. Martellotti in *Prose* (1955), 286–591.
Fam.	*Familiares. Le familiari,* vols. 1–3, ed. V. Rossi; vol. 4, ed. V. Rossi and U. Bosco. Edizione nazionale, vols. 10–13. Florence: Sansoni, 1933–1942.
Itin. syr.	*Itinerarium syriacum.* Itinerarium breue de Ianua usque ad Ierusalem et Terram Sanctam. Ed. G. Lumbroso in R. Accademia dei Lincei, *Rendiconti,* Classe di scienze morali, Ser. 4, 4 (1888), 390–403; also in his *Memorie italiane del buon tempo antico.* Turin: E. Loescher, 1889, 16–49.
Metr.	*Metricae.* In Francesco Petrarca, *Poesie minori,* Ed. D. Rossetti, vols. 2–3, Milan: Soc. tipogr. de' classici italiani, 3 vols., 1829–1834.
Ps. poen.	*Penitential Psalms.* Les psaumes pénitentiaux publiés d'après le manuscrit de la Bibliothèque de Lucerne. Ed. H. Cochin. Paris: L. Rouart, 1929.
Rer. mem. libri	*Rerum memorandarum libri iv.* Ed. G. Billanovich. Edizione nazionale, vol. 14. Florence: Sansoni, 1945.

Secretum	*Secretum.* Ed. E. Carrara, *Prose* (1955), 22–215.
Sen.	*Seniles.* Text of 1581.

Other Works

Baron (1968)	H. Baron. *From Petrarch to Leonardo Bruni.* Chicago: University of Chicago Press for Newberry Library.
Bernardo (1980)	A. S. Bernardo. *Francesco Petrarca: Citizen of the World.* Padua: Antenore.
Billanovich (1981)	G. Billanovich. *La tradizione del testo di Livio e le origini dell' umanesimo.* Padua: Antenore.
Bishop (1966)	M. Bishop. *Letters from Petrarch.* Bloomington: Indiana University Press.
Bolgar (1971)	R. R. Bolgar. *Classical Influences on European Culture AD 500–1500.* Cambridge: Cambridge University Press.
Curtius (1953)	E. R. Curtius. *European Literature and the Latin Middle Ages.* New York: Pantheon.
Fucilla (1975)	J. G. Fucilla. "The Present Status of Petrarchan Studies." In A. Scaglione, *Francis Petrarch, Six Centuries Later.* Chapel Hill: University of North Carolina and Newberry Library of Chicago.
Gerosa (1966)	P. P. Gerosa. *Umanesimo cristiano del Petrarca.* Turin: Bottega d'Erasmo.
Heitmann (1958)	K. Heitmann. *Fortuna and Virtus: Eine Studie zu Petrarcas Lebensweisheit.* Cologne: Boehlau.
IMU	*Italia medioevale e umanistica.*
Kristeller (1984)	P. O. Kristeller. "Petrarcas Stellung in der Geschichte der Gelehrsamkeit." In *Italien und die Romania in Humanismus und Renaissance,* ed. K. W. Hempfer and E. Straub. Wiesbaden: Steiner.
LCL	Loeb Classical Library
Lowenthal (1985)	D. Lowenthal. *The Past is a Foreign Country.* Cambridge: Cambridge University Press.
Mann (1971)	N. Mann. "The Manuscripts of Petrarch's 'De remediis': A Checklist." *IMU* 14 (1971): 57, n. 2.
Mann (1984)	N. Mann. *Petrarch.* Oxford: Oxford University Press.
Martellotti (1983)	G. Martellotti. *Scritti petrarcheschi.* Padua, Antenore.
Nolhac (1907)	P. de Nolhac. *Pétrarque et l'Humanisme.* 2 vols. Paris: H. Champion.
Petrarch Catalogue (1974)	*Petrarch: Catalogue of the Petrarch Collection in Cornell University Library.* Millwood, N.Y.: Kraus-Thomson.
Pfeiffer (1968)	R. Pfeiffer, *History of Classical Scholarship,* vol. 1, Oxford: Clarendon Press.
PL	J.-P. Migne. *Patrologia latina.*
Rawski (1967)	C. H. Rawski. *Petrarch: Four Dialogues for Scholars* [From *De remediis utriusque Fortune*]. Cleveland: Press of Western Reserve University.

Reynolds & Wilson (1974)	L. D. Reynolds and N. G. Wilson. *Scribes and Scholars: A Guide to the Transmission of Greek and Latin Literature*. Oxford: Clarendon Press.
Rico (1974)	F. Rico. *Vida u obra de Petrarca*. Vol. 1, *Lectura del Secretum*. Chapel Hill: University of North Carolina, Dept. of Romance Languages; North Carolina Studies in the Romance Languages and Literatures, Essays, 33. [Published separately, Padua: Antenore.]
Rico (1986)	"Philology and Philosophy in Petrarch." In P. Boitani and A. Torti. Cambridge: D. S. Brewer; Tuebingen: G. Narr.
Sabbadini (1905) and (1914)	See note 10.
Steiner (1975)	G. Steiner. *After Babel: Aspects of Language and Translation*. New York: Oxford University Press.
Ullman (1955)	B. L. Ullman. *Studies in the Italian Renaissance*. Rome: Ediz. di Storia e Letteratura.
Weiss (1977)	R. Weiss. *Medieval and Humanist Greek*. Padua: Antenore.
Wilkins (1958)	E. H. Wilkins. *Petrarch's Eight Years in Milan*. Cambridge, Mass.: Mediaeval Academy of America.
Wilkins (1959)	E. H. Wilkins. *Petrarch's Later Years*. Cambridge, Mass: Mediaeval Academy of America.
Wilkins (1961)	E. H. Wilkins. *Life of Petrarch*. Chicago: University of Chicago Press.
Wilks (1984)	M. Wilks, ed. *The World of John of Salisbury*. Oxford: Blackwell.
Yates (1966)	F. A. Yates. *The Art of Memory*. Chicago: University of Chicago Press.

Notes

1. Both 1554 and 1581 read:

FRANCISCI PETRARCHAE FLORENTINI, PHILOSOPHI, ORATORIS, ET POETAE CLARISSIMI, REFLORESCENTIS LITERATVRAE, LATINAEQUE LINGVAE, ALIQVOT SECVLIS HORRENDA BARBARIE INquinatae, ac pene sepultae, assertoris & instauratoris, OPERA quae extant omnia. In quibus praeter Theologica, Naturalis, Moralisque Philosophiae praecepta, liberalium quoque artium Encyclopediam, Historiarum thesaurum, & Poesis diuinam quandam uim, pari cum sermonis maiestate, coniuncta inuenies. . . .

Cf. *Petrarch Catalogue* (1974), 1. Note Martellotti (1983), chap. 40.

2. In 1554, pp. 1254–56; 1581, vol. 3:6–7. Cf. E. H. Wilkins, *The Making of the "Canzoniere" and Other Petrarchan Studies* (Rome: Ediz. di Storia e Letteratura, 1951), 9–69, esp., 53–61; Wilkins (1961), chap. 6; and Kristeller (1984), 104–5,

114-16. I am indebted to Professor Kristeller for his further commentary on this and the matter of the *De remediis fortuitorum* (note 52, below).

3. Boccaccio, *Opere latine minori*, ed. A. F. Massèra (Bari: Laterza, 1928), 195-244; idem, *Genealogia deorum*, as listed in C. Osgood, *Boccaccio on Poetry* (Princeton: Princeton University Press, 1930), 191 n. 12. Cf. W. Handschin, *Francesco Petrarca als Gestalt der Historiographie:* (Basel: Helbing & Lichtenhahn, 1964), chap. 1, 2; E. Bonnora in *I Classici Italiani nella storia della critica*, ed. W. Binni (Florence: Nuova Italia, 1962), 1:97-106.

4. On early humanistic activity, G. Billanovich, *I primi umanisti e le tradizioni dei classici latini* (Freiburg: Ediz. Universitarie, 1953); idem, "I primi umanisti e l'antichità classica" in Bolgar (1971), chap. 5; R. Weiss, *Il primo secolo dell'umanesimo* (Rome: Ediz. di Storia e Letteratura, 1949); idem, *The Renaissance Discovery of Classical Antiquity* (Oxford: Blackwell, 1969), chap. 2; B. Smalley, *English Friars and Antiquity in the Early Fourteenth Century* (Oxford: Blackwell, 1960), chap. 12; Reynolds & Wilson (1974), 110-13. On Petrarch and his position, among a large number of publications, Nolhac (1907); Ullman (1955), chaps. 6, 8; Gerosa (1966); R. R. Bolgar, *The Classical Heritage and Its Beneficiaries* (Cambridge: Cambridge University Press, 1954), chaps. 6, 7; Reynolds & Wilson (1974), 113-19; R. Pfeiffer, *History of Classical Scholarship* (Oxford: Clarendon Press, 1976), 2: 4; Martellotti (1983), esp. chaps. 1, 2, 7, 41, 47, and Bernardo (1980), 275-85; and the remarkable study on *la tradizione del testo di Livio e le origini dell'umanesimo* by Giuseppe Billanovich (Billanovich [1981]), now in progress.

5. Pfeiffer (1968), vii; Steiner (1975), 138.

6. Petrarch *Africa* 9.456-57:

> ... Poterunt discussis forte tenebris
> Ad purum priscumque iubar remeare nepotes.

On this, Th. Mommsen, "Petrarch's Concept of the Dark Ages," *Speculum* 17 (1942): 226; E. Panofsky, *Renaissance and Renascences in Western Art* (Stockholm: Almquist & Wiksell), 1960, 10-11; Steiner (1975), 132-38; note Lowenthal (1985), esp. 84-85, 372-73; and, most recently, L. Braudy, *The Frenzy of Renown* (New York: Oxford University Press, 1986), esp. 251-64.—Cf. also Petrarch, *Fam.* 20.8.11: *tantasque per tenebras stilum ferre.*

7. I.e., grammar, rhetoric, poetry, history, and moral philosophy. Cf. P. O. Kristeller, *Renaissance Thought and Its Sources* (New York: Columbia University Press, 1979), chap. 5. Note also the literature listed in Fucilla (1975).

8. Kristeller (1984); idem, *Eight Philosophers of the Italian Renaissance* (Stanford: Stanford University Press, 1964), chap. 1; here may also be noted the important papers by G. Constable, G. Billanovich, F. I. Murphy, Ch. Trinkaus, and G. Martellotti in Bernardo (1980); and Weiss (1977), esp. chaps. 10-13; and Rico (1986).

9. Pfeiffer (1968), 3.

10. Nolhac (1907); R. Sabbadini, *Le scoperte dei codici latini e greci ne' secoli xiv e xv.* 2 vols. (Florence: Sansoni, 1905, 1914; con nuove aggiunte e correzioni dell'autore a cura di E. Garin, 1967). Note U. Bosco, "Il Petrarca e l'umanesimo filologico (postille al Nolhac e al Sabbadini)," *Giornale storico della letteratura italiana* 120 (1942): 65-110.

11. On Billanovich, above, note 4, and the "Premessa bibliografica" in Bil-

Ianovich (1981), xii–xvi. For the works of Wilkins, cf. E. H. Wilkins, *Petrarch's Correspondence* (Padua: Antenore, 1960), "Publications of E. H. Wilkins," esp. xxiii–xxx; and idem, *Studies on Petrarch and Boccaccio,* ed. A. S. Bernardo, (Padua: Antenore, 1978). Ullman (1955). The entries in *Petrarch Catalogue* (1974), 534; and Mann (1971)—and, of course, the work of the editors of the Edizione Nazionale of Petrarch's works published thus far.

12. E. J. Kenney, "The Character of Humanist Philology" in R. R. Bolgar (1971), chap. 12. Cf. the relevant sections in J. G. Fucilla, *Oltre un cinquantennio di scritti sul Petrarca (1916-1973)* (Padua: Antenore, 1982); and Fucilla (1975).

13. Note Ch. Trinkaus, *In our Image and Likeness* (Chicago: University of Chicago Press, 1970), vol. 1; idem, *The Poet as Philosopher: Petrarch and the Formation of Renaissance Consciousness* (New Haven: Yale University Press, 1979); Rico (1974); Baron (1968), chap. 1; and Fucilla (1975) and (1982).

14. "Tra le opere del Petrarca, il *De remediis* è stata quella più abbandonata dagli studiosi." *Prose* (1955), 1169.

15. Mann (1971), 57 n. 2.

16. Heitmann (1958). Note also, C. N. J. Mann, "Petrarch and the Transmission of Classical Elements" in Bolgar (1971), chap. 22.

17. C. H. Rawski, *Petrarch's Remedies for Fortune Fair and Foul: A Modern English Translation of* De remediis utriusque Fortune, *with a Commentary*. Forthcoming from Indiana University Press.

18. Rawski (1967).

19. In his long, disparaging letter, *Homo quidam descendebat ab Hierusalem in Hiericho, & incidit in latrones* [Luke 10.30] (1581: 1060-68), in response to Petrarch's *Sen.* 9.1, *In exitu Israel de Egypto, domus Iacob de populo barbaro* [Ps. 113.1], written to Pope Urban V late in 1367 or early in 1368 (Wilkins [1959], 133), Jean de Hesdin (Wilkins [1961], 235-36; Nolhac [1907], vol. 2:303-12) cites carefully: e.g., *Lucan V;* [Iuvenal] *in III. Satyra; Pompeii Trogi breuiator Iustinus libro XXIII; Augustinus in III. de Ciuitate Dei, C[aput]. XIV* (1581: 1060, 1061, 1065, 1067). On *Contra eum,* Wilkins (1959), 237-41.

20. E.g.:

> quod in Libro uere religionis ait Augustinus (1581: 295); quibus in Libro sapientiae scriptum est (1581: 296); cum Sibyllas multas Varro numeret, studiosissimus Latinorum, quae a Lactantio sparsim posita, Institutionum eius libro primo [*Diu. inst.* 1.6, *PL* 6.140-48], ab Augustino autem collecta in Ciuitatis Dei libri [*De ciu. Dei* 18.23] disponuntur hoc ordine ... (1581: 304)

Note also the careful, patient citing in *Fam.* 17.1 (to Petrarch's brother Gherardo, Monza, November 7, 1353, Wilkins [1958], 43, 57-58).

21. I.e., an irksome wife. Our text continues:

> These are his words: *A wife's fault must be either put down or put up with.* He uses *tollendum*—to be put down in the sense of *corrigendum*—to be corrected, and offers, [30] briefly, but elegantly, this reason for his statement: *If a fault of that kind in a wife cannot be corrected, it should be tolerated, in so far of course as a man may endure it honorably; for faults are less serious than crimes.* But this commentary is not by Varro.

Both the quotation and the "commentary not by Varro" are supplied in Aulus Gellius *Noctes Atticae* 1.17.4-6. The quotation recurs in John of Salisbury, *Policraticus* 6.26, *PL* 199.629.

22. Lactantius *Diu. inst.* 2, 16, *PL* 6.335-36, on Hermes Trismegistus.
23. Seneca *Nat. quaest.* 6.1.1-2.
24. *Hist. Aug., Seu. Alex.*, 17.1-2, attributed to Aelius Lampridius.
25. E.g., Suetonius, 4 (*Calig.*), 30.1, referring to Accius as the tragic poet — while Boethius, *Cons. phil.* 3, pr. 6, 2 (echoing Aristotle, *Poet.* 1453a 29), uses the same epithet for Euripides.
26. On this, Curtius (1953), 453-57.
27. Cf. H. de Lubac, *Exégèse médiévale: Les quatre sens de l'Écriture*, (Paris: Aubier, 1961), 1:45-50.
28. Petrarch believed that Pliny, really a native of Como, was born in Verona (cf. *Rer. mem. libri* 1.19.1; *Fam.* 12.5.7; 24.8.6; *Metr.* 2.10.67-68 and 15.128; *Trionfi*, Tr. fame 3.42; *Itin. syr.* 61). Nolhac (1907), vol. 2:69 n. 2, speculates that Petrarch may have been misled by Pliny's referring to Catullus of Verona as *concerraneum meum* — my boon-companion. An old variant reading (Jahn-Mayhoff), *conterraneum meum*, indicates "my countryman," "my fellow citizen."
29. The line occurs in *Metr.* 2.14.273, and in *Africa* 7.292, where Hannibal addresses Scipio on "curbing Fortune's course." It is quoted by *Augustinus* in *Secretum* 3 (Prose [1955], 184), and, with an interesting explanation, in *Fam.* 7.7.5-6:

> Non queritur gratis clarum nomen nec seruatur quidem;
>   Magnus enim labor est magne custodia fame.
> Permitte michi meo uersiculo tecum uti, qui adeo michi placuit ut eum
> ex quotidianis epystolis non puduerit ad *Africam* transferre.

> A famous name is not sought freely, nor indeed is it preserved easily;
>   for it is great labor to guard a great fame.
> Permit me to use with you a short verse of mine, which I liked so much
> that I was not ashamed to extract it from my everyday letters and transfer
> it to my *Africa*.

(A. S. Bernardo, *Rerum familiarum libri I-VIII* [Albany: State University of New York Press, 1975], 350). On this, Rico (1974), 366 n. 399. Another self-quotation occurs 2.83.212-14. Note also the quotation from Petrarch's *Bucolicum carmen* in his invective *De sui ipsius* (1581: 1040).
30. Martial, 14.73 and 76; 3.95.1-2, quoted in Isidore *Etym.* 12.7.24 and 46 = Hrabanus Maurus *De uniuerso* 7, *PL* 3.246-47. On this, Nolhac (1907), 1: 209, and Martellotti (1983), chap. 24.
31. This is an omnipresent source of error for even the most painstaking scholarly reader; e.g., Baron (1968), 39 n. 69, quoting *DR* 2.118.179-89: *C. enim Caesar . . . clarificaret* is Lactantius, *Diu. inst.* 3, 18, *PL* 6.408-9, and not Petrarch.
32. Referred to in *Sen.* 15, 3 (1581: 934). Also quoted in John of Salisbury. *Policraticus* 5, 7, *PL* 199.557.
33. 1.2.52-59 (all *DR* texts are to 1492):

> Ad breuissimum tempus erit: quando oris habitus hic: colorque mutabitur.
> Cadet flaua cesaries: reliqua*albescent: teneras genas: & serenam frontem: squallentes arabunt rugae: laetas oculorum faces: & lucida sydera

moesta teget nubes: leue dentium ebur: ac candidum: scaber situs obducet atque atterret: ut non colore tantum: sed tenore alio sint: recta ceruix atque agiles humeri curuescunt.*Guttur leue*crispabitur. Aridas manus: & recuruos pedes suspiceris tuos non fuisse.
(*1581: reliquiae; curuescent; lene.)

And yet, within a very short time, this *comeliness* and glow of your face will change. These *blond locks* shall fall out, and what remains of your hair *shall become white,* ugly *lines will furrow* your soft cheeks and *the fair forehead* (Cicero, *De fin.* 3.17.56; Juvenal, 13.165; Horace, *Carm.* 3.14.25; Virgil, *Aen.* 7.417; Cicero, *Tusc. disp.* 3.15.31). The cheerful *brightness* and *the shining stars of your eyes* shall be covered by a melancholy cloud; and *rotten decay* (Propertius, 2.3.14, Statius, *Ach.* 1.164, also, Ovid, *Am.* 2.16.44 and 3.3.9–and Ovid, *Metam.* 8.802. On this, *Sen.* 7.2 1581: 830) shall consume and wear away the smooth white ivory of your teeth, not only changing their color, but also their regular array. The upright neck and nimble shoulders will be bent, the smooth throat wrinkled and those *withered hands* and crooked feet will not seem as your own (Matt. 12:10, Marc. 3.1; Ovid, *Ars am.* 2.670. Note *Sen.* 10.1 and *Ps. poen.* 5).

34. J. Huizinga, *Homo ludens: Versuch einer Bestimmung des Spielelementes in der Kultur* (Basel: Pantheon, 1938), 8.

35. E.g., "Do you remember the words of Lucan . . . ?" 2.114.313. Petrarch and his contemporaries admired the tenacious memory and sensitive ear this required—faculties still extolled and carefully discussed in the 1747 edition of Daniel Georg Morhof's *Polyhistor* (Luebeck: Peter Boeckmann), vol. 1, book 2. Cf. Petrarch, on the talents of his youthful amanuensis Giovanni Malpaghini, in *Fam.* 23.19 (also in *Prose* [1955], 1014–21; and Rawski [1967], 77–81).

36. Cf., e.g., Lowenthal (1985), 72, 81–84; Mann (1984), 18, 28; T. M. Greene, *The Light in Troy* (New Haven: Yale University Press, 1982), chaps. 5–7; Rawski (1967), 79–80; L. Spitzer, *Romanische Literaturstudien* (Tuebingen: Niemeyer, 1959), 923–44; Curtius (1953), 467. Note also A. Preminger, *Encyclopedia of Poetry and Poetics* (Princeton: Princeton University Press, 1965), s.v. "Imitation."

37. John of Salisbury, *Policrat.* 1, Prol., *PL* 199.387:

Quae uero ad rem pertinentia a diuersis auctoribus se animo ingerebant, dum conferrent, aut iuuarent, curaui inserere, tacitis interdum nominibus auctorum; tum quia tibi, utpote exercitato in litteris, pleraque plenissime nota esse noueram; tum ut ad lectionem assiduam magis ascenderetur ignarus. In quibus si quid a fide ueri longius abest, mihi ueniam deberi confido, qui non omnia, quae hic scribuntur, uera esse promitto; sed siue uera, seu falsa sunt, legentium usibus inseruire. . . . Haec quoque ipsa, quibus plerumque utor, aliena sunt, nisi quia quidquid ubique bene dictum est, facio meum, et illud nunc meis ad compendium, nunc ad fidem ac auctoritatem alienis exprimo uerbis. Et quia semel coepi reuelare mentis arcana, arrogantiam meam plenius denudabo. Omnes ergo qui mihi in uerbo aut opere philosophantes occurrunt, meos clientes esse arbitror, et quodque maius est, mihi uindico in seruitutem; adeo quidem ut in traditionibus suis se ipsos pro me linguis obiiciant detractorum.

On this, D. Luscombe in Wilks (1984), 30; E. Tuerk, *Nugae curialium:* Le *règne d'Henri II Plantagenêt (1154–1189) et l'éthique politique.* Centre de Recherches d'Histoire et de Philologie, IVe Sect., L'École pratique des Hautes Études, Hautes études médiévales et modernes, 28 (Geneva: 1977).

38. *Fam.* 17.3.3: Sepe de hac re sententiam meam dixi et sepe illam repetendo meam facio: "nusquam terrarum mora tranquilla est." Similar, *Fam.* 22.2.13.

39. Cf. esp. *Fam.* 22.2.12–17; and Mann (1984), 18–19.

40. *Fam.* 5.18.5–6:

> . . . adhuc enim integer, Domitiano principi credideram: "Nichil gratius decore, nil breuius." *Ad maiora* uero *genitus* sum, *quam ut sim mancipium corporis mei.* 'Seneca' inquis 'hoc dixit.' Quis negat? et ego dico, et multi dicent post me, et ante eum multi forte dixerunt, et quisquis id dixerit, modo ne mentiatur, egregium magnificumque uerbum dixerit. Ego et illud dixi, et quod sequitur dicam, et in utroque scio quod non mentior; utinam nec fallar. Absit a me ut amore corporis aut huius lucis desiderio diem mortis horrescam, quoniam et hoc ab alio uerissime dictum in usus meos uerti, quod hec nostra *que dicitur uita, mors est.*

On this letter, E. H. Wilkins, *Studies in the Life and Works of Petrarch* (Cambridge, Mass.: Mediaeval Academy of America, 1955), 10, 173–74.

41. Suetonius, 8 (*Dom.*), 18, 2, LCL, Rolfe, p. 381. Also quoted in *DR* 1.2.20; *Fam.* 1.3.10; *Secretum* 2, *Prose* (1955), 78; *Rer. mem. libri* 3.35.3.

42. Seneca *Ep.* 65.21; also quoted in Secretum 2, *Prose* (1955), 80. For a *subiectio* (*Ad Herennium* 4.23.33) similar to *You say, "Seneca said this,"* cf. e.g., Boethius *De consolatione Philosophiae* 5, pr. 6, 72–103.

43. Cicero *De re publ.* 6.14.14; *Tusc. disp.* 1.31.75; *Scaur.* 3.4; also, Seneca *Ep.* 77.18; Augustine *De ciu. Dei* 13.10–11, etc. Note the quotation in *Sen.* 13.1 (1581:915); and *De uita sol.* 2, *Prose* (1955), 128, referring to Cicero and Augustine. Cf. *DR* 2.117–18.

44. Cf. *Fam.* 3.18.3–4:

> libri medullitus delectant, colloquuntur, consulunt et uiua quadam nobis atque arguta familiaritate iunguntur, neque solum se se lectoribus quisque suis insinuant, sed et aliorum nomen ingerit et alter alterius desiderium facit. Ac ne res egeat exemplo, Marcum michi Varronem carum et amabilem Ciceronis *Achademicus* fecit; Ennii nomen in *Officiorum* libris audiui; primum Terrentii amorem ex *Tusculanarum questionum* lectione concepi. . . .

> But books thrill you to the marrow; they talk to you, counsel you, admit you to their living, speaking friendship. Nor do they insinuate themselves alone into the reader's spirit; they introduce other books; each one creates a desire for another. To give some examples, Cicero's *Academicus* made Marcus Varro my beloved friend [*Acad.* 1]; in the *De officiis* I first heard the name of Ennius [*De off.* 1.16.51; 24, 84, 2.7.23, etc.]; I first fell in love with Terence in the *Tusculan Disputations* [*Tusc. disp.* 3.14.29, 27, 65, etc.]. . . .

Bishop (1966), 40. Note the many other sources listed in the continuation of this letter, and carefully documented by V. Rossi in the Edizione nazionale, and the passage from Cicero's *Republic* quoted after Lactantius in *Fam.* 17, 1.29–31.

45. Attributions like 2.132.82:

> Incursus quoque serpentum atque immanium belluarum quarum impetum dicearchus docet: ut ait Cicero: quaedam hominum genera esse consumpta.
>
> The incursion of snakes and savage animals which, as Cicero says (*De off.* 2.5.16), Dicaearchus teaches, wiped out whole tribes of men

are rather uncommon. The problem is enhanced when the silently adopted source reference is cited or quoted in more than one key text. Cf. the Platonic *epigramma eroticum* in 1.69.169–74.

46. Cicero *Topica* 2.7–8:

> ... locos nosse debemus; sic enim appellatae ab Aristotele sunt eae quasi sedes, e quibus argumenta promuntur. Itaque licet definire locum esse argumenti sedem, argumentum autem rationem quae rei dubiae faciat fidem.
>
> ... we ought to know the places or topics: for that is the name given by Aristotle to the "regions," as it were, from which arguments are drawn. Accordingly, we may define a topic as the region of an argument, and an argument as a course of reasoning which firmly establishes a matter about which there is some doubt.

LCL, Hubbell, 387. Cf. Aristotle, *Rhetoric*, ed. F. Solmsen (New York: Modern Library, Random House, 1954), 30–31. I translate *the seats of an argument* with W. Ong, *The Presence of the Word* (New Haven: Yale University Press, 1967), 80–81.

47. Curtius (1953), 79; original German text (Bern: Francke, 1948), 87.

48. On topics (*loci communes*, commonplaces, Walter Ong's "purple patches") and related themes, maxims, and examples, cf. Curtius (1953), esp. chaps. 3, 7, and 5; W. Ong, *Ramus, Method, and the Decay of Dialogue* (Cambridge, Mass.: Harvard University Press, 1958), 116–18; J. M. Lechner, *Renaissance Concepts of the Commonplace* (New York: Pageant Press, 1962); and Ong, as above, note 46. On the indexes to the *sententiae* in the collected editions of Petrarch's Latin works, M. Fowler, *Cornell University Library: Catalogue of the Petrarch Collection* (London: Oxford University Press, 1916), 2–4, on Basel, 1496, Venice, 1501, and 1503; and, in considerable detail, A. D. Deyermond, *The Petrarchan Sources of La Celestina* (London: Oxford University Press, 1961), chap. 2, on 1496. On the "places" and "images" of artificial memory, see above.

49. Cf. Curtius (1953), chap. 5, 6; and C. H. Kahn in P. P. Wiener, *Dictionary of the History of Ideas* (New York: C. Scribner's Sons, 1973), 3:574–75.

50. C. S. Lewis, *The Discarded Image* (Cambridge: Cambridge University Press, 1964), 198–201; W. F. Bryan and G. Dempster, *Sources and Analogues of Chaucer's Canterbury Tales* (New York: Humanities Press, 1958), 550–59; Curtius (1953), 92–93.

51. Both works appear in Petrarch's lists of his favorite books, Ullman (1955), 122–23. Cf. Nolhac (1907), vol. 1, chap. 5; Sabbadini (1905), 26–28; Gerosa (1966), 38–40, 166–67; and G. Billanovich, "Petrarca e Cicerone," *Miscellanea Giovanni Mercati*, vol. 4 (Città del Vaticano, 1946), 88–106.

52. Cf., e.g., R. Harder, "Quelle oder Tradition?" (Fondation Hardt, 5 [1957], 327–33), as referred to in J. Gruber, *Kommentar zu Boethius* De consolatione

philosophiae (Berlin: De Gruyter, 1974), 40; and the discussions in E. de Bruyne, *Études d'Esthétique Médiévale*, 3 vols. (Bruges: De Tempel, 1946), esp. vol. 3. A special problem of parallelism and anonymous quotation in the *DR* concerns the *De remediis fortuitorum*, a brief, popular dialogue, for centuries ascribed to Seneca the Philosopher (*L. Annaei Senecae Opera*, ed. F. Haase [Leipzig: B. G. Teubner, 1886], 3:446–57), and often attributed to Martin of Braga (P. Toynbee, *A Dictionary of Proper Names & Notable Matters in the Works of Dante* [Oxford: Clarendon Press, 1968], arts. *"Fortuitorum remedia"* and "Martinus Dumiensis"). The work appears in the list of Petrarch's favorite books among the Seneca entries (Ullman [1955], 122, 124). Although seldom referred to by Petrarch (*DR* 1, Pref., 128; 2.18.17; *Fam.* 14.4.4), there obtain substantial contacts between the *DR* and both, the text of the *De remediis fortuitorum*, and the later *additiones*, which are frequently identical with passages in the *DR* (Nolhac [1907], 2:119–20). I hope to address these matters in another paper.

53. The same holds true for handbooks, such as Isidore's *Etymologies*, which originally furnished factual information, sequential patterns of subjects, and phraseology, that long since had become public knowledge. Cf. above, note 30; and A. J. Minnis, *Medieval Theory of Authorship*. 2nd ed. (Philadelphia: University of Pennsylvania Press, 1988), 213–14.

54. 1, Pref., 44–51:

> qui multis ante nos saeculis in terram uersi: diuinis ingeniis institutisque sanctissimis nobiscum uiuunt: cohabitant: colloquuntur. Interque perpetuos animorum fluctus: ceu totidem lucida sidera: firmamento ueritatis affixa: ceu totidem: suaues: ac foelices aurae: totidem industrii: ac experti nautae: et portum nobis quietis ostendunt: & eo uoluntatum nostrarum lenta carbasa promouent: & fluitantis animae gubernaculum regunt: quo ad tantis procellis agitata consilia tandem sistat: ac temperet:

Note also Petrarch *Met.* 1.6.181–83, 189–97, *Rime* (1951), 736, 738; and *Fam.* 3.18.3.

55. This list, at best, offers a crude approximation, both ordinally and numerically, of Petrarch's source apparatus in the *DR*. It must be considered in the light of the circumstances discussed in section 2 of this paper — and the high probability that I have overlooked text references, or have failed to recognize or identify them. The computerized index upon which this part of my paper is based, was designed and executed on the main frame system of Case Western Reserve University by Philip J. Boutros, to whom I am gratefully indebted.

56. Nolhac (1907), Ullman (1955), chap. 6, Reynolds & Wilson (1974), 116–17, and 236. Note also Gerosa (1966), as above (note 51), and the related studies cited there.

57. As summarized by Ullman (1955), 130–32.

58. Nolhac (1907), 1:247. In the *DR*, the Tusculans are also more extensively discussed and used than any other work. Cf., e.g., Reason's aperçu of Cicero's book 2 in 2.114.178–346.

59. Rawski (1967), 5–6; M. Galdi, "Boezio e Petrarca" in *Saggi boeziani* (Pisa: Giardini, 1938), 1–39.

60. [Boetius Seuerinus] . . . *uir sanctus ac doctus. Sen.* 11.12 (1581: 888), and Gerosa (1966), 162 n. 30.

61. *Sen.* 2.1 (*Prose* [1955], 1054): *Isidorus, quo auctore raro utor* . . .

62. As far as I know, the most frequent references to Boethius, *De cons. phil.* occur in the invective *Contra med.*, *Prose* (1955), 658-61. Among the many Boethian echoes in the *DR* are 1, Pref., 100; 1.8.2; 2.5.130; 2.9.2; 2.93.182; and 2.96.57. Some of these apparent echoes, however, turn out to be Boethian adoptions from older sources (e.g., *DR* 1.16.1-13; 1.92.1-14), foremost among them Cicero's *Tusculan Disputations*, which, of course, is a dominant key text in the *DR*. Cf. C. J. De Vogel, "Boethiana, II," *Viarium* 10 (1972): 10.

63. Nolhac (1907), 2:105.

64. On Petrarch and Vitruvius cf. L. A. Ciapponi, "Il *De architectura* di Vitruvio nel primo Umanesimo," *IMU* (1960): 59-99, esp. 80-81; and also Rico (1986), 49. My thanks to Professor Giuseppe Billanovich for his helpful remarks on the subject.

65. Ullman (1955), 181.

66. On Petrarch and Josephus Flavius, Nolhac (1907), esp. 2:154-56; Sabbadini (1905), esp. 28; Sabbadini (1914), esp. 264; V. Ussani, "Il Petrarca e Flavio Giuseppe," *Rendiconti della Pontificia accad. romana di archeologia* 20 (1943-1944): 447-65.

67. Ricci (1950), 66. On this Weiss (1977), 182.

68. Also quoted in 2.119.144.

69. 2.7.81-84: "& est illud quoque notissimum: ac necessitatibus humanis aptissimum consilium. Cupias quodcunque necesse est: sic uim ipsam necessitatis eluseris."

70. 2.121.11: "Sapiens sic instructus est ut quibus non possit obstare consentiat:"

71. Seneca *Ep.* 54.7: "nihil inuitus facit sapiens, necessitatem effugit, quia uult quod coactura est." LCL, Gummere, 364-65. Cicero, *Ad fam.* 4.9.2: ". . . tempori cedere, id est necessitati parere, semper sapientis est habitum." LCL, Williams, 292-93.

72. M. Pohlenz, *Die Stoa* (Goettingen, Vanderhoeck & Ruprecht, 1959), 1:101-6, 465. Note also Heitmann (1958), 85-87.

73. Reynolds & Wilson (1974), 120; B. L. Ullman, *The Humanism of Coluccio Salutati* (Padua: Antenore, 1963), 146.

74. P. G. Ricci has pointed out that the original dialogue 2.8 (entitled in the mss. I examined *De paupertate et damno*, or *De paupertate vel damno*) was split into dialogues 2.8 (*De paupertate*) and 2.9 (*De damno*) *sulla fede delle edizioni a stampa* (*Prose* [1955], 1171). However, the 1490 edition of the *DR* (D. W. Fiske, *Bibliographical Notices* 3, no. 7 [Florence: Le Monnier, 1888], p. 8, prints the text of the two dialogues as one.

75. Wilkins (1961), 205.

76. *Secretum* 2, *Prose* (1955), 122: "Tu uero, si suis locis Notas certas impresseris, fructum ex lectione percipies." *notae* relates to singling out when reading, writing down, and committing to memory. Petrarch may have read in his Martianus Capella (5.539, Dick [1925], 269):

> . . . ut scribamus ipsi quae facile uolumus retinere; deinde ut, si longiora fuerint, quae sunt ediscenda, diuisa per partes facilius inhaerescant; tum apponere notas rebus singulis oportebit in his, quae uolumus maxime retinere; nec uoce magna legenda sunt, sed murmure potius meditanda; et nocte magis quam interdiu maturius excitari memoriam manifestum est, cum et late silentium iuuat, nec foras a sensibus auocatur intentio.

... we should write down the things we wish easily to retain. Also, if the material to be remembered is rather lengthy, it sticks to the mind more readily if divided into sections. In that case it is useful to place *notae* against the specific items we wish to retain most. These should not be read out loud, but rehearsed with hardly a murmur. And, obviously, the memory is alerted more quickly at night rather than during the day—when we are aided by silence everywhere, and our attention is not distracted by other sense impressions.

Note also, J. Leclerq, *The Love of Learning and the Desire for God* (New York: Fordham University Press, 1961), 78, and M.-D. Chenu, *Nature, Man, and Society in the Twelfth Century* (Chicago: University of Chicago Press, 1968), chap. 8, esp., 301-9, on *lectio* and *meditatio*.

77. *Secretum* 2, ibid.:

Quotiens legenti salutares se se offerunt sententie, quibus uel excitari sentis animum uel frenari, noli uiribus ingenii fidere, sed *illas in memorie penetralibus* [Augustine, *De mag.* 12.39, *PL* 32. 1217] absconde multoque studio tibi familiares effice; ut, quod experti solent medici, quocunque loco uel tempore dilationis impatiens morbus inuaserit, habeas uelut in animo conscripta remedia. Sunt enim quedam sicut in corporibus humanis sic in animis passiones, in quibus tam mortifera mora est ut, qui distulerit medelam, spem salutis abstulerit.

On this, Rico (1974), 234-36.

78. Cf., e.g., the annotations in Petrarch's Pliny (*Nat. hist.* 25.79-91, Paris, B. N. lat. 6802, f. 256v.) and 1.40 and 1.41, as discussed in M. Baxandall, *Giotto and the Orators* (Oxford: Clarendon Press, 1971), 62-65; or the elaborate marginal notes and glosses in his Ambrosian Virgil (Nolhac [1907], vol. 1, chap. 3, Mann [1984], 31), and in the Suetonius, Oxford, Exeter Coll. 186 (G. Billanovich, "Nella biblioteca del Petrarca." *IMU* 3 [1960]: 28-58; N. Mann, *Petrarch Manuscripts in the British Isles* [Padua: Antenore, 1975], 494-95, no. 256; and fig. 1, above). In contrast to the *Franciscus* of the *Secretum,* excerpting, note taking, annotation, and studious immersion was a life-long habit of Petrarch's. Cf. *Fam.* 24.1 (to Philippe de Cabassoles, Bishop of Cavaillon, c. 1360; cf. Wilkins [1958], 239-41), 9-10:

Ego autem adolescens quanto his interlegendis ardore flagrauerim aliquot per annos, quando necdum aliud scriptorum genus tam familiariter noram, libelli indicant qui michi illius temporis supersunt et signa mee manus talibus presertim affixa sententiis, ex quibus eliciebam et supra etatem ruminabam presentem futurumque illico statum meum. Notabam certa fide non uerborum faleras sed res ipsas, misere scilicet uite huius angustias, breuitatem uelocitatem festinationem lapsum cursum uolatum occultasque fallacias, tempus irreparabile, caducum et mutabilem uite florem, rosei oris fluxum decus, irrediture iuuentutis effrenem fugam et tacite obrepentis insidias senectutis; ad extremum rugas et morbos et tristitiam et laborem et indomite mortis inclementiam implacabilemque duritiem.

As a youth I yearned to make an anthology of poetic beauties, when I had still little knowledge of other writers. The books that I still possess from those days, with my marginal notes referring to certain passages, make clear how precociously I chose to reflect upon my present and future state. I noted down not the verbal felicities but the substance of the thought — the distresses of this wretched life, its brevity, swiftness, haste, tumbling course, its hidden cheats, time's irrecoverability, the flower of life soon wasted, the fugitive beauty of a rosy face, the frantic flight of unreturning youth, the trickeries of stealthy age; and at the last the wrinkles, illnesses, sadness, toil, and the implacable cruelty of indomitable death.

Bishop (1966), 201.

79. Pliny *Nat. hist.* 7.24.89; Cicero *De orat.* 2.86; Quintilian 11.2.11. On this, Yates (1966), chap. 1.

80. Cicero *De orat.* 2.74.299 (cf. ibid., 2.86.357; *Acad.* 2.1.2; *De fin.* 2.32.104). Also told in Petrarch's *Rer. mem. libri* 2.9. On this, Yates (1966), 17.

81. 1.8.44–47:

fere tamen omnibus conuenit: ita omnes & dediscenda discitis: & discenda dediscitis. In his tantum quorum utilis esset obliuio memoriam exercentes. Inque id naturae finibus non contenti: insaniam arte laxatis.

In 2.101, Reason advises *obiectu contrarii* to plug up a leaky memory:

diligentia: & artificio . . . cunctis ingenii memoriaeque defectibus occurrit industria. Nil patitur industria perire: nil minui. Haec est quae philosophos et poetas senes: uirentissimo ingenio ac stilo: haec est quae decrepitos oratores uoce solida: ualidisque lateribus ac tenaci memoria seruare potest.

with industry and cunning devices. Diligent practice helps with all shortcomings of intellect and memory. Such practice permits nothing to be lost, nothing to be diminished. It is practice that provides aged philosophers and poets with a vigorous mind and style, senescent orators with a steady voice, strong lungs, and a retentive memory.

Reason's reference to *ingenium memoriaque*—intellect and memory invokes Hugh of St. Victor, *Didascalicon* 3, 6, *PL* 176.771: *ingenium inuenit et memoria custodit sapientiam*—aptitude gathers wisdom, memory preserves it (trans. J. Taylor, *The Didascalicon of Hugh of St. Victor* [New York: Columbia University Press, 1961], 91).

82. *Ad Herennium* 3.16.28, LCL, Caplan, 207. On *loci* note Aristotle, *Topics* 8, 163b, 27–31, and Boethius, *Cons. phil.* 1, pr. 5, 20–24 (*loci* . . . *sedem*). On medieval and Renaissance mnemonic theory, Yates (1966), chaps. 1–5. For a succinct overview of the subject, cf. J. D. Spence, *The Memory Palace of Matteo Ricci* (New York: Viking, 1984), chap. 1.

83. Azzo da Correggio, to whom the *DR* is dedicated and whom "Fortune . . . has caused . . . to be cast upon the turbulent deep sea of affairs and worries," has lost the "leisure to read, but not the desire to know. . . . To accomplish this, you have often used your memory, inferior to none, instead of books." 1, Pref., 56–62.

84. Macrobius *Saturn.* 2.7.4–5; John of Salisbury *Policrat.* 8, 14, *PL* 199.772.

85. Cicero *De off.* 2.7.23.

86. Dated Nov. 28, and written in 1373 (Wilkins [1959], 252–56).

87. Cicero *De off.* 1.28.97; Seneca *Dial.* 3, De ira 1.20.4, *De clem.* 1.12.4, and 2.2.2; Suetonius, 4, *Calig.* 30.1.

88. Cf. 2.55.41-43; 2.68.2-10; *Fam.* 22.14.64; *Sen.* 12.1 (1581: 898-99); etc.

89. On Spurina cf. 1.2.82; 1.72.23; 2.1.45; 2.77.28. The story comes from Valerius Maximus, 4.5.6, Ext. 1. On Diagoras, 1.29.37; 1.85.84; 1.90.41. Sources: Cicero *Tusc. disp.* 1.46.111; Aulus Gellius, 3.15.3. Cf. also, *DR* 1.23.28, and the echo in *Fam.* 8.1.8.

90. It is also an essential ingredient of any kind of argument by analogy—a form of expository logic for which we are poorly prepared today, but which for Petrarch certainly had not lost its relevance when it came to explore the *necessitas rationis.*

91. 2.82.46: "Sepe idem repeto: quia ita se res habet:"

92. 2.77.28: "An adolescentis illius obliuisceris: cuius mentio bis in hoc sermone incidit:"

93. A considerable area of oral practices remained in Petrarch's days. In the *DR,* as elsewhere in his writings (e.g., *Rer. mem. libri* 3.80.7), reference is made to *lecta uel audita*—having read or heard (2, Pref., 1). Such "hearing" is illustrated in *Fam.* 22.2, where Petrarch discusses his attempts to catch imperfections in his *Bucolicum carmen* by having parts of the poem read to him by Boccaccio and another friend (Wilkins [1958], 187-88). Yet, here as elsewhere, the text is his main concern. In 2.96.136, Reason, having told the story of the heroic death of blind king John of Bohemia in the Battle of Crécy (August 26, 1346), explains: "Rem narro notam omnibus: sed nisi mandata sit litteris obliuione perituram." ("I am telling you what everybody knows, but what will perish in oblivion, if it is not recorded.")

The basic aspect of "oral" and "written" are carefully analyzed in B. Stock, *The Implications of Literacy* (Princeton: Priceton University Press, 1983), esp. chaps. 1 and 4. Still to be explored with equal care remains Petrarch's contribution to a specific "literacy" that could be acquired and shared by every educated person—a mode of comprehension providing many of the contexts in terms of which the next generation of readers perceived and acted.

94. Cf. 1.44.49-56; 2.8.42; 2.132.88. Note also, *Secretum* 2, *Prose* (1955), 72.

95. Throughout the *DR* Petrarch's textual scholarship is nothing short of impeccable. In contrast to earlier scholars, such as, e.g., the remarkable John of Salisbury (cf. J. Martin, "John of Salisbury as Classical Scholar" in Wilks [1984], 179-201), he quotes with great accuracy, and accounts for any changes or adjustments. There are very few errors, and, more often than not, what appears as an error to the modern reader finds an explanation in Petrarch's exemplar—as in 2.39.11-13, where Reason observes:

> post hos magni nominis in hac arte discores*fuit: cuius cum opus*exprimeret nomen siluisse Plinium miror.
> (*1581: Dioscurides; opera.)

> After them (i.e., the Greek gemcutters Apollonides and Cronius), Dioscurides had a big reputation, and I am surprised that Pliny, when he described the work of this artist, was silent about his name.

This reads like an error: Pliny *Nat. hist.* 37.4.8-10, does not omit the name of

Dioscurides. But Petrarch's MS of Pliny, Paris, B. N. lat. 6802 (Nolhac [1907], 2:70-78), has a *lacuna* in the text. Petrarch got the name from Suetonius 2 (*Aug.*), 50. An exception is the historical lapse in 2.81.68-80, where Reason betrays Petrarch's preoccupation with Roman history when she confuses the earlier Greek tyrants of Syracuse, Gelo and Hiero (5th century BC), with Hiero II. and his son and co-regent Gelo, who figure in the history of the First Punic War (e.g., Livy 23.30.10-13), and wonders how Aristotle (*Polit.* 5.3.1302b, and 5.10.1312b) could possibly have known their names. The puzzling Catullus reference in 1.59.17 (Nolhac [1907], 1:165 n. 1) may indicate another error, according to Ullman (1955), 199-200.

96. 1.2.87-96:

> quamuis enim errare sibi uisum esse: qui ait gratior est pulchro ueniens in corpore uirtus. Scribit Seneca: mihi tamen iure reprehensus uideretur. Si dixisset maior: aut perfectior: aut altior. Nunc quia dicendo gratior non rem ipsam: sed spectantium iudicia respicit: non mihi uisus est errare. Vergilius qui hoc ait:

97. 2.93.150-53:

> Pronaque cum spectent animalia caetera terram. Os homini sublime dedit: caelumque uidere iussit. Et erectos ad sidera tollere uultus ut praeclare ait Naso: licet dictum prius a Tullio.

Ovid *Metam.* 1.84-86, LCL, F. J. Miller, p. 9; Cicero *De nat. deor.* 2.56.140; *De leg.* 1.9.26; *Tusc. disp.* 1.28.29.

PLENARY LECTURE

"Potens in opere et sermone": Philip, Bishop of Bayeux, and His Books*

R. H. ROUSE AND M. A. ROUSE

In contrasting the world of monastic learning with that of the cathedral schools, Sir Richard Southern said of the twelfth-century student, "He not only knew where to study, he also knew that his studies would have a market value." The schools, in Southern's words, "brought the idea of ... order and rationality into every area of human experience." In the early twelfth century, "slowly the ruling households of Europe, at all levels from the papal court to the household of a minor baron, were penetrated by men calling themselves *masters*, or as we should say, university men." This theme, the significant place of the schools in the formation of the twelfth-century state, permeates Southern's study of the period.[1]

The key role of the northern French cathedral schools in the growth of Anglo-Norman administration — civil and ecclesiastic — is a near textbook example, which no doubt was very much in Southern's thinking when he wrote these statements. Names come to mind almost unbidden: John of Salisbury, Arnulf of Lisieux, Hugh of Amiens, Rotrou of Rouen, Gilbert Foliot, Gerald of Wales — men whose ascent up the Anglo-Norman ladder depended on schooling as well as (or even instead of) birth. Today we know them — in some instances, know them best — for their writings. Their contemporaries knew and honored (or feared, or disliked) them as well for their positions as, respectively, bishop of Chartres, bishop of Lisieux, archbishop of Rouen, bishop of Evreux who became archbishop of Rouen, bishop of London, and bishop-elect of St. Davids. Although only two of these were major *literati*, all were learned, all had been "schooled."

In the present paper we want to pursue this theme through the life of one such man whose career has been neglected: Philip of Harcourt, bishop of Bayeux from 1142 to 1163.[2] He wrote nothing that survives, which explains why he receives scant notice in surveys of the twelfth-century Renaissance. His principal claim to notice has been his library, the 140 volumes that he left to the abbey of Bec.³ Although the books themselves, with slight exception, are not known today, the contemporary catalog of the collection provides much information.

Philip played a significant role in the transmission of ancient Latin authors. His library included such uncommon works as Cicero's *De academicis, De finibus,* Caesarian orations, and philosophical corpus; Seneca's Natural History, the Younger Pliny's letters, and Pomponius Mela's *De chorographia.* We have examined the list of Philip's books many times for what it may reveal about the transmission and dissemination of rare texts.⁴ Here we propose instead to examine it for the writings of Philip's contemporaries, and to use the books to illuminate the man.

We begin with the biographical information that can be assembled from the records, not a negligible quantity.⁵ Philip came from a significant though not princely Anglo-Norman family. His father Robert I fitz Anschetil was lord of Harcourt, a sizable holding midway between Evreux and Lisieux. Philip was one of, apparently, eight sons. In common with many Norman nobles, members of the Harcourt family held land on both sides of the Channel. The maternal side of Philip's ancestry is uncertain, but it seems likely that his mother was a sister of Philip of Briouze, lord of Bramber.⁶

Philip's life was ineluctably shaped by the patronage of Waleran, count of Meulan, who was overlord of Harcourt and (given his consistent fostering of Philip's career) doubtless a kinsman as well.⁷ Waleran is reputed to have been a learned man, who not only read Latin but composed Latin verse that was admired by contemporaries. Geoffrey of Monmouth sought his patronage, upon the publication of the *Historia regum Britanniae.* Waleran's twin brother Robert, earl of Leicester, enjoyed a similar reputation for learning.⁸ Philip's early formation, then, may have benefited from his association with this literate household.

Philip's library, as we shall see, reveals the schoolman in several specific ways, just as his success as an administrator betokens training in both laws. We have no explicit information about Philip's schooling, no mention in document or letter, and we must rely on a combination of deduction and analogy. Given his geographical location, it is likely that at least a part of his studies were at the cathedral school of Chartres. Philip's friend and contemporary Arnulf of Lisieux studied there in the late 1120s-early 1130s, it is thought,⁹ before going to Italy to study law; and Philip's and Arnulf's younger contemporary John of Salisbury later studied at Chartres.¹⁰ Count Waleran's cousin Rotrou, bishop of Evreux, archbishop of Rouen, and perhaps a distant kinsman of Philip's,[11] is known to have studied with Gilbert de la Porée; probably this also took place at Chartres, where Gilbert was chancellor.[12] At least one of Philip's books seems to have been written by Chartres scribes.[13] Orléans, too, is a good possibility for at least some of his schooling — again, to judge from the fact that some of the rarer texts that he owned were disseminated from twelfth-century Orléans.[14] As the contents of his library suggest, he was trained in the *artes,* including the study of formal composition in speaking and epistolary style based on the models of classical and patristic letters and orations; and he read as well in theology and both civil and canon law, whether or not he had formal schooling in these disciplines.

Philip's first living, the rectory of Sompting in Sussex, derived from his maternal uncle (?), Philip de Briouze, lord of Bramber. Thereafter, his rise in the church was rapid, aided almost entirely by his connection with Count Waleran of Meulan.[15] Before 1131, he became dean of Holy Trinity at Beaumont-le-Roger, burial place of the counts of Meulan and a dependency of Lincoln Cathedral, within the gift of Count Waleran. Thereafter, Philip became archdeacon of Evreux, Waleran's "neighborhood cathedral," and then dean of Lincoln Cathedral, during the episcopacy of Alexander (1123-1148). The precise dates are debatable, but these three steps must have been taken in very short order.[16]

Philip was in England in a time of civil war; and in 1139, as a protégé of King Stephen's supporter Count Waleran, he was made chancellor of Stephen's government. In December of that same year Roger, bishop of Salisbury, died; and Philip of Harcourt resigned the chancellorship, to free himself to fill the vacancy — to which, as anticipated, he was named by King Stephen, at Waleran's urging.[17] But support of the royal court was not adequate to overcome the objections of the cathedral chapter at Salisbury, who refused to elect Stephen's nominee Philip. The fact that Bishop Roger had died while imprisoned by King Stephen may have helped to make the Salisbury chapter a bit testy. At any rate, it was likely in the course of this melodrama that Philip became possessed of a reliquary, "an arm, gold plated and adorned with precious stones," from the treasury of Salisbury Cathedral — which he kept until he was persuaded to return it in 1148.[18] This was the arm-reliquary of St. Aldhelm that had been given to Salisbury in the eleventh century by St. Osmund.[19]

The setback in Philip's career was only temporary, for within three years he was elected bishop of Bayeux in Normandy, a position he held from 1142 until his death in 1163. With Stephen's capture by Angevin forces in 1141, Philip's patron Waleran had recognized that the future in Normandy lay with the Angevins, and had pragmatically shifted his

Continental allegiance to Geoffrey of Anjou in order to safeguard the family's Norman lands. Philip's election to Bayeux must have been part of an overall exchange of tokens between Waleran and Geoffrey. Subsequently, however, Waleran's relations with the Angevins cooled markedly as he flirted too openly with the French Crown.[20] Apparently, Philip successfully distanced himself from Waleran in this matter; his tenure at Bayeux was marked from beginning to end by civil, and ultimately cordial, relations with the House of Anjou.

Normandy during the English anarchy,[21] left largely on its own, had witnessed an upsurge in local autonomy, with the emphasis on survival of the fittest. The church, and especially the bishops, were for the most part faithful to Stephen. The turning point in the reestablishment of ducal authority in Normandy came, as we have seen, just before Philip took office. Geoffrey of Anjou, secure in his alliance with Robert of Gloucester, by 1141 dominated much of the south and west of Normandy; and by the spring of 1144 he received the submission of Rouen. Philip administered the see of Bayeux under Geoffrey duke of Normandy from 1144 until the spring of 1150, when Geoffrey gave the duchy to his son Henry, the future Henry II of England. At that time it was necessary for Philip once again to adapt to the court of a new ruler, though the adjustment was not so difficult as that in the period 1142–1144, no doubt; and for the last fourteen years of his life he worked effectively in and with Henry's court.

The Norman cathedral of Bayeux, consecrated in 1077 under Bishop Odo, had been burnt down in 1105 by Odo's nephew Henry I. Of Odo's cathedral, only the square towers and the crypt remained. The visible devastation of the building's fabric symbolized the financial ruin of the see itself. Philip's immediate predecessors, Bishop Richard II and his nephew Bishop Richard III, could not or would not withstand the encroachments of their assertive kinsman Robert, earl of Gloucester, who was the principal lay power in the diocese. This bastard son of Henry I was also the indispensable ally of Geoffrey of Anjou, who was not eager to alienate his supporter in order to benefit the new bishop of Bayeux whose political past was suspect, from an Angevin viewpoint. The great Norman abbeys like Fécamp and Troarn had also helped themselves to rights, privileges, and property at the expense of the bishops of Bayeux— no doubt largely a matter of self-preservation during the breakdown of authority.

Philip set about restoring his diocese. Much of the present cathedral was built or planned by him, with the six bays of the nave having been completed under his episcopacy and the gothic windows and buttresses in the time of his successors.[22] Along with his rebuilding in stone, Philip must have spent even more of his time and energy in rebuilding the episcopal authority, with the estates, rents, rights, and privileges pertaining to it; this was Philip's major undertaking, begun immediately and pursued relentlessly throughout his episcopacy.[23] All the techniques at his disposal were brought to bear in this matter: his influence with Rome, and with the duke, and his knowledge of law. He was so zealous in this area that Haskins considered him instrumental in the development of the jury of presentment or inquest.[24] Philip traveled back and forth to Rome at least three times, to secure the written instruments he needed. He was there in 1144 during the brief pontificate of Lucius II; we know, from the protocol of a trial held at the Curia, that he was present in Rome (still? again?), together with Archbishop Hugh of Sens and bishops Arnulf of Lisieux, Albero of Liège, Benedict of Orléans, and Bernard of Saragossa, on 15 February 1145 (N.S.) — the day when Lucius II died and the day of Eugenius III's election;[25] and he went twice more (in 1146 and in 1150 or 1151) during the term of Eugenius III. Three bulls from Lucius, reissued virtually unchanged by Eugenius, herald the upswing in Bayeux's fortunes:[26] (1) The first confirms to Philip all the possessions of the diocese (including rights and rents, as well as real property), itemized in prosaic detail;[27] Philip had obviously arrived in Rome well briefed, with his claims indisputably documented. (2) The second called upon all the faithful in the diocese — abbots, priors, clergy, laity — to help Philip in his task of recovering his rights, ordering them to hand over any of the bishop's property that they might hold illegally, and nullifying all exchanges, sales, or gifts of Bayeux property by all bishops since Odo — an attempt to roll back the clock forty-five years at one go.[28] (3) The third was addressed to Duke Geoffrey (just as a future one would be addressed to Duke Henry, as soon as he took the reins in Normandy), reminding him that Henry I in an earlier day had held inquests (or assizes, or *recognitiones*) to determine the possessions of the see, and asking Geoffrey to order a new *recognitio* to help restore Bayeux as it had been.[29] (The purpose of Henry I's inquests, by contrast, had been to benefit the Crown, a difference that the pope did not dwell on.) Geoffrey, in response, not only ordered *recognitiones* on Philip's behalf (i.e., juries of inquest taking sworn information from people who knew), but he even empowered Philip to order *recognitiones* on his own initiative, and to compel compliance as if the order had come from the duke.

Philip's methods were those of a schoolman: He went after his goals armed with the written word — the right, effective words, written by those (the pope, the duke) whose words had power among lesser lords, lay and ecclesiastic. Without an army, but simply by knowing how to use the written word and the law courts effectively, Philip persisted until he gradually established in law the see's rights, and secured the observation of those rights. (Actually, he never did quite compel submission from Robert of Gloucester, who made many promises but delivered nothing; but Philip outlived him, which had much the same effect.)

Philip's reliance on the power of documentation is visible in the well-known *Livre noir* of Bayeux, the cathedral cartulary that contains documents dating from the early eleventh century until the early fourteenth. As the *Livre noir*'s editor Bourrienne noted, the manuscript begins with a segment written in a single early thirteenth-century hand which has copied the first 213 charters, from the earliest (1035–1037) until 1205; later hands continued to record until the second decade of the fourteenth century.[30] If we look beneath the surface of the opening segment, however, we can recognize a unit within a unit: almost certainly, its kernel is the archive that Philip assembled to place the privileges, liberties, immunities, and possessions of his diocese on unassailable legal grounds. Roughly one hundred of these 213 charters date from the twenty-one years of Philip's episcopate, compared with only ninety-eight for the following forty-two years.[31] More distinctive still is the amount, and especially the nature, of the documentation in this segment that dates from before Philip's accession. There are only some fifteen of these earlier charters. Of them, nine are grants, or confirmations of grants, that date from Odo's day;[32] this reminds us that papal bulls nullified all sales, gifts, or exchanges "since the time of Bishop Odo." The one still earlier charter, dated 1035–1037, is an inventory of diocesan lands and possessions drawn up by Bishop Hugh II;[33] we recall that Philip's first concession from the papacy, in 1144, was papal confirmation of an inventory of Bayeux's possessions, which was itemized in terms similar to this. Of the only five charters in the *Livre noir* that date from the anarchic period between Odo's death and Philip's accession, all but one are *acta* of Henry I of England confirming or restoring rights of Bayeux as they had been at various previous times;[34] and here we recall that, although the papal bulls nullified any loss the diocese had suffered, nothing was said to disqualify any gains enjoyed "since the time of Bishop Odo." It does not stretch the imagination to see in these early charters the documentation that Philip had gathered up to take with him to Rome, when he first set out in 1144 to put his episcopal house back in order.

The twelfth-century prelates of Normandy comprised a small interwoven society of familiar faces. For example, two successive deans of Philip's cathedral became his colleagues as successive bishops of Coutances: Richard I de Bohun, seen in 1146 as dean of Bayeux, became bishop of Coutances in 1150; he was succeeded as bishop by William III de Tournebu, seen as dean of Bayeux in 1153 (his bishopric ends before 1183).[35] Philip himself belonged to the inner cadre of four who at mid-century firmly ran the Norman church and served the often absent king-duke in the government of the duchy: Hugh of Amiens, archbishop of Rouen 1130-1164; Rotrou, bishop of Evreux 1139-1165; Arnulf, bishop of Lisieux 1142-1184; and Philip, bishop of Bayeux 1142-1163. The four were colleagues, and perhaps something more, centering on the figure of the archbishop. Hugh of Amiens (b. ca. 1095) was successively prior of St-Martial of Limoges, abbot of Reading, and (during the whole of Philip's episcopacy) archbishop of Rouen. Trained at the cathedral school of Laon, Hugh wrote several works of theology and exegesis, including *Contra hereticos sui temporis, De fide catholica, In laudem memoriae, Questiones theologicae* (or *Dialogi*), and *Tractatus in hexaemeron* (or *In Genesim 1-3*).[36] It is not only by virtue of his office but by virtue of these writings that Hugh of Amiens links his three suffragans: two of Hugh's works—the *Dialogi* and *De fide*—appear on the list of books that Rotrou (Hugh's successor as archbishop) left to the cathedral of Rouen.[37] A third work, the Genesis commentary, which was praised by Bernard of Clairvaux,[38] bore a dedication to Hugh's "dearest son, the learned Arnulf, bishop of Lisieux."[39] Philip completes the circle, for he also owned something of Hugh's. We cannot tell which, since the booklist says simply *Liber Hugonis archiepiscopi;* perhaps it was the *Contra hereticos*, the most widely circulated of Hugh's works.[40] Assertive, capable, and learned, these four prelates in addition enjoyed the happy accident of exceptionally long tenures shared concurrently, providing an unexpected bedrock of stability beneath the agitated surface of Norman affairs through the middle of the twelfth century.

Philip was the first bishop of Bayeux since Odo to play an important role in the government of the duchy. He was one of the entourage of Norman bishops who accompanied the duke to England for his coronation as Henry II in 1154. Philip's role in Duke Henry's administration comes to the surface particularly for the period after the duke was crowned, because English records survive in much greater measure than do Continental ones. Following the coronation we see Philip attesting royal charters issued from every corner of Henry's sprawling domain, ranging from Périgueux down in Aquitaine to York in the north of England.[41] At least sixty-one of Henry II's *acta* have Philip as witness.[42] Not surprisingly, the largest group of these (fifteen) were issued at Rouen, capital of the duchy and seat of the Norman archdiocese, where both Henry and Philip were apt to find themselves, not necessarily on joint errands. Another three emanated from Bayeux itself. Of the remainder, seventeen were issued from various English sites, and twenty-six from different locales in Henry's Continental domains. Philip was joined as witness by Bishop Arnulf of Lisieux on forty-three occasions, and in nineteen instances by Bishop Rotrou of Evreux.[43] His appearance as a witness indicates, of course, that Philip was frequently in attendance upon the king and his itinerant court, and that the king found him reliable—just as, in 1161, the king is said to have entrusted Philip with taking a message to Pope Alexander III during the schism, although age ultimately prevented Philip from making the journey.[44]

Philip seems on occasion to have wielded extensive authority in Normandy on the duke's behalf. At the same time that Philip was employing the process of the sworn inquest to reestablish and maintain the rights of his see, Henry II was extending the use of this process throughout the duchy; a regularized procedure of ducal justice was especially necessary after the coronation in 1154, when Henry divided his time between the Continent and England. For this purpose he resurrected the post of justiciar of Normandy, to act as chief judicial officer of the duchy in the duke's absence. There were ordinarily two of these at one time, most often the seneschal of Normandy and a Norman bishop, or other combinations, on a rotating basis. Philip's confreres Arnulf, bishop of Lisieux, and Rotrou, then bishop of Evreux, served as justiciars during this period.[45] Not surprisingly, in at least two surviving documents Philip too seems to act in this capacity—once with Robert de Neubourg, seneschal of Normandy, and the second time in tandem with Bishop Rotrou, the seneschal's brother.[46]

Thus, Philip's ecclesiastical career, which crossed over the Channel and back, was paralleled by a career in civil administration on both sides of the water, as Stephen's chancellor in England in young manhood, as a member of Henry II's traveling entourage and witness to his charters in England in ca. 1154–1155 and on the Continent ca. 1156–1163, and perhaps as Henry II's justiciar in Normandy. Arnulf of Lisieux asserted that Philip was, "in the deliberations of the king, as in the affairs of the church, both welcome and effective."[47]

The full extent of his involvement in the Angevin administration can only be surmised, given the paucity of Continental records—which is a pity. To judge from what is known about him, Philip had both the nature and the training of a model civil servant, and was doubtless employed more frequently than the surviving evidence documents.

According to the *Chronicle* of Robert of Torigny (d. 1186), Philip had intended to retire at the end of his life to the abbey of Bec (just as his friend Arnulf of Lisieux was to end his days, and leave his books, with the abbey of St-Victor), but death intervened; however, Robert adds, Philip had already given the abbey 140 books.[48] A copy of the list of Philip's books survives, on the first flyleaf of Avranches Bibliothèque municipale MS 159 (fol. 1v), in a hand not much later than the date of his death. Also, beginning on the second flyleaf (fols. 2-3), a different hand of similar date has enrolled a list of books in the Bec library.[49] Avranches 159, written at Mont-St-Michel, is a book of histories that begins with Eusebius and his continuators and ends with the last redaction of Robert of Torigny's *Chronicle*. Robert was a monk at Bec from 1128 until he left in 1154 form Mont-St-Michel, where he was abbot until his death in 1186. He had been an avid builder of Bec's library, and after his move he commissioned books for Mont-St-Michel to be copied from Bec exemplars.[50] To all appearances, Avranches 159 is Robert's own copy of his *Chronicle*. His interest in securing copies of the books at Bec may explain the presence of the two Bec booklists on the flyleaves, but that point is uncertain.

Philip's list is headed "Tituli librorum quos dedit Philippus episcopus Baiocensis ecclesie Becci" ("Titles of the books that Philip bishop of Bayeux gave to the congregation of Bec"). The two opening words are written in display letters and the entire heading is slashed in red, with the next eight lines spaciously arranged. But then the writer decided that he wanted the whole text on one page, and he compressed the remainder of the list into forty-three long lines. Individual volumes (each of which may contain several works) are distinguished by the formula *In alio*, slashed in red. The body of the list appears to have been rapidly copied (presumably from the original at Bec), to judge from the minor slips of the eye. At the end of the list is the note, "Summa uoluminum .cxiii. exceptis .xxvii. uoluminibus quos [*sic*] dedit episcopus sed nondum habuerunt". ("Total number of volumes 113, not counting twenty-seven volumes which the bishop gave but which they [i.e., the Bec monks] do not yet have"). The flyleaf list describes the 113 volumes;[51] the missing twenty-seven, which would raise the total to the 140 cited by Robert of Torigny, have not been identified.

The second list, headed "Tituli librorum Beccensis almarii" ("Titles of the books in the Bec library"), is not as straightforward as it looks. It apparently represents an integration of Philip's books with other books at Bec, to judge from the frequent duplications of one list by the other.[52]

Indeed, in some instances it seems as if his volumes have been taken apart and rebound with other works at Bec to form new codices (containing the works of a single author, or works on a single topic);[53] any search for survivors from Philip of Harcourt's collection must take the possibility of rearrangement into account. The list does not appear to be a complete inventory of the Bec library, however, since a significant number of Philip's books do not reappear here; moreover, it seems to be a composite of an older list and of a partial revision with certain authors grouped together—which results in some duplication.

Unfortunately, history has not lent a helping hand in reconstructing Philip's library; neither he nor Bec's librarian left an ex libris mark on their books themselves, although a distinctive table of contents was entered in some of Bec's books before the end of the twelfth century.[54] No later Bec inventory survives. It is a hopeful sign that the surviving manuscripts thought to have been Philip's, few though they are, have been identified just within the last dozen years or so.[55] For now, however, the two lists contain the bulk of our knowledge of his books.

For Philip, the written word—instrument of the secular schools as represented in the *ars dictaminis* and in legal training, in collections of model letters and law codes—was the basis of his power. The list of his books vividly reflects this attitude.[56] Philip owned the books of the early twelfth century, books embodying the codification of subjects, books relevant to the professional ecclesiastical administrator: exegetical texts, law codes, dictaminal models, histories. His collections of ancient letters and orations—the Younger Pliny, a very great deal of Cicero, and even Ennodius, a rare find—would have served as models of style for a training in *dictamen*, a discipline of increasing formality though not as yet well served by manuals, and one that led to training in the law.[57] Like later generations, Philip saw books as useful instruments, part of the equipment of his profession; and throughout his life, it seems, he continued to acquire new works as they appeared.

Naturally, much of his library was commonplace. The standard works of the Fathers—Augustine, Jerome, Ambrose, Gregory, and others—comprise about a third of his collection; and he had kept, as one tends to do, a handful of very elementary schoolbooks—rhetoric, geometry, astronomy, arithmetic, and the like. What makes us value the collection, in contrast, is its indication that Philip kept abreast of what was new, and never ceased to acquire the very latest books that were of use. Thus he owned many works written by his contemporaries, both older and younger, such as Gerald of York (d. 1108), Petrus Alfonsus (d. ca. 1115), Gilbert Crispin (d. 1119), Hildebart of le Man (d. 1133), Hugh of St. Victor

(d. 1141), Adelard of Bath (d. ca. 1146), Bernard of Clairvaux (d. 1153), Gilbert de la Porrée (d. 1154), Zacharias Chrysopolitanus (d. 1156), Gratian (d. ca. 1160), Hugh of Amiens (d. 1164), Simon Chevre d'Or (d. 1170), and perhaps Geoffrey of Monmouth (d. 1155).

The Gospel harmony *Super unum ex quattuor* typifies Philip's acquisition of the up-to-date and the useful.[58] The work of Zacharias Chrysopolitanus, a Laon Premonstratensian who died in 1156, *Vnum ex quattuor* was compiled at Laon between 1140 and 1145; thus it is one of the many works that Philip acquired after he had become bishop. Like the later Bible history of Peter Comestor, which it clearly influenced, Zacharias's *Vnum ex quattuor* filled a need for an adequate cross-referenced merging of the Gospel accounts, and its popularity was immediate. In an era when the bishop was expected to do most of the preaching in his diocese, Philip no doubt found Zacharias' work an indispensable exegetical tool for the making of sermons. The text disseminated rapidly from Laon, with eleven of the 102 surviving manuscripts dating from the twelfth century. As is often the case, we can see that Philip's copy (pre-1164) must have been one of the earliest.

Although one would expect to find law books on Philip's list, given his involvement with legal matters for his diocese and with judicial matters for his duke, nevertheless his collection of law texts both civil and canon exceeds expectation. The study of civil law goes back to the late eleventh century in Bologna, and the influence of Roman law in northern Europe can be seen in the second quarter of the twelfth century; but mid-twelfth-century manuscripts of the whole corpus of civil law are not common. Philip's list represents the earliest documentable appearance in northern Europe of the full array of Roman law, in seven volumes—Codex, *Tres partes*, New Digest, *Inforciatum*, Old Digest, *Liber authenticorum*, and Institutes—in varying combinations and in duplicate.[59] More remarkable still, in the field of canon law, is the fact that (besides the old law, the letters and decretals of Ivo of Chartres and the decretals of Burchard of Worms) Philip owned not one but two copies of Gratian's *Decretum*.[60] Philip's copies of Gratian (nos. 69–70), like his manuscript of Zacharias, attest to the speed with which a new tool could be put to use: Gratian is thought to have finished his compilation only about 1140; and although the *Decretum* was known to the masters and students at Bologna, there is no evidence of its use in the papal chancery itself before 1160.[61] It is reasonable to suppose that Philip acquired both his Roman law manuscripts and his manuscripts of the *Decretum* in the course of his trips to Rome (1144, 1146, 1150/51).[62] Other evidence of early acquaintance with Gratian in the North includes an unmistakable quotation in a letter of John of Salisbury written at Canterbury in 1158–1160,[63] and a *Decretum* bequeathed to Lincoln Cathedral sometime between 1151 and 1158 by Hugh, archdeacon of Leicester.[64] Philip may well have played a significant role in the early and rapid dissemination of Roman and canon law among the Anglo-Norman jurists.

Like other contemporary princes of church and state—such as Henry the Liberal, count of Champagne—Philip collected histories.[65] No doubt he felt that a familiarity with the past was a fitting enlargement of his horizon—as well as a practical guide for behavior in the political world. He owned such venerable works as Florus' *Epitome* of Livy, Suetonius' *Lives of the Caesars*, a *Gesta Caesarum*, Pseudo-Clement, the *Historia tripartita*, Orosius, the early medieval historians Gregory of Tours and Freculf of Lisieux, the Jewish historian Josephus, and Nennius; and he owned contemporary works like the *Historia Normannorum* of William of Jumièges, doubtless with the revisions of Robert of Torigny, and Henry of Huntingdon.[66]

We should like in the concluding section to consider the information afforded by three particular titles on Philip's booklist. To say they illuminate "Philip's circle" would be an exaggeration. Certainly, however, they provide evidence about Philip's relationships with various contemporaries which is available from no other source.

The first of these is the *Historia* of Henry of Huntingdon, no. 95 in the list of Philip's books. The Bec catalog specifies that the *Historia* contained ten books,[67] which means that Philip must have owned Henry's last version, including events to the year 1147.[68] The possible source of Philip's text is a matter of some interest, since evidence of knowledge of the *Historia* on the Continent is narrowly limited to (1) a mid-twelfth-century manuscript, BN lat. 6042, containing the 1147 ten-book edition; (2) quotations in the *Chronicle* of Robert of Torigny, monk of Bec and (after 1154) abbot of Mont-St-Michel, based on a text similar to but not identical with MS lat. 6042; (3) a late twelfth- or early thirteenth-century manuscript, Rouen BM 1177, copied from BN lat. 6042 for the abbey of Jumièges; and (4) the mention in Philip of Bayeux's booklist.[69]

For our purposes, the unanswered question is where Philip could have laid hands on an exemplar from which to have his copy written, given the extreme rarity of this text in Normandy. An obvious possible source, within the duchy, is Robert of Torigny. Robert states, in the prologue to his *Chronicle*, that Henry of Huntingdon had sent him a copy of the *Historia*, to be one of his sources; but, according to this same statement, it was a version that ended with the year 1135—thus, a copy of the seven-book edition, which could not have been the exemplar for Philip's ten-book version. When one looks at Robert's use of the *Historia,* however, one sees that despite his description of the text he was given, he has in practice used the final version that extended to the year 1147 — hence, a different manuscript from Henry's gift.[70] One of the post-1135 elements that appear in Robert's *Chronicle* is a letter from Henry of Huntingdon to an unidentified Warinus Brito, mentioning inter alia Henry's stopover at Bec in 1139 on his way to Rome in the entourage of Theobald, the new archbishop of Canterbury (and, until his election, abbot of Bec). Curiously, a passage of the letter as quoted by Robert does not, in fact, occur in the text of this letter in manuscripts of Henry's *Historia;* Robert's version has Henry describing the occasion in these terms: "I met [at Bec] a certain Robert of Torigny, monk of that place, a seeker-out of sacred and secular books and a very learned collector. When he had asked me questions about my history of the English kings, and had eagerly listened to my answers, he brought me a book to read about the British kings who held our island before the English [i.e., Geoffrey of Monmouth]."[71] It is hard to ignore the possibility that Robert inserted this bit of flattery himself.[72] Apparently, this encounter with Henry of Huntingdon impressed Robert, for a miniature that depicts the meeting is included on fol. 174 of Avranches MS 159, Robert's own manuscript of his *Chronicles.*[73]

We think it likely, however, that Philip of Bayeux acquired his text of the *Historia* directly from Henry of Huntingdon. Certainly he did not require Robert of Torigny to serve as his link to Henry, archdeacon of Huntingdon: Huntingdon is an archdeaconry of the see of Lincoln, where Philip was dean in the 1130s. Alexander, bishop of Lincoln throughout Philip's deanship, was likewise Henry's patron who encouraged and supported his historical writing. Philip and Henry were contemporaries who would have known each other at that time. The acquaintance had an opportunity to be revived when Philip's attendance on Henry II in the months after the coronation led him again to Lincoln, where we see him witnessing royal charters (ca. 1155). The likeliest source of Philip's *Historia* is a text secured from Henry of Huntingdon himself during a trip to England, perhaps to be copied by scribes back in Normandy.

The second title we shall discuss, the *Ylias* of Simon Chevre d'Or, has a double-edged interest: Simon's work is the latest datable work on Philip's booklist (no. 112), and Philip's booklist is the earliest datable mention of Simon's work.[74] The *Ylias,* a Latin poem dealing with the Trojan War, was written at the behest of Henry the Liberal, count of Champagne — therefore after 1153, when Henry became count — and its appearance on Philip's list gives it a terminus ante quo of 1163. Not a great deal is known about Simon—that he wrote poetic epitaphs for contemporary figures who died in 1151 (Hugh of Mâcon, bishop of Auxerre), 1152 (Suger of St-Denis and Count Thibaut of Blois), and 1153 (Bernard of Clairvaux and Pope Eugenius III), presumably shortly after the dates of their deaths, and that he became, whether early or late in his life, a canon of St-Victor in Paris. Simon was still alive after 1170, for he wrote a poem on the death of Becket.[75] The appearance of this title on Philip's booklist accomplishes two things at once: it serves, as medieval booklists so often do, to help date the composition; and it documents in striking fashion that Philip, a busy administrator for church and state, could notice and acquire a work of contemporary poetry written for the court of Champagne shortly after it was completed. How it came to Philip's notice is not known—perhaps via Arnulf of Lisieux who, like Simon, had ties with both St-Victor and the comital house of Blois/Champagne; or perhaps Simon himself sent it to Philip in hopes of future patronage.

The booklist reveals that Philip's copy of the *Ylias* was part of a volume (no. 112) that included a number of other works; Seneca's *Natural Questions*, a work that had emerged from obscurity only in Philip's lifetime;[76] the *Natural Questions* of Adelard of Bath, composed in 1111–1116 and dedicated to Richard II, Philip's predecessor in the see of Bayeux;[77] the *Virgilian Cantos* of Proba, a fourth-century Christian poet; and poems and other works of Hildebert of Le Mans (d. 1133).

Philip's manuscript of this collection does not survive—though a fragment of it may exist. It seems, however, to have been the progenitor of a small but important body of manuscripts. Four manuscripts figure in this story, Escorial 0.3.2, Vatican Reg. lat. 585, Avranches 93, and Copenhagen Gl. Kgl. 546 fol. The Escorial manuscript, written in the early fourteenth century, is the only one to preserve the whole sequence of works reported to have comprised Philip's volume. Parrott, the editor of the *Ylias*, has demonstrated that, for that work, the Escorial manuscript is a direct copy of the Vatican manuscript, which was written in the second half of the twelfth century, perhaps late in the century. The Vatican manuscript now is just a fragment, containing only the poetry portions (Proba, Simon, Hildebert) of the collection that was in Philip's codex, the *Natural Questions* portion having been detached to go its own way. Vatican Reg. lat. 585 could possibly be the remains of Philip's own manuscript, but we are doubtful that it is old enough. A third echo of Philip's manuscript appears on the front and back flyleaves of the Avranches manuscript, whose medieval home was Mont-St-Michel: in the late twelfth century, someone at the Mont copied onto these flyleaves a text of Simon's *Ylias* from an exemplar closely related to the Vatican/Escorial version; the most logical source is Philip's manuscript, which by that date was at Bec, the source (it seems) of a number of Mont-St-Michel texts. The fourth witness to Philip's codex no. 112 is the Copenhagen manuscript, which is a fragment, a quire of eight leaves (Proba, Hildebert, and some unidentified *Carmina*). The extant quire does not contain either the *Ylias* or Seneca's *Natural Questions* — i.e., the only works in the group that have been sorted out by a modern edition; thus, its affiliation with the rest of the manuscripts is not yet established. It needs to be collated with the Vatican manuscript, for those texts that the two have in common. Until that has been done, one can only say that the Copenhagen fragment dates from the mid-twelfth century and, thus, it could on the basis of date be a fragment of Philip's codex. In any event, the existence of these four manuscripts and fragments, presumably descendants of Philip's codex, indicates that Bec could on occasion serve as a point of dissemination for the interesting texts left by Philip.

The last volume to consider (no. 57) contained the works of Ennodius, late fifth-/early sixth-century rhetorician and bishop of Pavia: letters, verses, *dictiones*, epitaphs, epigrams, and panegyrics.[78] His works were prized in Carolingian times primarily as purveyors of a variety of classical verse forms; and the brief flurry of interest produced three surviving ninth-century manuscripts. Thereafter — in a common enough pattern — Ennodius was not again heard from until the middle of the twelfth century. A number of witnesses survive from that time, including two surviving manuscripts, excerpts in the *Florilegium Angelicum,* and a mention in a letter. The record of Philip's Ennodius is as early as any of these, and earlier than most.

The discussion of Ennodius in a letter — the only medieval literary assessment of Ennodius — probably refers directly to Philip's manuscript. In 1160, Philip's colleague Bishop Arnulf of Lisieux wrote to Henry of Pisa, "I am sending you the book of Ennodius. It belongs to someone else, but if you decide that you like it, I shall have a transcript of it sent to you as soon as possible."[79] The indications are that it was Henry of Pisa, cardinal-priest of Sts. Nereus and Achilleus and a papal legate to France, who had inquired about Ennodius; for Arnulf remarks that he himself had never seen the work until Henry mentioned it. (Henry was often in Normandy in the late 1150s and 1160s and knew both Arnulf and Philip.)[80] Arnulf's letter continues with an oft-quoted diatribe on Ennodius's turgid style ("Once having seen the work, I was amazed that an author should have had the gall to publish it, or that anyone else should have been disposed to make copies of it. . . ." etc.) — concluding that the perpetrator of such writings should more aptly be called "Innodius" (complicated, tangled) than "Ennodius" (open, plain).

Was this Philip's book that Arnulf had in his hands? As we have mentioned, Arnulf and Philip were contemporaries, colleagues, and friends. By 1160, Philip and Arnulf had been associated with one another in the king's service on numerous occasions, and from one end of Henry's domains to the other—York, Lincoln, Oxford, Westminster, as well as Rouen, Caen, LeMans, Périgueux, and so on.[81] They had shared common adversaries who had usurped the rights of their respective sees, most notably the Benedictines of Fécamp; and in about 1153 Arnulf had petitioned Eugenius III on Philip's behalf in a strongly supportive letter.[82] Almost certainly, then, Philip of Harcourt was the "someone else" from whom Arnulf borrowed a rare copy of Ennodius to satisfy Henry of Pisa. Henry must thereafter have returned it, for it was included with Philip's gift to Bec.

If Arnulf had not heard specifically of Ennodius before, yet knew a good place to seek out a text when Henry of Pisa asked, the implication is that Arnulf knew Philip had a large and varied library. This in turn raises the intriguing possibility that some of the library which Arnulf left to St-Victor may have been copied from Philip's books, or that the two at least may have shared common sources of supply and common interests.

Medieval booklists have various uses for modern scholars, the most obvious being to date texts and authors, and to document the circulation of this or that work in a given area and time. Here we have seen, as well, that a booklist can add substance to an otherwise shadowy but important figure, and can document the use of codified learning in twelfth-century administration.

Robert of Torigny's epitaph for Philip is more than a little disapproving: "Philip, the bishop of Bayeux . . . was prudent and shrewd both at increasing, and at recovering, the property of his church, and he accomplished much there; but 'the wisdom of this world is foolishness, to God' [1 Cor. 3:19]." Proper, if uncharitable, sentiments for a Benedictine. But Philip's diocese, Philip's king, and Philip himself were well served by his share of the wisdom, and the learning, of this world, as contained in and attested by the books he owned.

Appendix: Charters of Henry II Witnessed by Philip

Philip attested at least sixty-one *acta* of Henry, count of Anjou, duke of Normandy, and (from 1154) king of England. A selection of Henry's acts were first sorted by Léopold Delisle; they were further edited, after Delisle's death, by Elie Berger, who published them in three volumes (*Recueil des actes de Henri II, roi d'Angleterre et duc de Normandie, concernant les provinces françaises et les affaires de France* [Paris, 1916-1927]). They are listed here in the order of the numbers assigned by Berger (occasionally different from Delisle's); documents numbered with asterisks date from before Henry's accession to the English throne.

Readers should recall that, although the arrangement of the acts in the edition follows the rules of chronology applicable to charters, the result is not necessarily convincing in historical terms. For example, no. 2 is dated March 1155 in London, while the only other London act, no. 231 (near the end of the present list), is dated 1155/1163 — which is to say, one can demonstrate with certainty only that the act was written after Henry's accession in 1154 and before Philip's death in 1163; but common sense suggests that Philip affixed his signature to both no. 2 and no. 231 during one and the same sojourn in London, in 1155.

As we have mentioned above, for some twenty-eight of these acts, Arnulf bishop of Lisieux joined Philip as a witness; for another four, Rotrou bishop of Evreux was co-witness; and for fifteen, Philip was joined by both Arnulf and Rotrou. The name of no other signatory, lay or ecclesiastical, is coupled with Philip's with any regularity (save, of course, the name of the king/duke's agents, English chancellor or Norman seneschal, who signed with Philip as without him). Consequently, we have noted those acts that bear the signatures of either or both of these bishops.

20.* Bayeux, 1151.
35.* Rouen, 1151-1153. Arnulf.
45.* Rouen, 1151-1153. Arnulf.
72.* Le Mans, 1154. Arnulf.
74.* Périgueux, 1154. Arnulf.
78.* Fontevrault, 1154. Arnulf.
 2. London, 1155. Arnulf.
25. Sauve-Majeure, abbey of, 1156. Arnulf.
26. Oxford, 1155 or 1157. Arnulf.
32. Chéci (near Orléans), 1156 or 1157. Arnulf.
33. Rouen, 1156-1157.
35. Falaise, 1157. Arnulf, Rotrou.
39. Barfleur, 1157. Arnulf.
40. ? n.p., ca. 1157.
44. Lincoln, 1155-1158. Arnulf.
48. Northampton, 1155-1158. Rotrou.

50. Northampton, 1155-1158.
56. Westminster, 1155-1158. Arnulf.
57. Westminster, 1155-1158. Arnulf.
58. Westminster, 1155-1158. Arnulf.
64. Westminster, 1155-1158. Arnulf.
65. Westminster, 1155-1158. Arnulf.
66. Westminster, 1155-1158. Arnulf.
67. Westminster, 1155-1158. Arnulf.
68. Westminster, 1155-1158. Arnulf.
76. York, 1155-1158. Arnulf.
77. York, 1155-1158. Arnulf.
95. Argentan, 1156-1159.
97. Argentan, 1156-1159.
98. Argentan, 1156-1159. Arnulf.
100. Argentan, 1156-1159. Arnulf.
101. Bayeux, 1156-1159. Arnulf, Rotrou.
104. Caen, 1156-1159.
108. Le Mans, 1156-1159. Arnulf.
112. Rouen, 1156-1159. Arnulf.
113. Rouen, 1156-1159. Arnulf.
116. Rouen, 1156-1159.
117. Rouen, 1156-1159. Arnulf, Rotrou.
122. ? n.p., 1156-1159.
123. Le Mans, 1157-1159. Arnulf.
134. Rouen, 1156-1160. Arnulf, Rotrou.
137. Lions, 1160.
138. Rouen, 1160. Rotrou.
141. ? n.p., 1160. Arnulf, Rotrou.
148. Argentan, 1156-1161. Arnulf, Rotrou.
152. Bayeux, 1156-1161. Arnulf, Rotrou.
153. Caen, 1156-1161. Arnulf, Rotrou.
154. Caen, 1156-1161. Arnulf, Rotrou.
180. Rouen, 1156-1161.
188. Rouen, 1156-1161. Arnulf, Rotrou.
198. Rouen, 1159-1161. Arnulf, Rotrou.
204. Les Andelys, 1156-1162. Rotrou.
205. Les Andelys, 1156-1162. Rotrou.
206. Argentan, 1156-1162.
208. Caen, 1156-1162. Arnulf, Rotrou.
215. Rouen, 1156-1162. Arnulf.
216. Rouen, 1156-1162. Arnulf, Rotrou.

223. Fécamp, 1162. Arnulf, Rotrou.
230. Lincoln, 1155-1163.
231. London, 1155-1163.
236. Rouen, 1157-1163. Arnulf, Rotrou.

Notes

*We thank Robert L. Benson, John F. Benton, and Margaret T. Gibson, who kindly read an earlier version of this essay and gave sound advice. We are grateful to Terry Nixon for his help over the years with the two Bec booklists, as well as for suggestions on specific aspects of this article. We are indebted to Patricia Stirnemann for generously sharing with us her detailed knowledge of many of the manuscripts mentioned below.

The title derives from epistle 8 of Arnulf of Lisieux (cited in n. 9 below), who says of Philip, "Homo enim consilii et fortitudinis est, potens in opere et sermone, in regalibus consiliis et negotiis ecclesiasticis acceptus et efficax...."

1. R. W. Southern, *The Making of the Middle Ages* (London, 1953), 209, and his *Medieval Humanism and Other Studies* (New York, 1970), 175.

2. Concerning Philip's life see V. Bourrienne, *Un grand bâtisseur: Philippe de Harcourt, évêque de Bayeux 1142-1163* (Paris, 1930), and Sarell Everett Gleason, *An Ecclesiastical Barony of the Middle Ages: The Bishopric of Bayeux, 1066-1204* (Cambridge, Mass., 1936). Bourrienne has amassed an impressive amount of information, but it is inextricably mixed with credulous borrowings from "romantic" earlier histories of the Harcourts and their region. Most recently, Philip's career can be followed as that of a recurring minor character in David Crouch, *The Beaumont Twins: The Roots and Branches of Power in the Twelfth Century* (Cambridge, 1986).

3. The catalog of Philip's books has been edited by Gustav Becker, *Catalogi bibliothecarum antiqui* (Bonn, 1885), 199-202; and, with slightly different numbering, by H. Omont, *Catalogue général des manuscrits des bibliothèques publiques* 2 (Paris, 1888), 394-98, the edition cited here. The collection is briefly discussed by Geneviève Nortier, *Les bibliothèques médiévales des abbayes bénédictines de Normandie* (Caen, 1966), 39-45. R. W. Hunt groups Philip's collection with the fifty-six volumes that belonged to the near-contemporary Celestine III (d. 1144), and with the libraries of two thirteenth-century churchmen, Cardinal Guala Bicchieri (d. 1227) and Bernard II archbishop of Santiago de Compostela (1223-1237), whose collections were similar in size to Philip's; see his "Universities and Learning," in *The Flowering of the Middle Ages*, ed. Joan Evans (London, 1985), 164ff.

4. See the index to *Texts and Transmission*, ed. L. Reynolds (Oxford, 1983), sub nom. "Philip, Bishop of Bayeux."

5. Unless otherwise noted, the events of Philip's biography given here are based upon the works cited in n. 2 above.

6. Crouch, *Twins*, 120-27 discusses the evidence for the individual Harcourts and their holdings; for a summary and genealogical table see 220-21. Abbé Bourrienne, 1-3, presents a genealogy that differs in most details, for which he offers nothing in the way of substantiation.

7. As Crouch recognizes, there is no concrete evidence that Philip is Robert fitz Anschetil's son (*Twins*, 220 n. 7)—nor even that Robert and Waleran were

cousins, though contemporary Bec historians record unspecified kinship (ibid., 120-21). Both assumptions are reasonable, and they explain much about Philip's career which would otherwise be perplexing. We are grateful to David Crouch for sharing with us his further thoughts on Philip's family.

8. See Crouch, *Beaumont Twins,* 207-11. Crouch is occasionally more willing than we are to accept at face value formulas in charters, such as *uidi et legi* or *legi et confirmaui,* as indications that Waleran "made it his business personally to research the archives of his dependent religious communities" (208).

9. Frank Barlow, ed., *The Letters of Arnulf of Lisieux,* Camden Third Series 61 (London, 1939), xiii-xv. The facts are three: (1) Arnulf, in letter no. 34, reveals that he had obtained his basic education at the cathedral school of Séez where his older brother John (bishop of Séez from 1124) was archdeacon—hence, before 1124; (2) in the introduction to his *Inuectiua in Girardum Engolismensem episcopum* written in the summer of 1133, he notes that he was then in Italy, for the study of law; and (3) the *Inuectiua* is dedicated to Geoffrey de Lèves, bishop of Chartres, whose clerk Arnulf had been—again, according to the introduction. Thus, Arnulf clearly spent some years in Chartres, between his earliest education at Séez and his legal studies in Italy; Barlow thinks it likely that those years were spent in schooling.

10. Such, at least, is the assumption of current study; see Olga Weijers, "The Chronology of John of Salisbury's Studies in France (Metalogicon, II.10)," in *The World of John of Salisbury,* ed. Michael Wilks, Studies in Church History Subsidia 3 (Oxford, 1984), 109-16, esp. 114-16.

11. Rotrou was first cousin to Count Waleran de Meulan; see Crouch, *Beaumont Twins,* 16 fig. 2, etc. Crouch elsewhere (45) suggests that Philip was a distant relative of the count.

12. When Gilbert was examined at Paris in 1147, and again at Reims in 1148, he alluded to his pupil Rotrou as evidence of the soundness of his teaching; see *Histoire littéraire de la France,* 14:296. Southern, *Medieval Humanism,* 67, argues that Gilbert's most important teaching probably occurred at Paris after he had left Chartres, which may well be correct. Gilbert is first documented at Paris in 1141, however, and by that date Rotrou was well past his school days, having become bishop of Evreux in 1138 or 1139.

13. The manuscript in question—Paris, B.N. lat. 5802, a collection of ancient historians—and the origins of Philip's library are discussed in T. Maslowski and R. H. Rouse, "Twelfth-Century Extracts from Cicero's *Pro Archia* and *Pro Cluentio* in Paris B.N. MS lat. 18104," *Italia medioevale e umanistica* 22 (1979): 97-122.

14. See R. H. Rouse, "*Florilegia* and Latin Classical Authors in Twelfth- and Thirteenth-Century Orléans," *Viator* 10 (1979): 131-60.

15. Concerning Philip's relationship with Count Waleran and his twin Robert of Leicester, see Crouch, *Beaumont Twins,* esp. 45 and 220.

16. For the documentation, such as it is, see Crouch, *Twins,* 45 and nn.

17. See the index sub nom. "Philip de Harcourt" in Crouch, *Beaumont Twins,* for the indications of consistent support from Waleran in the stages of Philip's career.

18. "Bracium unum, aureis lammis coopertum, et lapidibus preciosis adornatum"; see V. Bourrienne, ed., *Antiquus cartularius ecclesiae Baiocensis (Livre noir),* 2 vols. (Paris, 1902), 1:80-81, documents numbered 61 and 62, which record

all that we know about the incident: Hugh abp. of Rouen (no. 61) notifies the archbishops of Canterbury and York and all the English hierarchy that bishops Philip of Bayeux and Jocelin of Salisbury have reached agreement for return of the arm, along with a "gift"—doubtless some sort of amends—of ten silver marks. In fact, though only the arm is returned, the "quarrel" concerned "certain things [plural] carried off from the treasury of Salisbury Cathedral" (*controuersia . . . pro quibusdam absportatis de thesauro Salesburiensis ecclesiae*); perhaps the ten marks are payment for losses. For reasons unknown, an identical charter was addressed to the same recipients presumably at the same time by Rotrou, bishop of Evreux (no. 62). Neither document is dated; in both cases, Bourrienne has named the English archbishops as "Thomas of Canterbury" (1162-1170) and "Henry of York" (Henry Murdac, d. 1153), an impossible combination. R. H. C. Davis, *King Stephen, 1135-1154* (Berkeley, 1967), 47 and n., sensibly suggests that the manuscript must have said (or meant) "T[heobald]" rather than "Thomas" as archbishop of Canterbury—hence, that the agreement occurred between 1147 and 1153 (the tenure of Henry of York), probably in 1148 at the Council of Reims. This is the date accepted by Thomas G. Waldman, who is preparing an edition of "The *Acta* of Hugh 'of Amiens,' Archbishop of Rouen, 1130-1164" for the Royal Historical Society's Camden Series. We are grateful to Dr. Waldman for this information.

19. Previous mentions of this incident have not, to our knowledge, identified the relic at the center of the quarrel. The list of Osmund's gifts, ca. 1078-1099, is printed by C. Wordsworth, *Ceremonies and Processions of the Cathedral Church of Salisbury* (Cambridge, 1901), 183: "brachium sancti Aldelmi argenteum et deauratum." William of Malmesbury's *Vita* of Aldhelm explains how Osmund was given Aldhelm's left arm by Malmesbury in 1078; lodged in a sumptuous reliquary, it performed miracles of healing at Salisbury: see William of Malmesbury, *De gestis pontificum anglorum*, ed. N. E. S. A. Hamilton, Rolls Series (London, 1870), 428-29. The reliquary recurs in the inventory of ornaments found in the treasury at Sarum in 1214; Wordsworth, 169: "brachium sancti Aldelmi coopertum argento, cum multis lapidibus, continens alias reliquias." For a revisionist view of Norman regard for Anglo-Saxon relics see S. J. Ridyard, "*Condigna ueneratio*: Post-Conquest Attitudes to the Saints of the Anglo-Saxons," *Anglo-Norman Studies* 9, *Preeceedings of the Battle Conference* (1987): 179-206; we thank John Benton for this reference.

20. See Crouch, *Beaumont Twins*, 58-79.

21. Frank Barlow, *The Feudal Kingdom of England*, 2nd ed. (New York, 1961) provides a useful survey of the political and social history of Philip of Bayeux's lifetime; concerning the disputed succession of Henry I and the civil wars of King Stephen's reign, see 201-34; for Normandy, see esp. 208-9, 210, 221. For more recent bibliography see Davis, *King Stephen, 1135-1154*; W. L. Warren, *Henry II* (Berkeley, 1973), esp. chap. 2 (12-53), "The Pursuit of an Inheritance (1135-54)"; and Marjorie Chibnall, *Anglo-Norman England 1066-1166* (Oxford, 1986), and esp. 77-101 concerning civil war and succession.

22. Concerning the architecture of the new cathedral see J. Vallery-Radot, *La Cathédrale de Bayeux*, 2nd ed., rev. (Paris, 1958). It would be interesting to know if the famous bas-reliefs were placed on the walls of the new nave under Philip's direction. We have found no distinct connection between any of the scenes

depicted and any of the books in Philip's library. The bas-relief of a chained ape is particularly interesting, in that it is an early depiction of this subject in northern Europe according to H. Janson, *Apes and Ape Lore* (London, 1952), 49. E. Lambert, "Les écoinçons de la nef de la Cathédrale de Bayeux," in *Mélanges Henrick Cornell* (Stockholm, 1950), 262-71, did not explore potential literary sources.

23. Concerning Philip's renovation of his diocese, see Bourrienne, *Un grand bâtisseur* pt. 2, "L'évêque" (9-113); Gleason, *Ecclesiastical Barony*, 41-67; and C. H. Haskins, *Norman Institutions*, Harvard Historical Studies 24 (Cambridge, Mass. 1918), 203-16, 222-25.

24. Haskins, *Norman Institutions*, 148-50 and chap. 6: "The Early Norman Jury," 196 ff.

25. See Helmut Gleber, *Papst Eugen III. (1145-1153) unter besonderer Berücksichtigung seiner politischen Tätigkeit*, Beiträge zur mittelalterlichen und neueren Geschichte 6 (Jena, 1936), 11, who suggests that this group of northern prelates influenced the election. The protocol is printed by Paul Fridolin Kehr, Abh. Göttingen, N.F. 22.1, p. 345, no. 46. We are grateful to Robert L. Benson for this reference.

26. The bulls are preserved in the cartulary of Bayeux cathedral, the *Livre noir* edited by Bourrienne.

27. *Livre noir*, nos. 154 (16 May 1144, Lucius II); 155 (18 March 1145) and 156 (3 Feb. 1153, Eugenius III).

28. *Livre noir*, nos. 157 (16 May 1144, Lucius II = Jaffé-Löwenfeld #8612) and 173 (18 March ?1145, Eugenius III).

29. *Livre noir*, no. 206 (16 May 1144, Lucius II); cf. *Livre noir* no. 39 (ca. 1144) for the duke's allusion to the corresponding bull of Eugenius, which evidently does not survive. In these actions Philip was following a pattern visible in other North French dioceses of his time. See D. Lohrmann, *Kirchengut im nördlichen Frankreich*, Pariser historische Studien 20 (Bonn, 1983), and esp. 137-39; we are grateful to John Benton for this reference.

30. *Livre noir*, vol. 1, p. xiii, the charters numbered 1-214; nos. 33 *bis* and 168, which pertain to the 1260s, are later insertions.

31. Of the first 213 charters in the *Livre noir* (nos. 1-214, less the inserted no. 168), the following documents probably date from Philip's episcopacy: nos. 7, 9-10, 12-19, 24-28, 30-33, 35-37, 39-44, 52-54, 58-63, 71, 73, 76, 89-90, 99-101, 103-4, 106, 117-18, 127, 138-39, 148-51, 154-59 161-66, 173-75, 178-79, 181-95, 198- 203, 206-7, 210, 213.

32. *Livre noir*, nos. 1-6, 22-23, 172.

33. *Livre noir*, no. 21.

34. *Livre noir*, nos. 8, 29, 34, 38; no. 102 — confirmation of a gift of land to the cathedral's *succentor*, dated 1135-1142 — is the only charter that does not patently fit the mold.

35. See Bourrienne, 61, 70, and B. Gams, *Series episcoporum ecclesiae catholicae* (Regensburg, 1873-86; repr., Graz, 1957), 542.

36. Dom Martène's edition of Hugh's works is printed in Migne's *Patrologia Latina*, vol. 192; a modern edition of the Genesis commentary (of which Martène knew only a fragment) was produced by Francis Lecomte, "Un commentaire scripturaire du XIIe siècle: Le 'Tractatus in Hexaemeron' de Hugues d'Amiens (archevêque de Rouen 1130-1164)," *Archives d'histoire doctinale et littéraire du moyen âge* 33 (1958 [1959]): 227-94. For Hugh's biography see the article of

E. Vacandard in the *Dictionnaire de théologie catholique*; Lecomte's introduction; and the D.Phil. dissertation of Thomas G. Waldman, "Hugh 'of Amiens,' Archbishop of Rouen 1130-64" (Oxford University, 1970).

37. Edited by L. Delisle, "Documents sur les livres et les bibliothèques au moyen âge 1: Bibliothèque de la cathédrale de Rouen au XIIe siècle," *Bibliothèque de l'Ecole des chartes* 11 (1849): 218: "Liber Hugonis archiepiscopi ad Albanensem episcopum [= *Dialogi*]; libellus eiusdem de expositione fidei catholice et orationis Dominice." The second volume is now Geneva, Bibliothèque publique et universitaire MS lat. 41. Rotrou's list includes in addition Pliny, *Natural History*; Jerome, *Epistolae*; Augustine, *De ciuitate Dei*; Isidore, *Etymologies*; and Vitruvius, *De architectura*. Evreux Bibliothèque municipale MS 92, containing the *Confessions* and other Augustiniana—but not *De ciuitate Dei*—also bears Rotrou's ex libris, part of a bequest to his first cathedral, Evreux ("Hunc librum dedit dominus Rotrodus Rothomagensis archiepiscopus ecclesie Ebroicensi").

38. Cf. Lecomte, 227 and n. 6.

39. The letter is printed by Lecomte, 235-36. Arnulf wrote an epitaph on Hugh's death, printed in *PL* 201.200.

40. See Nortier, *Les bibliothèques*, 346. We are grateful to Thomas G. Waldman for confirming this suggestion.

41. See L. Delisle, *Recueil des actes de Henri II*, ed. E. Berger, 3 vols. (Paris, 1916-27), 1:80 and 1:180-81.

42. See Appendix below, for a list of the locations and the dates of the 61.

43. For a list of these acts, together with the dates and locations, see the Appendix below.

44. Gleason, *Ecclesiastical Barony*, 29.

45. See Haskins, *Norman Institutions*, 165-66.

46. Ibid., 167 and n. 63. Not surprisingly, the seneschal was also a frequent joint witness, with Philip, of royal acts (see above)—twenty of the sixty-two charters witnessed by Philip were also attested by Robert. We note, in passing, that Robert de Neubourg retired to the abbey of Bec (he had funded the building of the abbey's chapter house) at the end of his life in 1159, just as Philip was to do in 1163; ibid., 166 n. 57. Robert de Neubourg and Bishop Rotrou were brothers, first cousins of Waleran of Meulan, and thus probably distant kin of Philip; see Crouch, *Beaumont Twins*, 16, fig. 2.

47. Barlow, *Letters*, 11 ep. 8, "in regalibus consiliis et negotiis ecclesiasticis acceptus et efficax."

48. L. Delisle, ed., *Chronique de Robert de Torigni*, 2 vols. (Rouen, 1872-73), 1:344-45.

49. For a reproduction of fol. 1v see Nortier, *Les bibliothèques*, facing p. 66.

50. Concerning the library of Mont-St-Michel see Nortier, *Les bibliothèques*; F. Avril, "La décoration des manuscrits du Mont-St-Michel (XIe-XIIe siècles)," in *Millénaire du Mont-St-Michel* 2 (1967); and J. J. G. Alexander, *Norman Illumination at Mont-St-Michel* (Oxford, 1970). Scarcely any manuscripts survive from Bec, but a number of the surviving books from Mont-St-Michel correspond closely with descriptions in the Bec catalogs: Avranches Bibl. mun. MSS 83, 92, 93, 104, 113, 116, 157, 159-62, 225-26, 230, 235, 243; Paris, B. N. lat. 5997A; Vendôme, 189.

51. Numbered 115 by Omont's edition, which assigns numbers (69, 76) to two

entries written in the margins. Because the text of Becker's edition is inaccurate, being derived from F. Ravaisson's edition of 1841 rather than from the manuscript, we cite Omont's text and numbers here.

52. This list is printed with Philip's booklist (see n. 3 above): Becker 257–66, Omont 385–94. The possible merger of Philip's manuscripts with Bec books, suggested by Patricia Stirnemann, was worked out in detail by Terry Nixon; we are grateful to them both for lengthy discussions of this matter. David N. Dumville dates the Bec catalog "from the mid-twelfth century"; see his "An Early Text of Geoffrey of Monmouth's *Historia regum Britanniae* and the Circulation of Some Latin Histories in Twelfth-Century Normandy," *Arthurian Literature* 4 (1985): 1–36 at 7 and n. 26. Unfortunately, the appendix that was to present the evidence for this dating was not published with the article. We thank Dr. Dumville for calling this article to our attention.

53. For example, no. 95 (Omont, 397) on the list of Philip's books reads "In alio [uolumine] historia Henrici de Anglia, et liber Bede minor de temporibus et de natura rerum." The Bec catalog implies that the two Bede works were removed, and added to a manuscript containing Bede's *Ecclesiastical History* and some smaller works: no. 80 (Omont, 389), "In alio [uolumine] historia Anglorum libri V [= the *Ecclisiastical History*]. De temporibus liber I minor. De naturis rerum liber I. Liber Gilde sapientis de excidio Britannie. Vita sancti Neoti, qui in capite ponitur." The Henry of Huntingdon from Philip's no. 95 was left on its own, Bec catalog no. 132 (Omont, 393): "In alio [uolumine] historia Henrici de gente Anglorum libri X."

54. See, e.g., Leiden BPL 20, *Historia Normannorum* (Bec no. 120); Paris, B.N. MS lat. 1685, Athanasius (Bec no. 113); B.N. MS lat. 12211, Augustine (Philip no. 12 = Bec. no. 6); and possibly B.N. MS lat. 3808, Fulgentius (Bec no. 112?). Léopold Delisle, in *Bibliothèque de l'Ecole des Chartes* 71 (1910): 506–21, noted this feature of certain Bec manuscripts and suggested that the Bec catalog was compiled from these lists.

55. These manuscripts belonged, or possibly belonged, to Philip of Bayeux: Paris, B.N. lat. 152 fol. 32, Pomponius Mela (a leaf from no. 66 in the catalog of Philip's books); B.N. lat. 5802, Suetonius etc. (nos. 68 and 79); B.N. lat. 12211, Augustine (no. 12); and perhaps B.N. lat. 6042, Henry of Huntingdon (no. 95). Patricia Stirneman has recently suggested persuasively that MS 6042 was in fact Philip's manuscript of the *Historia*. This assumption provides a possible solution to the problem of the source of Robert of Torigny's second text of the *Historia*, discussed below: since Robert seems to have had copies of Bec exemplars made for Mont-St-Michel, it would be logical for him to have used a copy of lat. 6042 in writing his *Chronicle* if 6042 were a Bec manuscript (as a result of Philip's bequest).

56. Hunt ("Universities and Learning," 165) observed that Philip's collection was "remarkable for the relatively large number of Latin classical prose writers with not a single poet"—a reflection, surely, of his dictaminal training.

57. See the discussion in Rouse, "*Florilegia* and Latin Classical Authors," passim. For an example of the use of a dictaminal *florilegium* by a late twelfth-century scholar, see A. Goddu and R. H. Rouse, "Gerald of Wales and the *Florilegium Angelicum*," *Speculum* 52 (1977): 488–521.

58. Cat. # 113, "In alio Zacharias super 'Vnum ex quatuor.'" This does not

reappear in the Bec list. Regarding Zacharias and the composition and circulation of the concordance see: B. de Vregille, "Notes sur la vie et l'oeuvre de Zacharie de Besançon," *Analecta Praemonstratensia* 41 (1965): 293-309; and T. J. Gerits, "Notes sur la tradition manuscrite et imprimée du traité 'In unum ex quatuor' de Zacharie de Besançon," *Analecta Praemonstratensia* 42 (1966): 276-303 with brief descriptions of the 102 surviving manuscripts. See also the list in F. Stegmüller, *Repertorium biblicum medii aevi* (Madrid, 1940-), nos. 5699 and 8400.

59. Nos. 71-77 in the catalog of Philip's books. No. 76, "In alio [uolumine] Instituta Iustiniani," has been added by the scribe in the margin, presumably correcting an oversight. Concerning the spread of Roman law to the North, see R. C. Van Caenegem, *Royal Writs in England from the Conquest to Glanvill*, Selden Society Publications 77 (London, 1959), pt. 3, chap. 2, "Roman and Canon Law Influences on the Early Common Law," 360-90, especially 367-70.

60. One of these, no. 69, has been added in the margin by the scribe, presumably in correction of an omission.

61. For the dissemination of Gratian through the Anglo-Norman hierarchy, see the reference to Van Caenegem in the preceding note. Concerning the appearance and early knowledge of Gratian's *Decretum* in northern Europe see W. Holtzmann, "Die Benutzung Gratians in der päpstlichen Kanzlei im 12. Jahrhundert," *Studia Gratiana* 1 (1953): 325-49. See also Robert L. Benson, "Barbarossas Rede auf dem Reichstag von Roncaglia (1158): Zur Benutzung kanonischen und römischen Rechtes bei Rahewin," forthcoming; we are grateful to him for allowing us to see the relevant portion of this article in typescript.

62. Philip perhaps was the recipient of a decretal from Alexander III addressed simply "Baiocensi episcopo": see Walther Holtzmann, *Decretales ineditae saeculi XII*, ed. and rev. Stanley Chodorow and Charles Duggan, Monumenta iuris canonici B: Corpus collectionum 4 (Vatican City, 1982), 39, no. 21, which is a reply to a query about penances. Such a request implies canonistic knowledge, rather than ignorance; we thank Robert L. Benson for bringing this decretal to our attention.

63. See epistle 99 (1158-1160): *The Letters of John of Salisbury* 1: *The Early Letters (1153-1161)*, ed. W. J. Millor and H. E. Butler, rev. C. N. Brooke (London, 1955), 153. John also quotes from the *Decretum* in epistle 100 (ibid., 157), which is potentially earlier (ep. 100 can be dated only to the years 1147-1171, the tenure of its probable addressee). Like Philip, John had traveled to Italy; see the itinerary in this same volume of his letters, app. 1, "John of Salisbury at the Papal Curia," 253-56. W. Holtzmann has suggested that John brought a copy of the *Decretum* to England on his return from Rome in 1153-1154; see his review of S. Kuttner and E. Rathbone's "Anglo-Norman Canonists . . ." (*Traditio* 7 [1949-51]: 279-358), in *Savigny Zeitschrift für Rechtsgeschichte, Kan. Abt.* 39 (1953): 466; cited by Van Caenegem, *Royal Writs*, 366 n.

64. See Van Caenegem, *Royal Writs*, 368.

65. For an investigation of the books of twelfth-century French princes, in particular Henry the Liberal, see P. Stirnemann, "Quelques bibliothèques princières et la production hors scriptorium au XIIe siècle," *Bulletin archéologique du Comité des travaux historiques et scientifiques*, n.s.: 17-18A (Paris, 1984): 7-38, and "Les bibliothèques princières et privées aux XIIe et XIIIe siècles," forthcoming in *L'histoire des bibliothèques françaises*, vol. 1 (Paris, 1988); we thank her for allowing

us to read the latter in typescript. Dr. Stirnemann has discovered the inventory of Henry's library and is preparing an edition of it.

66. It has been said that Leiden BPL 20, a two-part composite manuscript that belonged to Bec and contains the *Historia Normannorum* of William of Jumièges, Geoffrey of Monmouth's *Historia regum Britanniae,* and an excerpt from Nennius's *Historia Britonum,* as well as some classical Alexander-lore, is a Bec rearrangement of two of Philip's codexes, nos. 43 and 44: "In alio, historia Normannorum. In alio, uita Alexandri et historia Britonum"; see Margaret Gibson, "History at Bec in the Twelfth Century," in *The Writing of History in the Middle Ages,* ed. R. H. C. Davis and J. M. Wallace-Hadrill (Oxford, 1981), 183 n. 1, and Crouch, *Twins,* 208, following Gibson. Although we should be glad if it were, we think BPL 20 is not Philip's, for two reasons: (1) The William of Jumièges portion of the manuscript is annotated in the hand of Robert of Torigny, creating what is known as Robert's continuation—therefore, rather than coming to the abbey with Philip's books in 1164, this part of BPL 20 must have belonged to Bec before Robert left to become abbot of Mont-St-Michel in 1154; and (2) the Alexander material (Julius Valerius, plus the *Epistola ad Aristotilem*), which in Philip's collection appeared in the same codex with the *Historia Britonum,* in the Leiden manuscript belongs to part 1, with William of Jumièges, rather than to part 2, with Geoffrey of Monmouth and Nennius, a division confirmed by the quire structure, quire signatures, and hands.

67. *Tituli librorum Beccensis almarii,* no. 132: "In alio [uolumine] historia Henrici de gente Anglorum, libri X."

68. See Thomas Arnold, ed., *The History of the English, by Henry, archdeacon of Huntingdon, from A.C. 55 to A.D. 1154...,* Rolls Series (London, 1879), x–xvi for a discussion of the versions, and xxxvi–xlii for a list of surviving manuscripts. It is possible that Philip instead owned Henry of Huntingdon's final version (through the year 1154), likewise in ten books; but this edition seems not to have circulated outside England. Recently Diana Greenway has taken a major step forward in bringing up to date the study of manuscripts of Henry of Huntingdon ("Henry of Huntingdon and the Manuscripts of His *Historia Anglorum,*" *Anglo-Norman Studies* 9, *Proceedings of the Battle Conference* (1986), ed. R. Allen Brown [Woodbridge, Suffolk, 1987]: 103–26); her description of the Bec/Mont-St-Michel manuscripts relies on assumptions, not always justified, of Delisle in the nineteenth century; see Greenway 113–14, and esp. nn. 56 and 58.

69. Concerning B.N. lat. 6042, see n. 55 above.

70. See Arnold's discussion of BN lat. 6042, *History,* xxxvii n. 2.

71. This long version, together with notice of the discrepancy between it and the *Historia* version, appears in Delisle's edition of Robert of Torigny's *Chronicle,* 1.97–98 and n. 2, and in Arnold's edition of the *Historia,* xxi and n. 1. Curiously, Léopold Delisle, Robert of Torigny's editor, ignored the fact that Philip of Bayeux had owned a manuscript of Henry of Huntingdon's *Historia* which was willed to Bec. Delisle supposed that B.N. lat. 6042 was copied, at Mont-St-Michel, from a Bec manuscript that Robert quoted. And he further suggests that that lost exemplar came to Bec from Henry of Huntingdon in gratitude for Robert's supposedly having introduced Henry to the work of Geoffrey of Monmouth.

72. Arnold, *History of the English,* xxi n. 1 makes this suggestion.

73. See Avril, *Millénaire* 2, 233 (the book Robert gives to Henry of Huntingdon is mistakenly identified as Nennius's *History*), and fig. 124.

74. Regarding Simon see A. Boutemy, "La Geste d'Enée," *Le moyen âge* 52 (1946): 243-56; J. Stohlmann, "Magister Simon Aurea Capra: Zu Person und Werk des späteren Kanonikers von St. Viktor," in *Hommages à A. Boutemy* (Brussels, 1976): 343-66. See also M. M. Parrott, "The *Ylias* of Simon Aurea Capra: A Critical Edition" (D. Phil. diss., University of Toronto, 1975), which contains a detailed examination of the manuscripts discussed above. We are grateful to George Rigg, who directed this thesis, for having helped us consult it.

75. See F. Swietek, "A Metrical Life of Thomas Becket by Simon Aurea Capra," *Mittellateinisches Jahrbuch* 11 (1976): 177-95.

76. Regarding the transmission of Seneca's Natural Questions see Reynolds, *Texts and Transmission*, 376-78.

77. The manuscripts of Adelard of Bath's *Natural Questions* are discussed by C. Burnett, "The Introduction of Arabic Science into Northern France and Norman Britain: A Catalogue of the Writings of Adelard of Bath and Petrus Alfonsi and Closely Associated Works, Together with the Manuscripts in Which They Occur," unpublished preprint, 25-27.

78. See R. H. Rouse and M. A. Rouse, "Ennodius in the Middle Ages: Adonics, Ps.-Isidore, Cistercians, and the Schools," in *Popes, Teachers, and Canon Law in the Middle Ages: Studies in Honor of Brian Tierney*, ed. S. Chodorow and J. Sweeney (Ithaca, forthcoming).

79. Barlow, *Letters of Arnulf*, 36-38, ep. 27; and F. Vogel, MGH Auct. Ant. 7 (Berlin, 1885), lx-lxi. The letter is printed and discussed by P. Von Moos, "Literarkritik im Mittelalter: Arnulf von Lisieux über Ennodius," in *Mélanges offerts à René Crozet* (Poitiers, 1966), 929-35.

80. Regarding Henry of Pisa see P. Clausen, "Aus der Werkstatt Gerhochs von Reichersberg," *Deutsches Archiv* 23 (1967): 47-56.

81. They jointly witnessed at least forty-four *acta*, at seventeen different locations; see Appendix.

82. Barlow, *Letters of Arnulf*, 11-12, ep. 8. The purpose and the circumstances of this letter are a mystery: In it Arnulf adds his voice to that of the Bayeux chapter in petitioning the pope to permit Philip to return home.

PLENARY LECTURE

The Classics in Medieval Education

ALDO SCAGLIONE

Allow me to begin with a rather cursory socio-anthropological look at the question from the vantage of audience- or reader-orientation. Whenever we think of a cultural system, we may wonder to what extent it is or was "popular." Ancient culture, especially in Greece, began as a popular culture at least within the central genres of epic and drama, which were collective, national, and popular. Gradually literature took a turn toward elitism, leaning on the differentiation, especially in Rome, between spoken language and learned literary language. Christianity restored a broad popular cultural basis, mostly oral. Renaissance humanism failed in course of time in its attempt to impose a learned, elitist culture on the educated public, yet it succeeded in establishing for more than four centuries a standard of "classicism" against which many matters of taste and behavior were to be measured in society.

It is worth noting how faithfully the schools reflected these differences and changes through the centuries. A main point that must be borne in mind is the difference between scholarly and intellectual appreciation of the classics and the widespread use of them in the practice of the schools. Here the difference between the Middle Ages and the Renaissance did amount to a true revolution. I shall have to return to this point later on, since a good deal of misunderstanding of the issues is often found in polemical findings as to the availability and appreciation of the classics or some classics in the medieval period.

Despite the wealth of specialized studies concerning the changes that occurred in the use of the classics between antiquity and the Renaissance, one of the most instructive, and still eminently readable, reconstructions of the crucial period between the fourth and the ninth century remains the 1905 book by Maurice Roger. The main lines in this book's thesis deserve recalling. Roger (438) found that ancient culture as inherited by the Carolingians did not come down to them directly from the late-ancient schools but through the intermediary of the Anglo-Saxon monks transplanted to the Continent at the time of Charlemagne, principally Alcuin; those monks, in turn, were working against the background of the Irish monks.

The way the Anglo-Saxon monks transmitted that heritage entailed, however, a profound change: based as it was on the system of the liberal arts, and especially the trivium, it relied heavily on the primacy of grammar, with rhetoric and dialectic being assigned a thoroughly secondary role as the two phases of a unified discipline of an essentially logical nature. Thus Alcuin defined dialectic and rhetoric as the two divisions of logic in his *De dialectica* 1, on the authority of Isidore of Seville (*Etymologiae* 2.24.7) who, in turn, had attributed this division to Plato (Roger 394).

Furthermore, grammar had been reduced to its didactic linguistic content and deprived of its vivifying classical purpose, that of establishing the necessary foundation for the explanation of the poets. This original purpose was replaced by the function of propaedeutics to the reading of the Scriptures. Similarly, rhetoric and dialectic, originally taught by the rhetor as a function of the understanding of the great orators and the formation of the new public speakers or civil servants, were equally reduced to ancillary instruments for the understanding of the figures of speech contained in the sacred writings (e.g., Roger 322). This general situation defines in its basic elements the difference between the use of the classics in the lower and higher Middle Ages on the one hand, and the systematic attempt of the Renaissance to revive ancient culture in its original form. More than with the Fathers of the Church, more than with St. Augustine and even Cassiodorus, the use of the classics had become consistently and completely subservient to the worship of God and to the study of the Scriptures or of theology: the *reductio artium ad sacram scripturam uel ad theologiam* was an accomplished fact (Roger 348). For these monks the work of the ancient philosophers and poets was nothing but a mass of splendid, mutilated fragments, comparable to the scattered shards of a broken mirror. But the Christian could rejoice in the consciousness of being able, thanks to this method, to make a coherent whole out of the disorder of these *disiecta membra* by giving them their true, *ex post facto* meaning. Had not St. Augustine himself discovered that he had become able to understand Plato only after his conversion (Roger 439)? And there was further coherence in the way to harmonize the whole of the past, the pagan and the Jewish of the Old Testament, with the Christian present. Christ had come not to wipe out the past but to bring it to fruition: Christianity brings to the full light of day what had been only imperfectly perceived in images by the prophets and in discursive arguments by the pagan philosophers (Roger 439).

Accordingly, in his *Ars grammatica* Alcuin did not require, as Martianus Capella had done, that grammar should teach a learned use of language, nor, as Cassiodorus had done, that it be esthetically adorned and beautiful. It was enough that it be correct (Roger 323). Even this criterion of correctness, the basic grammatical requirement ever since Aristotle, was no longer based on the examples of the classical authors, as it still was with Cassiodorus ("ex poetis illustribus oratoribusque," *Institutiones* 2.1), but on "natura, ratio, auctoritas et consuetudo" (Roger 324). This formula had its antecedents in such *artigraphi* as Charisius (Keil 1.1) and even in Quintilian (*Inst. orat.* 1.6), who had *uetustas* instead of *natura*. But aside from the fact that correctness had a different implication in Quintilian, i.e., one of choice between more and less approved examples among excellent literati, whereas with Alcuin it was simply a matter of achieving an intelligible expression with monks who started from a level of almost total ignorance of Latin, the more meaningful divergence came with the definition of authority and usage.

Quintilian had aimed at harmonizing the authority of the illustrious writers with the necessity of a lexicon with valid currency (*Inst. orat.* 1.6.3; 1.6.43); Alcuin's contemporaries had to cope with a language that was almost completely learned in school (more so in England than in France), hence the criterion of currency or *consuetudo* rested almost entirely with the usage, not of the ancient authors, but of the Roman Church, since, unlike the man of the street of Quintilian's days, the "people" of England or even France could not be invoked as an authority (Roger 325, 438).

Nevertheless, Roger (e.g., 396–98) appropriately warns us against assuming that Alcuin simply imported his compilation of the trivium system from York: his frequent ancient sources establish a new foundation for the system, and this new foundation was a result of his desire to adapt the arts to the secular needs of the palace. This applies especially to the rhetoric, which is differently focussed from what, say, a Bede had had to offer, with monastic education paramount in his mind. A truly Christian rhetoric had to wait until Rhabanus Maurus, notwithstanding St. Augustine's authoritative example in *De doctrina christiana*. For the time being, and even in later centuries, regardless of the further developments and enlargements, rhetoric remained restricted to an art of understanding the figures of speech in the Scriptures and of adding rhetorical *colores* to sermons or to bureaucratic correspondence (Roger 400).

Incidentally, St. Augustine's role in medieval culture and education remained a, shall we say, rather puzzling one, since, notwithstanding the unequalled power of his personality, his radicalism in indicting the whole of classical culture as inherently sinful and therefore dispensable made it too hard for even the most militant representatives of the Christian Church to follow his views literally.

The Council of Toledo, AD 527, and the Council of Vaison, AD 529, ordered the bishops and the parish priests, respectively, to establish episcopal and parochial schools, which, together with the monasterial schools, replaced the municipal schools of ancient Rome. They were designed to train future priests but without obligation of joining the clergy when the pupils would reach the age of decision. Some schools were established and financed by the king or emperor: see, for example, Lotharius' edict of Corteolona in 825 (Frova 18).

All types of schools that could be found in the Middle Ages before the twelfth century needed some degree of "pagan" culture at least in the form of grammar and, if they went that far, rhetoric, since these rudiments were based on the use of the ancient manuals and the ancient poets and prose writers as exemplary texts, even though in elementary form. Yet the ultimate goal was Christian formation; hence the basic texts remained the Christian ones. The Irish, for example, or more generally the Celts, imported to the Continent and even to Italy, starting with the monastic center of Bobbio (Columban, † 614), an ascetic culture based almost exclusively on the Scriptures and the Fathers. The only mentions of pagan classics came from quotations found in ancient grammatical manuals. The otherwise precious library of Bobbio apparently contained no classical texts.

Necessary as it ever had been as a foundation of literacy, the study of the classics produced a dilemma for the Christian, since it disclosed a puzzling divergence between the "regular" form of literary pagan writings and the glaring deviations apparent in the sacred texts. Should one accept the "barbarisms" and "solecisms" of the latter or correct them in the light of Donatus' teachings? One way of bypassing the difficulty was implied in Gregory the Great's opinion that it was "unbecoming to subject the words of the celestial oracle to Donatus's rules" (preface to the *Moralia in Job*: Riché 234).

In *The Gothic War* Procopius of Caesarea relates how Theodoric forbade the study of letters for the sons of the Gothic noblemen. Thereafter the Goths wanted a "barbaric education" for their sons, who should grow up in the company of their peers, accustoming themselves to using arms and to exercising force over their subjects, without the influence of old, effeminate wise men (Frova 74).

Raoul Glaber, *Historia Francorum*, book 2, chap. 12, tells the story of the grammarian Vilgardus in Ravenna around the year 1000 as a moral exemplum of the danger of falling from excessive love for letters into heresy:

> He nourished for grammar a passion more insane than prudent, as is typical of the Italians, who, for the sake of it, will neglect all the other arts. Filled with pride for his knowledge he came close to madness. So much so that one night the devils appeared to him in the shape of Virgil, Juvenal, and Horace, and thanked him for his enthusiasm in studying their books and extolling their authority among posterity. Thereafter, seduced by the devils' delusion, he started to teach their dogmas, asserting that the poets' words carry authority on all matters. At last he was judged to be a heretic and condemned by the bishop of the city, Peter. Everywhere in Italy there were found people who embraced this pestiferous belief: they too died from the iron and the fire. (Frova 64)

Nevertheless, the appreciation of classical culture, no matter how limited and qualified, was gradually growing, and the Burgundian cleric Wipo, preceptor of the future emperor Henry III, could hold up this very example of Italy while scolding the Germans for disdaining the education of other than future clerics; the Italians, or at least the Romans, all rushed from their youth to sweat in the schools as soon as they had passed the age of playing with childish toys. (Wipo, *Tetralogus*, ed. Breslau, vv. 187 ff., p. 81, cited by Riché 174, 387.)

Charlemagne's letter addressed to Baugulf of Fulda but meant for all bishops and abbots (Ceserani 1/2, 48 ff., from Frova 22 f.) states that "since in the Scriptures we find metaphors, tropes, and other figures of speech, it is clear to anyone that a reader will all the sooner be able to grasp the true spiritual sense the more instructed he has previously been in the letters."[1] Remarkable in this letter is the linking of knowledge and morals: "Although it is better to do well than to know, it is nevertheless true that knowing precedes doing" (Ceserani 49 f.). Lotharius' capitulary of 825, directed toward Italy, marks a new turn insofar as it entrusts the secular authorities with the task of providing for instruction, with the exception of Ivrea, which devolved to the local bishop.

When Gerbert of Aurillac became bishop of Reims, the emperor Otto III, son of Otto II of Saxony and of the Byzantine princess Theophano, was so impressed by his knowledge that he invited him to come to his court as a teacher. "Remove from us our Saxon uncouthness and allow the Greek refinement to grow in us. . . . A spark of the Greek spirit will then be found in us. . . . Arouse in us the lively genius of the Greeks." Gerbert accepted and, in his reply, asserted that "something divine manifests itself when a man of Greek origin and with Roman power in his person requests almost by hereditary right the treasures of Greek and Roman wisdom." (Cf. H. Lattin, trans., *The Letters of Gerbert* [New York, 1961], letters 153 and 154: Frova 65 f.) Gerbert had taught liberal arts at Reims for ten years (972–982) while councillor and secretary to the local bishop, and the chronicle (*Histoire*) of his pupil Richer, a monk at the monastery of Saint-Rémi in Reims, dedicated twenty-three chapters of book 3 to Gerbert's school, thus making it probably the best documented school of the early Middle Ages (Riché 180 f., 358 f.). This witness and Gerbert's own correspondence show clearly how keenly he relied on the direct reading of the classical texts for grammar, rhetoric, and dialectics, including Virgil, Statius, Terence, Juvenal, Persius, Horace, and Lucan for grammar and rhetoric, as well as Aristotle, Cicero, Porphyry, and Manilius for dialectics.

Peter of Blois (*Epistola* 101 in Migne, *PL* 27.312–14: Frova 66–68) criticized one of his pupils for being among those who presume to skip letters and particularly grammar to enter directly upon a course of dialectical studies. The rules of grammar must be studied solicitously, as did Donatus, Servius, Priscian, Isidore, Bede, and Cassiodorus, who recognized therein the necessary foundation of all science. Quintilian agreed, as did Caesar and Cicero: "It is written: knowledge resides in the ancients." He will have to undo the harm done to his new pupil by his previous teacher and send him back to the true foundation of science. He is glad that he "was obliged, when young, to memorize the epistles of Hildebert, which are models of style and elegance." Besides the customary school texts, he found profit in the intensive perusal of Pompeius Trogus, Flavius Josephus, Suetonius, Hegesippus, Curtius Rufus, Tacitus, and Livy, all authors who often intersperse their historical narratives with passages that are useful for morals and for learning the liberal arts.

We have more ample archival material available for Italy in the tenth and eleventh centuries. The presence there of large numbers of notaries, jurists, accountants, physicians, and exchange brokers has caused some historians to surmise that this proves the existence in those centuries of secular schools alongside the episcopal ones. Riché (174), for one, disputes this conclusion. The bishops were engaged in political struggles for the control of local governments that made such professionals very valuable to them. The episcopal library of Cremona, for example, contained a goodly number of secular manuals by Priscian, Martianus Capella, Rémi d'Auxerre, and others, as shown by the inventory redacted in 984 under Bishop Olderic (Riché 175).

Generally speaking, medieval education, when available in a non-exclusively ecclesiastic and religious form, was characterized by a type of encyclopedism which tended to show keen curiosity for medicine, law, and the quadrivium (music, astronomy, and mathematics), while the literary texts, when used and appreciated, tended to be kept on the level of necessary aids for the development of literacy (grammar and rhetoric) rather than as far-reaching goals in themselves. Alphanus, bishop of Salerno from 1058, is a good example of this typical cultural outlook on a high level. And once again, generally speaking, literary culture was available, if wanted, only at very great expense, since it required the more or less direct acquisition of very costly manuscripts. In 1044 the bishop of Barcelona had to sell a house and a plot of land in order to purchase two grammatical treatises of Priscian (Riché 179). We therefore stand in awe when coming across such unusual collections as that of Toul in Lorraine, where the monastery of Saint-Evre had a library of 270 volumes at the end of the tenth century (G. Becker, *Catalogi bibliothecarum antiqui*, no. 68 [repr., Brussels, 1969], 149-54; Riché 168).

The encyclopedism I have referred to was inherited, through the notion of liberal arts, from Hellenistic paideia, which was based on two basic tendencies: (1) the need to cater to larger, unspecialized audiences, hence to popularize the results of previous research by presenting them in a simplified and orderly organic form; (2) concomitantly and consequently, the desire to systematize large bodies of knowledge from various disciplines by presenting them as logical sequences, according to the hallowed principle of encyclopedism or ἐγκύκλιος παιδεία. It was in this form that most of ancient Greek knowledge was transmitted first to the Romans and then, through Rome, to the Middle Ages.

In addition to the names of standard classics that one often encounters in medieval quotations one must bear in mind that the most influential authors in the transmission of Greek culture first to the Romans and then, through the mediation of Roman compilations, to the Middle Ages had been, alongside Aristotle and Plato, the popularizing encyclopedists Posidonius (ca. 135-ca.51/50 BC) and Hermagoras (fl. ca. 150 BC). The former was the author, *inter alia*, of a vast treatment of universal history deeply imbued with systematic philosophical views on providential planning and control of world events. The latter had crystallized much of rhetorical theory, especially concerning the topics of invention. Varro's (116-27 BC) *Disciplinarum libri IX* and later the neoplatonic encyclopedists Macrobius (fl. ca. 400) and, more specifically for what concerns the system of the liberal arts, Martianus Capella (fl. 410-439) with his *De nuptiis Philologiae et Mercurii*, were the principal intermediaries that handed down Posidonius' (and Hermagoras') Greek compilations to the Middle Ages. These pagan authors were assisted in this momentous task by their Christian counterparts, principally Augustine, Boethius, Cassiodorus, and Isidore. Other compilers or the original and more creative authors and thinkers were mostly left behind because of their inherent complexity, as it happened to Archimedes and Euclid, who were only rediscovered in the Renaissance. This recovery required knowledge of Greek, which came slowly and was anticipated by the presence of Greek, Hebrew, and Arabic scholars at the courts of Toledo, after it was captured from the Moors in 1085, and Sicily, after its liberation from the Arabs in 1091 (Wagner, "The Seven Liberal Arts and Classical Scholarship," in Wagner 1983, 1-31 at 25 and passim).

On the more elementary level of grammar it must be noted that a restricted and rather surprising list of canonical authors remained popular in hundreds of schools from the ninth to the fifteenth century, namely the notorious *Liber Catonianus* extant in more than a hundred manuscripts and comprising the *Disticha Catonis*, (Gottschalk's) *Ecloga Theoduli*, the elegies of Maximianus, the fables of Avianus, Statius' *Achilleid*, and Claudian's *De raptu Proserpinae* (see e.g., Boas and Clogan). Despite some humanists' scornful assessments, it survived even in the course of the fifteenth century, when it became the equally notorious *Auctores octo* (printed in Lyon by Johannes de Prato, 1488).

This extremely popular manual exemplifies, with the extensive commentaries that accompanied its chosen texts, a trend that is supremely characteristic of medieval education and, in particular, the medieval use of the classics. This is the inherent bent toward a moral or moralizing interpretation of the literary texts, the use of which was ultimately justified precisely insofar as they could yield a moral lesson in a Christian key. Such a way of reading was not without a lingering impact even among humanistically-inclined readers in the Renaissance, and is found in the persistent habit of allegorization and "moralization" (signally evident in the long-lasting *Ouidius moralizatus* and *Ovide moralizé* of Pierre Bersuire) which lasted well into the sixteenth century and beyond. The humanistic revolution consisted essentially, in this context, of the attempt to rediscover the authentic meaning of literary fictions, ancient and modern, whereas in the Middle Ages the need was commonly felt to allow for educational reading only those texts that could lend themselves to a Christian exegesis.

It is therefore fair to say that classical culture could be accepted in the most responsible quarters only insofar as it could be seen as, first, a propaedeutical instrument to the reading and understanding of the Scriptures and the truly Christian doctrinal documents, and, second, as a sort of "prefiguration" of the moral and theological Christian truths.

In evaluating the prevailing medieval attitudes toward classical culture, a degree of confusion has been caused by the lack of distinction between general theoretical statements and the practice of the schools. Consequently, perhaps too much emphasis has been placed on the apparent double-mindedness of medieval authors, who accepted ancient culture as necessary while at the same time condemning it as pagan. Giuseppe Chiri (1954) made an interesting case of this difficulty in discussing and denying Antonio Viscardi's presentation of the matter (*Le Origini* [1939; 1950 2d ed.]). Chiri maintained that the medieval attitude toward the study of classical antiquity was not torn between contradictory attitudes of theoretical condemnation and constant practical use. Alcuin's and Gregory the Great's demurrers have been read out of context and either are humorous (Alcuin) or specifically limited to excesses at the hand of a bishop as a teacher (for Gregory see, especially, the famous letter to Desiderius bishop of Vienne, *Epist.* 11.34, ed. Hewald-Hartmann, *MGH, Epist.* 2.303). The school use of the classics was clearly propaedeutical and, as such, morally neutral — if the selections were wise and properly expurgated. Hence many *florilegia* had no moral end but were used as exempla of elegance, formal or prosodic (Chiri 409). At the same time, however, the most popular textbooks were morally oriented — witness the *Disticha Catonis* and the *Ecloga Theoduli* (cf. Mead).

All in all, it bears repeating that classical culture (for short, the Liberal Arts) was consistently justified and advocated as a necessary foundation and background to the reading and understanding of sacred culture, so that it was not accepted as an end in itself but only as a tool for higher ends. Cassiodorus and, at a significant chronological remove, Rhabanus Maurus are eloquent witnesses of this basic attitude: see the former's *Instit.* 1.28: "Nor did the most holy Fathers decree that the studies of secular letters must be despised and rejected, since our understanding of the Sacred Scriptures is built up considerably on that foundation."[2] And Rhabanus, *De cleric. instit.* 3.18: "Whenever we read the gentile poets, whenever books of secular wisdom come into our hands, if we find in them something useful *we turn it to our dogmas*, whereas if we find in them something superfluous concerning the idols, love, or worldly cares, we strike it out."[3] Hence the classics were accepted and welcomed but only, and this consistently and coherently, with the end of subordinating science and formal literary virtues to the absolute values of Christian formation and observance, theologically and morally.

The "system" of the Seven Liberal Arts was destined to a very long history and, even though it was more of an abstract intellectual schema of convenience than an actual pattern for precise organization of schooling and courses, it made its mark on every educational project for centuries, even to our own day. It derived ultimately from Varro's (lost) encyclopedia of the disciplines, with the subtraction of medicine and architecture (his eighth and ninth arts), as transmitted to the Middle Ages especially by Martianus Capella and then given its Christian form mainly by Cassiodorus and Isidore. It found new authoritative codifiers in the twelfth century in the persons of Hugh of St. Victor (*Didascalicon*), John of Salisbury (*Metalogicon*), and Thierry of Chartres (*Eptateuchon*). Hugh, in particular, insisted on the unity of the disciplines and on the necessity for encyclopedic comprehensiveness and synthesis, whereas most medieval scholars, either by necessity or by choice, limited themselves to cultivating one or two of the basic disciplines. Also, it bears noting, the order in which the disciplines were studied could vary, since the medieval curricula did not offer a graduated and logical sequence in their arrangement and in the way they were imparted to the students. A student often moved from place to place in order to attend the courses of a renowned master, and in any given university there was no set order in which to learn the various disciplines, despite the division into arts and faculties (on all the preceding, cf. Paré 94-108).

The gradual weakening of Latin made it necessary, in some regions more than in others, to resort to the vernacular to explain not only the sacred texts but also the ecclesiastical and monastic rules as well as all material used in the schools. In any event, it appears that it is precisely their enduring popularity in the schools that preserved the portions of pagan literature that were saved (Riché 249-51). The "classics" come from their having been regularly used in the "classes." The lists of textbooks in use in the early Middle Ages remained surprisingly similar through the centuries and all over Europe, with only partial differences, and the standard names are distributed by the way they were used in the curricula of the class sequences according to the system of the liberal arts. And the uniformity of curricula and basic textbooks extends beyond the Christian West well into the Greek Orthodox East and even the Arab world (Riché 251 f.). In the West not only the major poets and historians but also theorists (e.g., of rhetoric, like Cicero) and writers of model prose texts—typically, the collections of model letters, such as those of Sidonius Apollinaris, Avitus, Eginhardus, and Frotharius of Toul—were preserved thanks to their having become models to be imitated in school (Riché 256).

All in all I would venture the generalization that, besides the vastly expanded access to newly discovered texts after the onset of humanism, the most striking differences between medieval and Renaissance use of the classics in education are the following: (1) before the Renaissance the pagan authors were made subservient to the grammatical, rhetorical, and dialectical foundation that was felt to be necessary for the correct reading and intelligent interpretation of the Christian texts; (2) concomitantly, the Christian authors, including the poets (Arator, Avitus, Juvencus, Prudentius, Sedulius, etc.), were read together with the pagans, sometimes by contrasting their divergent validities but more often without any expressed feeling of inconsistency (Riché 249). One may find it rather surprising that often the schools of the Renaissance, signally those of the Jesuits, made hardly any room to the Christian literary writers.

The "authorization" for the reading of the pagans lay either in their "allegorization" and "moralization" (they contained hidden truths, as the prophecy of Christ's birth in Virgil's Fourth Eclogue) or in presenting them as necessary pillars of the liberal arts (signally for Macrobius and Martianus Capella). The teacher could eventually engage in a confrontation between the two cultures, as typically in the presentation of the *Ecloga Theoduli*, where the two interlocutors, the Greek shepherd Pseustis and the Hebrew shepherdess Alithia, were transparently introduced as engaged in an *altercatio* between defeated Falsehood and triumphant Truth (cf. R. P. H. Green). Bernard of Utrecht († 1099) used Fulgentius' (AD 467-532) *Mitologiarum libri* in the process of moralizing the *Ecloga Theoduli*, and Fulgentius' *Mitologiae* was the very source that most appealed to the moralists and allegorists of the time, including Bernard Silvestris for his *Commentum super sex libros Eneidos Virgilii*, dutifully endorsed, first of all, by John of Salisbury (Paré 120: cf. Hans Liebeschütz, *Fulgentius metaphoralis* [Leipzig, 1926], which includes an edition of the *Fulgentius metaphoralis*, a widely successful treatise on moralization by the English fourteenth-century Franciscan John Ridewall).

The changes that occur in the course of the medieval centuries concern in a visible way the distribution of the disciplines and the use of texts to serve the purposes of the various disciplines. The early Middle Ages is the age of grammar and rhetoric, whereas dialectics was left largely inoperative until the eleventh century. Grammar was "the art of interpreting the poets and the historians" (Rhabanus Maurus, *De institutione clericorum* 3.18), whereas rhetoric was the art of communicating the truth in an effective manner. In the meantime, the latter was another basic means whereby the ancient cultural patrimony was kept alive, since in their school exercises the pupils put on, even though temporarily, a classical personality: through his compositions, *controuersiae*, *suasoriae*, and *praeexercitamina*, the pupil of the high Middle Ages imagined himself wearing the Roman toga and addressing a Roman audience in the forum or in a tribunal (Riché 256). Rhetoric was, likewise, the foundation of official style (through what will become the *dictamen*) as well as of legal training, since the new schools of law were thoroughly grounded in the teaching of rhetoric.

Since the medieval mind was thoroughly imbued with the spirit of authority, schooling left permanent and indelible traces for the remainder of one's life, in action as well as in speech. The lack of spontaneity in literary and public expression is a direct result of the memorization and imitation of model formularies in the classrooms, ever since the times of the Roman Second Sophistic. At the same time, the earnest need for moralization induced into the medieval user of cultural documents a habit of investing technical precepts with a religious, metaphysical, and moral dimension. Gerbert d'Aurillac (letter to Ebrard, abbot of Tours: *Ep.* 44, Lattin 50, cited by Riché 257) says that "Since philosophy does not separate the ways of ethics from the ways of speech, I have always kept together the art of speaking and the art of living."

As to the role of logic or dialectic, if it is true that it did not come into its own until late in the eleventh century, it showed early on that sooner or later it would dominate the whole curriculum: in what was perhaps the most advanced and sophisticated curriculum of the early Middle Ages, Gerbert d'Aurillac's school at Reims, rhetoric itself was, in a way, already potentially subordinated to dialectic, since it was introduced last as a way of acquiring the right mode of presenting the truths and principles that had been learned through the study of the dialectical modes of thought (Richer, *Histoire* 3.46–49: Riché 358 f.). Gerbert turned, in a way, the trivium upside down, or at least reversed its order by starting with the texts of Aristotelian logic (*logica uetus*), then going on to the oratorical models, followed by rhetorical theory—all of this in order to teach how to communicate the higher truths effectively—and finally by reading the ancient poets and historians (in other words, ending with the grammatical level) in order to teach the proper style.

Still, up to 1150 or even later in some regions, grammar remained the dominant art of discourse, *ars sermocinalis par excellence*, and this was more a sign of the low level of cultural development than a clear-headed choice. But one could express the paradoxical situation of the "classics" in that long period in a somewhat excessive yet, I believe, basically correct and revealing manner by saying that the ancient predicament of grammar was somewhat reversed in the Middle Ages: instead of being the *ancilla* of literature (as it had been originally for the Alexandrian philologists), or of philosophy (as Aristotle and the Stoics saw it, namely as the framework for the expression of our thinking processes), it became itself the mistress of literature, since the reading of the classics was justified in order to learn grammar, which in turn would thus become the foundation of reading and understanding the Scriptures.

Education shared in the general process of gradual secularization which took place after the year 1000 (Ceserani 3.157–59). We have evidence from the thirteenth century to the effect that non-ecclesiastical schools developed gradually, especially for Florence, even though lay teachers appeared later in this city than elsewhere, from 1277 on. Frova (104) has published such documents which allow us to follow the movements of lay as well as clerical teachers from town to town. At times they were in possession of "licences" or graduate degrees granted by chartered institutions, sometimes not, but this official "licensing" was a new development and it marked the most conspicuous external function of the university.

Frova (102) thus summarizes the procedures:

> The classes are held in the house of the master, who also houses the externs or non-residents of the town as his pensioners. In this feature the medieval school resembles the ancient school of the grammaticus. The pupils' classes appear articulated into six levels in the extant documents. In the first grade the students "de carta" or "de tabula" learn how to read; in the second they continue this same process of learning and are designated as "de quaterno" or "de septem psalmis et uesperaliis" because they begin to read and memorize the Latin Psalms and the office of Vespers, though the study of Latin grammar has not yet started. The pupils of these two classes are known as "pueri" or "parui scolares" and are usually in the charge of the assistant or *repetitor*, while the *rector scolarum* busies himself with the more advanced ones. The "Donatists" comprise the third grade or class, and begin the rudiments of Latin grammar while learning by rote the *Disticha Catonis* and other grammatical texts as well as the Bolognese Rolando or Rolandino de' Passeggeri's *Ars notaria* of ca. 1255. The study of Latin composition follows in the fourth grade, articulated into the "minores," "mediocres," and "maiores." These last ones also learn arithmetic and geometry.

This pattern is fairly uniform among the free communes. One notes the preponderance, even in the lay schools, of the religious texts, mainly the Psalms, and the typically communal concern with the civic ingredient of the *ars dictaminis* in the form of Rolandino's manual. The lay school became progressively public, namely run and financed in part or in whole by the communes, which nominated and paid the teachers.

Giovanni di Paolo Morelli (*Ricordi* 270–73 [Ceserani 3.173 f.]) in a passage written in 1403 advises an orphan youth as follows:

> Science will lead you to the highest and honored positions in life: your virtue and wisdom will take you there even without your specific will to do so. You will have at your disposal all the men who matter: you will be able to spend all the time you want in the company of Virgil in your study room, he will never decline your entreaties, will answer all your questions, and will ask no fee of money to advise you and teach you, while taking you out of your grief, consoling you, and giving you pleasure. You will be able to keep company with Boethius, Dante, and the other poets, with Tully who will teach you eloquence, Aristotle who will teach you philosophy: you will know the reasons for things and how to derive pleasure from them, at least in part. You will be together with the prophets of the Holy Scriptures. . . .

A remarkable passage indeed, written in the eloquent mood of the famous passages of Petrarch and Machiavelli on the pleasures of meeting intimately with the good authors in the privacy of one's study room, and showing that secular culture is now on an equal footing with religious instruction, with the same effect of consolation, virtue, wisdom, knowledge, and psychological balance. At the same time, as Ceserani-De Federicis (3.174) appropriately points out, education and reading are now perceived as a screen between the individual and the rest of the world — an elitist stand which characterizes mature humanism but goes beyond it, insofar as Western education has consistently been based on the acquisition of certain patterns and bodies of knowledge that provide status even without guaranteeing any practical relevance. This characteristic prevails both in the Middle Ages and in the Renaissance, as well as in the later periods down to our own century.

Indeed, as it was for so long and under so different political and social circumstances, between the Middle Ages and the incipient Renaissance, the merchant, too, aspired to an education prevalently founded on the classics, understood as a sign of social status and "as a filter which avoids a direct cognitive rapport with the real" (Ceserani-De Federicis 3.175), at the same time that the differentiation between town and country in cultural opportunities became more acute.

The *Pseudo-Raniero*, a German treatise (1250–1300) against the errors of heretic sects, underlines with alarm that schools are more frequent among heretics in all the towns of Lombardy, Provence, and elsewhere, and that in such localities "all people, men and women, children and adults, night and day, do not cease to teach and learn; the workman who is at work by day learns and teaches at night. . . . Whoever has been learning for 10 days starts looking for someone to instruct in his turn". The female presence was characteristic of heresies, and it was favored by the adoption of the vernacular in the reading of the sacred texts in such milieus. Peter Waldo had started by asking theologians to supply vulgar translations for his use (Manselli 119).

It would be naive to assume that the classics were not read in university courses during the Middle Ages. Yet it is difficult to form an accurate picture of the situation, not only because our records are far scantier and more scattered before 1500, but also because the situation differed markedly from place to place. Let us take an example that is outstanding in its own right and particularly relevant as the site of an important polemic involving no lesser an authority than Petrarch (1304-1374). Petrarch had aroused the resentment of his learned Parisian admirers by asserting that rhetoric and poetry were taught much more in Italy than elsewhere. A number of important French humanists, soon after Petrarch's generation, rose to the challenge and came to the defense of the University of Paris. First the Rector of the University in 1393, Nicholas de Clemanges (1365-1437), entered the fray by countering that he himself had heard lectures at his university on the Rhetoric of both Aristotle and Cicero, and that such poets as Virgil, Horace, Terence, Ovid, and others were taught there (*Chartularium*, 3, no. 1650, pp. 589 f.). Of course the years he was referring to were later than the ones meant by Petrarch, and the situation might have changed in between, perhaps even under the impact of Petrarch himself. Yet in subsequent years an equally respectable observer, Pierre d'Ailly (ca. 1350-1420), Chancellor in 1389, reported on Priscian being studied within the grammar course and Cicero under rhetoric, both as part of the curriculum of rational philosophy (covering the whole trivium), while a host of ancient poets and prose writers were being read, including Virgil, Ovid, Fulgentius, Horace, Orosius, Juvenal, Seneca (tragedies), Terence, Sallust, Sidonius, Cassiodorus, Martial, Livy, and Valerius Maximus. Jean Gerson (1363-1429), Chancellor in 1395, and later on Guillaume Fichet (1433-ca. 1480), Rector of the University in 1467, appear by their very presence there as guarantors of the existence of classically oriented courses, since their tastes for humanistic fare are well attested (Kibre 220).

Yet, for all this, we must note that all these readings were imbedded within the trivium as propaedeutic to something else, something, at least by Petrarch's definition, not humanistic, namely the philosophical curriculum as part of the training, most often and most typically, of the theologian or the physician. Indeed, whereas grammar and dialectics are specifically testified to and spelled out time and time again, we have no apparent records, specifically, of rhetoric being an official part of the Paris statutes. This silence is significant: even though the texts were circulating and actually used, their role was not central and self-directed, as Petrarch would have wanted, and they were clearly subordinated or secondary to the more basic ingredients of the training of the logician or scientist. In fact, the whole trivium seemed to be conceived as a branch of philosophy, one of its three parts—rational philosophy—the other two being natural and moral philosophy (Kibre).

The use of the classics after 1500 by all sorts of writers and intellectuals can be understood more precisely if one has a clear picture of the change in the educational attitudes and practices around that time. We have read countless statements as to the general secularization brought about by the Renaissance; but as far as the writers are concerned, this secularization was most specifically a result of the new type of schooling they were receiving. "During the Middle Ages, Latin had predominantly been a specialized idiom, the language of scholarship [= "science"], diplomacy, and religion" (Kagan 36). In the course of the sixteenth century the municipal schools became firmly established on a regular basis in direct competition with the traditional, ecclesiastically-controlled episcopal and monastic schools. What this meant was that the Latin of the classics became the true staple of the new education, instead of being simply a prop for doctrinal formation and scriptural interpretation. The church managed to bring this new system partially under control again, at least in the Catholic areas, by placing religious orders, especially the Jesuits, in charge of most colleges, often taking them over from the municipalities that had established them and run them until the end of the sixteenth century. Yet this did not change much the nature of the new teaching, since it remained as classically oriented as it had become since 1500, and as it had never been before. Even the ecclesiastical control imposed by the Council of Trent on the lay teachers of the secular schools, in the form of official licensing of lay teachers by the local bishops, sanctioned by the civil authorities (a system that was accepted even by the proudly independent government of Venice), did not change the programs, since the questions that were put to the teachers for their licensing were cautiously generic and formal (see Baldo's documentation).

In conclusion I should like to quote a recent survey of European university life: "The available evidence suggests that Louis Paetow is correct when he asserts that the medieval universities were an obstacle to the study of the classics. Paetow argues that the universities actually delayed the coming of the humanistic renaissance . . ., that classical studies were 'smothered by the universities with their emphasis on logic, law, medicine, and theology' (namely, the very disciplines that the humanists, in strong reaction, generally despised). The medieval arts course . . . appears narrow and specialized. Not only were most of the ancient classics omitted, but there was also 'an entire lack of experimental sciences, of modern languages as well as history and the other so-called social sciences'" (Rudy 31; cf. Paetow 501 f.).

I should like to offer the following example of a school program in the ripe climate of the Renaissance. The typical curriculum of a French secular *collège* was eminently classical. Huppert (53 f.) gives the detailed example of a limited one, that of Auch (Gers), where there were no more than six classes rather than the full range of eight, but clearly divided and graduated, with one regent for each. (The division into graduated classes, which was to play such a major role in the Jesuit system, was considered part of the "Parisian style," even though it was not practiced in Paris.) In 1565 the consuls of Auch drew up an ambitious and rather expensive contract with an annual budget of 900 "livres" for the principal, Master Massé, who was to provide the six regents. There were two classes in the morning, then lunch at eleven, and classes again from one to five in the afternoon. The *sixième* was the abecedary class, teaching how to write words both in Latin and Greek. In the *cinquième* one studied Cato, Despautère, Donatus, and a bit of Cicero and Terence, with translations from Latin into French and vice versa. The *quatrième* continued with Cicero and Terence, then took up Virgil and Ovid, with the help of the more advanced grammatical manuals of Valla, Linacre, Clénard, and Pellisson. Latin and Greek grammar were continued in the *troisième*, which, however, more specifically took up rhetoric through the reading of Cicero's *De amicitia* and *De senectute*, the *Georgics*, and the *Metamorphoses*. The *deuxième* added to these poets Horace's *Odes* and *Satires*, Cicero's *De officiis*, and the *Aeneid*. The *première* concentrated further on rhetoric by adding Quintilian, Sallust, Livy, and Persius. The "modular" nature of the "Parisian style" made it possible to continue the six classes even when, at the expiration of the Massé contract, the wars drastically reduced the budget. Two regents were found, one for 144 "livres," the other for 120, who were able to run all six classes.

We must take note of this classical orientation of the *collèges* and keep in mind that it amounted to a reversal of an important feature of education from the very start of the medieval period, so that it exacted a considerable price for the enforcement of "classical" education. Gregory the Great's *Regula pastoralis*, cited in this context by both P. Riché and Frova

(70 f.), proposed different types of education for different social classes and groups. This was a sign of the medieval flexibility and sensibility to factual realities, and was a foundation of the social stability that characterized that long period. In this respect, the pedagogy of the humanistic Renaissance and, typically, the policies of the French colleges (like those of the Jesuits) were more like the idea of uniform schooling which characterizes modern democracies. The Renaissance grew in a comparatively open society; hence it was more abstract in its pedagogical ideas and less tied to the specific needs of individuals as members of concrete social groups. Furthermore, humanism's "new learning" flourished mostly outside the strongly conservative world of the established universities, even in Italy (perhaps less so in Germany and England, partly because of a polemical alliance between the humanistic circles and the antischolastic early Reformers). (Cf. Rudy, chap. 2 on the Renaissance, based mainly on Brucker, and chap. 3 on the Reformation.)

In sum, when we so often read about universities having been affected by Renaissance humanism only in a limited way, we must be aware that this observation can distort the true picture of the state of education in the age of the Renaissance. The fact is that education was then truly revolutionized by humanism in a deep and broad manner, not so much on the level of the traditional universities, but rather on the level of the secondary schools and the colleges. The Jesuit colleges, which were often a bridge between secondary school and university, were a signal example of this fact.[4]

Notes

1. Accordingly, realizing that ignorance had corrupted the transmitted form of the texts, scholars were impelled to emend them. Charlemagne's *Encyclica de emendatione librorum et officiorum ecclesiasticorum* (*MGH*, Leges 1:44 f.: Frova 91 f.) announces that Paulus Diaconus has been entrusted with the emendation of the Fathers of the Church and has compiled two volumes of offices for the liturgical year.

2. "nec illud Patres sanctissimi decreuerunt, ut saecularium litterarum studia respuantur, quia exinde non minime ad Sacras Scripturas intelligendas sensus noster instruitur." Cassiodorus, *Inst.* 1.28 (Migne, *PL* 70.1142).

3. "Quando poetas gentiles legimus, quando in manus nostras libri ueniunt sapientiae saecularis, si quid in eis utile reperimus, *ad nostra dogmata conuertimus*, si quid uero superfluum, de idolis, de amore, de cura saecularium rerum, haec radamus." Rhabanus Maurus, *De cleric. institutione* 3.18 (Migne, *PL* 107.396 [emphasis mine]).

4. See, for detailed documentation, A. Scaglione, *The Liberal Arts and the Jesuit College System*.

References

Baldo, Vittorio. *Alunni, maestri e scuole in Venezia alla fine del XVI secolo.* Como: Archivio Storico dei PP. Somaschi, 1966.
Boas, Marcus. "De librorum Catonianorum historia atque compositione." *Mnemosyne* 42 (1914): 17-46.
Brucker, Gene. *Renaissance Florence.* New York: J. Wiley, 1969.
Ceserani, Remo, and Lidia De Federicis. *Il Materiale e l'Immaginario.* 10 vols. Torino: Loescher, 1979-88.
Chiri, Giuseppe. "La cultura classica nella coscienza medioevale." *Studi Romani* 2.2 (1954): 395-410.
Clogan, Paul M. "Literary Genres in a Medieval Textbook." *Mediaevalia et Humanistica,* n.s., 11 (1982): 199-209.
Delhaye, Philippe. "L'enseignement de la philosophie morale au XIIe siècle." *Medieval Studies* 11 (1949): 77-99.
———. "Grammatica et ethica au XIIe siècle." *Recherches de théologie ancienne et mediévale* 25 (1958): 59-110.
Frova, Carla. *Istruzione e educazione nel Medioevo.* Torino: Loescher, 1973.
Gabriel, Astrik L. "The College System in the Fourteenth Century Universities." In *The Forward Movement of the Fourteenth Century,* ed. Francis F. Utley. Columbus: Ohio State Univ. Press, 1961, 79-124.
Gibson, Strickland. *Statuta antiqua Vniuersitatis Oxoniensis.* Oxford: Clarendon Press, 1931.
Green, R. P. H. "The Genesis of a Medieval Textbook: The Models and Sources of the *Ecloga Theoduli.*" *Viator* 13 (1982): 49-106.
Huntsman, Jeffrey F. "Grammar." In *The Seven Liberal Arts,* ed. Wagner, 58-95.
Huppert, George. *Les Bourgeois Gentilshommes.* Chicago: Univ. of Chicago Press, 1977.
———. *Public Schools in Renaissance France.* Urbana-Chicago: Univ. of Illinois Press, 1984.
Hyma, Albert. *The Christian Renaissance. A History of the 'Devotio Moderna.'* New York: The Reformed Press, 1924; New York and London: The Century Co., 1925.
———. *The Brethren of the Common Life.* Grand Rapids, MI: Eerdmans, 1950.
———. *Renaissance to Reformation.* Grand Rapids, MI: Eerdmans, 1951.
Ijsewijn, Jozef, and Jacques Paquet, eds. *The Universities in the Late Middle Ages.* Mediaevalia Lovaniensia, 1.6. Leuven: Leuven Univ. Press, 1978.
Kagan, Richard L. *Students and Society in Early Modern Spain.* Baltimore: Johns Hopkins Univ. Press, 1974.
Kibre, Pearl. "Arts and Medicine in the Universities of the Later Middle Ages." In *The Universities in the Late Middle Ages,* eds. Jozef Ijsewijn and J. Paquet, 213-27.
Le Goff, Jacques. *Les intellectuels au Moyen Age.* Paris: Editions du Seuil, 1957.
Lindberg, David C., ed. *Science in the Middle Ages.* Chicago: Chicago Univ. Press, 1978.
Manselli, Raoul. *L'eresia del male.* Napoli: Morano, 1963.
Mead, H. R. "Fifteenth Century Schoolbooks." *Huntington Library Quarterly* 3 (1939): 37-42.
Morin, Edgar. *L'industria culturale. Saggio sulla cultura di massa.* Trans. G. Guglielmi. Bologna: Il Mulino, 1974 (orig. ed. 1962).

Nada-Patrone, A. M. *L'ascesa della borghesia nell'Italia comunale.* Torino: Loescher, 1974.
Nardi, Bruno, ed. *Il pensiero pedagogico del Medioevo.* Classici della Pedagogia Italiana, 1. Firenze: Giuntine & Sansoni, 1956.
Padley, G. A. *Grammatical Theory in Western Europe, 1500–1700: Trends in Vernacular Grammar I.* Cambridge, Cambridge Univ. Press, 1985.
Paetow, Louis J. *The Arts Course at Medieval Universities with Special Reference to Grammar and Rhetoric.* Univ. of Illinois Studies in Language & Literature, 3.7. Urbana-Champaign: Univ. of Illinois Press, 1910.
Paré, Gérard M., A. Brunet, and P. Tremblay. *La Renaissance du XIIe siècle: Les écoles et l'enseignment.* Paris: J. Vrin-Ottawa: Inst. d'Etudes médiévales, 1933.
Quinn, Betty N. "ps. Theodolus." *Catalogus Translationum et Commentariorum*, II. Washington, DC, 1971, 383–408.
Rashdall, Hastings. *The Universities of Europe in the Middle Ages.* Ed. F. M. Powicke and A. B. Emden. 3 vols. Oxford: Clarendon Press, 1936 (1st ed. 1895).
Reynolds, L. D., and N. G. Wilson. *Scribes and Scholars. A Guide to the Transmission of Greek and Latin Literature.* 2nd ed. Oxford: Clarendon Press, 1974.
Riché, Pierre. *Les écoles et l'enseignement dans l'occident chrétien de la fin du Ve siècle au milieu du XIe siècle.* Paris: Aubier Montaigne, 1979.
Roger, Maurice. *L'enseignement des lettres classiques d'Ausone à Alcuin.* Introduction à l'histoire des écoles carolingiennes. Paris: A. & J. Picard, 1905; repr. Hildesheim: Georg Olms. 1968.
Rudy, Willis. *The Universities of Europe, 1100–1914: A History.* Rutherford, NJ: Fairleigh Dickinson Univ. Press; London; Cranbury, NJ: Associated University Presses, 1984.
Sanford, Eva M. "The Use of Classical Latin Authors in the Libri Manuales." *Transactions of the American Philological Association* 55 (1924): 190–248.
Scaglione, Aldo. *The Liberal Arts and the Jesuit College System.* Amsterdam: John Benjamins, 1986.
Schachner, Nathan. *The Medieval Universities.* London: George Allen & Unwin, 1938.
Schindling, Anton. *Humanistische Hochschule und freie Reichsstadt.* Wiesbaden: Steiner, 1977.
Stelling-Michaud, Sven, ed. *Les Universités européennes du 14e au 18e siècle. Aspects et problèmes.* Genève: Droz, 1967.
Wagner, David L. *The Seven Liberal Arts in the Middle Ages.* Bloomington, IN: Indiana Univ. Press, 1983.

Apuleius in the Middle Ages

CARL C. SCHLAM

Apuleius is best known today as a Roman novelist, author of the *Metamorphoses* of the *Golden Ass*. This novel, preserved together with the *Apology* and the *Florida,* came back into circulation in Italy in the fourteenth century.[1] Earlier in the Middle Ages these texts were virtually unknown. The *Philosophica* of Apuleius, however, were widely read and the strong reputation of the man from Madaura was as a *magus* and *philosophus Platonicus*. Our first concern in this paper is to examine the nature and basis of this reputation.[2] We will then focus on the novel. For the absence of direct knowledge of the text renders untenable the not infrequent claims for the influence of the *Metamorphoses* in the Middle Ages.

During his lifetime, in the second half of the second century of our era, Apuleius was honored and highly paid as a rhetor, a public speaker, and as a *philosophus Platonicus*. Apuleius was, at one point, brought to trial on charges of being a magician, of using magic to get Pudentilla, a rich widow, to marry him. His *Apology* is a literary version of the speech he delivered in his defense. He is much suspected by the foolish, he argues, who do not understand his religious seriousness and fail to comprehend the scientific character of his research. The suspicion of magic, however, persisted in later centuries and was reinforced by the reputation at least of the *Metamorphoses*. It is as a *magus* that Apuleius is most often cited in later antiquity by Christian polemicists, such as Lactantius and St. Jerome.[3] In this context he is joined to Apollonius of Tyana as a false or damnable worker of marvels, put forward as a supposed rival to Jesus.

St. Augustine, while he sometimes echoes this charge,[4] has a much fuller acquaintance with the thought and writings of his fellow North-African. He is well acquainted with the *Apology* and the *Metamorphoses*, and with several of the shorter works transmitted under the name of Apuleius, eventually grouped as the *Philosophica*. Of these, only the speech

De deo Socratis is accepted by modern scholars as unquestionably authentic.[5]

Apuleius is ranked by Augustine in the company of the most celebrated recent philosophers; for he groups thus "the renowned Plotinus, Iamblichus and Porphyry, who were Greeks, and the African Apuleius, *Platonicus nobilis*, learned in both Greek and Latin."[6] The *De deo Socratis* is much cited by Augustine in his extensive polemic against pagan daemonology in books 8 and 9 of the *City of God*. In this context, Augustine observes that the *Apology* of Apuleius, *copiosissima et desertissima oratio*, shows that even a pagan recognized the evil of using *daemones*.[7]

A reference to the *Golden Ass* — the source, in fact, of this alternative title to the *Metamorphoses* — later in the *City of God*, suggests that Augustine considered it possibly a true account of the author's experience. For Augustine argues that God-fearing Christians, whether or not they accept stories of demonic metamorphosis as true, must flee that evil Babylon. Examples include Circe changing men into beasts, or "Apuleius who, in a book he entitled the *Golden Ass*, either reported or fabricated that it happened to himself that, after he had been given a magic potion, while his spirit remained human, he became an ass."[8] The earliest medieval reference to the *Metamorphoses* is that of Vincent of Beauvais, in the mid-thirteenth century, followed shortly by two or three similar testimonies among French scholars. Vincent's remark, however, is a clear paraphrase of Augustine, and is not evidence of any further acquaintance with the novel.[9]

A certain acquaintance with the story of Cupid and Psyche, the longest and most artful of the subordinate tales in the *Metamorphoses*, was also transmitted by writers of late antiquity. Martianus Capella, writing in the first half of the fifth century, knows and draws upon the Apuleian text, for he echoes it in his account of the apotheosis of Philologia and her marriage in heaven. He is sometimes said to have provided an allegorization of the story of Cupid and Psyche, but this is not so. The Psyche whom Martianus describes as Mercury's first choice to be his bride, while an allegorical figure, is in no way Apuleian. Fulgentius passages, on the other hand, in the early sixth century, included in his *Mythologiae* a summary of at least the first half of the Apuleian tale, together with a loosely Christian allegorical interpretation of the figures.[10] The Martianus and Fulgentius passages, albeit that the latter was of less influence than is sometimes assumed,[11] are sufficient to explain the scattering of references in medieval literature to the figures of Cupid and Psyche.[12]

Two mid-fifth century letters of Sidonius Apollinaris make mention of Apuleius. One merely cites him as a figure of weighty eloquence: *pon-*

deris Apuleiani fulmen.[13] The other speaks of Apuleius and Pudentilla as husband and wife, but without specific mention of the *Apology*.[14] They are one of six couples in which the husband is a noted Roman prose author, supported by the devotion of his wife. Sidonius goes on to list six poets who he says were aided by their beloveds.[15] For the names of three of these women Apuleius' *Apology* 10 provided crucial testimony, though it was probably not the immediate source for Sidonius. In the twelfth-century satire, *Metamorphosis Goliae Episcopi*, Apuleius is said to burn for his Pudentilla.[16] They make the sixth pair, however, of which three are of the prose couples and three of the poetic given by Sidonius. It is a mistake to take this as any evidence for knowledge of the *Apology*.[17]

Augustine's more extended use of *De deo Socratis*, on the other hand, gave Apuleius an authoritative role as a *philosophus Platonicus* for the Middle Ages. Transmitted along with this lecture in the *Philosophica* are two treatises whose authenticity has been reasonably argued:[18] the *De mundo*, which Augustine quotes once,[19] and the *De Platone*, whose first chapters are the earliest extant biography of Plato. The *Asclepius*, a Latin version of a Greek Hermetic treatise, came to be attached to Apuleius' name and to be included in the collection. The earliest and best manuscript of this corpus, Brussels 10054-56, has now been securely dated to the third decade of the ninth century, having "sprung from the heart of the Carolingian revival."[20] The slightly earlier codex Salmasianus includes excerpts from these works.[21] Also preserved from the ninth century are two manuscripts of the *Herbarium*, now regarded as Pseudo-Apuleius, but reflecting his medieval reputation as a *magus* and/or scientist. Attribution to Apuleius of a treatise on logic, *Peri hermeneias*, or *De interpretatione*, has been recently reasserted.[22] It is preserved in at least four ninth-tenth century manuscripts together with other *dialectica*, in a tradition independent of the *Philosophica*.

In the high middle ages, Geoffrey of Monmouth has a wizard cite Apuleius' *De deo Socratis* as part of an explanation given for how it was possible for the mother of Merlin to have been impregnated by an *incubus daemon*.[23] This bare mention of the title seems, like the remark of Vincent of Beauvais on the *Golden Ass*, more a testimony to Augustine than to Apuleius. The texts, however, of the *Philosophica* and the *De interpretatione* become widely diffused from the eleventh century on. Excerpts from them are included in major *florilegia*.[24] The inaccessibility of Greek sources, along with the praise of Augustine, enhanced the authority of these texts and they served an important role in the transmission of Platonic concepts.[25] The *De mundo* was a major source for the *Cosmographia* or *De mundi uniuersitate* of Bernard Silvestris, who in other works drew upon

De Platone and the *Asclepius*.²⁶ John of Salisbury includes the closing chapters of *De deo Socratis* in his *Policraticus*,²⁷ not in the context of daemonology, but because of their charm of speech, giving eloquent expression to an ideal of the philosophic life.

The survival of the major Apuleian corpus, the *Metamorphoses*, the *Apology* and the *Florida*, depends on a single Beneventan manuscript, copied in the last quarter of the eleventh century—labelled F by the editors.²⁸ The only medieval citation from this corpus, of a line from the *Florida*, in a life of a Confessor at Monte Cassino, was, in all probability, drawn from this source.²⁹ A none-too-careful copy of F, labelled Φ in the manuscript tradition, was written at Monte Cassino in the thirteenth century, after a tear on one folio of F. There was at least one copy, now lost, made before the tear, which served as the archetype for Class 1 of the fourteenth-century manuscripts.³⁰ While interest in the *Philosophica* also flourished at Monte Cassino and its surroundings as well as in transalpine intellectual centers, direct knowledge of the major corpus is only attested in the Beneventan zone. Motifs parallel to elements in the *Metamorphoses* appear in a variety of northern literature of the high Middle Ages, but none are close enough in detail or language to substantiate claims for Apuleius as a source.³¹ Transformation into an ass was not unique to the *Metamorphoses*.³²

The fortunes of the Cupid and Psyche have been the subject of much separate research and controversy. The Apuleian Cupid and Psyche has been claimed as the principal source of a flourishing tradition of narrative patterns in French literature of the twelfth and thirteenth centuries.³³ The strongest claim for imitation of the Apuleian narrative has been made for the verse romance, *Partenopeus of Blois*. The sexual roles here are reversed: it is the man who comes to an empty palace, to a wife who must remain unseen. He violates the taboo under his mother's pressure to accept her choice of a bride, while the bulk of the work recounts the adventures he pursues to recover his beloved. Not a strong case; the parallel motifs could come from Fulgentius, or a folk narrative tradition.

It is further argued that the influence of Apuleius can be detected in the *Chevalier au cygne* and *Huon de Bordeaux*. There is no evidence, however, that the tale of Cupid and Psyche was ever transmitted independently of the rest of the *Golden Ass*. The Apuleian text was, we may conclude, unknown in the Middle Ages, outside the Beneventan zone. Huet's argument seems to me conclusive: No piece of medieval art or literature tells a story pairing the figures Cupid and Psyche. How could so forceful a text have been read and yet have left no direct reflection?³⁴

The question of medieval influence of the Cupid and Psyche became emeshed in the scholarly dispute over the essence of the Apuleian tale. Friedlander pioneered the arguments for a folk-tale basis of the story.[35] The parallels in medieval romance were taken as evidence of an ancient folk-tale tradition upon which Apuleius drew. The methodological problems of establishing a pre-modern oral tradition from later written sources have not yet been worked out sufficiently.[36] Folklorists have, however, amply shown that the Apuleian tale shares certain features with the folk-tale type, Aarne-Thompson 425, "The Search for the Lost Husband," and certain related types.[37]

Notable counter-arguments on the character of the ancient tale were developed by Richard Reitzenstein, beginning in 1912, who tried to establish a myth as the archetype of the tale.[38] An adequate treatment of the relationship of mythology and folklore is still very much wanting, and repudiation of one in favor of the other has not advanced our understanding. The characters Cupid and Psyche are, to be sure, mythological figures. My study, however, of the fairly abundant representations of them in ancient art and literature shows that there was no story at all told of the pair before that of Apuleius.[39] There was no classical myth of Cupid and Psyche.

Denial of a mythic basis of the tale does not, however, leave claims for its origin as a folk tale unqualified. The Apuleian text is, in any event, a sophisticated literary narrative. It elaborates all its motifs in a context full of rhetorical effects and playful allusions. Moreover, it is the only version cited by folklorists in which the principals are cast as Cupid and Psyche. It is highly misleading to label any folk tale type after them.

All that was known of the major works of Apuleius in the Middle Ages came through the testimony of Augustine, Fulgentius, and a handful of others in late antiquity. His fame, however, both as a magician and as a thinker, was great. The *Philosophica* and the *De interpretatione* were widely read and discussed. In the third decade of the fourteenth century the text of the major corpus, preserved at Monte Cassino, became known in Florence. Boccaccio, who later adapted two stories from the *Metamorphoses* into the *Decameron*,[40] composed a letter in 1339 adapting numerous phrases from the novel.[41] *Biblioteca Laurenziana* 54.32, a manuscript of Apuleius in Boccaccio's hand, includes the *De deo Socratis* as well as the major works. *Vaticanus Latinus* 2193, owned and annotated by Petrarch, includes more of the *Philosphica* together with the *Metamorphoses, Apology,* and *Florida*. The establishment of a now unified tradition, preserved in some twenty-two fourteenth-century manuscripts, may serve to close the subject of Apuleius in the Middle Ages.

Notes

1. L. D. Reynolds, *Texts and Transmission: A Survey of the Latin Classics* (Oxford, 1983), 15-18.
2. The most significant work in English on Apuleius in the Middle Ages remains E. H. Haight, "Apuleius in the Middle Ages," chapter 4 of his *Apuleius and his Influence* (London, 1927), 90-110. The most thorough treatments of the subject in more recent decades are those of S. Costanza, *La fortuna di L. Apuleio nell' età di mezzo* (Palermo, 1937) and C. Moreschini, "Sulla fama di Apuleio nella tarda antichità," in *Romanitas et Christianitas: Studia I. H. Waszink* (Amsterdam, 1973), 243-48, and "Sulla fama di Apuleio nel mediaevo e nel rinascimento," in *Studi filologici, letterari e storici in memoria di Guido Favati* (Padova, 1977), 2:457-76.
3. Lact. *Diu. Inst.* 5.3.7; Jer. *Tract. in Psalm. LXXXI.*
4. *Epist.* 138. 18- 19.
5. Apulée, *Opuscules Philosophiques,* ed. J. Beaujeu (Paris, 1973), vii-xxxv.
6. *CD* 8.12.
7. *CD* 8.19.
8. *CD* 18.18: "sicut Apuleius in libris, quos Asini Aurei titulo inscripsit, sibi ipsi accidisse ut, accepto ueneno, humano animo permanente, asinus fieret, aut indicauit aut finxit."
9. *Spec. nat.* 2.105; Costanza, 59.
10. Fulg. *Myth.* 3.6.
11. G. Huet, "Le roman d'Apuleé était-il connu au moyen-age?" *Le Moyen Age* 19 (1918): 45-46.
12. E.g., *Metamorphosis Goliae Episcopi* 161: "Nexibus Cupidinis Psyche detinetur"; 165: "Psyche per illecebras carnis captiuatur." (Father Synan, in his conference address, "The Classics: Episcopal Malice and Papal Piety," cites Apuleius as one of the sources of this poem.)
13. *Ep.* 4.3.1.
14. *Ep.* 2.10.5: "olim Marcia Hortensio, Terentia Tullio, Calpurnia Plinio, Pudentilla Apuleio, Rusticiana Symmacho legentibus meditantibusque candelas et candelabra tenuerunt."
15. *Ep.* 2.5.6: "saepe uersum Corinna cum suo Nasone compleuit, Lesbia cum Catullo, Caesennia cum Gaetulico, Argentaria cum Lucano, Cynthia cum Propertio, Delia cum Tibullo."
16. 183: "urit Apuleium sua Pudentilla."
17. So taken by M. Manitius, *Geschichte des lateinischen Literatur des Mittelalters* II (Munich, 1923); III (Munich, 1931), 269; Costanza, 73; Moreschini (1977), 467.
18. See above n. 5.
19. *CD* 4.2.
20. L. D. Reynolds, *Texts and Transmission*, 17.
21. Paris, Bib. Nat. Lat. 10318; *CLA* 5.593.
22. D. Londey and C. Johanson, *The Logic of Apuleius*, Philosophica Antiqua 47 (Leiden, 1987); cf. M. Sullivan, *Apuleian Logic* (Amsterdam, 1967), 9-14.
23. *Hist. reg. Brit.* 6.18.
24. R. and M. Rouse, "The Florilegium Angelicum: its Origin, Contents and Influence," in *Medieval Learning and Literature: Essays Presented to Richard W. Hunt* (Oxford, 1976), 70-74, 96.
25. E. R. Curtius, *European Literature and the Latin Middle Ages,* trans. W. R. Trask (Princeton, 1953), 112.

26. B. Stock, *Myth and Science in the Twelfth Century* (Princeton, 1972), 126-27, 150-62, 176-78.

27. 6.28-29.

28. E. A. Lowe, "The Unique Manuscript of Apuleius' *Metamorphoses* (Laurentian 68.2) and its Oldest Transcript," *CQ* 14 (1920): 150-55; reprinted in Lowe, *Palaeographical Papers* (Oxford, 1976), 1:92-98. Later, though we do not know when this manuscript was bound together with the famous Medici II of Tacitus, written at Monte Cassino some half century earlier than the Apuleius.

29. Walfarius of Salerno, *Vita Secundini*; M. Mantius, *Geschichte des Latineischen Literatur des Mittelalters* II (Munich, 1923), 489. Costanza, 87 n. 5 states that Radulfus de Diceto, in the twelfth century, included another citation from the *Florida* in his *Abbreuiationes chronicorum*, but this is in error. Three passages from *De deo Socratis* are cited by Radulf, *Opera historica*, ed. W. Stubbs, Rerum britannicorum medii aevi scriptores 68 (London, 1876) 1:46-47; cf. Manitius III (1931), 638. Costanza cites a later edition by R. Pauli, *MG SS* 27 (1925): 254-60, but these are only brief excerpts with no Apuleian material.

30. D. S. Robertson, "The Manuscripts of the *Metamorphoses* of Apuleius," *CQ* 18 (1924): 27-42, 85-99.

31. Manitius III (1931), 880, derives a story of incest in a poem by Petrus Pictor, a canon of St. Omer in the early twelfth century, from *Met.* 10.2-12. Henry and Renée Kahane argue that the account of the festival of Isis in book 11 of the *Met.* was a source for the treatment of the Grail legend by Chrétien de Troyes, "Proto-Percival and Proto-Parzival," *ZRPh* 79 (1963): 335-42; "On the sources of Chrétien's Grail Story," in *Festschrift Walter von Wartburg*, ed. K. Baldinger (Tübingen, 1968), 191-233.

32. William of Malmesbury, *Gesta Regum Anglorum* 2.171, tells a story of a young man made by witches to appear as an ass who dances. M. Kawczynski, "Ist Apuleius in Mittelalter bekannt gewesen?" in *Bausteine zur romanischen Philologie: Festgabe für Adolfo Mussafia* (Halle, 1905), 193-210, takes this as an example of the influence of the *Met* (196).

33. M. Kawczynski, "Ist Apuleius im Mittelalter bekannt gewesen," in *Bausteine zur romanischen Philologie: Festgabe für Adolfo Mussafia* (Halle, 1905), 193-210, is the prime presentation of this position. It is strongly reputiated by Huet (above, note 11).

34. Huet (1909), 26.

35. L. Friedländer, "Das Märchen von Cupid und Psyche," in *Amor und Psyche*, Wege der Forschung 126, ed. Binder and Merkelbach (Darmstadt, 1968), 16-43. The essay was originally published in 1871.

36. D. Fehling, *Amor und Psyche: Die Schöpfung des Apuleius und ihre Einwirkung auf das Märchen, eine Kritik der romantischen Märchentheorie* (Mainz, 1977); cf. *CP* 76 (1981): 164-66.

37. J. Swahn, *The Tale of Cupid and Psyche* (Lund, 1955).

38. R. Reitzenstein, "Das *Märchen* von Amor und Psyche bei Apuleius, " in Binder and Markelbach (above n. 35), 87-158.

39. C. Schlam, *Cupid and Psyche: Apuleius and the Monuments* (American Philological Assoc., 1976).

40. *Dec.* 5.10, from *Met.* 9.22-28, and 7.2, from *Met.* 9.5-7.

41. "Mauortis milex extrenue [= miles strenue]," G. Boccaccio, *Opere in Versi ... Epistole*, ed. G. Ricci (Milan and Naples, 1965), 1066-73.

Aeneas in Fourteenth-Century England

SHARON STEVENSON

Sir Gawain and the Green Knight opens with a reference to the destruction of Troy:

> Siþen þe sege and þe assaut watz sesed at Troye,
> Þe borg brittened and brent to brondez and askez,
> Þe tulk þat þe trammes of tresoun þer wrogt
> Watz tried for his tricherie, þe trewest on erthe;
> Hit watz Ennias þe athel and his highe kynde
> Þat siþen depreced prouinces and patrounes bicome
> Welnege of al þe wele in þe west iles.   (Silverstein 1-7)

The question is: who is "þe tulk" of line 3 who caused the destruction of Troy and was tried for his treachery?

Sir Israel Gollancz writes, "The reference is surely to Antenor, who was banished for his perfidy" (95). He argues that Antenor's treachery was so well known that the *Gawain* poet would not have to name him. According to this theory, then, Aeneas' name is attached only to the lines that follow his name, indicating that he subjugated provinces and became lord of nearly all the wealth—or "wele"—in the western realms.

However, Sir Frederic Madden indicates that all the lines, both those that refer to traitorous deeds and those that refer to subjugating provinces, are about Aeneas (308-9). Critics who interpret the lines in this way must prove that such a tradition of the character of Aeneas as traitor really did exist in England contemporaneously with or preceding the *Gawain* poet. Both Norman Davis (71) and Theodore Silverstein (112) attempt to prove just that by referring to a number of medieval versions of Troy which paint Aeneas as a traitor. The problem is that this character has never been delineated clearly so that modern readers can understand fully the differences between the glorious Aeneas we associate with Virgil and the traitorous Aeneas that the Middle Ages also seems to have known.

Roots

The tradition of Aeneas as traitor has its roots in the Dictys-Dares tale of Troy, which can be documented only as early as the first century AD (Frazer 7), but which comes to England through Benoit de Sainte-Maure and Guido delle Colonne (Meek xiv-xvi). Three English versions of the tale—*The "Gest Hystoriale" of the Destruction of Troy*, *The Laud Troy Book*, and Lydgate's *Troy Book*—all rely on Guido's thirteenth-century *Historia destructionis Troiae*.

The "Gest Hystoriale"

The "Gest Historiale" of the Destruction of Troy, finished in the fourteenth century (Gest liii–lxiv), best preserves Guido's material. The *Gest* purports to tell the historical truth of the fall of Troy as opposed to the fabulous stories of Homer and Virgil (1.51–52). Consequently we suspect that the *Gest's* Aeneas will be different than Virgil's heroic Aeneas.

The poet first mentions our subject as the husband of Creusa, Priam's eldest daughter, but then immediately identifies him as the hero of Virgil's work (1489–94). He is described as a small, broad, squinted-eyed man, fair of speech, learned, and very rich; in fact, no man in Troy is richer (3935–46).

Aeneas is depicted as a trusted counsellor to King Priam; unfortunately he does not always give good advice. When he is sent as advisor (2751–98) to accompany Paris to Greece to get Hesione back or to wreak some havoc on the Greeks, he becomes a source of the war. Priam, in the betrayal scenes, says to Aeneas: "Hade þou conceled the contrary [not to kidnap Helen], & comynd hit þan, / Should neuer lady of þat lede vnto þis lond comyn" (11336–37).

Although he does lead troops into battle, Aeneas is never portrayed as an especially good warrior. Diomedes has a special enmity for Aeneas because Aeneas advised Priam to put Diomedes to death. But when Diomedes bests Aeneas on the battlefield, it is Hector—not Aphrodite with her cloak of invisibility—who has to save Aeneas (7414–30).

When all significant Trojan warriors and allies are dead and the Trojans have no hope of doing battle, Aeneas, Antenor and Polydamas plot how they might save themselves, their families and their goods (11192–231). In Dictys and Dares, Antenor hatches the plan with others and they call in Aeneas only when the plan is full blown (Frazer 163–68). But here in the *Gest* and in Guido, Aeneas is a full partner in initiating the plan:

> Antenor & Eneas, with þaire avne sons,
> Serchid by hom-sluyn in sauyng hor lyues,
> . . . .
> To toune to be-tray, truly, þai thoght.
> And the gome to be-gyle, þat the ground aght,
> . . . .
> Therfore cast is hit cointly thies kene traytours,
> Vnder proffer of pes, pryam to lose;
> Hor cite to dissaiue in sauyng hor lyuis,
> And all Troy to be-tray, and the treit londis.
>   (11192-231)

Both Guido and the *Gest* poet underscore the strength of the traitors—they have many friends, much money, and large alliances (11385-92)—and their purpose is to save themselves, "hor sad fryndes, / Hor renttes, hor Riches, hor relikes also" (11385-96). The use of the ambiguous word "wele" in the opening lines of *Gawain* may indicate that the poet was playing on this tradition of Aeneas' wealth as part of his motivation for the betrayal.

The traitors subsequently meet with Priam and counsel him to sue for peace so that they—the traitors—may get outside the city gates to talk to the Greeks. Priam at once sees through their plan and refuses to agree. But when his plot to kill the traitors is foiled, he can do nothing except agree to talks, and Antenor is elected to go to the Greek camp (11428-31). Instead of asking for a real peace, however, he promises to betray Troy if the Greeks will promise to save him and Aeneas and their goods and families. Antenor deals first with the Greeks because he is the one who has been chosen by the Trojans to represent them, but Aeneas was a full partner in hatching the plot, and Antenor's request to the Greeks specifies that Aeneas is a co-conspirator (11451-57). Later, both Antenor and Aeneas eagerly visit the Greek camp to confirm the plan (11570-77). However, only Antenor is involved in stealing the Palladium (11582-716).

During the actual capture, Priam hesitates to take in the huge brass horse prepared by the Greeks, but Antenor and Aeneas, not Sinon, urge that it be taken in (11858-60) and so a portion of the city wall is pulled down to admit it. Dares does not include any account of a wooden, bronze, or brass horse. Instead he says the traitors, Antenor and Aeneas, let the Greeks in the Scaean gate, a wooden gate with the head of a huge horse carved in it (Frazer 165-66). Dictys, however, tells the story of the wooden horse which hides only Sinon, who emerges to signal the Greeks (Frazer 112).

In the *Gest* the Greek entourage emerge from the brass horse at night and slaughter the Trojans. At daybreak Antenor and Aeneas lead the Greeks to the palace where Priam is hiding (11956–58). In Dares, Antenor alone leads the Greeks to the palace (Frazer 166). In Dictys, neither Antenor nor Aeneas leads the Greeks to the palace (Frazer 112–13).

When Hecuba sees Priam killed, she flees with Polyxena. They meet Aeneas, who is alone, and Hecuba charges him with his crime:

"A! traytor vntrew, how toke þou on honde
þat trew to be-tray, þat trist in þe euer,—
Thy lege & þi lord, þat the louet wele,
And myche good hase þe gyffen of his gold red!
Thou hase led to þi lord, þat hym lothe was,
His fomen full fele thurgh falshed of the;
And done hym to dethe dolefully now,
Þat thy-selfe shuld haue socourd, hade þou ben sad tru.
The burgh, there þou borne was, baillfully distroyet,
To se hit leme on a low, laithis not þi hert?" (11972–84)

This is probably the height of pathos in the *Gest*, for medieval audiences undoubtedly knew that at the end of the poem Hecuba would be stoned to death, as a result of Aeneas' betrayal of the city. Thus Aeneas' role in this tale is much more prominent than Antenor's because Aeneas has greater stature in the poem. He is introduced in the catalog as part of the royal entourage and his actions depict him as a major advisor to the king. While other tales recognize Antenor as the chief traitor because he stole the Palladium, it is clear that, in this English translation of Guido, Aeneas' role is probably more heinous than Antenor's because Aeneas was the more trusted, being, after all, a son-in-law.

The city is set afire, except those buildings belonging to Aeneas and Antenor (12011–14), and the Greeks honor their promises to the traitors—Antenor and Aeneas and all their kin are saved; but when it is discovered that Aeneas has hidden Polyxena, the Greek council condemns him to banishment: "there þai demet þe duke, as by du right, / All his londes to lose, & launche out of towne" (12301–7). The use of "deemed" and "due right" here is an indication of legal judgment, the kind the *Gawain* poet mentions in his opening lines.

Before Aeneas leaves, he persuades the remaining Trojans to banish Antenor, who then leaves with his following. Aeneas defends the city from looters, but ultimately sets sail, too, with "Relikes full ryfe, & myche red gold" (12899). The *Gest* poet tells us to read Virgil if we want to know about Aeneas' glorious deeds (12910–12). Thus he ends his references to

Aeneas as he began them, by noting Virgil's story of the heroic Aeneas, but he himself portrays only the traitorous deeds.

The Laud Troy Book

The *Laud Troy Book*, another fourteenth-century Guido-based English version of the tale of Troy (Wulfing 374-96), presents only one side of Aeneas and never suggests the noble or heroic side. It claims to be a romance about Hector, the greatest knight in all history (11-64).

Like the *Gest* poet and Guido, the *Laud* poet first introduces Aeneas as Priam's son-in-law, but does not tell us that he went on to do marvellous deeds:

> The eldest, Clusa, weddid was
> Vnto that traytur Eueas,
> That afftirward trayed Troye;
> God geue him sorwe and neuere Ioye!
> (1877-80)

There is no mention of Virgil's work.

References to Aeneas in the *Laud* parallel those in the *Gest* and Guido. But the *Laud* poet misses no opportunity to curse the traitors: "Antenor and euel Eueas / Se thei neuerre god In the fas!" (17756-57) and ". . . Antenor and Eueas; / In helle mot be her wanyng-plas!" (18357-58). A portion of these epithets may have been done to facilitate the rhyme, but the instances are too numerous to be overlooked. The poet is obviously working to create an overwhelming image of the evils of treachery.

Midway through the tale, just after Achilles refuses to fight Hector in single combat, the poet stops to foreshadow the ending:

> . . . while he [Hector] leued, thei [Trojans] hadde no drede.
> When he was ded, than rose here bale;
> Alle thei died by oure tale,
> . . . .
> Saue Eueas and Antenor,
> Goddis curs haue thei ther-for!
> Thei were saued and alle theires,
> Seruaunt, mayden, wiff, and Ayres.
> For thei dissayued her lige lord,
> The deuel hem honge vpon a cord!
> Haue thei neuere so good pardoun,
> For thei wrougt suche a gret tresoun! (8582-94)

Just before the battle in which Achilles kills Hector, the *Laud* poet again foreshadows the end:

> But that [their end] schal be by fals tresoun;
> God geue hem his malesoun
> That the tresoun schope & wroght
> And that hit so aboute broght!
> That was Antenor & Eueas—
> God geue hem an euel gras!
> Come thei neuere In heuene riche,
> That thei wolde so her lord be-swyke
> And al that gentil nacioun!
> Schal be put In-to dampnacioun! (17049–70)

Although Guido is not above moralizing, this foreshadowing in the *Laud* is apparently the poet's unique embellishment done for the purpose of amplifying the treachery and creating a tragic effect.

The poet's final lament ends with the Greek judgment against Antenor and Aeneas:

> ... the traytoures bothe two
> For here ffalsnesse were afftir demed
> To be exiled & afftir flemed—
> With al here kyn & here lynage—
> For her wickednesse & her outrage. (18589–604)

The *Laud* poet never once in all 18,664 lines mentions Aeneas' glorious deeds after Troy. He does not even tell us to go read Virgil. He seems to have purposely omitted from his poem all references which would recall to his audience the figure of Aeneas as founding father or glorious hero, and he seems to have taken every opportunity to curse him for his treachery, denying him any redemption. By omitting the glorious deeds, the *Laud* poet has narrowed the character of Aeneas, making him an archtraitor, one who has committed the worst treachery of all times, the kind that the *Gawain* poet refers to in line 4, "tricherie, þe trewest on erthe." Thus the kind of tradition that Madden hints at and that Davis and Silverstein try to establish through reference seems best illustrated by the *Laud Troy Book*.

The Seege or Batayle of Troy

The Dares-based *Seege or Batayle of Troy*, an early fourteenth-century poem (lvi–lxxiv), also presents Aeneas as traitor only, but it is such a short work that characters are scarcely differentiated and little difference is made between Antenor and Aeneas. No scathing speeches by Priam and Hecuba are directed to their son-in-law and he is not given a more prominent role than Antenor. But Priam does deliver a moralistic speech on treachery which ends with the advice that all traitors should be drawn and quartered (1982–91). The direction is so specific we almost feel the poet had someone in mind.

Conclusion

Why such a portrait of Aeneas would have been so popular is something of an enigma. Norman Davis writes that the British were not embarrassed by the traitorous actions of Aeneas in Troy (71). But that does not explain why the medieval authors used it. Lydgate in his fifteenth-century *Troy Book* writes that Homer was "fauourable" to the Greeks because he was "allied" with them and that Virgil loved Aeneas, his founding father, so much that he, like Homer, told only part of the truth (Prol. 280–308). Lydgate evidently wanted in his own work to avoid the pagan error of biasing history to promote nationalism. He seems to justify propagating the story of the traitorous Aeneas as a means to avoid false glorification of Britain's founding father and to preserve a higher principle of historical truth.

The *Laud*, the *Gest*, and the *Seege* poets use the character of Aeneas to represent the reprehensible nature of treachery among those in high places. If we interpret all seven opening lines of *Gawain* as referring to Aeneas, then we see the *Gawain* poet doing something quite different. He is presenting Aeneas as a paradox: traitor in Troy, but founder of nearly all the provinces in Western Europe. His dual nature is the central analogy of the *Gawain* poem. Aeneas, who betrays his country to save his life and goods, is analogous to Gawain, who betrays his chivalric values to save his life. Because all Britains are presumably descendants of Aeneas, all suffer the same duality: they too have the potential for treachery or for heroism. Aeneas' role in the poem is an explanation for the human dilemma, and it offers hope, for while Aeneas was a traitor he was able to attain some measure of earthly redemption through his actions after Troy. We don't know whether Gawain goes on to do such great, though perhaps flawed, works afterward, but the Aeneas analogy and the Green Knight suggest that he may redeem himself. This redemption of course has religious overtones. Victor Haines argues that the entire poem contains a *mea culpa* theme ending in a kind of earthly redemption (*Fortunate Fall*).

The paradoxical Aeneas presented in the first seven lines of *Gawain* is certainly an emblem of such redemption.

So while the character of Aeneas as traitor presented in the fourteenth-century tales of Troy was done to paint reprehensible behavior, the *Gawain* poet seems to have used Aeneas as a paradox to present an explanation of the nature of mankind and a type of consolation. If the beginning seven lines of *Sir Gawain* are not understood as a reference to Aeneas, if the unnamed Antenor is the traitorous one and Aeneas the glorious one, then the poem loses its central metaphor, and the ingenuity of the *Gawain* poet is lost in what then appears to be an irrelevant, pseudo-epic introduction. Without the Dictys-Dares tradition, we would assume that the medieval understanding of Aeneas' character was the same as our understanding, which is derived from Virgil, and the Romans' attempt to "engineer history" would have been successful.

References

Benoit de Sainte-Maure. *Le Roman de Troie*. Ed. Leopold Constans. Société des Anciens Textes Français, 6 vols. Paris: Firmin Didot et Cie, 1904-12.

Borroff, Marie, ed. *Sir Gawain and the Green Knight*. New York: Norton, 1967.

Burrow, J. A., ed. *Sir Gawain and the Green Knight*. Middlesex, England: Harmondsworth, 1972.

Cawley, A. C., ed. *Sir Gawain and the Green Knight*. London: Everyman's Library, 1962.

Davis, Norman, et al., eds. *Sir Gawain and the Green Knight*. Oxford: Oxford Univ. Press, 1967.

Frazer, Richard, ed. and trans. *The Trojan War: The Chronicles of Dictys of Crete and Dares the Phrygian*. Bloomington: Indiana Univ. Press, 1966.

The "Gest Hystoriale" of the Destruction of Troy. Ed. G. A. Panton and D. Donaldson. EETS, nos. 39 and 56. 1869-74.

Gollancz, Sir Israel, ed. *Sir Gawain and the Green Knight*. EETS, no. 210. 1940.

Guido delle Colonne. *Historia destructionis Troiae*. Ed. and trans. Elizabeth Meek. Bloomington: Indiana Univ. Press, 1974.

Haines, Victor. *The Fortunate Fall of Sir Gawain*. Washington, D.C.: Univ. Press of America, 1982.

The Laud of Troy Book. Ed. J. E. Wulfing. EETS, nos. 121-22. 1902-3.

Lydgate's Troy Book. Ed. H. Bergen. EETS, nos. 97, 103, 106, and 126. 1906-35.

Madden, Sir Frederic, ed. *Syr Gawayne: A Collection of Ancient Romance-Poems*. London: Bannatyne Club, 1839. Reprint. New York: AMS Press, 1971.

The Seege or Batayle of Troy. Ed. Mary Barnicle. EETS, no. 172. 1927.

Silverstein, Theodore, ed. *Sir Gawain and the Green Knight*. Chicago: Univ. of Chicago Press, 1974.

Wulfing, J. Ernst. "Das *Laud Troy Book*," *Englische Studien* 29 (1901): 374-96.

PLENARY LECTURE

The Classics: Episcopal Malice and Papal Piety

EDWARD A. SYNAN

1

When the Dominican friar, Vincent of Beauvais, was bringing his *Speculum historiale* from the first verse of Genesis to the year 1244 of our calendar, he included a distressing notation for the year of grace 1148:

> Horum duorum magistrorum, Petri uidelicet Abaelardi et Gilberti Porretae, quidam discipuli nimium zelantes pro ipsis, beato Bernardo et toti Cisterciensi ordini postea detrahere coeperunt.[1]

A first document chosen to give its witness to a presence of the Latin classics in the Middle Ages verifies half the content of Vincent's notation. Thanks to its silence on the other half, that document can be dated with fair precision.

This first text is named the *Methamorphosis golye episcopi* in one of the two manuscripts in which it is extant, British Library Harleian 978.[2] "Bishop Goliath," anti-clericals will be disappointed to hear, is a fictitious person, a figment of the anti-clerical imagination rather than a justification for that contentious point of view. As Vincent of Beauvais has prepared us to expect, this poem, which arose in "goliardic" circles, defends the silenced Peter Abelard by attacking Bernard of Clairvaux and all his confreres. Abelard had been silenced by the Council of Sens in 1140 and Bernard took a large part in that action, strongly supported by other Cistercians, chief among them William of Saint-Thierry. A complaint that Bernard and his Cistercian armor-bearers had reduced Abelard to silence would have made no sense before 1140; the date is a solid *terminus ante quem non* for the *Methamorphosis*.

The date of Vincent's entry is the other extreme limit for the composition of the *Methamorphosis* because in that very year, 1148, Gilbert had indeed suffered embarrassment owing to the same Bernard and his monks, yet the poem is silent on that episode. Between 1140 and 1148—indeed between 1141 and 1146—would seem to be the most probable period for the composition of this poem. Gilbert, on whose troubles of 1148 the poem is silent, received a most favorable mention (stanza 43, lines 3 and 4); it is inconceivable that the unknown author could have neglected to support his case against the Cistercians with this second episode, had the event taken place by the time of writing. So precise a dating of an undated medieval work is seldom possible.

The poem is "goliardic" both in content and in manner. As to its manner, the *Methamorphosis* owes nothing to classical Latin prosody. Fifty-nine four-line stanzas, all four lines ending in an identical feminine rhyme, are written in a trochaic metre which is established by heavy stress rather than by quantity; each line is broken by a caesura after the fourth stressed syllable.

In content the *Methamorphosis* is equally "goliardic." The verses are witty, vituperative of the clerical establishment, knowledgeable, and catchy. A brief summary of the poem's burden may be welcome.

Gods, goddesses, satyrs, muses, and distinguished mortals had gathered in the spring at the palace of Jove for a divinely-sanctioned wedding. Eloquence, in the person of Mercury, who here is called "Cyllenius" from his birthplace, was the groom:

> Video Cyllenium superum legatum   20
> a predicti numinis sinistris locatum,
> ut nubentem decuit totum purpuratum,
> quadam pube tenera faciem umbratum.[3]

The bride was "Philologia," Love of Learning:

> Nupta sibi comes est de stirpe diuina,   22
> uestis de cyndalio, partim hyalina,
> uultus rutulancior rosa matutina
> quam nec nox[4] decoxerat nec lesit pruina.

Pallas Athēnē and Venus represented the dissident claims of erudition and of human love, to be so happily reconciled in this marriage:

> Sola soli Veneri Pallas aduersatur   39
> et pro totis uiribus usque nouercatur,
> nam quod placet Veneri, Pallas aspernatur,
> Venus pudiciciam raro comitatur.

Every classicist will recognize that the setting reflects the *De nuptiis Mer-*

curii et Philologiae by Martianus Capella, and a fair number of verbal borrowings from the *De nuptiis* reinforce that derivation. Bishop Goliath went well beyond this major source. Like a Renaissance painter representing figures from an incident in the Hebrew scriptures arrayed in the clothing and armor of the fourteenth or fifteenth century, Goliath has made two creative enlargements of the *dramatis personae* he had found in Martianus Capella.

First, a number of ancient philosophers and literary figures were introduced and these were culled, not from the *De nuptiis*, but from two letters of Sidonius Apollonaris.[5] (That Sidonius is a crucial source for Goliath was pointed out in my hearing by Professor John R. Clark of Fordham at a conference not unlike "Classics in the Middle Ages.") Sidonius, bishop of Clermont, was not shy about parading his knowledge of the classics, and Bishop Goliath was not shy about sharing what he found in the letters of Sidonius:

> Aderant philosophi, Tales udus stabat,   43
> Crisippus cum numeris, Zeno ponderabat,
> ardebat Eraclius, Perdix circinabat,
> totum ille Samius[6] proporcionabat.

In the same letter Sidonius named literary personalities and Goliath gave them a verse:

> Implicabat Cicero, explicabat Plato,   44
> hinc dissuadet Apius, hinc persuadet Cato,
> uacuus Archelias[7] tenuit pro rato
> esse quod inceperat undique locato.

In two more stanzas Goliath profited from another letter in which Sidonius listed intellectuals and the ladies they loved:

> Secum suam duxerat Getam Naso pullus[8]   45
> Cynthiam Propercius, Delyam Tibullus,
> Tullius Terenciam, Lesbiam Catullus,
> uates huc conuenerant, sine sua nullus.

> Queque suo suus est ardor et fauilla,   46
> Plinium Calpurnie succendit scintilla,
> urit Apuleium sua Pudentilla,[9]
> hunc et hunc amplexibus tenet hec et illa.

A second expansion on Martianus is a list of twelfth-century academics, for our author was well acquainted with the academic environment within which his hero, Peter Abelard, had functioned. This acquaintance is particularly visible in the twelve or thirteen explicitly named Masters that Goliath introduced at the wedding of Eloquence and the Love of Learning; from his verses can be derived one of the most complete rosters of academic personalities available to historians of the period.[10] Abelard was once referred to by name: *et professi plurimi sunt Abaielardum* (50.4); and in two other lines Bishop Goliath demonstrated his awareness of that scholar's contribution to philosophy and of his place of origin. The honorific epithet *nostrum Porphirium* (51.4) clearly alludes to Abelard's interventions on the famous "problem of the universal," a puzzle posed for logicians and philosophers by Porphyry of Tyre in his widely read and esteemed Eisagogē, his introduction to the *Categories* of Aristotle. The bride, Philologia, who in a secondary way seems to represent Heloise as well as erudition,[11] was represented as searching for where "her Palatine" might be: *Nupta querit ubi sit suus Palatinus* (54.1); thus, in the context of the poem, the term *Palatinus* is a pun in its meaning "an official in the palace," that is, in the palace of Jove where the wedding was celebrated, and its other meaning, "native of Le Pallet," where Abelard had been born.

Although designed to be a defense of Abelard against his persecution by a particularly sour monk named Reginald and by Bernard, the latter is never named. Bernard was, however, given a Russellian "definite description": *cucullati populi Primas cucullatus*, "cowled Abbot of a cowled people." If Saul Kripke is right to hold that such a description will not hold for all possible worlds, it was clearly valid in the world of Abelard and Bernard. Finally, Peter Abelard was also notorious for his disastrous love affair with Heloise.[12] In his clerical ambience, Bishop Goliath thought it right to make some place for celibacy. Deftly introduced, thanks to a chance phrase in Martianus Capella (*pellit coelibatum*), Goliath ascribed the renunciation of celibacy to Cupid's arrows (38.4), to the influence of Cupid's mother, Venus (39.1-4), and ended by remarking that this issue is yet to be settled: *adhuc est sub pendulo, adhuc est sub lite.* (40.4). To do him justice, Goliath presents both sides: the ancient exemplars of scholarship were often married, as we have seen above; hence there is no insuperable conflict between human love and the life of learning. On the other hand, a number of celibate clerics, contemporary with Abelard, are given full marks for their academic prowess.

When all has been said, Bishop Goliath produced a defense of Abelard that is richly evocative of the Latin classics and, like a French general before 1914, evidently considered the best defense an *attaque à outrance*. The Cistercians were given the harshest of characterizations:

> Grex est hic nequicie, grex perdicionis,   56
> impius et pessimus heres Pharaonis,
> speciem exterius dans religionis,
> set subest scintillula supersticionis.

Whatever the estimate of the academic propriety or of the aesthetic value of such verses, the *Methamorphosis golye episcopi* bears incontrovertible witness to a certain presence of the Latin classics in mid-twelfth century academic circles. Its pseudonymous author knew, and expected his readers to know, a respectable range of mythological and historical classical lore.

The very title *Methamorphosis,* assigned to the poem by the earlier of its two manuscript texts, guarantees this. As even a cursory reading will show, there is nothing in Goliath's verses to match the reasons customarily adduced to account for the choice of *Metamorphoses* to designate Ovid's encyclopedic presentation in poetic form of Graeco-Roman mythology.[13] Neither did Bishop Goliath have grounds such as those that make the *uariae fabulae* of Apuleius truly "books of transformations," *Metamorphoseon libri*. The hero of Apuleius, after all, underwent a dismaying transformation into the shape of an ass and then a blessed return to human form (whence the alternative title, *Asinus aureus*).[14]

To make another tack, "transformation" is so minor a theme in Goliath's primary source, the *De nuptiis,* that the term occurs there only once.[15] Neither, however, is there adequate source material in the *De nuptiis* for what Goliath has written on Psychē and Cupid. There may well be echoes of Ovid's descriptions of Cupid in those stanzas by Goliath:

> Nudus, nam propositum nequid sepelire,   37
> cecus, quia racio nequid hunc lenire,
> puer, nam plus puero, solet lasciuire,
> alatur, dum facile solet preterire.

Ovid may also have suggested that Goliath's remarks on Cupid's weaponry:

> Illius uibrabile telum est auratum   38
> et in summa cuspide modice curvatum,
> telum inuitabile, telum formidatum,
> nam qui hoc percutitur, pellit celibatum.[17]

Still, there can be no doubt but that Goliath's verses depend heavily upon the long account of Cupid and Psychē by Apuleius (41, 42). Those verses were termed a *Methamorphosis* neither because they deal with the way primaeval chaos had been changed by divinities into the cosmos of Ovid, nor because they deal with magicians and their ability to transmute humans into brute beasts, along with salvation sought through a mystery religion; it was rather because Ovid and Apuleius, in their respective *Metamorphoses,* provided material on Cupid and Psychē for the purposes of this twelfth-century goliard.

If Ovid surely and Apuleius possibly belong in the ranks of "classical" authors, not everyone will welcome the relatively late Martianus Capella into their company with equal confidence. No logician, however, can disallow the disjunction that Martianus either was an "ancient" or not; if not an ancient, then he must have been a "medieval." In either case, he deserves his passports for this consultation on the classics in the Middle Ages. Furthermore, it was thanks to Martianus that our twelfth-century versifier found warrants for his contention that eloquence and learning ought to be "married," for learning without eloquence is mute and eloquence without learning is vacuous — a position that neither Cicero nor Quintilian nor Virgil would have contested. In the words of Goliath:

> Nisi sapiencie sermo copuletur   23
> uagus, dissolutus est, infirmus habetur,
> et cum parum proficit, parum promeretur,
> eget ut remigio eius gubernetur.

We must allow that Goliath had more than a passing acquaintance with a broad range of classical literature and that he used it confidently in a most topical poem. Whether he knew classical prosody can neither be proved nor disproved from this poem and its form; this point may be clarified by the testimony of the second author chosen to illustrate medieval classical learning.

Our fictitious bishop has been introduced under the rubric of "malice." The stanza cited on the Cistercians indicates why that rubric was adopted. Goliath's anti-Cistercian malice reached its climax in the closing stanza which proclaims the judgment he claimed was the work of the dignitaries assembled for the wedding from which poor Abelard was missing:

> Quicquid tante curie sanctione datur   59
> non cedat in irritum, ratum habeatur:
> cucullatus igitur grex uilipendatur
> et a philosophicis scolis expellatur.   Amen.

The "court" he qualified as "so great," *tante curie,* is the council of divinities and heroic humans who passed sentence against Saint Bernard and his monks. We may note in passing that his use of technical legal terms, *sanctione, irritum,* and *ratum,* reveals that Bishop Goliath knew Roman law and its language as well as Latin literature.

It is difficult to think that Goliath wove together into so harmonious a whole disjointed scraps of classical learning, sentences memorized under the cane of a grammarian or found in *florilegia* only. Perhaps it is impossible to contrive an apodictic argument to show that a pseudonymous bishop had read the *Metamorphoses* of Ovid and Apuleius as well as the *De nuptiis* of Martianus Capella; all the odds, it seems to me, are that he had done so.

This conclusion will be less secure in the case of our second witness, but even on pope Innocent III, our dubieties may not survive comparison with a third witness. There can be no doubt but that John Henry Newman, for all his "under-the-line" performance in the Oxford schools of 1820, had read the classics *in extenso*.

2

In any event, to the episcopal malice exhibited by Bishop Goliath must now be added a pious use of the classics by Pope Innocent III. He was a son of the Count di Segni, head of the Conti family, and of an equally aristocratic mother; elected to the papacy in 1198 when he was about thirty-eight years old, Innocent died in 1216. The genuine Pope, here contrasted with a pseudo-bishop, was the greatest of medieval popes by the common consent of historians. Still, as one historian, S. C. Ferruolo, has lately remarked, "posterity has not conceded to him the merited title 'Innocent the Great.'"[18]

Before his election Lothario di Segni was given his first education in a Roman monastery. There he most certainly made contact with the classics in learning to read, to write, and to speak Latin. From Rome he went to Paris for theology and then to Bologna for the study of law. Innocent's sermons, his *Registers* of official correspondence, and a number of his treatises on moral, doctrinal, and liturgical issues are garnished with an important number of citations derived from Latin poets of the first rank.

Among those citations (it must be conceded immediately) there are three open to discussion. Innocent included proverbs that were ascribed during the middle ages to a "Dionysius Cato" who was then thought to be identical with Cato the Censor (or as he was also called, Cato the Elder), 234–149 BCE. Modern scholarship assigns this collection of proverbial wisdom, the *Disticha Catonis,* to the third or fourth century of our era. In circumstances such as these, however, Bishop Berkeley's *esse est percipi* enjoys a degree of validity. If Innocent thought he was citing the ancient Censor (who had, in fact, written a *Carmen de moribus*) then what he did with lines from the *Dionysii Catonis disticha de moribus ad filium* retains value, at least as witness to the esteem entertained for the classics by this not inconsiderable medieval author. To be a classic is an epistemic rather than an ontic affair; the notion of "classic" is primarily evaluative; it is descriptive in only a secondary way: *esse est percipi*.

Unlike Bishop Goliath, Pope Innocent III employed the poets of Latin antiquity in the interest of piety. Unlike Bishop Goliath in yet another mode, the Pope normally cited the *ipsissima uerba* of those poets, whether in full lines or in substantive fragments of their verses. Only once, to my knowledge, has he cited an isolated phrase, Horace's *ad unguem*.[19] Here and there the Pope omitted or inserted a word or two; as will be seen, these manipulations imply that he understood the quantitative metres of the ancients.

On the other hand, there is no need to rely on inference to establish that Innocent also esteemed the stressed and rhyming verse in which Goliath and so many other Latin versifiers of the twelfth century had engaged. The great Pope's use of the classical poets must be seen against his single surviving effort at writing Latin poetry. This is a hymn in eighty-four lines of which thirty-six praise Christ and forty-eight praise the Virgin Mary.[20] He followed this hymn with a prose prayer, addressed to the Lord Jesus, but asking that the mother of Christ might intercede in our behalf. Both prayer and hymn evoke the scriptural grounds for the Pope's theology of Mary's role as the uniquely effective intercessor with the Lord. Innocent was conscious of his own faults and, fearful of divine justice, felt he needed Mary's help. That he thought the same about us all is clear in an editorial parenthesis: the Pope attached various spiritual blessings to the use of his hymn and prayer. In this connection, he was also the author of a jeremiad on our human condition, heavily supported with classical quotations.[21] The hymn, however, is composed, not in classical metres, but in stressed, rhyming, couplets. Two lines, six and seventy-three, it is painful to report, seem somewhat skewed; all others forge ahead to end in feminine rhymes, each line composed of four jingling trochees. To cite only the first six lines:

> Aue mundi spes Maria,
> Aue mitis, aue pia;
> Aue charitatis plena,
>   Virgo dulcis et serena
> Sancta parens Iesu Christi;
> Electa sola fuisti. . . .

The Pope, you will have noticed, granted himself a generous poetic license for the last line quoted; read normally, *Electa sola fuisti* breaks his metrical pattern. Besides, if it is not too pedantic to mention a detail for which Innocent may bear no responsibility, the full stop after *fuisti* in the Migne text, presumably in Migne's source as well, will not wash. The infinitives *esse* and *lactare* in lines following are governed by the finite verb *fuisti*.

Should we admit the medieval Cato to the status of a classical author, a few statistics will convey the extent to which Pope Innocent III made use of Latin poetry from its golden age, more in his pessimistic *De miseria condicionis humane* than in any other work. There Juvenal is cited three times, Horace seven times, and Ovid four times. A control on this can be found in an intervention by L.-J. Bataillon, "Virgile chez les maîtres Parisiens." This scholar surveyed the classical citations made by Alan of Lille in his *Distinctiones;* that older contemporary of Innocent was all but obsessed by the Latin classics, as evidenced by his *Anti-Claudianus* and by his *De planctu naturae*. In the *Distinctiones,* Alan cited Virgil thirteen times, Lucan and Boethius seven times each, Statius five times, Ovid four, Claudian and Horace once each.[22]

Innocent quoted Juvenal four times, Virgil, Cato, and Ovid twice each, and Horace once in his extant sermons; in the formal letters of his Pontificate Horace appears twice and Ovid three times. The Pope adduced sayings from Cato twice in his *Commentarium* on the penitential psalms (the Migne text mal-ascribes one of those citations to Horace) and Ovid is there cited once.[23] In a study on the liturgy, *De sacrificii altaris mysteriis,* the Pope included a quotation of Virgil;[24] his *Liber de eleemosyna* quotes Horace once[25] and finally, not strictly a citation, a phrase Horace had himself used twice, *ad unguem,* is to be found in the Pope's *Encomium charitatis*.[26] To summarize this dull, but indispensable, numerical survey, our Pope has forty-eight times made use of one or another of forty classical *dicta,* fifteen from Horace, thirteen from Ovid, three each from Virgil, Cato, and Juvenal, two from Lucan, and one from Claudian. All were cited with substantial accuracy, but occasionally with the degree of freedom that was customary in the Middle Ages and which may have its roots in biblical exegesis. Since every line of the Bible is inspired by the Holy One, every line illumines every other line; an extracted verse from one context can function with verses from any other context without loss of truth.

One manifestation of that freedom is the Pope's willingness to collapse widely separated lines of a single poet into a composite text with no warning to the reader that the author's words have been rearranged in the very act of citation. Thus a composite of Horace, *Sat.* 1.1.68 and *Ep.* 1.2.56 appears as:

Tantalus sitit in undis [et]
<semper> avarus eget [in opibus][27]

Horace's word *semper* was suppressed; the phrase *in opibus* was added to clarify Innocent's intention; the *et*, it seems, is dubious and only *Tantalus* respects the text of the poet.

A more extreme instance of this freedom is the combination of phrases from two authors; an unwary reader might think them a smooth passage from one poet. Thus, Innocent linked one hexametre from Cato 3.6.2, *interpone tuis interdum gaudia curis,* to a line from Ovid, *Ep.* 4.89: *quod caret alterna requie durabile non est.*[28] The procedure may not meet our conventions, but the undamaged metre suggests that the freewheeling Pope understood the conventions of classical prosody. This impression is reinforced by his citation in two sermons[29] of a line from Virgil, *Aeneis* 6.733. In both places Pope Innocent thought it right to omit the last words of the line, *nec auras;* those words begin a new sentence, the burden of which is irrelevant to the Pope's intentions. What Innocent wanted to establish is that four emotion-laden responses mark human moral choices, *Quatuor sunt naturales mentis affectus: dolor, gaudium, timor et spes.* Virgil's four verbs in the verse cited, *metuunt, cupiuntque, dolent, gaudentque,* he read as supporting his own insight. Innocent was given to four-fold division; his essay on marriage, *De quadrapartita specie nuptiarum liber,*[30] for instance, proffers four sorts of marriage from a theological perspective. Only one is that between "a woman, licit to marry" and her husband. Virgil had given his four verbs a scope wider than the Pope wished to use. Expressing what might be termed a "Platonic" view of the ill consequences of material bodies, *noxia corpora* in Virgil's words, on all embodied souls (*Phaedo* 82D, E; *Timaeus* 30A), the poet applied his conception not only to us, but to brute beasts, to flying things, and to submarine monsters as well.[31] On the contrary, Innocent was interested exclusively in the human situation, in the *anima Christiana,* "milled," according to his metaphor, between "upper and lower millstones," that is, a present (*dolor* and *gaudium*) and a future (*timor* and *spes*), the first in each case an evil, and the second a good. On one of the two occasions when he used this line Innocent inserted the term *homines:*

Hinc [homines] metuunt, cupiunt, gaudentque, dolentque....[32]

An anapest, *homines* fills in the verse without disturbing its dactylic metre. Although he truncated the verse (and for a good reason), the Pope's manipulation of this line of classical poetry more than suggests that he knew his material and appreciated the literary consequences of his change.

More important than whether this medieval Pope, who had written rhyming Latin couplets, was competent to scan quantitative verse, is the aptness or the ineptitude of his citations. After these remarks on four human emotions that interest a preacher, one can advance to consider the application Innocent made of a *sententia* constructed by himself from passages taken from Cato's *interpone tuis interdum gaudia curis* and from Ovid's *quod caret alterna requie durabile non est*. The pope's theme was that no single emotion ought to prevail without let; cares ought to be tempered by joy; excess in either is disastrous. In the judgment of Innocent, Ovid's observation that, in order to perdure, a human must alternate rest with labor, seemed to match Cato's admonition that joys be interspersed among our cares; Ovid said as much. Innocent seems not to have strained the meaning he found.

Horace, *Ep.* 1.4.14, supplied the Pope with a line that parallels biblical wisdom:

>   grata superueniet, quae non sperabitur hora.[33]

Parallel is not identical; this is neither the first nor the last time that a Stoic aphorism has seemed to support a biblical perspective. Innocent thought that this one provides a suitable gloss of Psalm 30 (29):12: "You have transformed my desire into a joy for me." Repeating this image of the two millstones, Innocent reinforced the text of Horace just cited with a line from Ovid on the "median course" recommended in vain to Phaëton as he was about to drive the chariot of Phoebus between heaven and earth (*Metam.* 2.137):

>   inter utrumque uola, medio tutissimus ibis.[34]

It is not without interest that Lord Byron can be quoted[35] as having remarked on this very verse: "In short, the maxim for the amorous tribe is / Horatian: *Medio tu tutissimus ibis*" (*Don Juan* 6.17). Like Phaëton, Byron was incapable of following this excellent advice. English metre demanded *tu*, the author cited is Ovid, and in love the English poet failed by excess.

Before Innocent concluded his sermon he went once more to Ovid's well, this time also to the poet's *Metamorphoses*. Where Paul of Tarsus had assured the Corinthians that "the Lord loves a cheerful giver" (2 Cor. 9:7), the Pope remembered Ovid's story of gods travelling incognito and the hospitality extended to them by a humble couple with smiling faces, *Metam.* 8.677-78:

>   [et] super omnia uultus
>   accessere boni....[36]

Here too, Innocent's insertion of *et* in the fragment of the first line leaves Ovid's metre intact.

Innocent presented a mirror image of an important theological tradition when he three times cited two lines from Juvenal, 8.140–41, in his sermons. That tradition proposes the conception that a fault, or reparation for a fault, are proportionate to the dignity of the one offended and to the agent who compensates:

> omne animi uitium tanto conspectius in se
> crimen habet, quanto maior qui peccat habetur.[37]

Anselm of Bec and Canterbury had rung changes on such proportions and disproportions between the Holy One and sinners and had made a specialty of clarifying the work of human redemption after the rebellion of our race. His *Cur deus homo?* poses a theological question within an implicit affirmation of the Incarnation; God-made-man is alone proportional to man-offending-God. Juvenal had "anticipated," *sit uenia uerbo,* the Christian theologian in the eyes of this Pope.

It has been mentioned that before he became Innocent III, Lothario di Segni had cited the classics more frequently in *De miseria condicionis humane* than he would do anywhere else. On all counts, this treatise on human frailty — moral, physical, and intellectual — was his most successful literary venture. Realistic, not to say cynical, observations of our lot by Latin poets reinforce the side of Judaeo-Christian moralizing that turns a harsh light on human weakness. We are, for instance, beguiled by a love for money that feeds upon itself (Juvenal 14.139):

> crescit amor nummi, quantum ipsa pecunia crescit.[38]

Christians as well as pagans must recognize that those who live long are doomed to suffer innumerable indignities that afflict the old (Hor. *A.P.* 169):

> multa senem circumueniunt incommoda. . . .[39]

A biblical believer, no less than an exiled Roman poet, can be the victim of abandonment by fair-weather friends; in Ovid's verses (*Trist.* 1.9.5–6):

> cum fueris felix, multos numerabis amicos,
> tempora si fuerint nubila, solus eris.[40]

For the Bible and the Church, true wisdom is sanctity, and intellectual vagaries, in consequence, are vaguely touched with sinfulness. The young Cardinal thought it right to concede that, as Horace had put it (*Ep.* 1.2.14), our lack of wisdom approaches the madness often seen in kings:

> quicquid delirant reges, plectuntur Achiui.⁴¹

We can be so base as to be willing to live on another's pittance and Juvenal (5.2) had a sharply honed phrase for this:

> ... aliena uiuere quadra.⁴²

Our struggle against the inclinations that undo us will be in vain; those inclinations, corrupt though they may be, are "natural" and Horace had seen this (*Ep.* 1.10.24):

> naturam expellas furca, tamen usque recurret.⁴³

Envy, a capital sin in Christian tradition, had also attracted the attention of Horace, who had put his observations in three consecutive verses (*Ep.* 1.2.57–59), broken, to be sure, in the Cardinal's citation, by a *sed* which, one can argue, functions as a kind of rubric to sharpen the adversative relation between the first and the other two lines for, indeed, it does break the metre:

> inuidus alterius rebus marcescit opimis [sed]
> inuidia Siculi non inuenere tyranni
> maius tormentum. . . .⁴⁴

Australia with her black swans had not been discovered by Europeans when Lothario di Segni wrote, expanding on our miseries, and still less when Juvenal had composed the line that the Cardinal was to quote (6.165):

> rara auis in terris nigroque simillima cygno.⁴⁵

The Cardinal felt confident that in speaking of a "black swan" he spoke of the non-existent; medieval logicians were with him. "Whiteness," they held, although an "accident," is an "inseparable accident" from any and all swans.

Worry vies with fear (Ovid, *Her.* 1.12) even in love:

> res est solliciti plena timoris amor . . .⁴⁶

and it has been noted above that we resemble Tantalus in our avarice, thirsting, though surrounded by the sea, as he was. Avarice deceives us, leads us to see ourselves as "needy" in the midst of wealth; as we have seen, these notions called forth some extreme, not to say excessive, editorializing on the part of the future Pope Innocent.

Drunkenness is among the foremost themes of moralizers, and even Horace had provided a satiric comment that the Cardinal was glad to use (*Ep.* 1.5.19):

> fecundi calices quem non fecere disertum?⁴⁷

So too the most eminent of love poets wrote satirically of a foppish concern with impeccable grooming; where there is not so much as a hint of dust, we brush away—nothing! (Ovid *Ars am.* 1.151):

> et si nullus erit puluis, tamen excute nullum.⁴⁸

Human pain and disease in their inevitable recurrence merit the analogy of Tityus and his never-ending punishment (Ovid *Pont.* 1.2.39–40):

> sic inconsumptum Tityi semperque renascens
> non perit, ut possit saepe perire iecur.⁴⁹

In the *De miseria,* too, the future Pope engaged in a creative combination of two authors' texts in a complicated citation. Here, too, he preserved what the metre demands in a mosaic of fragments from Lucan (*Bell. civ.* and 1.70 and 81) and from Claudian (*In Ruf.* 1.22-23):

> in se magna ruunt| summisque negatum [est]
> stare diu| tolluntur in altum.⁵⁰

This comment on the fall of the mighty rounds out the reinforcement with Latin poets of the Cardinal's grim views on human misery; his world read them eagerly.

As Pope, our author on five occasions used snippets of classical verse in his day-by-day administration of Church affairs; all five quotations are defensible applications of poetic *dicta* to the matters at hand. In a letter to the Bishop of Ostia the Pope spoke of the ill consequences for the prestige of the Church should a disappointing result follow upon elaborate negotiations. Horace provided the well-worn line (*A.P.* 1.139):

> Turpe quidem existeret si, forsan, forte principium debilis sequeretur
> effectus, possetque Nobis illud improperari poeticum:
> parturiunt montes, nascetur ridiculus mus.⁵¹

By a happy coincidence Innocent gave what might count as a marginal gloss on the controversy beneath Bishop Goliath's *Methamorphosis.* In the course of refusing to approve the appointment of a Benedictine chaplain in a Cistercian house, the Pope reinforced two verses from the Book of Deuteronomy with a line from Ovid (*Ep.* 9.29):

> Cisterciensis ordinis monachi, etsi Regulam beati Benedicti sequantur, habent tamen propria instituta, et a uobis tam habitu quam ritu differunt in quibusdam, scientes quod non bene aratur "in boue

et asino" (Dt 22.10) nec induenda est uestis "ex lana linoque" (ibidem 11), et iuxta sententiam ethnici:
> non bene inaequales ueniunt ad aratra iuvenci.[52]

It will be remembered that Bernard and the Cistercians were pilloried by Bishop Goliath as persecutors of Abelard — and Abelard was a Benedictine. The "habit," the monastic gown, of the Cistercians was satirized by Goliath as the last layer of an "onion-like" costume and, above all, it differed in color from that of the Benedictines. Cistercians were called "white monks" from the color of their habit, Benedictines "black monks."

In a letter to the Archbishop of Sens, Innocent qualified a saying of "the poet" as "prophetic" and indeed, "moral"; the poet was Ovid, and the pope was citing that least likely of moral sources, the *Remedia amoris* (91):

> ... etsi poeticum sit, est tamen quasi propheticum et morale quod legitur in poeta:
> > principiis obsta, sero medicina paratur
> > cum mala per longas inualuere moras.[53]

Thus did the Pope reveal his fundamental attitude toward his classical sources. In the tradition of the *praeparatio euangelica,* Innocent saw in pagan wisdom a valid anticipation of his biblical and ecclesial faith.

A letter to the King of Hungary on that King's maltreatment of a papal Legate made use of a verse from the same poet (Ovid *Trist.* 5.6.13):

> ... dilectum filium L. tituli Sanctae Crucis presbyterum cardinalem, apostolicae sedis legatum, deuote receperis et honoraueris studiose, ita quod eum in osculo pacis benigne dimissum fecisti usque ad regni fines honeste conduci, ut iam non superesset nisi Danubii transitus de Vngaria in Bulgariam, quia, tamen, iuxta uerbum poeticum:
> > turpius eiicitur quam non admittitur hospes,[54]
> minus indecens exstitisset si non admi<si>sses euntem, quam admissum non sineres proficisci.

A last citation of a classical source in an official letter of Innocent occurs in one directed to church officials who were suffering unspecified difficulties at Cologne. Saint Paul, but Horace too (*Carm.* 3.37), the Pope was convinced, had something encouraging to say to them:

> ... uos quos "fidelis deus" tentari nullomodo patietur ultra quam ferre possitis (1 Cor. 10.13), augere animum, ac mentem conuenit ampliare, complendo illud de sapiente praeconium:

> si fractus illabatur orbis
> impauidum ferient ruinae.⁵⁵

Once more, in the view of the Pope, a pagan poet has known how to praise an authentically wise man; strength from the Holy One, announced by The Apostle, can be read as "completing" the insight of Horace. The wise man was a Stoic in misfortune and his praise was held worthy to be quoted in the same breath as Paul's assurance of divine mercy.

To my knowledge, one phrase alone in the *corpus* of Innocent refers to his esteem for classical Latin prose and its greatest master. In the very passage in which Innocent used the Horatian *ad unguem* he spoke of Cicero's eloquence:

> Ex his sic procedendum est: Quis praeditus Tulliana eloquentia, quis omniformatus sapientia, sufficit laudes charitatis exprimere, eiusque uirtutes ad unguem exponere?⁵⁶

There remains a metrical couplet, employed by the Pope in much the way in which he had used lines from the classics, but this one was evidently a Christian expansion of a line from Ecclesiastes 10:1. Preaching on an Ash Wednesday, the Pope's theme was Matthew 6:17: *Tu autem cum ieiunas unge caput tuum*. The Pope saw in "ointment" a figure of prayer:

> Per unguentum enim orat<i>o designatur secundum illud:
> > Ne tibi deperdant morientes figmata muscae
> > Ferueat assidue pectoris olla tui.
>
> "Muscae morientes perdunt suauitatem unguenti" (Eccl. 10.1), id est, importunae cogitationes tollunt deuotionem orationis.⁵⁷

The presumably Christian source of these two lines of verse I have not succeeded in locating.

If the Pope used a Christian paraphrase of Ecclesiastes 10:1 in his preaching, we have seen him invoke pagan poets as well in the pulpit. In addition to the texts discussed above, some used repeatedly in sermons and others used in his various treatises as well, there remain a number not yet discussed that occur only in sermons. Innocent railed against sloth in a sermon on texts assigned for the common of one confessor and there reinforced the moral to be drawn from the tragic case of Ishbosheth, 2 Kings (2 Samuel 4:5-12) with Ovid's observation on Aegisthus (*Rem. amor.* 161):

> quaeritis Aegisthus quare sit factus adulter
> in promptu causa est: desidiosus erat.⁵⁸

The same poet was right to warn that forbidden fruit is attractive precisely because forbidden, a perversity as old as the Garden of Eden (*Ars am.* 1.3):

> nitimur in uetitum semper, cupimusque negata.[59]

Pope Innocent III was neither the first nor the last preacher to admonish his hearers that a word, once spoken, cannot be recalled; he was borne out by a line from Horace (*Ep.* 1.18.71):

> et semel emissum uolat irreuocabile uerbum.[60]

"The Prophet," that is, the Psalmist, had spoken of the eternal divine Word; once born, that Word ever remains. Thus was the Roman poet authenticated by scriptural wisdom.

In a second Christmas sermon Innocent cited Virgil's *Eclogue* 4.7, long and widely held by Christians to be a pagan prophecy of Bethlehem's wonder:[61]

> en noua progenies caelo dimittitur alto.[62]

On a feast of Peter and Paul, the Pope noted that a preacher in choosing his theme and contriving his procedure instantiates the insight of Horace (*A.P.* 92):

> singula quaeque locum teneant sortita decenter.[63]

A last homiletic appeal to the improbable authority of Ovid (*Rem. am.* 94) urged that papal hearers not delay their repentance:

> Qui non est hodie, cras minus aptus erit.[64]

3

Somewhat as the great collection of medieval *dicta* amassed by Hans Walther[65] controls the use of the classics by Innocent III—about 70% of his citations are in Walther—so a block of correspondence by the Reverend John Henry Newman during his *iter Italicum* of 1832-1833 offer illuminating comparisons and contrasts with the medieval Pope. As Newman was preparing the journey, Archdeacon Lyall wrote to him concerning the manuscript of Newman's first book, *The Arians of the Fourth Century*. Two passages had given the Archdeacon pause:

> ... I see that at P 102 you speak of the "dispensation of Paganism," and consider it as proceeding from God ... at P 103 of the Heathen poets as having been "divinely illuminated"—a mode of expression

which would go far, *except stricly guarded,* to cast a doubt upon the whole doctrine of inspiration....⁶⁶

So much for one Anglican divine writing to another on the threshold of the Victorian Age, for the young Queen was in the sixth year of her long rule. As we have seen, Pope Innocent III (writing, as it happened, "in the sixth year of Our Pontificate" AD 1204) had not thought it wrong to cite a line of Ovid, a "poetic saying" to be sure, but "nevertheless, as it were, prophetic, indeed a moral saying."⁶⁷ That polyvalent *dictum* in Ovid's intention was a warning to Augustan rapscallions who might get in over their heads in affairs of the heart; hence his advice "to barricade the beginnings!" In his maturity, Newman was to return to what he had written in that first of his long shelf of books:

> Scripture was an allegory: pagan literature, philosophy, and mythology, properly understood, were but a preparation for the Gospel. The Greek poets and sages were in a certain sense prophets. There had been a divine dispensation granted to the Jews; there had been in some sense a dispensation carried on in favour of the Gentiles....⁶⁸

But there is more. We have seen Innocent freely inserting words in lines of classic poetry, provided that they scan, and as freely omitting words that did not advance a point he wished to convey. Newman was accustomed to cite fragments of classical poetry as did Innocent, but there are variations beyond incidental inaccuracy in quotation. One is that the Pope usually cited a full, or nearly full, verse, whereas Newman usually cited single phrases: *nemorosa Zacynthus* twice,⁶⁹ and twice also *inter uiburna cupressi* but with the variations that he changed *inter* to the correct *quantum* and spelled "cypress" *cypressi.*⁷⁰ So too, he cited the phrases *Barbarus segetes,*⁷¹ *ingenti percussus amore,*⁷² *en unquam,*⁷³ and (to leave his Virgil citations for the moment) *insanae molis,*⁷⁴ *disiecta membra,*⁷⁵ *fruges consumere nati,*⁷⁶ *si te diua potens,*⁷⁷ *Macte tua uirtute,*⁷⁸ this last a phrase inexactly remembered. In every case, it must be conceded, the short phrase made Newman's point. On some few occasions he matched Innocent's tendency to cite a line or two at length; thus:

> Actum, inquit, nihil est nisi Poeno milite portas
> Frangimus et media uexillum pone Suburra.⁷⁹
>
> Vrbem, quam dicunt Romam, Meliboee, putaui, stultus ego!⁸⁰
>
> O qui me gelidis in uallibus Haemi, etc.⁸¹

Despite a separation of more than six centuries between Innocent and Newman, both referred to the text of Ecclesiastes 10:1; the young Newman found in this text a metaphor to represent what he named:

> ... the lamentable mixture of truth with error which Romanism exhibits—the corruption of the highest and noblest views and principles, far higher than we Protestants have, with malignant poisons—as Solomon says. Dead flies cause the precious ointment to stink. . . .[82]

A last comparison can be made between Innocent III and John Henry Newman's 1832-1833 use of classical sources; this is with respect to the frequency with which particular authors appear in their writings.

Innocent cited Horace most frequently, Ovid next, and Virgil, Cato, Juvenal *ex aequo,* Lucan only twice and Claudian once. Against this, Newman had Virgil most frequently under his pen and Horace held second place; Terence he quoted twice, Juvenal and Cicero once each. It ought to be noted that Newman, unlike Innocent, cited Greek authors as well;[83] only once, in a letter to his mother, did he proffer a translation of a Greek term.[84]

Pope Innocent wrote in a culture that remained "oral" in important ways. The Gutenberg earthquake, as Marshall McLuhan taught us to see, had long transformed the world that dawned on Newman's consciousness. Goliath and Innocent, but Newman too, all quoted the classics from their capacious memories.

Beyond the happenstance of memory lies the more substantive zone of the convictions that condition, and either help or hurt, our natural capacities. All three authors held the Latin classics in honor, but all three also used them for their varied purposes. For Goliath, they validated his defense of eloquence and learning in Abelard against what he perceived as obscurantist religiosity. Pope Innocent III, dreaming bright dreams of a secure Christian polity on earth, as it were levied feudal dues upon the pagan poets to forward that enormous, doomed enterprise. Newman was not far from the medieval Pope in this, for Newman resisted in the name of faith the encroachments of the Whig ministry, and joined other Oxford theologians in decrying "national apostasy." He planned with Hurrell Froude to fulfill the great boast of Achilles in the Iliad, a boast which the two divines paraphrased rather than translated as:

You shall know the difference, now that I am back again![85]

Despite his Greek literature and his printed books, Newman was still using the classics in the spirit of a medieval schoolman. Given the Oxford of his time, that is exactly what he was.

Notes

1. Vincent of Beauvais, *Speculum quadruplex sive Speculum maius, Speculum historiale* (Duaci: B. Bellerus, 1624), liber 26, capitulum 86 (AD 1148), p. 1126; for Vincent's ambitious beginning, see cap. 56, p. 22: "Haec de continentia priorum partium epilogando transcurrimus: nunc ad historiam per uolumina temporum explicando transeamus. Adam et Eua (sicut creditur) ipsa die creationis suae. . . ." Vincent ended his survey, lib. 31, cap. 105, p. 1323: ". . . ad praesentem annum . . . qui est annus Christianissimi Regis nostri Ludouici 18. Imperii uero Friderici 33. Pontificatus autem Innocentii quarti 2 . . . ab Incarnationis Domini 1244. A creatione uero mundi 5105. . . ."

2. British Library, ms. Harley 978, fols. 100v–102v (13th century) designated H; St.-Omer ms 710, fols. 122v–124r (14th century) designated O; modern critical edition by R. B. C. Huygens, "Mitteilungen aus Handschriften III. Die Metamorphose des Golias," *Studi medievali* 3rd ser., 3 (1962): 764–72; this replaces the earlier edition of H only by Thomas Wright, *The Latin Poems Commonly Attributed to Walter Map* (London: Camden Society, 1841), 21–30.

3. For an isometric translation of the *Methamorphosis golye episcopi* see my "A Goliardic Witness: The *De nuptiis Philologiae et Mercurii* of Martianus Capella in the *Methamorphosis golye episcopi*," *Florilegium* 2 (1980): 121–45 (Carleton University Annual Papers on Classical Antiquity and the Middle Ages).

4. Stanza 22 is lacking (O); H, 22.4, has the misreading *sox*, noted by Huygens, but not emended to *nox* in his text, p. 768.

5. *Gai Sollii Apollinaris. Epistulae et carmina*, ed. C. Luetjohann, *Monumenta Germaniae Historica*, A. A. 8; lib. 2, ep. 10, p. 35, ll. 2–8 and lib. 4, ep. 2, p. 55, ll. 15–25.

6. *Samius*, "the Samian," is Pythagoras, cited by name in lib. 4, ep. 2, p. 55, l. 22.

7. Both *Archesilas*, the reading of O, and *Archelias*, the reading of H, neither found in Sidonius, may be corruptions of *Arcesilaus*, a figure well known through Augustine, *Contra Academicos*; his enigmatic characterization here does not help to identify him.

8. This line is the emendation suggested by S. T. Collins, "Who was Ysopullus?" *Speculum* 23, 1 (1948): 112, noted, but not adopted by Huygens; this brilliant emendation of a scribal lapse is confirmed by the text of Sidonius, lib. 2, ep. 10, p. 35, l. 6: ". . . quod saepe uersum Corinna cum suo Nasone compleuit," followed immediately by: "Lesbia cum Catullo,. . . Cynthia cum Propertio, Delia cum Tibullo" (11.6–8).

9. As noted by Huygens, O read: *Pradentilla*, whereas Wright had correctly named the wife of Apuleius *Pudentilla* in his transcription of this line from H.

10. Comparable lists are available in John of Salisbury, *Metalogicon* 2.10; ed. C. C. I. Webb (Oxford: Clarendon Press, 1929), 77–83 and in William of Tyre, ed. R. B. C. Huygens, "Guillaume de Tyre étudiant. Un chapitre de son 'Histoire' retrouvé," *Latomus* 12 (1962): 822–23; on those masters, see N. Häring, "Chartres and Paris revisted," *Essays in Honour of Anton C. Pegis*, ed. J. R. O'Donnell (Toronto: Pontifical Institute of Mediaeval Studies, 1974), 268–329.

11. This point has been the focus of debate; for J. F. Benton, "Philology's Search for Abelard in the *Metamorphosis Goliae*," *Speculum* 50, 2 (1975): 199-217, Heloise is not intended in this passage; the view followed here is that of W. Wetherbee, *Platonism and Poetry in the Twelfth Century. The Influence of the School of Chartres* (Princeton: Princeton University Press, 1972), 127-34.

12. "Vbi occasione quadam satis nota non bene tractatus, monachus in monasterio sancti Dionysii effectus est" is the terse notice, inserted in his account of Peter Abelard by Otto of Freising, *Gesta Friderici imperatoris,* lib. 1, cap. 47, *Monumenta Germaniae Historica, Scriptorum* t. 20 (Hanover: Hahn, 1868; repr., Leipzig: K. W. Hiersemann, 1925), 377; for an English translation see C. C. Meirow, *Otto of Freising, The Deeds of Frederick Barbarossa*, Records of Civilization, no. 49 (New York: Columbia University Press, 1953), 83.

13. "La croyance aux métamorphoses était aussi ancienne en Grèce que la mythologie . . . mais ce ne fut qu'à partir de l'époque Alexandrine qu'on eut l'idée de composer des recueils en prose ou en vers qui groupaient, sous un même titre, un grand nombre de fables relatives à des héros changés en bêtes, en plantes ou en rochers." G. Lafaye, *Ovide. Les Métamorphoses,* Collection des universités de France (Paris: Les belles lettres, 1928), iv; "In the *Metamorphoses* Ovid attempts no less a task than the linking together into one artistically harmonious whole all the stories of classical mythology. And this he does, until the whole range of wonders (miraculous changes, hence the name, *Metamorphoses*) is passed in review, from the dawn of creation, when chaos was changed by divine fiat into the orderly universe. . . ." G. P. Goold, *Ovid. Metamorphoses,* trans. F. J. Miller, Loeb Classical Library (London: W. Heinemann; New York: G. P. Putnam's Sons, 1916; revision, 1977), xi, xii.

14. This last preferred by its Elizabethan translator: ". . . these eleven books of the Golden Ass . . . worthily they may be enitituled [*sic*] The Books of the Golden Ass . . . Howbeit there may be many which would rather entitle it Metamorphosis, that is to say, a transfiguration or transformation, by reason of the argument and matter therein." See Apuleius, *The Golden Ass. Being the Metamorphoses of Lucius Apuleius,* trans. W. Aldington, revised by S. Gaselee, Loeb Classical Library (London: Heinemann; New York: G. P. Putnam's Sons, 1924), xxi.

15. "Cyllenius quoque in sidus uibrabile astrumque conuertitur. atque ita metamorphosi supera pulchriores per Geminos proprietate quadam signi familiaris inuecti augusto refulsere caelo ac mox Tonantis palatium petiuerunt." *De nuptiis* 1.29.30; *Martianus Capella,* ed. J. Willis, Bibliotheca scriptorum Graecorum et Romanorum Teuberiana (Leipzig: Teubner, 1983), 13, l. 16.

16. Parallels to Ovid in stanza 37 are : *Metham.* 37.3, "puer . . . lasciuire," Ovid *Metam.* 1.456: "lasciue puer . . ."; 37.4, "alatur . . . ," 1.466: "percussus aere pennis. . . ."

17. Parallels between stanza 38.1: "telum . . . auratum," Ovid 1,464: "meus arcus," 38.2: "cuspide modice curuatum," 1.470: "auratum est et cuspide." Similar verbal parallels can be identified elsewhere in Goliath's poem: e.g., 10.1: "regia columpnis elata" is matched by Ovid, 2.1: regia solis erat sublimibus alta columnis;" 12.4: "et Gradiui uincula et sue Dyonis" echoes Ovid 4.183: "arte uiri uinculisque;" 35.4: "atque risus excitat singulis deorum," and 4.188: ". . . superi risere, diuque," and these can be extended.

18. See entry "Innocent III, Pope," by S. C. Ferruolo, *Dictionary of the Middle Ages* (New York: Charles Scribner's Sons, 1985), 6:465.

19. See below, notes 26 and 56.

20. See *PL* 217.917-20: "Innocentii III papae hymnus de Christo et beatissima Virgine Maria dignissima Matre eius"; the source of this reprint by J. P. Migne is the *Opera Innocentii III* (Cologne: M. Cholinus, 1575), t. 1, 761, 762.

21. In addition to the *PL* 217.701b-746c reprint of the *De contemptu mundi siue De miseria conditionis humanae libri tres*, there are critical editions by M. Maccarrone, *Lotharii Cardinalis (Innocentii III) De miseria humane conditionis*, Thesaurus mundi Bibliotheca scriptorum latinorum mediae et recentioris aetatis (Lucani: In aedibus Thesauri mundi, 1955) and by R. E. Lewis, *Lothario dei Segni (Pope Innocent III) De miseria condicionis humane*, The Chaucer Library (Athens: University of Georgia Press, 1978).

22. L.-J. Bataillon, "Virgile chez les Maîtres Parisiens" (intervention). Lectures médiévales de Virgile. Actes du Colloque organisé par l'Ecole française de Rome, Rome, 25-28 octobre 1982. Palais Farnèse 1985. Collection de l'école française de Rome, 80, p. 143.

23. See *PL* 217.1000c for mal-ascribed citation from Cato 2.4.2 (Ps. 1), 1031c Ovid, *Metam.* 2.477 (Psalm 3), and 1071a Cato 1.30 (Psalm 4).

24. See *PL* 217.814d; Virgil *Eclog.* 8.75.

25. See *PL* 217.760b; Horace *Ars poetica* 1.2.

26. See *PL* 217.761c; Horace had used the phrase, *Ars poetica* 294 and *Sat.* 1.5.32.

27. The first line as Horace had written it is: "Tantalus a labris sitiens fugientia captat," and the second line in the poet's text is: "semper auarus eget; certum uoto pete finem." It is also worth noting that the *PL* citation does not include the non-Horatian "et"; the conjunction is to be found in the Maccarrone edition, p. 49, l. 18, and in the Lewis edition, p. 161, l. 1, *De miseria condicionis humane*.

28. See Sermon 6, third Sunday of Advent, *PL* 217.338b.

29. See Sermon 6, third Sunday of Advent, *PL* 217.337d and Sermon 5, Commemoration of one martyr, *PL* 217.615c.

30. See *PL* 217.921-68.

31.   inde hominum pecudumque genus uitaeque uolantum
et quae marmoreo fert monstra sub aequore pontus.
igneus est ollis uigor et caelestis origo
seminibus, quantum non noxia corpora tardant
terrenique hebetant artus moribundaque membra.
hinc metuunt cupiuntque, dolent gaudentque, nec auras
dispiciunt, clausae tenebris et carcere caeco.
                                  Aeneis 6.728-34.

32. *PL* 217.337d inserts *homines*, 615c does not; enclitic -que misplaced and the order of *dolent, gaudentque* reversed.

33. See Sermon 6, third Sunday of Advent, *PL* 217.339a.

34. Ibid., *PL* 217.339a.

35. F. Brittain, *Latin in Church. The History of its Pronunciation.* (London: A. R. Mowbray & Co., 1934; rev. 1955), 56; Brittain's argument is that Byron's rhyming indicates the pronunciation of Latin in early nineteenth-century England.

36. Sermon 6, third Sunday of Advent, *PL* 217.339b.

37. Sermons 1, 2, and 4 on successive anniversaries of his own consecration, *PL* 217.649c, 659c, and 666d.
38. Sermon 7, addressed to Lateran Council IV, *PL* 217.684b; also *De miseria* 2.6, *PL* 217.720a, Maccarrone ed. (henceforth "M") p. 44, l.7.
39. *De miseria* 1, 11; *PL* 217.706d; M 1, 10, p. 16, l. 17.
40. Ibid. 1, 16, *PL* 217.709a; M 1, 15, p. 21, ll. 4, 5.
41. Ibid. 1, 17, *PL* 217.709b; also Sermon 22 on feast of Saints Peter and Paul, *PL* 217.556c; M 1, 16, p. 21. l. 23.
42. Ibid. 1, 15; *PL* 217.709c: text given as *uiuere aliena praeda* by Migne; Juvenal's *aliena uiuere quadra* is given accurately by both M 1, 16, p. 22, l. 4 and Lewis, ed. cit. 1, 15, p. 117, l. 12.
43. Ibid. 1, 16; *PL* 217.709c; M 1, 17, p. 22, l. 22.
44. Ibid. 1, 19; *PL* 217.711c; M 1, 18, p. 25, ll. 23-25.
45. Ibid. 1, 22; *PL* 217.713b: text not set off by editor; M 1, 21, p. 29, l. 10.
46. Ibid. 1, 26; *PL* 217.714d; M 1, 25, p. 32, l. 14.
47. Ibid. 2, 19; *PL* 217.724b-c; M 2, 19, p. 53, l. 16.
48. Ibid. 2, 26, *PL* 217.727b; M 2, 26, p. 59, l. 13; it is noteworthy that both the Migne text and that of M carries *illum* in place of *nullum;* the Lewis text has the correct reading.
49. Ibid. 3, 11; *PL* 217.740d; M 3, 12, p. 87, ll. 16, 17.
50. Ibid. 2, 29; *PL* 217.728c; M 2, 29, p. 61, ll. 23-25 and p. 62, ll. 1, 2.
51. *Regestorum*, lib. 3; *PL* 214.895b.
52. Ibid. lib. 4; *PL* 215.264c.
53. Ibid. lib. 6; *PL* 215.268a.
54. Ibid. lib. 7; *PL* 215.415c.
55. Ibid. lib. 10; *PL* 215.1117b
56. *Encomium charitatis, PL* 217.761c.
57. Sermon 11, Ash Wednesday, *PL* 217.364b-c.
58. Sermon 10, common of one confessor, *PL* 217.740d.
59. Sermon 26, ninth Sunday after octave of Pentecost, *PL* 217.430b.
60. Sermon 1, Christmas, *PL* 217.451a.
61. See J. Pelikan, *Jesus through the Centuries. His Place in the History of Culture,* (New Haven and London: Yale University Press, 1985), chap. 3, "The Light of the Gentiles," 34-45.
62. Sermon 2, Christmas, *PL* 217.457c.
63. Sermon 22, feast of Saints Peter and Paul, *PL* 217.558a.
64. Sermon 9, feast of martyrs, *PL* 217.68d.
65. H. Walther, *Prouerbia sententiaeque latinitatis medii aevi* II/1-II/5, Carmina medii aevi posterioris latina (Göttingen: Vandenhoeck and Ruprecht, 1963-67).
66. Letter of 9 November 1832, *The Letters and Diaries of John Henry Newman,* ed. I. Ker and T. Gornall, S. J. (Oxford: Clarendon Press, 1979), 3:113; the two passages referred to occur in the first edition (*The Arians of the Fourth Century* [London: J. G. and F. Rivington, 1833]) on p. 91: "Accordingly, there is nothing unreasonable in the notion, that there may have been heathen poets and sages, or sibyls again, in a certain extent divinely illuminated, and organs through whom religious and moral truth was conveyed to their countrymen; though their knowledge of the Power from whom the gift came, nay, and their perception of the gift as existing in themselves, may have been very faint or defective." And

on p. 90 of the same edition: "The book of Genesis contains a record of the dispensation of natural religion, or paganism, as well as of the patriarchal." These correspond to Lyall's P 103 and 102 derived from Newman's manuscript before publication.

67. See above Innocent's words adducing Ovid, *Remedia amoris* 91 (. . . *quasi propheticum et morale quod legitur in poeta*), note 53.

68. J. H. Newman, *Apologia pro Vita Sua* (Garden City, N. Y.: Anchor Books, 1956), 145, 146.

69. *Aeneis* 3.270; *Letters and Diaries* 3:169, 254.

70. *Ecl.* 1.25; ibid., 234, 244.

71. *Ecl.* 1.71; ibid., 246.

72. *Geor.* 2.476; ibid., 476.

73. *Ecl.* 1, 68; ibid., 315.

74. Cicero, *Pro Milone* 31.85; ibid., 235.

75. Horace *Serm.* 1.4.62; ibid., 277 (*Inuenias etiam disiecti membra poetae*).

76. Horace *Ep.* 1.2.27; ibid., 242.

77. Horace *Carm.* 1.3.1; ibid., 255.

78. Horace *Serm.* 1.2.31 (. . . *Macte/ uirtute esto inquit sententia dia Catonis*); once more, Newman was imprecise; Horace has quoted Cato the Censor; ibid., 124.

79. Juvenal *Sat.* 10.155.156; ibid., 242.

80. Virgil *Ecl.* 1.19; ibid., 234.

81. *Geor.* 2.488; *Letters and Diaries*, 3:193.

82. Ibid., 280; on Pope Innocent's use of this text from Ecclesiastes see above, note 57.

83. Ibid., 125, 170, 176, 202, 235, 236, 245, 251, 255.

84. Ibid., 125; Newman cited Herodotus 1.74, νυκτομαχία, and translated it as "night engagement."

85. Text of *Iliad* 18.125; literally: "But let them know how much too long have I left the war!"

Rome as "Region of Difference" in the Poetry of Hildebert of Lavardin

CHARLES WITKE

Hildebert of Lavardin (c. 1055–1133), a Frenchman educated at Le Mans and later bishop of Tours, made probably three journeys to Rome after its destruction by the German soldiers of Henry IV and the Normans and Saracens of Robert Guiscard in 1084.[1] In two poems, numbers 36 and 38,[2] he sets forth his reactions to the ruined city and in the second poem presents Rome herself meditating on her state. Both poems are often cited as examples of a growing sense of individuality in expression in medieval Latin poetry, as well as examples of poetry using classical reminiscence more purposefully and successfully than poetry of the Carolingian revival. The present paper attempts to assess these two texts on Rome in two ways: first, in terms of their cultural significance, that is, how they handle the themes and organizational techniques of the type used by a stable body of antique and medieval Latin poetry, called the *laudes urbium*, or praises of cities;[3] and second, in terms of discourse analysis and the semiotic function of the texts as poems embodying some of the essential contrasts and tensions of twelfth-century Latin literary activity: in sum, the poetics of these two poems as encomia of Rome and as poems presenting Rome as a special place in special relationship to the space and time of these texts—Rome as "regio dissimilitudinis" or region of difference.

Rome can be praised because it is like no other city, different in that sense. Rome is also the center of these two poems because through Rome Hildebert is able to attain a metaphor for loss and alienation, and to make Rome a text which is read for its difference from and not for its imitation of the book of nature.

Literature constituting encomia of cities has a very long history in Greek and Latin literature. It is not my intention to survey this history but rather to present a few of the recurring features in descriptions of real, accessible cities, in order to show how Hildebert exploits the expectations his audience had for this kind of poetry. Rome herself has often figured in Latin poetry as the subject of poems of praise, and interestingly enough it is not only the pagan poets, such as Vergil,[4] Propertius[5] and Statius,[6] who do this, but also the late antique Christian poets, such as Prudentius on the martyr Lawrence, and on Hippolytus.[7] Also Paulinus of Nola, on Felix of Nola,[8] contains a famous passage on the city Rome and her civil life restated in Christian terms. Both Prudentius and Paulinus utilize enough of the commonplaces associated with Rome's description and praise according to the generic conventions of this kind of poetry to make their treatments fall into the pattern expected by literate audiences; basically, these two Christian poets use this pattern to facilitate their audience's recognition that the basis for praising Christian heroes rests on inverting the implications of traditional urban encomia while still employing the categories for such praises.

It is obvious that one could mention Rome turning to Christianity in terms which would not emphasize the physical aspects of the city encountered in these and other late antique Christian Latin poems, but evidently these poets are concerned with acknowledging the use of the *topos*, however brief. It is as if the Rome of the classical poets is the Rome that must turn into a Christian city, a Christian setting for acts of Christian martyrs and other heroic deeds. It is clear that there is no other way of presenting Rome, or better, no other Rome to present. On the level of literature as model of the world, it is, of course, exactly this with which the Christian poets were concerned. The classical rhetorical tradition directly confronted these poets; they made it their own, usurping the standard descriptive categories of the city, Rome in particular. Thus these poets demonstrated their awareness of the classical tradition, and their desire to make a new point in defining their relationship to it.

Turning to the early Middle Ages, we note an interesting fact. Many of the praises of cities are addressed to ones that are Italian. In his definitive treatment of this phase of the genre of the *laus urbis*, J. K. Hyde[9] identifies nineteen descriptions of cities, of which fifteen are Italian. Evidently the ancient epideictic oration and laudatory poetry became a powerful expression of Italian civic pride in the early Middle Ages; examples which are better known include the *Laudes* of Milan,[10] the *Versus de Verona*,[11] and one poem on Rome by Paulinus of Aquileia.[12]

This last text, an accentual poem by this prominent Carolingian writer, is as much hymn as encomium of Rome. In it Paulinus of Aquileia presents Peter and Paul in their cult center in Rome, and the city itself is only briefly mentioned in the seventh strophe. But one feature of it demands notice, for it adumbrates a development carried much further by Hildebert of Lavardin: unlike the traditional format, in which the given city is praised for its salubrious setting, its water supply, the industry of its citizens, the wondrous deeds performed by its local gods or saints, its splendid architectural monuments, its political stability, and so on, the basis for praising Rome in Paulinus' poem has been removed from its physical, and of course political grounding, to that of the merits of the saints whom it enshrines; this feature is also found in the just-mentioned poems on Milan and Verona but, unlike them, in the poem of Paulinus of Aquileia, the saints are the sole reason for this encomium of Rome. Unlike other Italian poems in praise of cities, this poem does not present Rome's physical aspects as basis for assigning praise. Probably this is because the text of Paulinus of Aquileia is a hymn as well as a kind of *laus urbis*; it is not so much an objectification of civic pride following programmatic outlines of the sort conventional in this kind of poetry; and it is not so much civic and ecclesiastical boosterism as a hymn to be sung by actual pilgrims in Rome visiting the sites associated with Peter and with Paul.

One should also mention one of the most well-known poems on Rome, the "O Roma nobilis" of the late tenth century,[13] for it marks a pivotal point in the external development of the encomium of a city—from the traditional methods of outward description of an accessible, physically palpable city, toward an individual response to a particular scene in a particular city. As another poem written, apparently, for pilgrims, "O Roma nobilis" shifts attention away from the physical to the spiritual connotations of Rome's fabric. It is a good example of an actual hymn or marching song, and on purely formal grounds it is a continuation of Carolingian rhythmic verse and its Lombard or Italian forebears.

This text makes no reference to Rome's earlier history and barely alludes to its physical fabric; perhaps the colors red and white in the first strophe may be taken to refer to brick and marble, but they are assigned quickly the expected spiritual significance. What is in the foreground is the relationship which the speaker has with the city as addressee. Hildebert of Lavardin, as we shall shortly see, carries this feature to its most complex development in Latin literature.

Hildebert, in his two poems on Rome, shows by citing a wide variety of precedent authors that he is operating very much with an awareness of the literary form we have been mentioning, the *laus urbis*. Martial, Claudian, Lucan, Vergil, Ovid, Horace as well as Prudentius form his sources. Likewise, his work is picked up by the *Carmina Burana*, William of Malmsbury, Hélinand, Vincent of Beauvais, Petrus Pictor, Bernard of Cluny and others, who cite him for a wide variety of purposes and attest to the widespread reception of these verses which, indeed, in the case of the first poem, "Par tibi Roma nihil," were regarded as late as 1825 as a late antique text. Thus these two poems seem to read the past texts on Rome and to be read as new texts on Rome in such a way as to constitute a recuperation of meaning from the past and to constitute a new reading of Rome for the future. Thus they are eminently worthy of detailed analysis and assessment, which here must be only tentative and partial.

First, a few formal observations on content and meter. In poem 36, "Par tibi Roma nihil," we note at the outset that the poet is addressing a ruined city, no longer accessible in its wholeness, and he exploits the paradox *integra/fracta* to set forth Rome's greatness even in decay. The classical penchant for mentioning buildings is fulfilled in *fastus, arces, superum templa*. Civic life is alluded to, and the quality as well as quantity of the city's fabric is presented in lines 15 ff. Something new is to be seen in lines 21 ff., the juxtaposing of the efforts of modern man to the physical fabric of Rome in order to demonstrate the city's grandeur and sheer size, and also in order to make the point so often found in Latin writing of this period concerning the relationship of man to the past: a kind of "dwarfs on the shoulders of giants" *topos*. Likewise new is the *cura hominum* in line 29, as against the *cura deum*: man is creative, powerful, far-seeing; the destructive aspect of the gods appears less powerful than man's creative potential, a reversal of the classical *topos*.

New too is the praise bestowed upon the sculpture of divinities and other powerful personages, many portraits of which must have confronted the visitor to Rome in the late eleventh century and precipitated in the sensitive beholder the romantic exaggeration of lines 31-32, where the gods wish to be like their artistic manifestations. As one might expect, when man and nature are compared, as in lines 33-34, man has pride of place, and the artistic level of existence has precedence over the natural order. Artistic perception is granted immense scope and put on a par with religious devotion itself in lines 35-36. There is nothing here about Rome's function as spiritual treasury or seat of a world religion, as in the earlier poems mentioned in passing. The engagement of this poet is entirely with the city's physical aspects and with intellectual constructions proceeding from his meditation on the ruins. Indeed, it would not be too much to say that the ruins need not have been visited at all (although they probably were). The poem is romantic, imaginative, reflective of certain humanistic and other values of the day, as we will presently see in detail.

The text is in end-stopped couplets, apart from lines 25-28, though a stop could easily be put at the end of line 26. Isosyllabism seems to be as carefully avoided as rhyme. Modularity of this sort is an important part of Carolingian aesthetic, as we are beginning to see, but the sentiments are very much those of the twelfth century. Further, the end-stopped couplets, though pervasive here, are in essence if not in rate not very different from those found in classical poets writing on Rome, such as Propertius (4.1) or Statius (*Siluae* 3.5.78 ff.).

In the second poem on Rome, number 38, "Dum simulacra mihi," Hildebert represents the city herself speaking, rather as she does to Julius Caesar in Lucan's *Pharsalia*, though for very different purposes. The city's physical fabric is once again prominent: *simulacra, moenibus, effigies, aras, palatia*, etc. Like the preceding text, this one modulates the alterations wrought by the passage of time, but here they are of a social and religious cast. Old and new leaders are vividly confronted, e.g., *Caesare Petrus* in line 11. The then/now contrast is exploited, but the ruined state of Rome is paradoxically made to encapsulate the height of control and of power, objectified by a renewal of site description, e.g., *templa, theatra, rostra*, in lines 20 ff. Paradox continues to dominate the concluding passage wherein the contrast between outward weakness and inward power is exemplified in the cross simultaneously enslaving and freeing the head of state; in the miser spending his fortune but gaining riches; and in lending money but keeping it. We recognize the paradoxes of Stoic philosophy energized by the unexpected juxtapositions and assertions of the Gospels. In very Roman terms, Hildebert concludes his poem with a summation presenting *Caesar, consul, rhetor, castra*, and the *studia* and *leges* associated with classical Rome; one solitary cross bestowed more than these.

End-stopped lines are noted again, together with another feature of post-classical and especially of Carolingian poetry, the line made up of blocks of words without connectives, as line 24, verb|verb|verb||noun|noun|noun.

It should be obvious that both poems do more than present different ways of perceiving and of organizing something very vast, Rome's fallen state. Hildebert's classical reminiscences enhance one's sense of his encapsulating Rome's physical past as well as Rome's literary past in his poetry, but they do not offer an organizing framework. It is his own perceptions that offer such a conceptual framework in the first of these texts, and interestingly enough in the second it is Rome herself, another "person" looking at Rome, who does the same thing. The modular units familiar in Carolingian literary practice are present, but do not have the shaping force which they display in poems composed without benefit of other organization in the Carolingian court. But more needs to be said about these two texts and their widely varying ways of approaching their statements.

First of all, why are there two poems? One may note that the first one is devoid of specific mention of Christianity, and indeed dwells lovingly on those aspects of the city most hated and feared by many Christian poets, including those poets exploited by Hildebert: namely, the statues of the gods. Hildebert's susceptibility to the aesthetic dimension, and — more important — his belief that he had an audience which shared this susceptibility, are the fruits of the culmination of the Carolingian recovery and stabilization of the classics that we call the renascence of the twelfth century. These values placed on human endeavor and on the relics of classical sculpture and architecture proceed from a more full and accurate recovery of the classical past through study of texts and autopsy of sites, buildings, statues, and paintings. But these endeavors of recovery and study were not carried out innocently in a scholarly vacuum.

Hildebert, unlike his forebears in this genre, is not addressing praise only to an accessible, material city, but also to a mental construct, a *regio dissimilitudinis* where different values prevail, where man's role is unchallenged in its supremacy over gods and where time cannot undo man's works. This city is indeed a region of difference because it contrasts so strongly with the world as we and Hildebert know it. By being "different" in this way, Rome in poem 36 functions to remind us of our loss, of our estrangement and alienation from a constant aesthetic, from an unchanging region of eternal value. A tension of opposites is created by writing of Rome in this way.

Rome's classical civilization has obviously been replaced by Rome as a religious center, by Rome as religion. The place has become internalized, as some of the poets working along these lines before Hildebert suggested. For them, the trajectory of time has brought about the destruction of the outer elements of Rome, and the consolidation of the inner elements. Hildebert uses this perception as his foundation, but goes farther in asserting that it was by no means necessary that this happen; the conditional clauses ending the poem leave open the possibility that things could have gone differently for the city in time; consolidation of its faith, not explicitly Christian, would have preserved its aesthetic integrity. By stressing the autonomous region of art and by showing how its perishing has impoverished the world to whom the text is addressed, Hildebert unmistakably reveals his valorization of nature, man, Rome, and religion: and the values he states obviously are not the expected ones for a bishop inspecting the ruins of Rome.

By regarding "Par tibi Roma nihil" as an example of allegory, or at least of what Isidore[14] calls *alieniloquium*, we can see some of the elements of Hildebert's extraordinary stance: what is a ruin can be a perfect structural whole in itself, not merely the container for a perfect religious faith; what was external and transitory can become internal and everlasting. The work of art that was Rome is undone, broken. Indeed, by abandoning that physical fabric the spiritual reality reveals itself and is attainable. The *aedificium* of Rome has become an *aedificium* of the spirit, much like Hugh of St. Victor's *aedificium scripturae*, in his *Eruditionis didascalicae* (4.4). The ruin is not merely the subject for romantic ruminations, but a *uia negatiua*, a paradox for perfect building.

Rome has acquired in Hildebert a fluidity in time; Rome is not a series of monuments but a state of history, caught in transience. As Walter Benjamin in another context wrote, "In the ruin history has physically merged into the setting. And in this guise history does not assume the process of an eternal life so much as that of irresistible decay."[15]

Rome is not a total construct; Hildebert, and through him, the audience, must give it what unity it possesses in this first poem. In the second poem Rome becomes a text speaking itself, reading itself with one voice. How to read the Rome of the first poem? Hildebert shows us in the second how Rome reads herself in a poem present to itself. In a sense, the second poem, "Dum simulacra mihi," deconstructs its deconstruction as presented in "Par tibi Roma nihil." This second poem is a kind of speculum reflecting the strands of meaning in the first poem. Poem 36 stressed continuity, poem 38 emphasizes, as in lines 11 ff., the discontinuity of its experience. The death and beauty of poem 36 are read as life and salvation when Rome speaks her own text in poem 38. Earlier poets like Prudentius had made Rome a storehouse of Christian culture, and Hildebert in poem 36 makes it a storehouse of pagan beauty. But in poem 38 Rome becomes a text, fulfilling the function of the pagan beauty of ancient Rome in the same way that Rome's mythologizing texts spoke to that beauty, classified it and made it totally meaningful. By writing such a text as this, Hildebert ranges himself with those classical poets like Vergil and Horace who sought to stabilize a myth for Rome.

Hildebert's statements about Rome in the first poem, "Par tibi Roma nihil," are dichotomizing in their address to past greatness, present ruin, past beauty and success in many areas of civic life, and present capacity to outstrip modern man's efforts to grasp and restore. Rome's statements about herself in poem 38, "Dum simulacra mihi," are totalizing, revealing Rome not as a container enveloping a content but as an example of textuality, a structuring process of words.

Rome has become an idea, not a place, but rather a *regio dissimilitudinis*. These two poems are composed in order to explain it, to made it accessible. The destabilized ruins become fixed sacrality; the concept of imitation as presented by Plato and Augustine is carried in poem 36 to absurd lengths, where the gods wish to resemble the Roman statues representing them; nor is Rome graphically represented in poem 38 where Rome writes her own script, as it were. Poetics is no longer in control of imitation or of the hermeneutic tradition. The authority for making sense out of Rome is ultimately the text which Rome writes, not the reader, or the poet with his manipulation of his *auctores*. The irony and paradox of poem 36 become in poem 38 a text whence meaning is recovered not from what is seen, the physical decay, but from what is not seen—very much unlike both the classical Roman poets on Rome, and also unlike Prudentius. This autonomy of the text, present to itself and commenting upon itself, should perhaps be sought in other twelfth-century Latin poetical productions as well.

Hildebert evidently found it impossible to reconcile in one poetic text these values of man-centered beauty coming to renewed life from the classical past, and at the same time the values of medieval clerical culture that were comfortable with presenting Rome either as a goal of pilgrimage or as a capital of a spiritual empire in poems composed along the lines provided by revamping the *laus urbis* tradition. Hence Hildebert composes in addition a text which Rome herself speaks, and where she employs very much the new literary aesthetic of personal relationship to the subject; poet reflecting on ruins becomes poem-ruin speaking. In re-establishing in the first poem the normative Roman values for poetry in praise of a city, Hildebert reveals his successful internalizing of the classical values abroad in his time; in going beyond these Roman norms and in composing the second poem as a text commenting in a very medieval way upon the first poem, and constituting a Rome which is very much a region of difference from other Romes, Hildebert may fairly be said to represent twelfth-century humanism at its highest.

Notes

1. See F. J. E. Raby, *A History of Secular Latin Poetry in the Middle Ages*, 2nd ed. (Oxford: Oxford University Press, 1957), 1:317; and *A History of Christian Latin Poetry*, 2nd ed. (Oxford: Oxford University Press, 1953), 265–66.
2. Edited by A. Brian Scott (Leipzig: Teubner, 1969); on pp. v and vi he also has information on Hildebert's life.
3. See the exhaustive treatment by C. J. Classen, *Die Stadt im Spiegel der* Descriptiones *und* Laudes Vrbium, Beiträge zur Altertumswissenschaft 2 (1980).
4. E.g., *Aeneid* 8.306–69.
5. E.g., book 4, 1.1–55.
6. *Siluae* 3.5.78–104 on Naples.

7. *Peristephanon* 2.469 ff., and *Peristephanon* 11, ed. J. Bergmann, Corpus Scriptorum Ecclesiasticorum Latinorum 61 (Vienna and Leipzig, 1926).

8. *Carmen* 19, ed. W. Hartel, Corpus Scriptorum Ecclesiasticorum Latinorum 30 (Vienna and Leipzig, 1893).

9. "Medieval Descriptions of Cities," *John Rylands Library Bulletin* 48 (1965–66): 308 ff.

10. *Monumenta Germaniae Historica, Poetae Latini Aeui Carolini* I, ed. E. Duemmler (Berlin, 1881), 24.

11. Ibid., 119.

12. Ibid., 136 ff.

13. Text in Raby, *Secular Latin Poetry*, 1:291.

14. *Etymologiae* 1.37.22.

15. *The Origin of German Tragic Drama*, trans. J. Osborne (London, 1977), 178.

Index

Aaron 231
Abelard, Peter 5, 6, 175, 183, 184, 379, 382, 384, 393, 397; —*Calamities* 5, 175, 183
Accius 291
Achaia 287
Achilles 29, 120, 226, 375, 376, 397
Adam 125
Adelard of Bath 325; —*Natural Questions* 328
Adlington, William 142
Aegisthus 394
Aegyptus 57
Aeneas 5, 29, 62, 117-19, 121, 122, 129-31, 133, 134, 137, 143, 147, 148, 175, 181, 183, 184, 186, 246, 254, 372-78
Aeneid (see Virgil)
Aeolus 29
Aeschylus 120
Aesop 116
Æthelward 165, 170
Afer, Constantine 132, 135
Agamemnon 62
Agricola, Rudolph 2
Alan of Lille, *Distinctiones* 387
Alaric 60
Albericus of London 142
Albert the Great 269, 277
Albertus Magnus 277
Alcibiades 53, 65
Alcuin 47, 81, 170, 201, 202, 344-45, 351; —*Ars grammatica* 345; —*De dialectica* 344

Aldheim, Abbot of Malmesbury, *Epistle to Acircius* 170
Aldhelm, St. 317
Alexander the Great 13, 14, 17, 48, 58, 59, 247
Alexander III, Pope 322
Alexander of Aphrodisias 268, 271, 276, 280; —*De anima* 268, 276
Alexander of Villedieu, *Doctrinale* 35, 36, 37
Alexandria 13, 16, 114
Alfred, King 6, 45, 47, 49-65; —*Boethius* 58-61, 63-65
allegory 113, 114, 116-18, 120, 129, 130, 141, 148, 176-79
Alonso, Amado 241, 243, 244
Alrica 60
Amata 135, 136
Amazon 59
Ambrose, St. 1, 5, 95, 97, 102, 103, 105-9, 291, 324; —*De officiis ministrorum* 97, 102-7
Ambrosian Library 87
"Ambrosian Virgil" 87, 89
Amiatine Bible 80
Ammianus 27
Amon 58
Anaximander 115
Anaxarches 50
Anchises 29, 119, 130
Angevins 317, 318
Anglo-Saxon Chronicle 165
Anglo-Saxons 5, 6
Anonymous of St. Gall 49

Anselm of Bec (and Canterbury) 167, 259, 390
Antenor 83, 122, 373, 374, 376-78
Antioch Chalice 17
Antony 13, 14
Aphrodite 16, 115, 372
Apollinaris, Sidonius 352
Apollo 55, 115, 146, 148, 184-86
Apollonius of Tyana 363
Apuleius 142, 291, 293, 363-67, 383-85; —*Apology* 363, 365-67; —*De deo Socratis* 364-67; —*De interpretatione* 365, 367; —*De mundo* 365; —*De Platone* 365-66; —*Florida* 363, 366-67; —*Golden Ass* 364-66, 383; —*Metamorphoses* 142, 363-64, 366-67, 383-85; —*Philosophica* 363, 365, 367
Apuleius (Pseudo), *Herbarium* 365
Aquinas, St. Thomas 120, 124, 125, 248, 259, 269
Aracoeli, Church of 231
Archbishop of Sens 393
Archimedes 350
Ares 115
Argentina 238
Arians 32
Ariosto, Ludovico 227
Aristippo 223, 230
Aristophanes 289, 292
Aristotle 3, 35, 53, 114, 120, 121, 125, 227, 228, 265-71, 273-80, 291-93, 345, 348, 349, 354, 356, 357, 382; —*Categories* 382; —*De anima* 275-76; —*De generatione animalium* 270; —*De incessu animalium* 270, 277; —*De motu animalium* 270, 277; —*De partibus animalium* 270, 277; —*Nicomachaean Ethics* 270; —*On Sense and Sensibles* 275; —*Parua naturalia* 270, 277-78; —*Politics* 270; —*Sophistical Refutations* 270, 277
Arlon 19
Arnulf of Lisieux 315, 316, 319, 321-23, 328-31
Ascalion 226
Ascanius 29
Ascension 17

Asclepius 365-66
Asser, Bishop 47, 49, 65, 166; —*Vita Alfredi* 166
Assisi 85
Asulanus, Evangelista Lungus 277
Athanasius 292
Athena 115
Athens 189
Atreus 57
Auch 359
Auerbach, Erich 27, 28, 124, 202; —*Dante as Poet of the Secular World* 124; —*Mimesis* 27, 93-94, 124
Augustine, St. 1, 27, 45, 48, 53, 54, 59, 65, 115, 116, 143, 145, 148, 179, 180, 184, 248, 259, 285, 289-94, 324, 344, 345, 349, 363-65, 367, 410; —*Confessions* 148, 294; —*De ciuitate Dei* 59, 289, 290, 294, 364; —*De doctrina christiana* 143, 180, 345; —*De uidendo Deo* 45; —*Soliloquia* 45
Ausonius 84
Auxerre, Cathedral of 19
Avignon 4, 85-89
Avitus 352-53

Babylon 64
Bacchus 14, 16, 18
Bamberg 4, 82, 85
Bandello, Matteo 227
Barzizza, Gasparino 38
Bartholomew 17, 18
Baugul of Fulda 347
Beatrice 175, 178, 185
Beautiful 191-94
beauty 288, 295, 298
Becket, Thomas 288
Bede 45, 84, 165, 170, 345, 348; —*De temporum ratione* 84; —*Historia ecclesiastica* 45
Benedict of Peterborough 170
Benedict, Canon of St. Peter's Basilica 209
Benedictines 393
Benoit de Sainte-Maure 372
Beowulf 5, 175, 182, 183
Berengarius of Tours 168

Bernard, St.(of Clairvaux) 292, 321, 325, 328, 379-80, 382, 393
Bernard of Cluny 405
Bernard of Utrecht 353
Bersuire, Pierre, *Ovide moralizé* 350; —*Ouidius moralizatus* 350
Bessarion, Cardinal 254
Billanovich, Giuseppe 4, 284
"Bishop Goliath" 6, 379, 381-86, 392, 393, 397; —*Metamorphosis* 392
Black Death 224
Blemmydes, Nicephorus 277
Boccaccio, Giovanni 1-3, 90, 141, 179, 223-31, 283, 367; —*Decameron* 223-31, 367; —*Filocolo* 226, 228; —*Genealogie deorum gentilium* 141
Boethius 3, 6, 35, 45-47, 49, 52-54, 56-61, 63-65, 86, 147, 183, 248, 259, 292, 294, 349, 356, 387; —*De consolatione* 6, 45, 46, 49, 51, 52, 54, 57, 60, 61, 64, 86, 294
Boethius of Dacia 35-36
Bolgar, R. R. 95
Bonaventure, St. 125
Boniface VIII, Pope 85, 126
Book of Revelation 31
Brescia 86
Brethren of the Common Life 37, 38, 39, 41
British Library 79, 84
Bruni, Leonardo 2
Brutus 46, 61, 182, 286
Burckhardt, Jakob 95
Busiris 54, 63, 64
Bussi, Giovanni Andrea, Bishop 91
Byzantium 96, 253, 257, 258, 259, 260, 268-70

Cadiz 84
Caesalpinus, Andreas 278
Caesar, Augustus 14, 54, 83, 168, 231, 286
Caesar, Julius 47, 58-59, 98, 169-71, 259, 348, 407
Camilla 135, 153-57, 159
Camille 153-57, 162
Canterbury 170
Capella, Martianus 28, 31, 114, 123, 172, 294, 345, 348, 349, 352, 353, 364, 381-85; —*De nuptiis Philologiae et Mercurii* 28, 349, 381, 383, 385
cardinal virtues 100, 104
Carmina burana 405
Carolingian Empire 199, 344
Carrara, Francesco da 298
Carthage 119, 246
Cassino, Monte 366, 367
Cassiodorus 60, 92, 172, 294, 344, 345, 348, 349, 352, 357; —*Chronicles* 60
Castro, Américo 249
cathedral schools 5
Cato the Elder (the Censor) 46, 51, 53, 58, 102, 172, 359, 385-89, 397; —*Carmen de moribus* 386
Catullus 65, 84, 292
Cavalcante 124
Celestina, La 240, 247
Celestine V, Pope 126
Centaur 59
Ceofrid, Abbot 80
Cerberus 29, 153
Cervantes 243, 246; —*Don Quixote* 246; —*La Galatea* 246
charity 181
Charlemagne 81, 166, 201, 202, 344, 347
Charles the Bold 80
Chartres 82, 88-90, 132, 316, 352
Chartres, cathedral school 316
Chatillon, Gautier de, *Alexandreis* 248
Chaucer 5, 145, 175, 178, 186, 187; —*Troilus* 175, 186, 187
Cherubim 18
Chevalier au cygne 366
Chrétien de Troyes 5, 175, 184-86; —*Erec* 175, 184, 186; —*Lancelot* 184
Christ 11, 15-19
Chrysopolitanus, Zacharias 325
Chrysostom, John 291
Church Fathers 2, 31, 48, 92, 95, 117, 141, 190, 193, 324, 344
Cicero, Marcus Tullius 2, 3, 5, 29, 31, 50, 52, 53, 55, 65, 95, 97-109, 116, 120, 166, 172, 225, 227-30, 248, 259, 285, 286, 289-95, 298, 299,

316, 324, 348, 352, 356-57, 359, 394, 397; —*Academica* 294, 316; —*Ad familiares* 295; —*De amicitia* 227, 228, 359; —*De diuinatione* 31, 286; —*De finibus* 98, 316; —*De legibus* 290; —*De natura deorum* 289, 290; —*De officiis* 97-100, 102, 103, 225, 228, 229, 298, 359; —*De senectute* 359; —*Tusculan Disputations* 98, 294

Cilicia 12
Cimbri 209
Cimone 230
Cincinnatus 50, 58, 59
Circe 55, 56, 364
Cistercians 393
City of Dis 124
Claudian 291, 293, 350, 387, 392, 397, 405; —*De raptu Proserpinae* 350
Claudius 121, 122, 168
Clemanges, Nicholas de 357
Clement III, Pope 85
Clement of Alexandria 13
Clement V, Pope 86
Clement X, Pope 214
Clement, Pseudo 326
Cleopatra 58
Codices Latini Antiquiores 92
Codrus 50
Colegio de México 239
Collatinus 61
Colonna, family 87
Colonna, Giacomo 89
Colonna, Giovanni, *De uiris illustribus* 88; —*Mare historiarum* 88
Colonna, Landolfo 88-90
Colonne, Guido delle 372
Colosseum 214
Comnena, Anna 270; —*Alexiad* 270
Constantine 16, 132, 135
Constantine, Baths of 210
Constantinople 12, 254, 255-56, 258, 260, 277
Corbie, monastery of 81
Corominas, Juan 239
Correggio, Azzo da 291
Council of Sens 379
Council of Toledo 346

Council of Trent 358
Council of Vaison 346
Courcelle, Pierre 148
Cratippus 229
Cremete 223, 230
Creusa 135, 372
Criseyde 186
Croesus 53, 54, 63, 64
Cupid 29, 184, 186, 364, 366-67, 382, 383
Curia 88, 89, 319
cursus 27
Curtius, Ernst Robert 96, 207, 243, 248, 289
Cybele 209
Cyriacus of Ancona 257
Cyrus 54, 64

d'Abano, Pietro 278
d'Ailly, Pierre 357
d'Arezzo, Simone 88, 89
da Piazzola, Rolando 86, 87
da Prato, Niccolò, cardinal 86-88
da Strada, Zanobi 226
Damocles 55, 56
Damon 226, 227
Danaus 57
Dante 1, 2, 5, 114, 116, 117, 119, 123-27, 175, 178, 182, 183, 185, 187, 230, 248, 356; —*Commedia* 123-27, 178, 182; —*Convivio* 123; —*De monarchia* 126; —"Donna gentile" 114; —*Vita nuova* 5, 123, 175, 185
Dares Phrygius 50, 62, 63, 121, 172, 294, 372, 374, 378
David 227
de Nolhac, Pierre 284
de Ridevall, John, *Fulgentius metaforalis* 142
de Soubiran, Raymond 88
de Vega, Lope 243, 247
De uiris illustribus 52, 53, 59, 65, 88
Dead Sea Fruit 48
Decoratus 51
Democritus 267
Despautère 359
Deucalion 58

Deventer 37
Diagoras of Rhodes 298
Diana 209
Dictys 121, 294, 372, 374, 378
Dido 29, 122, 130, 134-36, 143, 147, 148, 184, 186, 245, 246, 248
Diocletian's Edict 12
Diodorus 14
Diogenes the Cynic 119
Diomedes 57, 372
Dionysius Cato 385, 386; —*Dionysii Catonis disticha de moribus ad filium* 350-51, 385-86
Dionysius of Syracuse 226
Dionysius the Areopagite 190-94
Dionysos 11, 13-19
Damascenus the Studite 259
Domitian 14, 288
Domitius 171
Donatus, Tiberius Claudius 35, 38, 121, 122, 141, 346, 348, 359
Dronke, Peter 96, 146

Eadmer, *Historia nouorum* 165
Eallerica 59
Eberhard of Béthune 35-36
Ecclesiasticus 294
Ecloga Theoduli 351
Edward II 88
Egbert 170
Eginhardus 352
Egypt 11, 13-15, 18, 19, 180
Einhard, *Vita Caroli* 166-68
Eloquence 380
Elysium 117, 136
Empedocles, *On Nature* 266
Eneas 130, 153, 157
Ennius 48, 248, 289, 298
Ennodius 324, 329, 330
Epicureans 118
Epicurus 53, 292
Epistle to the Hebrews 210
Erasmus 40, 79, 91, 97
Erigena, Johannes Scotus 189, 192
Esquiline Hill 209
Etna 62, 63
Eucharist 17

Euclid 350
Eugenius III, Pope 319, 330
Eumenides 29
Euphorbus 172
Euphrates 52
Euripides 15-17, 53, 292; —*Bacchae* 15-17
Euryalus 226, 227
Eurydice 56, 57
Eusebius 189, 292, 323; —*Church History* 31
Eustratius 270
Eutropius 6, 46, 59, 65, 172, 294
Exeter, Joseph of, *De bello Troiano* 248
Exodus 124

Fabricius 46, 51, 52
Fabricius, Hieronymus, of Aquapendente 278; —*De uisione* 274
faith 1, 181
Farinata 124
Faunus, temple of 209
Felix III, Pope 91
Felix of Nola 404
Festus, Rufus 294
Fiammetta 228
Fichet, Guillaume 357
Filomena 225, 226
Florence 5
Florio 226
Florus, *Epitome* 326
Fortuna 53
Fortune 51, 284
Frangipani 85
Freculf of Lisieux 326
Frederick II, Emperor 85
Frontinus 59, 170, 172; —*Strategemata* 170
Frotharius of Toul 352
Fufetius, Mettus 49
Fulgentius 117-19, 122, 123, 127, 130, 141-43, 146, 148, 179-82, 184, 187, 353, 357, 364, 366, 367; —*De continentia Vergiliana* 117, 123, 142-43, 179, 181, 184; —*Mitologiarum libri* 141-42, 353, 364
Fulvus, Publius Quintius 224, 229

Galen 31, 133, 267, 268, 274, 276, 279, 280; —*De usu partium* 267, 274, 276; —*On His Own Books* 31; —*On the Order of His Own Books* 31
Ganymede 49, 58
Garden of Eden 1
Gawain 182, 185, 186, 371, 373, 377, 378; —*Gawain and the Green Knight* 182, 185, 371, 373, 377, 378
Gebert of Aurillac 347, 348
Gelasius II, Pope, *Aduersus Andromachum* 91
Gellius, Aulus 27, 289, 291
Genesis 177, 181
Genoa 86
Geoffrey of Anjou 318, 319
Geoffrey of Monmouth 170, 316, 325, 365; —*Historia regum Britanniae* 316
Gerald of Wales 315
Gerbert d'Aurillac 354
Gerson, Jean 357
Gesta Caesarum 326
"*Geste Historiale*" of the Destruction of Troy 372-75, 377
Ghibellines 85, 86
Ghismonda 224
Gildas 165
Gilson, Etienne 126
Giovio, Paolo 255
Girolamo, Abbot of Pomposa 84, 85
Gisippo 223-31
Good 191, 193, 194
Goths 59, 60
grammar 36
Gratian, *Decretum* 325
Greece 14
Greek 200, 203, 204
Gregory I The Great, Pope 190, 208, 214, 324, 346, 351, 359; —*Cura pastoralis* 45; —*Dialogues* 45, 63; —*Regula pastoralis* 359
Gregory V, Pope 82
Gregory IX, Pope 85
Gregory of Tours, St. 25-32, 326; —*History of the Franks* 25, 28, 31; —*Liber de gloria beatorum confessorum* 26, 28; —*Libri miraculorum* 29, 30; —*Life of Saint Martin* 28

Gregory, Master 209, 214, 217, 218
Griselda 223, 224
Grosseteste 270
Gualtieri 223, 224
Guelphs 86-87
Guido delle Colonne 372-76; —*Historia destructionis Troiae* 372
Guido di Città di Castello, Cardinal 209
Guido, St., Abbot of Pomposa 84
Guinevere 184
Guiscard, Robert 403

Hades 14
Hadrian 14, 286
Harvey, William 278
Haskins, Charles Homer 95
Hastings, Battle of 168, 169
Hector 372, 375, 376
Hecuba 374, 377
Hegesippus 48, 348
Hegius, Alexander 37-39; —*Inuectiua in modos significandi* 38
Heimskringla 170
Heldebert 348
Helen of Troy 18, 243
Helias 171
Héloise 183, 184, 382
Henry I, King 166-68, 318-20
Henry II, King 18, 82, 318, 321, 322, 327
Henry III, King 347
Henry IV, King 403
Henry VII, King 86
Henry of Huntington 170, 326, 327; —*Historia* 326
Hephaistos 115
Hera 115
Heraclitus 113, 115, 288, 291; —*Homerica Problemata* 113, 115
Hercules 13, 14, 19, 29, 46, 52, 54, 63, 227
Hermagoras 349
Hermes 115
hero 4, 5
Herodotus 14, 30, 255-58, 289, 291
Herophilus 280
Hesione 372

Higinus 55
Hildebald 91
Hildebert of Lavardin 403, 405, 407-10
Hildebert of Le Mans 328, 329
Hildebrand, Pope 168
Hippocrates 292
Hippolytus 404
Historia Augusta 86, 291
Holy Roman Empire 92
Homer 5, 53, 62, 63, 95, 114, 115, 119, 120, 176, 189, 254, 372, 377; —*Iliad* 62, 114, 119; —*Odyssey* 176
Honorius, emperor 60
hope 181
Horace 3, 143, 242, 285, 291, 293, 347, 348, 357, 359, 386-89, 391-95, 397, 405, 409; —*Epistles* 242; —*Epodes* 242; —*Odes* 242, 359; —*Satires* 242, 359
Horse Tamers of the Quirinal Hill 210
Hugh of Amiens 315, 321, 325
Hugh of Sens 319
Hugh of St. Victor 324, 352, 409; —*Didascalicon* 352
Humanism 1, 36, 38, 41, 201, 202, 243, 343
Humanities 1, 177
Huon de Bordeaux 366
Hyginus 50, 52-54, 294
Hylas 227
Hypermnestra 57

Iamblichus 364
Iarbas, King 246
Ibn Sina 268, 269, 279
India 53
Innocent III, Pope 6, 85, 92, 291, 385-90, 392, 393, 395-97; —*Commentarium* 387; —*De miseria condicionis humane* 291, 387, 390, 392; —*De quadrapartita specie nuptiarum liber* 388; —*Encomium charitatis* 387
Iphigenia 46
Irenaeus, St. 31
Isidore of Kiev, Cardinal 254
Isidore of Seville, St. 18, 48, 50, 52, 53, 55, 57, 141, 285, 292, 344, 348, 350, 352, 408; —*De poetis* 285;

—*Etymologiae* 18, 50, 57, 292, 344
Israelites 180
Italicus, Silius 65
Iulii Mausoleum 17

James of Venice 277
Janus 29, 214
Jean d'Outremeuse 116
Jean de Meun 180
Jerome, St. 29, 30, 45, 48, 291-93, 324, 363; —*Vita Malchi* 292
Jerusalem 113, 175, 181-84, 186
Joachim of Flora 5, 125, 126
Job 286, 294
John of Salisbury 288, 289, 292, 315, 316, 326, 352, 353; —*Metalogicon* 352; —*Policraticus* 288, 292
John VI Kantakouzenos, Emperor 254, 259
John XXII, Pope 87, 89
John, St. 16, 17, 29
Jonathan 227
Jordanes 172
Josephus, Flavius 48, 250, 291, 294, 326, 348
journey metaphor 5
Jove 29, 55, 58, 63, 380, 382
Julian the Apostate 14
Juno 18, 29, 133, 134, 217
Jupiter 18, 145
Justin 6, 15, 84, 85
Justin Martyr 15
Justin, *Epitome* 84
Justinian the Great 15, 189
Justinus 46
Juvenal (Decimus Iunius Iuuenalis) 50, 59, 248, 285, 291, 347, 348, 357, 387, 390, 391, 397
Juvencus 353

Khalkokondyles, Laonikos 255-58
Kilwardby, Robert 35
King of Hungary 393
Kristeller, Paul Oskar 283
Kritoboulos, Michael 256
Kydones, Demetrios 259

Laberius 298

Lactantius, Placidus 48, 59, 117, 285, 289, 291, 363; —*Institutions* 285
Lady Philosophy 147
Laelius, Gaius 227, 228
Lampridius, Aelius 285
Lancelot 5, 184
Landino, Cristoforo 38
Langland, William, *Piers Plowman* 5, 175, 177-78, 186
Laocoon 29
Latin 199-204, 207, 237, 240, 253, 345, 352, 359
Latin, Vulgar 204
Laud Troy Book 372, 375-77
Lavinia 135, 136
Lebuinus, St., gospel of 19
Legenda aurea 231
Leo III, Pope 81
León, Fray Luis de 250
Leonardo of Chios, Bishop 259
Lesbos 256
Leto 115
Liber Catonianus 350
Liber Pater 50, 58
liberal arts 6, 351
Liberius 50
Libro de Alexandre 247
Licinius 209
Life of St. Alexis 248
Linacre 359
Lincei, Academia de' 80
Lincoln Cathedral 317
Livy (Titus Liuius) 4, 6, 46, 48, 59, 79, 80, 82-85, 87-92, 248, 286, 291, 293, 326, 348, 357, 359; —*Ab urbe condita* 79, 80, 84, 85, 89-91; —*Periochae* 90, 91
logic 36
London 5, 142
Lothario di Segni 385, 390, 391
Lotharius 346, 347
Lovati, Lovato 4, 79, 83-87, 89, 91
Lucan 50, 51, 59, 144, 166, 170, 171, 291, 348, 387, 392, 397, 405, 407; —*Pharsalia* 170, 407
Lucius II, Pope 319
Lucretia 58, 59
Lucretius 248, 286, 291

Lupus of Ferrières 48
Lydgate, John 372, 377; —*Troy Book* 372, 375-77
Lydia 54
Lynceus 57

Machiavelli, Niccolò 356
Macrobius 56, 116, 141, 143, 144, 146, 147, 248, 291, 292, 349, 353; —*Commentum in Somnium Scipionis* 146; —*Saturnalia* 144
Maecenas 62
Mainardo, abbot 84
Malaxos, Manuel 259
Manilius, Marcus 348
Manutius, Aldus 254
Map, Walter, *De nugis curialium* 248
Marathon 59
Marble Horsemen 214
Maria in Fonte, Santa, church 209
Maria Maggiore, Santa, basilica 209
Marie de France 180
Marius, temple of 209
Mark Antony 13
Martial (Marcus Valerius Martialis) 292, 357, 405
Martin de Tours, St. 81
Martin, St., Pope 190
Mary 18, 386
Maurus, Hrabanus 18, 48, 141, 345, 353; —*De rerum naturis* 18; —*De institutione clericorum* 351, 353
Maximus the Confessor, St. 190
Medea 49
medieval university 35
Mela, Pomponius 59, 294, 316; —*De chorographia* 316
Mena, Juan de 249
Mercury 114, 184-86, 364, 380
Merlin 365
Met(h)amorphosis Goliae Episcopi 365, 369, 380, 383
Michael of Ephesus 265, 268-71, 274, 276-80
Minerva 154, 159, 229
Minotaur 57
Mirabilia urbis Romae 207-21, 231

Modists 35, 36, 38
Mommsen, Theodor, *Corpus inscriptionum latinarum* 80
Monophysitism 190
Morelli, Giovanni di Paolo, *Ricordi* 356
Munda, battle of 58
Muses 115, 147
Mussato, Albertino, *Ecerinis* 83, 87; — *Historia Augusta* 86
Mythographus I 52-53, 55-56

Nearchus 50
Nectanebus 58
Nennius 165, 326
Neoplatonists 268
Nepos, Cornelius 294
Nepotianus 170
Neptune 18, 29, 54
Nero 54, 61
New Albion 5, 175, 182
New Jerusalem 175
New Troy 5, 175, 186
Nicocreon 50
Nicomachi 80, 81
Nimrod 55
Nisus 226, 227
Noah 58
Nolhac, Pierre de 294
Nominalists 36

Octavian 223, 224, 230, 231
Odoacer 91
Odysseus 30, 115
Oedipus 57
Olaf, St. 170
Old English Orosius 60-65
Olderic, Bishop 348
Orestes 226, 227
Origen 292
Orléans 5
Orosius, Paulus 6, 45-48, 50, 53, 54, 57-65, 291, 326, 357; — *Historiarum aduersus paganos libri septem* 6, 45-46, 48, 53, 59-62, 64-65
Orpheus 46, 52, 56, 123
Osmund, St. 317
Otto I, Emperor 91

Otto II 91
Otto III, Emperor 82, 347
Ovid (Publius Ouidius Naso) 4, 6, 14, 19, 39, 50, 52, 55, 57, 59, 62, 65, 214, 217, 259, 291, 293, 298, 299, 357, 359, 383-85, 387-97, 405; — *Ars amatoria* 14, 39, 392; — *Fasti* 55, 59, 210, 214; — *Metamorphoses* 52, 55, 57, 65, 359, 384, 385, 389; — *Remedia amoris* 6, 39, 94, 393, 395

Padua 83-87, 237, 269, 277, 278
Palladium 373, 374
Pallas 136, 217
Pan 18
Panaetius 97-99, 102, 104, 107; — *On Duties* 9-98
Panofsky, Erwin 208-10, 214, 217
panther 16
Paraclete 184
Paradiso 5, 123, 125-27
Paris 5, 18, 35, 217, 269, 357, 372
Paris (of Troy) 372
Parmenides 53
Parnassus 2
Pasiphae 57
Patroclus 226
Paul, St. 6, 29, 62, 189, 286, 389, 393, 394
Paulinus of Aquileia 404, 405
Paulinus of Nola 404
Paulus 51
Pavia 237
pax Romana 231
Pelikan, Jaroslav 96
Pellisson 359
Pelops 49, 58
Pentheus 17
Perotti, Niccolò 37, 38; — *Cornucopiae* 37
Perses, King 51, 53
Persius (Aulus Persius Flaccus) 50, 248, 285, 292, 348, 359
Peter of Ailly, *Destructiones modorum significandi* 36
Peter of Blois 348
Peter, St. 62, 186, 286
Petracco di Parenzo 87, 88

Petrarca, Francesco 1-4, 6, 79, 83, 87-90, 119, 210, 246, 283-85, 288-91, 294, 296, 298, 299, 356-58, 367; —*Ad familiares* 3, 284; —*Contra eum* 285; —*Contra medicum* 294; —*Contra quendam* 298; —*De ocio* 284-85; —*De remediis utriusque Fortune* 284; —*De sui ipsius* 284; —*De uita solitaria* 284; —*Priuilegium lauree domini Francisci Petrarche* 283; —*Rerum uulgarium fragmenta* 90; —*Secretum* 284, 296; —*Seniles* 2, 284
Phaeton 58, 389
Pharoah 231
Phidias 210
Philip of Briouze 316
Philip of Harcourt, bishop of Bayeux 5, 315, 317, 324, 330
Philo of Alexandria (Philon) 114-15, 250
Philologia 380, 382
Philoponus, John 268, 277; —*Generation of Animals* 277; —*Parts of Animals* 277
philosophy 36, 55, 147
Phintias 226, 227
Phythias 227
Piccolomini, Aeneas Sylvius 254
Piccolomini, Franciscus 278
Pidal, Ramón Menéndez 241
Pietro in Vincoli, S., church 209
pilgrim 5
Pirithous 226, 227
Pius II, Pope 254
plague 2
Plato 114, 119, 129, 132, 190-94, 254, 266, 267, 270, 279, 289, 291, 293, 294, 344, 349, 365, 410; —*Kratylos* 190; —*Republic* 114, 294; —*Timaeus* 129, 132, 266
Platonism 179, 194, 268, 270
Plautus, Titus Maccius 292
Plethon, George Gemistos 257
Pliny (C. Plinius Secundus) 50, 53, 268, 285, 286, 291, 316, 324; —*Natural History* 268
Pliny the Younger (C. Plinius Caecilius Secundus) 316, 324
Plotinus 364

Plutarch (Mestrius Plutarchus) 14, 17, 242, 289, 291; —*De Iside et Osiride* 14; —*Parallel Lives* 242; —*Quaest. Conuiu.* 4 17
Pluto 29
Poliziano, Angelo 79
Polonus, Martinus 208
Polybius 14, 255-56
Polydamas 372
Polyphemus 46
Polyxena 374
Pomposa 4, 84, 85, 87, 89-91
Porphyry of Tyre 114, 115, 348, 364, 382, 384; —*De antro nympharum* 115
Poseidon 115
Posidonius 349
Praxiteles 210
Presbyter, Paulus, *Vita Ambrosii* 292
Priam 372-75, 377
Priscian 35-39, 348, 349, 357; —*Institutiones grammaticae* 35, 37, 39
Proba 328, 329; —*Virgilian Cantos* 328
Proclus 115, 190, 193
Procopius of Caesarea, *The Gothic War* 346
Propertius, Sextus 292, 404, 407
Proserpine 29
Prosper Tiro, *Chronicles* 60
Proverbs 294
Prudentius Clemens, Aurelius 114, 353, 404, 405, 409, 410; —*Psychomachia* 114
Psalms 294
Psalter 31
Pseudo-Dionysius 189
Psyche 364, 366, 367, 383
Ptolemies 11
Ptolemy (Claudius Ptolemaeus) 53, 287
Ptolemy Philadelphus 287
Publicius, Jacobus 39
Purgatorio 1, 124
Pylades 226, 227
Pyrrha 58
Pyrrhus 48
Pythagoras of Samos 172

quadrivium 146, 184

Quattrocento 207, 255, 260
Quintilian (M. Fabius Quintilianus) 121, 166, 292, 345, 348, 359, 384; —*Institutiones* 345

Radagaisus 60
Raedgota 59
Rand, E. K. 95
Ratherius, Bishop 81, 89, 91
Regulus 63–65
Remigius (Rémi d'Auxerre) 49, 54, 56, 348
Renaissance 1, 103, 114, 116, 141, 180, 185, 189, 199–202, 205, 207, 208, 223, 224, 227, 237, 238, 243, 245, 246–49, 253, 256, 259, 260, 269, 270, 277, 278, 316, 343, 344, 350, 352, 353, 356, 358–60, 381
Renaissance, Carolingian 199, 201
Renaissance, German 200
Renaissance, Italian 200
Renaissance, Twelfth-Century 199
Resurrection 17
Reynolds, L. D. 95
Rheims 48
Richard of Dyon 170
Ridewall, John 353
Robert of Gloucester 320
Robert of Harcourt 316, 318
Robert of Torigny, *Chronicle* 326, 327
Roger, bishop of Salisbury 317
Roland(in)o de' Passeggeri, *Ars notaria* 355
Roman de la Rose 5, 175, 178, 185, 248
Roman law 5
Rome 5, 231
Rotrou of Rouen 315, 321, 322, 331
Rufus, Q. Curtius 291, 348
Rufus, William 167, 168, 171, 172
Ruiz, Juan, *Libro de buen amor* 244, 249
Rushd, Ibn 279

S. Paolo fuori le Mura, basilica 80
Sabbadini, Remigio 284
Sabines 58, 59
Saela 170
Saladino 223
Salisbury Cathedral 317
Salisbury, John of 208, 366; —*Policraticus* 366

Sallust (C. Sallustius Crispus) 27, 39, 59, 285, 291, 357, 359; —*Bellum Catilinae* 39
Salutati, Coluccio 142, 295
Sansovino, Francesco 255
Sappho 243, 292
Saturn 29, 55
Scaevola, Mucius 58
Scholastics 19
Scipio, Publius 2, 58, 59, 116, 170, 227
Scot, Michael 277, 279
Scotus, John 53
Scythia 53, 60
Sedulius 353
Seege or Batayle of Troy 376–77
Semele 15, 16
Senate, Roman 231
Seneca, Lucius Annaeus 3, 55, 56, 62, 84–87, 285–89, 291, 293–95, 298, 299, 316, 328, 329, 357; —*Ad Lucilium* 85; —*De beneficiis* 85; —*De clementia* 85, 294; —*De tranquillitate animi* 287; —*Declamationes* 86, 87; —*Naturales quaestiones* 285, 287, 328–29
Seneca, Pseudo-, *Octavia* 62
Septuagint 240
Serra, Johannes 39
Servius 38, 48, 50, 52, 54, 55, 57, 117, 141, 348
Sibyl 117, 231
Sidonius Apollonaris 352, 357, 364, 365, 381
Sigebert of Gembloux 141
Siger of Brabant 5, 125, 126
Silverstein, Theodore 371, 376
Silvestris, Bernardus 123, 125, 127, 129–36, 142–48; —*Commentary on the First Six Books of the Aeneid of Vergil* 131, 133–34, 144–46; —*Cosmographia* 132–33, 147–48, 365; —*De mundi uniuersitate* 365
Simone d'Arezzo 86–87
Simonides of Ceos 297
Singleton, Charles, *Dante Studies* 124
Sinon 29, 373
Smaragdus of St. Michel 141
Sodom and Gomorrha 48
Sofronia 223, 224, 229, 230

Solinus 48, 50, 53, 292
Solomon 125, 126
Sophists 121
Spenser, Edmund 113, 114, 125, 227; —*Faerie Queene* 113, 114, 227
Speyer, cathedral 82
Sphrantzes, George 255, 256, 259; —*Chronicon Maius* 255, 259; —*Chronicon Minus* 255
St. John Lateran, basilica 80–82, 85, 89, 91
St. Peter's Basilica 17, 80, 209
Statius, Publius Papinius 50, 141, 144, 170, 291, 348, 350, 387, 404, 407; —*Achilleid* 350; —*Thebaid* 141
Stephen, King 317
Stileca 60
Stoa 5, 104, 107, 108
Stoicism 5, 95, 102-4, 109
Stoics 99, 100, 106-8, 229, 268, 354
Strabo 83
studia humanitatis 1
Sturlason, Snorri 170
Suetonius, Gaius 50, 56, 59, 166–71, 286, 291, 298, 326, 348; —*Lives of the Caesars* 167, 326; —*Titus* 169, 171
summum bonum 99, 101, 102, 104, 107, 108
Sybil 148
Sychaeus 246
Symmachi 80, 81, 92
Syria 12
Syrophanes 142

Tacitus, Cornelius 6, 17, 46, 55, 348; —*Annals* 55; —*Historiae* 17
Tancredi 224
Tantalus 391
Tarquinius Superbus 58, 61
Tarsus 12
Tasso, Torquato, *Jerusalem Delivered* 113
Tedaldo 224
Terence (Publius Terentius Afer) 144, 230, 285, 291, 293, 348, 357, 359; —*Andria* 230
Tertullian 48
Theagenes of Rhegium 115
Themistius 14
Themistocles 297

Theodoric, King 59, 60, 81, 91, 346
Theodosius I, Emperor 11
Theophrastus 267, 291
Theseus 59, 226, 227
Thessaly 13
Thetis 18
Thierry of Chartres, *Eptateuchon* 352
Thirty Years War 37
Thomaeus, Nicolas Leonicus 277
Thomas of Erfurt 36
Thomas, St. 1, 248, 259, 269
Thucydides 30, 255–58
Thyestes 57
Thyle (Thule) 53
Tiberius, Emperor 121, 122, 210, 286
Tibullus, Albius 294
Tigris 52
Titans 17
Tito 223-31
Titus, Emperor 168, 169, 171, 231
Tityus 392
Torello 223
Tortelli, Giovanni 38
Tower of Babel 55
Trajan, Emperor 14
Traube, Ludwig 82
Trevet, Nicholas 86, 87
Trinity 181, 187
Triumph of Dionysos 13, 15, 17, 18
trivium 6, 146, 184
Trogus, Pompeius 348; —*Philippic Histories* 84
Troilus 5, 175, 186, 187
Trojan cycle 52
Trojan War 52, 327
Trojans 122, 133, 372-74
Troy 5, 56, 61, 121, 122, 133, 175, 186, 243, 246, 258, 371-78
Turmair, Johannes (Aventinus) 40
Turnus 136

Ulysses (see Odysseus) 2, 29, 46, 52, 55, 56, 62
University of Alcalá 237
University of Basel 39
University of Basle 269
University of Bologna 87, 269
University of Chartres 132
University of Cologne 39

University of Erfurt 39
University of Frankfort 39
University of Freiburg-im-Breisgau 37
University of Ingolstadt 37, 40
University of La Plata 238
University of Louvain 39
University of Mainz 39
University of Montpellier 87
University of Oxford 269
University of Padua 83, 269, 277
University of Paris 35, 269, 357
University of Salamanca 237, 250
University of Salerno 132
University of Trier 39
University of Tübingen 37, 40
University of Uppsala 37, 48
University of Vienna 39
University of Würzburg 39
Utica 59, 102

Valerius Maximus 53, 59, 170, 225-26; 289, 291, 357
Valerius, Julius 48, 59; —*Res gestae Alexandri Macedonis* 48
Valla, Lorenzo 36, 38, 90, 91, 359; — *Antidotum in Facium* 90; —*Elegantiae linguae Latinae* 36; —*Emendationes in Liuium* 90
Varro, Marcus 285, 289, 291, 299, 349, 352; —*Disciplinarum libri IX* 349; —*On the Duty of a Husband* 285
Vatican Mythographers 141 (see Mythographer I)
Vegetius 172
Vegius, Mapheus 142
Venice 87, 277
Venus 134, 144, 209, 214, 217, 227, 380, 382
Venus, Capitoline 214
Venus, Temple of 227
Vergil (see Virgil) 27, 29, 116-19, 121-23, 129-37, 141-47, 175, 176, 179-83, 187, 404, 405, 409
Verona 81, 84, 88-90, 92, 286
Vesalius, Andreas 278
Vespasian (Titus Flauius Vespasianus) 168
vice 19
Victor, Aurelius 294

Vilgardus 346
Vincent of Beauvais 364, 365, 379, 405; —*Speculum historiale* 379
Virgil (see Vergil) 1, 3, 5, 19, 50, 53, 54, 57, 87, 89, 153-55, 157, 170, 242, 244-46, 291, 293, 294, 347, 348, 353, 356, 357, 359, 371, 372, 374-78, 384, 387, 388, 395, 397; —*Aeneid* 4, 27, 57, 117, 119, 123, 129, 131-36, 141-46, 153-55, 157, 170, 176, 179-82, 184, 187, 242, 246, 359; —*Eclogue IV* 395; —*Georgics* 57, 244, 359
Virgin 15, 16, 386
virtue 19
Vitalis, Ordoric 170
Vitruvius 291, 294
von Humboldt, Wilhelm 200
Voragine, Jacobus de, *Legenda aurea* 292
Vulgate 240

Wærferth, Bishop 45, 63
Waldo, Peter 357
Weland 51, 52
Wessex 45
Whitelock, Dorothy 59, 60
Widsith 60, 61
Wilkins, Ernest H. 284, 295
William II, King 166
William of Conche 144, 146
William of Jumièges 169, 326; —*Historia Normannorum* 326
William of Malmesbury 165-72, 405; —*Gesta regum* 165-69, 171, 172, 321, 342; —*Polyhistor* 170, 172; —*Vita Wulfstani* 167
William of Moerbeke 269, 277
William of Poitiers 169
William of Saint-Thierry 379
William the Conqueror 167-70
Wisdom 51, 53, 54
Worms, cathedral 91

Xenophon 292

York, library 170

Zabarella, Jacob 278
Zeno 50, 292
Zeus 13, 16, 122

The Classics in the Middle Ages, selected papers from the Twentieth Annual CEMERS Conference, examines the influence, direct or indirect, of classical writers on the culture of the Middle Ages. Covering a large variety of subjects and diverse fields—education, literature, the fine arts, linguistics, philosophy, and social institutions—these papers explore the myriad ways in which classical culture permeated the life, thought, and art of the Middle Ages. The topics range from allegory to zoology, from historiography to speculative grammar, from Dionysiac imagery in Coptic textiles to theories of medieval education. Among the authors discussed are Virgil, Cicero, Alfred the Great, Gregory of Tours, Fulgentius, Apuleius, Pseudo-Dionysius, Michael of Ephesus, Bernard Silvestris, William of Malmesbury, Hildebert of Lavardin, Petrarch, and Boccaccio. The contributors include Janet Bately, Giuseppe Billanovich, Marcia Colish, Philip Damon, Bernard F. Huppé, R. H. Rouse and M. A. Rouse, Aldo Scaglione, and Edward Synan.

Aldo S. Bernardo is Distinguished Service Professor of Italian and Comparative Literature Emeritus at the State University of New York at Binghamton. He is an internationally known Petrarch scholar and is an Honorary Member of the Accademia Arcadia of Rome. His publications include *Petrarch, Laura and the "Triumphs"* (1974) and three volumes of translations of Petrarch's *Rerum Familiarium Libri* (SUNY Press, 1975; Johns Hopkins, 1982 and 1984).

Saul Levin is Professor of Ancient Languages at the State University of New York at Binghamton. Among his numerous publications are *The Linear B Decipherment Controversy Re-examined* (1964), *The Indo-European and Semitic Languages* (1971), *The Father of Joshua/Jesus* (1978), and articles in *Journal of Biblical Literature, Transactions of the American Philological Association, Hebrew Studies, Studi Micenei ed Egeo-anatolici, General Linguistics, LACUS Forum, Aufstieg und Niedergang der römischen Welt, Kadmos,* and *Hermes Americanus.*